HOLY TREASURE AND SACRED SONG

Holy Treasure and Sacred Song

RELIC CULTS AND THEIR LITURGIES IN
MEDIEVAL TUSCANY

Benjamin Brand

OXFORD
UNIVERSITY PRESS

Oxford University Press is a department of the University of Oxford.
It furthers the University's objective of excellence in research, scholarship,
and education by publishing worldwide.

Oxford   New York
Auckland   Cape Town   Dar es Salaam   Hong Kong   Karachi
Kuala Lumpur   Madrid   Melbourne   Mexico City   Nairobi
New Delhi   Shanghai   Taipei   Toronto

With offices in
Argentina   Austria   Brazil   Chile   Czech Republic   France   Greece
Guatemala   Hungary   Italy   Japan   Poland   Portugal   Singapore
South Korea   Switzerland   Thailand   Turkey   Ukraine   Vietnam

Oxford is a registered trademark of Oxford University Press
in the UK and certain other countries.

Published in the United States of America by
Oxford University Press
198 Madison Avenue, New York, NY 10016

© Oxford University Press 2014

This volume is published with the generous support of the AMS 75 PAYS
Endowment of the American Musicological Society, funded in part by the
National Endowment for the Humanities and the Andrew W. Mellon Foundation.

All rights reserved. No part of this publication may be reproduced, stored in
a retrieval system, or transmitted, in any form or by any means, without the prior
permission in writing of Oxford University Press, or as expressly permitted by law,
by license, or under terms agreed with the appropriate reproduction rights organization.
Inquiries concerning reproduction outside the scope of the above should be sent to the
Rights Department, Oxford University Press, at the address above.

You must not circulate this work in any other form
and you must impose this same condition on any acquirer.

Library of Congress Cataloging-in-Publication Data
Brand, Benjamin David, 1977– author.
Holy treasure and sacred song : relic cults and their liturgies in medieval Tuscany / Benjamin Brand.
  pages cm
Includes bibliographical references and index.
ISBN 978–0–19–935135–0 (hardback : alk. paper)   1. Church music—Italy—Tuscany—500–1400.
2. Church music—Catholic Church—500-1400.   3. Christian saints—Cult—History of doctrines—
Middle Ages, 600–1500.   4. Catholic Church—Liturgy—History—Middle Ages, 600-1500.   I. Title.
ML3033.7.T87B73 2014
781.71'2009455—dc23
2013044969

9 8 7 6 5 4 3 2 1
Printed in the United States of America
on acid-free paper

To my friends and family

Contents

Acknowledgments   ix
Music Examples   xi
Figures   xiii
Tables   xv
Abbreviations   xvii
Timeline   xix

1. Introduction   1

PART I | DOMINUS ET CONSTRUCTOR   9

2. *The Bishop's Relics, 752–899*   17
   The Politics of Relic Cults: Bishop Giovanni I of Lucca   22
   Defenders of Ecclesiastical Treasure: Fiesole and Florence   36

3. *The Bishop's Clergy, 840–1039*   44
   Emperors—Canons—Bishops   47
   Arezzo: A Trio of Episcopal Builders   54
   San Miniato: A New Episcopal Center   61
   Fiesole: Between Episcopal and Monastic Reform   67

4. *The Bishop's Eclipse, 1032–1118*   72
   Florence: Reformed Monasticism and the Cathedral Canons   74
   Lucca: The Lord and Builder in the Age of the Reformed Papacy   84
   Pisa: The Rise of Civic Religion   102

PART II | ECCLESIA MATRIX   107

5. *The Cathedral Chapters, Their Churches, and Their Liturgies*   111
   Ordinals   116
   Altars, Relics, and Oblations   124
   Privatization   138

6. Public Drama in the Mass   144
    The Clergy and Populace Convene   148
    The Liturgy of the Word   150
    The Liturgy of the Eucharist   153
    The Dedication of the Church   156
    St. Martin   166
    St. Donatus   179

7. Sacred Narrative in the Divine Office   192
    St. Minias   200
    St. Zenobius   217
    St. Donatus   225
    Sts. Fridian and Regulus   233

APPENDIXES   247
    I. *Officium Sancti Miniatis*   247
    II. *Officium Sancti Zenobii*   251
    III. *Officium Sancti Donati*   253
    IV. *Officium Sancti Fridiani*   257
    V. *Officium Sancti Reguli*   259

References   261
    Manuscripts and Archival Documents   261
    Printed Books   263

Index   285
    Index of Manuscripts   294
    Index of Plainsong   295

Acknowledgments

The origins of this book lie in my dissertation, a study of music and liturgy at the cathedral of Lucca in the late Middle Ages. With its focus on a single church, that earlier project followed the now familiar path of exploring medieval and Renaissance music as it was created and heard at particular places and institutions. By the time of the completion of my dissertation, however, I knew that I wanted to fashion an equally illuminating but more distinctive approach with my book. This I did by narrowing its overall theme to liturgies inspired by relic cults, by shifting its chronological frame from the late to the early and central Middle Ages, and by broadening its geographic scope to include cathedrals and cities throughout Tuscany. This necessitated a considerable amount of new research, which was supported by a summer grant from the University of North Texas, as well as residential fellowships at the Villa I Tatti (Harvard Center for Renaissance Studies) in 2008–2009 and the American Academy in Rome in 2011–2012. I thank James Scott, Dean of the College of Music at the University of North Texas, for supporting these two leaves.

Many individuals provided assistance as I undertook the research for and the writing of this book. The archivists at the capitular and episcopal archives and libraries in Arezzo, Lucca, Fiesole, Pisa, Pistoia, Florence, and Siena made their collections available to me and answered my frequent queries. Kathy Bosi, F. Gordon and Elizabeth Morrill Music Librarian at the Villa I Tatti, greatly expedited my research by purchasing digital photographs of many of the liturgical manuscripts that are the foundation for much of this book. George Dameron, Joseph Dyer, Julian Gardner, Allen Grieco, Albertus Horsting, Patrick Nold, and Henry Parkes shared with me their expertise in art, ecclesiastical, and liturgical history. The meetings of the Interpreting Medieval Liturgy Network, organized by Helen Gittos and Sarah Hamilton, provided a stimulating venue in which to present portions of this book. Robert Lagueux and Maureen Miller graciously read and commented on particular chapters while Jennifer Davis, Tova Leigh-Choate, and Robert Upchurch did so for the entire manuscript. I am particularly thankful to these five and to the two anonymous readers from Oxford University

Press for their suggestions, which have improved its content and organization in a great many ways. Anna Celenza, Thomas Kelly, Anne Robertson, David Rothenberg, Guido Ruggiero, Marica Tacconi, and Kate Van Orden offered advice and encouragement at various points in the research and writing process, while Suzanne Ryan shepherded this project through the submissions process at Oxford with consummate professionalism. Finally, I thank my former mentor, Craig Wright, whose scholarship, in its intellectual breadth and rigor, continues to be a model for my own.

Music Examples

3.1. *Ignis ardore* (*Officium Sancti Donati*, V-Am) 59
4.1. *O gemma fulgens presulum* (*Officium Sancti Zenobii*, V-R) 80
6.1. *Organicis Christo.* Trope of *Terribilis est locus iste* (Introit for the Dedication of the Church) 163
6.2. *Invisibilis Deus.* Trope of *Terribilis est locus iste* (Introit for the Dedication of the Church) 164
6.3. Alleluia *Oculis ac manibus* (Alleluia for the *dies natalis* of St. Martin) 169
6.4. *Sacerdotem Christi Martinum* (Sequence for the *dies natalis* of St. Martin) (first three of nine verses) 177
6.5. Comparison of *Confractum vitreum* and *Stetit angelus* (Offertories for the *dies natalis* of St. Donatus of Arezzo and the feast of St. Michael) 185
7.1. *Tecum principium* (Nativity, V2-A1), *Tunc iratus* (*Officium Sancti Miniatis*, M-A9) and *Tunc imperator* (*Officium Sancti Miniatis*, L-A3) 205
7.2. Comparison of *Beatus Christi miles* (*Officium Sancti Miniatis*, M-R5) and *Ministri presidis* (*Officium Sancti Miniatis*, M-R2) 206
7.3. *Pretiosus Christi* (*Officium Sancti Miniatis*, M-R10) and *Vox de caelo* (*Officium Sancti Miniatis*, M-V10) 211
7.4. *Martyrialis honor* (*Officium Sancti Miniatis*, V-A3) and *Pervigil o pastor* (*Officium Sancti Zenobii*, V-A3) 212
7.5. *Illuminata Siranna* (*Officium Sancti Donati*, M-A5), *Antime frater et levita* (*Officium Sancti Donati*, M-A9), and *Pontifices almi* (*Officium Sancti Nicolai*, M-A7) 230
7.6. Comparison between *Cum beatus Donatus* (*Officium Sancti Donati*, M-R5) and *Hodie cum exultatione* (*Officium Sancti Donati*, M-R9) 245
7.7. Incipits of Four Antiphons: *Frigianus pontifex* (*Officium Sancti Fridiani*, M-A7), *Frigianus namque pontifex* (*Officium Sancti Fridiani*, L-A1), *Beatus Regulus* (*Officium Sancti Reguli*, L-A1), and *Beatus Regulus* (*Officium Sancti Reguli*, L-Ab) 239

7.8. *Hodie sacer sumus* (*Officium Sancti Reguli*, V2-Am) 240

7.9. *Laudanda est Trinitas* (*Officium Sancti Reguli*, V-Am) and *Ejectus a propriis* (*Officium Sancti Reguli*, M-A2) 241

N.b. Quotations of chant texts denote in italics the words drawn from a hagiographic source; the alignment of particular pitches with individual syllables is indicated in boldface type.

Figures

1.1. The Dioceses of Medieval Tuscany. 5
2.1. Fiesole viewed from the northern suburbs of Florence, ca. 1520. 20
2.2. Translation of St. Martin. 34
4.1. Plan of Santa Reparata, Florence. 82
4.2. Plan of San Martino, Lucca. 88
4.3. Tunc elevant (rubric for the elevation of the relics) and Surgite sancti (antiphon). 94
5.1. Santa Maria Assunta, Pisa. 113
5.2. Façade (saec. XIII^{in}) and portico (ca. 1233–1250) of San Martino, Lucca. 114
5.3. Raised presbytery and crypt of San Miniato, Florence (saec. XI^{ex}). 125
5.4. Nave of San Cristoforo of Barga (diocese of Lucca) (saec. XII). 127
6.1. Pulpit, San Cristoforo of Barga (saec. XII$^{3/4}$; attr. Guido Bigarelli da Como). 152
6.2. St. Martin and the Pauper (saec. XII$^{1/2}$). Retrofaçade of San Martino, Lucca. 170
6.3. Life of St. Martin (ca. 1233–1250). Portico of San Martino, Lucca (north panel). 171
6.4. Life of St. Martin (ca. 1233–1250). Portico of San Martino, Lucca (south panel). 171
6.5. St. Donatus (saec. XII$^{1/4}$). 189
6.6. St. Donatus (above) and St. Hylarian (below). 190
7.1. Façade Mosaic, San Miniato al Monte, Florence (saec XII^{in}). 214
7.2. Apse Mosaic, San Miniato al Monte, Florence (1297). 215
7.3. Altarpiece of St. Zenobius (ca. 1230; attr. Master of the Bigallo). 224
7.4. Life of St. Regulus (ca. 1233–1250). Portico of San Martino, Lucca. 238

Tables

5.1. The Tuscan Ordinals 118
6.1. The Structure of High Mass 146
6.2. Service Books for the Mass 155
6.3. Mass for the Dedication of the Church 157
7.1. Textual Borrowing from the *Passio Sancti Miniatis I* into the *Officium Sancti Miniatis* 201

Abbreviations

BIBLIOGRAPHIC

AAF	Archivio Arcivescovile, Florence
AAL	Archivio Arcivescovile, Lucca
ACA	Archivio Capitolare, Arezzo
ACL	Archivio Capitolare, Lucca
ACFie	Archivio Capitolare, Fiesole
ACP	Archivio Capitolare, Pisa
ACPist	Archivio Capitolare, Pistoia
AVPist	Archivio Vescovile, Pistoia
AH	*Analecta Hymnica Medii Aevi*, 55 vols. (Leipzig, 1886–1922).
AS	*Acta Sanctorum*, 69 vols. (Antwerp, 1643–1940).
BAV	Biblioteca Apostolica Vaticana
BCL	Biblioteca Capitolare, Lucca
BCT	Biblioteca Capitolare, Toledo
BCR	Biblioteca Casanatense, Rome
BCIS	Biblioteca Comunale degli Intronati, Siena
BLF	Biblioteca Laurenziana, Florence
BGV	Biblioteca Guarnacci, Volterra
BHL	*Bibliotheca Hagiographica Latina Antiquae et Mediae Aetatis*, 3 vols. (Brussels: Société des Bollandistes, 1900–1901). *Novum Supplementum*, ed. H. Fros (Brussels: Société des Bollandistes, 1986).
CAO	René Hesbert. *Corpus Antiphonalium Officii*, 6 vols. (Rome: Herder, 1975).
CCCM	Corpus Christianorum Continuatio Mediaevalis
MDL	*Memorie e documenti per servire all'istoria del ducato di Lucca*, 16 vols. (Lucca, 1813–1933).
MGH	Monumenta Germaniae Historica
AA	Auctorum Antiquissimorum

____C	Concilia	
____DK	Diplomata Karolinorum	
____DRIG	Diplomata regum et imperatorum Germaniae	
____EPMC	Epistolae Merowingici et Carolini Aevi	
____L	Legum	
____Q	Quellen zur Geistgeistesgesch des Mittelalters	
____SS	Scriptores	
____SRM	Scriptores rerum Merovingicarum	
Mores	Florence, Archivio dell'Opera di Santa Maria del Fiore, I.3.8 (*Mores et Consuetudines Ecclesiae Florentinae*)	
ODL	Opera del Duomo, Lucca	
OOES	Trombelli, Giovanni Crisostomo, ed. *Ordo Officiorum Ecclesiae Senensis Ab Oderico Eiusdem Ecclesiae Canonicus Anno Mccxiii Compositus* (Bologna: Longhi, 1766).	
OOL	Lucca, Biblioteca Capitolare, 608 (*Ordo Officiorum* of Lucca)	
OOP	Bologna, Biblioteca Universitaria, 1758 (*Ordo Officiorum* of Pisa)	
OOPIST1	Pistoia, Archivio Capitolare, C114	
OOPIST2	Pistoia, Archivio Capitolare, C102	
PL	Patrologiae Cursus Completus Series Latina, ed. J. P. Migne, 217 vols. (Paris, 1844–1845).	
PM	*Paléographie Musicale*, 22 vols. (Solesmes, 1889–2001).	
PRG	Romano-German Pontifical	
Ritus	Florence, Biblioteca Riccardiana, 3005 (*Ritus in ecclesia servandi*)	

LITURGICAL

A	antiphon
B	Benedictus
L	lauds
LX	lesson
M	matins
R	responsory
V	vespers
V	verse

Timeline

The following timeline includes key events and texts discussed in the book. Dates refer either to a precise event or, in the case of bishops and popes, to the beginning and ending of an episcopate or pontificate. Arrows indicate the probable impetus for the writing of a hagiographic text or for the composition of a liturgy.

700

    713: King Liutprand legalizes pious donations to the church
    ca. 730–754: Bishop Walprando, Lucca
    752–757: Pope Stephen II
        Confirms Aretine claims on Sant'Ansano (752)
        Translates St. Crescentius from Rome to Siena
    755–780: Bishop Peredeo of Lucca
    757–767: Pope Paul I
        Translates relics of fifty saints *intra muros*
    774: Charlemagne conquers Italy
    780–800: Bishop Giovanni I, Lucca
        Translates St. Regulus to cathedral (780)
        → *Translatio Sancti Reguli I*
        Translates St. Pantaleon to Santa Reparata
        Translates St. Fridian in San Frediano
        → *Vita Sancti Fridiani II*
    786: Charlemagne donates property to San Miniato

800

    801–818: Bishop Jacopo of Lucca
        Translates St. Pontianus to Sts. Jacopo e Filippo in Lucca
        Restores Santa Maria ad Praesepe and San Pietro in Vincoli

816: Rule of Aachen
†823: St. Alexander, Bishop, Fiesole
ca. 823–876: Bishop Romano, Fiesole translates St. Alexander in San Pietro
829–876: St. Donatus, Bishop, Fiesole
ca. 840: Bishop Pietro, Arezzo, founds cathedral chapter

900

ca. 950–1000: Romano-German Pontifical (PRG)
966: Bishop Zenobio, Fiesole, founds cathedral chapter
→ *Passio Sancti Alexandri* (?)
970: Otto II translates relics of St. Minias to Metz
987–1010: Bishop Elemperto, Arezzo
    Reforms cathedral chapter (966)
    Rebuilds canonry and cathedral

1000

1008–1024: Bishop Ildebrando, Florence
    Founds monastery at San Miniato (1018)
    Builds outer crypt at San Miniato
    → Drogone, *Passio Sancti Miniatis II*
    → *Officium Sancti Miniatis* (Layer 2) (1030s [?])
†1025/1027: St. Romualdo founds hermitage at Camaldoli (1012)
1014–1023: Bishop Alberto, Arezzo, begins construction of San Donato
    → *Passio Sancti Donati II* (before 1026)
    → *Missa Sancti Donati* (before 1026)
    → *Officium Sancti Donati* (before 1026)
1023–1036: Bishop Teodaldo, Arezzo
    Consecrates San Donato (1032)
    → *Translatio Sancti Donati* (after June 1036)
    Consecrates Chapel of St. John the Evangelist, cathedral of Florence
1023–1036: Guido of Arezzo, *Micrologus*
1024–1039: Bishop Jacopo, Fiesole
    Builds San Romolo (ca. 1028–1032)
    Reforms the cathedral chapter (1032)
    → *Translatio Sancti Romuli et sociorum*
    → *Passio Sancti Romuli*
1023–1056: Bishop Giovanni II, Lucca
    Translates St. Lucine from Rome to San Martino

1030s: Cathedral canons of Florence
    Obtain financial independence and papal protection (1036)
    Rebuild Santa Reparata (?)
    → *Vita Sancti Zenobii* by Lorenzo of Amalfi (ca. 1039)
    → *Officium Sancti Zenobii* (1030s [?])
1038: St. Giovanni Gualberto founds Vallombrosan Order
1046: Augustinian canons resident at San Frediano
    → *Vita Sancti Fridiani III*
    → *Officium Sancti Fridiani*
1057–1073: Bishop Anselmo I, Lucca
    Translates St. Senesius in San Pietro (before 1061)
    Elected Pope Alexander II (1061)
    Translates St. Alexander from Rome to San Alessandro Maggiore (after 1061)
    Reforms cathedral chapter (after 1061)
    Translates Sts. Jason, Maurus, and Hilaria from Rome to cathedral (after 1061)
    Consecrates San Martino (1070)
    → Rangerio (?), *Sermo in dedicatione ecclesie*
1063–1100: Reconstruction of San Miniato (Phase 1)
1064–1118: Construction of cathedral, Pisa
    Translation of Sts. Ephysius and Potitus from Sardinia to cathedral (1088)
    Consecration of cathedral by Pope Gelasius II (1118)
1073–1086: Bishop Anselmo II, Lucca
ca. 1096–1112: Bishop Rangerio, Lucca
    Vita metrica Sancti Anselmi (ca. 1100)
    Translatio Sancti Reguli II (?)
    Translates St. Regulus and Sts. Jason, Maurus, and Hilaria in San Martino (1109)
    → *Translatio Sanctorum Reguli, Iasonis, et Mauri*
    → *Officium Sancti Reguli* (?)

1100

ca. 1100: *History of the Custodians of Arezzo*
1107: Translation of St. Ansanus from Dofana to cathedral, Siena
1118–1161: St. Ranierius of Pisa
ca. 1120: Honorius Augustodunensis, *Gemma animae*
ca. 1125–1150: Reconstruction of San Miniato (Phase 2)
ca. 1140–1160: Rolando, *Ordo Officioum*, Pisa (*OOP*)
1144: Translation of relics of St. James from Compostella to cathedral, Pistoia
ca. 1150–ca. 1190: Façade of cathedral, Pisa, by Rainaldo

ca. 1160–1164: Johannes Beleth, *Summa de ecclesiasticis officiis*

ca. 1180–ca. 1190: *Ritus in ecclesia servandi,* Florence (Ritus)

1181: Settlement between Opera di Santa Croce, Lucca, and cathedral chapter concerning oblations on high feast days

1190: Settlement between bishop, cathedral, and Opera del Duomo, Siena, concerning oblations on high feast days

1197: Cathedral canons of Pisa elect nine new colleagues without the permission of their bishop

late 12th century: Pseudo-Simplician, *Vita Sancti Zenobii II*

1200

early 13th century: First ordinal of Pistoia (OOPist1)

early 13th century: Sicardo of Cremona, *Mitralis de officiis*

early 13th century: Façade mosaic, San Miniato

ca. 1200–1120: Façade of cathedral, Lucca, by Guidetto

1202: Reduction of cathedral canons, Lucca, to sixteen

1203: Reduction of cathedral canons, Florence, to twelve

1203: Cathedral canons, Arezzo, transfer their residence to San Pietro

1215: Oderigo, *Ordo officiorum ecclesie senensis* (*OOES*)

1219: Reduction of cathedral canons, Arezzo, to fourteen

1227: Reduction of cathedral canons, Pistoia, to twelve

1205–1230: Bishop Giovanni da Velletri, Florence

    Reconsecrates high altar of Santa Reparata over newly enlarged crypt (ca. 1230)

1230–1249: Bishop Ardingo, Florence

    Mores et Consuetudines Canonice Florentine (Mores) (ca. 1231)

    Leges Ardinghi (1231)

ca. 1230: Altarpiece of St. Zenobius, cathedral, Florence, attr. Master of the Bigallo

ca. 1233–1250: Portico of cathedral, Lucca, Guido Bigarelli

1248–1289: Bishop Guglielmino Ubertini, Arezzo

    Capitular constitutions (1263)

ca. 1250–1275: Pulpit, San Cristoforo of Barga, attr. Guido Bigarelli

before 1275: Endowed chaplaincies of St. Augustine and for the magister scholarum, cathedral, Pisa

1276–1300: Bishop Paganello, Lucca

    Capitular constitutions (1281, 1284, 1294)

    Ordo Officiorum of Lucca (ca. 1292) (*OOL*)

†1278: St. Zita of Lucca

1290: Davino endows two chaplaincies at the cathedral of Pistoia

1296: Construction of new cathedral, Florence, begins

1297: Apse mosaic, San Miniato

late 13th century: Second ordinal of Pistoia (OOPist2)

HOLY TREASURE AND SACRED SONG

> Since it was a matter of usefulness to the church, your authority decreed that this way of training in the art of music—for which I am mindful that with God's help I have toiled not in vain—be published. Just as you completed by an exceedingly marvelous plan the church of St. Donatus, the bishop and martyr, whom you protect by the will of God and as his lawful vicar, so likewise by a most honorable and appropriate distinction you would make the ministers of that church beacons for all clerics throughout almost the whole world. In very truth it is sufficiently marvelous and desirable that even boys of your church should surpass in the practice of music the fully trained veterans of all other places; and the height of your honor and merit will be very greatly increased because, though subsequent to the early fathers, such great and distinguished renown for learning has come to this church through you.
>
> —Guido of Arezzo, Dedicatory Letter to Bishop Teodaldo, *Micrologus* (ca. 1023–1036)

I

Introduction

Few musicians cultivated the support of powerful men to greater effect than Guido of Arezzo.[1,2] His dedicatory letter to his *magnum opus*, the *Micrologus*, hails his patron, Bishop Teodaldo of Arezzo (1023–1036), who had welcomed Guido into his entourage after his departure from the Benedictine abbey at Pomposa under a cloud of discontent. Teodaldo was a scion of one of the preeminent families of central and northern Italy, the Canossa, and was himself lord of a large and wealthy bishopric, and key supporter of an influential movement of eremitic monasticism that had taken root in his diocese at the hermitage of Camaldoli. While in this bishop's service, moreover, Guido acquired a supporter of even higher rank, Pope John XIX (1024–1032), who invited him to Rome and endorsed his innovative method of sight-singing. The backing of such prelates as Teodaldo and John was instrumental in encouraging the widespread adoption of Guido's pedagogy, which became the foundation of practical music theory throughout Latin Christendom until the sixteenth century.

---

[1] Joseph Smits van Waesberghe, ed. *Guidonis Aretini Micrologus* (n.p.: American Institute of Musicology, 1955), 82–83: "Qua de re cum de ecclesiasticis utilitatibus ageretur exercitium musicae artis, pro quo favente Deo non incassum desudasse me memini, vestra iussit auctoritas proferri in publicum, ut sicut ecclesiam beatissimi Donati episcopi et martyris, cui Deo auctore iure vicario praesidetis, mirabili nimium schemate peregistis, ita eiusdem ministros ecclesiae honestissimo decentissimoque quodam privilegio cunctis pene per orbem clericis spectabiles redderetis. Et revera satis habet miraculi et optionis, cum vestrae ecclesiae etiam pueri in modulandi studio perfectos aliorum usquequaque locorum superent senes vestrique honoris ac meriti perplurimum cumulabitur celsitudo, cum post priores patres tanta ac talis ecclesiae per vos studiorum provenerit claritudo." Translation after Claude V. Palisca, ed., *Hucbald, Guido, and John on Music*, trans. Warren Babb (New Haven: Yale University Press, 1978), 57–58.

[2] For the most recent evaluation of Guido's career, see Christopher Page, *The Christian West and its Singers: The First Thousand Years* (New Haven: Yale University Press, 2010), 443–464.

If the dedicatory letter to the *Micrologus* acknowledges the debt of a client to his patron, it also underscores the power of holy relics to inspire music and architecture. Teodaldo, we learn, was not only righteous and erudite but also a builder of a magnificent church in which lay the body of St. Donatus. By divine consent, the bishop guarded the basilica and its precious relic even as he spurred its clergy to ever greater virtue. Teodaldo's efforts on behalf of San Donato and its saint provide the artistic and religious context for Guido's education of its choirboys. No religious house demanded expertly trained singers to adorn its solemn liturgy more than a splendid, well-administered church endowed with the body of a saint and overseen by a wise, munificent bishop. Music, Guido implied with a substantial measure of self-interest, was of the upmost importance to the projects of such ambitious prelates as Teodaldo.

Holy Treasure and Sacred Song explores the critical role of the liturgy and its music in the development of medieval relic cults, focusing on the region where Guido spent his most productive years. In Tuscany there flourished vibrant, well-documented cults devoted to local saints, holy men buried in the cathedrals and suburban shrines (*martyria*) of its principal cities. These were products less of spontaneous devotion on the part of the Christian faithful and more of concerted campaigns by ecclesiastic authorities like Teodaldo, campaigns that reflected the political and economic interests of such powerful men. The promotion of a relic cult was a multifaceted project, involving the writing of the saint's hagiography, the building and decoration of his burial church, and the creation of solemn liturgies. Celebrated at his tomb on the saint's feast by the resident clergy of his church, these solemn rites were visual as well as olfactory spectacles due to their ritual gestures, ecclesiastical vestments, and burning incense. Yet at their heart, one must add following Guido, was their plainsong. With its sung rather than recited or spoken texts, this music offered an affecting mode of discourse by which singers recounted the miracles, virtue, and heroism of a saint; exhorted the faithful to venerate him or her; and pleaded for him or her to intercede with God on behalf of their community. At once literary and musical in nature, plainsong was central to the manifold campaigns that rendered the holy men buried in Tuscan churches objects of veneration.

A full and nuanced evaluation of medieval relic cults demands that we consider their artistic, architectural, literary, and liturgical components in light of one another while situating them within their proper historical context. That this holistic approach remains rare reflects boundaries that have often divided musicology from other disciplines. In past decades, music historians have responded to a growing interest in medieval relic cults with numerous case studies of plainsong composed for individual saints.[3] Yet the technical character of most musical analysis ensures that such scholarship makes

---

[3] Exemplary are the essays in Roman Hankeln, ed. *Political Plainchant?: Music, Text, and Historical Context of Medieval Saints' Offices* (Ottawa: Institute of Mediaeval Music, 2009); and Margot E. Fassler and Rebecca A. Baltzer, eds., *The Divine Office in the Latin Middle Ages: Methodology and Source Studies, Regional Developments, Hagiography, Written in Honor of Professor Ruth Steiner* (Oxford: Oxford University Press, 2000), 401–520.

little impact on the broader field of medieval studies.[4] Meanwhile, art, architectural, and ecclesiastical historians have expressed an ever greater interest in the medieval liturgy, but have eschewed its central dimension, its music, owing to the notorious complexity of this medium.[5] The present study bridges this disciplinary divide, developing music-analytic techniques in a manner accessible to nonspecialists and placing the aural riches of the liturgy at the heart of a broader examination of medieval relic cults.

Holy Treasure and Sacred Song comprises two parts that reflect its holistic approach through their divergent focus and organization. Part I presents a historical narrative centered on early medieval bishops like Guido's patron, Teodaldo, who asserted and displayed their authority as "lords and builders" (*domini et constructores*) by establishing the most important relic cults in Tuscany. It concomitantly traces the ascent of cathedral canons from subordinates of the bishop to quasi-independent actors who, by the eleventh century, were able to usurp his role as guardian of local relic cults. Organized chronologically and into case studies focused on individual prelates, part I draws on rich and varied nonmusical evidence—hagiography, charters, and archeology—known to specialists in the relevant disciplines but rarely if ever studied in concert. Examinations of plainsong and ritual punctuate its narrative in order to support its historical arguments and thus make a broader methodological point: the liturgy reflected and reinforced the claims of bishops and canons to their relics, as did the aforementioned literary, legal, and physical sources. The stories of these clerics are not the ones that musicologists are accustomed to tell, but they form a critical entrée into the examination of music, ritual, visual art, and architecture in the second, longer part of this book.

---

[4] There remain, of course, prominent exceptions, including Margot E. Fassler, *The Virgin of Chartres: Making History Through Liturgy and the Arts* (New Haven: Yale University Press, 2010); Susan Rankin, "*Terribilis est locus iste*: The Pantheon in 609," in *Rhetoric Beyond Words*, ed. Mary Carruthers (Cambridge: Cambridge University Press, 2010), 281–310; and Susan Boynton, *Shaping a Monastic Identity: Liturgy and History at the Imperial Abbey of Farfa, 1000-1125* (Ithaca, NY: Cornell University Press, 2006). See also the volume of collected essays, Robert A. Maxwell, ed. *Representing History, 900-1300: Art, Music, History* (University Park: Pennsylvania State University Press, 2010).

[5] Salient examples include Franklin Toker, *On Holy Ground: Liturgy, Architecture, and Urbanism in the Cathedral and the Streets of Medieval Florence* (Turnhout: Brepols, 2009); Augustine Thompson, *Cities of God: The Religion of the Italian Communes, 1125-1325* (University Park: Pennsylvania State University Press, 2005); and Sible De Blaauw, *Cultus et Decor: Liturgia e architettura nella Roma tardoantica e medievale*, trans. Maria Beatrice Annis, 2 ed., 2 vols. (Vatican City: Biblioteca Apostolica Vaticana, 1994). More distant, chronologically and geographically, to the present study but nonetheless exemplary in its use of liturgical evidence is Eamon Duffy, *The Stripping of the Altars: Traditional Religion in England 1400-1580* (New Haven: Yale University Press, 1992). On the architectural setting of the medieval liturgy in general, see Allan Doig, *Liturgy and Architecture from Early Church to the Middle Ages* (Burlington: Ashgate, 2008); and Elizabeth C. Parker, "Architecture as Liturgical Setting," in *The Liturgy of the Medieval Church*, ed. Thomas J. Heffernan and E. Ann Matter (Kalamazoo, MI: Medieval Institute Publications, Western Michigan University, 2001), 273–326.

Part II reveals that cathedral canons employed the liturgy as a means by which to consolidate control of relic cults at the expense of their rivals, including local bishops, monasteries, and civic authorities. Entitled *"Ecclesia Matrix"* (Mother Church) in reference to the feminine image with which the canons replaced the masculine one of lord and builder, part II proceeds thematically rather than chronologically to facilitate substantial yet accessible analyses of three types of evidence. The first is the canons' ordinals and constitutions—collections of liturgical and ecclesiastical prescriptions that give pointed expression to these clerics' desires to amplify their influence by codifying the liturgical traditions of their own churches and imposing them on other religious houses throughout the diocese. The second and third are the liturgies of the Mass and Divine Office, respectively—ones enacted by the canons on the feasts of saints whose relic cults were once associated with early medieval bishops. Part II presents detailed reconstructions of these holy rites in their aural and visual splendor and shows how their plainsong and ritual shaped (and was shaped by) the architecture, sculpture, and altarpieces of the churches in which they unfolded. Moreover, part II uncovers the diverse meanings ascribed to the Mass and Divine Office on these solemn occasions by the clergy and laity who flocked to the cathedral to venerate its holy treasure.

Holy Treasure and Sacred Song concomitantly reevaluates the relative importance of individual Tuscan cities and churches as religious and musical centers. Just as relic cults were rooted in discrete places, so too this book is delimited geographically, yet without adhering to the focus on single cities and institutions characteristic of many studies of medieval and Renaissance music.[6] Instead, its scope includes no fewer than seven Tuscan dioceses, a rarely used comparative approach that yields many benefits (fig. 1.1).[7] This method distinguishes between liturgical practices that were in fact unique to a particular church or diocese and ones that were common to the entire region. It also mitigates against the uneven survival of primary sources by assembling evidence that is much greater than what exists for a single institution. Finally, this regional approach belies the presumed dominance of a city like Florence, which, before becoming a regional

---

[6] On the importance of place in the development of relic cults, see Alan Thacker, *"Loca Sanctorum*: The Significance of Place in the Study of Saints," in *Local Saints and Local Churches in the Early Medieval West*, ed. Alan Thacker and Richard Sharpe (Oxford: Oxford University Press, 2002), 1–43. Tuscany has been particularly well represented by studies on music and place: Frank D'Accone, *A Documentary History of Music at the Florentine Cathedral and Baptistery During the Fifteenth Century*, Ph.D. diss., Harvard University, 1960; Frank D'Accone, *The Civic Muse: Music and Musicians in Siena During the Middle Ages and the Renaissance* (Chicago: Chicago University Press 1997); and Marica S. Tacconi, *Cathedral and Civic Ritual in Late Medieval and Renaissance Florence: The Service-Books of Santa Maria del Fiore* (Cambridge: Cambridge University Press, 2005).

[7] With its regional approach, Jean-François Goudesenne, *Les Offices historiques ou historiae composés pour les fêtes des saints dans la province ecclésiastique de Reims (775-1030)* (Turnhout: Brepols, 2002) provides a rare precedent for the present study.

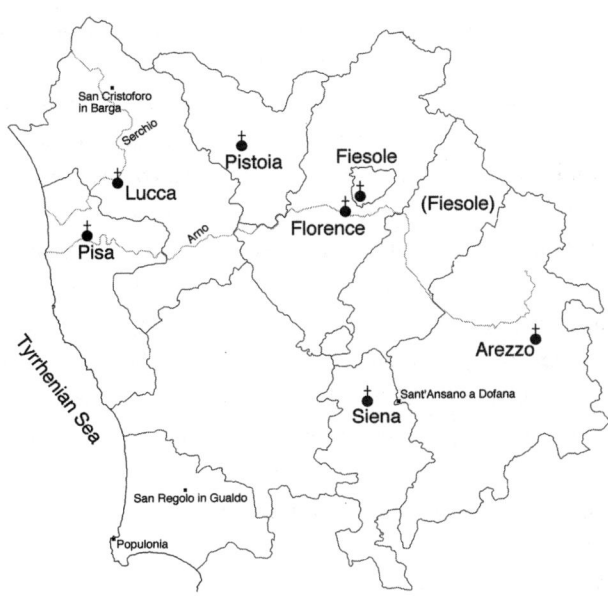

FIGURE I.I. The Dioceses of Medieval Tuscany (after Guidi [1932]).

hegemon, shared the stage with such vital centers as Arezzo and Lucca.[8] As we shall see, all three cities (and not just Florence) supported major relic cults that inspired integrated programs of architecture, hagiography, and liturgy.

If Tuscany offers fertile ground for an interdisciplinary study of relic cults and their liturgies owing to its political prominence and wealth, it also illustrates the role of such cults in fueling alliances and rivalries between cities and churches. One of three Lombard duchies in central and northern Italy, Tuscany became an imperial margravate after Charlemagne's conquest of Italy in 774. With the emergence of autonomous city-states in the late eleventh century, it remained an arena for artistic, cultural, and economic exchange. Writing around 1100, Bishop Rangerio of Lucca captured the sense of civic pride associated with this new political order, as well as the enduring importance of the region as a geographical horizon for its inhabitants. The liturgical traditions of his city, he boasted, were descended from Rome and "unknown to all other churches in Tuscany."[9] Despite such expressions of parochialism, or *campanilismo*, ecclesiastic and

---

[8] The title of Thomas W. Blomquist and Maureen F. Mazzaoui, eds., *The "Other Tuscany": Essays in the History of Lucca, Pisa, and Siena during the Thirteenth, Fourteenth, and Fifteenth Centuries* (Kalamazoo: Medieval Institute Publications, Western Michigan University, 1994) succinctly captures the privileged position of Florence within Tuscan historiography.

[9] *Vita Metrica Sancti Anselmi*, ed. MGH SS, vol. 30, 1171–1172, vv. 706–708: "Contulit et mores festivos et staciones, | Quod non est Tuscis omnibus aecclesiis."

civil authorities were acutely aware of the campaigns enacted by their neighbors in the service of local relic cults. In gestures of emulation or competition, they adopted each others' building practices and liturgical customs to promote their own patron saints.

The diverse institutional and religious character of Tuscan churches, as well as their geographic proximity, provoked such alliances and rivalries between them. *Holy Treasure and Sacred Song* explores a selection of cities and churches based on their historical significance and surviving documentation. It focuses on the three richest bishoprics of the Tuscany—Arezzo, Florence, and Lucca—but draws considerable evidence from their neighbors: Fiesole, Pisa, Pistoia, and Siena (fig. 1.1).[10] This approach yields a geographically cohesive area that comprises the wealthier and more prominent northern half of the region. Its most important institutions were the cathedrals, the sites of the most vibrant relic cults of Tuscany owing to the efforts of early medieval bishops. In this respect, the region contrasts with others in Italy and north of the Alps, where monasteries rivaled, if not outstripped, local bishoprics in temporal and spiritual wealth.[11] Nonetheless significant, however, were the Augustinian canonry of San Frediano (Lucca) and the Benedictine monastery of San Miniato al Monte (Florence). Although their prominence likewise derived from episcopal patronage in the early Middle Ages, these two religious houses subsequently engaged in fierce competition with the canons of their local cathedrals—rivalries that found pointed expression in the liturgies devoted to their relics.

Finally, the horizons of this study extend beyond central Italy to reveal the impact of broader political dynamics on local relic cults and their liturgies. Tuscany derived its considerable significance not only from its wealth of churches but also from its status as an arena of influence from the two preeminent European powers, the Carolingian (and later) Holy Roman Empire on the one hand and Rome on the other. Its strategic position facilitated exchange from both north and south of the Alps: the principal pilgrimage route, the Via Francigena ("Frankish Way"), passed through Lucca and Siena, while a secondary one followed the Via Cassia through Florence and Arezzo.[12] The partnership between the Carolingians and the papacy in the eighth and ninth centuries rendered imperial and papal models of architecture and plainsong complementary if not indistinguishable objects of emulation. Its subsequent dissolution in turn forced Tuscan bishops

---

[10] The relative wealth of the Tuscan bishoprics and cathedral chapters is quantified in the tithes paid by these ecclesiastical foundations in the 1270s: Pietro Guidi, *Tuscia*, 2 vols., vol. 1 (Vatican City: Biblioteca Apostolica Vaticana, 1932).

[11] See, for instance, the abbeys of Farfa and Montecassino, of which the liturgies are treated in Boynton, *Shaping a Monastic Identity;* and Nicola Tangari, ed. *Musica e liturgia a Monatecassino nel medioevo. Atti del Simposio internazionale di studi (Cassino, 9-10 dicembre 2010)* (Rome: Viella, 2012).

[12] Debra J. Birch, *Pilgrimage to Rome in the Middle Ages: Continuity and Change* (Woodbridge, Suffolk, and Rochester, NY: Boydell, 1998), 48. On the Tuscan portion of the Via Francigena in particular, see Stella Patitucci Uggeri, "La via Francigena in Toscana," in *La via Francigena e altre strade della Toscana medievale*, ed. Stella Patitucci Uggeri (Florence: All'Insegna del Giglio, 2004), 9–134.

and canons to signal their loyalty to one party or another. The initial cooperation and subsequent competition between the empire and papacy number among the most important issues of medieval history; however, the effects of these political forces on the liturgy, including textual and melodic features of its plainsong, in territories north of Rome and south of the Alps remain entirely unexplored. In Tuscany, hagiography, architecture, and liturgy became prisms that refracted not only local and regional politics but also competing alliances with the great European powers. Through its interdisciplinary approach and multiple geographical frames, *Holy Treasure and Sacred Song* reveals the diverse shades that colored the literary, artistic, and musical aspects of the rich veneration inspired by medieval relic cults.

PART I
Dominus et Constructor

FEW IF ANY liturgies communicated the dominion of a local bishop over a church and its relics more than the consecration of that house of worship. This solemn rite was codified in a "rule" (*ordo*) preserved in the so-called Romano-German Pontifical (henceforth PRG), a collection of liturgical prescriptions and commentary disseminated throughout the Holy Roman Empire.[1] The rule instructed the bishop to bless the interior of the church before joining the clergy and laity awaiting him at its front door. Together with this assembly, he retrieved the saints' relics, which, according to ancient custom, were the

---

[1] Cyrille Vogel and Reinhard Elze, *Le Pontifical romano-germanique du dixième siècle*, 3 vols. (Vatican City: Biblioteca Apostolica Vaticana, 1963-1972), vol. 1, ch. 40, nos. 126–129, 168–169. The recent research of Henry Parkes calls into question not only the scholarly consensus that traces the origins of the PRG to Mainz in the mid-tenth century but also the extent to which medieval scribes conceived of the PRG as a stable, unified collection of texts as implied by Vogel and Elze's edition. He outlines this second finding in "Questioning the Authority of Vogel and Elze's Pontifical Romano-Germanique," in *Understanding Medieval Liturgy: Essays in Interpretation*, ed. Sarah Hamilton and Helen Gittos (Aldershot: Ashgate, forthcoming). I thank Dr. Parkes for allowing me to read this essay in advance of its publication and for discussing his broader research on the PRG with me. On pontificals in general, see Sarah Hamilton, "The Early Pontificals: The Anglo-Saxon Evidence Reconsidered from a Continental Perspective," in *England and the Continent in the Tenth Century. Studies in Honour of Wilhelm Levison (1876-1947)*, ed. David Rollason, Conrad Leyser, and Hannah Williams (Turnhout: Brepols, 2010), 411–428, who explores the diverse functions and characters of this type of liturgical book with particular reference to the PRG (415–418); as well as Niels Krogh Rasmussen, *Les pontificaux du haut moyen âge: Genèse du livre de l'évêque*, ed. Harcel Maverlas (Leuven: Spicilegium Sacrum Lovaniense, 1998). Dana M. Polanichka, "Transforming Space, (Per)forming Community: Church Consecration in Carolingian Europe" *Viator* 43 (2012), 85–88, illustrates the similarities of this particular *ordo* with earlier ones concerning the consecration of a church. For a broader survey of the liturgical and literary sources for the rite throughout the Middle Ages, see Didier Méhu, "*Historiae et Imagines* de la consécration de l'église au moyen âge," in *Mises en scène et mémoires de la consécration de l'église dans l'occident médiéval*, ed. Didier Méhu (Turnhout: Brepols 2008), 15–48.

sine quibus non of a properly consecrated altar.[2] As they processed around the exterior of the edifice, the clerics sang six chants known as antiphons, with which they enjoined their saints to enter their new home, cast as a New Jerusalem. Meanwhile, the laymen, women, and children responded "Lord have mercy" (*Kyrie eleison*). Finally, the bishop paused to address his flock before entering the church where he was to bury the holy treasure:

> Let [him] talk to the congregation concerning ecclesiastical honor, the peace of those coming and leaving, the tithes and offerings of churches, and also the anniversary of the dedication of this church. Let him announce to both the clergy and to the people in whose honor the church has been constructed and dedicated, and also the names of the saints resting there. Moreover, let the lord and builder (*dominus et constructor*) of this church be advised concerning the endowment of it and the honor and care he ought to show to the priest and to the church.[3]

The consecration of the church was but one of many episcopal rites codified in the PRG, ones that collectively underscored the bishop's centrality to the religious and political administration of the Ottonian dynasty.[4] In this particular moment, the prelate adopted his traditional role as pastor, one emphasized earlier in the rite when he had privately inscribed in ash the Greek and Roman alphabets onto the pavement of the nave. Disposed into two perpendicular lines to form a cross, these letters symbolized the rudiments of holy doctrine. Yet the address to the faithful also cast the bishop as guardian of the treasure of the new church, both its *spiritualia* and *temporalia*. He identified the saints whose relics he proceeded to bury in its altar, thus establishing their patronage

---

[2] The interment of relics as part of the consecration of a church had become a standard practice by sixth century: G. G. Willis, *Further Essays in the Early Roman Liturgy* (London: Society for Promoting Christian Knowledge, 1968), 149–152. Of particular importance was the eighty-third canon, "De falsis memoriis martyrum," of the Fifth Council of Carthage (401), which ruled that all altars or shrines dedicated to martyrs must contain authentic relics of their dedicatees: Giovanni Domenico Mansi, *Sacrorum Conciliorum Nova et Amplissima Collectio*, 31 vols. (Venice: Antonio Zatta, 1759–1798), vol. 3, col. 782. On the significance and enduring influence of this canon throughout the Middle Ages, see Eric Waldram Kemp, *Canonization and Authority in the Western Church* (Oxford: Oxford University Press, 1948), 15 and 39–42, respectively.

[3] Vogel and Elze, *Le Pontifical*, vol. 1, ch. 40, nos. 128–129, 169: "habeat pontifex verbum ad plebem de honore ecclesiastico et de pace venientium ad redeuntium et de decimis vel oblationibus aecclesiarum, ac de anniversaria ipsius aecclesiae dedicatione, et annuntiet tam clero quam populo, in cuius honor constructa et dedicata sit aecclesia vel etiam nomina sanctorum ibi quiescentium. Ipse autem dominus et constructor ipsius ecclesiae ammoneatur de dote illius et qualem honorem vel curam ecclesiae et presbitero exhibere debeat." Translation after Brian V. Repsher, *The Rite of Church Dedication in the Early Medieval Era* (Lewiston, NY: Edwin Mellen, 1998), 169.

[4] Eric Palazzo, "The Image of the Bishop in the Middle Ages," in *The Bishop Reformed: Studies of Episcopal Power and Culture in the Central Middle Ages*, ed. John S. Ott and Anna Trumbore Jones (Aldershot: Ashgate, 2007), 88. Since the fifth century, synodal legislation and papal policy had cast the rite of consecration as the exclusive purview of local bishops: Willis, *Further Essays*, 142–144.

over the new edifice. The bishop likewise provided for the material well-being of the church: its coffers were to remain full, he decreed, by the requisite tithes and oblations, and it was to be maintained with the continued support of the lay lord who had built it. The *ordo* of consecration in the PRG applied to any church, from a modest chapel to a large cathedral; however, the bishop was almost invariably the lord and builder in the case that the edifice was to serve as his seat.

The bishop's role as *dominus et constructor* is the central theme of part I of this study and, as most literate Tuscans knew, had originated in late Antiquity, when prelates throughout the Roman Empire distinguished themselves as patrons of church building.[5] Among the most celebrated of such builders were the popes who had founded and decorated churches throughout Rome after the cessation of Christian persecution and had established a model of patronage for their papal successors through the central Middle Ages. Such munificence was chronicled in the official papal biographies, the *Liber pontificalis*, of which one of the earliest extant copies was produced at the episcopal scriptorium in Lucca between 787 and 816.[6] Of equal renown was St. Ambrose (†397), who had built three basilicas in the suburbs of Milan, including his burial church, the Basilica Ambrosiana.[7] Memory of him remained particularly strong in Florence, as he had founded that city's first cathedral, San Lorenzo.[8] For episcopal builders of medieval Tuscany, such Roman and Milanese prelates had set a venerable precedent.

Yet more obscure, local bishops joined these widely known figures as models for subsequent lords and builders in their particular dioceses. In Italy as throughout western

---

[5] Claudia Rapp, *Holy Bishops in Late Antiquity: The Nature of Christian Leadership in an Age of Transition* (Berkeley: University of California Press, 2005), 220–223; and Peter Brown, *Power and Persuasion in Late Antiquity: Towards a Christian Empire* (Madison: University of Wisconsin Press, 1992), 120–121.

[6] Louis Duchesne and Cyrille Vogel, eds., *Le Liber pontificalis*, 2nd ed., 3 vols. (Paris: E. de Boccard, 1955), vol. 1, no. 34, 170 ff., trans. Raymond Davis, *The Book of Pontiffs (Liber Pontificalis): The Ancient Biographies of the First Ninety Roman Bishops at AD 715*, 3rd ed. (Liverpool: Liverpool University Press, 2010), 14 ff. Davis (xxvii–xli) surveys the building projects ascribed to popes in the fourth and early fifth centuries. BCL, 490, fols. 137–160v (787–800), preserves the first ninety chapters of the *Liber pontificalis* (through the pontificate of Pope Constantine [708–715]), and fols. 161–210 (795–816) the subsequent seven chapters (through that of Pope Hadrian I [772–795]). On the dating and contents of the manuscript, see Luigi Schiaparelli, *Il codice 490 della Biblioteca Capitolare di Lucca e la scuola scrittoria lucchese (sec. VIII-IX)* (Vatican City: Biblioteca Apostolica Vaticana: 1924), 1–20, whose findings are summarized and supported in Amadeo Petrucci, "Il codice n. 490 della Biblioteca Capitolare di Lucca: Un problema di storia della cultura medievale ancora da risolvere," *Actum Luce* 2 (1973): 160–162.

[7] Neil B. McLynn, *Ambrose of Milan: Church and Court in a Christian Capital* (Berkeley: University of California Press, 1994), 226–237.

[8] Paulinus, *Vita Sancti Ambrosii* (BHL 377), ed. PL, vol. 14, no. 29, col. 37; cf. Anna Benvenuti, "Stratigrafie della memoria: Scritture agiographiche e mutamenti architettonici nella vicenda del 'Complesso cattedrale' fiorentino," in *Il bel San Giovanni e Santa Maria del Fiore: Il centro religioso di Firenze dal tardo antico al Rinascimento*, ed. Domenico Cardini (Florence: Le lettere, 1996), 110. On Ambrose's Florentine residence in general, see Carlo Nardi, "La fortuna di Ambrogio nelle memorie medioevali di Zanobi, vescovo di Firenze," in *Le radici cristiane di Firenze*, ed. Anna Benvenuti, Franco Cardini, and Elena Giannarelli (Florence: Aliena, 1994), 77–116.

Christendom, the construction of tombs and churches, and the consecration of such monuments, were crucial events in depicting prelates as protectors of ecclesiastical treasure, both temporal and spiritual. As related in chapter 2, Tuscan bishops of the eighth and ninth centuries reshaped the topography of their cities by translating (or transferring) relics from suburban or rural shrines to urban basilicas, typically the cathedral. According to literary accounts, these occasions provoked joyous celebration marked by the singing of psalms, hymns, and other musical praises of the sort later prescribed in the PRG. Moreover, translations of relics underscored bishops' authority in two ways: first, by showcasing their prerogative to exhume and rebury holy treasure; and second, by enriching cathedrals at the expense of extramural sites. If the bishop's seat was to become a magnificent treasury of *spiritualia*, it would surely attract pilgrims who would fill its coffers with donations. Finally, early medieval bishops of Tuscany embraced the role of the ambitious builder in the mold of their late Antique predecessors, as well as that of valiant defenders of ecclesiastical wealth. Hence, they grounded their achievements in the legendary histories of their individual cities in addition to the precedents set by the celebrated bishops of Rome and Milan. In so doing, these local prelates often acquired an aura of holiness in the manner of their saintly precursors, thus entering the holy pantheon of their respective dioceses.

From the ninth through the early twelfth century, the development and finally the decline of the role of Tuscan bishops as *domini et constructores* was equally important in shaping local relic cults and, by extension, their liturgies. Chapters 3 and 4 focus on the relationships between these prelates and the chapters of canons resident at their cathedrals. Because these communities took as their primary duty the veneration of saints buried in these churches, they were often responsible for documenting the activities of the related episcopal lord and builders via the writing of legal or hagiographic texts (of which more will be said presently). In so doing, canons evinced a range of attitudes toward such bishops. They remembered most of these prelates as virtuous founders, protectors, and reformers of their chapters. But others they condemned as rapacious bishops who joined unscrupulous laymen in usurping their capitular patrimony, on which rested the canons' increasing autonomy. Among the upright bishops, the most significant were loyal clients of the Ottonian emperors who rebuilt their cathedrals and other basilicas in the decades around 1000. These treasuries of holy relics belonged to the "white mantle of churches" that, according to the oft-cited chronicler, Rodulfus Glaber, enveloped France and Italy at the millennium.[9] By the end of the eleventh century, however, the rise of monastic and papal reformers, as well as of the civic governments known as communes, resulted in the eclipse of local bishops as translators of relics and builders of churches.

The scope and character of part I of *Holy Treasure and Sacred Song* is shaped by its function as a historical entrée into the analysis of music, ritual, art, and architecture in part II. Rather than providing a comprehensive account of episcopal authority and patronage in

---

[9] Rodulfus Glaber, *The Five Books of the Histories*, trans. John France (Oxford, 1989), bk. 3, ch. 4, no. 13, 117.

early medieval Tuscany, it focuses on bishops associated with the cults that inspired the most prominent and distinctive liturgies in the region.[10] The narratives of episcopal power told in part I, moreover, illustrate and inflect but do not substantially recast broader historical themes familiar to medievalists of various disciplines. For instance, chapter 3 shows that the cults of St. Donatus of Arezzo and St. Minias of Florence acquired imperial associations due to the fealty of their episcopal promoters to the empire. This particular discovery illustrates that the veneration of relics acquired political subtexts and explains the similarities in the devotion to these two saints. Moreover, it illuminates important literary and musical characteristics of the plainsong composed for them, including their shared "post-Gregorian" melodic style discussed in chapter 7. Recognizing the political affinities in the cults of St. Donatus and St. Minias, however, does not alter the current scholarly perception of imperial influence in central and northern Italy and is not intended to do so. Part I of *Holy Treasure and Sacred Song* presents an independent historical narrative that draws selectively on liturgical evidence to support its claims; however, it serves first and foremost to contextualize the liturgical analyses in part II.

The diverse, nonmusical sources treated in part I mirrors its predominantly historical (rather than musicological) concerns. Little of medieval Tuscan cathedrals stands today, although physical evidence recovered by archeologists and architectural historians enables the tentative reconstruction of the spaces that served as treasuries for relics and stages for the related liturgies. The production and preservation of such legal texts as charters and capitularies were crucial to the formation of successful religious houses and witness the evolving relationships among bishops, cathedral chapters, and their lay patrons.[11] Equally if not more relevant are the Lives (*vitae*) and Passions (*passiones*) of the holy men buried in Tuscany, the accounts of their postmortem transfer from one grave to another (*translationes*), and sermons written in commemoration of such events.[12] Lives and Passions first appeared in late Antiquity and were written (and rewritten) throughout the Middle Ages; however, Translations emerged as a distinct genre only in the eighth century and were less often subject to revision.[13] Although the dating and authorship of such hagiography in Tuscany as elsewhere is often notoriously

---

[10] For a broader survey of episcopal building in medieval Tuscany, see Romano Silva, "*Dilexi decorem domus tuae*: Il ruolo dell'episcopato nello sviluppo dell'architettura in Toscana dall'XI secolo alla prima metà del XII," *Arte medievale* 10 (1996): 23–38.

[11] Cf. Julia Smith, "*Aedificatio Sancti Loci*: The Making of a Ninth-Century Holy Place," in *Topographies of Power in the Early Middle Ages*, ed. Mayke De Jong, Frans Theuws, and Carine Van Rhijn (Leiden: Brill, 2001), 361–396, which provides an exemplary case study of the role of charters and related forms of written documentation in the establishment and expansion of a Carolingian monastery.

[12] Thus the terms "life," "martyrdom," and "translation" refer to the lived experience, execution, and transfer of relics attributed to a saint. By contrast, the capitalized "Life," "Passion," and "Translation," or the Latin *vita*, *passio*, and *translatio*, denote their respective literary accounts.

[13] Patrick J. Geary, *Furta Sacra: Thefts of Relics in the Central Middle Ages*, 2nd ed. (Princeton, NJ: Princeton University Press, 1990), 10–12.

difficult to establish, it is usually ascribable to a member of the bishop's household or to one belonging to the religious house (usually the cathedral chapter) that oversaw the cult of the saint in question.

Hagiography yields particularly rich and manifold insights into the sacred history of its cathedrals, cities, and dioceses. Lives, Passions, and Translations are highly formulaic texts, employing literary topoi intended to illustrate their subject's sanctity rather than a precise historical reality. If historians have rightly emphasized the literary character of such narratives, they have also, quite justifiably, treated them as historical documents, albeit highly stylized ones, which illuminate both the moments in which their narratives occur and those in which they were actually written.[14] The Passion of St. Alexander, Bishop of Fiesole (†823), illustrates the challenges associated with such texts. Perhaps written in 966 in connection with the establishment of the cathedral chapter of Fiesole, it relates St. Alexander's murder on account of his staunch defense of ecclesiastical property, the looting of his first grave, and the building of a second, magnificent tomb for him immediately thereafter.[15] Like many *vitae* and *passiones* of Carolingian saints, the Passion underscores the importance of protecting ecclesiastical treasure, a theme of crucial relevance to the formation of the cathedral chapter of Fiesole in the 960s. Nevertheless, it also remains the only surviving account of the establishment of St. Alexander's cult under the auspices of his successor, Romano, and is thus an invaluable witness to the events that transpired one hundred and thirty years before its probable writing. Although the author of this text undoubtedly invented or borrowed some of its details, he was surely intent on producing a narrative that was plausible to its present and future readers.

The most important of such readers were bishops and cathedral canons, who, from the mid-eleventh century, preserved their Lives, Passions, and Translations in hagiographic lectionaries (or passionaries) similar to the "Giant Bibles" widely produced in this period.[16] They placed these large and (often) sumptuously illuminated books alongside

---

[14] While Geary, *Furta Sacra*, 9–15, distinguishes between the relative historicity of Passions, Lives, and Translations in general, his *Living with the Dead in the Middle Ages* (Ithaca, NY: Cornell University Press, 1994), 9–29, surveys and critiques historians' treatment of hagiographical texts since the mid-1960s. The historical literature on medieval hagiography is vast, but see in particular the recent case study, Samantha Kahn Herrick, "Studying Apostolic Hagiography: The Case of Fronto of Périgeux, Disciple of Christ," *Speculum* 85 (2010): 235–270. Chris Wickham, *The Inheritance of Rome: A History of Europe from 400 to 1000* (London: Penguin 2009), presents a general history of late Antiquity and the early Middle Ages that likewise makes frequent use of saints' Lives as historical documents.

[15] See chapter 2, on the events related in the *Passio Sancti Alexandri*, and chapter 3, on its plausible authorship in the tenth century.

[16] Charles Buchanan, "Spiritual and Spatial Authority in Medieval Lucca: Illuminated Manuscripts, Stational Liturgy and the Gregorian Reform," *Art History* 27 (2004): 729–732. On the diverse impetus behind the production of Giant Bibles, see Lila Yawn, "The Italian Giant Bible, Lay Patronage and Professional Workmanship (11th-12th centuries)," in *Les usages sociaux de la Bible, XIE-XVE siècles* (Paris: Laboratoire de Médiévistique Occidentale de Paris, 2011), 162–255.

their charters in their libraries for safekeeping. Despite the differences between hagiographic and legal texts, part I shows that both served to support the claims of the local clergy to its property, whether it be holy relics buried in the cathedral or the lands belonging to the bishopric or chapter. Equally important, in the absence (with but one exception) of the sort of chronicles written for and about monastic institutions, both were key vehicles for the creation and preservation of institutional memory. The canons emerge as the crucial actors in the telling and perpetuation of the early histories of their churches and relics, but the protagonists of their narratives were almost invariably local bishops such as St. Alexander.

Nevertheless, the relevance of medieval hagiography, Tuscan and otherwise, exceeds the concerns of ecclesiastical historians owing to its function as a literary source for sacred art and the liturgy. The most extravagant hagiographic lectionaries, for instance, feature illuminated initials depicting the protagonists of their texts (e.g. figs. 2.2 and 6.6). Likewise directly inspired by hagiography, we shall learn, are the scenes from the lives of St. Martin, St. Regulus, and St. Zenobius depicted in the sculptural reliefs at the cathedral of Lucca (figs. 6.2, 6.3, 6.4 and 7.4) and the altarpiece of that of Florence (fig. 7.3). Their diverse media notwithstanding, each of these images emphasizes or modifies certain aspects of their saint's biography in ways that served the interests of the bishops, canons, and/or other clerics who oversaw that saint's cult. Finally, hagiographic lectionaries not only were compendia intended for the edification of clerical readers but also, as their modern title indicates, divided their texts into lessons to be recited at the night office on the appropriate feast.[17] Indeed, the ties of such text to the liturgy went even further, for, as shown in part II, portions of the text were set to music and chanted on the aforementioned feasts. Much like the illuminators, sculptors, and painters of the aforementioned works of visual art, the canons and other clerics who composed such plainsong excerpted and edited the Lives and Passions according to the concerns of their religious communities.

Like the hagiography on which it draws, part I of *Holy Treasure and Sacred Song* is intended as an exercise in textual *aedificatio* in the dual sense of the term.[18] As *vitae* and *passiones* served to educate (or edify) their readers by telling the tales of saints, so part I aims to introduce a diverse, interdisciplinary audience to the stories of those bishops, the lords and builders, who established the most significant relic cults in Tuscany. As

---

[17] During the Merovingian period, the Frankish clergy commonly recited hagiography to largely illiterate lay audiences at Mass or other public services. From the eighth century, by contrast, such literature evidently catered to a more circumscribed, clerical readership. See Katrein Heene, "Audire, legere, vulgo: An Attempt to Define Public Use and Comprehensibility of Carolingian Hagiography," in *Latin and the Romance Languages in the Early Middle Ages*, ed. Roger Wright (University Park: Pennsylvania State University Press, 1996), 147–149.

[18] On the term, "textual *aedificatio*," see Smith, "*Aedificatio Sancti Loci*," 262–263.

hagiography was the literary foundation for visual and liturgical expressions of veneration associated with such cults, moreover, so part I lays the historical groundwork for the analyses of plainsong and ritual in part II. In so doing, it aims to capture a measure of the dramatic flair and evocative detail with which medieval hagiographers wrote of their saints.

2

The Bishop's Relics, 752–899

NO CASE FROM Tuscany more succinctly illustrates the purview of bishops over holy relics than the dispute between the dioceses of Arezzo and Siena. On 19 May 752, Pope Stephen II (752–757) issued a bull to Bishop Stabile of Arezzo in which he recounted the longstanding controversy over churches situated in the latter's diocese but in the political territory of Siena.[1] In 715, the rectors of these contested foundations had testified before a notary, sent by King Liutprand (712–744), that their churches in fact belonged to the Aretine and not the Sienese diocese.[2] Liutprand's ruling in favor of Arezzo, however, did not end the dispute: during the pontificate of Zachary (741–752), a Sienese gastald named Guasperto had built an altar in one of the contested churches, Sant'Ansano, located in the village of Dofana just east of Siena (fig. 1.1). Without Stabile's knowledge much less his presence, Guasperto had moved the body of the titular saint from an old altar to the new one, which he had compelled Bishop Ansifredo of Siena, under threat of violence, to consecrate. Zachary had condemned this infringement of canon law and had convened the bishops of nearby Città di Castello, Volterra, and Clusina (present-day San Casciano dei Bagni), before whom Ansifredo, after some denial, had admitted his offense. Having related this tortured story, Pope Stephen concluded his own bull by

---

[1] Ubaldo Pasqui, *Documenti per la storia della città di Arezzo nel medio evo*, 4 vols. (Florence: G.P. Vieusseux, 1899, 1904, 1916, and 1937), vol. 1, no. 11, 26–27 (19 May 752). On Stephen's bull and the broader controversy between Arezzo and Siena, see Alfredo Maroni, *Prime comunità cristiane e strade romane nei territori di Arezzo—Siena—Chiusi (dalle origine al secolo VIII)*, 3rd ed. (Siena: Cantagalli, 2001), 270–280; Jean Delumeau, *Arezzo: Espace et sociétés, 715-1230* (Rome: École française de Rome, 1996), vol. 1, 475–487; and Diana Webb, *Patrons and Defenders: The Saints in the Italian City-States* (London: Tauris Academic Studies, 1996), 37–39.
[2] Pasqui, *Documenti*, vol. 1, no. 5, 9–17 (20 June 715).

confirming the judgments of both Liutprand and Zachary: Sant'Ansano was to remain under the jurisdiction of the Aretine bishop.

The perceived gravity of Guasperto's crime reflected less the importance of St. Ansanus in particular and more the conviction that the right to translate any saint belonged exclusively to the local bishop. Ansanus was a Roman who had fled his native city during the Great Persecution (ca. 303–313) and had briefly preached in Siena before his execution in nearby Dofana. It was little wonder that such a civil authority as Guasperto wished to honor the local martyr by burying him in a new, more magnificent altar: through his heroic sacrifice, the latter tied the sacred history of Siena to that of the Eternal City. By the eighth century, however, the translation of relics had become the primary means by which local bishops officially recognized a saint's holiness and provided new momentum to his cult, all in an age before the papacy reserved for itself the right of canonization.[3] Equally relevant, the privilege of consecrating an altar had for centuries belonged to the prelate in whose diocese it was located.[4] Thus Guasperto elicited the opprobrium of two popes for having denigrated the episcopal office by disregarding the jurisdiction of the Aretine bishop and by compelling the Sienese to consecrate the new altar. Meanwhile, Ansifredo of Siena and Stabile of Arezzo emerge as exemplars of episcopal vice and virtue, the former a weak and equivocating bishop, the latter an assertive one tirelessly defending the prerogatives of his office.

If the Aretines were justifiably outraged by Guasperto's disregard for contemporary norms of ecclesiastical jurisdiction, the Sienese were surely infuriated by such "foreign" jurisdiction over Sant'Ansano and its titular saint. The relative wealth of relics buried in other Tuscan dioceses could have only added injury to insult. The Aretines claimed the protection of their own evangelizer, St. Donatus, likewise a Roman who had fled the persecutions of Julian the Apostate (†363) and was buried outside their city walls. Other cities in the region claimed the relics of early evangelizers who were natives such as Sts. Minias and Zenobius of Florence and St. Romulus of Fiesole, although the latter was later recast by local clerics as a Roman apostle of St. Peter whose very name evoked the legendary founder of the Eternal City.[5] Lucca, by contrast, would come to venerate the relics of two foreigners who had come to Tuscany in the sixth century: St. Fridian was an Irish pilgrim elected bishop of Lucca and St. Regulus was an archbishop who fled the Vandal conquest of North Africa only to find equally vicious antagonists, the Ostrogoths, in Tuscany. This wealth of relics in nearby cities made their absence in Siena all the more conspicuous and likely encouraged Pope Stephen to grant Bishop

---

[3] Eric Waldram Kemp, *Canonization and Authority in the Western Church* (Oxford: Oxford University Press, 1948), 29. Carolingian legislation of the ninth century would confirm local bishops' monopoly over the translation of relics: Martin Heinzelmann, *Translationsberichte und andere Quellen des Reliquienkultes* (Turnhout: Brepols, 1979), 36.

[4] See introduction to part I, n. 4, this volume.

[5] On this revision of St. Romulus's dossier in the eleventh century, see chapter 3, this volume.

Ansifredo relics of another young martyr. St. Crescentius was a Roman contemporary of St. Ansanus buried just outside the Eternal City on the Via Salaria.[6] Anticipating the translations of relics *intra muros* in the late eighth and ninth centuries, Ansifredo deposited such treasure in his church within the confines of the city walls and thus safe from claims of neighboring bishoprics.[7]

These saints emerged not only as protagonists in the legendary history of their respective dioceses but also as powerful models for local Tuscan prelates. All were men and many were bishops who embodied virtues associated with their ecclesiastical office. According to their Lives and Passions, they were zealous evangelizers, defenders of Christian orthodoxy, compassionate healers, upright administrators, and protectors of their flock. Early medieval bishops were further encouraged to follow the conduct of their holy predecessors due to the common location of the respective graves of these saints. In Tuscany as throughout western Christendom, and in accordance with the pattern established by the Roman catacombs, early Christian bishops and martyrs alike lay outside the city walls. And just as popes had been buried at the suburban basilica of St. Peter's in Rome since the late seventh century, so Tuscan bishops favored such extramural martyria as their own gravesites.[8] The church situated below Fiesole and toward its neighbor, Florence, was exemplary (fig. 2.1). Dedicated to St. Peter, it was "decorated with the honor of many saints and distinguished with the tombs of many bishops."[9] These prelates formed an episcopal lineage that purportedly stretched back to late Antiquity and thus their martyrium was the natural choice as the bishop's seat. The arrangement of an extramural cathedral likewise characterized Arezzo, Florence, and perhaps other Tuscan dioceses, although from the ninth century, as related later, local bishops favored urban churches.[10] Due to

---

[6] The translation of St. Crescentius to Siena coincided with the earliest acquisitions of Roman relics by Frankish collectors north of the Alps: Julia M. H. Smith, "Old Saints, New Cults: Roman Relics in Carolingian Francia," in *Early Medieval Rome and the Christian West: Essays in Honour of Donald A. Bullough*, ed. Julia M. H. Smith (Leiden: Brill, 2000), 321–322, 335.

[7] *Passio Sancti Crescentius* (BHL 1986), ed. *AS* September, vol. 4, 353. The date of St. Crescentius's translation to Siena has been a point of debate since the sixteenth century. Ferdinando Ughelli, *Italia Sacra*, 8 vols. (Rome: Bernardino Tano, 1644–1662), vol. 3, col. 540, argued that it had occurred under Pope Stephen IX in 1058. That the only Sienese bishop known to have been named Ansifredo is the eighth-century prelate in question makes him the likely instigator of the Crescentius translation: Franca Ela Consolino, "Un martire 'Romano': Crescenzio," *Bullettino senese di storia patria* 97 (1990): 47–48.

[8] Franz Alto Bauer, "La frammentazione liturgica nella chiesa romana del primo medioevo," *Rivista di Archeologia Cristiana* 75 (1999): 401–406.

[9] "Predictus locus multorum sanctorum remanserat honore decoratus, multorumque episcoporum tumulis insignitus," quoted from the diploma of 27 March 1028 of Bishop Jacopo of Fiesole, ed. Ughelli, *Italia Sacra*, vol. 3, col. 224, on which see chapter 3, this volume. Jean-Charles Picard, *Le Souvenir des évêques: Sépultures, listes épiscopales et culte des évêques en Italie du Nord des origines au Xe siècle* (Rome: École Française de Rome, 1988), 271–325, 388–391, surveys the broader phenomenon of episcopal burial at extramural martyria.

[10] Scholars long viewed the extramural cathedral as the norm in early medieval Italy, as seen in Cinzio Violante and Cosimo Damiano Fonesca, "Ubicazione e dedicazione delle cattedrali dalle origini al periodo romanico nelle città dell'Italia centro-settentrionale," in *Il romanico pistoiese nei suoi rapporti con l'arte*

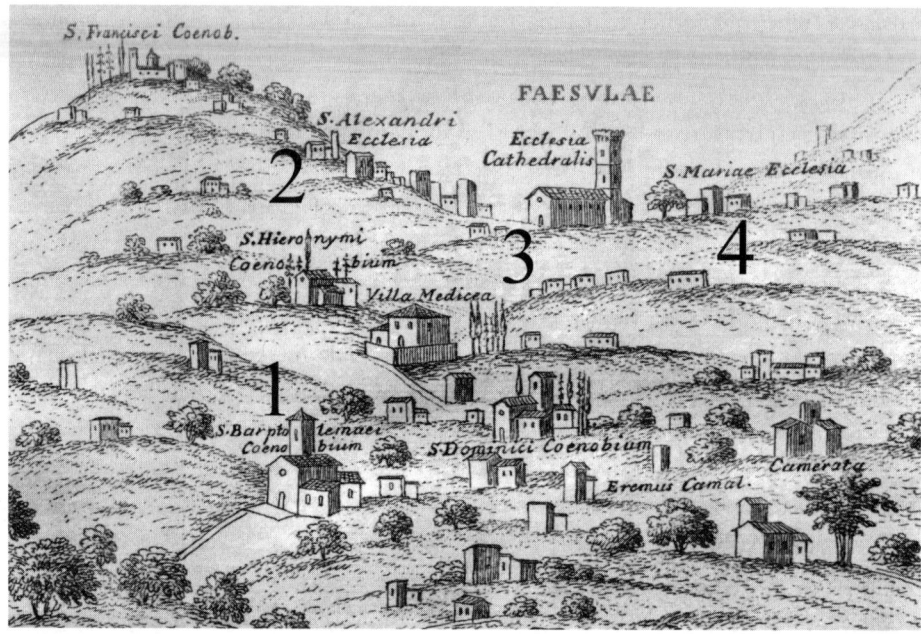

FIGURE 2.1. Fiesole viewed from the northern suburbs of Florence ca. 1520 (from Lami [1758]). 1 = the old cathedral of Fiesole (San Pietro/San Romolo/San Bartolomeo). 2 = San Pietro in Gerusalemme/San Alessandro. 3 = the new cathedral of Fiesole (San Romolo). 4 = Santa Maria.

their exemplarity in life and proximity in death, local saints were a primary source of emulation for Tuscan bishops.

Whether or not they served as his seat, extramural martyria offered the bishop a potentially lucrative source of revenue in the form of oblations from visitors traveling from near and far. Early-medieval Lives and Passions typically concluded with a brief allusion to their protagonist's postmortem miracles, which not only attracted pilgrims but also were the impetus for the construction of small churches at their graves.[11] Unusually detailed in this respect was the Passion of St. Regulus, a "cephalophore" who, according to the narrative conventions of this holy type, chose his own resting place after

---

romanica dell'Occidente. Atti del primo convegno internazionale di studi medioevali di storia e d'arte, Pistoia, Montecatini Terme, 27 settembre-3 ottobre 1964 (Pistoia: Ente provinciale per il turismo, 1966), 303–346. Nevertheless, more recent archeological evidence reveals that urban cathedrals were in fact equally if not more prevalent: P. Testini, G. Cantino Wataghin, and L. Pani Ermini, "La cattedrale in Italia," in *Actes du XI Congrès international d'archéologie chrétienne* (Rome: École française de Rome, 1989), 5–229. For instance, in such cities as Lucca and Pisa, the cathedral had always stood within the old Roman walls.

[11] See, for instance, the brief mention of the "many benefits" available at the grave of St. Ansanus: *Passio Sancti Ansani* (BHL 515), in Giovanni Domenico Mansi, ed. *Stephani Baluzii Tutelensis Miscellanea*, 4 vols. (Lucca: Vincentius Junctinius, 1761), vol. 4, 63. The *Vita Sancti Fridiani I*, ch. 8.3 (BHL 3177b), in Gabriele Zaccagnini, *Vita Sancti Fridiani: Contributi di storia e di agiografia lucchese medievale* (Lucca: Fazzi, 1989), 184, includes a similar notice of the "miracles" that unfolded at its subject's extramural tomb.

his decapitation. He picked up his head and carried it two hundred and fifty paces to a site near the old Etruscan city of Populonia on the southern coast of Tuscany. Having discovered him, his disciples cried, "Arise, arise, holiest father, that we might be able to bury your body in a place of your choosing," to which St. Regulus obliged by selecting a site a stone's throw away.[12] His burial in turn occasioned a second miracle: one of his executioners visited the grave in search of respite from a demon, which the saint mercifully banished. This act of clemency, noted his Passion, inspired the local populace to build an oratory that soon attracted pilgrims in search of relief for their own afflictions, as news of this and subsequent miracles spread.[13] The offerings made to such a martyr in return for his intercession with God provided local bishops with great incentive to exercise their dominion through the translation of relics and the construction of new, more magnificent burial churches.

The most prominent examples of lords and builders in early medieval Tuscany come from Lucca, Fiesole, and Florence. In the first city, as related below, Bishop Giovanni I (780–800) was an enterprising acquirer of holy relics who self-consciously followed the venerable precedents of relic translation and church building set by bishops in such disparate locales as Rome, Milan, and Tours. In so doing, he deftly navigated shifting political landscapes as his city adjusted to its newfound status under Carolingian dominion. In Fiesole and Florence, by contrast, three bishops—St. Alexander (†823), St. Donatus (829–876), and Andrea (869–893)—responded to rising insecurity engendered by local and foreign marauders by becoming defenders of ecclesiastical *spiritualia* and *temporalia*. Hagiographic texts reveal in a detailed if stylized manner that such diverse impulses drove Bishop Giovanni of Lucca and Bishop Andrea of Florence to the same course of action: the translation of relics from extramural shrines to intramural cathedrals. In so doing, these two prelates not only emerged as protagonists in the sacred history of their dioceses, as did St. Alexander and St. Donatus of Fiesole, but also established urban cults that inspired sumptuous liturgical commemorations later, in the central Middle Ages.

---

[12] *Passio Sancti Reguli*, ch. 8 (*BHL* 7102), in Manlio Simonetti, "Note sulla tradizione agiografica di S. Regolo di Populonia," in *Atti del convegno "Il Paleocristiano nella Tuscia," Viterbo, Palazzo dei Papi, 16-19 giugno 1979* (Viterbo: Consorzio per la gestione delle bibliotheche comunale degli ardenti e provinciale "Anselmo Anselmi," 1981), 124: "Surge, surge, sanctissime pater, ut in loco voluntatis tuae valeamus tuum sepellire cadaver."

[13] *Passio Sancti Reguli*, ch. 9, in Simonetti, "Note sulla tradizione," 124–125. Cf. the *Passio Sancti Cerbonii* (*BHL* 1728), *AS* October, vol. 5, col. 81, which omits such postmortem miracles and notes only that St. Regulus's disciples, St. Cerbonius and Felix, "extraordinarily" buried him after his execution. On the figure of the cephalophore in medieval hagiography, see Adele Simonetti, "Santi cefalofori altomedievali," *Studi medievali* 28 (1987): 67–121; and Edmund Colledge and J. C. Marler, "*Céphalologie*: A Recurring Theme in Classical and Medieval Lore," *Traditio* 37 (1981): 411–426. Scott B. Montgomery, "*Mittite capud meum. . . ad matrem meam ut osculetur eum*: The Form and Meaning of the Reliquary Bust of Saint Just," *Gesta* 36 (1997): 62, n. 40, provides further bibliography on the subject.

THE POLITICS OF RELIC CULTS: BISHOP GIOVANNI I OF LUCCA

The exemplary *dominus et constructor* of early medieval Tuscany was Bishop Giovanni, whose immortalization in the liturgies of his favored saints, Regulus and Fridian, secured him the exalted status in the ecclesiastical history of his city. Three historical conditions, which are outlined in this and the subsequent three paragraphs, made Lucca particularly fertile ground for the rise of such an ambitious lord and builder. The first lay in the history of that city during the previous two centuries. In 713, King Liutprand had initiated the dramatic expansion of ecclesiastical patrimony throughout Italy by legalizing pious donations to the church.[14] Lucca was a major (and unusually well-documented) beneficiary of the new legislation by virtue of its political prominence as the capital of the Lombard Duchy of Tuscany.[15] Two hundred and fifty years later, Bishop Rangerio of Lucca judged the sixth-century episcopate of St. Fridian to have been his city's golden age, a claim that can be traced back to the saint's first Life. Composed sometime before the eighth century, this *vita* was exceptional among early Tuscan hagiography for depicting its subject as a builder of churches, including the extramural basilica, San Frediano, which became St. Fridian's resting place.[16] Yet Rangerio also described a second, silver age, one evocative of the eighth and early ninth centuries, when clerical and lay patronage funded the construction and restoration of at least twenty-five churches in Lucca and its diocese: "The Lucchese populace exhibited a certain honor of light [*lux*] in their acts, on which account they have their name. The clergy and populace, joined as if mind to body, aspired to sanctify its streets."[17] The implied image of wholesale urban renewal is misleading, as the broader fabric of early-medieval Lucca and cities throughout Italy remained poor by the standards of the preceding and subsequent periods.[18] Yet the disposition

---

[14] Chris J. Wickham, *Early Medieval Italy: Central Power and Local Society 400-1000* (Totowa, NJ: Barnes & Noble, 1981), 43.

[15] Duane J. Osheim, *An Italian Lordship: The Bishopric of Lucca in the Late Middle Ages* (Berkeley: University of California Press, 1977), 10-15, traces the expansion of episcopal territories in eighth-century Lucca, while Susan Wood, *The Proprietary Church in the Medieval West* (Oxford: Oxford University Press, 2006), 48-65, examines the patterns of land grants throughout Lombard Italy. Finally, Bryan Ward-Perkins, *From Classical Antiquity to the Middle Ages: Urban Public Building in Northern and Central Italy, AD 300-850* (Oxford: Oxford University Press, 1984), 51-84, surveys the construction of Italian churches from the fourth to the mid-ninth century.

[16] *Vita Sancti Fridiani I*, ch. 2, no. 4 (on St. Fridian's architectural projects in general) and ch. 8, no. 3 (on San Frediano), in Zaccagnini, *Vita*, 159 and 184.

[17] "Sic populus quondam Lucensis lucis honorem, | Ex quo nomen habet, actibus exhibuit. | Clerus cum populo quasi mens cum corpore iuncta | Certabant proprias sanctificare vias." Rangerio recounted the golden and silver ages of his city in the rhymed Life (*BHL* 540) devoted to his predecessor, Bishop Anselmo II of Lucca (1073-86), in MGH SS, vol. 30, 1249, vv. 4373-4428. The present quotation derives from vv. 4425-4428. The precise number of twenty-five churches comes not from Rangerio but, rather, from the surviving charters of the eighth and ninth centuries: Ward-Perkins, *From Classical Antiquity*, 245-247.

[18] Wickham, *Framing*, 644-656, discusses the scholarly debates surrounding the decline of urbanism in early medieval Italy and makes particular reference to Lucca at pp. 652-653.

among the Lucchese toward pious giving, one Rangerio related to the very name of their city, was in fact a hallmark of Giovanni's lifetime. The precedent of local episcopal building ascribed to St. Fridian and the enrichment of the church made possible by Liutprand laid the ground for Giovanni's own relic translations and building projects.

The distinctive hierarchy of Lucchese churches and uneven distribution of holy treasure among them provides a second historical backdrop to Giovanni's emergence as a paradigmatic lord and builder. Before departing Lucca on an ill-fated military campaign, an earlier bishop named Walprando (ca. 730–754) had prudently drafted a will dividing his property among the three most venerable churches in the city.[19] One-fourth of his estate went to the aforementioned basilica of San Frediano, the resting place of St. Fridian, and another one-fourth went to an old cathedral of the city situated within its walls and dedicated to the virgin and martyr Reparata. The latter retained an adjoining baptistery dedicated to John the Baptist and thus remained the baptismal church (*pieve*) of the city.[20] By this bishop's lifetime, Santa Reparata had ceded its position as the episcopal seat to the nearby church of San Martino, and he signaled the preeminence of this second church by leaving it the remaining half of his estate. Despite their central location within the city walls, as well as their status as the former and current cathedral, respectively, Santa Reparata and San Martino nonetheless retained a secondary position with respect to the extramural basilica of San Frediano, owing to their lack of relics. This conspicuous absence Giovanni would ameliorate through the acquisition of new *spiritualia* for the two urban churches.

A third and final historical condition that encouraged and inflected Giovanni's activities was the challenge to local episcopal authority provoked by the passage of the Kingdom of Italy from Lombard to Carolingian control. Giovanni's immediate predecessors, Bishops Walprando and Peredeo (755–780), had overseen the enrichment of their diocese through their cultivation of lay patrons and consecration of churches.[21] Not

---

[19] Luigi Schiaparelli, *Codice diplomatico Longobardo*, 2 vols. (Rome: Istituto Storico Italiano, 1929–1933), vol. 1, no. 114, 134–145 (July 754). Hansmartin Schwarzmaier, *Lucca und das Reich bis zum Ende des 11. Jahrhunderts: Studien zur Struktur einer Herzogstadt in der Toskana* (Tübingen: M. Niemeyer, 1972), 14–38, provides a broader survey of Lucca and its churches before the Carolingian period.

[20] An act of Walprando's predecessor, Bishop Talesperiano, is the earliest surviving document to identify San Martino rather than Santa Reparata as the cathedral (*ad ecclesiam Sancti Martini in episcopio*): Schiaparelli, *Codice*, vol. 1, no. 35, 126 (724). Walprando's testament is in fact the first documentary witness to Santa Reparata. The earliest notice of its function as the urban *pieve* (*ecclesiae plebis vestre Sancte Reparate et Sancti Johannis Baptiste*) dates from the tenth century (*MDL*, vol. 4, pt. 2, no. 68 [967]); however, Santa Reparata had likely functioned in this manner since Walprando's time: Letizia Ermini Pani, "La fasi altomedievali," in *La chiesa dei Santi Giovanni e Reparata in Lucca: Dagli scavi archeologici al restauro*, ed. Giovanna Piancastelli Politi Nencini (Lucca: Fazzi, 1993), 49–53.

[21] On Walprando and Peredeo, see Schwarzmaier, *Lucca und das Reich*, 74–85; Almerico Guerra and Pietro Guidi, *Compendio di storia ecclesiastica lucchese dalle origini a tutto il secolo XII* (Lucca: Cooperativa Artigiana Editrice, 1924), 71–86; and Luca Bertini, *Peredeo vescovo di Lucca* (Pisa: Pacini, 1973). Chris Wickham, "Economic and Social Institutions in Northern Tuscany in the 8th Century," in *Istituzioni*

coincidentally, they enjoyed particularly close ties with the Lombard kings who had succeeded Liutprand. The son of the duke of Tuscany, Walprando, joined the aforementioned royal expedition against the Frankish army, which had descended into Italy to defend the papacy from Lombard aggression. The affinities between the Lucchese bishopric and the Lombard aristocracy endured after his death in battle. By 768, Peredeo had perhaps assumed the temporal duties of a duke owing to the extinction of Walprando's family.[22] Such political ties probably explain why Peredeo was among the three Italian bishops whom Charlemagne obliged to return with him to Francia after having conquered Italy in 774.[23] The privileged position of Lucca and its bishops under Lombard rule had become a distinct liability, depriving the city of its prelate, Peredeo, and leaving its church open to despoliation during these turbulent times. For a newly consecrated bishop such as Giovanni, the recognition of preexisting relic cults, or institution of new ones via that translation of relics and the building of tombs, undoubtedly served as a clear reassertion of episcopal authority.

The newfound position of Lucca within the Carolingian Empire transformed the city's relationship not only with the Franks but also with Rome in ways that would likewise reshape local relic cults and their liturgies. Charlemagne's conquest of Italy was the culmination of a fifty-year-long struggle between the papacy and the Lombards, a contest in which the former had forged an alliance with the Franks in order to counterbalance the military superiority of the latter. If the dioceses of Lombard Tuscany had accordingly maintained a studied distance from Rome before 774, their assimilation into the Carolingian Empire provided an incentive for them to signal their spiritual fidelity to the Eternal City.[24] Lucca provides the best evidence for this new posture via the copy of the *Liber pontificalis,* produced in its episcopal scriptorium during Giovanni's episcopate and with his active participation.[25] Circulating throughout Latin Christendom,

---

ecclesiastiche della Toscana medieovale (Galatina: Congedo, 1980), 23, likewise signals the importance of these three bishops as builders.

[22] Bertini, *Peredeo*, 22.

[23] In a letter to Charlemagne, Pope Hadrian I (772–795) requested that the former allow the bishops of Lucca, Pisa, and Regio to return to their respective bishoprics: MGH, EPMC, vol. 1, ch. 8 ("Codex Carolinus"), no. 50, 568–570 (774^{ex}). Peredeo's immediate successor, Bishop Giovanni I, similarly noted that "my predecessor had been detained in Francia in the service of the lord king" (*Peredeus episcopus decessor meus in Francia erat detentus in servitio domini regis*): *MDL*, vol. 5, pt. 2, no. 189 (17 January 783). Peredeo had returned to Lucca by March 777, when he is documented as having purchased various properties for the cathedral: *MDL*, vol. 4, pt. 1, no. 84, 134–135.

[24] Hence no bishops from Lombard Tuscany attended the synods organized by Pope Gregory II in 721 and Stephen II in 769: Giovanni Domenico Mansi, *Sacrorum Conciliorum*, vol. 12, cols. 264–65 and 714–15, respectively.

[25] BCL, 490, fols. 161–210, on the dating of which see introduction to part I, n. 6. Luigi Schiaparelli, *Il codice 490 della Biblioteca Capitolare di Lucca e la scuola scrittoria lucchese (sec. VIII-IX)* (Vatican City: Biblioteca Apostolica Vaticana, 1924), 23–32, argues that one of its most prominent copyists (i.e., "Scribe B") was none other than Giovanni, while Amadeo Petrucci, "Il codice n. 490 della Biblioteca Capitolare di Lucca: Un problema di storia della cultura medieval ancora da risolvere," *Actum Luce* 2 (1973), 172–173, draws attention to the political background to the creation of the manuscript.

these official papal biographies were not merely a work of local, Roman history but also served to inform a broader, clerical readership about the great architectural and liturgical initiatives of the popes since late Antiquity.[26] This pedagogical function finds particularly concrete but largely unexplored expression in Lucca. It explains the distinctly papal overtones to Giovanni's institution of relic cults, by which this local prelate, as we shall see, amplified his standing by styling himself as a papal *dominus et constructor* writ small.

Of the three historical conditions outlined above—the local tradition of episcopal building stretching back to the sixth century, the dearth of relics in urban basilicas of Lucca, and the Frankish conquest of Italy—the second and third conditions illuminate Giovanni's acquisition of the bodies of saints with no preexisting connection with the city.[27] In this respect, his actions recalled those of Bishop Ansifredo of Siena, who had obtained the relics of the Roman martyr St. Crescentius, perhaps in response to his inability to control the cult of a local one, St. Ansanus. Giovanni, however, did not look to the Eternal City for holy treasure. He was likely responsible for the translation of St. Pantaleon of Nicomedia to the old cathedral of Santa Reparata.[28] And he certainly brought about the acquisition of St. Regulus, whose church near Populonia had fallen under the dominion of the Lucchese bishopric despite its position outside its diocese (fig. 1.1). Under the guidance of rectors appointed by Giovanni's predecessors, San Regolo had attracted many pious gifts and became home to a community of monks.[29] Indeed, Bishop Peredeo himself had left two houses to "our monastery of St. Regulus in Gualdo, where his holy body lies," in his will of 778; however, such relics had migrated to San Martino by 781.[30] With the translations of St. Pantaleon and St. Regulus, Giovanni

---

[26] Thomas F. X. Noble, "A New Look at the *Liber Pontificalis*," *Archivium Historiae Pontificiae* 23 (1985): 352–353; and Pierre Riché, *Education and Culture in the Barbarian West: From the Sixth through the Eighth Century*, trans. John Contreni (Columbia: University of South Carolina Press, 1976), 408.

[27] On Giovanni, see Schwarzmaier, *Lucca und das Reich*, 85–87; and Guerra and Guidi, *Compendio*, 86–96. Schwarzmaier (335–338) similarly emphasizes the Carolingian background to Giovanni's relic translations but neglects the particular dynamic between urban and suburban basilicas emphasized here.

[28] Ermini Pani, "La fasi," 63–65.

[29] The earliest record of San Regolo is a donation of 744/745: Schiaparelli, *Codice*, vol. 1, no. 84, 248–250. In 749 or 750, its rector in turn acknowledged the subjugation of his church and his office to Bishop Walprando: Schiaparelli, *Codice*, vol. 1, no. 99, 285–287. Simone Collavini, "Da società rurale periferica a parte dello spazio politico lucchese: S. Regolo in Gualdo tra VIII e IX secolo," in *"Un filo rosso," Studi antichi e nuove richerche sulle orme di Gabriella Rossetti in occasione dei suo settanta anni*, ed. Gabriella Garzella and Enrica Salvatori (Pisa: ETS, 2007), 231–247, examines the political dynamics by which San Regolo became subject to the Lucchese bishopric.

[30] "Ecclesia monasterii nostri Sancti Reguli in Waldo, ubi sanctum corpus eius requiescit" (*MDL*, vol. 4, pt. 1, no. 86, 137 [778]). Other donors of the 770s called attention to the presence of a monastery and St. Regulus's body at San Regolo, e.g., Schiaparelli, *Codice*, vol. 2, no. 240, 309 (24 May 770), and *MDL*, vol. 4, pt. 1, no. 10, 15 (778). By contrast, the donation of the nun Godiperga to San Martino in 781 denotes San Martino as St. Regulus's burial site (*MDL*, vol. 4, pt. 1, no. 88, 141), and that of Ramingo of Volterra to San Regolo, in the following year, described San Regolo as "the church in which his body had recently [*iam in antea*]

not only exercised his right to institute new cults but also reoriented the sacred topography of his city away from the suburban martyrium of San Frediano and toward Santa Reparata and San Martino, the current and former cathedral, respectively.

A Translation, perhaps written during Giovanni's lifetime, furthered the bishop's political aims by casting him as a virtuous prelate motivated by piety alone and thus justifying his acquisition of holy treasure.[31] If the removal of St. Regulus from Gualdo accorded with the established dominion of the Lucchese bishopric over San Regolo, it nonetheless contravened the cephalophore's own postmortem preferences for his burial site.[32] In a manner characteristic of its hagiographic genre, the Translation described Giovanni as a model of episcopal virtue—handsome, eloquent, wise, charitable, powerful, pure in faith, and holy in deeds—who made an annual pilgrimage to St. Regulus's grave. He visited the holy site not "on account of a passion for treasure" but instead to venerate the saint who had cured him of a childhood illness.[33] Inspiration for the translation came not from this well-intentioned bishop but from an angel who appeared to him in a dream. God's messenger revealed the precise location of St. Regulus beneath the ground of the martyr's shrine and ordered the bishop to rebury him in his cathedral of San Martino. Thereafter, noted the angel, St. Regulus would be the protector of Lucca, that Tuscan capital or "province of provinces." Such civic rhetoric was not atypical of early medieval Translations, but it appears particularly pointed when set against the uncertain political position of Lucca under Carolingian rule. It complements the broader aim of the Translation, namely to insulate Giovanni from charges of being a rapacious acquirer of relics by portraying him as a righteous bishop armed with celestial authority.

---

rested" (*MDL*, vol. 4, pt. 1, no. 90, 144). On the precise date of St. Regulus's translation, see Guerra and Guidi, *Compendio*, 86–89, n. 1.

[31] *Translatio Sancti Reguli I* (*BHL* 7104), in *AS* September, vol. 1, cols. 238–240, transmits the text transcribed in Ughelli, *Italia Sacra*, vol. 1, 847–848, from the passionary compiled for the convent of San Matteo of Pisa, BAV, Vat. Lat. 6453, fols. 106v–107 (saec. XII[in]). That it concludes with four verses from the Martyrology of Wandelbert of Prüm but ones erroneously attributed in the Translation to Bede suggests a *terminus post quem* of ca. 850: Simonetti, "Note sulla tradizione," 112–113, n. 17. Nevertheless, the poetry was perhaps a later addition to the original text as noted by Collavini, "Da società rurale," 239, n. 24. On the Translation of St. Regulus, see Webb, *Patrons*, 64; Raffaele Savigni, *Episcopato e società cittadina a Lucca: Da Anselmo II (†1086) a Roberto (†1255)* (Lucca: S. Marco 1996), 317–318; and Collavini, "Da società rurale." Patrick J. Geary, *Furta Sacra: Thefts of Relics in the Central Middle Ages*, 2nd ed. (Princeton, NJ: Princeton University Press, 1990), 112–118, outlines various justifications for the transfer of relics commonly employed in *translationes*.

[32] Graziano Concioni, *Vescovi e canonici a Lucca tra Longobardi e Franchi* (Pisa: ETS, 2007), 22–27, argues that the Lucchese bishops had likewise promoted the cult of St. Regulus at Gualdo as a means by which to stamp out the vestiges of Arian heresy in southern Tuscany. The saint's translation to San Martino, according to Concioni's hypothesis, served to underscore the success of their efforts.

[33] *Translatio Sancti Reguli I*, BAV, Vat. Lat. 6453, fol. 106v: "In suo namque tempore per singulos annos pergebat locum maritime, non tantum propter passionem prædii, sed tantum ut adoraret ad sepulchrum beati Reguli."

Behind the literary topoi of the *Translatio Sancti Reguli* lay an ambitious strategy that reflected local priorities but held regional implications. The precedents (and perhaps models) for Giovanni's translation of St. Regulus and St. Pantaleon to Lucca included not only Bishop Ansifredo's acquisition of St. Crescentius for Siena in the 750s but also the translation of no fewer than fifty saints from the catacombs outside the Aurelian walls of Rome into intramural churches by Pope Paul I (757–767). Copied at San Martino toward the end of Giovanni's episcopate or just after his death, the pontiff's official biography would have invited comparisons between Giovanni and Paul.[34] Just as the Translation of St. Regulus portrays its protagonist in the most flattering of lights, so the *Liber pontificalis* depicts the pope as "a most blessed bishop" deeply solicitous of saints' ancient graves in the catacombs but moved to act on account of their present-day neglect. And as in Lucca so in Rome, there lay a political subtext just beneath this account of episcopal virtue: Pope Paul's relic translations responded to the insecurity wrought by a Lombard siege of the city in 756 and allowed him to reassert papal authority over the Roman *campagna*.[35] The acquisition of St. Regulus and St. Pantaleon for Lucca in turn foreshadowed subsequent translations of relics *intra muros* elsewhere in Tuscany in the ninth and tenth centuries.[36] Bishop Giovanni thus set the stage for the emergence of Tuscan cathedrals as veritable storehouses of relics and, by extension, the subsequent creation of liturgies in honor of such *spiritualia* by the canons of these urban basilicas.

Indeed, Giovanni himself demonstrated an impeccable sense of ecclesiastical ceremony and a canny appreciation for liturgical memorial in his orchestration of the transfer of holy relics. Having recounted his celestial vision to his priests, deacons, and minor clerics, notes the *translatio,* he led them in three days of fasting and prayer before exhuming St. Regulus. The bishop even participated in the messy work of unearthing the body: he was "the first digger of earth" among his clergy! The Translation then proceeded with two set pieces, the *inventio* (discovery) and the *elevatio* (elevation) of the holy corpse. Giovanni and his clerics marveled at its perfectly preserved state and its sweet scent of "cinnamon, balsam, and precious incense."[37] They wrapped their prize in linen, placed him on a bier, and carried him to Lucca while singing psalms and hymns. By doing so, they removed St. Regulus from the relatively isolated site of Gualdo to

---

[34] Louis Duchesne and Cyrille Vogel, eds., *Le Liber pontificalis*, 2nd. ed., 3 vols. (Paris: E. de Boccard, 1955), vol. 1, no. 95, 464. The biography of Pope Paul I was one of the seven added to the Lucchese copy of the papal biographies, BCL, 490, fols. 161–210, sometime between 795 and 816: introduction to part I this volume, n. 6.

[35] Caroline J. Goodson, *The Rome of Pope Paschal I (817–824): Papal Power, Urban Renovation, Church Rebuilding and Relic Translation* (Cambridge: Cambridge University Press, 2010), 208–215.

[36] Webb, *Patrons*, 34–47, surveys numerous cases of translations of relics *intra muros* in ninth- and tenth-century Italy while Maureen C. Miller, *The Bishop's Palace: Architecture and Authority in Medieval Italy* (Ithaca, NY: Cornell University Press, 2000), 125–145, esp. 129–130, contextualizes them within the centralization of cathedrals within the urban topography of Italian cities.

[37] *Translatio Sancti Reguli I*, BAV, Vat. Lat. 6453, fol. 106v.

the preeminent urban center of Tuscany, where they might more easily convene large audiences for the martyr's veneration. The conclusion of the *translatio* underscored this desideratum: so many miracles unfolded after the masses celebrated by the bishop in the saint's honor that it was decreed that "all Lucchese from far and wide were to celebrate with joy and devotion" not at their respective parishes but instead together at San Martino.[38] Finally, Giovanni subtly linked his own story to that of St. Regulus by translating him to Lucca on the day of the saint's martyrdom (1 September). Henceforth, the local clergy commemorated the saint's translation not as a separate feast, as was typical, but instead on his *dies natalis*, reciting both the *Passio* and *Translatio Sancti Reguli* on that day. Memory of St. Regulus's choice of his original gravesite thus became intertwined with Giovanni's divinely inspired selection of a new one.

If Giovanni's institution of the cults of St. Regulus and St. Pantaleon in Lucca buttressed his authority in part by raising the profile of his former and current cathedral, his promotion of that of St. Fridian served this same purpose by strengthening his dominion over a suburban martyrium. Once home to a community of Benedictine monks who elected their own abbot, St. Fridian's burial church had fallen under the authority of an episcopally appointed rector by the mid-eighth century.[39] Giovanni ensured his influence at San Frediano by appointing his brother, Jacopo, to the position.[40] Even more important, he gave the cult of his episcopal predecessor, St. Fridian, his official approbation as documented in a revised and expanded *Vita Sancti Fridiani*. Perhaps written during Giovanni's lifetime, this narrative ends with an account of the bishop's exhumation and reburial of St. Fridian.[41] Although less effusive in its praise of Giovanni than the Translation of St. Regulus, it shares the basic format and many of the literary topoi of that aforementioned text. Having miraculously discerned the precise location of St. Fridian beneath the pavement of San Frediano, Giovanni unearthed and reburied him

---

[38] *Translatio Sancti Reguli I*, BAV, Vat. Lat. 6453, fol. 107: "Ex [h]ac ergo consuetudine decretum est ut omnes sancte Dei eccleise lucensium longe lateque solempnia beati Reguli devotissime cum gaudio celebrent et omnes plebes ibi veniant adorare et missarum sollempnitatem celebrare in die qua prediximus Kl. Septembris." Chris Wickham, "Topographies of Power: Introduction," in *Topographies of Power in the Early Middle Ages*, ed. Mayke De Jong, Frans Theuws, and Carine Van Rhijn (Leiden: Brill, 2001), 6–7, similarly notes the advantages of urban sites for such public displays of power, liturgical and otherwise.

[39] The single documentary witness to the Benedictine monastery at San Frediano is an accord between its abbot, Babbino, and Bishop Felice of Lucca concerning the rights and responsibilities of the former's community: Schiaparelli, *Codice*, vol. 1, no. 7, 16–19 (20 January 685). The first known rector of that church was Guasperto, who witnessed the aforementioned testament of Bishop Walprando in 754 (see above, n. 19).

[40] *MDL*, vol. 5, pt. 2, no. 539, 321 (April 838), records the testimony of various Lucchese witnesses concerning the ownership of San Frediano. While all noted that Jacopo had governed San Frediano in his capacity as bishop—he was his brother's episcopal successor—a cleric named Giovanni implied that he was also its rector. If the testimony was indeed accurate, Bishop Giovanni thus appointed his brother rector of San Frediano in 788, thirty years before the latter's death in 818. See Enrico Coturri, "La canonica di S. Frediano di Lucca dalla Prima Istituzione (metà del sec. xi) alla unione alla congregazione riformata di Fregionaia (1517)," *Actum Luce* 3 (1974): 50–51, n. 8; and Schwarzmaier, *Lucca und das Reich*, 89.

[41] *Vita Sancti Fridiani II* (*BHL* 3175), ch. 10, nos. 1–2, in Zaccagnini, *Vita*, 187.

in a more prominent site beneath the high altar. By thus bestowing episcopal recognition on the cult of St. Fridian, whose suburban martyrium had once enjoyed significant autonomy from the bishop, he once again demonstrated his power during a tumultuous period of political transition.

The similarities between the Translation of St. Regulus and the new Life of St. Fridian include not only their narratives of episcopal authority but also their celebration of the local tradition of episcopal building. Extending back through Giovanni's immediate predecessors, Bishops Walprando and Peredeo, to St. Fridian, this tradition was the first of those three historical conditions that made Lucca such fertile ground for Giovanni's ascent as a *dominus et constructor*. The original *Vita Sancti Fridiani*, as noted above, was exceptional among early Tuscan hagiography for its depiction of its saint as a builder. The *Translatio Sancti Reguli* enriched this portrait by ascribing to St. Fridian the construction of the cathedral of San Martino. The text justified this novel claim by ascribing it to no less an authoritative figure than the angel who appeared to Giovanni in a dream and authorized St. Regulus's translation from Gualdo to Lucca.[42] The revised and expanded Life of St. Fridian, in turn, described other architectural projects of its protagonist with newfound detail and drama. Landowners, it related, beseeched St. Fridian to build churches on their property, an anecdote redolent of the enrichment of the Lucchese bishopric in the eighth century. Their donations allowed him to build its twenty-eight *pievi*, the administrative backbone of the diocese corresponding to his twenty-eight-year episcopate. Finally, the new Life told of St. Fridian's building of his future burial church, San Frediano, just north of Lucca. Workmen found themselves without sufficient marble and hastened to a field where, according to recent reports, there lay an enormous piece of such material. Unable to move the marble due to its weight, they called upon their bishop, who, with God's aid, effortlessly lifted it and ordered it to be laid in the pavement directly in front of the high altar, which he dedicated to Sts. Vincent, Stephen, and Lawrence.[43] Collectively, the *Translatio Sancti Reguli* and new *Vita Sancti Fridiani* thus amplified St. Fridian's stature of a lord and builder in the mold (one might add) of

---

[42] The angel orders Bishop Giovanni to bury St. Regulus "inside the basilica of the blessed Martin, confessor of Christ, which the blessed bishop Fridian built from its foundations" (*intus in basilica beati Martini confessoris Christi, quam beatus episcopus Frigidianus a fundamentis edificavit*): Translatio Sancti Reguli I, BAV, Vat. Lat. 6453, fol. 107. On the historical evidence for St. Fridian's involvement in the building or rebuilding of San Martino, see Zaccagnini, *Vita*, 41–44.

[43] *Vita Sancti Fridiani II* (*BHL* 3175), ch. 2, nos. 9–10 (on the donations of land and the *pievi*) and ch. 4 (on the miracle of the marble), ed. Zaccagnini, *Vita*, 159 and 166–168, respectively. Savigni, *Episcopato e società*, 332–334, notes that the emphasis on such building projects reinforced the ties between St. Fridian and his city and thus underscores the gradual evolution of a civic consciousness in early medieval Lucca. A massive, rectangular piece of white limestone believed to have been the piece of "marble" in question is now displayed in the aisle to the left of the presbytery of the current basilica of San Frediano: Romano Silva, *La basilica di San Frediano a Lucca: Immagine simbolica di Roma Cristiana* (Lucca: Maria Pacini Fazzi, 2010), 73–78; and Zaccagnini, *Vita*, 33.

St. Ambrose of Milan, who had likewise constructed his own martyrium, the Basilica Ambrosiana.[44]

Perhaps written during the episcopate of Giovanni, such hagiography legitimized that bishop's own architectural projects by casting him as the inheritor of the local tradition of episcopal building inaugurated two centuries earlier by St. Fridian. Having ascribed the building of the original edifice of San Martino to St. Fridian, the Translation of St. Regulus credits its reconstruction to Giovanni.[45] Moreover, both the *Translatio Sancti Reguli* and the revised *Vita Sancti Fridiani* provide detailed descriptions of the crypts in which the bishop deposited the relics of their two saints. According to these two texts, these monuments bore a marked resemblance to each other. Both lay beneath the high altar of their respective churches and were surrounded by an enclosure. St. Regulus's crypt was spacious enough to accommodate a separate altar and its enclosure was inscribed with the story of the saint's translation to Lucca.[46] Similarly, St. Fridian's crypt contained a burial urn, of which the surviving cover features an inscription commemorating the saint's exhumation.[47] Until their destruction in the early twelfth century, the crypts with their inscriptions served the same function as the Translation and Life that document their construction.[48] Both crypts and hagiography were thus monuments to their respective saints as well as to Giovanni, whom they depict as taking up the mantle of the Lucchese *dominus et constructor* established by St. Fridian.

The marked similarities between the crypts of St. Fridian and St. Regulus reflected not only their common builder but also their shared model that served the practical purpose of enticing and accommodating the pilgrims attracted, as noted in St. Fridian's Life and St. Regulus's Translation, by the newly installed relics.[49] The prototype in question

---

[44] Neil B. McLynn, *Ambrose of Milan: Church and Court in a Christian Capital* (Berkeley: University of California Press, 1994), 226–237.

[45] *Translatio Sancti Reguli I*, BAV, Vat. Lat. 6453, fol. 107 notes that Giovanni "built the church and confessional" (*fabricavit ecclesiam et confessionem*). Taken in isolation, the term "ecclesia" might refer not to the cathedral but instead to the ciborium that stood atop the confessional of St. Regulus, on which more will be said below. When read in its entirety, however, the phrase encourages a more literal reading because medieval documents typically cited an entire building before one of its architectural features: Silva, *La basilica*, 44.

[46] *Translatio Sancti Reguli I*, BAV, Vat. Lat. 6453, fol. 107, which transmits the inscription, albeit in garbled form: "Sic legitur in postibus iuxta aram beati Martini: Metallo presul Iohannes solo cum gradibus postibus fecit, hic corpus beati Reguli deduxit, et altare sursum erexit et construxit. Ad eius caput iacet humatus Pascentius archdiaconus suus: ibi namque legitur et cernitur in brevi tabula lapidea." The archdeacon Pascentius presumably served Giovanni rather than St. Regulus, as nobody of that name is mentioned in the latter's Passion.

[47] The cover of the urn is now affixed to the interior wall of the left nave of San Frediano. Its inscription is datable on paleographic grounds to the eighth century but is almost illegible due to subsequent embrasures: "†HOC SCI TVMULUM FRICIANI F.CIT MAULAM PRE […] S.CCE IOHANN.S […] C.IVS SIC SA[…]NTI LUCAN" (Zaccagnini, *Vita*, 53–55).

[48] On the destruction of the crypt of St. Regulus see chapters 3 this volume. The crypt of St. Fridian was dismantled in the twelfth century with the reconstruction of San Frediano: Silva, *La basilica*, 42–49.

[49] *Vita Sancti Fridiani II*, ch. 10.3, in Zaccagnini, *Vita*, 188; and *Translatio Sancti Reguli I*, BAV, Vat. Lat. 6453, fol. 107.

was the annular confessional at St. Peter's in Rome. Supporting a presbytery and high altar raised above the nave, the apostle's magnificent tomb immediately signaled the importance of the saint buried therein. It also gave pilgrims access to his relics through a grille in front and a curved passage along the inside of the apse in back, of which the latter approximated the narrow corridors of the catacombs.[50] Archeological and literary evidence suggests that the Lucchese crypts emulated this arrangement. The apse of the early-medieval basilica of San Frediano, uncovered in the course of nineteenth-century excavations, seems designed to accommodate a curved passage analogous to that at the St. Peter's.[51] Equally suggestive is the more recently uncovered crypt of St. Pantaleon, whose relics Giovanni likely translated to the old cathedral of Santa Reparata. Located below the high altar, it featured a straight passage that ran from north to south along the entrance to the apse rather than a curved one along the outer wall, but otherwise it resembled the confessional of St. Peter.[52] Finally, the *Translatio Sancti Reguli* explicitly noted the similarity between the third and final crypt attributable to Bishop Giovanni, that of St. Regulus, with St. Peter's.[53] As in Rome so in Lucca, this distinctive type of confessional encouraged and facilitated veneration of relics by those pilgrims whose pious offerings promised to enrich the local church.

The function of the Lucchese crypts *a la romana* was not only practical but also political: the precise form of these structures allowed Bishop Giovanni, once again, to take up the mantle of earlier, papal builders and thus signal his fidelity and that of his city to Rome and the Carolingian Empire. The Lucchese prelate and his clergy would have attributed the construction of the original crypt of St. Peter to Pope Gregory I, as did his official biography in the *Liber pontificalis*, a text copied at San Martino during Giovanni's episcopate.[54] Gregory's successors to the seat of St. Peter followed him by building annular confessionals in other Roman churches. Meanwhile, Frankish bishops and abbots adopted the arrangement as their kings, first Peppin and then Charlemagne, forged an alliance with Rome in the second half of the eighth century.[55] By building the

---

[50] Bauer, "La frammentazione liturgica," 390–393 and 398; and Sible De Blaauw, *Cultus et décor: Liturgia e architettura nella Roma tardoantica e medieval*, trans. Maria Beatrice Annis, 2nd. ed., 2 vols. (Vatican City: Biblioteca Apostolica Vaticana, 1994), 539–542.

[51] Silva, *La basilica*, 44–45.

[52] John Crook, *The Architectural Setting of the Cult of Saints in the Early Christian West, c.300-1200* (Oxford: Oxford University Press, 2000), 120–122; and Ermini Pani, "La fasi," 53–66.

[53] *Translatio Sancti Reguli I*, BAV, Vat. Lat. 6453, fol. 107.

[54] Duchesne and Vogel, eds., *Le Liber pontificalis*, vol. 1, no. 66, 312.

[55] Margherita Cecchelli, "La cripta semianulare vaticana e le sue derivazioni romane," in *L'Orbis Christianus Antiquus di Gregorio Magno*, ed. Letizia Ermini Pani (Rome: Società alla Biblioteca vallicelliana, 2007), 118–120; and Bauer, "La frammentazione liturgica," 394–397, examine Roman imitations of St. Peter's crypt through the mid-ninth century. Crook, *The Architectural Setting*, 80–109; Werner Jacobson, "Saints' Tombs in Frankish Church Architecture," *Speculum* 72 (1997): 1107–1143, esp. 1134–1139; and M. Angelini et al., "L'uso e la diffusione delle cripte nell'Europa carolingia," in *Roma e l'età carolingia. Atti delle giornate di studio, 3- maggio 1976* (Rome: Multigrafica, 1976), 319–323, trace the broader diffusion of the model.

crypts of St. Regulus, St. Fridian, and St. Pantaleon, Bishop Giovanni was not simply following in the footsteps of a single, celebrated pope (i.e., Gregory the Great) but in fact participating in a broader pattern of architectural emulation that had gained currency in Rome and Francia.

When read together and in concert with the *Liber pontificalis* and archeological evidence, the Translation of St. Regulus and the revised Life of St. Fridian thus engender a rich web of associations that placed Giovanni, implicitly or explicitly, in the company of such prominent Italian bishops as St. Ambrose, St. Gregory, and Pope Paul I. To these celebrated figures the Lucchese added a Frankish one, St. Martin of Tours, the original and arguably most influential exemplar of episcopal virtue throughout Latin Christendom.[56] The Translation of St. Regulus, as noted above, attributed to St. Fridian the building of the cathedral of Lucca and, by implication, its intitulation to St. Martin. Bishop Giovanni strengthened the perceived ties between this local Lucchese saint and the universally venerated one by interring St. Fridian in his new confessional at San Frediano on 18 November, just four days after St. Martin's *dies natalis*. The Lucchese bound the episcopal father of Lucca even closer to St. Martin and Giovanni by treating the annual commemoration of this event as St. Fridian's principal feast rather than, as was typical, his original *dies natalis* (18 March).[57] Historical anecdote in the *Translatio Sancti Reguli* and the proximity of the two November feasts thus drew these three bishops together in the minds of the local faithful.

St. Martin's inclusion in the constellation of prominent bishop saints outlined above offered the Lucchese a final, particularly apposite precedent for Giovanni's ascent as a *dominus et constructor* in the person of Bishop Perpetuus of Tours (461–491). Yet again, the political conditions of the late eighth century loomed large, as Perpetuus belonged neither to the local history of Lucca (as did St. Fridian) nor to the Eternal City but instead to the territories of the city's new Frankish overlords. In his *De virtutibus Sancti Martini*, Gregory of Tours (538–594) wrote how Perpetuus had built a new burial church for St. Martin "with wise enthusiasm and marvelous workmanship."[58] The author proceeded to Perpetuus's elevation of his episcopal predecessor from his original grave and transfer of him to the new edifice on the occasion of its consecration. Gregory's text offers one of the earliest literary accounts of a relic translation and anticipates topoi evident in Lucchese hagiography. Like Giovanni and his clergy, Perpetuus and his retinue undergo three days of prayer or fasting before elevating St. Martin from his original resting place. Similarly, an angel appears at a critical moment, helping the Touraine clerics to lift the miraculously heavy body.[59] In both its broader trajectory and its narrative

---

[56] On the cult of St. Martin, see chapter 6, this volume.
[57] Zaccagnini, *Vita*, 3–4, 89–103.
[58] *Translatio Sancti Martini* (*BHL*, 5623), ed. MGH, SRM, vol. 1, pt. 2, bk. 2, ch. 6, 591–592: "Quod sagaci insistens studio, mirifice mancipavit effectui." Translation after Raymond Van Dam, *Saints and their Miracles in Late Antique Gaul* (Princeton, NJ: Princeton University Press, 1993), 208.
[59] *Translatio Sancti Martini*, in MGH, SRM, vol. 1, pt. 2, bk. 2, ch. 6, 591–592.

details, Gregory's account of Perpetuus's construction of a church dedicated to St. Martin, and his translation of relics therein, thus foreshadowed Giovanni's promotion of San Martino in Lucca. Were Bishop Giovanni to have known *De virtutibus Sancti Martini*—a probability given the renown of its author, Gregory of Tours—he would have undoubtedly drawn inspiration from his Touraine counterpart.

Indeed, the exceptional place that Perpetuus obtained in the Lucchese liturgy in the central Middle Ages highlighted his similarities with Giovanni. The diocese of Lucca was the only one in the region to commemorate the anniversary of St. Martin's translation (4 July).[60] On that day, the local clergy recited Gregory's account in *De virtutibus Sancti Martini*, which accordingly appears in two Lucchese passionaries, of which one was compiled for San Frediano.[61] The manuscript ornaments the text with a rare historiated (as opposed to merely inhabited) initial that depicts the moment of entombment at the conclusion of the rite of consecration (fig. 2.2). Clothed in episcopal regalia and aided by his acolyte, Perpetuus leans over and censes the open sarcophagus.[62] The image reminds the viewer that such liturgies engaged multiple senses: candles illuminated the holy body, incense perfumed it, and (one might add) the clergy sang antiphons celebrating its new home. In the absence of any reference or allusion to the distinctive details of *De virtutibus Sancti Martini*, the initial presents a generic scene of episcopal authority by situating any bishop as the orchestrator of relic translation and church consecration. Among the Lucchese, the image undoubtedly called to mind Giovanni, who had so elevated St. Fridian, his own episcopal predecessor and the titular of the church for which the passionary was produced.

Giovanni's illustrious example exerted a palpable influence on subsequent Lucchese prelates and in particular on his younger brother, Jacopo, whose funeral epitaph reveals that this former rector of San Frediano continued his elder sibling's elevation of the urban cathedral of San Martino after his own consecration as bishop in 800. Similar in style to the accounts of papal building in the *Liber pontificalis*, this text celebrates Jacopo's restoration of two churches near San Martino, one dedicated to St. Peter in Chains and another to the Virgin Mary of the Crib. Despite the shared dedication of

---

[60] Among the Tuscan ordinals inventoried in table 5.1, only that of San Martino, *OOL*, fol. 56, features the feast of St. Martin's *translatio*.

[61] BCL, C, fols. 212v–213 (1180s) and BCL, D, fols. 55–55v (saec. XII^ex); cf. Baudouin de Gaiffier, "Catalogue des passionaires de la Bibliothèque Capitulaire de Lucques," in *Recherches d'hagiographie latine* (Brussels: Société des Bollandistes, 1971), 99 and 103. On the precise dating and provenance of the first manuscript, see Charles Buchanan, "Evidence of a Scriptorium at the Reformed Canonry of S. Frediano in Lucca," *Scriptorium* 57 (2003): 3–26.

[62] Charles S. Buchanan, "An Illustrated Romanesque Hagiographic Lectionary (Lucca: Biblioteca Capitolare, Passionario C): Inspiration, Formulation, and Reception," *Studies in Iconography* 28 (2007): 155–156; and Charles S. Buchanen, "Spiritual and Spatial Authority in Medieval Lucca: Illuminated Manuscripts, Stational Liturgy and the Gregorian Reform," *Art History* 27 (2004), 723, presents a more detailed description of the initial.

FIGURE 2.2. Translation of St. Martin, BCL, C, fol. 212v (1080s).

these local Lucchese churches with the Roman basilicas of San Pietro in Vincoli and Santa Maria Maggiore, the epitaph eschews overt reference to the Eternal City in order to illustrate the proper relationship of the cathedral to other churches in its city:

> [Jacopo] was the restorer of the church that is called *ad Praesepe*, which had recently been destroyed. He made it an altar with wood columns. Due to the filthiness, the office and the lighting of candles did not occur even on Sundays. But now Mass is celebrated there in the summer just as in the winter and priests complete the full office day and night, just as in the church of San Martino. And [the bishop] established a library of books, just as befitted the mother church.[63]

---

[63] *MDL*, vol. 5, pt. 3, no. 1759, 663, with corrections from Guerra and Guidi, *Compendio*, 100–101, n. 2, and quoted in full in Ward-Perkins, *From Classical Antiquity*, 247–248: "et restaurator ecclesie que dicitur ad Praesepe, quae nuper diruta fuerat, et cum columnis ligneis altare ipsum fecit, et multas spurcitias ibi fiebant, nec officium, nec luminaria, nisi tantum in die dominico. Aestivo tempore missa celebratur sicut in hyeme. Modo vero sacerdotes ibidem diurno et nocturno officium plenum peragunt, scilicet in ecclesia Sancti Martini, et libri bibliothecarum instituit, sicut decebat in matrice ecclesia." The restoration of Santa Maria al Praesepe likely dates back to the first decade of the ninth century, when a lay patron and local abbess made donations to that church under Jacopo's direction: *MDL*, vol. 4, pt. 2, no. 6, 9 (13 November 805) and no. 9, 13 (12 February 807), respectively.

By the end of Giovanni's episcopate, San Martino had boasted a library, the body of St. Regulus, and a community of clerics who faithfully chanted the liturgy. Under his brother, it became a true *ecclesia matrix*, the model for the reconstruction and restoration of its daughter churches throughout Lucca.

The epitaph further establishes Jacopo's credentials as a lord and builder in ways that signal the enduring importance of extramural martyria in Lucca as well as the bishop's continuation of his brother's philo-Roman posture. This text ascribed to him the foundation of Ss. Jacopo e Filippo, of which the first of its two titulars was the bishop's name saint. Situated just west of the city walls and home to a community of nuns, it became the resting place of the second-century martyr Pontianus, whose body Jacopo had acquired from Rome.[64] By establishing an entirely new suburban martyrium, the prelate strengthened the ties between Lucca and the Eternal City already established in various ways by his brother, while also following in the footsteps of Bishop Ansifredo of Siena, who had similarly acquired Roman relics in the wake of a delicate moment in relations with the papacy fifty years earlier.

The image of Bishop Giovanni as *dominus et constructor* obtained a central, enduring, and influential place in the historical imagination of his city via literature, liturgy, and architecture. A rich and complex portrait of episcopal virtue and initiative emerges, first and foremost, from the *Translatio Sancti Reguli* and the new *Vita Sancti Fridiani*, which the local clergy solemnly recited on the principal feasts of their holy subjects. Likewise important to the perpetuation of Giovanni's memory were the crypts that once housed the relics of these saints and that were described in detail in these hagiographic texts. Yet few would have mistaken Giovanni as an unprecedented case of episcopal initiative or virtue, one isolated from contemporary events beyond his diocese. Following in the footsteps of earlier, more prominent bishops in such diverse locals as Rome, Milan, and Tours, he deftly reinforced his episcopal authority while navigating the political landscape transformed by Charlemagne's conquest of Italy. In so doing, Giovanni cast himself as inheritor of a local tradition of episcopal building of which the origins lay in the sixth century with St. Fridian. It was thus eminently appropriate that despite his promotion of urban basilicas, he was buried outside the city walls at San Frediano, where, according to local tradition, he performed miracles in the manner of its titular saint.[65]

---

[64] The Lucchese were not alone in claiming such relics: Ado of Vienne (†875) noted in his martyrology that during the pontificate of Nicholas I (858–867), St. Pontianus and his companions, Sts. Eusebius, Peregrinus, and Vincentius, were transferred from their original resting place between the Via Aurelia and Via Triumphalis outside of Rome to monasteries located in Gaul and dedicated to St. Peter (PL, vol. 123, col. 337).

[65] A manuscript that perished in a fire of 1596 catalogued these miracles: Guerra and Guidi, *Compendio*, 95–96; and Cesare Franciotti, *Historia delle miracolose imagini e delle vite dei santi, i corpi dei quali sono nella città di Lucca* (Lucca: Ottavio Guidoboni, 1613), 513.

DEFENDERS OF ECCLESIASTICAL TREASURE:
FIESOLE AND FLORENCE

If Giovanni and Jacopo lived through peaceful and prosperous times, subsequent generations of Tuscan bishops faced new and greater threats, both internal and external, with the gradual dissolution of the Carolingian Empire in the ninth century. As embellished by hagiographers, the careers of three bishops of Fiesole—St. Alexander (†823), Romano (fl. 820s), and St. Donatus (829–876)—illustrate the challenges posed by such villains as rapacious noblemen and Viking marauders. These three prelates accordingly emerge as heroic defenders of holy relics, both in life and, miraculously, in death. Unfortunately, less evidence, hagiographic and otherwise, survives for the translations of relics from extramural shrines to the future cathedral situated within the city walls in Florence than in Fiesole. Yet these translations were also motivated by an energetic bishop, Andrea (869–893), concerned for the safety of such treasure. The breakdown in central authority and resulting insecurity in Tuscany thus not only enriched the image of the region's bishops by bestowing upon them the role of defender of holy relics but also accelerated the sanctification of their cities with such treasure.

Likely written in the 960s by a cathedral canon of Fiesole, the Passion of St. Alexander captures the patron-client relationship forged in the previous century between the Carolingian emperors and the Tuscan bishops as a means, albeit an imperfect one, to protect ecclesiastical property from depredation.[66] The story begins neither with its protagonist's childhood nor with his episcopal election but, rather, *in medias res*, with his appearance as a full-fledged bishop at the royal court at Pavia. There, St. Alexander requested aid from Charlemagne's grandson, Emperor Lothair I (817–855), in his efforts to recoup lands stolen from his church. Recognizing the bishop's holiness, Lothair issued a charter granting St. Alexander's request and enriched his diocese with new lands. Determined that this document never reach Fiesole, a band "of most wicked knights," who (one assumes) had wrongfully appropriated property of the bishopric, intercepted St. Alexander as he departed from Pavia and drowned him in a river.

Even as the narrative introduces the phenomenon of imperial patronage as secured via legally binding (albeit physically vulnerable) charters, it concomitantly presents models of episcopal sanctity and virtue far different from the ones traditional to late Antiquity. St. Alexander was neither a thaumaturge nor a martyr in the classic sense: the first sign of his holiness emerged only after his murder as his companions carried his body through the city of Fiesole. According to an alternate version of the Passion, they intended to

---

[66] *Passio Sancti Alexandri I* (*BHL* 277b), in Giovanni Lami, *Sanctae Ecclesiae Florentinae Monumenta*, 4 vols. (Florence: Angelo Salutatae, 1758), vol. 3, xxxvii–xxxviii. This text identifies the current king as Rotari, a sixth-century Lombard and an Arian heretic; however, "Rotarius" was surely conflated for "Lotarius," or Lothair I, whose reign coincided with Alexander's tenure as bishop. On the authorship and dating of the *Passio Sancti Alexandri*, see chapter 3, this volume.

bury him, as was customary, at the extramural cathedral of San Pietro (fig. 2.1); however, the Holy Spirit intervened by making his body so heavy that they were unable to reach that distant church.[67] Both versions of the Passion agree that St. Alexander came to rest in the basilica of San Pietro in Gerusalemme, located within the old fortress of Fiesole. The fortified position, however, did not hinder the scavengers who presented St. Alexander's successor, Romano, with a royal diploma of dubious authenticity that authorized them to raid graves of gold and silver.[68] The Passion describes Romano as a deeply pious bishop but hardly a commanding figure like Giovanni of Lucca: the former remained speechless with grief as the looters proceeded to plunder St. Alexander's tomb. Indeed, the deceased bishop, St. Alexander, accomplished what the living one, Romano, could not: when the scavengers forced open his grave, his luminous body struck them down with terror. Upon regaining their senses, they fled the church only to slaughter each other with their swords. The miracle thus showed St. Alexander to be as staunch a defender of the church's *spiritualia* in death as he had been of its *temporalia* in life.

Despite his passivity in the face of greedy bandits, Bishop Romano emerges from the Passion as a defender of liturgical propriety, a model of episcopal virtue only implicit in previously discussed hagiography. St. Alexander's miraculous slaying of looters had established his reputation for sanctity, on which account Romano decided to transfer him to a new, more prominent tomb near the high altar of San Pietro in Gerusalemme. When a group of almost fifty enthusiastic laymen attempted to carry St. Alexander to this more prominent position, however, God intervened by once again making him too heavy to move. Understanding that the business of translations belonged to the clergy, Romano waited for the laity to disperse at sunset and convened his "priests, primates, and singers of the church to chant psalms and lessons continually until they had completed the office of matins."[69] Even under normal circumstances, the night office of matins was a long and demanding service and, by dawn, the majority of the clerics had returned to their dwellings to sleep.[70] Romano and a robust few were left to move St. Alexander to his burial site with ease. The lay men and women who returned at the hour of terce were thus amazed to find him occupying the holiest position in the church, directly beneath the high altar in a tomb that surely resembled the annular crypts built by Bishop Giovanni in Lucca in the previous century. Armed with its liturgical and musical expertise, the clergy had exercised its monopoly over the translation of relics under the direction of its bishop.

---

[67] *Passio Sancti Alexandri II* (*BHL* 277d), in Francesco Cignoni, "Le officiature dei santi Alessandro e Romulo, vescovi di Fiesole. Edizioni e studio," *Rivista internazionale di musica sacra* 22 (2001): 82.

[68] The following summarizes *Passio Sancti Alexandri I*, in Lami, *Sanctae Ecclesiae*, vol. 3, xxxviii–xxxx; cf. *Passio Sancti Alexandri II*, in Cignoni, "Le officiature," 82–84, for a briefer account of these same events.

[69] *Passio Sancti Alexandri I*, in Lami, *Sanctae Ecclesiae*, vol. 3, xxxx: "Denique autem maturius suos convocavit sacerdotes, primates, et cantores ecclesiae, ut sine intermissione in psallentia [sic], et lectionibus canerent, et usque ad matutinum lucubrationes decantarent. Et ita fecerunt sine cessatione."

[70] On the length and demanding character of the night office, or matins, see chapter 7, this volume.

Like the Passion of St. Alexander, the *vita* of Romano's successor, St. Donatus, likely dates from the 960s but vividly conveys the anxiety over the threats posed to the church by unscrupulous laymen.[71] The worst assaults came from beyond Tuscany: in 825, Norman marauders sailed up the Arno River and sacked the extramural cathedral and its archives. With their church in ruins, their imperial charters destroyed, and their diocese leaderless, the Fiesolani implored their saints to intercede with God to send them a new bishop. Aid came in the person of St. Donatus, a learned Irishman on pilgrimage to St. Peter's in Rome. His residence in the Eternal City was brief: Christ soon called him to Fiesole, where he revitalized the local church during a lengthy episcopate of approximately fifty years. In life, St. Donatus proved more effective than St. Alexander in recouping its property, as seen in his confrontation with a local landowner whom the bishop had repeatedly accused of appropriating ecclesiastical land. An exasperated St. Donatus finally urged his deceitful interlocutor to repeat "with your twisted tongue that which you have twisted around with your obstinacy."[72] The latter's head, we read, turned around to face backwards and remained so until he returned his ill-begotten lands. The bishop had become a staunch protector of ecclesiastical property in his capacity as a vessel for such divine intervention.

St. Donatus amplified his profile as a defender of the church by posthumously guarding his gravesite, albeit in a more prosaic manner than St. Alexander. The former was buried, as ancient custom dictated, in the extramural cathedral rather than the urban church of San Pietro in Gerusalemme. His tomb featured an epitaph attributed to the deceased and recorded in his Life, one evocative of the erudition and eloquence expected of episcopal clients of the empire from the tenth century.[73] "I am devoured by dust and vermin in this tomb," it began, before lauding his lengthy episcopate, loyalty to the emperors, and teaching of grammar and versification. The epitaph concluded with a plea addressed to "the pilgrim or whoever approaches in the Christ's service: be not reluctant to become familiar with my grave and to pray to God, who rules the highest heavens, so that he will allow me to enter his blessed realm."[74] Those who flocked to St. Donatus's grave heeded the admonition, but the clergy proved to be less solicitous. When water began to leak onto his sepulcher, St. Donatus appeared to the night watchman of the

---

[71] This paragraph summarizes the *Vita Sancti Donati* (BHL 2305), ch. 9, ed. *AS* October, vol. 9, col. 656, no. 9 (on the Norman attack and Donatus's arrival in Fiesole), col. 657, no. 17 (on the destruction of the episcopal archives), and col. 657, no. 17 (on Donatus's encounter with the usurper of ecclesiastical land).

[72] *Vita Sancti Donati*, ch. 1, ed. *AS* October, vol. 9, col. 657, no. 15: "Perge torto ore, quod tua obstinatione torsisti."

[73] C. Stephen Jaeger, "The Courtier Bishop in the *Vitae* from the Tenth to the Twelfth Century," *Speculum* 58 (1983): 300–307.

[74] *Vita Sancti Donati*, ch. 2, in *AS* October, vol. 9, col. 662, no. 27: "Hic ego Donatus, Scotorum sanguine cretus, | Solus in hoc tumulo, pulvere, verme voror [...] | Posco viator, adis quisquis pro munere Christi, | Te, homo, non pigeat cernere busta mea, | Atque precare Deum, regit qui culmina cæli, | Ut mihi concedat regna beata sua."

cathedral and urged him to cover his tomb. The guard did nothing and so the deceased appeared to him a second and even a third time, finally striking him for his indolence. Only then did the bruised and contrite watchman report the leak.[75] If St. Alexander's slaying of the looters of his tomb illustrated a bishop's ability to defend the *spiritulia* of his church with deadly violence, St. Donatus's reprimand of the guard did so with a lighter, more humorous touch.

In Florence, the defense of holy treasure likewise motivated a translation of relics *intra muros*, an obscure event nonetheless ascribable to the city's late-ninth-century bishop, Andrea. Written around 1039, the earliest surviving Life of St. Zenobius narrates the Florentines' transfer of the relics of its protagonist from the old suburban cathedral of San Lorenzo to the current episcopal seat and urban baptismal parish, San Giovanni.[76] Much as the Holy Spirit had rendered the body of St. Alexander inordinately heavy, thereby compelling its burial in a fortified urban church, so St. Zenobius refused to be carried over the threshold of the pieve until the presiding unnamed bishop appointed twelve clerics who would perpetually guard and venerate his body in prayer. Like the *Passio Sancti Alexandri*, this Life signals the necessity of protecting holy relics, albeit from external rather than internal threats. Recalling the Normans who had sailed up the Arno in 825 and pillaged the extramural cathedral of Fiesole, it ascribes St. Zenobius's translation to the occupation of the surrounding territories by foreign tribes. Less convincingly, the *Vita Sancti Zenobii* dates this event to the years just after its subject's death in 417, as does a subsequent, revised Life written in the twelfth century. Yet the identification of the presiding bishop as "Andrea" in this second text suggests that the translation had in fact occurred much later: the only Florentine prelate known to have been so named lived in the late ninth century.[77]

Further and hitherto unrecognized evidence for Andrea's involvement in the translation of St. Zenobius emerges in connection with his fidelity to the Carolingian Empire. An imperial legate, Andrea traveled to Pavia in 875 for the coronation of Charles the Bald (875–877). On this occasion, the new emperor accelerated the decline of extramural martyria already seen in Lucca and Fiesole by decreeing that all cathedrals and canonries

---

[75] *Vita Sancti Donati*, ch. 2, in *AS* October, vol. 9, col. 662, no. 28.

[76] *Vita Sancti Zenobii I* (*BHL* 9014), ch. 3, no. 13, in *AS* May, vol. 6, col. 61, on the authorship and dating of which see chapter 4, this volume. The earliest surviving evidence for the dedication of the pieve to St. John the Baptist and the status of this church as the seat of the bishop appears in an imperial confirmation of Florentine episcopal property rights: Renato Piattoli, *Le carte della canonica della cattedrale di Firenze (723-1149)* (Rome: Istituto storico italiano per il Medio Evo, 1938), no. 2, 6–7 (852).

[77] Anna Benvenuti, "Stratigrafie della memoria: Scritture agiographiche e mutamenti architettonici nella vicenda del 'Complesso cattedrale' fiorentino," In *Il bel San Giovanni e Santa Maria del Fiore: Il centro religioso di Firenze dal tardo antico al Rinascimento*, ed. Domenico Cardini (Florence: Le lettere, 1996), 113–114. The account of St. Zenobius's translation appears in the *Vita Sancti Eugenii* (*BHL* 2682), which is appended to the *Vita Sancti Zenobii II* (*BHL* 9015) in the passionary of San Lorenzo of Florence, BLF, Pluteo 27.1, fol. 143 (saec. XII), and in Giovanni Lammi, *Charitonis et Hippophili hodeoporicon*, 4 vols. (Florence: Viviani, 1741-1754), vol. 2, 574–575. On the authorship and dating of both Lives, see chapter 7, this volume.

henceforth be located within their city's walls.[78] Andrea's transfer of his episcopal seat from the suburban basilica of San Lorenzo to the urban pieve may have been a direct response to Charles's legislation, in which case the transfer of St. Zenobius to that same church presumably occurred in 875 or soon thereafter as well.

That Andrea followed not only current imperial policy but also earlier precedents established in the Tuscan capital of Lucca makes his involvement in the translation of St. Zenobius all the more credible. By interring the body of this sanctified Florentine in the pieve, Andrea confirmed the transfer of his seat from San Lorenzo to this urban church and thus the centralization of episcopal authority within the walls likewise encouraged by Bishop Giovanni in Lucca a century earlier. Moreover, the Florentine pieve already resembled its Lucchese counterpart by comprising a basilica and freestanding baptistery.[79] Tradition ascribes to Andrea the rededication of its high altar to St. Reparata, who had no previous association with this city, and thus joined John the Baptist as the titulars of that church.[80] This double-dedication, distinctive of if not unique to Lucca, endured in Florence until the late tenth century, when the basilica became associated exclusively with St. Reparata and its baptistery with St. John.[81] Bishop Andrea's translation of St. Zenobius would have conformed to a broader pattern of emulation as did the very crypt in which that saint came to rest: situated beneath the high altar of the

---

[78] Ludovico Antonio Muratori, *Rerum italicarum scriptores*, 25 vols. (Milan: Typ. Societatis Palatinae, 1723–51), vol. 2, pt. 2, col. 153. On the development of the Tuscan canonries and their chapters of canons, see chapter 3, this volume. As emperor and king of West Francia (840–877), Charles further signaled the rise of urban cathedrals and other churches via the itinerary of his court. Unlike his predecessors, he preferred urban rather than rural sites, either episcopal residences or (later) royal or episcopal monasteries: Janet L. Nelson, "Charles the Bald and the Church in Town and Countryside," in *The Church in Town and Countryside: Papers Read at the Seventeenth Summer Meeting and the Eighteenth Winter Meeting of the Ecclesiastical History Society*, ed. Derek Baker (Oxford: Oxford University Press, 1979), 111–112.

[79] The early medieval baptistery of Florence was a relatively small octagonal structure, of which the foundations survive beneath its much larger, twelfth-century successor: Franklin Toker, "A Baptistery Below the Baptistery of Florence," *Art Bulletin* 58 (1976): 163–165. See also the more recent discussions of the early medieval baptistery in Domenico Cardini, "Ipotesi sulle fasi trasformative del Centro religioso dalla formazione della cinta difensiva carolingia alla sua sostituzione," in *Il bel San Giovanni e Santa Maria del Fiore: Il centro religioso di Firenze dal tardo antico al Rinascimento*, ed. Domenico Cardini (Florence: Le lettere, 1996), 151–156.

[80] See most recently Benvenuti, "Stratigrafie," 109–114.

[81] An act of 987, issued "in atrio ecclesie Sancte Reparate," constitutes the earliest such reference to the basilica dedicated to that virgin and martyr: Piattoli, *Le carte*, no. 19, 57 (6 June 987). Meanwhile, in his foundation charter of San Miniato (on which see chapter 3, this volume), Bishop Ildebrando identified the urban parish as the *plebs Sancte Reparate*: Luciana Mosiici, ed. *Le carte del monastero di S. Miniato al Monte (secoli IX-XII)* (Florence: Leo S. Olschki, 1990), no. 5, 71 (27 April 1018). On the broader disassociation between the basilica and the baptistery, see Benvenuti, "Stratigrafie," 118–120; Mauro Ronzani, "La 'plebs' in città. La problematica della pieve urbana in Italia centro-settentrionale fra IX e il XIV secolo," in *Chiesa e città: Contributi della Commissione italiana di storia ecclesiastica comparata aderente alla Commission international d'histoire écclesiastique comparée al XVII Congresso internazionale di scienze storiche (Madrid, 26 agosto-2 settembre 1990)*, ed. Cosimo Damiano Fonseca and Cinzio Violante (Galatina: Congedo 1990), 35–36; and Toker, "The Baptistery," 165.

Florentine pieve and likewise ascribable to Andrea, it was an annular confessional of the type introduced from Rome to Tuscany by Bishop Giovanni.[82] In conjunction with the persisting threats to local security and Charles the Bald's preference for urban cathedrals, the similarities between Lucca and Florence argue strongly in favor of Andrea's translation of St. Zenobius.

The desire to safeguard relics in urban, fortified locations so characteristic of the ninth century provoked the transfer of a second Florentine saint *intra muros*, albeit one from which the local bishop was conspicuously absent. St. Minias lay atop the Monte Fiorentino to south of the Arno, the purported site of his execution upon the order of Emperor Decius (249–251). His shrine had obtained distinction as the only religious foundation in Tuscany to receive a donation of land from Charlemagne. In 786, the Frankish king had celebrated Christmas in Florence and gave four houses to a single priest named Haderisus, in residence at San Miniato.[83] The attack on Florence by a band of Magyars (or Hungarians) a year after Bishop Andrea's death in 894 surely called into question the wisdom of leaving St. Minias in such a vulnerable site.[84] His body still lay atop the Monte Fiorentino in May of 898, when an imperial charter cited nine unidentified saints buried at this shrine; however, a revised version of the charter issued in the following April mentions only eight saints, but names St. Minias as well as John the Baptist as titular of the urban pieve.[85] An eleventh-century inventory of the pieve provides further evidence that the Florentines had translated the martyr to their pieve by identifying him among the relics of that church.[86] Lacking any mention of the participation of a

---

[82] Franklin Toker, "Excavations Below the Cathedral of Florence," *Gesta* 14 (1975): 30–32. More recently, Franklin Toker, *Archeological Campaigns Below the Florence Duomo and Baptistery, 1895-1980* (Turnhout: Brepols, 2013), 177–180, has suggested that the "tomb 46" discovered under the nave of Santa Reparata had served as St. Zenobius's temporary burial place before the construction of the confessional by Bishop Andrea. By contrast, Cardini, "Ipotesi," 130–131, argues that the confessional dates from the fifth or sixth century and thus antecedes St. Zenobius's translation. According to this latter hypothesis, sometime in the ninth or tenth century, the Florentines (and perhaps Andrea) transformed the annular confessional into a larger hall crypt of the sort documented in the cathedrals of Arezzo and Fiesole in the decades around 1000, a development Toker (p. 35) dates to the thirteenth century.

[83] MGH DK, vol. 1, no. 55, 210. An earlier witness to St. Minias's cult is the foundation of a church in his honor by seventeen individuals on a site now occupied by the town of San Miniato in the province of Pisa. In 783, Bishop Giovanni I of Lucca reported that the nomination of its first rector occurred with the consent of his episcopal predecessor, Balsari (fl. 700): *MDL*, vol. 5, pt. 2, no. 189, 111.

[84] Robert Davidsohn, *Storia di Firenze*, trans. Giovanni Battista Klein, 7 vols. (Florence: Sansoni, 1956-1965), vol. 1, 145.

[85] Piattoli, *Le carte*, no. 7, 22 (21 May 898) and no. 8, 24 (25 April 899). Cf. Benvenuti, "Stratigrafie," 116–118, who ascribes the translation of St. Minias to the pieve to Bishop Andrea.

[86] See the eleventh-century inventory of the cathedral that survives in a seventeenth-century copy, ASF, Carte Strozziane II, 56, fols. 22v–23v, on which see Marica S. Tacconi, *Cathedral and Civic Ritual in Late Medieval and Renaissance Florence: The Service-Books of Santa Maria del Fiore* (Cambridge: Cambridge University Press, 2005), 94–97.

local bishop, however, these scattered documentary sources provide no richly detailed narratives of episcopal authority so prominent in Lucchese and Fiesolane hagiography.

The cases of Fiesole and Florence thus show how, in response to the insecurity of the ninth century, Tuscan bishops adopted the role of defender as well as those of lord and builder. Indeed, the heroic protection of ecclesiastical *temporalia* and *spiritualia* ascribed to St. Alexander and St. Donatus earned these bishops inclusion in the ranks of the holy. External threats such as Vikings or Magyars also accelerated the migration of Tuscan relics *intra muros*. Through such translations, local bishops recognized the holiness of such long-dead saints as Zenobius and Minias, as well as the recently deceased St. Alexander. They concomitantly elevated urban basilicas at the expense of suburban or rural shrines. San Pietro in Gerusalemme in Fiesole and the pieve of Florence emerged with newfound treasure and thus a potential source of lucrative income from pilgrims. Driving these developments were not only such local dynamics but also regional and supra-regional ones, including the precedents set by Bishop Giovanni I of Lucca in the eighth century and concerted imperial involvement in Italian affairs.

* * * * *

While the aforementioned Lives, Passions, and Translations of early medieval Tuscany feature diverse protagonists and settings, they reflect with striking unanimity the interests of bishops and their clergy by presenting narratives of episcopal authority. These texts strongly imply that the lawful transfer of holy relics was the exclusive purview of a local prelate. Only Bishop Giovanni (when directed by an angel) and Bishop Romano (after having celebrated matins with his clerics) were able to disinter the relics of St. Regulus and St. Alexander without facing divine retribution. Although such episodes belong to a common stock of hagiographic topoi, they appear particularly pointed given the conspicuous absence of alternate models. Early Tuscan hagiography featured few if any accounts of monastic translations of relics—narratives that proliferated elsewhere and naturally evinced little episcopal orientation.[87] Moreover, it shows no discernible trace of the influential measures taken at the Council of Mainz in 813 to curb the license of individual bishops and to bolster the authority of the empire. The legislators ruled that legitimate translations of relics necessitated not only the presence of the local prelate but also the assent of a secular ruler, as well as an entire synod of bishops.[88]

In Tuscany, by contrast, a translation became a "theft" when temporal authorities were involved in the transfer of relics. The gastald of Siena, Guasperto, learned this lesson when he moved St. Ansanus to a new altar without leave from Bishop Stabile of Arezzo

---

[87] See, for instance, the cases of monastic translations discussed in Geary, *Furta Sacra*, 56–86.
[88] The fifty-first canon of the Council of Mainz (813), "Ne corpora sanctorum transferantur de loco ad locum," in MGH C, vol. 2. pt. 1, 272, on the substance and subsequent influence of which, see Kemp, *Canonization*, 39–42.

in the early eighth century. So too did Margrave Adalbert I of Tuscany (ca. 847–886), who in 878 laid siege to the city of Narni (near Viterbo in Umbria) in retaliation for its loyalty to his adversary, Pope John VIII. A Translation written from the Narniense perspective tells how the patron saints of the city—Juvenal, Cassius, and Fausta— prevented Adalbert from penetrating its walls by force, thus obliging him to enter by trickery.[89] Having promised the citizens to depart in peace if his army was allowed to march through their city unmolested, he permitted his soldiers to loot the city and carry away the relics of its three saints. Adalbert brought the spoils to his capital of Lucca and interred them in San Frediano. The Lucchese recension of the Translation concludes with a joyful call to venerate the newly acquired saints, but the Narniense one ends on a less victorious note. A series of natural disasters punished the Lucchese for their misbegotten relics and moved Adalbert to return St. Juvenal (but not Sts. Cassius and Fausta) to Narni. Without episcopal license, by implication, the margrave was little more than a common relic thief.

If bishops thus played the central role in establishing the most prominent relic cults of early medieval Tuscany, they shared the stage with their clerics, who not only witnessed their decrees and served as episcopal vicars but also were essential to the translation of relics and consecration of churches.[90] They were the priests and deacons who sang psalms and hymns as they bore St. Regulus from Populonia to Lucca, the singers who chanted matins before laying St. Alexander below the high altar of San Pietro in Gerusalemme, and the clerics appointed to venerate St. Zenobius in his new home in Florence. Even the Translation of Sts. Juvenal, Cassius, and Fausta underscored the key musical role of this supporting cast. In a clever reversal, Adalbert's brutal soldiers (implausibly) sang the requisite musical praises as they carried away their illicitly acquired relics. From the ninth century, the bishops' clerics gradually emerged from the shadow of their episcopal lords to form communities distinct from their households and dubbed "congregations," "colleges," or finally, "chapters" (the term adopted here). As shown in chapter 3, these communities laid claim to diverse patrons and protectors: emperors and bishops as well as the saints buried in their churches. As they amplified the effect of transalpine politics on local ecclesiastical affairs, the evolving relationships between these varied actors—ultramontane and Italian, lay and clerical, living and dead—indelibly shaped the development of Tuscan relic cults from the mid-ninth through the mid-eleventh centuries.

---

[89] The following summarizes the *Translatio Iuvenalis et Cassii episcoporum Narniensium Lucam* (*BHL* 4615), in MHG SS, vol. 30, 976–83, on which see Savigni, *Episcopato e società*, 319–320; and Adolfo Simonetti, "Alberto I Marchese di Toscano e il saccheggio di Narni nell'878," *Bollettino della Deputazione di Storia Patria per l'Umbria* 7 (1901): 1–17.

[90] The earliest surviving documentary witness to the bishop's clergy in Tuscany is the decree of Bishop Felice of Lucca witnessed by an archpriest and four priests: Schiaparelli, *Codice*, vol. 1, no. 7, 16–9 (20 January 685). On the early history of the bishop's clergy in Lucca, see Concioni, *Vescovi*.

3

The Bishop's Clergy, 840–1039

FROM THEIR VERY inception, cathedral chapters elicited a broad measure of scrutiny that signaled the diverse authorities to which these foundations would answer. Although clerical communities had served cathedrals since late Antiquity, their consolidation into chapters distinct from their bishop's household necessitated a "rule" (*canon*), to which its members signaled their subordination by adopting the title of "canon" (*canonicus*). This rule was provided by Emperor Louis the Pious (813–840), who, with his son Lothair I, was remembered in Tuscany as the original champion of such communities.[1] The two sovereigns followed Louis's father, Charlemagne, in styling themselves as the protectors and legislators of the church, and shared his belief that vibrant religious communities loyal to the empire fostered both political stability and spiritual well-being.[2] In 816, Louis issued thirty-three capitularies mandating the formation of cathedral chapters. Known collectively as the Rule of Aachen, they provided the template for the governance of cathedral chapters in Tuscany and throughout the Carolingian Empire and its successor states.[3] The Rule prescribed a quasi-monastic arrangement to ensure that canons performed their most important duty: the celebration of the liturgy. They were

---

[1] Thus the *Vita Sancti Donati*, in *AS* October, vol. 9, col. 656, situates its protagonist's pilgrimage to Rome during the reign of Louis and Lothair, "who had together instituted the holy canonical rule at the palace of Aachen in 816" (*qui sanctam in eorum coadunatione apud Aquisgrani palatium canonicam instituerunt regulam sub anno Dominicæ Incarnationis Domini CCCXVI*).

[2] Rosamond McKitterick, *The Frankish Church and the Carolingian Reforms, 789-895* (London: Royal Historical Society, 1977), 1–16, surveys the ecclesiastical legislation of Charlemagne and his successors, noting the premium it placed on political stability, as well as the emperor's role as defender of churches (9–10).

[3] In fact, the Council of Aachen issued no fewer than 145 capitularies, of which the first 113 present quotations from patristic sources or early conciliar legislation concerning the life and obligations of the clergy. The final 33 provide concrete prescriptions, or "rules" (*regula canonicorum*) in question. The latter appear in MGH C,

to live in a "canonry" (*canonica*) situated near the cathedral and comprising a dormitory, refectory, and storeroom around an enclosed cloister.[4] Although frequent references to the local bishop underlined his role in overseeing canons, the Rule left no doubt that the ultimate arbiter of canonical life was the emperor.

A third class of patron of cathedral chapters comprised local saints whose relics aided in the accumulation of the wealth upon which these communities depended. In contrast with bishops, who were increasingly outsiders appointed by the emperor, canons were usually locals drawn from the minor aristocracy or from families of judges or notaries.[5] They naturally styled themselves as protectors and venerators of saints buried in their churches: the Florentines, for instance, traced the origins of their community to the translation of St. Zenobius from an extramural shrine to their urban cathedral.[6] Once established, a chapter needed a shared income that would free its members from indigence and distraction, thus allowing them to dedicate themselves to the celebration of the liturgy. The Rule of Aachen made such common wealth all the more necessary by encouraging (but not requiring) canons to follow monks in renouncing personal property.[7] Pious offerings made to cathedrals and their relics provided the traditional source of revenue and thus amplified the importance of holy treasure to canons.[8] Equally if not more significant was land given directly to a chapter in perpetuity, either at the moment of its foundation or during the early centuries of its history. Such donations

---

vol. 2, pt. 1, 396–421, and were themselves based on the 34 capitularies issued by Bishop Chrodegang of Metz around 755 for the clergy of his cathedral: Julia Barrow, "Chrodegang, his Rule and its Successors," *Early Medieval Europe* 26 (2006): 203–204; cf. M. A. Claussen, *The Reform of the Frankish Church: Chrodegang of Metz and the Regula Canonicorum in the Eighth Century* (Cambridge: Cambridge University Press, 2004). Barrow, "Chrodegang," 204, notes that the Rule of Aachen "was used by cathedral communities to provide general guidance rather than a strict rule." Indeed, evidence for its adoption in Tuscany remains uneven and limited to allusions in legal and narrative sources such as the *Vita Sancti Donati* cited above in n. 1. On the early development of cathedral chapters in Italy, see Maureen C. Miller, *The Bishop's Palace: Architecture and Authority in Medieval Italy* (Ithaca, NY: Cornell University Press, 2000), 81–83, who expresses reservations about their adherence to the Rule and notes (81) that the majority of manuscript sources for the Rule in Italian libraries date from the eleventh or twelfth centuries.

[4] MGH C, vol. 2, pt. 1, no. 117, 398 (on the canonry) and no. 123, 398 (on residence in the dormitory).

[5] Miller, *The Bishop's Palace*, 85; and Hagen Keller, "Origine sociale e formazione del clero cattedrale dei secoli XI e XII nella Germania e nell'Italia settentrionale," in *Le istituzioni ecclesiastiche della 'societas christiana' dei secoli XI-XII. Diocesi, pievi, parrocchie. Atti della VI settimana internazionale di studi (Milano, 1-7 settembre 1974)* (Milan: Vita e pensiero, 1977), 155–158. Raffaele Savigni, *Episcopato e società cittadina a Lucca: Da Anselmo II (†1086) a Roberto (†1225)* (Lucca: S. Marco, 1996), 150–153, discusses the origins of the cathedral canons of Lucca in particular while Anscar Parsons, *Canonical Elections* (Washington, DC: Catholic University of America Press, 1939), 43–45, notes the ubiquity of imperial selection of bishops from the ninth through the early eleventh century.

[6] See chapter 2, this volume.

[7] MGH C, vol. 2, pt. 1, nos. 115–116, 397.

[8] Pope Gelasius I (492–496) had long ago established the principle of dividing offerings to the bishopric into four equal parts to be allocated to the bishop, to his clergy, to the poor, and for the renovation of churches. See the twenty-seventh decree of his ninth letter, in PL, vol. 59, col. 56, which was incorporated into the capitularies issued by the Council of Tribur in 895 and by the Council of Nantes of approximately

produced capitular patrimonies that promised a stable income in the form of rents. The largest and most significant of such gifts came from emperors and bishops, who invariably named the holy relics venerated by the canons as they justifying their largesse. The holy men buried in and around Tuscan cathedrals were not only spiritual patrons to whom the canons directed liturgical prayers but also generators of the temporal wealth that allowed them to do so.

The history of the cathedral chapters and their patrons emerges through close readings of an even richer and more varied collection of sources than was available for chapter 2. The legal charters pertaining to the creation or reform of these communities provide the evidentiary foundation for chapter 3. The authors of these documents were local bishops and emperors who sought, *inter alia*, to obtain spiritual salvation via the canons' intercessory prayers. The charters are highly formulaic and usually include three elements: a confirmation of preexisting property of the chapter, an offering of new property, and a pledge of protection against the expropriation of the resulting capitular patrimony. Some also include narrative excursus that raise matters beyond the economic sphere by addressing the motivations of the canons and their patrons.[9] Traditionally the purview of ecclesiastical historians, the charters under consideration have rarely been studied in light of hagiographic, much less liturgical, texts; however, reading these three types of sources together and in tandem with archeological evidence yields two major benefits. First, it uncovers thematic correspondences between charters and hagiography and thereby provides new interpretive contexts for the anonymous and undated Lives and Passions. Second and more important, this holistic approach reveals that the evolving relationships between emperors, bishops, and canons shaped local relic cults in all their architectural, literary, and musical splendor.

Through a sequence of historical vignettes that unfolded in Arezzo, Fiesole, and Florence from the 840s to 1030s, chapter 3 demonstrates three long-recognized developments in Italian ecclesiastical history that shaped the interactions between cathedral chapters and their patrons. First, the dissolution of Carolingian power in the late ninth century deprived the chapters of their imperial protectors, resulting in a decline in their wealth and discipline. Furthermore, the lack of central authority encouraged bishops to expropriate the canons' land in the manner of unscrupulous laymen. Such prelates thus became anti-heroes in the religious history of their dioceses. Second, the reestablishment of imperial dominion under the Ottonian dynasty in 962 begat the return of ambitious bishops who added the foundation or reform of cathedral chapters as per the Rule of Aachen to the more traditional activities of an episcopal lord and builder: the translation of saints,

---

the same year: Giovanni Domenico Mansi, *Sacrorum Conciliorum Nova et Amplissima Collectio*, 31 vols. (Venice: Antonio Zatta 1759–1798), vol. 18, ch. 13, cols. 139–140 and ch. 10, col. 169, respectively.

[9] Sarah Foot, "Reading Anglo-Saxon Charters: Memory, Record, or Story?," in *Narrative and History in the Early Medieval West*, ed. Elizabeth M. Tyler and Ross Balzaretti (Turnhout: Brepols, 2006), 41–46, surveys recent research on narrative elements in legal charters of the central Middle Ages.

the building of tombs and churches, and the writing of hagiography. The political loyalties of such philo-imperial bishops, moreover, shaped their promotion of relic cults more thoroughly and explicitly than in the past. The third development was the emergence of Tuscany as a central arena for monastic reformers in the eleventh century, ones whose austere ideals of clerical virtue challenged and influenced local bishops. If episcopal *dominus et constructor* remained the protagonist in the history of Tuscan relic cults, his actions were nonetheless more constrained by an increasingly varied cast of characters.

EMPERORS—CANONS—BISHOPS

The foundation of the cathedral chapter of Arezzo demonstrates that relic cults provided emperors with a key incentive to promote the consolidation of such corporate communities by local bishops. The most distinctive witness to this event is the *History of the Custodians of Arezzo*, a chronicle written around 1100. The only surviving chronicle to pertain to a Tuscan cathedral, it synthesizes and quotes an unusually rich collection of charters in the capitular archives of its city.[10] As related in the *History*, Lothair I undertook a tour of the empire in 840 after the death of his father, Louis the Pious, with whom he had issued the Rule of Aachen twenty-five years earlier.[11] He was the first of many emperors drawn to Arezzo because of its holy treasure, as well as by its convenience as a way station on one of the principal routes to Rome, the Via Cassia. Just southwest of the city, atop the hill named Pionta, stood the cathedral of Ss. Maria e Stefano and the nearby shrine of the fourth-century Aretine bishop and martyr named Donatus (not to be confused with the ninth-century Fiesolane bishop of the same name). According to the *History*, Lothair visited the city in order to pray at the tomb of this saint, whose inclusion (one might add) in such influential works as the *Dialogues* of Gregory the Great (ca. 593) and the martyrology of Bede (ca. 731) made him the only Tuscan martyr widely venerated beyond the region and north of the Alps.[12] Lothair's anger at the

---

[10] *Historia Custodum Aretinorum*, in MGH SS, vol. 30, 1468–1482, on which see William North, "The Fragmentation and Redemption of a Medieval Cathedral: Property, Conflict, and Public Piety in Eleventh-Century Arezzo," in *Conflict in Medieval Europe: Changing Perspectives on Society and Culture* (Aldershot: Ashgate, 2003), 109–130; and Jean Delumeau, *Arezzo: Espace et sociétés, 715–1230* (Rome: Ecole française de Rome, 1996), vol. 1, 475–562. The incorporation of material from charters into chronicles was common in monastic histories of the ninth through the twelfth centuries: John Van Engen, "The 'Crisis of Cenobitism' Reconsidered: Benedictine Monasticism in the Years 1050-1150," *Speculum* 61 (1986): 287–288; and Marjorie Chinball, "Charter and Chronicle: The Use of Archive Sources by Norman Historians," in *Church and Government in the Middle Ages: Essays Presented to C. R. Cheney on his 70th Birthday*, ed. Christopher Nugent Lawrence Brooke (Cambridge: Cambridge University Press, 1976), 1–17. See, for instance, the case discussed in Julia Barrow, "William of Malmesbury's Use of Charters," in *Narrative and History in the Early Medieval West*, ed. Elizabeth M. Tyler and Ross Balzaretti (Turnhout: Brepols, 2006), 67–89.

[11] *Historia Custodum Aretinorum*, in MGH SS, vol. 30, no. 1, 1471.

[12] See chapter 6, this volume.

absence of a chapter of canons at Ss. Maria e Stefano stemmed not only from the failure of his host, Bishop Pietro, to implement the Rule of Aachen but also, by implication, from the resulting neglect of St. Donatus. Faced with his sovereign's displeasure, Pietro founded a chapter and built it a canonry adjacent to the cathedral. As documented in contemporary charters and synthesized much later in the *History*, the Aretines ascribed the origins of their cathedral chapter to the devotion of an emperor (and not a local bishop) to its most prized relic.

Lothair's power and initiative contrasts with the profile of Bishop Pietro, whose motivations appear to have derived from his loyalty to his imperial patron rather than a desire to establish his own reputation, in life and in death, as a lord and builder. In an undated charter upon which the *History of the Custodians* based its account of the foundation of the chapter, Pietro bestowed upon twelve inaugural canons four plots of episcopal land, which would free them "from indigence, so that they might pray delightfully for the stability of the kingdom and empire of our lords."[13] He thus stands as the nominal founder of the chapter, of which the number of canons (twelve) cast them as apostles loyal to their Christ-like bishop; however, as Pietro himself acknowledged, he was simply (and belatedly) complying with imperial legislation as the personal behest of his lord, Lothair. In endowing the chapter, moreover, he created a new community of clerical landowners subject to his authority but whose property, as stipulated in the charter, remained exempt from episcopal interference for as long as it pleased the emperor. The fiscal autonomy bestowed upon the canons reinforces the impression of Pietro as less commanding a figure than those episcopal *domini et constructores* discussed in chapter 2.

Subsequent Aretine prelates likewise proved less active than lay donors, and emperors and kings in particular, in rewarding the cathedral chapter for discharging its key mission of liturgical prayer. Indeed, the canons soon became competitors with their bishop for lay donations: in 843, Lothair confirmed Pietro's grant of protection and enlarged their nascent patrimony.[14] Thus began a virtuous cycle recounted in the *History of the Custodians*: news of the canons' strict adherence to the Rule of Aachen spread and provoked many devout men to enrich these clerics with their own gifts.[15] If a reputation for clerical discipline proved to be a lucrative source of income, so too did a much venerated relic. In 936, for example, King Hugh of Italy (926–945) visited St. Donatus's shrine just as Lothair had done almost a century before. He enlarged the canon's properties and reminded them of their liturgical duties to their heavenly and earthly patrons, under whose protection they were to serve God and pray for the safety of Hugh's realm and

---

[13] Ubaldo Pasqui, *Documenti per la storia della città di Arezzo nel medio evo*, 4 vols. (Florence: G. P. Vieusseux, 1899, 1904, 1916, 1937), vol. 1, no. 30, 44–45: "quatenus ipsi cannonici et sacerdotes, qui ibidem consistunt et Domino famulantur, absque indigentia vivere possint et delectabiliter exorare valeant, pro stabilitate regni et imperii domnorum nostrorum." On this charter in general, see Delumeau, *Arezzo*, vol. 1, 490–491.

[14] Pasqui, *Documenti*, vol. 1, no. 34, 48–49 (29 August 843).

[15] *Historia Custodum Aretinorum*, in MGH SS, vol. 30, no. 1, 1471.

that of his soul.[16] In concert with Tuscan donors, emperors and kings rather than local prelates played the starring role in the early history of the cathedral chapter.

A local relic cult could nonetheless limit as well as encourage imperial influence over local bishops and cathedral chapters. As related in chapter 2, Charles the Bald had issued an edict at his imperial coronation in 875 that all cathedrals and canonries be located within their city's walls, thus accelerating the broader pattern of favoring urban shrines at the expense of suburban or rural ones. One attendee, Bishop Andrea of Florence, obeyed, moving his seat from San Lorenzo to the baptismal parish of his city; but another, Bishop Giovanni of Arezzo, proved less compliant. When Charles soon passed through Arezzo en route to Rome, the emperor acknowledged that its cathedral quite appropriately stood near St. Donatus's extramural shrine, the location of which, he admitted, the saint had perhaps chosen before his death; however, Charles made clear his preference that Arezzo "glitter with the gables of its church within its walls." He thus donated the city forum as the site of a new cathedral and canonry so that there would resound "canonical celebrations of divine praise where until now there were aired legal disputes."[17] That the local bishops and canons nonetheless remained outside the city at Pionta in flagrant disregard of the directive reveals the enduring appeal of extramural martyria and the waning of imperial authority even in Arezzo, an ally of the empire throughout the Middle Ages.[18] More broadly, it illustrates that relic cults attracted the interest but did not necessarily yield to the desires of powerful outsiders.

With the collapse of imperial dominion in Italy in the late ninth century, cathedral chapters struggled to protect their spiritual and temporal wealth from various threats, external and internal. The former included Viking and Magyar incursions that, as previously noted, encouraged the Florentines to translate St. Zenobius and St. Minias to their urban pieve. More deleterious was the confiscation of capitular property by local landowners and thus the impoverishment of cathedral canons, a cruel blow to religious communities of which the identities were so intimately tied to their patrimonies. Among the witnesses to their resulting decline was the aforementioned King Hugh, whose stepfather and mother, Margrave Adalbert II (884/6–915) and Bertha (d. 925), had patronized the canons of Lucca and Pisa much as Emperor Lothair had once championed their Aretine counterparts.[19] Hugh likewise supported such communities in Lucca, Pisa, and, as noted

---

[16] Pasqui, *Documenti*, vol. 1, no. 61, 86 (17 January 936). Cf. *Historia Custodum Aretinorum*, in MGH SS, vol. 30, no. 1, 1471–1472.

[17] Pasqui, *Documenti*, vol. 1, no. 43, 61–63 (1 March 876): "et cur intra moenia civitatis, more ceterarum, domus Dei sede pollens antistitis non emineret, perspicacius inquisisse. . . ut episcopo in sua sede apud sanctum Donatum residente, ibi nihilominus per eius ordinationem divina laudis canonicae fiant concelebrationes ubi actenus mallationum ventilatae sunt lites," on which see Delumeau, *Arezzo*, vol. 1, 493–494.

[18] That the author of the *History of the Custodians* likewise considered the exchange between Charles the Bald and Bishop Giovanni of Arezzo an anomalous one in his city's history is confirmed in his decision to include no mention of it in his chronicle.

[19] Adalbert and Bertha made their first recorded donation of land to the cathedral canons of Lucca: Pietro Guidi and O. Parenti, eds., *Regesto del capitolo di Lucca*, 3 vols. (Rome: Ermanno Loescher, 1910–1933), vol. 1,

above, Arezzo, but indicated in his charters that the usurpation of capitular land was not the fault of unscrupulous laymen alone. That he felt obliged to forbid the appropriation of such wealth by local bishops clearly indicates that such prelates numbered among the potential culprits.[20] Most deleterious to the spiritual unity and discipline of the canons, however, was their own financial mismanagement: many encouraged the alienation of their property by issuing perpetual leases (*livelli*), which Hugh acidly described as a veritable Tuscan tradition.[21] From foreign marauders to corrupt bishops and incompetent canons, many actors threatened capitular *spiritualia* and *temporalia* in this time without a strong, central authority.

Conversely, the return of imperial power in Italy under the new Ottonian dynasty provided impetus for the creation and preservation of cathedral chapters as per older, Carolingian policies. In 962, Pope John XII crowned Otto I of Germany (936–973) Holy Roman Emperor at St. Peter's in Rome, which provides the immediate political background for the establishment of the cathedral chapter of Fiesole four years later. The foundation charter issued by Bishop Zenobio is novel in its depiction of such prelates as both heroes and anti-heroes. Zenobio quoted his clerics' reports of their indigence due to the "destruction and dissipation of our church" and the "malign and unjust decree made by that most wicked Vinizzone," evidently his predecessor.[22] The precipitous decline of the canons' wealth had in turn led to their abandonment of the major basilica of

---

no. 3, 3–4. Adalbert meanwhile supported the efforts of the bishop of Pisa to save his canons from poverty, as recalled in the charter of Bishop Grimaldo of Pisa (fl. 958–965), in Natale Caturegli, ed., *Regestum pisanum* (Rome: Istituto storico italiano per il Medio Evo, 1938), no. 49, 28; and Ferdinando Ughelli, *Italia Sacra*, 8 vols. (Rome: Bernardino Tano, 1644–1662), vol. 3, cols. 353–354, which is itself based on an earlier but now lost exemplar by Bishop Zenobio (fl. 930–954): Emma Falaschi, *Carte dell'Archivio Capitolare di Pisa 1 (930-1050)* (Rome: Edizioni di storia e letteratura, 1971), no. 1, 1–4 (December 930).

[20] Pasqui, *Documenti*, vol. 1, no. 63, 87–88 (21 March 939), on which see Delumeau, *Arezzo*, 495–496.

[21] Pasqui, *Documenti*, vol. 1, no. 61, 84–86 (17 January 933), on which see Delumeau, *Arezzo*, 495–497; and Mauro Ronzani, "Vescovi, canoniche e cattedrali nella 'Tuscia' dei secoli X e XI: Qualche considerazione a partire dall'esempio di Fiesole," in *Un archivio, una diocesi: Fiesole nel medioevo e nell'età moderna*, ed. Maura Borgioli (Florence: Leo S. Olschki, 1996), 7–13. On the role of such long-term leases in the dissipation of ecclesiastical land around Florence and throughout Italy in the tenth century, see Chris Wickham, *Early Medieval Italy: Central Power and Local Society 400–1000* (Totowa, NJ: Barnes & Noble, 1981), 142–143; and Robert Davidsohn, *Storia di Firenze,* trans. Giovanni Battista Klein, 7 vols. (Florence: Sansoni, 1956–1965), vol. 1, 212–213.

[22] "Propter destructionem et dissipationem ecclesiae nostrae, et propter tam gravem intentionem, et malignam, et iniustamque ordinatem, quam ille pessimus Venizanes egit contra te, et contra nostram matrem ecclesiam, quae in praesenti est modo desolata, et in ruinis posita." The following discussion summarizes Zenobio's charter, edited in Ughelli, *Italia Sacra*, vol. 3, cols. 215–217 (966), from which the present quotation derives (col. 215). Yoram Milo, *Tuscany and the Dynamics of Church Reform in the Eleventh Century*, Ph.D. diss., Stanford University, 1979, 67–71, characterizes the bishop as refounding the cathedral chapter and reinstituting the Rule of Aachen; however, Zenobio gives no indication that the cathedral clergy had formed a corporate community subject to a Rule before his arrival. This would explain why in 890 Margrave Adalbert II made a donation of land to the bishopric of Fiesole rather than to a cathedral chapter as he did in Lucca: Ughelli, *Italia Sacra*, vol. 3, col. 214 (7 June 890).

their city, San Pietro in Gerusalemme, as well as the extramural cathedral dedicated to the same saint (fig. 2.1). In order to ensure the proper celebration of the liturgy at both churches, Zenobio endowed a chapter of fifteen canons with episcopal properties, marking the belated implementation of the Rule of Aachen in Fiesole exactly one hundred and fifty years after the promulgation of that imperial legislation. He followed the policy established by Emperor Charles the Bald in 877 by building a canonry within the city walls at the church of Santa Maria rather than at the cathedral. Finally, Zenobio signaled his allegiance to the new imperial line, entrusting this new religious community to "our lords," Otto I and his son and co-regent, Otto II (961–983). Once again, transalpine politics inflected a local Tuscan story, in which a virtuous bishop atoned for the crimes of his corrupt predecessor by implementing imperial policy.

In Fiesole unlike in Arezzo, imperial influence over local ecclesiastical affairs accompanied an assertive posture on the part of the bishop as Zenobio styled himself as a steadfast defender of the cathedral chapter. This model of episcopal virtue finds vivid expression in the wealth of biblical allusions that supplement the conventional legalese of his foundation charter. Zenobio relates the canons' financial rights to their moral life by paraphrasing First Corinthians (9:13–14): not only "should those who preach the gospel, live by the gospel," but also "those who serve the altar, should partake of the altar."[23] With Vinizzone surely in mind, he concludes the charter with an impassioned warning to future bishops to respect the canons' property: the earth would swallow such malefactors as it had Dathan and Abiron for their defiance (Numbers 16:31). He meanwhile invokes the apostolic ideal of shared property, one first established in the Acts of the Apostles but frequently cited in the ninth and tenth centuries by those who sought to protect ecclesiastical wealth from alienation.[24] Zenobio portrays the canons (albeit fifteen rather than twelve) as latter-day apostles whose common property underscored their spiritual unity and virtue. Rapacious bishops, he promises, would die as had Ananias and Sapphira (Acts 5:3), who "cheated the apostles of their money" rather than handing it over for the benefit of the Christian community (Acts 4:32 and 4:35). In contrast with Bishop Pietro of Arezzo, another imperial client who cut a distinctly passive figure in founding a cathedral chapter, Zenobio conveyed a learned self-confidence by adopting the mantle of protector of the church.

That precisely this ideal of episcopal virtue acquired great prominence in the hagiography devoted to two local saints, the *Passio Sancti Alexandri* and *Vita Sancti Donati*, suggests that Zenobio followed the well-established practice of justifying his own

---

[23] Ughelli, *Italia Sacra*, vol. 3, col. 215: "De qua re scriptum est: Qui evangelium annuntiant, de evangelia vivant, et qui in altari participant, de altari participentur."

[24] David Ganz, "The Ideology of Sharing: Apostolic Community and Ecclesiastical Property in the Early Middle Ages," in *Property and Power in the Early Middle Ages*, ed. Wendy Davies and Paul Fouracre (Cambridge: Cambridge University Press, 1995), 26–30.

actions by promoting the cults of his episcopal predecessors.[25] Recall that these texts provide the earliest surviving accounts of the ninth-century bishops of Fiesole—St. Alexander and St. Donatus—who lay in the two churches dedicated to St. Peter where the cathedral chapter celebrated its liturgy. As the Passion and Life depicted their protagonists as loyal clients of the Carolingian Empire, so the foundation charter issued by Zenobio curried favor with a new imperial order. As St. Alexander and St. Donatus had protected episcopal lands from predatory laymen, so Zenobio warned future bishops of Fiesole against appropriating his canons' patrimony. Tellingly, the foundation charter, *passio*, and *vita* all address the fragility of the legal documents upon which rested the rightful claims of bishops and canons to their ecclesiastical land. Villainous knights had murdered St. Alexander to prevent his imperial privilege from arriving at Fiesole; Norman raiders had destroyed the episcopal archives shortly thereafter. Zenobio sought to avoid such loss by ordering that a copy of his own document be sent to the cathedral canonry of Florence for safekeeping.[26] The manifold affinities between the charter and hagiography invite the ascription of the *Passio Sancti Alexandri* and *Vita Sancti Donati* to Zenobio or to a member of his circle.[27] By commissioning or even writing these stories of episcopal virtue, this bishop would have not only promoted local relic cults with a potential to attract pilgrims and their pious gifts but also highlighted two flattering precedents, St. Alexander and St. Donatus, for his loyalty to the empire and care for the cathedral chapter.

Transcending the particulars of local history, the developments in Fiesole in the 960s mark the return of the emperor as the disciplinarian and protector of the Italian clergy, a role envisioned in the Rule of Aachen and exemplified, as noted above, in Arezzo in the 840s. All the Ottonian emperors through Henry II (1004–1024) spent significant time in Italy, where they reestablished a measure of the imperial authority that had crumbled a century earlier. In Tuscany as elsewhere, they appointed such loyal men as Zenobio as bishops and richly patronized their dioceses in order to foster the loyalty of local actors, as well as their newly exalted ideal of a sacral kingship.[28] Among the greatest beneficiaries of this imperial largesse were cathedral chapters, which received new donations and grants of immunity.[29] Ottonian charters nonetheless indicate that the condition of these communities

---

[25] This paragraph draws on the analysis of the *Passio Sancti Alexandri* and *Vita Sancti Donati* in chapter 2, this volume.

[26] Ughelli, *Italia Sacra*, vol. 3, col. 217.

[27] The manuscript tradition of these hagiographic texts neither supports nor contradicts such an ascription. The earliest surviving sources for the *Passio Sancti Alexandri* and the *Vita Sancti Donati* are the Fiesolane passionaries, ACFie, II.B.1, fols. 50v–52v (ca. 1100) and ACFie, XXII, 1, 277–280 (saec. XII^{in}), respectively, on the dating of which see Giovanni Nino Verrando, "I due leggendari di Fiesole," *Aevum* 74 (2000): 452.

[28] Nigel Hiscock, "The Ottonian Revival: Church Expansion and Monastic Reform," in *The White Mantle of Churches: Architecture, Liturgy, and Art Around the Millennium*, ed. Nigel Hiscock (Turnhout: Brepols, 2003), 5–8, provides an overview of and relevant bibliography concerning the political and religious contexts for Ottonian patronage of religious foundations.

[29] Otto I's charters to Lucca and Arezzo are published in MGH, DRIG, vol. 1, no. 238, 330–31 (13 March 962); and Pasqui, *Documenti*, no. 71, 97–99 (10 May 963), respectively. Otto II's charters to Fiesole, Lucca, Florence, and Arezzo are published in MGH DRIG, vol. 2, no. 276, 320 (27 July 982); MGH DRIG, vol. 2,

had deteriorated even further since the time of King Hugh. In 983, for instance, Otto II condemned the cathedral canons of Florence for having "distributed canonical property as benefices or, even worse, given it to prostitutes," by whom he was perhaps alluding to their wives or concubines. As a result, noted the emperor, "their church is destroyed and utterly abandoned by its clerics."[30] In Pisa, by contrast, the chapter grew too large to be supported by their patrimonies and thus Henry II limited its size to eighteen canons.[31] Hence imperial intervention into the affairs of Tuscan bishops and canons documented and potentially curbed some of the worst excesses of these clerics.

Despite the newfound prominence of the Ottonians, the decisive figures in the resurgence of cathedral chapters were in fact their clients, namely local bishops. Over the subsequent half-century, prelates in Arezzo, Florence, and Fiesole followed Zenobio in reforming canons and promoting cults of local saints. The latter involved not only the writing of new hagiography but also the construction of new churches, part of a building campaign around the millennium elegantly described in an oft-cited passage from the *History* of Rodulfus Glaber (ca. 985–1046): "But it seems as though each Christian community were aiming to surpass all others in the splendor of construction. It was as if the whole world were shaking itself free, shrugging of the past, and cladding itself everywhere in the white mantle of churches."[32] These were magnificent shrines for holy

---

no. 289, 340–42 (21 December 982); Renato Piattoli, *Le carte della canonica della cattedrale di Firenze (723–1149)* (Rome: Istituto storico italiano per il Medio Evo, 1938), no. 18, 54–56 (25 January 983); and Pasqui, *Documenti*, no. 82, 116–117 (12 July 996), respectively. Emperor Conrad II would later cite a now-lost charter of Otto II to the Pistoiese chapter as he confirmed the property and immunity of that institution: MGH DRIG, vol. 4, no. 254, 353–354 (7 February 1038). Otto III's charter to Pisa and Arezzo are published in MHG DRIG, vol. 2, no. 224, 637–638 (August 996); and Pasqui, *Documenti*, no. 85, 119 (2 May 998), respectively. Henry II's charter to Pisa is published in MGH DRIG, vol. 3, no. 291, 355–357 (March 1014).

[30] Piattoli, *Le carte*, no. 18, 54–55 (25 January 983): "videlicet eiusdem sancte Florentine ecclesie pastores terram canonice Sancti Iohanis sive in beneficio distribuendo seu, quod detrius est, meretricibus dando, sancta Dei ecclesia esset diruta et etiam a clericis ibidem servientibus omnino derelicta." I thank Susan Boynton for the suggestion that the "prostitutes" (*meretrices*) in question may have been a reference to clerical marriage.

[31] MGH DRIG, vol. 3, no. 291, 355–357 (1014), on which see Cinzio Violante, "Appunti per lo studio delle canoniche regolari a Pisa al tempo della riforma gregoriana," in *Studi in onore di Mons. C. Castiglioni* (Milan: Dott. A Giuffrè, 1957), 256, who suggests that the Pisan canons numbered at least twenty during this period and probably more.

[32] Rodulfus Glaber, *The Five Books of the Histories*, trans. John France (Oxford: Oxford University Press, 1989), bk. 3, ch. 4, 117. Indeed, the translation of relics and construction of churches in Tuscany paralleled contemporary developments at monastic institutions in Burgundy and Aquitaine, as related in Bernhard Töpfer, "Reliquienkult und Pilgerbewegung zur Zeit der Klosterreform im burgundische-aquitanischen Gebiet," in *Vom Mittelalter zur Neuzeit: Zum 65. Geburtstag von Heinrich Sprömberg*, ed. Hellmut Kretzschmar (Berlin: Rütten & Loening, 1956), 420–439, trans. János Bak as "The Cult of Relics and Pilgrimage in Burgundy and Aquitaine at the time of the Monastic Reform," in *The Peace of God, Social Violence and Religious Response in France around the Year 1000*, ed. Thomas Head and Richard Landes (Ithaca, NY: Cornell University Press, 1992), 41–57. For a particularly vivid example, see the consecration of Saint-Martial of Limoges in 1028, as recounted by Ademar of Chabannes: Richard Allen Landes, *Relics, Apocalypse, and the Deceits of History: Ademar of Chabannes, 989-1034* (Cambridge, MA: Harvard University Press, 1995), 199–204.

relics, magnets for pilgrims, and impressive stages for the liturgy of reformed chapters. In building and consecrating them, the Tuscan bishops once again embraced their traditional role as *dominus et constructor*.

AREZZO: A TRIO OF EPISCOPAL BUILDERS

In Tuscany, not one but three Aretine bishops provide the *locus classicus* of the episcopal lord and builder in the Ottonian age. Elemperto (987–1010), Alberto (1014–1023), and Teodaldo (1023–1036) were exceptionally well-placed men: the first and third were brothers of Tuscan margraves or margravines and all three were particularly close allies of the emperors.[33] Such aristocratic affinities, as related below, shaped their architectural legacy: the reconstructed cathedral complex situated outside the city walls atop the hill of Pionta. Abandoned in the thirteenth century and demolished in 1561, this center included the canonry, the episcopal palace, the cathedral of Ss. Maria e Stefano, and the shrine of an early bishop and martyr, St. Donatus, of which the last was transformed from a small oratory into an imposing church dedicated to that saint. Finally, a wall surrounded these edifices in order to protect their temporal and spiritual wealth.[34] The three Aretine prelates attributed, however obliquely, inspiration for rebuilding their extramural seat to their holy predecessor. Their efforts provoked the rewriting of his Passion and the composition of new plainsong, of which the latter expresses their desire that St. Donatus be an object of popular veneration despite his burial in a now fortified complex outside his adopted city. Finally, the themes of imperial patronage, episcopal building, and public worship all found expression in his minutely described translation to the newly built church of San Donato in 1032.

Elemperto laid the groundwork for this new episcopal lineage of *domini et constructores* as witnessed in his charter issued in the penultimate year of his life. Learned in style but modest in tone, it dramatically enriched the capitular patrimony and recounted how he had rebuilt the canonry and, with "prayer, exhortations, and even threats," had reinstituted the Rule of Aachen among the canons.[35] The document formed the basis for the related discussion in the *History of the Custodians*, which describes Elemperto as the

---

[33] Wilhelm Kurze, "Nobiltà toscana e nobiltà aretina," in *I ceti dirigenti in Toscana nell'età precommunale. Atti del I Convegno, Firenze, 2 dicembre 1978* (Pisa: Pacini, 1981), 260–261. The archdeacon of the cathedral, Wilielmo, succeeded Elemperto as bishop by 1011, but his episcopate was brief and poorly documented: Delumeau, *Arezzo*, vol. 1, 504–506.

[34] The cathedral complex appears in a late-sixteenth-century mural located in the current episcopal palace of Arezzo and attributed to Pietro Buonamici, on which see Guglielmo De Angelis D'Ossat, "Il 'Duomo Vecchio' di Arezzo," *Palladio* 27 (1978): 8–13.

[35] Pasqui, *Documenti*, vol. 1, no. 94, 129–131 (12 February 1009), on which see Delumeau, *Arezzo*, 498–504; and Giovanni Tabacco, "Canoniche Aretine," in *La vita comune del clero nei secoli XI e XII. Atti della settimana di studio, Mendola, settembre 1959* (Milan: Vita e pensiero, 1962), 245–257.

"good father" of the canons. The chronicle tells how he played the part of loyal imperial client when, in 996, he presented these clerics to Otto III, who was following in the footsteps of previous emperors by visiting the shrine of St. Donatus.[36] In 1015, Alberto likewise extolled his predecessor as a virtuous and learned reformer, due to whose efforts the canons now fulfilled their liturgical duties to their holy patrons, "communally and under the discipline of the canonical rule, as soldiers of God and of the holy martyrs Stephen and Donatus."[37] Only five years after his death, Elemperto had become a beacon for future Aretine bishops.

Reading Alberto's charters in light of the archeological record shows that this prelate played a critical role in fashioning this new episcopal lineage by amplifying his predecessor's activities as a builder. Elemperto's credentials in this regard were likely more extensive than he himself had acknowledged in 1009. Six years later, Alberto ascribed to him the wholesale reconstruction not only of the canonry but also of the cathedral.[38] Ss. Maria e Stefano was a traditional basilica with a nave framed by single aisles and its eastern apse set into the defensive wall. While archeological evidence suggests Elemperto renovated rather than rebuilt the edifice, his modifications to the older structure were nonetheless significant. They included the addition of a crypt larger than the annular confessionals hitherto favored in Tuscany, one comprising four aisles extending from the apse beneath the transept.[39] The earliest Italian examples of such hall crypts date to the eighth century, but they became widespread on the peninsula only in the eleventh.[40] The

---

[36] *Historia Custodum Aretinorum*, in MGH SS, vol. 30, no. 1, 1472, which is based on a charter issued to the cathedral canons by Otto III at the shrine of St. Donatus: Pasqui, *Documenti*, vol. 1, no. 82, 116–117 (12 July 996).

[37] Pasqui, *Documenti*, vol. 1, no. 106, 146–147 (March 1015): "Renovata igitur sua a fundamento basilica et mansione constructa, clericos ibidem ordinavit, qui simul communiter et sub disciplina canonice regule Deo sanctisque martiribus Stefano et Donato militarent." Cf. the *Historia Custodum Aretinorum*, in MGH SS, vol. 30, no. 1, 1477, which similarly ascribes the construction of Ss. Maria e Stefano to Elemperto.

[38] See above, n. 37.

[39] Caterina Tristano and Alessandra Molinari, eds., *Arezzo: Il Pionta. Fonti e materiali dall'età classica all'età moderna* (Arezzo: Rotary Club, 2005), 143–144; and Alessandra Melucco Vaccaro, ed., *Arezzo. Il colle del Pionta. Il contributo archeologico alla storia del primitivo gruppo cattedrale* (Arezzo: Provincia di Arezzo, Progetto archeologia, 1991), 52–55. In 1078, Bishop Constantino of Arezzo alluded to the hall crypt in distinguishing between the "superior" and "inferior" levels of Ss. Maria e Stefano (*aecclesiae Sancte Marie et Sancti Stephani superiores et inferiores*): Pasqui, *Documenti*, vol. 1, no. 228, 319 (11 November 1078). For an overview of the excavations at Pionta, see Elisabetta De Minicis and Alessandra Molinari, "I nuovi scavi sulla collina del Pionta ad Arezzo: Una cittadella vescovile tra alto e bassomedioevo. Notizie preliminari," *Archeologia Medievale* 30 (2003): 299–301.

[40] Charles B. McClendon, "Church Building in Northern Italy around the Year 1000: A Reappraisal," in *The White Mantle of Churches: Architecture, Liturgy, and Art Around the Millennium*, ed. Nigel Hiscock (Turnhout: Brepols, 2003), 223–224; and Maria Clotilde Magini, "Cryptes du haut Moyen age en Italie: Problèms de typologie du IX jusqú au début du XI siècle," *Cahiers Archeologiques* 28 (1979): 56–85. Thomas E. A. Dale, *Relics, Prayer, and Politics in Medieval Venetia: Romanesque Painting in the Crypt of Aquileia Cathedral* (Princeton, NJ: Princeton University Press, 1997), 12–16, presents a case study of one of the earliest Italian hall crypts, one built between 811 and 823 and later enlarged in the 1030s. John Crook, *The*

History of the Custodians makes no mention of the novel Aretine structure but elaborates Alberto's claims of wholesale reconstruction. It asserts that no less than the pope consecrated his newly rebuilt cathedral at some unspecified date.[41] By inflating but not fabricating Elemperto's architectural legacy, Alberto acquired in this respected bishop of recent memory a valuable precedent for his even more ambitious reconstruction of the remainder of the cathedral complex.

This episcopal citadel atop Pionta not only represented an impressive legacy for a trio of episcopal builders but also announced their fidelity to their imperial patrons.[42] Alberto began the church of San Donato, which his successor, Teodaldo, finished and consecrated while rebuilding the episcopal palace. Any visitor to the cathedral complex would have understood the local significance of new shrine of St. Donatus: towering over the cathedral, it signaled through its sheer size the renewed commitment of the bishop and cathedral chapter to the saint's cult. The cosmopolitan would have also discerned a political subtext in the centralized, octagonal plan, of San Donato, one that differed from the rectangular one of a traditional basilica such as the cathedral and recalls the form of the sixth-century church, San Vitale, in Ravenna. That city had been identified with imperial authority in late Antiquity and once again since the eighth century, when Charlemagne modeled his palatine chapel at Aachen on the venerable Ravennate edifice.[43] An imperial appointee who had served as archbishop of Ravenna for ten years before his arrival in Arezzo, Alberto sent his architect, Maginardo, to that city in order to study San Vitale. Maginardo returned and duly recreated its form at Pionta.[44] The crowning architectural achievement of the cathedral complex, San Donato bore witness to a new line of *domini et constructores* in Arezzo, one loyal to the recently established Ottonian dynasty.

In Arezzo as elsewhere in Tuscany, episcopal lords and builders furthered their priorities by recasting local saints in their own image. An early medieval Passion of St. Donatus identified its protagonist as a bishop of Arezzo executed in the penultimate year of the

---

Architectural Setting of the Cult of Saints in the Early Christian West, c.300–1200 (Oxford: Oxford University Press, 2000), 135–160, traces the broader development of hall crypts from the ninth to eleventh century.

[41] *Historia Custodum Aretinorum*, in MGH SS, vol. 30, no. 1, 1472. The unnamed pope in question was perhaps John XV (985–996), who evidently fled to Tuscany following his expulsion from Rome in 995 (p. 1472, n. 4).

[42] This paragraph draws on Romano Silva, "*Dilexi decorum domus tuae:* Il ruolo dell'episcopato nello sviluppo dell'architettura in Toscana dall'XI secolo alla prima metà del XII," *Arte medievale* 10 (1996), 25–26; and De Angelis D'Ossat, "Il 'Duomo Vecchio,'" 17–33.

[43] Romano Silva, "Chiese e cappelle palatine in Toscana: Origine e tradizione," *Prospettiva* 24 (1981), discusses centralized, or "palatine," churches throughout Tuscany. Delumeau, *Arezzo*, vol. 1, 508, considers San Donato a synthesis of Tuscan and Ravennate traditions given that its octagonal plan is elongated along the east-west axis and its exterior ornamentation resembles that of the cathedral of Pisa, consecrated nearly a century later in 1118.

[44] See Teodaldo's payment to Maginardo, in which the bishop also described the latter's service to both Elemperto and Alberto, as well as his current work on the episcopal palace: Pasqui, *Documenti*, vol. 1, no. 125, 176–178 (December 1026).

reign of Julian the Apostate (355–363).[45] A revised and expanded *passio* datable to the episcopate of Elemperto or to the first two years of that of his successor, Alberto, places the saint's death in 404 and recasts him as an ally of the Christian emperor, Theodosius I (379–395).[46] The old Passion ascribed the selection of his gravesite at Pionta to those who buried him after his execution. The new one, by contrast, tells that St. Donatus chose that site before his death because he had once miraculously brought rain to a thirsty populace there. Having obtained a grant of land from Theodosius, he constructed an oratory to serve as his future resting place.[47] Unmentioned in previous scholarship, this literary transformation has all the signs of being the work of Bishop Alberto, who had similarly amplified the architectural legacy of his more recent predecessor, Elemperto. Regardless of its precise origins, the portrayal of St. Donatus as an imperial client who had chosen Pionta as his future gravesite and built his own shrine there corroborated the Aretines' longstanding refusal to abandon that holy place in favor of an urban cathedral as per imperial policy. Equally important, the refashioning of this fourth-century bishop and martyr made him a model for the trio of episcopal lords and builders who championed his cult in the early eleventh century.

As they enlisted St. Donatus in their manifold efforts of clerical reform and ecclesiastical building, these three Aretine prelates confronted the challenge of fostering his public cult. The new shrine of San Donato illustrated their problem: visible from the city center and, like most churches its size, designed as a setting for solemn liturgies to which the populace would flock, the edifice nonetheless stood in a fortified, suburban complex that accentuated the division between its clerical residents and the laity beyond its walls. The desire on the part of the bishops and cathedral canons to ensure that St. Donatus remained an object of public veneration finds pointed expression in their plainsong sung on the saint's *dies natalis* (7 August).[48] Contemporaneous with the revised Passion, these

---

[45] *Passio Sancti Donati I* (*BHL* 2289), in Corrado Lazzeri, *La donazione del tribuno romano Zenobio al vescovo d'Arezzo San Donato (sec. IV)* (Arezzo: Reale Accademia Petrarca, 1938), 117–121, which was likely in circulation by the late seventh or early eighth century: Pierluigi Licciardello, *Agiografia aretina altomedievale: Testi agiografici e contesti socio-culturali ad Arezzo tra VI e IX secolo* (Florence: SISMEL—Edizioni del Galluzzo, 2005), 286–287.

[46] *Passio Sancti Donati II* (*BHL* 2294), in Giovanni Alpigiano and Pierluigi Licciardello, *Officium Sancti Donati I: L'ufficio liturgico di san Donato di Arezzo nei manoscritti toscani medievali* (Florence: Edizioni del Galluzzo, 2008), 363–378, on the dating of which see Licciardello, *Agiografia aretina*, 325.

[47] *Passio Sancti Donati II*, in Alpigiano and Licciardello, *Officium Sancti Donati*, ch. 14, no. 33, 375 and ch. 16, no. 14, 377. Cf. *Historia Custodum Aretinorum*, in MGH SS, vol. 30, no. 6, 1477, which instead ascribed the construction of the oratory to Donatus's successor, Bishop Gelasius. The possibility that Donatus had selected his own gravesite was not in itself new. In 876, Emperor Charles the Bald acknowledged it even as he ordered Bishop Giovanni of Arezzo to transfer the bishopric within the city walls (see above, n. 17 this volume). See De Minicis and Molinari, "I nuovi scavi," 301–303, on the descriptions of St. Donatus's burial site in these two and other recensions of St. Donatus's Passion.

[48] Chapters 6 and 7 discuss the mass and office chants for St. Donatus, respectively, and the latter chapter likewise treats the public character of vespers to which the final sentence of this paragraph alludes. Chapter 7 also analyzes the mode and formulaic construction of such chants as *Ignis ardore fatigatus* (ex. 3.1), technical aspects of this musical repertoire not considered here.

chants set passages from that narrative that emphasize his evangelization and thaumaturgy in Arezzo, as well as his relationship with Emperor Theodosius. Of particular prominence, however, is St. Donatus's felling of a dragon and purification of a well polluted by that beast, miracles by which he became not simply a curer of individual souls but also a defender of the entire city. Sung at the conclusion of the public hour of vespers, the antiphon *Ignis ardore fatigatus* sets a heartfelt plea that it ascribes to the local populace, a petition to which the Passion merely alludes via indirect speech (ex. 3.1).[49] In a manner typical of its genre, the chant features a simple melody due to its persistent alternation between the pitches, d and f, and to its largely neumatic declamation, by which syllables of text are set to one, two, or three notes. The narrow ambitus and spare declamation throw into relief the melisma (i.e., a single syllable set to more than three notes) ascending to b (*Donate*). Placed on the final syllable of the proper noun, this comparatively florid gesture emphasizes its vocative case and, by extension, the direct, second-person appeal to the saint. Although attributed to the Aretine populace by the chant text, this petition was in reality sung by the cathedral chapter due to its liturgical performance at vespers. As *Ignis ardore fatigatus* celebrates St. Donatus as a defender of the Aretine people, or *defensor civitatis*, it also channels the kind of pleas that local bishops and canons hoped would be made by the lay men and women who would gather at the shrine of St. Donatus on their patron's feast.

The consecration of San Donato reveals that the equilibrium between private and public, clerical and lay devotion was in fact more delicate than this plainsong suggests. This great festivity unfolded on 12 November 1032 and marked the culmination of the rebuilding of the cathedral complex, the reform of its chapter, and the refashioning of its patron saint by Elemperto, Alberto, and Teodaldo. As codified by Frankish liturgists in the Romano-German Pontifical (PRG), the requisite prelude to this solemnity was the transfer of the titular saint from his original tomb to the new basilica. A detailed Translation documents this consecration, one traditionally ascribed to the longtime canon and primicer of the cathedral, Gerardo, and perhaps written soon after the death of the presiding bishop, Teodaldo, in June 1036.[50] It employs the themes so prominent in Tuscan hagiography of the early Middle Ages: Teodaldo was the authoritative lord and builder who exercised his sole authority to translate a local saint. The prelate was a virtuous man "elected by God to translate the body of blessed Donatus and to dedicate his church."[51] Under Teodaldo's supervision, the canons painstakingly exhumed the

---

[49] V-Am: "Ignis *ardore fatigatus populus*: "Aquam," inquit, "salutarem nobis, pater Donate, tribue, *quia* mors in fonto isto latitat" horum ille inclinatus precibus fontem sanavit." Cf. *Passio Sancti Donati II*, in Alpigiano and Licciardello, *Officium Sancti Donati*, ch. 13, no. 1, 372.

[50] Licciardello, *Agiografia aretina*, 336–347; Pasqui, *Documenti*, vol. 4, 12, of which the latter dates the text to the episcopate of Teodaldo's successor, Bishop Immone (1036–1051). The following discussion summarizes the *Translatio Sancti Donati* (BHL 2295–2296), in Pasqui, *Documenti*, vol. 4, 12–14.

[51] Pasqui, *Documenti*, vol. 4, 12: "Dictus Theodaldus, Dei electus ad translationem corporis beati Donati ad dedicationem eiusdem ecclesie." Cf. the accounts of the translations of St. Regulus and St. Fridian in Lucca, as well as that of St. Alexander in Fiesole (see chapter 2, this volume).

EXAMPLE 3.1 *Ignis ardore* (Officium Sancti Donati, V-Am).

saint's body, "a celestial treasure more precious than all gold and gems."[52] This elevation occurred in the dead of night, and thus without the interference of the laity, as the clerics bore St. Donatus away, singing the requisite hymns with lofty voices. Thus far, the Translation presents a traditional story of clerical and, more specifically, episcopal prerogative concerning local relic cults.

Nevertheless, the *Translatio Sancti Donati* differs from earlier accounts of such events in Tuscany by focusing on the public character of the next phase of the rite and on the resulting accumulation of wealth in the form of pious donations. This novelty surely reflected the altered circumstances of the early eleventh century, when unprecedentedly large crowds flocked to holy relics that were displayed in the magnificent new churches, as described so memorably by Rodulfus Glaber.[53] Among the many visitors to Arezzo were the bishops of five neighboring dioceses and such nobles as Count Raineri, whose father had been a patron of the cathedral chapter and whose grandfather was a Tuscan margrave and brother to Bishop Elemperto: "it was as if all of Tuscany had convened to

---

[52] Pasqui, *Documenti*, vol. 4, 13: "sacrumque tumulum aperientes, intus celestem thesaurum omni auro et gemmis pretiosorem reperiunt."
[53] Louis Hamilton, *A Sacred City: Consecrating Churches and Reforming Society in Eleventh-Century Italy* (Manchester: Manchester University Press, 2010), 57–65; and Barbara Fay Abou-El-Haj, "Audiences for the Medieval Cult of Saints," *Gesta* 30 (1991): 3–15.

celebrate a mystery of such solemnity with sacrifices, gifts, and much ornament."[54] Following his private, nocturnal elevation, St. Donatus was placed on the high altar of Ss. Maria e Stefano for public, diurnal viewing. There he perhaps inspired greater devotion than even Teodaldo had wished, for a "great throng" broke down the doors of the church in its eagerness to behold the holy patron. The faithful were "incessant in pouring forth their prayers, in wetting [his] holy feet with their tears, [and] in piling the altars with gifts."[55] The dramatic scene undoubtedly exceeded the canons' expectations of public veneration as intimated by the vespers antiphon, *Ignis ardore fatigatus*, and recalls the rowdy and even violent displays of such piety documented in contemporary France.[56]

Indeed, rivalries between Arezzo and its Tuscan neighbors amplified clerical ambivalence toward intensely public response to holy relics. It was surely with much relief that Teodaldo and the canons removed St. Donatus from his exposed position at Ss. Maria e Stefano and bore him to his final resting place inside the high altar in the central apse on the second floor of San Donato.[57] According to the Translation, however, its consecration provoked a heated disagreement. The altar housed two confessionals of which one faced west toward the nave and was sculpted with lifelike scenes from the Old and New Testaments, while the other was concealed in its middle. The Aretine clergy favored the first, more impressive option, the visiting bishops the second, more discreet one. The latter were perhaps disturbed by the raucous display at Ss. Maria e Stefano and had little incentive to encourage a relic cult that might compete for oblations with those in their own dioceses. According to the Translation, an unknown priest appeared and noted that although "the disciples of Christ reign in hidden places, these exalted men nonetheless triumph in heaven."[58] The Aretines capitulated and lay St. Donatus in the second confessional only to discover that their mysterious visitor had disappeared. Yet the visiting prelates were surely disappointed if they had hoped that the obscurity of the tomb would discourage pilgrims: according to the *History of the Custodians*, in subsequent years, "all of Tuscany assembled with infinite offerings" at the basilica of San Donato on account of the many miracles performed by its titular saint.[59]

---

[54] Pasqui, *Documenti*, vol. 4, 12: "totaque quasi Tuscia ad celebranda tante solemnitatis misteria cum hostiis et muneribus copiosoque apparatu convenit." The donation of Ranieri's father, Gualfredo, to the cathedral chapter appears in Pasqui, *Documenti*, vol. 1, no. 114, 163–164 (February 1022). On Ranieri's grandfather and his deposition by Conrad II in retaliation for his insubordination, see Davidsohn, *Storia*, vol. 1, 192–193, 232–233. On his familial relationship with Bishop Elemperto, see Kurze, "Nobiltà," 260.

[55] Pasqui, *Documenti*, vol. 4, 13: "totaque die illa et nocte non cessant preces effundere, sanctos pedes lacrimis rigare, altaria donis cumulare, nec quiescunt more fluctuantium segetum, seu modo procellarum certatim littori applicantium."

[56] Compare, for instance, the more than fifty men and women who were reportedly trampled to death in 1018 as they crowded into Saint-Martial in Limoges to worship at the tomb of its titular saint during nocturnal vigils of Lent: Abou-El-Haj, "Audiences," 4.

[57] De Angelis D'Ossat, "Il 'Duomo Vecchio,'" 14.

[58] Pasqui, *Documenti*, vol. 4, 14: "docens Christi discipulos in abditis regnare, in excelsis vero sublimes triumphare."

[59] *Historia Custodum Aretinorum*, in MGH SS, vol. 30, no. 7, 1477–1478: "propterea concurrit tota Tuscia cum infinitis oblationibus ad eius impetranda suffrage."

A healthy sense of *campanilismo* thus accentuated those distinctions—public/private, clerical/lay, and intra-/extramural—illustrated so clearly by the early-eleventh-century development of the cult of St. Donatus.

The achievements of the trio of lords and builders—Elemperto, Alberto, and Teodaldo—carried ramifications beyond their lifetimes and their diocese. The fortified complex at Pionta remained a potent symbol of episcopal prestige that harkened back to the old imperial order. In 1052, Emperor Henry III (1046–1056) conferred committal authority upon the local bishop, rendering him the only bishop in Tuscany to acquire such temporal powers.[60] About thirty years later, however, his successor, Henry IV (1084–1106), destroyed the walls surrounding San Donato after the local bishop had angered him but allowed the latter to rebuild the fortifications after the prelate's apology.[61] The episcopates of Elemperto, Alberto, and Teodaldo in turn marked a critical juncture in the broader development of Tuscan relic cults. In the 960s, Bishop Zenobio of Fiesole had promoted the cults of his predecessors, St. Alexander and St. Donatus, in order to bolster his profile as defender of the church. Approximately fifty years later, these Aretine bishops similarly enlisted their episcopal father, St. Donatus, in a far more ambitious program that included the building of entirely new churches and the composition of new plainsong. In so doing, they provided a model for their counterparts elsewhere in Tuscany, Ildebrando of Florence (1008–1024) and Jacopo of Fiesole (1024–1039), imperial clients who likewise promoted the cults of local saints through these same means.

SAN MINIATO: A NEW EPISCOPAL CENTER

In the second and third decades of the eleventh century, the cult of St. Minias of Florence became the most controversial of its kind in medieval Tuscany, owing to the dubious claims and questionable reputation of its most enthusiastic supporter, Ildebrando. This bishop, as we shall see, strove to establish a new episcopal center at the extramural shrine of San Miniato, one analogous to the complex at Pionta. Unlike the Aretine bishops, however, Ildebrando found it necessary to refute persistent doubts that St. Minias currently occupied his ancient burial place. As has long been recognized, the primary instrument by which he made this case was a heavily revised Passion of St. Minias that transformed the Florentine martyr into a cephalophore who chose his own grave in the mold of the celebrated apostle of the Gauls, St. Denis. Archeological and liturgical evidence presented here for the first time strengthens this connection with St. Denis as

---

[60] Pasqui, *Documenti*, vol. 1, no. 177, 251–252 (17 June 1052); George W. Dameron, *Episcopal Power and Florentine Society, 1000-1320* (Cambridge, MA: Harvard University Press, 1991), 24, notes that while bishops in neighboring Lombardy frequently acquired comital status, those of Arezzo were the only ones in Tuscany to do so.

[61] Pasqui, *Documenti*, vol. 1, no. 258, 357–358.

well as its political subtext, namely the alliance between Ildebrando and Emperor Henry II. Yet the promotion of St. Minias was political in another way, one equally specific to its Florentine context: Ildebrando intended it to blunt criticism of his conduct by a new generation of monastic reformers. Despite a marked resemblance to the cult of St. Donatus in Arezzo, then, that of St. Minias remained far more polarizing by virtue of the particular challenges faced by its episcopal champion.

The obscure yet undeniably troubled history of San Miniato provided Ildebrando with an unstable foundation on which to rebuild the cult of its titular saint. Situated south of the Arno atop the Monte Fiorentino, this shrine was the gravesite of the first recorded martyr of Florence, St. Minias. Moreover, it was the only religious foundation of Tuscany known to have received a gift of land from Charlemagne. Yet San Miniato seems not to have attracted a resident community of monks or canons: there remains no recorded protest lodged by such clerics upon the translation of St. Minias's relics to the cathedral that evidently occurred around 899.[62] The precise location of this martyr became more uncertain because his name appears among those saints whose relics Otto II purportedly acquired during a military campaign in Italy in 970 and subsequently deposited in Metz.[63] If Otto were to have in fact acquired relics from Florence, they would have more likely come from San Miniato rather than from the cathedral. Unlike the latter, the former stood exposed to external threats outside the city walls and was guarded by a solitary anchoress who could have hardly refused the sovereign's demands for relics.[64] The claim of San Miniato to possess the body of its titular was thus tenuous indeed.

Ildebrando responded to this problem with a bold act of historical revisionism buttressed by imperial support. With a charter issued in 1018, he established at San Miniato a Benedictine monastery and richly endowed it with episcopal property, which he justified with a story fraught with dubious claims. While making an inspection of local churches, the reader learns, Ildebrando discovered San Miniato to be "neglected by too much age" and "a virtual ruin."[65] He determined to rebuild the church and to reestablish

---

[62] See chapter 2, this volume.

[63] Life of Bishop Deodericus of Metz: MGH SS, vol. 4, 476. The clergy of Metz was evidently familiar with the earliest surviving Passion of St. Minias, the *Passio Sancti Miniatis I* (BHL 5965), which appeared in an unnamed Messine manuscript cited in *AS* October, vol. 11, col. 428.

[64] See the charter issued to San Miniato by Otto II's father just one year after the former's presumed translation of St. Minias: Luciana Mosiici, ed. *Le carte del monastero di S. Miniato al Monte (secoli IX-XII)* (Florence: Leo S. Olschki, 1990), no. 3, 63 (1 March 971). Mosiici (p. 7) notes that the anchoress, Ermergarda, may have been at the head of a community of nuns resident at San Miniato, but that it was more likely that she lived alone. On the likelihood that the relics acquired by Otto II belonged to one of the eight unnamed martyrs whose bodies were thought to remain at San Miniato, see Anna Benvenuti, "Stratigrafie della memoria: Scritture agiographiche e mutamenti architettonici nella vicenda del 'Complesso cattedrale' fiorentino," in *Il bel San Giovanni e Santa Maria del Fiore: Il centro religioso di Firenze dal tardo antico al Rinascimento,* ed. Domenico Cardini (Florence: Le lettere, 1996), 116.

[65] Mosiici, *Le carte,* no. 5, 70 (27 April 1018); translation after George Dameron's in Katherine L. Jansen, Joanna Drell, and Frances Andrews, eds., *Medieval Italy: Texts in Translation* (Philadelphia: University of

the monastery that (he alleged) had once flourished there. Inspired by news (from unnamed sources) that St. Minias's body remained on site, he elicited the financial support of his patron (*meum senior*), Henry II, on which account Ildebrando dedicated the new monastery to the salvation of the emperor's soul and those of his heirs. Finally, the bishop returned to San Miniato, where he discovered its titular and other martyrs, buried "visibly yet inappropriately," and translated them to a newly built confessional. This unlikely story facilitated the relaunch of the cult of St. Minias in three ways. First, it posited a historical antecedent for the otherwise novel foundation of a monastery and, second, it sustained the very real tradition of imperial patronage of that shrine established by Charlemagne. As Ildebrando undoubtedly envisioned, San Miniato indeed became an enduring symbol of loyalty to the empire much like the centralized plan of San Donato at Pionta.[66] Third and most important, the narrative addressed the problem of the whereabouts of St. Minias by simply ignoring the rival claims to his relics, which, it implied, had never left the Monte Fiorentino.

As in the 960s in Fiesole and in the 1010s in Arezzo, so in the 1020s in Florence did the local bishop reinforce the objectives presented in his charter by (re)telling the heroic life and death of his chosen saint. This literary project fell to Drogone, whom that bishop had selected as the first abbot of San Miniato and who dedicated it to his episcopal patron.[67] In the process of revising the existing *Passio Sancti Miniatis*, which had circulated since the ninth century, Drogone harmonized its subject's biography with Ildebrando's charter in two ways previously noted in the scholarly literature.[68] First, he

---

Pennysylvania Press, 2009), 33–36. Dameron in turn follows Ughelli, *Italia Sacra*, vol. 3, col. 47, in mistakenly dating the charter to 1013 rather than 1018.

[66] Thus Monte Fiorentino was known as the "Mons Regis" until the late twelfth century: Mosiici, *Le carte*, 5.

[67] Ildebrando appointed Drogone abbot of San Miniato in his foundation charter: Mosiici, *Le carte*, no. 5, 74 (27 April 1018). Only one copy of the *Passio Sancti Miniatis II* (*BHL* 5967) (alternatively known as the *Passio Drogonis*) survives along with its dedicatory prologue to Ildebrando, namely the late-twelfth-century addition to the passionary BLF, Mugell. 13, fols. 233–236 (saec. XII$^{2/4}$), compiled at the Florentine monastery of Santa Maria degli Angeli for the pieve of Santa Maria dell'Impruneta: Rossana E. Guglielmetti, *I testi agiografici latini nei codici della Biblioteca Medicea Laurenziana* (Florence: SISMEL—Edizioni del Galluzzo, 2007), 413–414; and Knut Berg, *Studies in Tuscan Twelfth-Century Illumination* (Oslo: Universitetsforlaget, 1968), no. 77, 273–274. It is partially edited in Giovanni Felice Berti, *Cenni storico-artistici per servire di guida ed illustrazione alla insigne Basilica di S. Miniato al Monte e di alcuni dintorni presso Firenze* (Florence: Baracchi, 1850), 161–171; however, all subsequent citations to this text refer to the aforementioned manuscript.

[68] *Passio Sancti Miniatis I*, on which more will be said in chapter 7, this volume. The earliest surviving source for this text is the passionary compiled for the abbey of Farfa between 842 and 898, Rome, Biblioteca Nazionale, Farfa 29, fols. 150–153: Eugenio Susi, "Strategie agiografiche altomedievali in un leggendario di Farfa," *Christianesimo nella Storia* 18 (1997): 300. Subsequent quotations from the Passion nonetheless derive from the version of the text in the cathedral passionary of Florence, BLF, Edili 139, fols. 102–103v (saec. XII$^{2/4}$), as well as from the edition in *AS*, October, vol. 11, cols. 428–430. On the relationship between the *Passio Sancti Miniatis II* and Ildebrando's foundation charter, see Scott B. Montgomery, "*Quia venerabile corpus redicti martyris ibi repositum*: Image and Relic in the Decorative Program of San Miniato al Monte, Florence," in *Images, Relics, and Devotional Practices in Medieval and Renaissance Italy*, ed. Sally

asserted that St. Minias had died not alone but with fellow Christians, thereby justifying the bishop's discovery of multiple martyrs at San Miniato. Second, he eschewed reports of St. Minias's translation to Florence and to Metz and further buttressed Ildebrando's claims to have discovered the saint's relics atop the Monte Fiorentino by ascribing the choice of that burial site to St. Minias himself. Recall that the new Passion of St. Donatus of Arezzo had achieved this same goal by casting its protagonist as the builder of his own martyrium. Drogone followed a more dramatic course, transforming St. Minias into a cephalophore beheaded north of the Arno, a mile east of the city and (perhaps not coincidentally) at the future site of its gallows.[69] His subsequent ascent, head in hand, up the Monte Fiorentino involved an audacious elaboration of St. Minias's biography that well suited the needs of Ildebrando: a martyr who so miraculously chose his final resting place and, by implication, would hardly have allowed himself to be moved neither to the local cathedral nor to Metz without divine sanction. As reimagined by Drogone, St. Minias thus joined Emperor Henry II in sanctioning Ildebrando's monastic foundation at San Miniato.

The likely source of inspiration for St. Minias's transformation into a cephalophore in turn reinforced the imperial associations of the new monastery. This literary conceit immediately recalls the postmortem perambulation of St. Regulus, whose subsequent translation to Lucca in 780 had purportedly occurred only with the permission of God. A more likely point of inspiration for the newly refashioned St. Minias, however, was St. Denis, the great evangelizer buried just north of Paris in the royal abbey dedicated to him. The cathedral canons of Florence and their counterparts throughout Tuscany commemorated the *dies natalis* of St. Denis (9 November) by reciting an anonymous Passion datable to the late eighth or early ninth century, one that recounted his solitary journey to an unspecified location after his death.[70] A revised narrative by Abbot Hilduin of Saint-Denis (†840), by contrast, told how an angel led the decapitated martyr to his future burial place, the royal abbey.[71] That such a celestial messenger guided St. Minias (but not St. Regulus) on his miraculous journey suggests that Hilduin's narrative was a model for the Drogone's despite its conspicuous absence from Tuscan passionaries.[72]

J. Cornelison and Scott B. Montgomery (Tempe: Arizona Center for Medieval and Renaissance Studies, 2005), 11–12; and Dameron, *Episcopal Power*, 33.

[69] *Passio Sancti Miniatis II*, BLF, Mugell. 13, fol. 236.

[70] *Passio Sancti Dionysii II* (*BHL* 2178), in *AS* October, vol. 4, no. 13, col. 794, on the dating and for a brief description of which, see Tova Ann Leigh Choate, *The Liturgical Faces of Saint Denis: Music, Power, and Identity in Medieval France*, Ph.D. diss., Yale University, 2009, 6–7. Although this Passion is not identified as the nine lessons recited by the cathedral canons of Florence in their twelfth-century ordinal (Ritus, fol. 94v), it nonetheless appears in their passionary, BLF, Edili 139, fols. 94–96v, as well as in many others from the region: Guglielmetti, *I testi agiografici*, 111 and 882; Verrando, "I due leggendari," 468 and 498; and Baudouin de Gaiffier, "Catalogue des passionaires de la Bibliothèque Capitulaire de Lucques," in *Recherches d'hagiographie latine* (Brussels: Société des Bollandistes, 1971), 138.

[71] *Passio Sanctissimi Dionysii III* (*BHL* 2175), in PL, vol. 106, ch. 32, col. 47,

[72] Cf. *Passio Sancti Miniatis II*, BLF, Mugell. 13, fol. 236, and *Passio Sancti Reguli*, in M. Simonetti, "Note sulla tradizione," no. 8, 124. Montgomery, "*Quia venerabile corpus*," 13, esp. n. 14, identifies St. Denis as the

This particular similarity between the two texts hints that Ildebrando sought not simply to render San Miniato a major pilgrimage center in the mold of the royal abbey but more specifically to signal once again the allegiance of his new monastery to the current imperial dynasty.

Two hitherto unrecognized connections between San Miniato and Saint-Denis, one liturgical and another architectural, strengthen this otherwise tenuous relationship between the two monasteries and in so doing reveal how transalpine politics shaped the cult of the Florentine martyr. The first connection is a responsory, *Pretiosus Christi*, one of eight chants composed by the monks of San Miniato for their titular's *dies natalis* (25 October; see ex. 7.3).[73] It sets St. Minias's final prayer before his execution as told in the revised Passion by Drogone: "I give thanks to you, hope of gladiators, that you allowed me to defeat the tyrant. Order, I beg, only that my spirit be received in peace."[74] Introducing this direct speech are words taken from a responsory for St. Denis, *Preciosus Domini*, that similarly sets the French saint's last words to God: "Christ's precious martyr, Minias [originally: "the Lord's precious Denis"] prayed in the newest agony, saying."[75] The Dionysian chant belongs to a collection of plainsong based on Hilduin's revised Passion of St. Denis and often ascribed to that abbot; however, the words quoted above, and the distinctive phrase "in agone novissimo" in particular, are unique to the two responsories.[76] The correspondence between the Florentine and Parisian chants does not extend to their melodies, which are completely different, but it nonetheless suggests that the monks of San Miniato had access to the text (if not the music) of *Preciosus Domini*, which was not previously known to have circulated south of the Alps.[77]

The second connection between San Miniato and Saint-Denis concerns the crypt built by Bishop Ildebrando at the Florentine monastery. It was likely a partially subterranean

---

probable model and notes the common figure of the angel in their revised Passions. Adele Simonetti, "Santi cefalofori altomedievali," *Studi medievali* 28 (1987), 114–117, by contrast, situates St. Minias's transformation into a cephalophore within the broader tradition of Italian saints of that type originating with the cult of St. Regulus.

[73] On the genesis as well as musical and literary style of these eight chants, see chapter 7, this volume.

[74] M-R10: "Pretiosus Christi martyr Minias in agone novissimo dicens: *Gratias tibi ago spes certantum. Iube precor* modo in pace recipi *spiritum meum*." Cf. *Passio Sancti Miniatis II*, BLF, Mugell. 13, fol. 236.

[75] Compare the text of *Preciosus Domini Dyonisius*: "Preciosus Domini Dyonisius in agone novissimo oravit dicens: Nunc iam Domine per coronam martyriicum fratribus meis servis tuis suscipe me" (transcribed in Leigh Choate, *The Liturgical Faces*, 103). I thank Dr. Leigh Choate for bringing this textual correspondence to my attention.

[76] Leigh Choate, *The Liturgical Faces*, 62–73, reviews the evidence for and against Hilduin's authorship of the plainsong for St. Denis.

[77] The plainsong for St. Denis appears neither in the Italian sources inventoried in "Cantus: A Database for Latin Ecclesiastical Chant," http://publish.uwo.ca/~cantus/, nor in Giacomo Baroffio, "Sanctorum Officia. Ufficiature liturgiche del Santorale tramandate in fonti italiane," *Rivista internazionale di musica sacra* 21 (2000): 270–295. That the monks of San Miniato had access to both Hilduin's *Passio Sancti Dionysii* and the related Office of St. Denis finds a measure of confirmation in the fact that the aforementioned solitary angel who accompanies the cephalophore to his grave appears only in the Passion but not in the Office.

space appended to the apse of the preexisting church and thus a variation on the hall crypt recently adopted at Ss. Maria e Stefano at Pionta by Bishop Elemperto.[78] It has gone unnoticed that such "outer crypts" were largely new to Tuscany but not to northern Europe, where the most prominent example had been built by Hilduin at Saint-Denis around 832.[79] The Florentine crypt, moreover, housed the relics of St. Minias purportedly rediscovered by Ildebrando and was surely the site of the night office sung by the Benedictine monks on the martyr's feast. As they sang *Pretiosus Christi* before the altar of their holy patron, both music and architecture reinforced the newfound similarities between St. Minias and St. Denis and, by extension, the shared royal or imperial associations of their churches and cults.

Although the revival of the cult of St. Minias atop the Monte Fiorentino resembled that of St. Donatus at Pionta in its topography and politics, the ultimate motivation behind the first (unlike the second) lay in the personal criticism leveled at its episcopal champion. Ildebrando's conduct notoriously ran afoul of a new generation of ecclesiastical reformers, of which the most influential was Romualdo (†1025/1027). Around 1012, the latter founded a hermitage at Camaldoli (in the diocese of Arezzo), which became a model for an austere form of monasticism associated with the eremitical life, one later championed by his biographer, Peter Damian. Romualdo found an enthusiastic ally in the local bishop, Teodaldo, who richly endowed the hermitage on the condition that its brothers maintain the solitary, contemplative life mandated by its founder.[80] Romualdo's fierce opposition to simony nonetheless brought him into conflict with many other prelates, of whom some were reported to have sought his pardon for this crime.[81] Ildebrando was exactly the type of bishop against whom such reformers as Romualdo and his followers railed: he had not only purchased his office from Henry II but also had married and fathered children.[82] In this context, a religious foundation governed by the Benedictine Rule, as was San Miniato, moreover, furthered two priorities: first, to insulate Ildebrando from charges of moral turpitude, and second, to protect episcopal land from alienation by rivals among prominent Tuscan families allied with the reformers. Indeed, Ildebrando intended San Miniato to function as a proprietary monastery of the

---

[78] Walter Horn, "Romanesque Churches in Florence. A Study in their Chronology and Stylistic Development," *Art Bulletin* 25 (1943): 122–123.

[79] Sumner McKnight Crosby, *The Royal Abbey of Saint-Denis from its Beginnings to the Death of Suger, 475-1151*, ed. Pamela Z. Blum (New Haven: Yale University Press, 1987), 87–94; cf. Crook, *The Architectural Setting*, 147, on outer crypts of the ninth century in general.

[80] Pasqui, *Documenti*, vol. 1, no. 127, 180–182.

[81] Peter Damian, *Vita Sancti Romualdi*, ch. 35 (*BHL* 7324), in PL, vol. 144, cols. 986–987, describes these encounters but claims to have known no simoniacal bishops who actually relinquished their offices as promised. Cf. Henrietta Leyser, *Hermits and the New Monasticism: A Study of Religious Communities in Western Europe, 1000-1150* (New York: St. Martin's, 1984), 70–72, on the keen opposition to simony among such reformers as Romualdo.

[82] This and the subsequent two sentences draw on Dameron, *Episcopal Power*, 24–31.

sort often established by laymen, safeguarding such property for the benefit of his own offspring rather than for that of successive bishops.

If the foundation of San Miniato presents an episcopal lord and builder characteristic in many respects of the Ottonian age, it reminds us that the personal concerns of particular bishops inevitably shaped broader historical patterns. The reestablishment of an extramural martyrium in 1018 and the promotion of its saint by an enterprising prelate along philo-imperial lines mirrored the revival of the cult of St. Donatus of Arezzo in the same period. As advanced by diverse media—the foundation charter, revised Passion, outer crypt, and new plainsong—the relaunch of the cult of St. Minias also reflected the peculiar history of the martyr's shrine and the behavior of his champion, Ildebrando, criticized by monastic reformers. Indeed, their indirect role in the Florentine bishop's emergence as a *dominus et constructor* anticipated the more prominent part of such actors in the rise of a new episcopal cult in Fiesole ten years later.

FIESOLE: BETWEEN EPISCOPAL AND MONASTIC REFORM

Jacopo of Fiesole (1024–1039) was one of the last of the Tuscan bishops under consideration who adhered to that distinct Ottonian profile: an energetic founder (or reformer) of religious communities and loyal imperial client who embraced his traditional role as lord and builder. His translation of relics *intra muros* to a newly built, urban cathedral conforms to the longstanding migration of bishoprics and their holy treasure into city centers, even as it contrasts with the contemporaneous building campaigns atop the Monte Fiorentino and at Pionta. His promotion of a hitherto obscure saint named Romulus, moreover, exceeded in its scope that of St. Minias and St. Donatus at those hilltop shrines insofar as it bestowed upon Fiesole a holy protector who linked its legendary history with that of Apostolic Rome. Finally, Jacopo was unusual in that he was a native of Bavaria rather than of his diocese, for which reason he seems to have been acutely sensitive to local and regional concerns. To a far greater degree than the Florentine and Aretine prelates discussed in chapter 3, this foreigner heeded the criticism and adopted the rhetoric of the monastic reform movement in central Italy. In this respect, he marks less a continuation of an established pattern and more a turning point in the history of Tuscan bishops, cathedral chapters, and relic cults.

Jacopo embraced the image of an intrepid imperial client whose transfer of his episcopal seat within the walls furthered a broader campaign of clerical reform mandated by his patron, Emperor Henry II. As he recalled in a charter issued in 1028, Jacopo was an outsider whom Henry had appointed four years earlier in order to repair the damage wrought upon Fiesole by the preceding bishop, Raimbaldo (1017–1024).[83] The latter's

---

[83] The remainder of the paragraph draws on Jacopo's charter in Ughelli, *Italia Sacra*, vol. 3, cols. 224–227 (27 February 1028). On Raimbaldo in particular, see George W. Dameron, "The Cult of St. Minias and the

efforts to transform ecclesiastical lands into a patrimony for his sons mirrored those of Ildebrando of Florence and, noted Jacopo, impoverished the entire diocese. Particularly troubling, continued this bishop, was the desertion of the extramural cathedral by the chapter of canons instituted by Bishop Zenobio nearly seventy years earlier. Comfortably installed in their canonry near Santa Maria in Fiesole, these clerics rarely if ever made the inconvenient trip to the old episcopal seat (fig. 2.1). As per imperial policy favoring urban bishoprics, Jacopo had already transferred his seat to Santa Maria. Looking forward, he formally announced his plan to build a new urban cathedral in order to provide the canons with a safer, more convenient house of worship.

Although done in the name of clerical discipline, this foreigner's transfer of the bishopric *intra muros* elicited a negative reaction from the local populace, one that monastic reformers exploited for the sake of extending their own influence. A history of the Camaldolese order tells that a hermit and follower of Romualdo named Azzo had traveled to Fiesole in order to denounce Jacopo for having forsaken the old cathedral. As he approached the city in the middle of the night, passing by the deserted church, Azzo saw a procession of martyrs and bishops, buried therein, sadly chanting matins in the absence of the cathedral canons.[84] This vision of a postmortem liturgy suggests that relic cults at the old cathedral retained a significant constituency among the Fiesolani, whose resistance to change an outsider like Jacopo might easily have underestimated. Indeed, it offered a pointed rebuke to which Jacopo probably alluded in his aforementioned charter: "I accepted the council of prudent men [Azzo?] and was admonished many times through revelation [the vision of the deceased bishops and martyrs?] to establish a monastery in that same place."[85] The bishop justified his foundation in purely local terms as a means by which to ensure that the memory of those buried at the old cathedral endured. Yet the new monastery clearly served the aims of Azzo and his brethren as a center of reformed monasticism in stark contrast (one might add) with the propriety monastery of San Miniato. By championing local relic cults, Tuscan reformers thus persuaded a foreign prelate to further their spiritual ideals.

A subsequent charter of 1032, in which Jacopo turned his attention from founding a religious community to reforming one, provides further evidence for the influence of monastic reform.[86] With the new cathedral and its canonry complete, he addressed the

---

Struggle for Power in the Diocese of Florence, 1011-1018," *Journal of Medieval History* 13 (1987): 130; and Davidsohn, *Storia*, vol. 1, 222–224.

[84] Agostino Fortunio, *Historiarum Camaldulensium, libri tres.*, 3 vols. (Florence: Bibliotaeca Sermartelliana, 1575), vol. 2, 16–20, cited in Davidsohn, *Storia*, vol. 1, 237–238.

[85] Ughelli, *Italia Sacra*, vol. 3, col. 224: "A prudentibus ergo viris consilium accepi, atque multis vicibus per revelationem admonitus sum, ut in eodem loco monasterium facerem, ubi episcopatus honorem, simulque cathedram abstuleram." Cf. Ughelli, *Italia Sacra*, vol. 3, cols. 224–227 (26 February 1028), in which Jacopo officially founded the monastery at the old cathedral of Fiesole.

[86] The remainder of the paragraph draws on Ughelli, *Italia Sacra*, vol. 3, cols. 229–231 (1032), on which see Milo, "Tuscany," 77–80.

poor state of discipline among its canons by reinstituting the Rule of Aachen. In promoting such imperial legislation, Jacopo celebrated his now deceased patron, Henry II, who, "pained by the grave poverty of our church, granted to it many [lands], restored certain ones stolen long ago, and confirmed some for the sake of its renovation."[87] Yet juxtaposed with such expressions of political fealty characteristic of the Ottonian period was a deep ambivalence toward temporal wealth typical of monastic reformers: "It is necessary to remove the soul from worldly goods and strive to obtain the rewards of eternal beatitude through just works."[88] Jacopo underscored the profound consequences of the canons' choices, admonishing them to remember the words ascribed to Solomon: "whatsoever thy hand is able to do, do it earnestly: for neither work, nor reason, nor wisdom, nor knowledge shall be in hell, whither thou art hastening" (Ecclesiastes 9:10).[89] The bishop sounded such themes surely not because he expected the canons to embrace poverty by giving up their personal property, which the Rule of Aachen encouraged but did not demand. Instead, he undoubtedly employed such rhetoric in order to reaffirm his own support for the broader ideals of monastic reform.

Jacopo buttressed his program of clerical reform via a strategy more typical of a lord and builder: the promotion of a local saint, one whose undefined biography made him an unusually attractive canvas on which a bishop might paint, in keeping with his particular concerns and aspirations. This Bavarian bishop surely gained credibility among his flock by elevating the profile of St. Romulus, whom an ancient funeral inscription in the old cathedral cast as a local deacon but not a saint. In his foundation charter of 966, Bishop Zenobio made three passing comments that suggest this biographical profile had evolved: first, Romulus was a confessor rather than a deacon; second, he was a holy man instead of an ordinary man; and third, the cathedral was dedicated to him rather than to St. Peter.[90] A historical anecdote related by Giovanni Villani provides further evidence that St. Romulus was the object of a burgeoning cult around the millennium. According to this late medieval chronicler, Fiesole suffered a humiliating defeat on St. Romulus's feast, 6 July, in 1010, when the Florentines attacked because the city's gates were left open and its men were unarmed due to the festivities.[91] An object of popular devotion

---

[87] Ughelli, *Italia Sacra*, vol. 3, col. 230: "praecipue Henrici imperatoris... qui praecepti serie nostrae Ecclesiae paupertati compatiens, multa contulit, quaedam longo tempore privata restituit, nonnulla vero renovando confirmavit."

[88] Ughelli, *Italia Sacra*, vol. 3, col. 230: "necessarium est a temporalibus bonis animum removere, atque eam in beatitudinis praemia per iustitae operae assequi studere."

[89] Ughelli, *Italia Sacra*, vol. 3, col. 230: "quodcumque potest manus tua facere, instanter operare, quia nec opus, nec ratio, nec scientia valet apud inferos, quo tu properas."

[90] Ughelli, *Italia Sacra*, vol. 3, col. 215 (966).

[91] Giovanni Villani, *Nuova Cronica*, 3 vols. (Parma: Fondazione Pietro Bembo, 1990), vol. 1, bk. 5, ch. 6, 172, on which see Anna Benvenuti, "Il *Bellum Fesulanum* e il mito delle origini fiorentine," in *Un archivio, una diocesi: Fiesole nel medioevo e nell'età moderna*, ed. Maura Borgioli (Florence: L.S. Olschki, 1996), 23–39; and Davidsohn, *Storia*, vol. 1, 196–197.

whose biography remained fluid and evidently unmoored by a written Life or Passion, St. Romulus presented a more or less blank slate on which a bishop could project a message of his choosing.

In championing this saint, Jacopo demonstrated unusual restraint by appealing to local sympathies rather than transforming St. Romulus into a vehicle for his personal aspirations. He numbered among those Tuscan prelates who, in 1032, aided in the solemn translation of St. Donatus of Arezzo to a new martyrium at Pionta. These visitors insisted that this martyr be buried in a plain, inconspicuous confessional rather than a sculpted, more visible one, surely in order to discourage the emergence of relic cult that might draw pilgrims and pious gifts away from their own local saints.[92] Jacopo's visit to Pionta provides an illuminating, hitherto unrecognized context for his translation of St. Romulus from the old, extramural cathedral to a crypt beneath the new, urban one dedicated to him. "Built with columns and vaults," this subterranean space measured thirty-one meters long by eight meters wide, thereby surpassing its likely model: the thirty-year-old hall crypt beneath the cathedral of Arezzo that Jacopo undoubtedly saw in 1032.[93] In its size and design, the Fiesolane crypt signaled the holiness of St. Romulus not only in absolute terms but also in comparison with such competitors as St. Donatus of Arezzo.

This spirit of *campanilismo* adopted by a foreign bishop extended to the portrait of St. Romulus in his Translation and Passion. Hagiography associated with episcopal initiatives, as multiple Tuscan examples have now shown, often casts its long-dead protagonist in the self-image of the current bishop: St. Fridian of Lucca had become a builder of churches; St. Alexander of Fiesole, a protector of ecclesiastical wealth; and St. Donatus of Arezzo, an imperial client. The *Translatio* and *Passio Sancti Romuli*, by contrast, capitalized on their saint's namesake, the legendary founder of the Eternal City, in portraying him as the embodiment of a privileged relationship between Fiesole and Rome. These two texts elaborate the biographical sketch of St. Romulus provided by Bishop Zenobio approximately sixty years earlier: he was now a bishop and martyr (not a mere confessor) who founded the local diocese at the behest of St. Peter.[94] Unlike Siena and

---

[92] *Translatio Sancti Donati*, in Pasqui, *Documenti*, vol. 4, 12.

[93] *Translatio Sancti Romuli et sociorum*, in Cignoni, "Le officiature," 213; Cecilia Camici and Debora Giorgi, eds., *La Cattedrale di San Romolo a Fiesole e lo scavo archeologico della cripta* (Florence: A. Pontecorboli, 1995), 131, fig. 6.

[94] *Passio Sancti Romuli* (*BHL* 7330), in Giuseppe Raspini, *San Romolo vescovo di Fiesole* (Florence: Giampiero Pagnini, 1997), 23–41, on the dating and authorship of which see Francesco Cignoni, "Le officiature di San Donato vescovo di Fiesole (†876). Edizione e studio," *Rivista internazionale di musica sacra* 24 (2003), 95–96; and Giuseppe Raspini, *San Romolo vescovo di Fiesole* (Florence: Giampiero Pagnini, 1997), 43. Christiane Klapisch-Zuber, "San Romolo: Un vescovo, un lupo, un nome alle origini dello stato moderno," *Archivio Storico Italiano* 155 (1997): 28–30, provides the most recent discussion of the transformation of St. Romulus into a disciple of St. Peter, while H. E. J. Cowdrey, "The Structure of the Church, 1024-1073," in *The New Cambridge Medieval History. Vol. 4: c. 1024-c. 1198*, ed. David Luscombe and Jonathan Riley-Smith (Cambridge: Cambridge University Press, 2004), 256–257; and Jean-Charles Picard, *Le Souvenir des*

Arezzo, whose holy evangelizers, St. Ansanus and St. Donatus, were believed to have arrived only in the fourth century, the Fiesolani now traced the origins of their church through St. Romulus to the prince of the apostles.

Evidence for Jacopo's role in the transformation of St. Romulus emerges in newly discovered similarities between the bishop's charters and the aforementioned hagiography. Jacopo refers to St. Romulus as a martyr, the first datable description of the saint as such and one that agrees with the Translation and Passion.[95] That this bishop repeatedly associates St. Romulus with St. Peter, moreover, accords with the biographical connection between the two made in the hagiographical texts. Jacopo reminds his readers that St. Peter was the titular of the old cathedral and St. Romulus that of its secondary altar. He reforms the cathedral chapter in the name of both saints and invokes their authority as he places the abbot of the new monastery under his jurisdiction.[96] His conception of St. Peter and St. Romulus as an indivisible pair contrasts with Zenobio's charter of 966, which makes no such mention of St. Peter. The affinities between Jacopo's charters and St. Romulus's hagiography indicate that the evolution of the saint into the apostle's representative occurred after Zenobio's episcopate and before or during Jacopo's. Considered alongside the latter's promotion of St. Romulus via the construction of his crypt, moreover, the textual correspondences suggest that Jacopo himself may have been responsible for reimagining St. Romulus as a first-century Roman evangelizer and martyr.

Jacopo's episcopate marked a turning point in the development of relic cults in medieval Tuscany. He embodied a familiar type of bishop who had emerged in the ninth century and traced its origins and development to imperial patronage. Like earlier or contemporaneous prelates in Arezzo, Fiesole, and Florence, he was not simply a traditional lord and builder who promoted a local relic cult but also a founder and reformer of religious communities, canonries, and monasteries, which existed in large part to sustain that cult through their liturgy. Yet even as Jacopo recouped ecclesiastical land, built lofty churches, and (perhaps) commissioned or wrote hagiography, he expressed some doubt concerning the traditional consensus that wealth was crucial to the spiritual unity and well-being of his clergy. His anxiety reflected the influence of monastic reformers, who would continue to shape the consolidation of cathedral chapters in the eleventh century. Furthermore, the literary turn toward Rome in the person of St. Romulus anticipates the entrance of the popes, previously marginal figures in the present story, who came to displace the emperor and even, at times, the local bishop in the development of Tuscan relic cults.

évêques: Sépultures, listes épiscopales dt culte des évêques en Italie du Nord des origines au Xe siècle (Rome: Ecole Française de Rome, 1988), 689–699, provide a broader one of such "protobishops" in general.

[95] Ughelli, *Italia Sacra*, vol. 3, cols. 224–225 (1028).
[96] Ughelli, *Italia Sacra*, vol. 3, cols. 230 (1032) and 226 (1028).

4

The Bishop's Eclipse, 1032–1118

FEW INDIVIDUALS EMBODIED the challenges to the philo-imperial bishops of early-eleventh-century Tuscany more than Giovanni Gualberto (†1073). Sometime in the middle of the 1030s, this pious youth entered the monastery of San Miniato, an emblem of imperial influence founded by Bishop Ildebrando of Florence in 1018. Since Ildebrando's death in 1024, subsequent bishops had curtailed the influence of his descendants over the monastery's assets, but had reinforced its ties to the Florentine episcopate and the empire.[1] That the new abbot of San Miniato had purchased his office from Bishop Attone (1032–1046) was particularly troubling to Giovanni. On the advice of a local hermit named Teuzo, he appeared in the Mercato Vecchio of Florence and denounced his abbot and bishop as simoniacs. The local populace was unsympathetic as an angry mob drove him from the city.[2] He settled briefly at the renowned hermitage established by Romualdo at Camaldoli before founding his own monastery closer to Florence at Vallombrosa, where he combined the hermit's asceticism with the strict observance of the Benedictine Rule. His new house soon attracted the support of pious donors and acquired dependent churches, forming a network of monasteries not unlike that established in France by Cluny. The Vallombrosans remembered Giovanni's early days at San Miniato and regarded that rival house as an emblem of the corruption bred in proprietary monasteries based on an unholy alliance between the church and crown.[3]

---

[1] George W. Dameron, *Episcopal Power and Florentine Society, 1000–1320* (Cambridge, MA: Harvard University Press, 1991), 39–42.

[2] *Vita Sancti Iohannes Gualberti* (*BHL* 4397), written in 1092 by the Vallombrosan abbot, Andrea da Strumi (†1106), in PL, vol. 146, cols. 769–720; cf. Robert Davidsohn, *Storia di Firenze,* trans. Giovanni Battista Klein, 7 vols. (Florence: Sansoni, 1956–1965), vol. 1, 248–250.

[3] Anna Benvenuti, "Giovanni Gualberto e Firenze," in *I Vallombrosani nella società italiana dei secoli XI e XII: Primo colloquio vallombrosano, Vallombrosa 3-4 settembre 1993,* ed. Giordano Monzio Compagnoni (Florence: Edizioni Vallombrosa, 1995), 92.

In establishing his new order, Giovanni emerged as a prominent lord and builder whose foundations underscored the enduring concern with poverty among monastic reformers and thus marked an implicit critique of the Ottonian *domini et constructores* examined in chapter 3.[4] He condemned not only simony and clerical marriage, like the older Romualdo, but also the clergy's widespread failure to build hospitals for pilgrims and for the poor. Such charitable institutions contrasted with the larger, more impressive basilicas built by bishops to house holy relics in Arezzo, Florence, and Fiesole in previous decades. Though mandated in the Rule of Aachen in 816, these more humble buildings become closely identified with eleventh-century reformers.[5] By example and exhortation, noted his biographer, Giovanni ensured that "so many hospitals were built and so many of the most dilapidated churches were renovated throughout Tuscany."[6] Equally important, Giovanni inspired clerics to forsake their concubines and, "following the apostolic rule," to adopt common life. Such rhetoric was not in itself new: cathedral chapters in Arezzo and Florence, as we have seen, alluded to the Apostles by claiming to have been founded by twelve clerics. In Fiesole, moreover, the Ottonian client, Bishop Zenobio, had explicitly likened the members of his new chapter to the apostles from whom Ananias and Sapphira had withheld their property in Acts 5:1–5. Yet Giovanni and his contemporaries instead cited the fourth book of Acts: "The multitude of believers had but one heart and one soul: neither did anyone say that aught of the things which he possessed, was his own; but all things were common unto them" (4:32).[7] Such reformers thus proscribed personal property among the secular clergy as the Rule of Aachen had not. Like Tuscan bishops, Giovanni was a lord and builder, but one inspired by new ideals of clerical virtue rather than old ones of episcopal authority.

The reformed monasticism of Romualdo, Giovanni Gualberto, and others comprises the first of three historical developments that encouraged the eclipse of bishops in the development of Tuscan relic cults in the eleventh century. First, Giovanni contributed to making Tuscany a center of clerical reform, and his ideals shaped the evolution of cathedrals and their chapters in the region. In Florence in the 1030s, as related below, the canons embraced the spirit of his ideals by establishing their independence and that of their spiritual patron, St. Zenobius, from an imperially appointed bishop. Second, an invigorated papacy adopted the mantle of reform and, under the leadership of Pope Gregory VII (1073–1085), engaged in a bitter conflict with the empire. In Tuscany, papal influence culminated in Lucca in the 1060s in the person of Bishop Anselmo I, whose

---

[4] This paragraph draws upon Andrea da Strumi's *Vita Sancti Iohannes Gualberti*, ch. 3, nos. 34–35, in PL, vol. 146, col. 779, on which see Sofia Boesch, "Giovanni Gualberto e la vita comune del clero nelle biografie di Andrea da Strumi e di Atto da Vallombrosa," in *La vita comune del clero nei secoli XI e XII. Atti della settimana di studio, Mendola, settembre 1959* (Milan: Vita e pensiero, 1962), 229–232.
[5] MGH C, vol. 2, pt. 1, no. 39, 416–417: "CXLI. Cui committi debeant stipendia pauperum."
[6] *Vita Sancti Iohannes Gualberti*, in PL, vol. 146, col. 779: "Hospitalia tot et tanta hujus exemplo et exhortatu jam videmus nunc per Tusciam aedificata, et ecclesias vetustissimas tot renovatas."
[7] Giovanni Miccoli, "Ecclesiae primitivae forma," *Studi medievali* (1959): 470–498.

concurrent role as Pope Alexander II shaped his campaigns on behalf of local relic cults and made him a less traditional episcopal lord and builder than he might at first seem to have been. Third, the emergence of a new temporal authority, the communes, in the decades around 1100, marginalized local bishops—first in Lucca and most conspicuously in Pisa—as they became the defining political feature of Italian city-states. By virtue of these religious and political developments of the eleventh century, Tuscan bishops could no longer plausibly claim to monopolize the promotion of relic cults.

Despite the importance of these novel historical developments, patterns in the evolution of relic cults uncovered in chapters 2 and 3 endured in Florence, Lucca, and Pisa. With or without the intervention of a local bishop, Tuscan clerics and laymen continued to promote local saints via architectural, literary, and liturgical means. They built cathedrals and wrote Lives and Passions, of which the architectural iconography and narrative details conveyed the influence not of the local bishop but of newly emerging players such as monastic reformers or the pope. Moreover, cathedral canons celebrated public liturgies that can be analyzed in greater detail than previously discussed instances due to the survival of liturgical sources. The best example is the consecration of the cathedral of Lucca by Bishop Anselmo I in 1070, reconstructed here in its visual and aural riches for the first time. Even the widely disseminated, ostensibly standardized liturgy of consecration illustrates that Tuscan relic cults became vehicles (once again) for political and religious agendas, both local and regional ones and those emanating from north and south of the Alps. Hence the reformed monasticism, papal ambitions, and communal government characteristic of the eleventh century provided crucial impetus to the otherwise traditional development of relic cults in medieval Tuscany.

FLORENCE: REFORMED MONASTICISM AND THE CATHEDRAL CANONS

Giovanni Gualberto's influence was most immediately felt in his native city of Florence, where the cathedral canons underscored his ideals in order to establish their house as a rival to the monastery to which he had once belonged, San Miniato. In contrast to that Benedictine community, the chapter of Santa Reparata obtained an unusual degree of independence from its bishop, Attone, an imperial appointee, who had elicited Giovanni's criticism by selling the office of abbot of San Miniato to its current incumbent. The most explicit witness to this novel dynamic between bishop and chapter is a charter of 1036 addressed to the canons by Attone: traditionally interpreted as merely one more instance of episcopal reform of a religious community, this document, upon closer inspection, in fact underlines the unusually strong position of the canons vis-à-vis that of their bishop.[8] Its text derives largely from the act with which Jacopo of Fiesole

---

[8] Renato Piattoli, *Le carte della canonica della cattedrale di Firenze (723–1149)* (Rome: Istituto storico italiano per il Medio Evo, 1938), no. 38, 106 (November 1036), on which see Elena Rotelli, *Il capitolo della cattedrale*

had reformed his cathedral chapter four years earlier.[9] Attone included Jacopo's prologue so critical of worldly property but otherwise struck a more humble tone in recognition of his canons' success in maintaining discipline among their own number.[10] While Jacopo had described the Rule of Aachen as hopelessly corrupted in Fiesole, Attone had "decided on the canonical *ordo*, which he recognized served the Lord properly, partly by virtue of its rule [of life] and partly indeed because it upheld the ancient custom of the church." Whereas Jacopo had grieved at the state of his chapter, Attone, surely eager to rebut Giovanni's aforementioned critique, "rejoiced, because the canonical rule pleased me from the beginning."[11] Finally, while Jacopo styled himself as the canons' disciplinarian in order to ensure their adherence to the Rule, Attone's posture was that of a friend who offered them assistance and granted their request to restore their alienated property.

The Florentine bishop not only ceded his traditional role as disciplinarian of the chapter but also sidelined the emperors, prominent patrons of San Miniato and the traditional protectors of Tuscan cathedral canons, by placing the chapter under the protection of an ecclesiastical authority higher than himself. In his charter, Attone (unlike Jacopo) made little reference to the emperors, although both bishops were imperial appointees. Instead, he successfully petitioned Pope Benedict IX (1032–1045) to extend papal protection to the local capitular patrimony. His charter acquired the status of a papal bull as it consequently bore the signature of the pope in addition to the bishop and (yet again) the twelve canons.[12] If Attone's request marked a watershed that diminished the emperor's influence in local ecclesiastical affairs, as per the priorities of ecclesiastical reformers, it likewise responded to the sheer proximity of the papal court at that

---

di Firenze dalle origini al XV secolo (Florence: Firenze University Press, 2005), 4–5; Dameron, *Episcopal Power*, 49–50; Yoram Milo, *Tuscany and the Dynamics of Church Reform in the Eleventh Century*, Ph.D. diss., Stanford University, 1979, 132–135; and Davidsohn, *Storia*, vol. 1, 255–256.

[9] Ferdinando Ughelli, *Italia Sacra*, 8 vols. (Rome: Bernardino Tano, 1644–1662), vol. 3, cols. 229–231 (1032), discussed in chapter 3, this volume.

[10] Although the Florentine canons had abandoned their church in the 980s, they had evidently reconstituted their community by the turn of the eleventh century. The imperial charter of Otto II included the stinging indictment of them for their financial mismanagement and moral failings: Piattoli, *Le carte*, no. 18, 54–55 (25 January 983) (discussed in chapter 3, this volume). By contrast, its revision in 998 (by Otto III) omits any reference to such faults: Piattoli, *Le carte*, no. 22, 65.

[11] Piattoli, *Le carte*, no. 38, 106 (November 1036): "Iter diversas igitur ac varias curas positus, dum ad meliorem statum reparare omnia studerem, ordinata regere, inordinata ordinare, ad canonicorum ordinem usque deveni, quem partim regulari tramite, partim vero, ut antiquus aecclesie mos optinuit, Domino decenter militare cognovi; quod ego videns valde letatus sum, quoniam canonicus ordo ab initio michi placuit."

[12] The *Translatio Sancti Romuli et sociorum*, in Francesco Cignoni, "Le officiature di San Donato vescovo di Fiesole (†876). Edizione e studio," *Revista internazionale di musica sacra* 24 (2003), 211–212, 214, asserted that Jacopo similarly received an indulgence from Benedict IX for the building of San Romolo as well as the pope's permission to divide the income of the bishopric among his three foundations, namely the cathedral and monasteries at San Bartolommeo and San Gaudenzo. Such claims were perhaps made to counter the impression of undue favor on the part of the papacy toward the Florentine church. In fact, no papal intervention on behalf of Fiesole is recorded before the twelfth century: Paul Fridolin Kehr, *Regesta Pontificum Romanorum. Italia Pontificia*, 10 vols. (Berlin: Weidmann, 1908), vol. 3, no. 6, 75, and no. 1, 78.

particular time.[13] In 1035, Benedict settled in Florence after his expulsion from Rome and, in November of 1037, organized a synod in an effort to reassert his authority over the church. In attendance were thirty-three bishops, including Jacopo, Attone, and their counterparts from Lucca and Siena.[14] The topics of discussion remain unknown but probably included clerical reform as Benedict sought to dispel his own reputation as an ineffective and corrupt pope.[15] As the imperially appointed bishop relinquished his own role as key protector of the cathedral chapter, so too did the emperor.

If the cathedral canons of Florence acquired a new patron in the pope, they also turned to an old one, the sixth-century bishop St. Zenobius, championing him with a determination equal to that with which Bishop Ildebrando had reestablished the cult of St. Minias atop the Monte Fiorentino twenty years earlier. As Abbot Drogone had revised the *Passio Sancti Miniatis*, so the canons asked Lorenzo of Amalfi (†1049) to pen a new Life for their saint. Lorenzo was a former monk at the abbey of Montecassino and a reformer who maintained a close friendship with Abbot Odilo of Cluny. Literate in Greek and Latin, Lorenzo elicited praise for both his piety and learning and was an early tutor to Hildebrand, the future Pope Gregory VII.[16] He served as archbishop of Amalfi before being driven from his archdiocese by the prince of Salerno in 1039 and settling in Florence. During his brief stay, he cultivated close ties with the cathedral canons, for whom he wrote a Life of St. Zenobius. Indeed, Lorenzo may have resided at their canonry: he addressed the prologue of this eloquent text to the canons, his "amiable brothers," and concluded by describing himself as "an exile who has experienced [Zenobius's] protection."[17] The author noted that the loss of earlier Lives dedicated to this Florentine saint had obliged him to rely on references to St. Zenobius in Paulinus's Life of St. Ambrose, an early supporter of the saint, and on reports from "most serious people," among whom surely numbered the canons.[18]

The *Vita Sancti Zenobii* furthered the interests of Lorenzo's hosts in ways previously undetected: in a manner analogous to the Passion of St. Minias, it reinforced their

---

[13] Note, however, that the request did not mark the end of imperial involvement in business of the Florentine cathedral chapter. In the following two years, Emperor Conrad II joined Benedict IX in confirming the community's ownership of lands restored to it by Attone: Piattoli, *Le carte*, no. 39, 109–111 (10 July 1037) and no. 40, 111–113 (24 March 1038).

[14] Giovanni Domenico Mansi, *Sacrorum Conciliorum Nova et Amplissima Collectio*, 3 vols. (Venice: Antonio Zatta, 1759–1798), vol. 19, cols. 579–582, describes the synod as a "Roman council"; however, its location in fact remains unknown and was likely Florence: Davidsohn, *Storia*, vol. 1, 252–253.

[15] Rodulfus Glaber, *The Five Books of the Histories*, trans. John France (Oxford: Oxford University Press, 1989), bk. 4, ch. 6, 198–199, and ch. 9, 210–211; bk. 5, ch. 5, 252–253.

[16] *Vita Sancti Odilonis* (BHL 6281), in *AS*, January, vol. 1, no. 48, 70. See Lorenzo of Amalfi, *Opera*, ed. Francis Newton, MGH Q 7 (Weimar: H. Böhlaus Nachf, 1973), 1–9; and Davidsohn, *Storia*, vol. 1, 253–254, on Lorenzo's residence in Florence.

[17] *Vita Sancti Zenobii* I, nos. 1 and 15, in *AS*, May, vol. 6, cols. 58 and 62, respectively; cf. Davidsohn, *Storia*, vol. 1, 254.

[18] *Vita Sancti Zenobii* I, nos. 1 and 7, in *AS*, May, vol. 6, cols. 58–59.

claims to his relics while tying the foundation of their community to such treasure. This text reflected a broader impulse characteristic of the eleventh century, namely to document the miracles performed by saints after their deaths. Unlike early medieval hagiography, which typically concluded with brief allusions to such posthumous acts, the entire final third of the Life of St. Zenobius is devoted to four miracles of this sort.[19] The first two occurred during his translation from the old suburban cathedral of San Lorenzo to Santa Reparata.[20] When his bier brushed against a dead elm, the tree miraculously sprouted leaves; when it reached the door of his new home, it could not be carried inside until the presiding bishop deputized no fewer than twelve clerics to honor him with perpetual prayer. Marking the establishment of the cathedral chapter, this second miracle ascribed the genesis of that community to divine will expressed by its patron saint. It was surely no coincidence that the number of clerics (twelve) was not only apostolic but also accorded with the number of canons who signed the aforementioned charter of Attone. The final two miracles recounted in the Life involved the curing of ailing supplicants before St. Zenobius's new altar. As retold by Lorenzo of Amalfi, all four miracles emphasized the saint's bodily presence at Santa Reparata and thus the canons' privileged claim to his patronage.

Although St. Zenobius was himself a bishop, his Life was redolent of the newfound autonomy of the canons from episcopal jurisdiction, in three ways. First, Lorenzo minimized the role of the bishop who oversaw the translation of St. Zenobius by referring to him merely as "the prelate who presided over this city at that time."[21] This absence of secure identification may have simply resulted from the dearth of textual sources on which Lorenzo was able to base his Life. It nonetheless suggests an anti-episcopal agenda in light of the predominance of named, well-documented bishops (e.g., Giovanni of Lucca, Romano of Fiesole, and Teodaldo of Arezzo) in accounts of relic translations in Tuscan hagiography in general. Second, Lorenzo further limited the profile of the bishop in the Life by mentioning the canons but not their prelate in connection with St. Zenobius's final two miracles. Third, he implied that the cathedral chapter rivaled the Florentine bishopric in its antiquity: the translation of St. Zenobius, he asserted, and by extension the legendary foundation of the chapter, had occurred shortly after the saint's death in 417. This contention contradicts the (admittedly meager) historical record, which places the transfer of St. Zenobius *intra muros* during the ninth-century

---

[19] In this respect, the *Vita Sancti Zenobii* resembles the eleventh-century *Vita Sancti Fridiani III* (*BHL* 3175b), which similarly recounts the miracles that unfolded at the annular confessional of its protagonist at San Frediano of Lucca (see chapter 7, this volume). A more distant yet nevertheless evocative point of comparison is Bernard of Angers's *Liber miraculorum Sancte Fidis* (1010–1020), which detailed the miracles of its subject, St. Foy, at her shrine in Conques: Kathleen M. Ashley and Pamela Sheingorn, *Writing Faith: Text, Sign and History in the Miracles of Sainte Foy* (Chicago: University of Chicago Press, 1999), 5–6.

[20] *Vita Sancti Zenobii I*, nos. 13–17, in *AS*, May, vol. 6, cols. 61–62.

[21] *Vita Sancti Zenobii I*, no. 14, in *AS*, May, vol. 6, col. 61: "quamdiu Pontifex, qui tunc temporis huic præerat urbi."

episcopate of Bishop Andrea.²² With the approval of his hosts, Lorenzo fashioned a Life that effaced Andrea and other local bishops from the literary history of their cathedral and its chapter.²³

A newly discovered instance of literary borrowing in the *Vita Sancti Zenobii* strengthens the impression that St. Minias and his episcopal champion, Ildebrando, were foils against which Lorenzo and, by extension, the canons of Santa Reparata promoted St. Zenobius. In the foundation charter of San Miniato of 1018, Ildebrando had claimed to have rediscovered St. Minias's relics, which he described as "most precious gems."²⁴ This was not an unusual phrase and, in this context, underscored widely recognized affinities between spiritual and temporal wealth; however, medieval hagiographers appear to have used the metaphor of holy relics as *gemma pretiosissima* rarely, if at all.²⁵ Hence its occurrence in the *Vita Sancti Zenobii* is almost certainly a case of deliberate borrowing from the foundation charter of San Miniato. In his account of St. Zenobius's translation to Santa Reparata, Lorenzo referred to the elm that had miraculously flowered when touched by the holy body and asked:

> Does it not seem that this tree demonstrated the flowering virtues of blessed Zenobius and indicated that the city of Florence reflowered beyond many others by various rewards that resulted from its relics? Thus let the Florentine populace happily rejoice and exult in the Lord, since it deserved to accept through divine intervention this *most precious gem* excellent with respect to all the riches of the land.²⁶

The appearance of the phrase *gemma pretiosissima* indicates that the foundation charter of San Miniato was a point of reference for Lorenzo. In its author, Ildebrando,

---

²² See chapter 2, this volume. That the canons were eager to exaggerate the age of their community finds confirmation in their forgery in 1037 of a charter, dated to 723/724, by which Bishop Specioso of Florence had ostensibly made the first recorded donation of land to their community: Piattoli, *Le carte*, no. 1, 3-6 (September 723–June 724), on which see Davidsohn, *Storia*, vol. 1, 502.

²³ Memory of Bishop Andrea nevertheless endured as evidenced in a tomb-altar dedicated to him, situated near that of St. Zenobius in the crypt of Santa Reparata, but first documented only in the fourteenth century: Franklin Toker, *On Holy Ground: Liturgy, Architecture, and Urbanism in the Cathedral and the Streets of Medieval Florence* (Turnhout: Brepols, 2009), 74–75.

²⁴ Luciana Mosiici, ed. *Le carte del monastero di S. Miniato al Monte (secoli IX–XII)* (Florence: Leo S. Olschki, 1990), no. 5, 71 (27 April 1018).

²⁵ A keyword search of the hagiographic texts archived in Acta Sanctorum Database, accessed 23 July 2013, http://acta.chadwyck.co.uk, yielded no instances of *gemma pretiosissima* (or variants thereof) applied to saints' relics besides that of the *Vita Sancti Zenobii I* quoted below in no. 26.

²⁶ *Vita Sancti Zenobii I*, nos. 13, in *AS*, May, vol. 6, col. 61: "Nonne videtur, lector, hæc arbor et flores virtutum beati Zenobii demonstrasse, et Florentinam civitatem indicasse, pre multis aliis urbibus ob ejus reliquias variis gratiis reflorere? Letabiliter itaque gaudeat Florentinus populus, et exultet in Domino: quia divinitus accipere meruit hanc *gemmam pretiosissimam*, excellentem cunctis terræ opibus" (italics added).

he and the cathedral canons surely saw a parody rather than a model of episcopal virtue: an imperial client of dubious repute who promoted a relic cult in order to further his personal priorities. In the passage quoted above, Lorenzo intimates this negative view of Ildebrando by appropriating the bishop's words but associating them with the Florentine people, whose civic pride echoes in wordplay (*flores, Florentina, reflorere*). As they enlisted Lorenzo in their campaign on behalf of St. Zenobius, the canons thus presented their community vis-à-vis Ildebrando as a more virtuous albeit less orthodox *dominus et constructor*.

The prominent place that the image of the gem obtained in the sung liturgy of cathedral chapter provides further evidence that the use of the phrase *gemma pretiosissima* in the Life of St. Zenobius was not as innocuous as it might otherwise seem. In the early-morning hours on the anniversary of St. Zenobius's translation (26 January), the cathedral canons gathered to celebrate their private hour of matins, at which one of their number recited the portion of Lorenzo's *vita* that included the two key words in question. With this phrase fresh in their ears, their entire community sang the last (and thus the most important) of nine responsories assigned to this service, *O gemma fulgens presulum* (ex. 4.1).[27] Composed by the canons as early as the 1030s and perhaps in coordination with the Life, the chant recalled the Life of St. Zenobius recited moments beforehand through its textual incipit, "radiant gem of bishops."[28] Due to its prominent position at the private hour of matins, the ninth responsory drew attention to this image originally drawn from the foundation charter of San Miniato.

Yet *O gemma fulgens presulum* did more to advance the anti-episcopal program of the cathedral canons when these clerics sang it at the public hour of vespers on the vigil of St. Zenobius's feast. The chant text presents an unidentified "we" imploring St. Zenobius to intercede on behalf of Florentine citizens. In the context of its performance at the cathedral of Santa Reparata, this third-person singular denoted the canons, of whom all chanted the responsory, but not their bishop, who did not normally join them in the celebration of their liturgical hours. At the private hour of matins, the *cives Florentiae* named in the chant would in turn have brought to mind the *populus Florentinus*, whom Lorenzo of Amalfi had urged to celebrate St. Zenobius's bodily

---

[27] This sentence, the remainder of the present paragraph, and the entirety of the subsequent one draw on liturgical prescriptions for the feast of St. Zenobius, which provide the model for the anniversary of the saint's translation. These prescriptions appear in the Florentine ordinals of the twelfth and thirteenth centuries, Ritus, fols. 73, and 82v–83, and Mores, fols. 8 and 9v–10. Chapter 5, this volume, provides a detailed examination of these two sources while chapter 7 discusses the private character of matins vs. the public one of vespers, as well as the origins of the plainsong composed for St. Zenobius.

[28] The incipit, *O gemma fulgens presulum*, also recalls the texts of two chants not sung on the feast of St. Zenobius: the antiphon *O gemma clara martyrum* (sung on the feasts of martyrs) and the responsory, *Martinus Abrahae sinu laetus* (for St. Martin), of which the latter describes its subject as a *gemma sacerdotum*. These two chants appear in the Florentine antiphoner, AAF, n.s., fols. 226 and 191, respectively (saec. XII^{med}).

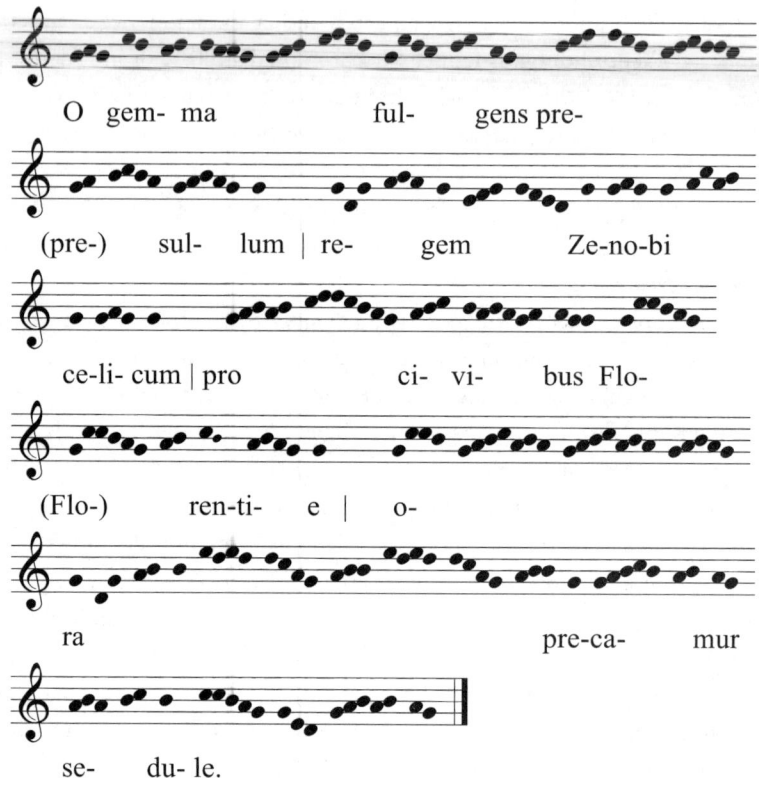

EXAMPLE 4.1 *O gemma fulgens presulum* (*Officium Sancti Zenobii*, V-R).

presence in the cathedral in his Life, recited earlier in the service. At the public hour of vespers, by contrast, the "Florentine people" evoked the laity in attendance in the nave. By virtue of its liturgical performance on the vigil of St. Zenobius, *O gemma fulgens presulum* thus portrayed the canons as the exclusive intermediaries between the Florentines and their saint.

The music of the responsory enriched this portrait of the canons as intercessors in a manner discernible to the lettered and unlettered alike. The two longest melismas of the chant fall on the word *pray* (*ora*) and demand a measure of vocal agility that invited the singers, namely the canons, to demonstrate the strenuous, heartfelt character of their pleas. The narrow, repetitive trajectory of the first melisma throws into relief the more expansive, linear shape of the second one. The former ascends no less than three times through the same interval, the fourth between g and c′, once by leap and twice by scalar (or stepwise) motion. The latter, by contrast, immediately outlines a full ninth (d to e′) via leaps (d to g and b to e′) and thereafter remains in the higher reaches of the singers' tessitura. Assuming that the canons navigated this difficult melodic line with the requisite skill, they demonstrated to the populace that they (and not their bishop) were carrying out the hard work of securing St. Zenobius's patronage.

The marginalization of the Florentine bishop obtained pointed expression not only in legal, hagiographic, and liturgical media but also in the reconstruction of Santa Reparata, which would henceforth provide a glorious stage on which the canons might celebrate their liturgy. The rebuilding of this edifice occurred during the first half of the eleventh century; however, the absence of foundation charters of the sort issued by bishops in Arezzo and Fiesole obscures the precise chronology of this project, as well as the identity of those behind it.[29] Indeed, this dearth of episcopal documentation hints that the canons rather than their bishop took the initiative in the rebuilding of Santa Reparata. So too does the depiction of St. Zenobius in his new Life by Lorenzo of Amalfi. Since the eighth century, as we have seen, Tuscan hagiographers had repeatedly depicted holy bishops (e.g., St. Fridian of Lucca and St. Donatus of Arezzo) as intrepid builders, thus amplifying the resemblance of these legendary figures to contemporary bishops who in fact constructed their tombs and churches.[30] Lorenzo, by contrast, ascribed no such activities to St. Zenobius, presumably because his allies, the cathedral canons, had no interest in celebrating their patron saint as a *dominus et constructor*. Hence the absence of episcopal oversight of the reconstruction of Santa Reparata in the 1030s (one suspects) shaped the literary portrait of its saint as one similarly uninvolved in the building of churches.

In the new Florentine cathedral, architectural iconography once again underscored political affiliations that were both local and transalpine in character: whereas the centralized plan of San Donato signaled the loyalty of the Aretine bishops to the Ottonian dynasty, the layout of Santa Reparata alluded to a northern monastic order and thus to local reformers who had accused Florentine bishops of corruption. The foundations of the medieval structure of Santa Reparata lie beneath the present cathedral of Santa Maria del Fiore. Their east end adheres to a stepped (or *en échelon*) plan formed by the central apse flanked by the two apsidioles and two lateral chapels (fig. 4.1). Completed, as we shall see, by 1036, this arrangement was exceptional among Tuscan cathedrals, rare in Italy, but common in northern Europe, where it was particularly evocative of the abbey of Cluny.[31] Since its foundation in 910, Cluny had acquired a vast network of dependents

---

[29] Florentine tradition ascribed the dedication of the baptistery of San Giovanni to Bishop Gerardo (1046–1061) on 6 November 1059 and thus shortly after his election as Pope Nicholas II earlier that same year: Toker, *On Holy Ground*, 109. The twelfth-century Florentine ordinal, Ritus, fols. 96–96v, likewise places the consecration of the "ecclesia Sancti Johannis baptiste" on 6 November. Guido Tigler, *Toscana romanica* (Milan: Jaca Book, 2006), 132–134, argues that the notice in fact indicates the consecration of the cathedral of Santa Reparata rather than its baptistery. He accordingly situates the rebuilding of the basilica between 1036, the year in which Bishop Attone reformed its chapter, and 1059.

[30] For instance, the rewriting of the *Vita Sancti Fridiani* evoked the rebuilding projects of Bishop Giovanni I of Lucca in the late eighth century (see chapter 2, this volume); that of the *Passio Sancti Donati* recalled those of Bishops Elemperto, Alberto, and Teodaldo in the decades around 1000 (see chapter 3, this volume).

[31] Domenico Cardini, "Ipotesi sulle fasi trasformative del Centro religioso dalla formazione della cinta difensiva carolingia alla sua sostituzione," in *Il bel San Giovanni e Santa maria del Fiore: Il centro religioso di Firenze dal tardo antico al Rinascimento*, ed. Domenico Cardini (Florence: Le lettere, 1996), 140; Franklin Toker, "Excavations Below the Cathedral of Florence," *Gesta* 14 (1975): 33–34. Prominent examples of the *en*

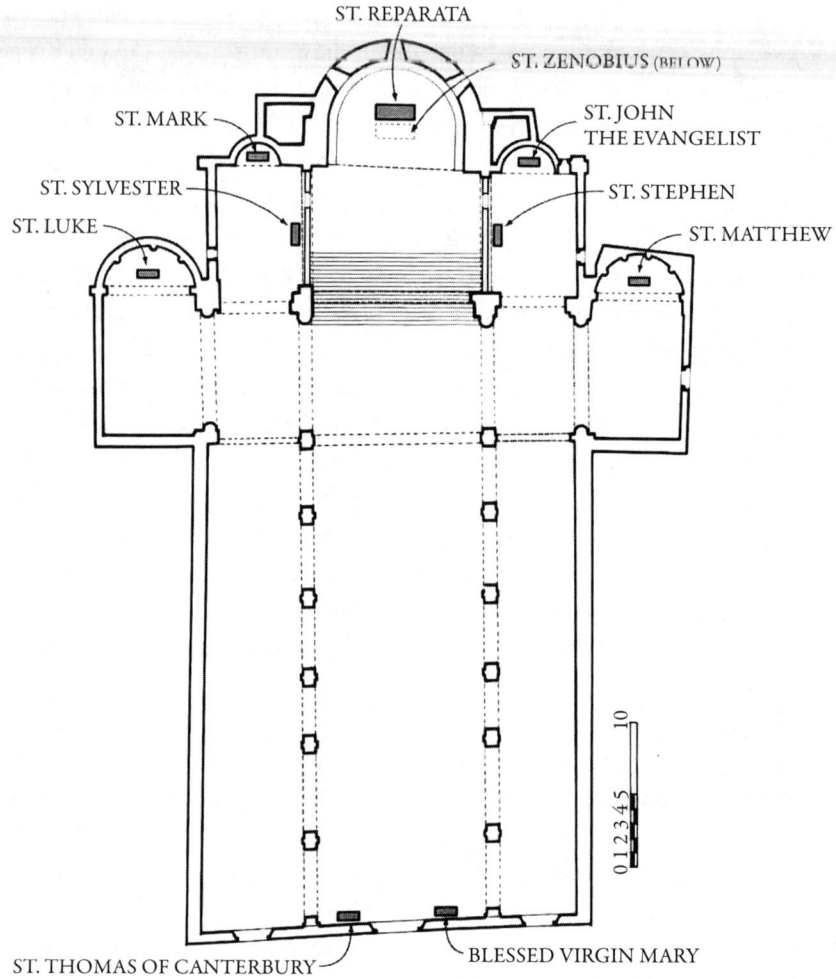

FIGURE 4.1. Plan of Santa Reparata, Florence (from Toker [2009]).

and acclaim for its strict adherence to the Benedictine Rule.[32] There were few Cluniacs in Italy, but the cathedral canons of Florence surely associated the order with clerical virtue due to its connection with local monastic reformers.[33] Recall that Lorenzo of Amalfi was a friend of its abbot, Odilo, a suggestive link with Cluny to which another can be

---

échelon plan include the eleventh-century Cluniac abbey of Fruttuaria (near Turin), founded around 1000 by William of Saint-Bénigne: Luisella Pejrani Baricco, "I risultati dell'indagine archeologica sulla chiesa abbaziale di Fruttuaria: Prime considerazioni," in *Dal Piemonte all'Europa: Esperienze monastiche nella società medievale*, ed. Renato Bordone (Turin: Deputazione subalpine di storia patria—regione Piemonte, 1988), 587–606.

[32] Dominique Iogna-Prat, *Agni immaculati: Recherches sure les sources hagiographieques relatives à Saint Maieul de Luny (954-994)* (Paris: Cerf, 1988).

[33] Pejrani Baricco, "I risultati," 592, n. 24, counts only six Italian churches, including Santa Reparata in Florence, that adopted the Cluniac plan.

added: Giovanni Gualberto, the outspoken critic of the Florentine bishop Attone, and of San Miniato, turned to a Cluniac monk to consecrate his monastery of Vallombrosa.³⁴ Redolent of the kind of reformed monasticism that criticized the conduct of Florentine prelates, the plan of Santa Reparata marked one more gesture of independence on the part of the canons from their bishop.

This political interpretation of the architectural iconography of Santa Reparata obtains support in the minor yet suggestive part played by Teodaldo of Arezzo in its reconstruction. As portrayed in the Translation of St. Donatus, Teodaldo was an episcopal lord and builder in the traditional Ottonian mold whose ambitions culminated in the consecration of San Donato at Pionta in 1032; however, he also allied himself with monastic reformers as the preeminent patron of Romualdo, whose hermitage at Camaldoli was located within his diocese. These two credentials provide the background for an act made by the cathedral canon, Rolando, at the altar of St. John the Evangelist in the east end of Santa Reparata. With the support of his fellow canons, Rolando endowed a hospital at Santa Reparata, the first such institution recorded at a Tuscan cathedral and just the sort of charitable establishment promoted by such monastic reformers as Giovanni Gualberto. The act also recalls the consecration of the altar of St. John not by the local Florentine prelate, Attone, but instead by Teodaldo, "a glorious and most reverent bishop of good memory."³⁵ The death of the Aretine bishop in 1036 provides a *terminus ante quem* for the consecration and, by extension, the rebuilding

---

³⁴ Davidsohn, *Storia*, vol. 1, 263–264. Toker, "Excavations," 34, by contrast, relates the plan of Santa Reparata to the aforementioned Bishop Gerardo, who was born in Burgundy and was a supporter of Cluny; however, his arrival in Florence postdated the completion of the east end of Santa Reparata by 1036 as established by the canon Rolando's charter cited below in n. 35. More recently, Toker has argued that the stepped plan responded to the cult of the evangelists at Santa Reparata, of which the likely impulse was the acquisition of their relics in a Byzantine ivory casket around the turn of the millennium. Hence the unusual arrangement of an altar dedicated to each evangelist and located in each of the apsidioles and chapels of the east end: Franklin Toker, "A Gap in the Liturgical History of Florence Cathedral, and a Byzantine Casket Rich Enough to Fill It," in *Arte d'Occidente: Studi in onore di Angiola Maria Romanini*, ed. Antonio Cadei et al. (Rome: Edizioni Sintesi Informazione, 1999), 767–779.

³⁵ Piattoli, *Le carte*, no. 42, 118 (4 November 1040). A marginal note in the twelfth-century Florentine ordinal, Ritus, fol. 69v, indicates that the consecration of the altar of St. John occurred on the feast of St. Lucy (13 December). On Rolando's act and its significance, see Toker, *On Holy Ground*, 71–72; Mauro Ronzani, "Vescovi, canoniche e cattedrali nella 'Tuscia' dei secoli X e XI: Qualche considerazione a partire dall'esempio di Fiesole," in *Un archivio, una diocesi: Fiesole nel medioevo e nell'età moderna*, ed. Maura Borgioli (Florence: Leo S. Olschki, 1996), 116–117; and Davidsohn, *Storia*, vol. 1, 266–267. See also Anna Benvenuti, "Stratigrafie della memoria: Scritture agiographiche e mutamenti architettonici nella vicenda del 'Complesso cattedrale' fiorentino," in *Il bel San Giovanni e Santa Maria del Fiore: Il centro religioso di Firenze dal tardo antico al Rinascimento*, ed. Domenico Cardini (Florence: Le lettere, 1996), 120; and Cardini, "Ipotesi," 140–141, who nonetheless mistakenly asserts that Teodaldo in fact consecrated the altar of St. John in 1040. Finally, the *terminus ante quem* of 1036 argues against the hypothesis, articulated in Toker, "Excavations," 34, and repeated in Maria S. Tacconi, *Cathedral and Civic Ritual in Late Medieval and Renaissance Florence: The Service-Books of Santa Maria del Fiore* (Cambridge: Cambridge University Press, 2005), 2, that the impetus for the reconstruction of Santa Reparata came from Bishop Gerardo.

of the entire east end evocative of Cluny. In light of the foundation of the hospital, the selection of Teodaldo rather than Attone as consecrator by (one presumes) the canons provides further evidence that the cathedral chapter sidelined its own bishop by affiliating itself with the Aretine one, as well as with the sort of monastic reformers whom Teodaldo patronized.[36]

The case of the Florentine cathedral in the 1030s marked a dramatic departure from the previous history of Tuscan dioceses: inspired by a new generation of reformers, its canons denied their bishop his traditional role as *dominus et constructor* and promoted the cult of St. Zenobius in opposition to that of St. Minias and his champion, Ildebrando. In so doing, the canons of Santa Reparata claimed the pope as the protector of their fiscal independence, thus placing themselves under the patronage of an ecclesiastical rather than a temporal authority such as the emperor. Indeed, the papacy itself adopted many of the priorities of monastic reformers under Pope Leo IX (1049–1054) and his successors. It usurped the emperor's traditional role as patron and protector of cathedral chapters, bestowing grants of immunity on such communities in Tuscany and beyond.[37] Yet papal influence was most pronounced not in Florence but rather in Lucca, where it elevated the profile of individual bishops but gradually eroded episcopal authority over local relic cults.

LUCCA: THE LORD AND BUILDER IN THE AGE OF THE REFORMED PAPACY

The episcopates of four Lucchese bishops—Giovanni II (1023–1056), Anselmo I (1057–1073), St. Anselmo II (1073–1086), and Rangerio (ca. 1096–1112)—illustrate how papal influence at times bolstered but ultimately circumscribed the role of such prelates in the promotion of local relic cults. The most distinctive witness to this period of Lucchese history is the rhymed Life of St. Anselmo II by Rangerio: composed in elegiac couplets and

---

[36] The connection between Bishop Teodaldo and the cathedral canons of Florence finds a faint yet perceptible echo in the Translation of St. Donatus. In recounting the elevation of its saint by that Aretine bishop and the cathedral canons, this text describes his relics as "a celestial treasure more precious than all gold and gems" (*celestem thesaurum omni auro et gemmis pretiosorem*): Ubaldo Pasqui, *Documenti per la storia della città di Arezzo nel medio evo*, 4 vols. (Florence: G.P. Vieusseux, 1899, 1904, 1916, 1937), vol. 4, 13. The phrase *gemmis pretiosorem* recalls that of *gemmae pretiosissimae* employed, as noted above, in the foundation charter of San Miniato (1018) and Life of St. Zenobius (ca. 1039). Written sometime after Teodaldo's death in June 1036, the Translation may have provided another point of inspiration for the use of "most precious gems" in the Life. Given the uncertainty surrounding its precise dating, however, the opposite scenario is equally plausible.

[37] Leo IX to Lucca (12 March 1051): Kehr, *Regesta*, vol. 3, no. 1, 397–398. Victor II to Pisa (1055–1057): no. 15, 334; Victor II to Arezzo (1055–1057): no. 2, 157; Nicholas II to Siena (1059–1061): no. 1, 206; Alexander II to Pistoia (1061–1073): no. 1, 124. Note, however, that the canons of Pisa had been particularly precocious in obtaining papal protection of their properties from John XVIII (May 1007): no. 12, 333–334. On papal influence over the Tuscan dioceses in general, see H. E. J. Cowdrey, "Pope Gregory VII and the Bishoprics of Central Italy," *Studi Medievali* 34 (1993): 51–64.

replete with classical allusions, it was intended not for liturgical recitation but, rather, to edify learned readers.[38] Previously unrecognized similarities between the *vita* and more traditional hagiographic texts—two Translations and a sermon—support the ascription of these three anonymous works to Rangerio as well. All four texts, as demonstrated below, bear witness to the emergence of a new type of *dominus et constructor* in the person of Anselmo I, whose relic translations and building projects were, first and foremost, displays of fidelity to Rome rather than of local episcopal authority. Serving concurrently as bishop of Lucca and pope, Anselmo I marked the apogee of papal influence in the entire region. Yet the ultimate consequence of papal intervention in Lucchese affairs proved to be the marginalization of local prelates vis-à-vis local relic cults in a manner far more extreme than in Florence forty years earlier.

Although the first of this quartet of Lucchese prelates, Giovanni II, conformed to the traditional mold of the Ottonian lord and builder, his very name evoked an older, Carolingian model in the person of Bishop Giovanni I. A member of a wealthy Milanese family, Giovanni II was a traditional, philo-imperial *dominus et constructor*, founding canonries and building churches in Lucca and throughout its diocese.[39] Yet he also followed in the footsteps of his eighth-century namesake in enriching the treasury of his cathedral with holy relics. Giovanni I had acquired the body of St. Regulus from a site within his episcopal dominion (i.e., Populonia in southern Tuscany) in the inaugural year of his episcopate. Similarly, Giovanni II obtained relics of St. Lucine perhaps as early as 1027, when he traveled to Rome in the company of Emperor Conrad II.[40] The choice of this Roman matron of late Antiquity intimates the latter bishop's desire to style himself as a protector of relics: St. Lucine had cared for Christian martyrs during their lifetime and tended to their bodies after their execution.[41] Her *vita*, which was probably written in Lucca, concludes with a brief account of her transfer to San Martino and underscores the similarities

---

[38] *Vita Metrica Sancti Anselmi*, in MGH SS, vol. 30, 1152–1307, on which see Raffaele Savigni, *Episcopato e società cittadina a Lucca: Da Anselmo II (†1086) a Roberto (†1255)* (Lucca: S. Marco, 1996), 345–376; and Gabriella Severino, "La 'Vita metrica' di Anselmo da Lucca scritta da Rangerio: Ideologia e genere letterario," in *Sant'Anselmo vescovo di Lucca (1073-1086). Nel quadro delle trasformazioni sociali e della riforma ecclesiastica*, ed. Cinzio Violante (Rome: Istituto Palazzo Borromini, 1992), 223–271.

[39] Graziano Concioni, *Contributi alla storia del Volto Santo* (Pisa: ETS, 2005), 171–174; Irene Scaravelli, "Giovanni da Besate," in *Dizionario Biografico degli Italiani* (Rome: Istituto dell'Enciclopedia Italiana, 2000), 716–717; and Romano Silva, "*Dilexi decorem domus tuae:* Il ruolo dell'episcopato nello sviluppo dell'architettura in Toscana dall'XI secolo alla prima metà del XII," *Arte medievale* 10 (1996): 28–29.

[40] Almerico Guerra and Pietro Guidi, *Compendio di storia ecclesiastica lucchese dalle origini a tutto il secolo XII* (Lucca: Cooperativa Artigiana Editrice, 1924), 135.

[41] St. Lucine was a recurring figure in early *gesta* of Roman martyrs of the first through the early fourth centuries: Kate Cooper, "The Martyr, The Matrona and the Bishop: The Matron Lucina and the Politics of Martyr Cult in Fifth- and Sixth-Century Rome," *Early Medieval Europe* 8 (1999): 308–315. The martyrology of Ado of Vienna (†875), likewise associates Lucine with early Christian martyrs and described her as a "discipulae aposotolorum" in connection with her own feast day (PL, vol. 123, col. 296). The Lucchese probably knew St. Lucine via her appearance in the papal biography of St. Cornelius in the *Liber Pontificalis*, of which a copy, BCL, 490, they had possessed since the late eighth century: Louis Duchesne and Cyrille Vogel, eds., *Le Liber pontificalis*, 2nd. ed., 3 vols. (Paris: E. de Boccard, 1955), vol. 1, ch. 150–151.

between her translation and that of St. Regulus more than two centuries earlier. It describes the second Giovanni, like the first, as a pious suppliant to the saint's grave and conflates two bishops by identifying him with the equivocal phrase as "a certain Giovanni."[42] According to Carolingian and Ottonian standards, Giovanni II was thus a thoroughly conventional *dominus et constructor.*

In retrospect, the translation of St. Lucine from Rome was nonetheless a harbinger of Tuscany's prominent place in the reform movement championed by the papacy even after the aforementioned residence of Pope Benedict IX in Florence in the 1030s. In 1055, Pope Victor II (1055–1057) convened a synod at Santa Reparata of Florence attended by 120 bishops, a watershed at which some of these prelates were deposed for simony or dissipation.[43] Tuscany remained a major arena for papal action as Bishops Gerardo of Florence (1046–1061) and Anselmo I of Lucca (1057–1073) ascended to the chair of St. Peter under the names Nicholas II (1059–1061) and Alexander II (1061–1073), respectively. Neither was native to Tuscany—the first was Burgundian, the second Milanese—but both signaled their enduring commitment to their adopted cities by retaining their local episcopal offices throughout their pontificates. During the Lenten season of his first year as pope, Gerardo convened a synod in Rome where the archdeacon (and future Pope Gregory VII) Hildebrand championed the priorities of older monastic reformers. With the support of Anselmo I, he criticized the Rule of Aachen for allowing secular canons to hold private property and for bestowing upon them extravagant amounts of food and drink. The final legislation of the Lenten synod proved to be more moderate than he had desired, ordering only these clerics remain chaste, eat and live together, and not divide ecclesiastical income among themselves; however, the sentiment of his critiques remained in its exhortation that all clerics "take pains exceedingly to arrive at the apostolic, namely common life."[44] In the middle decades of the eleventh century, Tuscan bishops thus acquired particularly prominent roles in the emergence of the reformed papacy.

---

[42] That the *Vita Sancte Lucine* (*BHL* 5021m) survives only in the Lucchese passionaries, BCL, B, fols. 205–206v (1175–1200) and BCL G, fols. 129–130 (saec. XII^{ex}/XIII^{in}), suggests that it was written by a local cleric.

[43] Mansi, *Sacrorum Conciliorum*, vol. 19, cols. 835–838; and Davidsohn, *Storia*, vol. 1, 296–297.

[44] Mansi, *Sacrorum Conciliorum*, vol. 19, cols. 897–920, on which see Fermino Poggiaspalla, *La vita comune del clero* (Rome: Storia e Letteratura, 1968), 158–166; and H. E. J. Cowdrey, "The Gregorian Papacy and Eremetical Monasticism," in *San Bruno e la Certosa di Calabria. Atti del convegno internazionale di studi per il IX centenario della Certosa di Serra S. Bruno. Squillace, Serra S. Bruno, 15-18 settembre 1991*, ed. Pietro De Leo (Catanzaro: Soveria Mannelli, 1995), 34. The latter study also outlines the sympathies of Pope Gregory VII with such Italian monastic reformers as Giovanni Gualberto (34–37). Cosimo Damiano Fonseca, "Il capitolo di San Martino e la riforma canonicale nella seconda metà del sec. XI," in *Sant'Anselmo vescovo di Lucca (1073-1086). Nell quadro delle trasformazioni sociali e della riforma ecclesiastica*, ed. Cinzio Violante (Rome: Istituto Palazzo Borromini, 1992), 54, discusses Anselmo's role at the synod; Tilmann Schmidt, *Alexander II (1061-1073) und die römische Reformgruppe seiner Zeit* (Stuttgart: Hiersemann, 1977), 134–216, addresses his broader ties with papal reformers.

The papal synods of the 1050s find distinct echoes in the relic translations and building projects of Anselmo I, whose exclusively philo-Roman approach to such initiatives not only accorded with his dual office as bishop and pope but also differentiated him from traditional lords and builders. Before ascending to the chair of St. Peter in 1061, he interred the relics of St. Senesius, previously acquired from Rome, in a new crypt beneath San Pietro Maggiore, a church situated just south of the city walls.[45] After ascending to the papacy, Anselmo I deposited relics of his papal namesake, St. Alexander I, in the urban basilica of San Alessandro Maggiore.[46] Yet these were minor achievements in comparison to the reconstruction of cathedral, San Martino, a project completed at breakneck speed between 1060 and 1070. Thirty years later, in his rhymed Life of St. Anselmo II, Bishop Rangerio drew attention to the edifice, and in particular to the massive columns dividing its nave into five rather than three aisles (fig. 4.2). He intimated the unmistakable model for this distinctive arrangement, St. Peter's in Rome, by identifying Anselmo I according to his papal name, Alexander, and by describing him as "ruler of Rome and Lucca."[47] Anselmo I himself accentuated the Roman iconography of San Martino by translating therein three martyrs from the Eternal City: the brothers Jason and Maurus and their mother, Hilaria.[48] Earlier in the eleventh century, as we have seen, *domini et constructores* in Arezzo, Fiesole, and Florence had championed the cults of local saints and drew on imperial patronage in order to buttress their episcopal authority. This bishop and pope, by contrast, appears less parochial, enlisting the support of Roman martyrs and emulating the plan of a Roman basilica so as to bind Lucca tighter to the Eternal City.

The distinctive portrait of Anselmo I in two of the aforementioned four hagiographic texts strengthens the impression that Rangerio perceived in him a new kind of lord and builder. When that author described the reconstruction of San Martino in his rhymed Life, he lauded Anselmo I as a "new Solomon," perhaps the earliest instance

---

[45] *Passio Sancti Senesii* (*BHL* 7576), partially in *AS,* May, vol. 1, col. 473, and preserved in the Lucchese passionary likely compiled for San Pietro Maggiore, BLF, Pluteo 20.30 (saec. XII$^{3/4}$), fols. 13–13v.

[46] Cesare Franciotti, *Historia delle miracolose imagini e delle vite dei santi, i corpi dei quail sono nella città di Lucca* (Lucca: Ottavio Guidoboni, 1613), 361. On Anselmo I's relic translations in general and his acquisition of St. Alexander in particular, see Schmidt, *Alexander II*, 37–42 and 98–100, respectively.

[47] *Vita Metrica Sancti Anselmi,* in MGH SS, vol. 30, 1251, vv. 4503–4508: "Aspice nunc edem primam, mirare columnas, | Ordine quas gemino ducit utrumque latus. | Aspice structuram lapidum, quas [sic] arte decora | Docta manus posuit sub Salomone novo, | Quae sub Alexandro Romam | Lucamque regente | Grande sed angusto tempore fecit opus." Cf. Romano Silva, "La ricostruzione della cattedrale di Lucca (1060–1070): Un esempio precoce di architettura della riforma gregoriana," in *Sant'Anselmo vescovo di Lucca (1073-1086). Nel quadro delle trasformazioni sociali e della riforma ecclesiastica,* ed. Cinzio Violante (Rome: Istituto Palazzo Borromini, 1992), 297 and 306, on the papal associations of the plan of San Martino.

[48] *Sermo in dedicatione ecclesie Sancti Martini,* in Pietro Guidi, "Per la storia della cattedrale e del Volto Santo," *Bollettino storico lucchese* 4 (1932): 183, on which see below, n. 50.

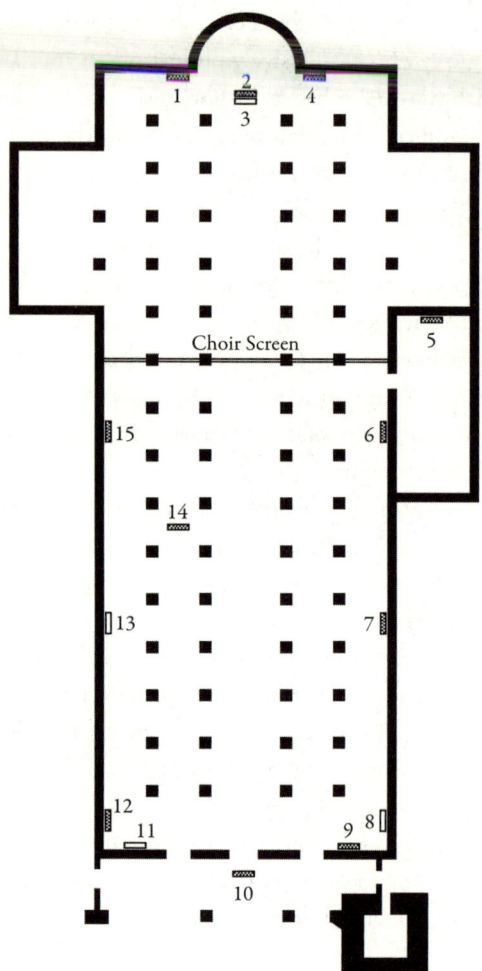

FIGURE 4.2. Plan of San Martino, Lucca (after Ridolfi [1882]). 1 = Altar of Sts. Jason, Maurus and Hilaria (after 1109). 2 = Altar of St. Martin (above). 3 = Altar of St. Regulus in confessione (before 1109). 4 = Altar of St. Regulus (after 1109). 5 = Altar of St. Apollinaris. 6 = Altar of St. Michael. 7 = Altar of St. Agnellus. 8 = Altar of Sts. Jason, Maurus, and Hilaria (before 1109). 9 = Altar of St. Blaise. 10 = Altar of St. Edmund supra porticum (after 1165). 11= Altar of the Holy Cross (before 1120 [?]). 12 = Altar of St. Lucine. 13 = Altar of Sts. Agatha and Agnes (until 1109 [?]). 14 = Chapel of the Holy Cross (after 1120 [?]). 15 = Altar of the BMV.

of a Tuscan bishop being likened to the great builder of the Old Testament.[49] Three similar references appear in the sermon recited by the cathedral canons on the anniversary of Anselmo I's consecration of San Martino on 6 October 1070, strengthening

---

[49] See above, n. 47. Previous citations of Solomon in episcopal documents from Tuscany usually occurr in connection with ecclesiastical reform—e.g., when Bishop Jacopo of Fiesole's quoted Solomon's presumed admonition to virtue from Eccles. 9:10 in 1032 (see chapter 3, this volume).

the (hitherto speculative) attribution of this second text to Rangerio.⁵⁰ First, the local populace made donations equal to "Solomon's riches," thereby facilitating the remarkably swift building campaign. Second, Anselmo I deposited Sts. Jason, Maurus, and Hilaria in San Martino in the cathedral "so that its treasury was in no way inferior to that preserved in the tabernacle by Moses or those in the temple by Solomon."⁵¹ Third, he instituted the anniversary of the consecration "in the manner of Solomon." The prominent naming of Solomon in the *vita* and the *Sermo in dedicatione ecclesie Sancti Martini* provides concrete evidence that both texts were written by Rangerio. Moreover, the comparison of the current bishop of Lucca and of Rome to that Old Testament figure suggests the appeal to that author of a *dominus et constructor* who embodied and promoted the aims of the reformed papacy.

The *Sermo in dedicatione* nonetheless shows that local ecclesiastical history and contemporary religious politics clarified the reconstruction of San Martino in equal measure. The text emphasizes the similarities between Anselmo I and his immediate predecessor, Giovanni II: as the latter had transferred St. Lucine from Rome and, "with great devotion," interred her in the northwest corner of the cathedral, so the former translated Sts. Jason, Maurus, and Hiliaria from the Eternal City and "honorably" buried them in the southwest corner of that same church (fig. 4.2). Applied to both men, the hagiographic trope of the bishop as a pious translator of relics provides a literary parallel to the identical source (Rome) and destination (the west end of San Martino) of the relics in question. That Anselmo I placed Sts. Jason, Maurus, and Hilaria opposite St. Lucine, moreover, indicates the meaning that he himself ascribed to the translation of the latter saint earlier in the eleventh century. This arrangement underscored biographical similarities between St. Lucine and St. Hilaria, both of whom buried their sons after the execution of these young men on account of their faith.⁵² More important,

---

⁵⁰ The *Sermo in dedicatione ecclesie Sancti Martini* survives as an unicum in the passionary of San Martino, BCL, P†, fols. 132–32v, and is partially edited in Guidi, "Per la storia," 182–184. Guidi, p. 174, n. 1, attributes the sermon to Rangerio without citing supporting evidence. Without endorsing this ascription, Anna Rosa Calderoni Masetti, "Anselmo da Baggio e la cattedrale di Lucca," *Annali della Scuola Normale Superiore di Pisa, Serie III* 1 (1977): 95–96, notes that the author of the sermon was evidently writing at some chronological distance from the consecration of San Martino in 1070 and was demonstrably interested in the architecture of the new edifice. Both characteristics (one might add) apply to Rangerio.

⁵¹ *Sermo in dedicatione ecclesie Sancti Martini*, BCL, P†, fol. 132v, in Guidi, "Per la storia," 183: "Ut autem etiam de thesauris nichil minus esse potuisset vel ad illa que in tabernaculo per Moysen vel que in templo sunt reposita per Salomonem, Romam detulit memoratus pontifex et prelibate ecclesie obtulit sanctorum corpora Iasonis et Mauri et eorum matris Hylarie."

⁵² *Passio Sanctorum Chrysanthi et Dariae*, chs. 20–21 (*BHL* 1787), in *AS* October, vol. 11, cols. 481–482. Anselmo I was undoubtedly aware of the biagragraphical similarities between St. Lucine and St. Hilaria. On the wall of the west transept of Santa Prassede in Rome, whence he translated St. Jason and Maurus to Lucca, appears an early-ninth-century fresco that depicts St. Hilaria's burial of her two sons: Caroline J. Goodson, *The Rome of Pope Paschal I (817–824): Papal Power, Urban Renovation, Church Rebuilding and Relic Translation* (Cambridge: Cambridge University Press, 2010), 240.

it accentuated the Romanophilic architectural iconography of San Martino by transforming its west end into a shrine of Roman relics. Whatever her original significance to a traditional *dominus et constructor* like Giovanni II, St. Lucine had thus become subsumed into a more innovative, philo-Roman program.

Anselmo I differed from earlier lords and builders not only in his overriding focus on the Eternal City but also in the surprisingly hands-off approach ascribed to him by contemporary sources. Accounts of episcopal building projects typically used active verbs to describe their bishops—for example, "he built" (*fabricavit*) or "he made" (*fecit*).[53] An inscription located in the northernmost arcade of the portico of San Martino combines passive and active constructions in order (one suspects) to clarify Anselmo I's varied roles: "The radiant gables of this lofty temple were *constructed under* Pope Alexander II, to the care of which [temple] and for the prelate's use, he himself *built* the surrounding buildings—houses, chapels, and a hospital—over which he established [his] earthly authority under pain of excommunication."[54] The inscription emphasizes Anselmo I's authority over the entire cathedral complex, but makes a distinction between the church and its outbuildings, of which the first was built "under him" and the second by him. Rangerio's description of the cathedral in his rhymed Life of St. Anselmo II employs a similar construction: "marvel at its columns, which a skilled hand positioned with practical knowledge of beauty *under* the new Solomon."[55] Read against accounts of traditional *domini et constructores*, these two passages suggest that Anselmo I was not the hands-on builder that one might have otherwise assumed.

---

[53] E.g., the account of the construction of San Martino and its confessional by Bishop Giovanni I around 780 in the *Translatio Sancti Reguli I*, BAV, Vat. Lat. 6453, fol. 107: "Post hec autem diligentissime et cum omni studio et universo populo Lucensi *fabricavit* ecclesiam et confessionem similem beati Petri apostoli urbis Rome" (italics added). Similarly, the inscription on the confessional of Regulus, one reported in the *Translatio Sancti Reguli I* and presumably visibile during Anselmo I's lifetime, tells that Giovanni I "made" (*fecit*) the structure and "erected and constructed" its altar (BAV, Vat. Lat. 6453, fol. 107). Written in the late eleventh century, the *Historia Custodum Aretinorum*, in MGH SS, vol. 30, 1477, recounts the building projects of the trio of early-eleventh-century bishops of Arezzo in similarly active terms: "A follower of his predecessor, Elemperto, who had *renovated* Santa Maria from its foundations, [Alberto] *constructed* the church of San Donato from its foundations and brought it half way [to completion]. Having been prevented by his death, his successor, Teodaldo, *completed* it" (Denique ipse secutus antecessorem suum Helpertum, qui ecclesiam Sancte Marie a fundamentis renovaverat, sic etiste a fundamentis ecclesiam construxit Sancti Donati eamque ad medietatem deduxit, sed preventus morte, successor quidem Teodaldus perfecit) (italics added).

[54] "Huius que celsi radiunt fastigia templi | Sunt *sub* Alexandro papa *constructa* secundo | Ad curam cuius proprios et presulis usus | Ipse domos sedes presentes *struxit* et edes | In quibus hospitium faciens terrena potestas | Ut sit in eterno statuens anathemate sanxit | Milleque sex denis templum fundamine iacto | Lustro sub bino sacrum stat fine peracto" (italics added). The present epigraph belongs to the ornamentation of the portico of San Martino, executed between 1233 and 1250 and attributed to Guido Bigarelli, on which see chapter 5, this volume. While this epigraph thus dates from the middle thirteenth century, it is likely a copy of an eleventh-century original: Riccardo Ambrosini, "Le iscrizioni del Duomo e della Curia," *Rivista di archeologia, storia, costume* 26 (1998): 12; and Enrico Ridolfi, *L'arte in Lucca studiata nella sua cattedrale* (Lucca: Canoventti, 1882), 10, n. 2.

[55] See above, n. 47.

The "skilled hand" to which Rangerio referred likely alludes to the cathedral canons, with whom Anselmo I evidently forged a partnership that finds little if any precedent in medieval Tuscany. A twelfth-century hagiographic text ascribable to one of these clerics provides a different yet not contradictory account of the reconstruction of San Martino from the above-quoted sources. With no mention of Anselmo I, it lauds the archpriest and archdeacon, Lamberto and Blancardo, "wise, pious men, and most worthy men, born of the same mother, [who] built the present church from its foundations and, with amazing labor, perfected it in honor of blessed Martin."[56] This passage has led some to deny Anselmo I any role in the reconstruction of the cathedral, a hypothesis that accords better with the sidelining of a local bishop that (we now know) had occurred in Florence in the 1030s.[57] A more plausible scenario envisions a collaboration between the bishop and the cathedral canons. After his election to the papacy in 1061, as related below, Anselmo I was largely absent from Lucca and thus unable to supervise the rebuilding of San Martino. The *Sermo in dedicatione* hints that the canons acted as his surrogates, bringing to fruition the project that he had initiated: its opening lines praise the "dearest brothers," before signaling out those among them "who *completed* this work in St. Martin's name and honor and with such speed [i.e., in ten years] and dedicated it with such devotion."[58] Hence Anselmo I's double office, episcopal and papal, not only mirrored the philo-Roman iconography of San Martino but also contributed to the distinct impression of Anselmo I as a new kind of *dominus et constructor*. By delegating responsibility to Lamberto and Blancardo, he departed in yet another way from the model of episcopal building promoted in hagiography from the Carolingian and Ottonian periods.

The moderation that characterized Anselmo I's broader relationship with the cathedral chapter strengthens the case for his collaboration with its canons in the

---

[56] Blancardo is documented as archdeacon of San Martino from 1057 to 1078, Lamberto as one of its deacons from 1044 to 1059, and its archpriest from 1065 to 1086: Savigni, *Episcopato e società*, 419–420 and 443–444, respectively. The present quotation derives from *De inventione, revelatione ac traslactione* [sic] *Sanctissimi Vultus*, BCL, 626, fol. 11v (saec. XIII^(1/2)), edited in Concioni, *Contributi*, 29: "Nam tempore Lamberti archiprebiteri et Blancardi archidiaconi qui fratres uterini viri sapientes et religiosi Deo et homini acceptissimi funditus presentem ecclesiam edificaverunt et ad honorem beati Martini." See chapter 5, this volume, on the origins of *De inventione* and the cult of the wooden sculpture known as the Volto Santo.

[57] Guido Tigler, "Maestri lombardi del Duecento a Lucca: Le sculture della facciata del duomo," in *I magistri commacini: Mito e realtà del medioevo lombardo. Atti del XIX Congresso internazionale di studio sull'alto medioevo, Varase-Como, 23-25 ottobre 2008* (Spoleto: Fondazione Centro italiano di studi sull'alto medioevo, 2009), 886–887, follows the hypothesis set forth in Telesforo Bini, "Di chi promovesse la reidificazione della Cattedrale di Lucca dal 1060 al 1070," *Atti della Reale Accademia Lucchese di Scienze, Lettere e Arti* 7 (1860): 179–197, that the brothers and not their bishop were responsible for the project. Silva, "La ricostruzione," 300, by contrast, describes the archdeacon and archpriest as the "financers," of Anselmo I's architectural vision. Finally, Concioni, *Contributi*, 171, speculates that the brothers played an important role in the rebuilding of San Martino but does not attempt to define their contribution.

[58] *Sermo in dedicatione ecclesie Sancti Martini*, in Guidi, "Per la storia," 182, "qui eius nomini et honori tantum opus tanta caeleritate *consumarunt* tanta devotione dedicarunt" (emphasis added).

reconstruction of San Martino. In the second year of his pontificate, as related in the *Annales* of Tolomeo of Lucca (ca. 1307), he bestowed upon these clerics the right to wear mitres during solemn processions, a dignity typically reserved for Roman cardinals.[59] He adopted a more adversarial posture in an undated bull, harshly accusing the canons of simony and forbidding them from buying and selling their offices. Yet Anselmo I did not attempt to impose upon them the strict standards of clerical virtue that he had advocated at the Lenten synod of 1055.[60] He even refrained from urging them to "lead the common life" and to "live canonically," admonitions that did not necessarily proscribe private property but that nonetheless belonged to the rhetoric of monastic and papal reformers.[61] The head of the reformed papacy thus asked nothing more from his cathedral chapter than episcopal reformers in the Ottonian mold had required of theirs. By adopting a posture conciliatory in substance, if not in tone, one suspects that he fostered cordial relations with those clerics upon whose archpriest and archdeacon he depended to complete the rebuilding of San Martino.

The portrait of Anselmo I as a lord and builder tailored to the age of the reformed papacy obtained its greatest expression neither in literary *vitae* nor in papal bulls but instead in a liturgical ceremony: the consecration of San Martino on 6 October 1070. Three sources facilitate the reconstruction of this sumptuous rite in the following paragraphs. The first two are preserved in a Lucchese copy of the Romano-German Pontifical (PRG) compiled by 1000.[62] The *ordo* of consecration codifies the textual, musical, and ritual aspects of this rite as celebrated throughout Latin Christendom, while the commentary, *Quid significent*, provides the canonical interpretation of the consecration of a church as a spiritual journey of the humble Christian.[63] Third, the *Sermo in dedicatione*

---

[59] Tolomeo of Lucca, *Annales*, in MGH SS, n.s., vol. 8, 5.

[60] *MDL*, vol. 5, pt. 3, no. 1794, 665–666. The rhetoric (if not the substance) of the bull impressed Rangerio, in whose rhymed Life Anselmo I delivers a soliloquy that summarizes the entire charter: *Vita metrica Sancti Anselmi*, in MGH SS, vol. 30, 1166, ll. 415–426.

[61] By contrast, Anselmo I conceded a piece of adjacent land to the Lucchese church of San Donato on the condition that each of its canons "consent to lead the common life and to live canonically" (*ibi communem vitam ducere voluerint et canonice vixerint*): PL, vol. 146, col. 1284 (1063). On Anselmo I's broader efforts to reform religious communities in Lucca and its diocese, see Schmidt, *Alexander II*, 37–42.

[62] BCL, 607, of which a description and inventory appear in Michel Andrieu, *Les Ordines Romani du Haut Moyen Age*, 5 vols. (Louvain: Spicilegium Sacrum Lovaniense, 1931–1961), vol. 1, 156–165. While Andrieu (p. 157) dates the manuscript to the second half of the tenth century, Roger E. Reynolds, "The Ritual of Clerical Ordination of the Sacramentarium Gelasium Saec. VIII: Early Evidence from Southern Italy," in *Rituels mélanges offerts à Pierre-Marie Gy, o.p.*, ed. Paul De Clerck and Eric Palazzo (Paris: Editions du Cerf, 1990), 439, suggests, on paleographical evidence, that it might date from as late as the turn of the eleventh century. On the PRG in general, see introduction to part I, this volume.

[63] The *Ordo ad benedicendam ecclesiam* and the related commentary, *Quid significent duodecim candelae*, are edited in Cyrille Vogel and Reinhard Elze, *Le Pontifical romano-germanique du dixième siècle*, 3 vols. (Vatican City: Biblioteca Apostolica Vaticana, 1963–1972), vol. 1, ch. 35, 90–123 and ch. 40, 124–173, respectively. An English translation of the *Ordo* appears as Appendix A of Brian V. Repsher, *The Rite of Church Dedication in the Early Medieval Era* (Lewiston, NY: Edwin Mellen, 1998), 139–195. Repsher (esp. 121–128); and Lee Bowen, "The Tropology of Mediaeval Dedication Rites," *Speculum* 16 (1941): 469–479 (esp. 470),

ascribed above to Rangerio yields a specific, historical reading of the consecration of San Martino that complements the general, moral one in *Quid significet*. Read together for the first time, these texts remind us that the execution and interpretation of ostensibly "universal" (i.e., uniform) rites varied from one place to another in response to local conditions, political and otherwise.[64] In Lucca, the *ordo*, commentary, and sermon reveal, the consecration of the cathedral publically conveyed the Romanophilia and collaborative spirit that made Anselmo I so distinctive a *dominus et constructor.*

To a degree hitherto unrecognized, the political context surrounding the consecration of San Martino in 1070 shaped the significance of this event before it had even begun. Six years earlier, Anselmo I had passed through Lucca en route from Rome to Mantua. According to Tolomeo, his adopted city had received him with great joy and its army had accompanied him to his final destination.[65] At Mantua, Anselmo I attended a synod that endorsed his claims to the papal throne and dismissed those of the anti-pope, Honorius II.[66] This victory surely provoked great celebration upon his return to Lucca in 1070 and ensured that his consecration of San Martino attracted an unusually large and distinguished audience. The consecrations of San Donato (in Arezzo) and San Romolo (in Fiesole) earlier in the century had drawn ecclesiastical dignitaries from throughout Tuscany; by contrast, that of San Martino, according to the *Sermo in dedicatione*, was attended by twenty-two bishops, many abbots, and an "infinite multitude" of clerics "said to have flown together not only from nearby cities but all the way from France."[67] Tolomeo added that many of these foreigners were members of the papal court who (one presumes) had attended the council of Mantua.[68] Few would have appreciated the cathedral, with its five-aisle plan evocative of St. Peter's and its treasury of Roman martyrs, more than these partisan witnesses to Anselmo I's triumph over Honorius II. The consecration of this particular church had acquired a political significance that extended well beyond its own city and region.

---

examine the moral interpretation of latter text, while Repsher (35–39) traces the relationships between the *Ordo* and *Quid significet* and notes the enduring influence of the latter on subsequent commentators. Dana M. Polanichka, "Transforming Space, (Per)forming Community: Church Consecration in Carolingian Europe," *Viator* 43 (2012): 91–93, shows how *Quid significet* tied the object of consecration, namely the physical church, to the community of faithful defined as the *ecclesia*. As illustrated by Louis Hamilton, *A Sacred City: Consecrating Churches and Reforming Society in Eleventh-Century Italy* (Manchester: Manchester University Press, 2010), 89 ff., other interpretations of the rite proliferated with the ecclesiastical reforms of the eleventh century, but the moral one remained the most influential throughout the Middle Ages.

[64] Hamilton, *A Sacred City*, 20–26, demonstrates the variability of the rite of consecration in particular via a comparative study of six sources from southern Italy.

[65] Tolomeo of Lucca, *Annales*, in MGH SS, n.s., vol. 8, 9.

[66] Mansi, *Sacrorum Conciliorum*, vol. 19, cols. 1029–1032. On the schism between Alexander II and Honorius II, see Schmidt, *Alexander II*, 104–133.

[67] *Sermo in dedicatione ecclesie Sancti Martini*, in Guidi, "Per la storia," 183: "Tacemus clericorum multitudinem infinitam, qui non modo de vicinis urbibus, sed ab usque ipsa Francia affuisse memorantur."

[68] Tolomeo of Lucca, *Annales*, in MGH SS, n.s., vol. 8, 9.

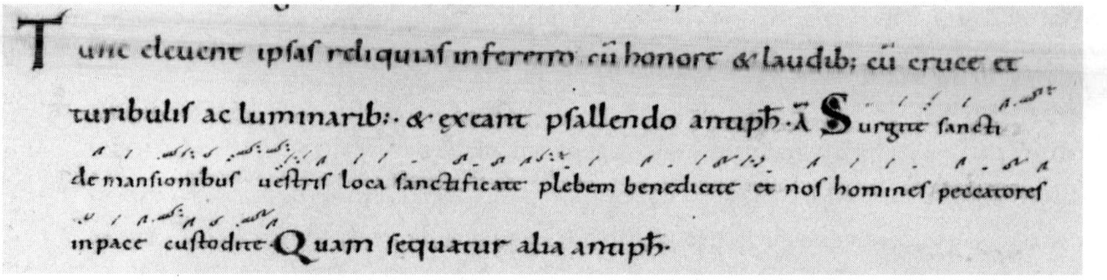

> Tunc elevent ipsas reliquias inferetro cu honore & laudib; cu cruce et turibulis ac luminarib: & exeant psallendo antiph. A. Surgite sancti de mansionibus vestris loca sanctificate plebem benedicite et nos homines peccatores in pace custodite Quam sequatur alia antiph.

FIGURE 4.3 *Tunc elevant* (rubric for the elevation of the relics) and *Surgite sancti* (antiphon). From the *Ordo ad benedicandam ecclesiam*, Romano-German Pontifical, BCL 607, fol. 51v (Lucca, by 1000). The musical notation is a later addition to the manuscript.

As the consecration of San Martino showcased Anselmo I's philo-Roman initiatives, so it underscored his dependence on the cathedral canons in their capacity as musicians. According to the aforementioned *ordo*, these clerics sang twenty-nine antiphons during this long and complex rite, and their bishop surely expected them to perform their part with solemnity and skill. His concern for liturgical ceremony in general found expression in the same bull in which he had accused the canons of simony: Anselmo I noted disapprovingly that the canons lacked a fixed order for singing Mass and worried that their liturgy might one day fall to the lowest of the Holy Orders, doormen and lectors.[69] Circumstantial evidence suggests that the canons prepared themselves to assist Anselmo I in the consecration of San Martino with the competence that he demanded. Among the many liturgical texts preserved in the Lucchese copy of the PRG, only the *ordo* presents antiphon texts fully overlaid with musical notation, which was added to the manuscript sometime in the eleventh century (fig. 4.3).[70] The "unheightened" neumes denote the general contour but not the precise pitches of the chants and served as an *aide-mémoire* to experienced singers familiar with similar melodies. A canon of San Martino (one might reasonably speculate) added the notation to the *ordo* in order to assist his brethren as they prepared to join their bishop in what was, by any measure, the liturgical performance of their ecclesiastical careers.

From the beginning, the consecration of San Martino signaled the philo-Roman character and collaborative spirit that Anselmo I brought as lord and builder. The bishop and canons gathered in front of a tent that housed the relics of St. Lucine, the Roman matron

---

[69] *MDL*, vol. 5, pt. 3, no. 1794, 665.

[70] While such musical notation appears in various sections of the Lucchese copy of the PRG, the only instances of fully notated chants (as opposed to the melodic incipit [or intonation]) appear in the *ordo* for consecration: BCL, 607, fols. 51v–72v. That the copyist of the original text did not provide extra space for melismas (i.e., singles syllables set to multiple notes), e.g., "mansioni**bus**" and "sanctifica**te**" (fig. 4.3), indicates that the notation postdates his work. Suggestive of an eleventh-century date for the notation is its similarity to the neumes in a notated breviary likely compiled in the diocese of Arezzo but now preserved in Lucca, BCL, 605 (saec. XI). On the dating of such notation in general, see Solange Corbin, *Die Neumen* (Cologne: Arno Volk, 1977), 155.

translated to the cathedral by Bishop Giovanni II and at whose altar Anselmo I had chosen to consecrate San Martino (fig. 4.2).[71] Her ancient ties to Rome and more recent ones to Lucca inflected the meaning of the ostensibly generic texts recited and sung by the bishop and canons in an alternating fashion that underscored their partnership. First, Anselmo I said a prayer that cast this Roman native as a local protector: "Allow us, Lord, to have contact with the limbs of your saints consecrated especially to you, whose patronage we unceasingly desire to have."[72] He proceeded to exorcise and bless the water and the salt used later in the rite. Afterwards, the canons lifted St. Lucine's bier and accompanied their bishop to the cathedral, chanting an antiphon that once again enlisted her patronage: "Rise up from your abodes, you saints, sanctify these places, bless the people, and guard us sinners, in peace. Alleluia" (fig. 4.3).[73] As the focal point for the consecration, St. Lucine underscored the emergence of this new model of *dominus et constructor* by virtue of her origins in the Eternal City.

With the arrival of the bishop and canons at San Martino, the moral associations of the rite overshadowed the historical ones. The clerics processed around the new edifice three times as he sprinkled its exterior with holy water, the first of many moments in the rite redolent of baptism. While the majority of canons guarded the bier outside, the bishop and several of their number entered San Martino and blessed its interior. Anselmo I inscribed the pavement with ash, writing the Greek and Roman alphabets in two perpendicular lines extending the length of the nave. These letters formed the arms of a cross and symbolized the rudiments of holy doctrine imparted to the laity. Moreover, they underscored the role of the bishop as pastor to both clergy and laity, reforming the former and instructing the latter on matters of Christian doctrine.[74] Finally, the prelate made a mortar of holy water with salt, ash, and wine—four ingredients signifying, respectively, the populace, divine doctrine, Christ's crucifixion, and his divinity. Through this purification, explained the commentary, *Quid significent*, the

---

[71] The Lucchese ordinal notes that on the feast of the Dedication of the Church, High Mass was celebrated at Lucine's altar, "which alone had been consecrated on that day" (*OOL*, fol. 63). Anselmo I's decision not to consecrate San Martino at its high altar probably reflected the fact that this altar had remained intact throughout the building campaign due to its position over the crypt of St. Regulus and thus did not need to be consecrated again: Silva, "La ricostruzione," 300. Such practical considerations, however, do not explain the selection of the altar of St. Lucine, which was but one of multiple side altars from which Anselmo I might have chosen as shown in fig. 4.2.

[72] Vogel and Elze, *Le Pontifical*, vol. 1, ch. 40, 129, n. 4, translation after Repsher, *The Rite*, 141: "Fac nos, domine, sanctorum tuorum tibi specialiter dicata membra contingere, quorum cupimus patrocinia incessanter habere."

[73] Vogel and Elze, *Le Pontifical*, vol. 1, ch. 40, 131, n. 10: "Surgite sancti de mansionibus vestris loca sanctificate plebem benedicite et nos homines peccatores in pace custodite alleluia."

[74] *Quid significent*, in Vogel and Elze, *Le Pontifical*, vol. 1, ch. 35, 97–98. The Lucchese redaction of *Quid significent* lacks its first fourteen chapters and thus begin with the explanation of the bishop's inscription of the church pavement with the Greek and Latin alphabet.

bishop "educates, corrects, consoles, and encourages the populace."[75] In the seclusion of a nearly empty cathedral, Anselmo I embraced a model of episcopal virtue older and more and universal than his particular brand of lord and builder.

The bishop fulfilled his pedagogical duty when he delivered a public discourse that returned holy relics to center stage and invited, once again, an historical interpretation evocative of Lucca. Having exited through the main doors of San Martino, he joined the cathedral chapter as well as the other clergy and laity that had since flocked to the cathedral to witness its consecration. This grand assembly processed around the edifice, the canons bearing the bier of St. Lucine and singing antiphons that cast their church as the New Jerusalem. Upon returning to the main doors, Anselmo I gave his address, of which the essentials were prescribed in the *ordo*: the decorous behavior of visitors to the church, the tithes and donations owed to it by its "lord and builder," and the veneration of the saints buried therein. The *Sermo in dedicatione*, by contrast, claims to preserve the particularities of Anselmo I's discourse, employing the first person as if quoting the bishop's words. As represented in the sermon, he artfully wove together the three themes mandated in the *ordo*, proscribing violence at San Martino, affirming the right of lawful sanctuary therein, and underscoring the power of its martyrs to foster social harmony. The bishop urged all those present to guard the holy "riches" of the cathedral: "What use to you is the possession of the martyrs' relics, which are almost hidden manna, when you reject their life, abhor their labors, and do not care for their crown?" The examples set by the saints, he continued, encourage peace and virtue: "let us redirect our efforts, do away with discord, and correct our frauds and perjuries." Failure to do so, he concluded, would only elicit God's wrath.[76] By casting relics as promoters of peace and harmony, these words fortify our impression of Anselmo I as a bishop who not only ascribed particularly great significance to such holy treasure but also maintained cordial relations with such clerics as the cathedral canons.

The conclusion of the consecration of San Martino returned the Roman matron, St. Lucine, to center stage and recapitulated the moral and historical themes sounded at different moments in the rite. After the clergy and laity had entered the church, Anselmo deposited her relics in the designated altar, enclosing them beneath a stone tablet affixed with the holy mortar. The canons chanted the antiphon, *Sub altare*, once again aiding their bishop with a sung gloss on his ritual action even as they addressed St. Lucine as a local patron: "you accepted the seats under the Lord's altar. Intercede for us to the Lord, who elected you."[77] The historical themes of cooperation between bishop and chapter,

---

[75] *Quid significent*, Vogel and Elze, *Le Pontifical*, vol. 1, ch. 35, 107: "cum populum se audientem, quantum sibi possibile est, erudit, castigat, consolatur et fovet et contra omnes inimici insidias armari docet."

[76] Guidi, "Per la storia," 184: "Quid valet vobis eorum habere reliquias, quasi quaddam manna reconditum, quorum vitam spernitis, labores aborretis, coronam non curatis?... Si Christus nobis iratus est, irati sunt et martyres... Quamobrem mutemus studia, discordias omittamus, fraudes, periuria corrigamus."

[77] Vogel and Elze, *Le Pontifical*, vol. 1, ch. 40, 171; BCL, 607, fol. 67: "Sub altare Domini sedes accepistis intercedite pro nobis ad Dominum qui vos elegit."

Lucca and Rome, accompanied the moral ones established by the canonical interpretation of the consecration rite. Sicardo of Cremona, a twelfth-century liturgist whose writings were read in Lucca and throughout Tuscany, made explicit what *Quid significent* only implied: just as the church signified Man, so too did the altar signify his heart. The enclosure of St. Lucine marked the faithfuls' embrace of her example as per their pastor's exhortation and the end of the spiritual journey.[78] From a historical point of view, moreover, it signaled the completion of the relic translations and building project that had rendered Anselmo I so distinctive a *dominus et constructor*.

If Anselmo I conveyed the benefits of papal influence upon Lucca in the form of holy relics and a rebuilt cathedral, his nephew and local episcopal successor, Anselmo II, illustrated the limits of such influence due to his antagonism of the cathedral canons. A protégé of his uncle's successor to the chair of St. Peter, Gregory VII, this second Anselmo is portrayed in his rhymed Life by Rangerio as a virtuous yet uncompromising "Gregorian" bishop caught up in the struggle between the empire and papacy.[79] He attempted precisely what his uncle had not: exhorting the canons of San Martino to follow the Apostles by renouncing their private property and their comfortable lifestyle.[80] In response, a sizable faction of them drew upon the support of local laymen and drove Anselmo II into exile, for which Gregory VII excommunicated them in 1079.[81] The dissident canons promptly elected a new bishop drawn from their own ranks and, in classic Ottonian fashion, loyal to the emperor, Henry IV (1056–1106). The emperor rewarded the Lucchese by recognizing their right to govern their city and its environs at the expense of their traditional sovereign (and a staunch supporter of the pope), Countess Matilda of Tuscany (1076–1115). His grant numbers among the earliest pieces of evidence for the emergence of the communes in Italy and thus, in retrospect, signaled nothing less than a political sea change.[82] The first unambiguous indication that the chapter had returned to the pope's good graces was the election of the papal ally, Rangerio, to the Lucchese episcopate in 1096, an entire decade after Anselmo II had died in exile.[83]

---

[78] Sicardo of Cremona, *Mitralis de Officii*, ed. Gábor Sarbak and Lorenz Weinrich (Turnhout: Brepols, 2008), bk. 1, ch. 10, 39–40. On the ubiquity of this line of interpretation in the twelfth and thirteenth centuries, see Bowen, "Tropology," 478. That the cathedral canons of Lucca owned a copy of Sicardo's *Mitralis* is but one indication of its influence in Tuscany (see chapter 5, this volume).

[79] Savigni, *Episcopato e società*, 345–376; and Severino, "La 'Vita metrica,'" 223–271.

[80] *Vita Metrica Sancti Anselmi*, in MGH SS, vol. 30, 1188, vv. 1497–1500, quoted in Fonseca, "Il capitolo di San Martino," 60–61.

[81] Kehr, *Regesta*, vol. 3, no. 11, 399–400 (1 October 1079). Fonseca, "Il capitolo di San Martino," 54–59, provides the most recent account of Anselmo II's failed reform of the Lucchese chapter. Gregory VII's bulls in support of Anselmo II are inventoried in Kehr, *Regesta*, nos. 8–11, 399–400.

[82] MGH, DRIG, vol. 6, no. 334, 437–439 (1081), on which see Chris Wickham, *Courts and Conflict in Twelfth-Century Tuscany* (Oxford: Oxford University Press, 2003), 20–21; and Savigni, *Episcopato e società*, 34–47.

[83] While a bishop named Goffredo (fl. 1091) preceded Rangerio, he probably did not reside permanently in Lucca and his episcopate remains almost entirely undocumented: Savigni, *Episcopato e società*, 401.

Rangerio and the cathedral canons reacted to the traumatic break with Rome through literary and liturgical means and in ways that reflected their divergent perspectives. The recently arrived bishop, as related above, wrote the *Vita metrica Sancti Anselmi* and (most likely) the *Sermo in dedicatione*, which together reflected his loyalty to the papacy by celebrating Anselmo I as a philo-Roman builder and Anselmo II as an ardent ecclesiastical reformer. The canons naturally endorsed the first but not the second of these portraits. On the anniversary of the consecration of San Martino (6 October), they commemorated the first Anselmo by reciting the sermon at the night office.[84] In the thirteenth century, moreover, they supervised the decoration of the portico of their church and preserved the inscription that lauded Anselmo I in connection with its rebuilding.[85] By contrast, the canons simply ignored the second Anselmo and his reputation outside of Lucca as a holy man and the first canonist of the reformed papacy.[86] The absence of his feast day (18 March) from their liturgical calendar was an implicit condemnation of his treatment of their community. If Rangerio offered detailed, highly partisan portraits of both Anselmos in his voluminous hagiographic output, the canons simply consigned the memory of the younger one to oblivion.

Nevertheless, the remarkable literary project by which Rangerio told the history of his cathedral, its clergy, and its relic cults was not limited in scope, as is generally thought, to his immediate episcopal predecessors, but in fact included a much earlier bishop of Lucca, Giovanni I. Evidence for Rangerio's interest in this early medieval prelate emerges in the third (of four) hagiographic texts attributable him, the *Translatio Sanctorum Reguli, Iasonis, Mauri, et Hilarie*, which documents Rangerio's translation of its four titular saints to two new altars in the east end of San Martino on 12 August 1109 (fig. 4.2).[87] The previous position of Sts. Jason, Maurus, and Hilaria opposite St. Lucine, as demonstrated previously, had created a shrine of Roman martyrs in the east end of the church and had drawn a parallel between the bishops responsible for the translation of all four saints from Rome to Lucca, Anselmo I and Giovanni II. According to the same logic, their new location opposite St. Regulus elevated the status of that saint's original translator, Giovanni I, at the expense of his eleventh-century namesake. Through this new arrangement of altars and its hagiographic witness, the sermon, Rangerio signaled his concern for Lucchese lords and builders of the distant as well as the recent past.

---

[84] *OOL*, fol. 63.

[85] On the inscription and the decoration of the portico of San Martino, see above, n. 47, and chapter 5 this volume, respectively.

[86] Kathleen G. Cushing. *Papacy and Law in the Gregorian Revolution: The Canonistic Work of Anselmo of Lucca* (Oxford: Oxford University Press, 1998).

[87] *Translatio Sanctorum Reguli, Iasonis, Mauri, et Hilarie* (BHL 7105a), BCL, 47, fols. 1–6, in Guidi, "Per la storia," 184–184, who convincingly argues for the attribution of this text to Rangerio on account of the similarities of its literary style with the *Vita metrica Sancti Anselmi*, as well as its use of the first-person plural in connection with Rangerio's translation of the four saints in question (p. 184, n. 1).

Indeed, in a newly discovered development, Rangerio celebrated Giovanni I in a more direct fashion by revising the early medieval account of the latter's translation of St. Regulus to Lucca in 780. The revised *Translatio Sancti Reguli* is the fourth (and final) hagiographic text under consideration and has never before been associated with Rangerio.[88] It adopts the narrative structure and substance of the original Translation, leaving unchanged the portrait of Giovanni I as a pious venerator of relics and ambitious builder of tombs. Yet the expressions of civic consciousness that frame this new text evoke the political climate of the early twelfth century and thus provide one (of several) pieces of evidence for its attribution to Rangerio.[89] Near its beginning, the revised Translation lauds the "wisdom," "judgment," and "glory" of Lucca and celebrates the city's victory over unidentified enemies, possibly an allusion to the war with Pisa between 1105 and 1110.[90] It concludes with the exclamation, "O happy Lucca, which so greatly deserved to have such a patron [i.e., St. Regulus] whose intercession both defends it from enemies and protects it from all other evils."[91] Such rhetoric evokes the emergence of the Italian communes at the turn of the twelfth century, a political development for which Lucca and Pisa provide the earliest evidence on the entire peninsula.[92] The *Translatio Sancti Reguli* thus couches the signature achievement of an early medieval bishop, Giovanni I, in terms concordant with the more recent political developments of its day.

---

[88] On the *Translatio Sancti Reguli I*, see chapter 2, this volume. The *Translatio Sancti Reguli II* (*BHL* 7103a) is edited in Manlio Simonetti, "Note sulla tradizione agiografica di S. Regolo di Populonia," in *Atti del convegno "Il Paleocristiano nella Tuscia," Viterbo, Palazzo dei Papi, 16-19 giugno 1979* (Viterbo: Consorzio per la gestione della bibliotheche comunale degli ardewnti e provinciale "Anselmo Anselmi," 1981), 128–130, and its earliest surviving source is the passionary of San Martino, BCL, P†, fols. 92–92v (saec. XII²/⁴). M. Simonetti (p. 119) lists further sources for St. Regulus's Passion and revised Translation, among which two eleventh-century manuscripts conspicuously preserve the former but not the latter. Among those sources that include both narratives is the cathedral passionary of Pistoia, BCR, 719. Once thought to date from the eleventh century, this manuscript has more recently been dated to the subsequent one: Sara Francesconi, "Storia della miniatura a Pistoia dall XII al metà del XIII secolo,"Tesi di laurea, University of Pisa, 2008, 714; Natale Rauty, *Il culto dei santi a Pistoia nel medioevo* (Florence: SISMEL—Edizioni del Galluzzo, 2000), xxi.

[89] The attribution of the *Translatio Sancti Reguli II* to Rangerio revises my previous contention that it was written during the episcopate of Bishop Anselmo I: Benjamin Brand, "John Hothby and the Cult of St Regulus at Lucca," *Early Music History* 27 (2008): 10–11.

[90] Tolemeo of Lucca, *Annales*, in MGH SS, n.s., vol. 8, 29–30.

[91] *Translatio Sancti Reguli II*, ch. 20, in M. Simonetti, "Note sulla tradizione," 130: "O felix Luca, quae tantum meruit habere patronum, cuius intercessione et ab hostibus defenditur et a pluribus aliis malis protegitur."

[92] See above, n. 82, for the aforementioned diploma issued by Emperor Henry IV in 1081. Rangerio likewise alluded to the nascent commune in his rhymed Life by speaking of the "consuls" before whom supporters of Anselmo II were tried in 1081: *Vita Metrica Sancti Anselmi*, in MGS SS, vol. 30, 1267, v. 5311. The civic rhetoric in the *Translatio Sancti Reguli II* similarly led Simone Collavini, "Da società rurale periferica a parte dello spazio politico lucchese: S. Regolo in Gualdo tra VIII e IX secolo," in *"Un filo rosso": Studi antichi e nuove recherché sulle orme di Gabriella Rossetti in occasione dei suo settanta anni*, ed. Gabriella Garzella and Enrica Salvatori (Pisa: ETS, 2007), 238, n. 22, to date it to the communal period.

The *Translatio Sancti Reguli* features prominent, repeated instances of wordplay that amplify its civic overtones and provide more concrete evidence for its attribution to Rangerio. In the *Vita metrica Sancti Anselmi*, this same author punned on the name of his adopted city while celebrating its wealth and glory. The literary strategy was hardly new to Tuscan hagiography but acquired a distinctive ideological function in the rhymed Life.[93] Ever the papal partisan, Rangerio used it to underscore an ancient, enduring bond between Lucca and Rome that (by implication) had survived the recent excommunication of the canons of San Martino:

> Peter's seat in Rome [is] preeminent throughout the world, but Lucca [is] not inferior in its sacred seats. Rome was loftier than any city in its power and wealth, illustrious in its title and throne of faith. Lucca was bright (*lucens*) and leading by the path of light (*lux*), called by the nobility of Rome. The nobility of faith from the first tradition gave form to the Lucchese church. It conferred festal traditions and stations unknown to all other churches in Tuscany.[94]

The revised Translation of St. Regulus likewise uses wordplay to ground the history of Lucca in that of the Eternal City. First, it ascribes its city's name to its glittering fame (*lucendo*) and to a distinguished Roman consul, "Lucius," who was believed to have rebuilt Lucca. Second, it proceeds immediately from this ancient builder to the early medieval one, Bishop Giovanni I, whom it introduces with words not in the original *translatio*: he "brought light (*lucem*) into the world" and followed Christ's admonition to his disciples, "let your light (*lux*) shine before men," and "you are the light (*lux*) of the world" (Matt. 5:16 and 5:14).[95] Employed in both the *Vita metrica* and the revised *Translatio Sancti Reguli* to similar ideological ends, this luminous, Romanophilic wordplay suggests not simply a common political outlook but in fact a common author.

Even as Rangerio granted Giovanni I a prominent place in his philo-Roman history of Lucca, he obscured, ironically enough, that bishop's own legacy vis-à-vis the Eternal City. According to the original *Translatio Sancti Reguli*, Giovanni I had

---

[93] Cf. the wordplay in the Life of St. Zenobius of Florence written approximately sixty years earlier (n. 26 above).

[94] *Vita Metrica Sancti Anselmi*, in MGH SS, vol. 30, 1171–1172, vv. 688–708: "Roma Petri Sedes et rerum prima per orbem, | Sed nec Luca sacris sedibus inferior. | Roma viris, opibus omni sublimior urbe | Et fidei titulo claruit et solio. | Lucca fuit lucens et lucis tramite ducens | Et de Romana nobilitate cluens. | Nobilitas fidei de prima tradicione | Lucensi formam contulit aecclesiae. | Contulit et mores festivos et staciones, | Quod non est Tuscis omnibus aecclesiis." Later in the rhymed Life, Rangerio engaged in such wordplay again in ascribing his citizens' name, "Lucchese," to the "honor of light" acquired through their pious giving since the eighth century (see chapter 2 this volume, n. 17).

[95] *Translatio Sancti Reguli II*, ch. 18, in M. Simonetti, "Note sulla tradizione," 129: "lucem mundo intulerat, iuxta dominicam sententiam qua dicitur: *Luceat lux vestra coram hominibus*; et illud: *Vos estis lux mundi*."

interred St. Regulus in a newly built confessional beneath the high altar of San Martino, one "similar to that of the blessed apostle Peter in the city of Rome."[96] This annular crypt, as demonstrated in chapter 2, numbered among the most prominent examples of the bishop's emulation of papal builders in response to the Frankish conquest of Italy in 774. The elevation of St. Regulus to his new altar in the south tribune of San Martino in 1109 honored Giovanni I by drawing a parallel between him and the more recent *dominus et constructor*, Anselmo I. Yet it also resulted in the closing up of the old confessional, which Rangerio justified on practical grounds. The crypt, he claimed, had recently become a place of idle chatter rather than of pious veneration.[97] Whatever the veracity of this assertion, Rangerio clearly felt compelled to downplay the Roman associations of the monument that he had effectively destroyed: his revised Translation of St. Regulus follows the original *translatio* by lauding the beauty of the confessional but excises the mention of its similarity to the crypt of St. Peter.[98] With this telltale omission, Rangerio demonstrated himself to be just as selective as the cathedral canons in his telling of the history of Lucca and its relic cults.

The rhymed Life, two Translations, and sermon formed an exceptional literary oeuvre that collectively documents the history of relics cults in Lucca in the eleventh century. Although their probable author, Rangerio, declined to style himself as an authoritative *dominus et constructor*, he so lionized his predecessors, Giovanni I and Anselmo I, albeit in markedly different ways. The former, Rangerio misleadingly implied, was a lord and builder of merely local importance because his relic translations and building projects were unshaped by the broader political and religious developments of his time. The latter, by contrast, emerges as a new kind of *dominus et constructor*, whose initiatives unfolded on a grander stage of papal politics. As illustrated in the episcopates of Anselmo I and his nephew, Anselmo II, papal influence in fact diminished local episcopal authority. The election of the first Anselmo to the chair of St. Peter obliged him to cede oversight of the rebuilding of the cathedral to its canons, who in turn drove the second Anselmo from his church in retaliation for his unrelenting commitment to the ideals of papal reformers. Hence political and religious developments that extended north and south of the Alps not simply inflected but also curtailed the traditional figure of the lord and builder in the development of Tuscan relic cults.

---

[96] See above, n. 53.
[97] *Translatio Sanctorum Reguli, Iasonis, Mauri, et Hilarie*, in Guidi, "Per la storia," 185. Silva, "*Dilexi decorem*," 31, argues without justification that the motives attributed to Rangerio in the Translation were a mere pretext for destroying the annular crypt and thus adopting an arrangement evocative of late antique basilicas in Rome.
[98] *Translatio Sancti Reguli II*, n. 19, in M. Simonetti, "Note sulla tradizione," 130. Cf. *Translatio Sancti Reguli I*, BAV, Vat. Lat. 6453, fol. 107.

PISA: THE RISE OF CIVIC RELIGION

If the emergence of monastic and papal reformers did not supplant the *dominus et constructor* in Lucca, the rise of the local citizenry and its nascent government did exactly that in its nearby rival, Pisa. That the archbishop played little discernible role in the reform of the cathedral chapter in the 1070s is one sign of the prelate's marginalization. Impetus came instead from local lay benefactors, who made gifts to the canons on the condition that they abandon private quarters and live together in their canonry as per the Rule of Aachen.[99] Even more conspicuous was the archbishop's understated role in the rebuilding of the cathedral, which commenced in 1064, only four years after Anselmo I began the reconstruction of San Martino. The nearly fifty-year campaign produced the largest cathedral in Tuscany to predate the fourteenth-century edifice of Santa Maria del Fiore in Florence. Its size, architectural plan, and rite of consecration on 26 September 1118, as related below, reflected the civic consciousness and political priorities of an established maritime power and its communal government.

The rise of civil authority and marginalization of the archbishop found literary expression in three inscriptions in the lower level of the first arcade of the twelfth-century façade of the cathedral.[100] While an analogous inscription in the portico of San Martino of Lucca celebrated Anselmo I as its lord and builder, those in Pisa ascribed that role to the local citizenry and the architect, Buschetto († after 1110). One inscription locates the building program during the archiepiscopate of Guido († 1076), a native of Pavia and imperial appointee known to both Emperor Henry IV and Pope Alexander II. The latter was a fellow Lombard probably familiar with Guido before their respective elections to the bishoprics of Rome and Pisa around 1060.[101] Prominent features of the edifice underscored the imperial and papal affinities noted in the inscription. Its five-aisle plan recalled that of San Martino and, by extension, that of St. Peter's in Rome; its massive dome resembled the imperial Kaiserdome in Speyer and Pavia.[102] Yet the text credits the construction of the new church to the Pisan citizens while a second one amplifies the

---

[99] This tradition of reform-minded largess culminated in a major donation of land from Matilda of Canossa: Matilde Tirelli Carli, *Carte dell'Archivio Capitolare di Pisa 3 (1076-1100)* (Rome: Edizioni di storia e letteratura, 1977), no. 4, 8–12 (27 August 1077), on which see Ronzani, "Vescovi," 20. On the broader pattern of pious donations to the Pisan chapter in the preceding decades, see Mauro Ronzani, *Chiesa e civitas di Pisa nella seconda metà del secolo 11: Dall'avvento del vescovo Guido all'elevazione di Daiberto a metropoita di Coriscia, 1060-1092* (Pisa: GISEM-ETS, 1997), 38–58.

[100] On the façade of the cathedral of Pisa, see chapter 5, this volume.

[101] Adriano Peroni, ed., *Il Duomo di Pisa*, 3 vols. (Modena: F.C. Panini, 1995), vol. 1, 338, no. 9b. Giuseppe Scalia, "Ancora intorno all'epigrafe sulla fondazione del duomo pisano," *Studi Medievali* 10 (1970): 494–495, establishes the identification of the unnamed pontiff with Alexander II rather than his successor, Gregory VII.

[102] Christine Smith, "East or West in 11th-Century Pisan Culture: The Dome of the Cathedral and its Western Counterparts," *Journal of the Society of Architectural Historians* 43 (1984): 195–208. Tigler, *Toscana*, 41–46, presents an overview of the Romanesque edifice.

note of civic pride by narrating the victories of their navy in the early eleventh century.[103] Directly above was the tomb of Buschetto, an architect and administrator (*operaio*) of the organization known as an *opera*, charged with the construction of the edifice.[104] According to the inscription, he overcame the obstacles erected by the devil in order to bring the construction of the cathedral to completion.[105] In the place of an episcopal lord and builder, then, stood an architect, *opera*, and the local citizenry renowned for its military prowess.

Civic overtones likewise displaced the traditional figure of the *dominus et constructor* in connection with a campaign of relic acquisition that anticipated the consecration of the cathedral. Much like San Martino of Lucca, this episcopal seat never possessed the relics of truly local bishops or martyrs such as St. Donatus of Arezzo or St. Zenobius of Florence. The Pisans were obliged to look beyond their immediate environs in the manner of the Lucchese. If the latter underscored their alliance with the Eternal City by acquiring Roman martyrs, the former emphasized their military dominion by looking to Sardinia. The island had fallen under their influence after they had expelled its Saracen rulers in a joint campaign with the Genoese in 1015. In 1088, the Pisans transferred Sts. Ephysius and Potitus from Nora (south of Cagliari) to their city.[106] These martyrs came to reside in an altar in the south transept of the cathedral, where its canons celebrated the date of the saints' transfer (13 November) as their new *dies natalis*.[107] As occurred on the liturgical commemorations of St. Fridian and St. Regulus in Lucca, the conflation of feasts of translation and martyrdom integrated the history of a Tuscan city and the sacred biography of two saints.[108] In Pisa, however, the archbishop played no role in the resulting historical narrative.

As related in an *Historia dedicationis*, the consecration of the cathedral distinguished itself not in the particular dignity and virtue of its celebrant (as in Lucca) but instead in the magnitude of its ceremonial trappings, which mirrored the expansive dimensions

---

[103] See the transcriptions and translations in Peroni, *Il Duomo di Pisa*, vol. 1, 337–338, no. 9a. On the political background to the construction of the cathedral of Pisa, see Mauro Ronzani, "Da aula cultuale del vescovo a 'Ecclesia Major' della città: Note sulla fisonomia istituzionale e la rilevanza pubblica del Duomo di Pisa," in *La cattedrale e la città nel medioevo: Atti della giornata di studio Pisa, giugno 1991* (Pisa: Pacini, 1993), 77–89.

[104] Buschetto numbered among the "rectors and procurators or operaii of Santa Maria" (*rectoribus et procuratoribus sive operariis Sancte Marie*), to whom Lamberto di Specioso made a donation: Pio Pecchiai, *L'opera della Primaziale pisana. Notizie storiche e documenti. Elenco degli Operai. Regesto di diplomi a tutto il XIV secolo* (Pisa: F. Mariotti, 1905), no. 1, 61–62 (2 December 1104).

[105] See the transcriptions and translations in Peroni, *Il Duomo di Pisa*, vol. 1, 336–337, no. 8.

[106] Maria Luisi Ceccarelli Lemut, "Santi nei Mediterraneo dalla Sardegna a Pisa," *Bolletino Storico Pisano* 74 (2005): 206–208. Notice of the translation of Sts. Ephysius and Potitus to Pisa appears at the conclusion of the *Passio Sancti Ephysii*, ch. 38 (*BHL* 2567), in *AS* January, vol. 1, col. 1004. Its dating to 1088 is reported in *AS* January, vol. 1, cols. 753–754, a claim that Ceccarelli Lemut (p. 207) calls into question.

[107] See the Pisan ordinal, *OOP*, fol. 53 (on which see chapter 5, this volume). The canons memorialized the dedication of the altar of Sts. Ephysius and Potitus on their traditional *dies natalis*, June 13 or 14 (fol. 46).

[108] See Chapter 2, this volume.

of the edifice.¹⁰⁹ The participants, whose number rivaled those who attended the consecration of San Martino, included Roman cardinals and a "multitude of clerics, laymen, and women, one larger than any that our age remembered to have convened in one day."¹¹⁰ Surely present though conspicuously unmentioned was the local archbishop, Pietro, who ceded the role of celebrant to Pope Gelasius II (1118–1119).¹¹¹ Even longer than the list of prominent personages was that of thirty saints whose relics the pontiff donated to the cathedral. He deposited them in the high altar dedicated to the Virgin Mary because the church featured no crypt in accordance with the new aversion to such subterranean shrines evidenced in St. Regulus's elevation at San Martino in 1109. As with the relic acquisitions of recent Lucchese bishops, most of the saints donated by Gelasius were Roman martyrs, popes, and others whose cults were based in the Eternal City. Succinctly catalogued in the *Historia*, however, these relics underscored less the ties that bound Pisa to Rome and more the sheer wealth of holy treasure now preserved in its massive cathedral.

If the aforementioned participants recorded in the *Historia* impressed by virtue of their status and number, their presence also reflected contemporary politics concerning the maritime dominion of Pisa, the end of its recent hostilities with Lucca, and the rise of the Pisan commune. Among the visiting bishops were those of Sardinia, whose attendance reflected the place of their island within the Pisan sphere of influence. Pope Gelasius used the occasion to elevate its diocese to metropolitan status, which similarly involved the submission of Corsica to the archdiocese.¹¹² Equally significant was the participation of Lucchese clerics, alone among the many attendees whom the *Historia* precisely identified. It depicted a scene of striking unanimity given the strife between the neighboring cities that had ended only eight years earlier in 1110: "The Lucchese church assisted, with its vicars and other canons, priors, abbots, its vigils of relics, and remaining

---

¹⁰⁹ The Pisan *Historia dedicationis* survives as an *unicum* in the fourteenth-century lectionary ACP, C150, fols. 179v–80v, partially edited in Giuseppe Scalia, "La consacrazione della cattedrale pisana," *Bollettino storico pisana* 61 (1992): 12–13. The surviving recension represents an elaborated version of a now lost text perhaps written just after the consecration and itself dates from no earlier than the early thirteenth century (Scalia, "La consacrazione," 13–14).

¹¹⁰ Scalia, "La consacrazione," 12: "Tanta siquidem clericorum, laicorum, necnon et mulierum multitudo die illa convenit, quantam nullius nostre etatis una die in unum convenisse meminit".

¹¹¹ The *Historia Dedicationis* nonetheless alluded to Pietro by office if not by name in recording that Gelasius allowed the archbishop to make processions on horseback on the anniversary of the consecration, the Monday after Easter, and the Assumption of the Virgin: Scalia, "La consacrazione," 13. That Pietro attended the consecration, as one would expect, finds further support in the act that he drafted three days after the solemn rite in the episcopal palace and with the support of the pope: Fedor Schneider, ed., *Regestum Senese* (Rome: Ermanno Loescher, 1911), no. 280, 117 (29 September 1118).

¹¹² Pope Urban II had already bestowed this honor on the archdiocese of Pisa in 1092 but it had subsequently been revoked: Scalia, "La consacrazione," 1–3.

offices of the dedication as if it were the Pisan church."[113] Finally, Gelasius donated the Roman relics to "the canons and consuls of Pisa," a display of unanimity between the cathedral chapter and a new class of civil authorities all the more unprecedented because it excluded the archbishop.

Pisa illustrates the newfound impact of communal politics on the otherwise familiar phenomena of ecclesiastical building, relic acquisition, and clerical reform. The conflict between the papacy and empire had accelerated the development of the Lucchese commune, and Bishop Rangerio in turn adopted the rhetoric of civic pride in his hagiography. Nevertheless, only in Pisa did the local citizenry and its nascent government effectively replace the archbishop in driving the evolution of the cathedral, its clerics, and its holy treasure. This foreshadows lay participation in cathedrals throughout Tuscany via the *opere* that flourished from the twelfth century. As related in part II, such civic organizations were a third actor who joined the bishop and cathedral canons in shaping the liturgical and artistic life of these churches.

* * * * *

The diverse phenomena traced in part I of this book—the migration of cathedrals and their relics into cities; the promotion of those relics via the creation of hagiography, tombs, and churches; and the consolidation of cathedral chapters—shaped the establishment and evolution of relic cults throughout medieval Tuscany. Typically local or regional in scope, these phenomena nonetheless reflected broader political and religious agendas of which the origins usually lay with the empire or the papacy (or both). As related in part II, they were the invariable impetus to the development of equally local liturgies, of which the creation and codification fell to the cathedral canons. Their burgeoning chapters displaced the bishop as the overseers of the cathedrals during the twelfth and thirteenth centuries. Consequently, the image of the *dominus et constructor* gave way to that of the *ecclesia matrix*, the mother church and magnificent stage upon which the canons enacted their sacred rites before a large, unified populace. Memory of the episcopal lords and builders who had laid the foundations of such liturgies nonetheless persisted in the sung and recited texts, as well as the ritual action, sculpture, and altarpieces associated with such rites. Through aural and visual media, then, the early foundational histories of the Tuscan cathedrals endured.

---

[113] Scalia, "La consacrazione," 12: "Lucana autem ecclesia, cum suis locopositis aliisque canonicis, sed et cum prioribus, abbatibus, et reliquiarum vigiliis, et reliquis dedicationis officiis, tanquam ipsa Pisana ecclesia, astitit." The "vicars" in question are surely the canons deputized to serve as in the bishop's stead in the case of his absence. As noted by Scalia, "La consacrazione," 20, Pope Gelasius himself referred to the "consent of the bishop and priors, who are named substitutes" (*consensu episcopi et priorum, qui locopositi nominantur*), in a bull that he directed to the cathedral canons of Lucca during his residence in Pisa: Kehr, *Regesta*, vol. 3, no. 20, 401 (13 September 1118).

This book belongs to the Lucchese episcopate of blessed Martin. If one were to steal it or fraudulently keep it, by the authority of this mother church, the head of all churches of the Lucchese episcopate, and by the canons' consent, there would be a perpetual anathema unless he returned it. Amen, amen, amen.

PART II
Ecclesia Matrix

This *ex libris* illustrates the rise of the cathedral chapter as a guardian of its church at the expense of its bishop.[1] Entered at the turn of the twelfth century into a collection of canon law, it employs the epithet, *ecclesia matrix*, to signal the preeminence of the cathedral within the diocese. The phrase had characterized the Universal Church since late Antiquity, but commonly described cathedrals only from the central Middle Ages.[2] The *ex libris* juxtaposes the authority of the mother church with that of its canons, implicitly grounding the latter in the former. It accordingly construes the chapter as the defender of the treasure of its cathedral, as represented in this case by the codex itself. The position of the *ex libris* within the codex nonetheless suggests that the canons' purview extended beyond this single manuscript: on the preceding verso and recto appears a complete

---

[1] BCL, 124, fol. 4v (saec. XI^{ex}), quoted in Raffaele Savigni, *Episcopato e società cittadina a Lucca: Da Anselmo II (†1086) a Roberto (†1255)* (Lucca: S. Marco, 1996), 343: "Iste liber est beati Martini Lucensis episcopatus, quem si quis fueratus fuerit aut fraudulenter retinuerit ex auctoritate huius matricis ecclesie que caput est omnium ecclesiarum lucensis episcopatus et canonicorum consensu anathema sit in perpetuum nisi reddiderit. Amen, amen, amen." The majority of the codex (fols. 5–167v) is devoted to Burchard's *Decretum* (1012) while the remainder contains synodal and other ecclesiastical legislation (fols. 167v–197).

[2] Joseph C. Plumpe, "Ecclesia Mater," *Transactions and Proceedings of the American Philological Association* 50 (1939): 535–555, especially 542, traces the general use of "ecclesia matrix" to the mid-third century, while Augustine Thompson, *Cities of God: The Religion of the Italian Communes, 1125–1325* (University Park: Pennsylvania State University Press, 2005), 116–133; and Cosimo Damiano Fonesca, "'Ecclesia matrix' e 'Conventus civium': L'ideologia della Cattedrale nell'età comunale," in *La Pace di Costanza, 1183. Un difficile equilibrio di poteri fra società italiana ed impero. Milano-Piazenza, 27-30 aprile 1983* (Bologna: Cappelli, 1984), 139–141, examine its narrower application to cathedrals in communal Italy. Nevertheless, the latter usage can occasionally be found in earlier periods, as in the ninth-century funeral inscription of Bishop Jacopo of Lucca (see chapter 2 this volume, n. 63).

inventory of the altars and relics preserved in San Martino.³ With the ascendance of the image of the mother church, the role of the bishop as protector of the cathedral had yielded to that of the canons as overseers of its *temporalia* and *spiritualia*.

Yet the *ex libris* rightly suggests that memory of episcopal *domini et constructores* endured despite the canons' claims to the cathedral. It highlights the dedication of the church to St. Martin of Tours, the most influential model of episcopal sanctity in Latin Christendom. Furthermore, the first verso of the codex presents a list of fourteen Lucchese bishops of late Antiquity and the early Middle Ages.⁴ The most important of them was St. Fridian, who had overseen his city's golden age and inspired his episcopal predecessors, Giovanni I and Jacopo, to glorify Lucca through the construction of new relics, tombs, and churches.⁵ The interest in such bishops accorded with the persistent appeal of the cults of local saints in central-medieval Italy.⁶ Canons remembered and venerated those early bishops who had transformed cathedrals into *ecclesie matrices* by positioning these edifices at urban sites and enriching them with relics. Belonging to the distant past, these lords and builders did not threaten the canons' more recent ambitions to control their cathedrals.

With its feminine associations, the notion of the *ecclesia matrix* paradoxically underscored the holy men buried therein. The cathedrals of Pisa and Siena, for instance, were dedicated to the Assumption of the Virgin Mary, on the anniversary of which the subjects of the cities demonstrated their political allegiance by offering candles to their mother church.⁷ The liturgy associated with the feast in turn amplified the traditional characterization of the cathedral as a holy treasury: it shared many of its psalms with the anniversary of the consecration of the church, a rite centered on the translation and burial of relics. According to the twelfth-century liturgist Johannes Beleth, this correlation was appropriate because "the church is mother of all saints and holds the name of virginity."⁸ By implication, a cathedral constituted a womb for the bishops and martyrs interred therein, complementing rather than obscuring their traditional roles as holy protectors of the city and diocese.

The *ecclesia matrix* was mother not only to its saints but also to the local populace via its traditional monopoly on baptism. The twelfth century witnessed the construction of

---

³ BCL, 124, fols 3v–4, of which transcriptions and analysis appear in Anna Rosa Calderoni Masetti, "Anselmo da Baggio e la cattedrale di Lucca," *Annali della Scuola Normale Superiore di Pisa, Serie III* 1 (1977): 91–94; and Pietro Guidi, "Per la storia della cattedrale e del Volto Santo," *Bollettino storico lucchese* 4 (1932): 169–177.

⁴ BCL, 124, fol. 1v; cf. fol. 3 for two fragmentary lists of bishops. Gabriele Zaccagnini, *Vita Sancti Fridiani: Contributi di storia e di agiografia lucchese medievale* (Lucca: Fazzi, 1989), 13–18, summarizes the scholarly debate on the authenticity and significance of all three lists.

⁵ See chapter 2, this volume.

⁶ Fonesca, "'Ecclesia matrix,'" 146–149.

⁷ Thompson, *Cities of God*, 166–174, 278–280.

⁸ Johannes Beleth, *Summa de Ecclesiasticis Officiis*, ed. Heribert Douteil, 2 vols. (Turnhout: Brepols, 1976), vol. 2, ch. 146, 284–285: "Ecclesia namque mater est omnium sanctorum et nomen tenet virginitatis."

a new generation of large, octagonal baptisteries in Italy, ones typically situated directly west of the cathedral and dedicated to John the Baptist. Perhaps the most celebrated examples stand in Florence and Pisa and are massive edifices that underscore the ambitions of their burgeoning communes.[9] Because baptism marked one's admission into the city's Christian community, these buildings were magnets for civic pride.[10] As the baptistery of Florence physically overshadowed the nearby cathedral, so its titular, John the Baptist—and not that of the bishop's seat, St. Reparata—became the preeminent patron of the city. Florentine citizens and their subjects accordingly made their tribute of candles on the feast of St. John (24 June).[11] Yet Florence was unusual in this respect: elsewhere in Tuscany, baptisteries and baptism reinforced rather than detracted from the status of the cathedral as mother church.

Part II of *Holy Treasure and Sacred Song* explores Tuscan relic cults and their liturgies in the age of the *ecclesia matrix*. Chapter 5 traces the interactions between bishops, chapters, and the *opere* through which the laity exercised influence over cathedrals. Through the compilation of collections of liturgical prescriptions known as ordinals, canons not only consolidated oversight of the sacred rites of their cathedrals but also buttressed the preeminence of these churches throughout the dioceses. These sources also show how canons adapted to a new generation of relic cults located in their churches but promoted by the laity rather than the clergy. These new objects of veneration were among the most important relics situated in the east and west ends of the cathedrals, where they were immediately visible to the populace rather than hidden away in crypts. Although canons vied with bishops and *opere* for the copious offerings made to such relics, the resultant income proved insufficient to meet the financial challenges of the late twelfth and thirteenth centuries. Such hardships thus compelled the canons to privatize their communities: governed by financial incentives rather than principles of common life, cathedral chapters became corporations designed to ensure the celebration of the liturgy with the solemnity due the *ecclesia matrix*.

Chapters 6 and 7 situate the liturgies of Tuscan relic cults against the historical backdrop outlined in previous ones. Chapter 6 casts the public drama of the Mass as a classic

---

[9] Enrico Cattaneo, "Il battistero in Italia dopo il Mille," in *Miscellanea Gilles Gerard Meersseman* (Padua: Antenore, 1970), 173–177, surveys Italian baptisteries and their dates of construction, while Guido Tigler, *Toscana romanica* (Milan: Jaca Book, 2006), 55–64, 137–145, discusses the Pisan and Florentine examples. The baptistery of Pistoia resembles those two structures in its shape and position if not its size and dates only from the fourteenth century. In the twelfth century, the Lucchese, by contrast, built a large, square baptistery over the early medieval one attached to the former cathedral of Santa Reparata: Giovanna Piancastelli Politi Nencini, "Le ultime fasi costruttive del Battistero," in *La chiesa dei Santi Giovanni e Reparata in Lucca: Dagli scavi archeologici al restauro*, ed. Giovanna Piancastelli Politi Nencini (Lucca: M. P. Fazzi, 1993), 138–139. The Aretines utilized the baptismal font located in the pieve of their city rather than the extramural cathedral at Pionta while the Fiesolani used a font located in their cathedral of San Romolo rather than a free-standing baptistery.

[10] Thompson, *Cities of God*, 26–33.

[11] Cattaneo, "Il battistero," 188–189; Robert Davidsohn, *Storia di Firenze*, trans. Giovanni Battista Klein, 7 vols. (Florence: Sansoni, 1956–1965), vol. 1, 510–511.

"ritual of association" that obscured the often tense relationship between bishops and chapters. Before an audience of congregants drawn to the mother church, the bishop reenacted Christ's crucifixion, underscoring his sacramental authority rather than that of a traditional lord and builder. Meanwhile, the canons played the part of his faithful ministers. On three occasions—the feasts of St. Martin and St. Donatus of Arezzo, as well as the Dedication of the Church—the clergy sang plainsong proper (or specific) to the day that reinforced its image as an angelic choir and that of the bishop as a divinely inspired celebrant. Chapter 7, by contrast, studies the plainchant sung at the private hours of the Divine Office in honor of saints whose cults had been promoted by early episcopal lords and builders. Such music often formed richly textured narratives that retold the lives and deaths of its holy subjects. Literary and musical analysis uncovers the chronology of this plainchant and shows how its composition coincided with turning points in the history of its respective cults. Even as the public liturgy of the Mass at times obscured the legacy of early medieval bishops, the private one of the office indirectly celebrated it.

Focused on the central rather than early Middle Ages, part II benefits from a wealth of primary sources not available for earlier periods. The most important are the service books by which the cathedral canons codified the liturgies of their mother churches. The ordinals aided in the coordination between ritual action and recited and sung texts, of which the latter are preserved in missals, graduals, tropers, and sequentiaries (for the Mass), as well as breviaries and antiphoners (for the Divine Office). Meanwhile, acts and legislation reveal the ecclesiastical politics that Tuscan liturgies at times reflected and at others obscured. Finally, visual evidence shows that these rites often echoed or complemented the sacred spaces in which they unfolded. Of the Romanesque cathedrals of Tuscany, those of Lucca and Pisa survive largely intact, as do two extramural martyria, San Miniato (in Florence) and San Frediano (in Lucca). The cathedrals of Fiesole and Pistoia, by contrast, underwent subsequent renovations that have obscured the central medieval edifices, while those of Arezzo, Florence, and Siena were destroyed entirely.[12] Nevertheless, the relative wealth of surviving visual sources joins the trove of documentary ones in facilitating the reconstruction of political, religious, and artistic contexts in which flourished the Tuscan relic cults and their liturgies.

---

[12] For overviews of the Romanesque cathedrals of Pisa and Pistoia, see Tigler, *Toscana*, 128–129, 167–172. That of Siena likely dated from the second half of the twelfth century and was replaced by the current Gothic structure in the subsequent one between the 1220s and 1260s: Max Seidel, "Tradizione e innovazione. Note sulle scoperte architettoniche nel duomo di Siena," in *Sotto il duomo di Siena: Scoperte archeologiche, architettoniche e figurative*, ed. Roberto Guerrini (Siena: Silvana, 2003), 41–47. Similarly, the cathedral of Santa Reparata of Florence was dismantled in the course of the building campaign of its successor, Santa Maria del Fiore, begun in 1296 but consecrated only in 1436: Walter Paatz and Elisabeth Valentiner Paatz, *Die Kirchen von Florenz, ein kunstgeschichtliches Handbuch*, 6 vols. (Frankfurt: V. Klostermann, 1952–1955), vol. 3, 324–334. On the history and demolition of the episcopal complex at Pionta outside of Arezzo, see chapter 3, this volume.

5

The Cathedral Chapters, Their Churches, and Their Liturgies

DURING THE CENTRAL Middle Ages, Italian communes came to exercise an unusual degree of influence over cathedrals through the *opere* charged with the construction, upkeep, and decoration of these churches.[1] The equivalent of cathedral "works" or "fabrics" in England, the *opere* in Italy were organizations governed by a chief builder (*operaio*) and distinct from the bishop's household and the cathedral chapter. Pisa, Siena, and Lucca provide the evidence for the early development of these corporations in Tuscany. The earliest documented example was the Opera di Santa Maria of Pisa, which oversaw the construction of the massive cathedral of Santa Maria Assunta in the decades around 1100.[2] In Pisa and Siena, the local bishop selected the *operaio* until the thirteenth century, when this prerogative passed to the commune.[3] In Lucca, by contrast, the cathedral canons nominated the chief builder until 1274, when the *opera* became a fully autonomous organization.[4] All three cities thus illustrate the broader pattern of increasing lay control over the mother church, a reminder that the *ecclesia matrix* belonged to the local citizenry.[5]

---

[1] Wim Vroom, *Financing Cathedral Building in the Middle Ages: The Generosity of the Faithful*, trans. Elizabeth Manton (Amsterdam: Amsterdam University Press, 2010), 47–68, surveys the formation of cathedral *opere* throughout the medieval West and focuses on the distinctive pattern of communal control in Italy in pp. 65–68.

[2] See chapter 4, this volume. Mauro Ronzani, "Dall'*edificatio ecclesiae* all' 'Opera di S. Maria': Nascita e primi sviluppi di un'istituzione nella Pisa dei secoli XI e XII," in *Delle fabbriche cittadine fino all'inizio dell'età moderna. Atti della tavola rotonda, Villa I Tatti, Firenze, 3 aprile 1991*, ed. Margaret Haines and Lucio Riccetti (Florence: Leo S. Olschki, 1996), 17–24, traces the early history of the Pisan *opera*.

[3] Ronzani, "Dall'*edificatio*," 5 and 61–64 (on Pisa); Andrea Giorgi and Stefano Moscadelli, *Costruire una catatedrale: L'Opera di Santa Maria di Siena tra XII e XIV secolo* (Munich: Deutscher Kunstverlag, 2005), 112–115 and 124–125 (on Siena).

[4] Graziano Concioni, "San Martino di Lucca: La cattedrale medioevale," *Rivista di archeologia, storia, costume* 22 (1994): 38–41.

[5] In at least one instance, a Tuscan commune overstepped its bounds in extending its control over the cathedral. Bishop Attone of Pistoia (1133–1153) excommunicated the consuls of his city for having taken possession

If the structure most associated with old episcopal *domini et constructores* was the subterranean crypts that mediated worshipers' access to their relics, the pride of new *operaii* were the marble façades that announced the dignity of the mother church to the public. Only the cathedrals of Pisa and Lucca retain their original Romanesque faces, which were both executed in the decades around 1200 and signaled the rivalry between the two cities through their marked similarities (figs. 5.1 and 5.2).[6] Both feature seven arcades punctuated by three doors (below) and multiple registers supported by small columns (above). San Martino differs from Santa Maria in its incorporation of a portico and campanile, of which the latter disturbs the symmetry of the ensemble. Both carry inscriptions in their northern arcade celebrating those responsible for the original edifice, Bishop Anselmo I (in Lucca) and the *operaio* Buschetto (in Pisa); however, the façades also memorialize a newer generation of builders responsible for their own construction. In the spandrels just above and to the right of the central door of Santa Maria, an inscription attributes "this extraordinary work" to the "prudent *operaio* and master, Rainaldo."[7] On the southernmost column in the first register of San Martino appears a sculpture of a bearded man holding a scroll that proclaims, "the right hand of the excellent Guidetto set these beautiful [columns]."[8] Once applied to episcopal *domini et constructores*, such adjectives as *prudens* and *electus* now described laymen who either guided or were employed by *opere*.

Even as the *opere* established lay control over the physical edifices of the Tuscan cathedrals, canons consolidated their role as guardians of these churches and their liturgies

---

of San Zeno, its treasury, and its bell tower, in response to which the communal officials relinquished their claims: Natale Rauty, ed. *Regesta Chartarum Pistoriensium: Canonica di S. Zenone Secolo XII* (Pistoia: Società Pistoiese di Storia Patria, 1995), no. 418, 90–91 (9 January 1138), on which see Natale Rauty, "Società, istituzioni, politica nel primo secolo dell'autonomia comunale," in *Storia di Pistoia. L'età del libero comune. Dall'inizio del XII alla metà del XIV secolo*, ed. Giovanni Cherubini (Florence: Felice Le Monnier, 1998), 17–19.

[6] Work on the Pisan façade likely began in the middle decades of the twelfth century and concluded in the 1190s: Antonio Milone, "Il Duomo e la sua facciata," in *Il Duomo di Pisa*, ed. Adriano Peroni (Modena: F.C. Panini, 1995), 198–202; and Guido Tigler, *Toscana romanica* (Milan: Jaca Book, 2006), 50–51. While the Lucchese had formed an "Opera del Frontespizio" by 1190, the building of their façade likely occurred only in the first two decades of the subsequent century: Guido Tigler, "Maestri Lombardi del Duecento a Lucca: Le sculture della facciata del duomo," in *I magistri commacini: Mito e realtá del medioevo lombardo. Atti del XIX Congresso internazionale di studio sull'alto medioevo, Varase-Como, 23–25 ottobre 2008* (Spoleto: Fondazione Centro italiano di studi sull'alto medioevo, 2009), 842–856; and Concioni, "San Martino di Lucca," 38. An analogue to the Lucchese and Pisan façades is the surviving atrium situated below and northeast of the presbytery of the Romanesque edifice of Santa Maria Assunta of Siena. Decorated in fresco with scenes from the Old and New Testaments, it faced the city center and offered the faithful a convenient entrance to the cathedral: Roberto Guerrini, ed. *Sotto il duomo di Siena: Scoperte archeologiche, architettoniche e figurative* (Siena: Silvana, 2003).

[7] Adriano Peroni, ed. *Il Duomo di Pisa*, 3 vols. (Modena: F. C. Panini, 1995), vol. 1, no. 56, 345: "Hoc opus eximium tam mirum tam pretiosum | Rainaldus prudens operator et ipse magister | constituit mire sollerter et ingenioso."

[8] Riccardo Ambrosini, "Le iscrizioni del Duomo e della Curia," *Rivista di archeologia, storia, costume 26* (1998): 8: "MC-IIII. Condidit electi ta[m] pulchras dextra Guidecti."

FIGURE 5.1. Santa Maria Assunta, Pisa (Alinari / Art Resource, NY).

in particular. Since the early Middle Ages, the chapters had been natural defenders of their cathedrals because their members were usually natives to their dioceses rather than foreign appointees, as were many bishops. The Pisans conveyed a sense of proprietorship undoubtedly shared by their Tuscan counterparts in styling themselves as "rectors and custodians" of their church.[9] The distinction between local canons and their foreign prelates abated in the twelfth century, when the former came to elect the latter and invariably chose candidates from their own ranks. Without ending conflicts between bishops and chapters, such capitular elections yielded prelates who had obtained their positions via their service to their cathedral rather than their ties to the emperor.[10] Yet

---

[9] Mauro Ronzani, "Da aula cultuale del vescovo a "Ecclesia Major' della città: Note sulla fisonomia istituzionale e la rilevanza pubblica del Duomo di Pisa," in *La cattedrale e la città nel medioevo: Atti della giornata di studio Pisa, giugno 1991* (Pisa: Pacini, 1993), 84. The earliest surviving witness to this appellation documents the exchange of land between layman and five canons, including the archdeacon, archpriest, primicer, and cantor, all described as "rectoribus adque custodibus eclesie episcopatui sancte Marie Pisense." See Emma Falaschi, *Carte dell'Archivio Capitolare di Pisa 1 (930–1050)* (Rome: Edizioni di storia e letteratura, 1971), no. 9, 27 (4 May 975).

[10] Mauro Ronzani, "Vescovi, capitoli e strategie famigliari nell'Italia comunale," in *Storia d'Italia. Annali 9. La Chiesa e il potere politico dal medioevo all'età contemporanea*, ed. Giorgio Chittolini and Giovanni Miccoli (Turin: Einaudi, 1986), 103–120, of which pp. 108–109, address the conditions throughout Tuscany. On conditions in Lucca in particular, see Raffaele Savigni, *Episcopato e società cittadina a Lucca: Da Anselmo*

FIGURE 5.2. Façade (saec. XIII[in]) and portico (ca. 1233-1250) of San Martino, Lucca (Alinari/ SEAT / Art Resource, NY).

even these truly local bishops spent significant amounts of time away from their cities and, when they were in residence, often worshiped in private chapels located in their palaces rather than with their former colleagues in the cathedral.[11] By the twelfth century,

---

II (†1086) a Roberto (†1255) (Lucca: San Marco, 1996), 126–137; and Martino Giusti, "Le elezioni del vescovo di Lucca specialmente nel secolo XIII," *Rivista di storia della chiesa in Italia 6* (1952): 205–230. For a broader discussion of capitular election of bishops, see Anscar Parsons, *Canonical Elections* (Washington, DC: Catholic University of America, 1939), 47–55.

[11] H. E. J. Cowdrey, "The Structure of the Church, 1024–1073," in *The New Cambridge Medieval History, Vol. 4: c. 1024–c. 1198,* ed. David Luscombe and Jonathan Riley-Smith (Cambridge: Cambridge University Press, 2004), 247, emphasizes the itinerancy of bishops in the central Middle Ages. On the construction and significance of private episcopal chapels in general, see Maureen C. Miller, *The Bishop's Palace: Architecture and Authority in Medieval Italy* (Ithaca, NY: Cornell University Press, 2000), 215–252, esp. 222–223. Such

the liturgy of the mother church had thus become the uncontested purview of the canons rather than their bishop.

The most elegant witnesses to the canons' role as guardians of liturgical tradition are their ordinals. As related below, these books codified the sacred rites of their *ecclesiae matrices* in order not only to preserve them for posterity but also to impose them on the daughter churches of their dioceses. The ordinals cast these liturgies as ancient and authoritative while concomitantly witnessing the rise of a new generation of relic cults, of which the most aggressive promoters were laymen rather than clerics. St. Ansanus (in Siena), the Volto Santo (in Lucca), and St. James (in Pistoia) became magnets for public devotion and were thus among the most prominent of many relics to acquire newfound visibility and accessibility in altars situated in the east or west end of their cathedrals. Canons nonetheless staked claims to these new objects of civic pride as they did to the old bishops and martyrs buried in the crypts. With varying degrees of success, they competed with bishops and *opere* for shares of oblations made to these relics while concomitantly incorporating them into the liturgies prescribed in the ordinals.

An overriding concern for the proper celebration of the liturgy prompted canons to reorganize their communities in ways that contradicted the religious values associated with their original foundation. In response to financial challenges in the early Duecento, they implemented a three-pronged process of privatization that signaled the end of the ideals of common property and life that had shaped the identities of their communities since the ninth century. Canons divided their patrimony among themselves and instituted cash payments for service in choir. They likewise hired chaplains to maintain the large number of clerics necessary for the celebration of solemn rites. These junior employees came to derive their income from private benefices often made by laymen and thus another avenue for lay influence at the cathedral. By the late thirteenth century, the cathedral chapters of Tuscany had thus evolved into complex, heterogeneous organizations governing the musical and ritual life of their churches, analogues to the *opere* that oversaw the building, renovation, and ornamentation of these edifices.

---

chapels are documented in Florence from the eleventh century and in Lucca, Pisa, and Pistoia, and Siena in the twelfth: Franklin Toker, *On Holy Ground: Liturgy, Architecture, and Urbanism in the Cathedral and the Streets of Medieval Florence* (Turnhout: Brepols, 2009), 112 (on San Salvatore al Vescovo in Florence); Pietro Guidi and O. Parenti, eds., *Regesto del capitol di Lucca*, 3 vols. (Rome: Ermanno Loescher, 1910–1933), vol. 1, no. 860, 371 (27 December 1128) (the first documentary witness to the episcopal chapel of Lucca); Natale Caturegli, ed. *Le carte arcivescovili pisane del secolo 13*, 4 vols. (Rome: Istituto storico italiano per il Medio Evo, 1974–1993), no. 425, 309–310 (15 June 1157) (the first documentary witness to the episcopal chapel of Pisa); Natale Rauty, *L'antico palazzo dei vescovi a Pistoia: Storia e restauro*, 2 vols. (Florence: Leo S. Olschki, 1981), vol. 1, 124–135 (on the episcopal chapel of San Niccolò in Pistoia); Giorgi and Moscadelli, *Costruire*, 61, n. 61 (on the episcopal chapel of San Giacomo of Siena).

ORDINALS

Since the early Middle Ages, the organization of a religious community's ritual life and the preservation of its liturgical customs had fallen to its chief singer, the cantor or primicer, whose musical gifts bestowed upon him a charismatic authority.[12] According to the Rule of Aachen, he was to be "distinguished and illustrious both in voice and skill, to such an extent that the pleasures of his sweetness inspire his listeners' minds."[13] The Rule directed the cantor to use his God-given talents with humility as he guided the voices of his brethren and thus ensured their decorous singing.[14] Such restraint in musical performance, it noted, would elicit pious devotion rather than vain praise from the attendant populace. In Tuscany as elsewhere, moreover, the cantor usually oversaw the instruction of choirboys, thus initiating new generations of cathedral clerics into the liturgical customs of his community.[15] A funeral inscription on the façade of the Lucchese church,

---

[12] Christopher Page, *The Christian West and its Singers: The First Thousand Years* (New Haven: Yale University Press, 2010), 214–218, traces the office of cantor from its inception to the sixth century while Margot Fassler, "The Office of the Cantor in Early Western Monastic Rules and Custom Rites: A Preliminary Investigation," *Early Music History* 5 (1985): 29–51, its subsequent development in monastic communities.

[13] MGH C, vol. 2, pt. 1, can. 137, 414: "et voce et arte praeclarum inlustremque esse oportet, ita ut oblectamenta dulcedinis animos incitent audientium, et caetera." Translation from James Grier, "Adémar de Chabannes, Carolingian Musical Practices, and 'Nota Romana,'" *Journal of the Americal Musicological Society* 56 (2003): 76. Another canon of the Rule of Aachen concerns reading and singing and is more explicit about the identity of such listeners. It admonishes the canons to "persuade the learned and edify the less learned with the sweetness of lessons and melodies, [to] desire the edification of the people in lesson or song rather more than its vain adulation." (*Tales ad legendum, cantandum et psallendum in ecclesia constituantur, qui non superbe, sed humiliter debitas Domino laudes persolvant et suavitate lectionis ac melodiae et doctos demulceant et minus doctos erudiant plusque velint in lectione vel cantu populi aedificationem quam popularem vanissimam adulationem.*) See MGH C, vol. 2, pt. 1, can. 133, 409.

[14] The Rule thus echoed Augustine's oft-cited pronouncement on the spiritual perils of beautiful music in his *Confessions*, translated in W. Oliver Strunk and Leo Treitler, eds., *Strunk's Source Readings in Music History (Revised Edition)* (New York: W. W. Norton, 1998), 132–134.

[15] For instance, the cathedral canon of Arezzo, Suaverico, identified himself as the primicer and teacher of grammar (*sapiens grammatico*) in 961. He retained the former dignity even after becoming archpriest two years later, but presumably ceded his pedagogical duties to his fellow canon, Sigezone, identified first as *maior scole* (in 963) and later as *cantor scole* (in 996 and 998): Ubaldo Pasqui, *Documenti per la storia della città di Arezzo nel medio evo*, 4 vols. (Florence: G. P. Vieusseux, 1899, 1904, 1916, 1937), vol. 1, no. 61, 85; no. 69, 95 (28 February 961); no. 71, 98 (10 May 963); no. 82, 116–117 (12 July 996); and no. 85, 119 (2 May 998). The case of the Sienese canon named Ugolino demonstrates that Tuscan cantors continued to serve as teachers into the late twelfth century, for he is variously identified as cantor in Antonella Ghignoli, ed. *Carte dell'Archivio di Stato di Siena: Opera Metropolitana (1000-1200)* (Siena: Accademia senese degli intronati, 1994), no. 79, 178 (5 April 1177) and no. 91, 206 (21 April 1190) and *maior scolis* in no. 83, 186 (19 June 1182); no. 86, 195 (18 March 1185); no. 88, 199 (19 October 1189); no. 96, 213 (30 October 1193); and no. 100, 230, (10 February 1196). According to the list of canons documented at the cathedral of Siena between 1000 and 1300 in Mino Marchetti, *Liturgia e storia della chiesa di Siena nel XII secolo: I calendari medioevali della chiesa senese* (Siena: Istituto storico diocesano di Siena, 1991), 121–126, the cantors had often (though not always) served as the schoolmaster since the mid-eleventh century. On the pedagogical role of the cantor in Italian collegiate churches of this period generally, see Giuseppe Vecchi, "L'insegnamento e la pratica musicale nella

Ss. Vincenzo e Anastasio, underscored the learning and decorum expected of a chief singer: "presbyter Enrico, wise and modest grammarian, cantor, and master who taught lessons, the honor, dignity, and rector of this church."[16] According to early medieval ideals of canonical life, the chief singer maintained not only the liturgical traditions but also the intellectual life and moral standing of his chapter.

Nevertheless, the emergence of ordinals as written repositories of liturgical knowledge coincided and perhaps even contributed to the decline of this single, alluring figure in the late twelfth and thirteenth centuries. Aretine documents witness the musical activities of a primicer through the 1260s; however, chief singers are conspicuously missing from the archival record in every other Tuscan center under consideration after approximately 1200.[17] Their absence from Sienese and Lucchese acts is particularly conspicuous given that these sources regularly mention the cantor up until 1196 and 1207, respectively.[18] In this same period, cathedral chapters began to preserve via written prescriptions in ordinals the liturgical customs once passed down from one cantor to another (table 5.1).[19] That the two known authors of these codices were members of the chapter

---

comunità dei canonici (sec. XI—XII)," in *La vita comune del clero nei secoli XI e XII. Atti della settimana di studio, Mendola, settembre 1959* (Milan: Vita e pensiero, 1962), 29–31.

[16] "Presbyter Henricus sapiens atque pudicus, | Gramaticus, cantor, scolas tenuitque Magister, | Histius Ecclesiae splendor decus atque minister." Quoted in Cesare Lucchesini, *Della storia letteraria del ducato lucchese*, 2 vols. (Lucca: Francesco Bertini, 1825-1831), vol. 1, 20. Enrico was evidently neither a canon of the cathedral nor the cantor of that church as he is not identifiable with the homonymous canons documented at San Martino: Savigni, *Episcopato e società*, 435–436.

[17] For instance, the capitular constitutions of Arezzo, on which more will be said below, indicated that the duties of the primicer were identical to those traditionally associated with a cantor: Pasqui, *Documenti*, vol. 2, no. 623, 366, con. 5 (21 October 1268).

[18] Marchetti, *Liturgia*, 124–126; and Savigni, *Episcopato e società*, 466–467.

[19] Subsequent citations of the *OOL*, *OOP*, OOPist1, and OOPist2 refer to the original manuscript source. Those of the Ritus and Mores refer to the transcription of these two texts in Toker, *On Holy Ground*, 160–264, 268–284. Finally, citations of the *OOES* refer to the edition, Giovanni Crisostomo Trombelli, ed., *Ordo Officiorum Ecclesiae Senensis ab Oderico eiusdem Ecclesiae canonicus anno MCCXIII compositus* (Bologna: Longhi, 1766). The following studies establish the dating of the Tuscan ordinals: Marica S. Tacconi, *Cathedral and Civic Ritual in Late Medieval and Renaissance Florence: The Service-Books of Santa Maria del Fiore* (Cambridge: Cambridge University Press, 2005), 94–98 (Ritus and Mores); Giulio Cattin, "'Secundare' e 'Succinere.' Polifonia a Padova e Pistoia nel duecento," *Musica e storia 3* (1995): 70 (OOPist1 and OOPist2); Raffaele Argenziano, *Agli inizi dell'iconografia sacra a Siena: Culti, riti e iconografia a Siena nel XII secolo* (Florence: Edizioni del Galluzzo, 2000), 54–58 (*OOES*); and Benjamin Brand, *Liturgical Ceremony at the Cathedral of Lucca, 1275–1500*, Ph.D. diss., Yale University, 2006, 6–7 (*OOL*). OOP was discovered by Augustine Thompson, who dates it to the late twelfth century in Thompson, *Cities of God: The Religion of the Italian Communes, 1125-1325* (University Park: Pennsylvania State University Press, 2005), 9; however, that the ordinal makes no mention of St. Ranierius, who was buried in the cathedral in 1160, suggests an earlier date of compilation. Moreover, its self-identified author is surely the same Rolando whose name appears in several acts drafted in the 1140s and 1150s and published in Caturegli, *Regestum pisanum*: an eponymous deacon and cathedral canon consecrated the church and hospital of San Marco in 1141 (no. 381, p. 256) and witnessed three public acts, two at the episcopal palace in 1147 (no. 407, p. 274) and 1154 (no. 433, p. 297), and one in Pisa in 1158 (no. 457, p. 318). While the author of Mores remains unknown, its copyist was probably Salvo, who included the notice (fol. 14) that "I presbyter Salvo, chaplain of said canonry" was to

TABLE 5.1
THE TUSCAN ORDINALS

City	Incipit	Abbreviation	Compiler	Date	Manuscript
Pisa	Liber de ordine officiorum	OOP	Rolando, deacon	1140–1160	Bologna, Biblioteca Universitaria, 1758
Florence	Ritus in ecclesia servandi	Ritus		1180–1190	Florence, Biblioteca Riccardiana, 3005
Pistoia	Ordo in divinis officiis Pistoriensis ecclesie	OOPist1		Saec. XIII[in]	ACPist, C114
Siena	Ordo Officiorum Ecclesiae Sensensis	OOES	Oderigo, canon	1215	BCIS, G.V.8
Florence	Mores et consuetudines canonice Florentine	Mores		1231	Florence, Archivio dell'Opera di Santa Maria del Fiore, I.3.8
Pistoia	Ordo in divinis officiis Pistoriensis ecclesie	OOPist2		Saec XIII[ex]	ACPist, C102
Lucca	Cum in primitiva ecclesia	OOL		Ca. 1292	BCL, 608

but not cantors is yet another sign of the decline of the office of chief singer. The ordinals were modest books, small and typically without musical notation or illuminations, with the exception of the Sienese *ordo*. They comprised two essential elements: textual incipits of chants, readings, and prayers and rubrics specifying their ritual context.[20]

---

receive foodstuffs from the church of Sant'Andrea in Percussina on the feast of St. Reparata. That this is the only use of the first personal singular in Mores suggests that Salvo was indeed its scribe. Finally, the ascription of *OOES* to Oderigo is based on his obituary in a thirteenth-century martyrology that identified the year of his death as 1225 and ascribed to him the composition of an "ordinal" (*ordo officiorum*): Argenziano, *Agli inizi*, 55. Marchetti, *Liturgia e storia*, 45–56, has argued that *OOES* was in fact compiled ca. 1140, an hypothesis never accepted among other scholars and now invalidated by the textual borrowings of the Sienese ordinal from Sicardo of Cremona's *Mitralis* (ca. 1205), as discussed in Lorenz Weinrich, "Der *Ordo officiorum Senensis ecclesie* des Oderigo und Sicards *Mitralis de officiis*," *Sacris Erudiri* 42 (2002): 375–389.

[20] On ordinals in general, see Tillman Lohse, "Stand und Perspektiven der *Liber ordinarius*-Forschung," in *Liturgie in mittelalterlichen Frauenstiften*, ed. Klaus Gereon Beuckers (Essen: Klartext Medienwerkstatt,

The earliest *ordines* present cursory rubrics, the later ordinals longer ones that specify in greater detail the ritual actions of the clergy. The growing desire to codify this dimension of the liturgy was one reason for the creation of new ordinals, as illustrated in the brief rubrics of the first Pistoiese ordinal and the expansive ones of the second.[21] Finally, the only Tuscan cathedral that demonstrably maintained the office of chief singer, that of Arezzo, is also the only one for which no ordinal survives. This is further evidence, albeit circumstantial, that the decline of the cantor and emergence of ordinals were interrelated phenomena.

The diminished profile of chief singers in central medieval Tuscany hardly connoted a lack of musical expertise among select members of the cathedrals chapters. Among the heirs to the cantor were those who sang the extemporized polyphony known as organum or discant, a virtuosic art prescribed in the ordinals.[22] According to pedagogical treatises of the central Middle Ages, the latter term denoted a style of music produced as one or more singers improvised against a preexisting chant, forming consonant intervals with its successive pitches.[23] Able performances of organum amplified the solemnity

---

2012), 215–255, Aimé-Georges Martimort, *Les "Ordines," les Ordinaires et les Cérémoniaux* (Turnhout: Brepols, 1991), 62–85; and Edward Foley, "The 'Libri Ordinarii.'" *Ephemerides liturgicae 102* (1988): 129–137.

[21] The Florentine Ritus and Lucchese *ordo* were likewise revisions of earlier, now-lost ordinals. The antiquarian Carlo Tommaso Strozzi (1587–1670) transcribed passages from a Florentine "Ritual antico" preserved in a now-lost manuscript of the twelfth century, but the text of which perhaps dated from an eleventh-century one: ASF, Carte Strozziane, II, 56, fols. 13–23v, on which see Tacconi, *Cathedral*, 94–96. An inventory of the sacristy of San Martino of Lucca drafted in 1297 similarly includes an "Ordo vetus" that was likely the model for *OOL*: Pietro Guidi and Ermenegildo Pellegrinetti, *Inventari del vescovato, della cattedrale e di altre chiese di Lucca* (Rome: Poliglotta vaticana, 1921), 190, on which see Martino Giusti, "L'*Ordo Officiorum* della Cattedrale di Lucca," in *Miscellanea Giovanni Mercati* (Vatican City: Biblioteca Apostolica Vaticana, 1946), 528–530.

[22] On the citations of improvised polyphony in the Tuscan ordinals, see Tacconi, *Cathedral*, 128–131; and Giulio Cattin, "Novità dalla cattedrale di Firenze: Polifonia, tropi, e sequenze nella seconda metà del XII secolo," *Musica e storia 6* (1998): 29–34 (on Ritus); Brand, *Liturgical Ceremony*, 178–189; and Agostino Ziino, "Polifonia nella cattedrale di Lucca durante il XIII secolo," *Acta musicologica 47* (1975): 16–30 (on *OOL*); Cattin, "'Secundare' e 'Succinere,'" 63–86 (on OOPist1 and OOPist2); Frank D'Accone, *The Civic Muse: Music and Musicians in Siena During the Middle Ages and the Renaissance* (Chicago: University of Chicago Press, 1997), 93–97; Gemma Gonzato, "Alcune considerazioni sull' 'Ordo Officiorum Ecclesiae Senensis,'" in *Le polifonie primitive in Friuli e in Europa. Atti del congresso internazionale (Cividale del Friuli, 22-24 augusto 1980)*, ed. C. Corsi and P. Petrobelli (Rome: Torre d'Orfeo, 1989), 247–293; and Kurt Von Fischer, "Die Rolle der Mehrstimmigkeit am Dome von Siena zu Beginn des 13 Jahrhunderts," *Archiv für Musikwissenschaft 18* (1961): 167–182 (on *OOES*).

[23] Michael Beiche, "Discantus / Diskant," in *Handwörterbuch der musikalischen Terminologie*, ed. Hans Heinrich Eggebrecht (Stuttgart: Franz Steiner, 1997). On the musical style of Tuscan organum/discant, see in addition to the studies cited above in n. 22, the examination of the handful of notated examples of Italian polyphony from the thirteenth century: Susan Rankin, "Between Oral and Written: Thirteenth-Century Italian Sources of Polyphony," in *Un millennio di polifonia liturgica tra oralità e scrittura*, ed. Giulio Cattin and F. Alberto Gallo (Bologna: Il mulino, 2002), 93–95. Sarah Fuller, "Early Polyphony," in *The New Oxford History of Music. The Early Middle Ages to 1300*, rev. ed., ed. Richard Crocker and David Hiley (Oxford: Oxford University Press, 1990), 485–528, provides a useful survey of medieval organum and discant in general.

of a liturgy and showcased the musical skill of the soloists singing *ex tempore*. Indeed, talented "organists" were evidently in short supply and undoubtedly demanded greater recognition for their service.[24] In 1244, Bishop Ardingo of Florence (1230–1249) denied them extra pay, ruling that those who sang with organum deserved no more remuneration than those who merely chanted plainsong.[25] The decline or outright disappearance of the position of the cantor hardly removed the potential, signaled in the Rule of Aachen, for vanity or ambition among the musically skilled.

If the ordinals were thus written repositories of liturgical custom, expertise in which had once belonged to a single cathedral cleric, they also served a broader readership of diocesan clergy, as revealed in the prologue to the Pisan *ordo*:

> Because many brothers, both parish rectors and chaplains, have asked me how the divine office is celebrated in our church, I will compile a book of the divine offices with the help of God. Indeed, this work seemed to me difficult and very weighty on account of my imbecility. But since charity lifts that which an insupportable burden weighs down, I could by no means refuse: for during my repeated travels through the diocese I have recognized the diversity and ignorance of many. And so out of love of brotherhood I have devoted myself to the compilation of a book on the order [of the divine office] throughout the entire cycle of the year. As for the rest, every diversity will be removed from all the churches of the Pisan diocese and the general ignorance will vanish. Then all the rectors of the churches and their brothers will be able to know manifestly in this book how they must celebrate the office for the entire year in God's church. I thus ask you, brothers, to remember me in your prayers, namely Rolando the deacon, a sinner who nevertheless trusts in God's mercy, because just as I have expressed myself to you, so may I be aided (with God granting it), by your kindnesses and prayers before the merciful and severe judge in his strict consideration. Amen.[26]

---

[24] *OOL*, fol. 30, confirms that skilled performers of organum were not always available. It notes that on Holy Saturday, the third lesson of matins might be sung by "three good clerics inducted into holy orders, who know organum very well. If neither good nor a sufficient number of ordained singers can be found, others can be accepted if they are found" (*vel a tribus bonis clericis in ordinis sanctis constitutis qui optime sciant organum. Et si consecrati boni nec sufficientes possint inveniri accipiantur de aliis si inveniuntur*).

[25] ACF, Dipl. 434 (12 March 1244), in Giovanni Lami, *Sanctae Ecclesiae Florentinae Monumenta*, 4 vols. (Florence: Angelo Salutatae, 1758), vol. 3, 1657: "And further that singers, who sing broken song and melodies [i.e., organum], may not have something more on that feast [of St. Pancras] than those, who sing with one voice" (*Item quod cantores, qui cantant cantum ruptum et melodias non habeant ulterius ad illud festum nisi solummodo tales, qui cantum una voce cantent*). For a different interpretation of this passage, see Tacconi, *Cathedral*, 130–131.

[26] *OOP*, fol. 1v: "Rogatus a multis fratribus plebanis videlicet et cappellanis ut quemadmodum in ecclesia nostra divinum officium fieret, eo ordine adiuvante deo divinorum officiorum librum componerem, labor quidem michi videbatur difficilis et propter meam inbecillitatem nimium gravis. Verum quia caritas sublevat quod sarcina importabilis gravat, honus subire nullatenus recusavi. Diversitatem namque et ignorantiam

Indeed, the surviving redaction of the Pisan *ordo* was perhaps copied for just such a cleric eager to conform his liturgy to that of his mother church, a scenario that might explain why the codex now resides in Bologna rather than in the capitular library of its cathedral.[27] Elsewhere in Tuscany, rectors of daughter churches likewise procured the ordinals of their cathedral: even the chapel of San Giorgio of Sorbano del Giudice (near Lucca) could afford one of these relatively inexpensive books.[28]

Yet neither Rolando's self-deprecating tone nor his impression of clerical brotherhood should obscure the ordinals' purpose in reinforcing the preeminence of the *ecclesia matrix*. Oderigo was more candid about this political function in his prologue to the Sienese *ordo*. He characterized his diocesan clerics not as "brothers" but as "good sons" (*boni filii*) required to follow the liturgy of their "holy mother church," an apt allusion to the status of Santa Maria Assunta as cathedral and its dedication to the Virgin.[29] Oderigo reinforced the point by concluding his ordinal with a passage from Gratian's *Decretum* (ca. 1140) ordering that clerics follow the liturgical customs of their cathedral.[30] The enforcers of such uniformity were evidently the canons and not their bishop, whom neither Rolando nor Oderigo mentions. The latter spoke for his entire chapter by declining to name himself in his preface and instead using the first-person plural on behalf of his canons. The proprietary attitude of such clerics vis-à-vis the liturgy of their church found blunter expression in the incipit of the second Florentine ordinal, by which it claimed to preserve the "customs and traditions" of neither the city nor the cathedral but instead "the Florentine canonry" (table 5.1).

Concurrent with their political aims, the ordinals bestowed upon their prescribed liturgies a patina of antiquity that amplified the perceived authority of these rites. Oderigo characterized the liturgy of his cathedral as an "ancient use passed down from

---

multorum eundo per episcopatu[m] sepe numero agnovi. Ideoque ad conponendum de ordine librum per totum anni circulum fraternitatis amore me contuli. De cetero igitur ab universis pisane diocesios ecclesiis omnis removeatur diversitas et universa pereat ignorantiam [sic]. Denique cuncti rectores ecclesiarum et eorum fratres in hoc libro poterunt manifeste cognoscere qualiter in ecclesia Dei per totum anni circulum debeant officium celebrare. Rogo ergo vos fratres ut in orationibus vestris memineritis mei, Rolandi videlicet diaconi peccatoris, sed tamen de Dei misericordia presumseretis. Quatinus sicut pro vobis elaboravi, ita beneficiis et orationibus vestris apud misericordem et severum iudicem in districto eius examine, ipso donante adiuvari possim. Amen."

[27] Alternatively, *OOP* may have been the "ordinarium officii" listed in the late-thirteenth-century inventory of the cathedral: Riccardo Barsotti, ed., *Gli antichi inventari della cattedrale di Pisa* (Pisa: Istituto di storia dell'arte, Universita di Pisa), 22.

[28] An "ordinarium officii lucane ecclesie" appears in the inventory of San Giorgio: ACL, LL 45, fol. 35v (18 November 1300). The modest wealth of this church is reflected in the small tithe of £2.20 that its rector paid in 1276–1277: Pietro Guidi, *Tuscia*, 2 vols., vol. 1 (Vatican City: Biblioteca Apostolica Vaticana, 1932), 211.

[29] *OOES*, pt. 1, prologue, 1–2.

[30] *OOES*, pt. 2, ch. 106, 514; cf. the "Decretum Gratiani," in *Corpus iuris canonici*, ed. Emil Albert Friedberg (Leipzig: Bernhardus Tauchnitz, 1879), vol. 1, dist. 12, ch. 13. In 1258, Archbishop Frederico Visconti of Pisa (1254–1277) signaled the enduring importance of liturgical uniformity by ordering all secular churches of his diocese to conform to the liturgy of the cathedral: Antonio Felice Mattei, *Ecclesiae Pisanae Historia*, 2 vols. (Lucca: Leonardo Venturini, 1768–1772), appendix to vol. 2, no. 1, 2.

our forbearers in our church," such that one learned through experience in choir as well as through consultation of other *ordines*.³¹ Indeed, the inclusion of deliberately anachronistic material amplified the conservatism of the ordinals. The most conspicuous of such cases were the frequent references to cantors in their capacity as chief singers of the choir in the ordinals of Siena and Lucca, the very cities of which archival documents abruptly cease to mention the cantor after 1196 and 1207, respectively.³² Oderigo devoted an entire chapter to the cantor that recalled the authoritative and virtuous cleric portrayed in the Rule of Aachen: "In the manner of a good exhorter in the Lord's camp, he awakens the slumbering, stimulates the lazy, restrains the tempestuous, sets an example for the less expert. Like God's trumpet of beaten metal, which sounds loud or soft at the right time, he seeks to bring all together into a well-tempered whole."³³ If this image of the cantor evoked an earlier age, the rhetoric of ecclesiastical concord remained an opportune metaphor for a diocese in which the musical and ritual life of its daughter churches accorded with that of its cathedral.³⁴

Every Tuscan ordinal save the Florentine ones further enhanced the perceived authority of their prescribed rites by including glosses from legal or literary sources.³⁵ These, noted Oderigo, enhanced the utility of the ordinals because they illuminated the doctrinal foundations of the liturgy.³⁶ Among the oft-cited works was Burchard's *Decretum* (1012), a convenient source for papal letters and conciliar legislation concerning the

---

[31] *OOES*, pt. 1, prologue, 2: "Sicut igitur audivimus et vidimus et ab antiquioribus nostris accepimus in nostra ecclesia fuisse antiquitus usitatum."

[32] Unlike the Sienese and Lucchese ordinals, the Pisan ordinal, *OOP*, fol. 25, mentions a "weekly cantor" (*cantor ebdomadarius*), and its Florentine counterpart, Ritus, fol. 29v, a "cantor whom we call the *hebdomadarius* of the offices" (*cantor quem hebdomadarius officiorum vocamus*). This "weekly cantor" or hebdomadary, however, was not a chief singer in the traditional sense but rather a canon who performed the solo portions of the plainchant on a one-week rotating basis. Another probable instance of deliberate antiquarianism includes the prescriptions in *OOL*, fols. 36v–38, for the processions on the Monday, Tuesday, and Wednesday before the feast of the Ascension (i.e., the Minor Litanies). They described two churches as extramural that had nonetheless been enclosed by a new circuit of city walls in the first half of the thirteenth century: Giusti, "L'Ordo," 528–529.

[33] *OOES*, pt. 2, ch. 17, 417: "tamquam bonus exhortator in castris Domini, dormientes excitat, pigros stimulat, effrenatos retinet, omnibus minus peritis modum inponit, et velut ductilis tuba Dei pro congrua opportunitate quandoque submisse, quandoque alte, temperate omnes studet insimul concordare." Translation after D'Accone, *The Civic Muse*, 71. On this chapter as a whole, see D'Accone, *The Civic Muse*, 70–74; and Von Fischer, "Das Kantorenamt," 167–182.

[34] Oderigo's chapter devoted to the cantor likely sounded another antiquarian note in directing the cantor to consult the bishop, if the latter be present, in his selection of canons to sing and recite items at the night office: *OOES*, pt. 2, ch. 17, 418. By the twelfth century, the bishop celebrated the night office with his canons rarely and only on the highest feasts (see chapter 7, this volume).

[35] The remainder of the paragraph is based on my own study of the Tuscan ordinals as well as the systematic examination of literary sources in *OOL* by Giusti, "L'Ordo," 530–532, and in the critical apparatus to the edition of *OOES* by Trombelli; and in Weinrich, "Der *Ordo officiorum*."

[36] *OOES*, pt. 2, ch. 17, 417.

liturgy, a copy of which was owned by the cathedral chapter of Lucca.[37] Equally important were liturgical commentaries designed for the instruction of clerics.[38] The oldest and most influential of such treatises was the *Liber officialis* by Amalarius of Metz († ca. 850); however, the Lucchese *ordo* likewise borrowed from the most prominent works of a later generation of ultramontane liturgists, the *Gemma animae* (ca. 1120) of Honorius Augustodunensis (i.e., "of Regensburg") and *Summa de ecclesiasticis officiis* (ca. 1160–1164) of Johannes Beleth of Paris.[39] Its Sienese counterpart, by contrast, drew on the *Mitralis* of Bishop Sicardo of Cremona (†1215), a massive tract likewise owned by the cathedral canons of Lucca, which integrated the work of the three transalpine liturgists with its author's detailed knowledge of Italian customs.[40] Once again, the ordinals thus reinforced the status of the cathedral as *ecclesia matrix*, the exclusive sources of a local liturgies grounded in Catholic orthodoxy and guarded by the canons.

Finally, the Tuscan *ordines* were ideological documents in yet another way: they bear witness to the relics preserved in the cathedrals and upon which the claim of these churches to be *ecclesiae matrices* was partially based. When read in concert with documentary and archeological evidence, these liturgical sources illustrate the strategies adopted by bishops, canons, and *opere* to encourage the veneration of relics, including the construction of monumental crypts and the burial of relics in altars located throughout the church. While the old cults of local bishops and martyrs remained the purview of the cathedral chapter, newer ones often associated with universal objects of veneration became identified with the populace and its commune. Both types attracted considerable revenue in the form of pious offerings, to which bishops, canons, and opere alike laid claim.

---

[37] See introduction to part II, this volume.

[38] Christina Whitehead, "Columnae... sunt episcopi. Pavimentum... est vulgus: The Symbolic Translation of Ecclesiastical Architecture in Latin Liturgical Handbooks," *The Medieval Translator / Traduire au Moyen Age 8* (2003): 32.

[39] Honorius's cryptic surname, "Augustodunensis," probably referred to Regensburg, where he spent much of his productive life from ca. 1103–1140: Valerie I. J. Flint, "Place and Purpose in the Works of Honorius," *Revue Bénédictine 87* (1977): 97–127; and Valerie I. J. Flint, "The Career of Honorius Augustodunensis. Some Fresh Evidence," *Revue Bénédictine 82* (1972): 81–86. Johannes Beleth is not known to have been a Parisian native, but nonetheless taught in Paris as a master of theology and drew upon his knowledge of its local liturgy in his *Summa de Ecclesiasticis Officiis*, ed. Heribert Douteil (Turnhout: Brepols, 1976): Paolo Masini, "Magister Johannes Beleth: Ipotesi di una Traccia Biografica," *Ephemerides Liturgicae 107* (1993): 252–259.

[40] The *Mitralis* (1205) appears in the earliest surviving inventory of the cathedral sacristy of Lucca: Guidi and Pellegrinetti, *Inventari*, 122 (1239). That *OOL* does not quote it in the manner of *OOES* may reflect the fact that the former was largely copied from an earlier Lucchese exemplar, perhaps the *Ordo vetus* cited in the cathedral inventory of 1297 (see above, n. 21). If this "old ordinal" was compiled during the late twelfth century, it would have predated the *Mitralis* but not Honorius's *Gemma animae* and Beleth's *Summa de ecclesiasticis officiis*, of which passages indeed appear in *OOL*. On Sicardo's life and work, see Ercole Brocchieri, "Sicardo di Cremona e la sua opera letteraria," *Annali della Biblioteca Governativa e Libreria Civica di Cremona 11* (1958): 1–115.

ALTARS, RELICS, AND OBLATIONS

Throughout the Middle Ages, no physical structures signaled the rise of Tuscan cathedrals as holy treasuries more conspicuously than their crypts. The annular confessional was the preferred arrangement in the Carolingian period while the hall crypt supplanted it in the decades around the millennium.[41] The reconstruction of San Miniato al Monte just south of Florence one hundred years later, for instance, embellished the latter model (fig. 5.3).[42] Incorporating the outer crypt built by Bishop Ildebrando in the 1010s, the present one extends across the full width of the church rather than its apse alone and occupies a full third of its interior. This "monumental" crypt dominated lay worshipers' view from the nave, intimating the wealth of relics preserved therein.[43] Moreover, it would (one hoped) draw them down the central flights of stairs and to St. Minias's altar, a more direct route than the narrow semi-circular passageways characteristic of old confessionals. Yet if this arrangement streamlined congregants' access to relics, it also accentuated their division from the clergy, which sang its liturgy in the presbytery and choir above, undisturbed by lay worshipers in the nave and crypt below.[44]

The monumental crypt at San Miniato was perhaps the model for those of the cathedrals of Siena and Florence. The twelfth-century church of Santa Maria Assunta boasted a crypt large enough to accommodate the bishop, cathedral chapter, and the city clerics—approximately sixty to seventy individuals.[45] After the rebuilding of the cathedral in the second half of the thirteenth century, the crypt lay buried beneath the pavement of the transept and

---

[41] See chapter 2, this volume (on the annular confessional), and chapter 3, this volume (on the hall crypt).

[42] Francesco Gurrieri, Luciano Berti, and Claudio Leonardi, *La Basilica di San Miniato al Monte a Firenze* (Florence: Giunti Barbèra, 1988), 15–31, summarizes the chronology set forth in Walter Paatz and Elisabeth Valentiner Paatz, *Die Kirchen von Florenz, ein kunstgeschichtliches Handbuch*, 6 vols. (Frankfurt: V. Klostermann, 1952–1955), vol. 4, 211–293; and Walter Horn, "Romanesque Churches in Florence. A Study of Their Chronology and Stylistic Development," *Art Bulletin* 25 (1943): 112–131, according to which the reconstruction of San Miniato unfolded in two campaigns, one in the final third of the eleventh century and another in the second quarter of the twelfth. The monumental crypt belongs to the first campaign. San Miniato is the most famous but not necessarily the first Florentine church to feature such a structure. Others include San Pier Scheraggio, consecrated in 1068 but largely destroyed in 1560, and the eleventh-century church of San Godenzo, located north of Florence in the Mugello Valley: Tigler, *Toscana*, 147–148; and Toker, *On Holy Ground*, 14–15, respectively.

[43] George W. Dameron, "The Cult of St. Minias and the Struggle for Power in the Diocese of Florence, 1011-1018," *Journal of Medieval History* 13 (1987): 144, notes that the crypt bolstered the dubious claims of the monks of San Miniato to possess the relics of their titular saint, an argument elaborated in chapter 7, this volume. The construction of the Chapel of the Holy Cross in 1448 obscured the view of the crypt from the nave.

[44] Indeed, the facades of such crypts functioned as de facto choir screens, as noted in Jacqueline Elaine Jung, "Beyond the Barrier: The Unifying Role of the Choir Screen in Gothic Churches," *Art Bulletin* 82 (2000): 624–625.

[45] *OOES*, pt. 1, ch. 168, 147, prescribes the bishop's blessing of the paschal candle in the crypt and before the clerical assembly on Holy Saturday, as signaled in Max Seidel, "Tradizione e innovazione. Note sulle scoperte architettoniche del duomo di Siena," in *Sotto il duomo di Siena: Scoperte archeologiche, architettoniche e figurative*, ed. Roberto Guerrini (Siena: Silvana, 2003), 74; and Argenziano, *Agli inizi dell'iconografia*, 84.

FIGURE 5.3. Raised presbytery and crypt of San Miniato, Florence (saec. XI[ex]) (Alinari / Art Resource, NY).

directly below the cupola. When excavations temporarily uncovered it two hundred years later, the provost of Santa Maria described it as "more beautiful than any in Italy, supported by fifteen columns with three rows of decorated and painted vaults. The walls [were] painted quite graciously."[46] Such ornamentation surely magnified the allurement of the crypt for lay worshipers and perhaps inspired the Florentines to remodel the east end of their cathedral. Bishop Giovanni da Velletri (1205–1230) marked the end of the reconstruction of Santa Reparata by consecrating its high altar around 1230. Its crypt now occupied the full width of the basilica and was accessible via a wide, central staircase in the manner of that of San Miniato.[47]

---

[46] Bartolomeo Benvoglienti, *Trattato de l'origine et accrescimento de la citta di Siena. Composto da M. Bartolomeo Benvoglienti proposto di Siena, e professor di filosofia & teologia. A l'Ilustriss. et reverendiss. Cardinale Sforza Legato di Bologna e Romagna*, trans. Fabio Benvoglienti (Rome: Giuseppe degli Angeli, 1571), 12–13, quoted in Seidel, "Tradizione," 74: "Hebbe dunque la nostra Chiesa una confessione piu bella di tutte l'altre d'Italia sostentata da quindici colonne con tre ordini di volte rilevata & illustre. I muri de la qual pochi anni inanzi si videro dipinti assai gratiosamente." On the position of the crypt with respect to the present, late medieval edifice, see Seidel, "Tradizione," 74–76. Seidel convincingly refutes the identification of the crypt with the aforementioned atrium, noted above in n. 6, by Kees Van Der Ploeg, *Art, Architecture, and Liturgy: Siena Cathedral in the Middle Ages* (Groningen: Egbert Forsten, 1993), 54.

[47] Franklin Toker, "Excavations Below the Cathedral of Florence," *Gesta* 14 (1975): 35. Domenico Cardini, "Ipotesi sulle fasi trasformative del Centro religioso dalla formazione della cinta difensiva carolingia alla sua sostituzione," in *Il bel San giovanni e Santa Maria del Fiore: Il centro religioso di Firenze dal tardo antico al*

By the thirteenth century, monumental crypts had nonetheless become old-fashioned with respect to an alternate arrangement that brought congregants into even greater proximity with the clergy, as well as with holy treasure. In 1109, Bishop Rangerio of Lucca dismantled the confessional of St. Regulus in San Martino and moved the martyr's relics and those of Sts. Jason, Maurus, and Hilaria to altars in the east end of the church (fig. 4.2). The cathedral of Pisa, consecrated eight years later, likewise featured no crypt. At both churches, the canons worshiped in choirs and presbyteries elevated only several steps above the nave and separated by a low enclosure.[48] While none of the screens survive in situ, extant fragments indicate that they resembled the arrangement in the pieve of San Cristoforo of Barga (fig. 5.4).[49] Comprising a series of rectangular marble *plutei* that span the entire width of the basilica, the enclosure stands approximately one meter tall and thus allows congregants an unobstructed view of the clergy and altars in the east end.[50] Unlike the monumental crypt, however, this arrangement reduced the accessibility of holy relics by obliging laymen and women to worship at the eastern altars only when choir and presbytery were otherwise unoccupied so as not to disturb the celebration of the liturgy.[51]

Rinascimento, ed. Domenico Cardini (Florence: Le lettere, 1996), 137–146, by contrast, ascribes the enlargement of the crypt of Santa Reparata to the eleventh-century reconstruction of that church (on which see chapter 4, this volume), in which case it would have anticipated rather than followed the building of that of San Miniato. Mores, fol. 12, records Bishop Giovanni's consecration of the high altar on the first Sunday after the feast of All Saints (1 November).

[48] Iacopo Lazzareschi Cervelli, "L'arredo scultoreo," *Rivista di archeologia, storia, costume* 26 (1998): 31–32 (on Lucca); Adriano Peroni, "Funzionalità architettonica, configurazione e arredo dell'area liturgica: Il caso del duomo di Pisa," in *Medioevo: La chiesa e il palazzo*, ed. Arturo Carlo Quintavalle (Milan: Electa, 2007), 372–373; Anna Rosa Calderoni Masetti, "L'abside maggiore del duomo, dalle origini al Quattrocento," in *La tribuna del Duomo di Pisa, capolavori di due secoli*, ed. Roberto Paolo Ciardi (Milan: Electa, 1995), 13–15; and Adriano Peroni, "Architettura e decorazione," in *Il Duomo di Pisa*, ed. Adriano Peroni (Modena: Modena: F.C. Panini, 1995), 100–102 (on Pisa).

[49] One *pluteus* of the Romanesque enclosure of San Martino of Lucca survives in the Museo Nazionale di Villa Guinigi: Giorgio Monaco, Lucia Bertolini Campetti, and Silvia Meloni Trkulja, *Museo Nazionale di Villa Guinigi, Lucca: La villa e le collezioni* (Lucca: Ente provinciale per il turismo, 1968), no. 434, 81. Nine plutei of the cathedral of Pisa survive in the Museo dell'Opera del Duomo: Peroni, Il Duomo di Pisa, vol. 1, nos. 1801–1802, 1865–1866, and 1868, 589–590, and 613–615.

[50] The Romanesque screens of the cathedrals were nonetheless more ornate than the unadorned marble at San Cristoforo, featuring geometric designs similar to those in the taller screen at San Miniato (fig. 5.3) as noted in the studies cited above, n. 49.

[51] That Pope Leo IV (847–855) felt obliged to ratify the "ancient custom" by which the laity refrained from entering the presbytery during the celebration of Mass suggests that congregants were not always so solicitous: Louis Duchesne and Cyrille Vogel, eds., *Le Liber pontificalis*, 3 vols. (Paris: E. de Boccard, 1955), vol. 2, ch. 105, no. 499, 108. Indeed, Pope Eugene II (824–827) issued a similar admonition in a council convened in Rome in 826 and attended by sixty-two bishops, among whom numbered those of Arezzo, Lucca, Fiesole, Florence, Pisa, Pistoia, and Siena: Giovanni Domenico Mansi, *Sacrorum Conciliorum Nova et Amplissima Collectio*, 31 vols. (Venice: Antonio Zatta, 1759–1798), vol. 14, 1008, con. 33. This and the remaining capitularies issued by Eugene appear in the collection of ecclesiastical legislation that belonged to the cathedral canons of Lucca and was discussed in the introduction to part II: BCL, 124, fols. 191–193v, esp. 193 (saec.

FIGURE 5.4. Nave of San Cristoforo of Barga (diocese of Lucca) (saec. XII) (Alinari / Art Resource, NY).

Translations of holy treasure to Tuscan cathedrals in the late eleventh and twelfth centuries further illustrate the declining appeal of crypts while concomitantly underscoring the rise of lay influence over the mother church. The relics of St. Ansanus (in Siena), the Volto Santo (in Lucca), and St. James (in Pistoia) came to reside in altars located in the east end or in side aisle of their respective cathedrals, where they were visible and accessible to the many lay men and women who flocked to these churches on high feast days.[52] Accounts of their

---

XI[ex]). That the laity entered the east end of the cathedral at the prescribed times in turn finds confirmation in the *Translatio Sancti Ansani* (*BHL* 517b), Giovanni Domenico Mansi, ed., *Stephani Baluzii Tutelensis Miscellanea*, 4 vols. (Lucca: Vincentius Junctinius, 1761), vol. 4, 66, on which more will be said below. It describes a woman tormented by a demon who found relief at the altar of St. Ansanus, located in the east of Santa Maria Assunta of Siena. Finally, the veneration of relics was not the only reason that congregants entered the east end of their churches. For instance, women gave thanks for the delivery of their children and couples elicited the blessing for their nuptials in the presbytery: Thompson, *Cities of God*, 39.

[52] Cf. Bernhard Töpfer, "The Cult of Relics and Pilgrimage in Burgundy and Aquitaine at the Time of the Monastic Reform," trans. János Bak, in *The Peace of God, Social Violence and Religious Response in France around the Year 1000*, ed. Thomas Head and Richard Landes (Ithaca, NY: Cornell University Press, 1992), 52, who identifies congregants' desire to see relics as the reason behind the interment of such treasure in above-ground altars in eleventh-century Aquitaine and Burgundy.

translations, as related below, highlight the popular impetus behind their arrival at their respective churches and foreshadow the role of civic officials rather than of the bishop or canons in the promotion of their cults. While the local saints championed by early medieval bishops usually remained in crypts, these newer arrivals thus obtained even greater proximity to the lay public.

The transfer of St. Ansanus from his rural shrine of Dofana to Santa Maria Assunta of Siena harkened back to a dispute of the early Middle Ages and, in its broad outlines, resembled the episcopal translations of relics of that period. In the eighth century, this Roman evangelizer had become a flashpoint in the struggle over the churches located in the diocese of Arezzo but in the political territory of Siena. A Sienese gastald had interred his relics in a new altar without the Aretine bishop's leave, an insult to episcopal authority that earned a rebuke from the pope.[53] Almost four centuries later, Bishop Gualfredo of Siena (1085–1127) sought to extend his jurisdiction over all the contested churches, an audacious plan that the translation of St. Ansanus in 1107 was intended to bolster. The transfer undoubtedly occurred without permission of the Aretine bishop and thus reprised the illicit translation of the saint's relics in the eighth century. In another act of bravado, Gualfredo later presented to the newly installed pope, Honorius II (1124–1130), a forged decree in favor of Sienese claims to the disputed churches, one attributed to Pope Leo IV and Emperor Louis II.[54] In his acquisition of holy relics to underscore his episcopal dominion and his translation of them *intra muros*, Gualfredo resembled early medieval lords and builders such as Bishop Giovanni I of Lucca.

The account of the translation of St. Ansanus nonetheless tells a different story that elevates the role of the laity at the expense of the bishop and his canons. It makes no mention of Gualfredo in connection with the event and ascribes the impetus to the Sienese citizens (*cives*), who desired to protect their patron saint upon learning that unnamed enemies (presumably the Aretines) were about to abscond with his body.[55] Clerics played their traditional role, disinterring the saint's miraculously preserved and fragrant corpse; however, local knights preceded them in order to put flight to their antagonists and other lay people accompanied them to the shrine. Yet they arrived too late to thwart unidentified "butchers" (*carnifices*) who had stolen St. Ansanus's head at some unknown date. This was another allusion to the Aretines, who in fact claimed to possess St. Ansanus's skull in the late Middle

---

[53] See chapter 2, this volume.
[54] Michele Pellegrini, *Chiesa e città: Uomini, comunità e istituzioni nella società senese del XII e XIII secolo* (Rome: Herder, 2004), 246–250; and Alfred Maroni, *Prime comunità cristiane e strade romane nei territori di Arezzo-Siena-Chiusi (dalle origine al secolo VIII)*, 3rd. ed. (Siena: Cantagalli, 2001), 280–291.
[55] *Translatio Sancti Ansani*, in Mansi, *Stephani Baluzii*, vol. 4, 65–67, which postdates both the construction of St. Ansanus's new altar in the cathedral in 1110 and Gualfredo's death in 1127: Francesco Barcellona Scorza, "Un martire locale: Ansano," in *I santi patroni senesi*, ed. Franca Lea Consolino (Siena: Accademia Senese degli Intronati, 1991), 26–27. Diana Webb, *Patrons and Defenders: The Saints in the Italian City-States* (London: Tauris Academic Studies, 1996), 62–64, discusses the civic overtones of the *Translatio* likewise explored below.

Ages.⁵⁶ The loss nonetheless failed to quell the exclamation of joy upon the assembly's return to Siena, which in turn overshadowed the traditional psalms and hymns sung by the clergy in procession, according to conventional *translationes* of the early Middle Ages:

> The entire Sienese populace, men and women of every age and condition, who had remained [in the city], hurried to meet the most holy relics, all exclaiming with one voice, "Come, Father Ansanus, return to us, O Lord, wish not to delay your return to your city, which you instructed in the first beginnings of its faith. Protect the place established by you in the name and title of Jesus Christ. Here, O Father, return here, and accept our offerings, which we, your devotees, so desire to give."⁵⁷

In the place of an authoritative bishop returning home in triumph with his holy treasure, the *Translatio Sancti Ansani* presents the voice of an assertive citizenry jubilant on account of the homecoming of its patron saint.

The Translation likewise illustrates the civic overtones infusing the development of St. Ansanus's cult at the expense not merely of the bishop but even of the cathedral itself. It explains that Siena divided itself into five sectors, representatives of each of which guarded their newly acquired treasure on a rotating basis. Henceforth the relics would never go "without the constant protection of the city and people. In order to carry out these vigils, there convened with pious devotion the monasteries of monks and nuns, pievi, and chapels with their congregants as they pertained to one of the five aforementioned parts."⁵⁸ Such collective devotion normally reinforced the image of a cathedral as *ecclesia matrix*; however, the Translation never even alludes to, much less names, Santa Maria even as it cites Gualfredo's consecration of the martyr's altar in 1110 and recounts miracles that St. Ansanus performed there. This conspicuous omission puts the Sienese laity front and center by obscuring the sacred stage, namely the burial church, in which such postmortem dramas conventionally unfolded.

Yet the cathedral canons hardly ceded the role of protectors of St. Ansanus to their Sienese compatriots, as they staked their claim to the newly arrived martyr through liturgical ceremony. Their ordinal, compiled roughly a century after his translation, included

---

⁵⁶ Barcellona Scorza, "Un martire locale," 25–26.

⁵⁷ *Translatio Sancti Ansani*, in Mansi, *Stephani Baluzii*, vol. 4, 65–66: "Omnis autem populus virorum et mulierum Senensium cuiuscumque aetatis vel condictionis qui remanserant, velocissima festinatione obviam ibant sacrosanctis reliquis, omnes una voce pariter conclamantes: Veni Pater Ansane, redi ad nos Domine, noli amplius tardare ad tuam regredi civitatem, quam fidei primordiis instruxisti, et conserva locum per te nomini, et titulo Jesu Cristi consignatum. Huc Pater, huc redeas, hic munera suscipe nostra, qua tibi devoti reddere concupimus."

⁵⁸ *Translatio Sancti Ansani*, in Mansi, *Stephani Baluzii*, vol. 4, 66: "et sancte relique numquam vacarent a frequenti cleri et populi custodia. Ad has etiam vigilias supplendas conveniebant cum integra devotione monasteria monacorum et monialium, plebs, et capelle cum populis suis, sicut unicuique predictarum quinque partium adiacebant."

an unusually long rubric emphasizing the importance of his cult at Santa Maria and their longstanding observance of his *dies natalis* (1 December).[59] On the previous evening, they organized an act of collective devotion, calling the entire Sienese clergy and populace to the mother church. With their clerical brethren, the cathedral canons celebrated a service known as a vigil under the direction of their archpriest (not the bishop), reciting a portion of the saint's Passion.[60] The canons surely selected the second half of the *passio*, which recounted St. Ansanus's activities in Siena rather than in Rome—namely his evangelism, trial, and execution. Indeed, this third episode is the subject of a small historiated initial at the beginning of the liturgical prescriptions for the vigil of St. Ansanus in the ordinal: a Roman executioner raises his sword over the kneeling saint as an angel waits to receive God's hero into heaven.[61] The canons articulated their claims to the martyr's cult by emphasizing the ties forged by him with their city in life and thus long before the translation of his relics to Siena in 1107. This they did through the medium over which they enjoyed near complete control: the liturgy celebrated at their cathedral.[62]

Finally, the cult of St. Ansanus reveals a broader tendency among Tuscan cathedrals: saints whose cults were civic in origin obtained visual prominence in altars above ground while those who owed their arrival to early medieval bishops remained in the crypts of which the construction was attributed to those lords and builders. The Sienese interred St. Ansanus in an altar in the east end of Santa Maria Assunta, where it seems to have formed an arrangement analogous to (and perhaps inspired by) the one established at San Martino of Lucca a year earlier (fig. 4.2). In Siena as in Lucca, altars dedicated to local patrons, Sts. Ansanus and Savinus, evidently flanked a high altar of which the titular, the Virgin Mary, was an object of universal veneration.[63] These three altars were the "major altars" of the cathedral because of the wealth of oblations that they attracted, as well as (one presumes) their privileged position within the church.[64] The

---

[59] *OOES*, pt. 1, ch. 295, 273.

[60] *OOES*, pt. 1, ch. 295, 273–274.

[61] *Passio Sancti Ansani* (BHL 515), in Mansi, *Stephani Baluzii*, vol. 4, 60–63, of which the incipit, "Revertur in scripturis divinis," is cited in *OOES*, pt. 1, ch. 296, 274, in connection with the night office of matins. The historiated initial appears in *OOES*, BCIS, G.V.8, fol. 117v.

[62] Nevertheless, the cathedral canons hardly refuted the account of St. Ansanus's arrival in Siena provided in the Translation. Indeed, they recited the text at another vigil on the evening before the saint's *translatio* (6 February): *OOES*, pt. 1, ch. 328, 304.

[63] Savinus was an early Christian bishop martyred in Spoleto but who had passed through Siena: Elena Giannarelli, "Savino, Bartolomeo e l'alternanza dei patroni," *Bullettino senese di storia patria 97* (1990): 64–75.

[64] The phrase, "three major altars," derives from an agreement between Bishop Bono and the cathedral canons, on which more will be said below: Ghignoli, *Opera Metropolitana*, no. 21, 203 (21 April 1190). On the disposition of all the altars in the Sienese cathedral, see Raffaele Argenziano, "Corpi sancti e immagini nella Siena medievale: I santi patroni," *Bullettino senese di storia patria 60* (2004): 216–222; and Argenziano, *Agli inizi*, 71–73, of which both base their discussions in part on the description of the crypt and altars in *OOES*. Moreover, they substantially revise the reconstruction of the east end of the cathedral by Van Der Ploeg, *Art, Architecture*, 63–81.

Sienese nonetheless departed from the Lucchese precedent by preserving rather than destroying the old crypt of their cathedral. Their course of action intimates a measure of respect for an episcopal initiative of the distant past: the crypt was the burial place of St. Crescentius, the Roman martyr whose relics Bishop Ansifredo had obtained from Pope Stephen II in the 750s, after the debacle of St. Ansanus's unauthorized translation within his martyrium at Dofana. As in Siena so in Florence the crypt remained the site of the oldest relic cult of the cathedral—namely that of St. Zenobius, whose original confessional had been built in the late ninth century by Bishop Andrea. The altars located in the east and west end of the church, by contrast, purportedly contained the relics of more than fifty saints acquired by the mid-twelfth century (fig. 4.1).[65] As related below, the Volto Santo (in Lucca) and relics of St. James (in Pistoia) likewise resided in new chapels located in or just off the nave, thereby conforming to the pattern seen in Siena and Florence by which crypts were reserved for older, episcopal cults.

The Volto Santo illustrates how the memory of an authoritative bishop might become associated with an object of civic pride in a city distinguished by its august line of episcopal lords and builders. First documented in the late eleventh century, this wooden sculpture of the crucified Christ, one believed to have been fashioned in Palestine, stood at an altar against the retro-façade of San Martino and later in a chapel in its north aisle of San Martino (fig. 4.2).[66] Like John the Baptist in Florence, it found its most enthusiastic promoters among civic officials, who similarly required citizens and subject communities to offer candles to the cathedral and commune on the Exaltation of the Cross (14 September).[67] The Volto Santo was the subject of a Translation datable to the first half of the twelfth century, one that, as noted in chapter 4, praised the archpriest and archdeacon of San Martino, Lamberto and Blancardo, respectively, for rebuilding their church in the 1060s. This anomalous attribution conflicts with the canonical one, promoted first and foremost by Bishop Rangerio, to Bishop Anselmo I (i.e., Pope Alexander II), and suggests that the author of the Translation

---

[65] As summarized in Tacconi, *Cathedral*, 118–121, two saints (Nicholas and Zenobius) appear in the original text of Ritus, the remaining fifty-one in marginal additions added soon after its compilation. Mores, by contrast, noted the presence of fifteen saints, of which only one (Mary Magdalene) was not specified in Ritus.

[66] Diana Webb, "The Holy Face of Lucca," *Anglo-Norman Studies 9* (1986): 228–237. See also Romano Silva, "La datazione del Volto Santo di Lucca," in *La santa croce di Lucca: Il Volto Santo: Storia, tradizione, immagini: Atti del Convegno, Villa Bottini, 1-3 Marzo 2001* (Lucca: Editori dell'Acero, 2003), 76–81, which dates the sculpture to the second half of the eleventh century on stylistic grounds. Graziano Concioni, *Contributi alla storia del Volto Santo* (Pisa: ETS, 2005), 11–16, provides a survey of the considerable bibliography on the Volto Santo, to which must be added Hansmartin Schwarzmaier, *Lucca und das Reich bis zum Ende des 11 Jahrhunderts: Studien zur Struktur einer Herzogstadt in der Toskana* (Tübingen: Bibliothek des Deutschen Historischen Instituts in Rom 41, 1972), 336–368.

[67] Concioni, *Contributi*, 40–48. The political overtones of this so-called *Luminaria* are apparent in an edict of 1261, by which the Lucchese commune required those parishes and communes falling under its jurisdiction to participate in the event: ASL, Opera di Santa Croce, 2, fols. 15v–20.

was a member of the cathedral chapter.[68] In a pattern to be encountered elsewhere in Tuscany, however, episcopal lords and builders of the distant past proved less threatening to canons than those of recent memory. In fact, the Translation shrouds the Volto Santo in legendary history by crediting its acquisition to that esteemed prelate of the early Middle Ages, Giovanni I. Borrowing from the *Translatio Sancti Reguli* revised by Rangerio, this text casts him as a pious and divinely inspired acquirer of relics.[69] Hence the cathedral canons incorporated a new civic cult into the longstanding veneration of local episcopal lords and builders.

The integration of the Volto Santo into the holy treasury of San Martino found ritual expression in an elaborate procession, or suffrage, enacted by the canons on weekdays outside of Lent (fig. 4.2).[70] First, these clerics processed to the Chapel of the Holy Cross, where they sang an antiphon for its secondary titulars, the Twelve Apostles, recited a versicle (or brief reading) for God the Father, and prayed to the Holy Trinity. Next, they split into two halves, of which one made such commemorations at the altars on the north side of the church and the other at those on the south side. Each half stopped at three altars but honored five saints: one lingered at the Mary altar to honor the co-titulars, Agnes and Agatha, the other at that of St. Michael for John the Baptist and the Evangelist. The two halves of the chapter were thus to enter the choir at the same moment and commemorate the titular of the high altar, St. Martin.[71] The arrangement of three "major altars" situated in the east end and established by Bishop Rangerio in 1109 had privileged the martyrs Sts. Regulus, Jason, Maurus, and Hilaria, whose translations were the work of those esteemed bishops, Giovanni I and Anselmo I. The suffrage, by contrast, acknowledged the Chapel of the Holy Cross as the preeminent holy site of the cathedral. Marking the beginning of this daily rite just as St. Martin did its end, the Volto Santo was the only relic to elicit the veneration of the entire chapter at once. This

---

[68] *De inventione, revelatione ac traslactione Sanctissimi Vultus*, transcribed in Concioni, *Contributi*, 20–39, from BCL, 626, fols. 1–39 (saec. XIII$^{2/2}$). On the origins of *De inventione*, see Webb, "The Holy Face," 229–230, whose suggestion that the author of the Translation was a member of Bishop Rangerio's circle seems unlikely given its conspicuous failure to mention Bishop Anselmo I in connection with the reconstruction of San Martino.

[69] *De inventione*, BCL, 626, fols. 4v–5, transcribed in Concioni, *Contributi*, 23, recounts Bishop Giovanni I's purported involvement in the translation of the Volto Santo to Lucca. On the parallels with the *Translatio Sancti Reguli II*, see Schwarzmaier, *Lucca und das Reich*, 343–344.

[70] OOL, fols. 10v, 18v–19, 41v, and 45; Giusti, "*L'Ordo*," 537, n. 74. The other Tuscan ordinals do not prescribe such suffrages with the possible exception of Ritus, fol. 4v, which directs that a versicle, prayer, and antiphon be declaimed in honor of the Virgin and then for "the patrons" of the cathedral during Advent. On suffrages in general, see John Harper, *The Forms and Orders of Western Liturgy from the Tenth to the Eighteenth Century* (Oxford: Oxford University Press, 1991), 130–131.

[71] The suffrage eschewed the altar of St. Edmund (above the portico) and the chapel of St. Apollinaris presumably because they were not easily accessible. Furthermore, the omission of the altar of St. Blaise likely reflects the desire to commemorate an equal number of five titulars on each side of the cathedral before returning to the choir.

exercise in intercessory prayer thus incorporated an object of popular devotion into the storehouse of relics that was the cathedral while implying its preeminence among them.

In a manner exceptional among Tuscan cathedrals, the exterior decoration of San Martino confirmed the place of the Volto Santo with St. Martin and St. Regulus as a patron of the church. The portico, of which the decoration was supervised by Guido Bigarelli da Como (†1257), is one of the greatest examples of sculpture from medieval Tuscany (fig. 5.2).[72] Reliefs in mezzo-relievo adorning the three doors signal the intitulation of the corresponding altars in the east end. Over the central portal appear Christ in Majesty (in the lunette) and the Virgin and the Apostles (in the architrave); however, the flanking registers depict four episodes from the Life of the dedicatee of the high altar, St. Martin (figs. 6.3 and 6.4). Likewise, above the right door leading to St. Regulus's altar are two scenes from his Passion (fig. 7.4). By the same logic, images of Sts. Jason, Maurus, and Hilaria should grace the left door; instead there appears Christ's Deposition (in the lunette) and the Adoration of the Magi (in the architrave) in recognition of the Chapel of the Holy Cross, which disrupts the line of sight from the western door to its corresponding eastern altar.[73] As with the suffrage, inspiration for this visual program likely came from the canons, who, in what was perhaps an exceptional arrangement in Tuscany, shared responsibility for building projects with the cathedral *opera* before the latter acquired full autonomy in 1276.[74] As with the Translation and the suffrage, so with the decoration of the portico, the cathedral chapter acknowledged the significance of the Volto Santo as it integrated this object of popular veneration into the sacred topography of its church.

In contrast with the cult of the Volto Santo in Lucca, that of St. James in Pistoia reveals how communal influence and popular devotion might circumscribe the actions of the bishop and canons in their own cathedral. Translated from Compostella in 1144, James's relics lay in a small chapel in the south aisle west of the choir, one divided from the interior of the church, accessible only by an external door in the west end and supplied by its own sacristy.[75] Its upkeep fell to a dedicated *opera* dedicated to St. James, of which the chaplain worshiped at its altar and separately from the cathedral chapter.[76] On the *dies natalis* of

---

[72] Work on the portico began in 1233 and was largely completed around 1250. See most recently Laura Cavazzini, "La decorazione della facciata di San Martino a Lucca e l'attivita di Guido Bigarelli," in *Medioevo: Le officine. Atti del Convego internazionale di Studi, Parma, 22-27 settembre 2009* (Milan: Electa, 2010), 481–493; and Tigler, "Maestri lombardi," 912–935, of whom the later discerns a second workshop under the supervision of another master and distinct from that of Guido.

[73] Christ's Deposition and the Adoration of the Magi were later additions to the portico datable to the late 1250s and attributed to Nicola Pisano: Cavazzini, "La decorazione," 482; and Clara Baracchini and Antonino Caleca, "Il duomo di S. Martino in Lucca: Urbanistica, architettura, arredo fisso." In *Il duomo di Lucca*, ed. Clara Baracchini and Antonino Caleca (Lucca: Baroni, 1973), 25.

[74] Concioni, "San Martino di Lucca," 38–41.

[75] Webb, *Patrons*, 78–81.

[76] Natale Rauty, *Il culto dei santi a Pistoia nel medioevo* (Florence: SISMEL - Edizioni del Galluzzo, 2000), 178–179; Rauty, *L'antico palazzo*, vol. I, 111–120. The earliest surviving inventory of the sacristy of the chapel

St. James (25 July), the bishop and canons occupied the chapel to celebrate High Mass; however, they could not orchestrate the shared devotion typical of such services by inviting the city clergy to join them. Such a magnanimous gesture would have reinforced the status of the cathedral as mother church, but the chapel was too small to accommodate such a large assembly.[77] Likewise problematic were the laymen and women who audibly prayed at St. James's altar earlier on the eve and morning of his feast rather than standing in respectful silence in the nave while the canons chanted a vigil, matins, and Low Mass in their choir. In an act of exceptional forbearance, the clergy abbreviated its solemnities due to the murmuring of the people.[78] The layout of the chapel and popular devotion to its relic thus diminished rather than augmented the liturgy of the *ecclesia matrix*.

Despite the differences between older, episcopal cults and newer, civic ones, they shared a potential to unify or divide their clerical and lay overseers owing to the oblations that they attracted. Both scenarios are illustrated in the *History of the Custodians of Arezzo* (ca. 1100), discussed in chapter 3 for its relevance to the early history of the local cathedral chapter.[79] Its focus was nonetheless other clerics charged with cleaning and guarding Ss. Maria e Stefano in return for three-quarters of the oblations made to its altars. Over the course of the eleventh century, such income corrupted these custodians, who neglected their duties, forsook celibacy, and fathered offspring. Shares of the altars become progressively fragmented as they passed from one generation to another. Following the consecration of the basilica of San Donato in 1032, the custodians divided its four altars among themselves and harassed pilgrims who came to venerate the relics of its titular. The heroes of the *History* were naturally the cathedral canons. United by their common property and commitment to clerical virtue, they gradually purchased the altars from the custodians in a process of reintegration completed in 1078. With

---

of San Jacopo dates from 1276 and is edited in Sabatino Ferrali, *L'Apostolo S. Jacopo il maggiore e il suo culto a Pistoia* (Pistoia: Opera dei Santi Giovanni e Zeno, 1979), no. 2, 137–143. On the history of the Opera di San Jacopo, see Ferrali, *L'Apostolo*, 97–119; and Diana Webb, "St. James in Tuscany: The Opera di San Jacopo of Pistoia and Pilgrimage to Compostela," *Journal of Ecclesiastical History 50* (1998): 207–234.

[77] On the feast of the titular of the cathedral, St. Zeno, the bishop, chapter, and city clergy (*cappellani et plebani plebalibus*) convened in the procession to High Mass (OOPist2, fol. 45v). By contrast, only the "clergy" was to join the bishop on the feast of St. Jacob, a reference to the cathedral chapter (OOPist2, fol. 61v). On the participation of city clerics in the celebration of High Mass at Tuscan cathedrals in general, see chapter 6, this volume.

[78] OOPist2, fol. 61v.

[79] *Historia Custodum Aretinorum*, in MGH SS, vol. 30, 1471–1482, on which see William North, "The Fragmentation and Redemption of a Medieval Cathedral: Property, Conflict, and Public Piety in Eleventh-Century Arezzo," in *Conflict in Medieval Europe: Changing Perspectives on Society and Culture* (Aldershot: Ashgate, 2003), 118–127; Jean Delumeau, *Arezzo: Espace et societies, 715–1230* (Rome: Ecole française de Rome, 1996), vol. 1, 514–519; and Gabriella Rossetti, "Origine sociale e formazione dei vescovi del 'Regnum Italiae' nei secoli XI e XII," in *Le istituzioni ecclesiastiche della "Sociatas Christiana" dei secoli XI e XII: Diocesi, pievi e parrocchie. Atti della VI settimana di studio, Milano 1-7 settembre 1974* (Milan: Vita e pensiero, 1977), 66–70.

the blessing of the bishop, they had brought peace to the cathedral and San Donato by consolidating control over their altars.

Capitular monopoly over altars nonetheless remained rare as canons competed with bishops and *opere* for their income. The cathedral *opera* of Lucca, named the Opera di Santa Croce in honor of the Volto Santo, brokered a particularly advantageous settlement with the canons in 1181. On five high feasts of the year and others if they so chose, its *operaii* were to elicit oblations from lay men and women who flocked to San Martino on such days and were to divide the proceeds with the chapter. On the Exaltation of the Cross, however, they would retain two-thirds of such offerings and nearly all candles offered to the mother church by the Lucchese and their subjects. The remaining third of the oblations would in turn go to an "old *operaio*," perhaps the administrator of an old cathedral *opera* ultimately replaced by the Opera di Santa Croce.[80] That neither the bishop nor the canons made claims to the wealth generated by the Volto Santo on its feast indicates (once again) that such objects of popular veneration were regarded as the purview of the laity.

In Siena, disputes over the altars of Santa Maria Assunta broke out between the bishop and canons rather than between the canons and the *opera*, a sign of the relative weakness of the *opera* in that particular city. In 1190, the chapter brokered a far-reaching settlement with the recently elected bishop, Bono (1189–1216), in order to resolve the "controversies" between them.[81] The bishop recognized the canons' oversight over the "relics and treasure" of the cathedral and ceded to them all oblations, with three key exceptions. First, he laid claim to the candles donated on the feast of the Assumption, that expression of civic dominion of which the beneficiary was more usually the cathedral *opera*. Second, Bono and the canons divided the offerings made to the high altar and the altar of St. Savinus, two of the three "major altars" located in the east end. Third, the bishop, canons, and the *opera* would each receive a third of the offerings made to the remaining "major altar," that of St. Ansanus. Again, the *opera* staked claim to the newest and most popular cult of the cathedral, although it negotiated a less lucrative arrangement than had its counterpart in Lucca. Despite such local variation, all three centers discussed above—Arezzo, Lucca, and Siena—illustrate the tendency of relic cults to fuel

---

[80] *MDL*, vol. 4, pt. 2, no. 113, 144–145; Concioni, "San Martino di Lucca," 37–38, n. 10 (3 January 1181). The feasts in question were the *dies natales* of St. Regulus and St. Martin, the Dedication of the Church, Holy Saturday, and the Minor Litanies (or Rogation Days).

[81] Ghignoli, *Opera Metropolitana*, no. 91, 202–207 (21 April 1190), on which see Luigi Nanni, "La canonica della cattedrale senese nei secoli XI-XII," in *La vita comune del clero nei secoli XI e XII. Atti della settimana di studio, Mendola, settembre 1959* (Milan: Vita e pensiero, 1962), 258–259. Bono had served as archpriest of the cathedral chapter before his election as bishop in 1189. Disagreements likewise broke out between the cathedral canons of Florence and their bishop, Giovanni da Velletri, concerning, *inter alia*, offerings made to their church and its baptistery: ACF, Dipl. 328/C16 (1 June 1210), on which see Elena Rotelli, *Il capitolo della cattedrale di Firenze dalle origini al XV secolo* (Florence: Firenze University Press, 2005), 16–17.

rivalries between bishops, canons, and *opere* and, in so doing, to reveal the relative influence of these three actors vis-à-vis each other.

The emergence of distinctly popular cults in Tuscan cathedrals associated with St. Ansanus, the Volto Santo, and St. James thus coincided with the elevation of altars and relics from crypts to positions throughout their churches. From such visible and accessible positions, holy treasure (it was hoped) would offer reliable sources of income to bishops, canons, and opere. By the turn of the Duecento, however, capitular patrimonies and pious oblations no longer supported the large chapters of canons consolidated in earlier centuries. In 1202, the Lucchese were obliged to reduce their number from thirty to sixteen in response to their economic challenges.[82] One year later, the Florentines gathered before the altar of St. Zenobius to fix theirs at twelve members, a measure brought about, they noted, by legitimate expenses as well as their financial mismanagement.[83] In the 1210s and 1220s, the canons of Arezzo and Pistoia followed suit by reducing their membership to fourteen and twelve, respectively.[84] With such greatly reduced numbers, clergy and laity alike undoubtedly wondered how they would manage to celebrate the liturgies of their *ecclesia matrix* with requisite solemnity.

That the holy rites of the cathedral were to be the model for daughter churches of the diocese made the shrinking chapters a particularly delicate problem, as revealed in a case from Pisa. In 1197, Archbishop Ubaldo (1176–1208) returned from a voyage at sea to discover that seven cathedral canons had elected nine new colleagues in his absence and without his permission.[85] Before a large assembly of clerics and laymen, he demanded an explanation from the offenders, who assured him that they had had no wish to diminish the prelate's authority. Instead, the canons explained, they had acted to quell "the murmur and complaint" among the diocesan clergy that their number was insufficient to celebrate the liturgy as tradition demanded. In a corollary that confirms the local and often exalted backgrounds characteristic of cathedral canons since the early Middle Ages, the Pisans described their new colleagues as "wise, literate, and noble" men. Three were aristocrats and all but one locals already familiar (one presumes) with the liturgical customs of the mother church.[86] A mollified Ubaldo confirmed the election of the nine

---

[82] The bull of Pope Honorius III, ACL, Dipl. BB 44 (22 May 1225), not only cites the inability of the cathedral chapter of Lucca to maintain thirty canons, but also specifies that the community should comprise eight priests, four deacons, and four subdeacons. ACL, Dipl. BB 43 (5 December 1202) preserves the canons' original decision to reduce their number.

[83] ACF, Dipl. 310/16 (27 February 1203), on which see Rotelli, *Il capitolo*, 15.

[84] Pasqui, *Documenti*, vol. 2, no. 485, 159 (25 October 1219); and ASF, Diplomatico, Capitolo della cattedrale di Pistoia (2 August 1227).

[85] The following paragraph summarizes ACP, Dipl. 728 (14 August 1197), in Mattei, *Ecclesiae Pisanae Historia*, vol. 1, appendix, no. 22, 65–68, which mistakenly transcribes "expeditio ultramarina" as "expeditio ultramontana" (p. 65).

[86] ACP, Dipl. 728 (14 August 1197), in Mattei, *Ecclesiae Pisanae Historia*, vol. 1, appendix, no. 22, 65, identifies three of the candidates as clerics associated with two local churches, San Giorgio a Porte a Mare in Pisa and the Pieve San Pietro di Rigoli situated just northeast of the city. Two others were counts and one the son of a vice-count. Only "magister Lotterius de Cremona" was a foreigner.

candidates, who duly prostrated themselves at his feet. The necessity of a chapter fully staffed by learned, cultivated clerics thus trumped the bishop's desire to maintain his traditional prerogatives.[87]

Nevertheless, cathedral chapters found a more durable solution to financial challenges through "privatization." A modern (rather than medieval) term hitherto used to describe the supposedly private rather than communal experience of the Mass by lay elites in the late Middle Ages, here "privatization" denotes broader yet interrelated developments that characterized cathedral chapters in the thirteenth century.[88] As related below, these communities encouraged their canons' service in choir by dividing their patrimony into shares, or prebends, and offering extra income in the form of distributions. Meanwhile, the chapters augmented their size by hiring "chaplains," a title previously reserved for rectors of small churches (*capelle*) that were neither baptismal parishes nor home to entire collegiate or monastic communities.[89] Many of these junior clerics were employees of the canons, but by the late Duecento, others drew income from private endowments. Such administrative and financial measures were characteristic of cathedrals and collegiate churches throughout late medieval Europe and, in their transalpine manifestations, are familiar to musicologists. Yet the impetus behind their creation (e.g., financial hardship) and their broader religious significance have heretofore remained obscure.[90] With the emergence of prebends and chaplains, the celebration of the liturgy began to resemble labor deserving of remuneration rather than a religious duty. Meanwhile, chapters were no longer homogenous communities united in their common property, as envisioned in the Rule of Aachen. Instead, they had become complex communities, veritable corporations of which the administration was codified in capitular constitutions. So removed from the principles of common life, the chapters would have

---

[87] The election of new canons did not, however, solve the long-term staffing problems at the cathedral of Pisa. Approximately twenty-years later, Pope Honorius III issued a bull in which he noted the lack of a sufficient number of canons at that church and the resulting scandal among the local populace. He thus ruled that henceforth up to sixteen canons would serve the cathedral: ACP, Dipl. 842 (4 August 1218).

[88] For a critique of scholarship positing the "privatization" of the Mass in late medieval England, see, with references, Eamon Duffy, *The Stripping of the Altars: Traditional Religion in England 1400–1580* (New Haven: Yale University Press, 1992), 121–123.

[89] Thus Bishop Bonfilio of Siena (1216–1252) ruled that the Divine Office be celebrated "in pievi, canonries, and chapels of the city" (*in plebibus, canonicis, et capellis civitatis*): Ferdinando Ughelli, *Italia Sacra*, 8 vols. (Rome: Bernardino Tano, 1644–1662), vol. 3, cols. 556–557 (13 March 1232). Likewise the cathedral canons of Lucca entered into negotiations with Arrigo, "chaplain" of the local church of San Concordio: Guidi and Parenti, *Regesto*, vol. 2, no. 1530, 344–345 (13 November 1185). Similarly Bishop Bono of Pisa arbitrated between the cathedral canons of his city and the "presbiter Sismundus cappellanus suprascripte ecclesie Sancti Salvatoris de Putignano": ACP, Dipl. 800 (30 April 1208).

[90] See especially Barbara Haggh, "Foundations or Institutions? On Bringing the Middle Ages into the History of Medieval Music," *Acta Musicologica 68* (1996): 87–128, who argues for a more nuanced historical understanding of late medieval foundations, albeit without presenting the same arguments concerning "privatization" made here.

surely distressed ecclesiastical reformers of earlier eras even as their mission remained the preservation of the liturgical traditions of the *ecclesia matrix*.

PRIVATIZATION

The primary witnesses to the privatization of the Tuscan cathedral chapters were their constitutions, regulations that illustrate the enduring centrality of the liturgy to these communities and the resurgent role of bishops as their reformers. The latter were probably inspired by the decree of the Fourth Lateran Council (1215) that prelates must discipline cathedral canons if chapters proved unable or unwilling to correct their own members.[91] Sixteen years later, Bishop Ardingo of Florence imposed new constitutions upon the canons of Santa Reparata, now known as the *Leges Ardinghi*.[92] In Arezzo, the cathedral chapter drafted its own legislation but "with the consent and express authority" of Bishop Guglielmino Ubertini (1248–1289).[93] Finally, Bishop Paganello of Lucca (1276–1300) coauthored one of three sets of constitutions issued and adopted by the canons during his episcopate.[94] Ardingo was a papal appointee from Pavia rather than a former cathedral canon like Guglielmino and Paganello, and his status as an outsider perhaps encouraged the canons of Santa Reparata to later accuse him of disregarding their traditional prerogatives.[95] Of the three Tuscan bishops, he nonetheless most succinctly articulated the impetus behind the privatization of cathedral chapters. His last constitution ordered the canons and their Florentine brethren to observe "all approved customs concerning processions, litanies, and

---

[91] Mansi, *Sacrorum Conciliorum*, vol. 22, no. 7, col. 991.

[92] ACF, Dipl. 392 (18 November 1231), in Lami, *Sanctae Ecclesiae*, vol. 3, 1653–1654, on which see Rotelli, *Il capitolo*, 20–21; and Brunetto Quilici, *La chiesa di Firenze nei primi decenni del secolo XIII* (Florence: Salesiana, 1965), 5–6.

[93] Pasqui, *Documenti*, vol. 2, no. 623, 364 (21 October 1263). On Guglielmino's episcopal career, see Corrado Lazzeri, *Guglielmino Ubertini, vescovo di Arezzo (1248-1289) e i suoi tempi* (Florence: Libreria editrice fiorentina, 1920), 45–46, 147–150.

[94] The first set of Lucchese constitutions appear in the original diploma, ACL, Dipl. S 160 (1 April 1281), as well as the contemporary register, ACL, LL 40, fols. 31–33v.; ACL, LL 40, fols. 39–42 (14 March 1284); and ACL, LL 43, fols. 191–193 (25 June 1294), preserve the second and third sets of Lucchese constitutions, respectively. Elsewhere in Tuscany, the earliest surviving constitutions of the cathedral date from the fourteenth and fifteenth centuries. These include the *Pacta et capitula vetera* (April 1364), the *Pacta et Capitula Nova* (1397), and the constitutions (1459) of Siena, *Constitutiones Sacri Capituli Metropolitanae Senensis Ecclesiae* (Siena: Luca Bonetto, 1579), 57–65, 70–80, and 1–42, respectively. The first and second sets of legislation are partially transcribed in Stefano Moscadelli, ed. *L'Archivio dell'Opera della Matropolitana di Siena* (Munich: Bruckmann, 1995), no. 46, 310–311 and no. 47, 311–312, respectively. See also the constitutions from Pistoia, ACPist, C117 (1435–1436, with later additions through 1564) and a second set from Florence, ACF, P238 (Florence, 1483, with later additions from 1504).

[95] ACF, Dipl. 406/C17 (30 January 1237), in Lami, *Sanctae Ecclesiae*, vol. 3, 1656. On Ardingo's tenure as bishop, see Rotelli, *Il capitolo*, 19–20; and P. Umberto Betti, "Il maestro Ardengo, vescovo di Firenze," *Divinitas 9* (1965): 161–164.

high feasts of the *ecclesia maior*."⁹⁶ Even a foreigner understood that the mother church derived its preeminence in large part from its local liturgical traditions.

The constitutions underscored the privatization of cathedral chapters by their division of the capitular patrimony into prebends and of the canonry into private dwellings, of which both contravened the tenets of common life.⁹⁷ Prebends promised to foster collegiality by providing canons with a guaranteed share of its income and thus resolving internal disputes over the administration of common property.⁹⁸ They also encouraged canons to maintain residence and to attend to their liturgical duties, as prolonged absences from the cathedral triggered the temporary loss of the share.⁹⁹ The division of the canonry into private quarters accompanied that of the capitular patrimony into prebends. The *Leges Ardinghi* futilely attempted to reverse this process. Ardingo ordered the canons to live and eat together in the dormitory and refectory, and demanded that five of them relinquish private rooms or small houses that they had carved out of their

---

⁹⁶ ACF, Dipl. 392 (18 November 1231), in Lami, *Sanctae Ecclesiae*, vol. 3, 1654: "Tandem consuetudines omnes approbatas de processionibus, litaniis, festivitatibus precipuis maioris ecclesie." The *consuetudines* in question were perhaps those codified in the second Florentine ordinal, Mores, just before or after Ardingo's appointment as bishop: Tacconi, *Cathedral*, 98; and Lorenzo Fabbri and Marica Tacconi, eds., *I libri del duomo di Firenze codici liturgici e biblioteca di Santa Maria del Fiore (secoli XI-XVI)* (Florence: Centro Di, 1997), no. 61, 164.

⁹⁷ The Florentine canons had already established the division of their property when they reduced their number to twelve in 1203 and referred to the "prebend" owed to resident canons (see above, n. 83). By contrast, the Aretines and Lucchese established such shares with their constitutions: Pasqui, *Documenti*, vol. 2, no. 623, 371, con. 25, and ACL, LL 40, fol. 31, con. 1. The Lucchese also drafted a separate list of the properties tied to each prebend: ACL, LL 40, fols. 2–29v (4 April 1281), in Guidi and Pellegrinetti, *Inventari*, 129–178. By the late thirteenth century, the cathedral chapters of Fiesole and Pisa had likewise assigned prebends to their canons as indicated in the separate tithes paid by their recipients in 1275–1267: Guidi, *Tuscia*, vol. 1, 41–42 (on Fiesole) and 177 (on Pisa). On the division of capitular patrimonies at cathedrals throughout Italy in the twelfth and thirteenth centuries, see Cosimo Fonesca, "Canoniche regolari, capitoli cattedrali, e 'cura animarum,'" in *Pievi e parrocchie in Italia nel basso medioevo (sec. XIII-XV). Atti del VI convegno di storia della chiesa in Italia (Firenze, 21-25 Settembre 1981)* (Rome: Herder 1984), 267–268.

⁹⁸ Hence, the cathedral canons of Lucca elected their archdeacon and three of their number to draft their first set of constitutions, which divided their property into prebends and would, they declared, resolve the heated disputes among themselves over the financial administration of their community: ACL, LL 38, fol. 180v (13 September 1280).

⁹⁹ The Florentines moved aggressively against absenteeism by withholding prebends from errant canons: ACF, Dipl. 447/C22 (18 December 1253). The Aretines and Lucchese allowed three and four months of annual absence: Pasqui, *Documenti*, vol. 2, no. 623, 365, con. 3; ACL, LL 40, fols. 31–31v, con. 3 (1 April 1281), of which the latter sanctioned unlimited absence for canons enrolled at a *studium generale* and for those serving the chapter, bishop, or pope. Even such generous provisions did not satisfy the Lucchese canons, for whom Bishop Paganello expanded their allotted absence to a full seven years (!): ACL, LL 40, fols. 232–232v (23 September 1285). Finally, the Lucchese proscribed canons from holding multiple benefices that might conflict with their duties at the cathedral. When, for instance, Tomasino da Loppia (north of Lucca) received his canonicate at San Martino of Lucca, he "renounced all the ecclesiastical benefices and churches that he had in Tuscany according to the constituted form of this chapter" (*iam renuntiavit omnibus benis ecclesiasticis et ecclesiis que habet in Tuscia secundum formam constitutionem ipsius capituli*) (ACL, Dipl. +8 [27 November 1299]).

canonry.[100] The Lucchese constitutions, by contrast, mandated the privatization of the canonry via its partition into single rooms assigned to the individual canons.[101] The model of a clerical community united in its common property and its living quarters had clearly lost its currency among the cathedral canons of Tuscany.

The prebends struck at the ideals of common life in yet a second way: by transforming the celebration of the liturgy from a religious obligation into a task that merited payment. So too did the distributions mandated by the Aretine and Lucchese constitutions. For instance, an Aretine canon received five *denarii* for attending matins, three for Mass or vespers, and one for any of the five remaining hours of the day.[102] Documented in Francia since the eighth century, such payments seem to have been a far more recent phenomenon in Tuscany and are thus best understood here as but one aspect of the broader trend toward privatization in the thirteenth century.[103] Like the withholding of prebends from absent canons, they provided an incentive for clerics to honor their duties in choir. In so doing, they assigned a financial value to the liturgy in a process of "monetization." Together, the prebends and distributions inverted the views of earlier generations of reformers such as Peter Damian. In a letter to Pope Alexander II, Peter had doubted that clerics distracted by material needs could properly discharge their choral duties, for "whoever is a slave of money, finds only disgust in the Church's liturgy."[104] By the late Duecento, Tuscan bishops and cathedral canons had come to the opposite conclusion as they attempted to harness the profit motive in order to ensure the proper celebration of the liturgy.

Indeed, this transformation in sentiment found its greatest expression in the appointment of chaplains as "hired hands," who compensated for the reduction in the number of canons in the early thirteenth century. Their number steadily grew throughout

---

[100] ACF, Dipl. 392 (18 November 1231), in Lami, *Sanctae Ecclesiae*, vol. 3, 1653–1654, on which see Toker, *On Holy Ground*, 96. Toker also illustrates the privatization of the cathedral canonry despite such legislation (p. 107).

[101] ACL, LL 40, fols. 32v–33v (1 April 1281), con. 23–33, 38–42, 45, and 52, on which see Concioni, "San Martino di Lucca," 111–112.

[102] Pasqui, *Documenti*, vol. 2, no. 623, 365, con. 3. Cf. the similar system of distributions established in ACL, LL 40, fol. 31v, con. 5 (1 April 1281). By contrast, the *Leges Ardinghi* implied a more ad hoc approach with its reference to the "punishment which it will please us the bishop to apply" (*aliqua pena quam nobis episcopo inferre placebit incurrat*) for canons absent from one of the principal services of the day: ACF, Dipl. 392 (18 November 1231), in Lami, *Sanctae Ecclesiae*, 1653–1654.

[103] A particularly early precedent for such distributions from beyond the region is the list of payments from Bishop Angilram of Metz (768–791) to singers for their service at his cathedral during Lent and at Easter: Jean Baptiste Pelt, *Etudes sur la cathédrale de Metz: Textes extraits principalement des registres capitulaires (1210-1790)* (Metz: Imprimerie du Journal de Lorrain, 1930), 38–39. The earliest evidence for distributions in Tuscany is perhaps the episcopal act of 1244 ruling that Florentine singers of organum should receive no more than those of plainsong (see above, n. 25).

[104] Peter Damian, *Letters, 91-120*, trans. Owen J. Blum (Washington, DC: Catholic University of America Press, 1998), no. 22, 98.

Tuscany: documentary sources record two in Pisa (in 1197) and two in Florence (in 1231), four in Lucca (in 1259), three in Arezzo (in 1263), and eight in Siena (in 1280).[105] San Martino of Lucca offers the most detailed portrait of the chaplains, who were usually of modest means and unexceptional lineage in contrast to the canons.[106] Senior officials such as the archpriest and primicer oversaw the appointment of chaplains, who in turn received a fixed salary and distributions for their service in choir but not a permanent share of the capitular patrimony.[107] These junior clerics slept in dormitories, ate in the refectory, and were forbidden from leaving the cloister for more than one day and night at a time without permission.[108] The chaplain's place, by implication, was in the choir, where he augmented the now reduced forces of the canons. In an ironic twist, the very clerics whose positions were so symptomatic of privatization at Tuscan cathedrals lived according to the standards of common life forsaken by their superiors, the canons.

In the late Duecento, another phase of privatization accelerated the growth in chaplains' numbers as these junior clerics became recipients of benefices established by private patrons, both clerical and lay.[109] The cathedral of Pisa was perhaps the earliest beneficiary

---

[105] Two chaplains of Santa Maria Assunta of Pisa witnessed the aforementioned act of Bishop Ubaldo in 1197: ACP, Dipl. 728, in Mattei, *Ecclesiae Pisanae Historia*, vol. 1, appendix, no. 22, 67. The *Leges Ardinghi* ordered that two "vicars" temporarily replace four canons currently away from Florence: ACF, Dipl. 392, in Lami, *Sanctae Ecclesiae*, vol. 3, 1653–1654. While four "cappellani capituli Lucani" witnessed a capitular act, ACL, LL 32, fol. 31 (8 April 1259), the canons later fixed the number of such priests at six in ACL, LL 46, fol. 7v (16 July 1302). The cathedral chapter of Arezzo employed three chaplains as mandated by its constitutions: Pasqui, *Documenti*, vol. 2, no. 623, 367, con. 9. Around 1270, its bishop, Guglielmino, permanently diverted the income of two vacant prebends to support four "vicars" on account of the canons' persistent absence: ACA, Dipl. 694 (undated). In 1280, the cathedral canons of Siena elected the priest, Palmerio, to the chaplaincy founded by Master Cavalcante, rector of the pieve of Lucignano in the diocese of Siena. They promised him the distributions for choral service and a room in the canonry, benefits enjoyed by "eight of the other chaplains" (*sicut viii ex aliis cappellanis*): ASS, Diplomatico, Archivio dell'Opera Metropolitana (17 April 1280).

[106] Nevertheless, at least one chaplain, Silvestro, amassed a library of twenty volumes as rector of the church of Santa Maria in Via. These appear in the inventory, ACL, LL 32, fol. 125v (1260), which indicates that he donated the codices to the sacristy of San Martino of Lucca upon his appointment as cathedral chaplain.

[107] In 1260, for instance, the archpriest and primicer of San Martino of Lucca, appointed the aforementioned Silvestro a "perpetual chaplain" of their chapter, promising him a salary of £0.6: ACL, LL 32, fol. 122v (28 July 1260). Their capitular constitutions fixed the distributions received by chaplains, e.g., ACL, LL 40, fol. 32v, con. 20 (1 April 1281).

[108] ACL, LL 43, fol. 192, con. 10 (25 June 1294); ACL, LL 40, fol. 32v, con. 22 (1 April 1281); ACL, LL 40, fol. 40v, con. 19 (14 March 1284).

[109] Such benefactors were sometimes clerics and even cathedral canons but other times laymen. For instance, the cathedral canon of Siena, Rinaldo Malavolti, founded a chaplaincy at his own church: ASS, Diplomatico, Archivio dell'Opera Metropolitana (27 April 1288); cf. ASS, Diplomatico, Archivio dell'Opera Metropolitana (4 March 1284), in which Rinaldo had already promised to donate various properties in support of not one but two chaplaincies upon his death. Four years earlier, the Florentine doctor, Roberto Aldobrandini, had likewise established two such positions at Santa Reparata. ACF, Dipl. 533 (21 July 1280) preserves the testament in which Roberto declared his intention to found one or two chaplaincies at an unspecified church. ACF, Dipl. 534/C29 (7 August 1280) in turn presents the accord made after his death between his executors and the canons of Santa Reparata in which both parties agreed to locate the two chaplaincies in the cathedral.

in Tuscany of such foundations. Already by 1275, it boasted two endowed chaplaincies, one dedicated to St. Augustine and another reserved for the master of the choirboys.[110] Like the chaplains employed directly by the chapters, the recipients of such private benefices participated in the corporate liturgy of their church in return for distributions.[111] Nevertheless, they also celebrated votive services for their patron or his family and were usually selected by him, his heirs, or the *operaio*.[112] If these foundations increased the involvement of private benefactors in the ritual life of the cathedral, they occasionally brought spiritual benefits to the bishop and canons. In 1290, the rector of the Ospedale della Misericordia of Pistoia, Davino, made a substantial donation of £1200 to San Zeno in order to endow two chaplaincies.[113] The incumbents, whose election would fall to bishop and provost rather than the *operaio*, were to celebrate three weekly Requiem Masses, of which each would feature a prayer for Davino, one for deceased bishops, and another for similarly departed "provosts, archpriests, canons, and clerics" of the cathedral. Such concern for the deliverance of the clergy of the mother church was nonetheless unusual among private donors, whose primary concern was their own salvation and that of their family.

The endowed chaplaincies thus marked the culmination of the process of privatization that had begun a century earlier. Just as canons had split their patrimony into prebends, divided their canonries into personal rooms, and equated the celebration of the liturgy with mere labor, so chaplaincies married the interests of the *ecclesia matrix* with those of private benefactors. The number of beneficed chaplains would grow dramatically in the Trecento as wealthy donors, guilds, and communes increasingly sought to earn their place in heaven through the intercessory prayer of such priests.[114] Yet as bishops and canons oversaw the demise of common life, they did so not (or not only) for financial reward but also in order to support large communities of clerics capable of

---

[110] Guidi, *Tuscia*, vol. 1, 179.

[111] The foundation of Presbyter Davino of Pistoia, cited below in n. 113, prescribes chaplains' participation in the canonical liturgy with unusual clarity and detail.

[112] On such votive services in late medieval Italy in general, see Samuel K. Cohn, *The Cult of Remembrance and the Black Death: Six Renaissance Cities in Central Italy* (Baltimore: Johns Hopkins University Press, 1992), 205–211.

[113] ASF, Diplomatico, Capitolo della cattedrale di Pistoia (8 July 1290).

[114] For instance, the Sienese constitutions, the "Pacta et capitula vetera" (April 1364), in *Constitutiones*, 59, identified no fewer than eight beneficed chaplaincies, of which four had been endowed by an unidentified bishop and four by other patrons including the aforementioned canon, Rinaldo Malavolti (see above, n. 109). By this same year, moreover, seven beneficed chaplaincies had been founded at the cathedral of Lucca: Brand, *Liturgical Ceremony*, 290.

celebrating with requisite solemnity the sacred rites codified in their ordinals. Whatever the costs to the religious ideals that had inspired the foundation of cathedral chapters in the early Middle Ages, Tuscan canons thus strove to maintain their liturgical traditions in a manner befitting the *ecclesia matrix* and its holy treasure.

* * * * *

The central Middle Ages thus witnessed the rise of municipal and lay influence over Tuscan cathedrals, as seen in the emergence of the *opere*, the development of civic relic cults, and the role of private patrons in the privatization of the chapters. Cathedral canons bolstered their position by casting themselves as protectors of the diocesan liturgy, incorporating objects of popular devotion into their holy rites and claiming a share of oblations to their mother church. As related in chapter 6, they also orchestrated public displays of ecclesiastical ceremony via the liturgy of the Mass. On solemn feasts, this service became a public drama by which the bishop and canons performed their roles of divinely inspired celebrant and faithful ministers, thus replacing the episcopal ideal of the lord and builder with a more collegial model and obscuring their sometimes adversarial relationship. Meanwhile, the civic dimension of the mother church came into sharper focus as cathedral clergy enacted their drama before large audiences of fellow citizens drawn to the sacred rites of their *ecclesia matrix*.

6

Public Drama in the Mass

IN CENTRAL MEDIEVAL Tuscany, the bishop, canons, and laity rarely joined in celebrating Mass. Lay people who worshiped at the cathedral usually attended Low Mass (or *missa popularis*), which was conveniently positioned at the beginning of the work day at prime (ca. 6:00).[1] This was a modest service that involved few if any canons, much less the bishop: in Lucca as perhaps elsewhere, it merited the participation of only a chaplain, acolyte, and choirboy.[2] The entire chapter celebrated a more solemn, High Mass (or *missa conventualis*) at terce (ca. 9:00) on Sundays and feasts, but did not necessarily encourage lay attendance.[3] The canons of Santa Reparata of Florence celebrated such dominical masses in the baptistery, which accommodated fewer congregants than the cathedral despite its considerable size.[4] Moreover, lay men and women who did attend

---

[1] The term *missa popularis* appears in Mores, fol. 1v, in Franklin Toker, *On Holy Ground: Liturgy, Architecture, and Urbanism in the Cathedral and the Streets of Medieval Florence* (Turnhout: Brepols, 2009), 268; and *OOES*, pt. 1, ch. 10, 11.

[2] That neither the Lucchese nor the Aretine constitutions penalized canons for their absence from Low Mass indicates that their attendance was not mandatory. Indeed, the cathedral canons of Lucca required that all junior clerics attend Low Mass only on solemn feasts: ACL, LL 40, fol. 32v, con. 20 (1 April 1281); and ACL LL 40, fol. 39, con. 1; fol. 40v, con. 16; fol. 41v, con. 30 (14 March 1284). The *Leges Ardinghi* of Florence are more ambiguous, prescribing the canons' attendance at all "solemn masses before the people" (*misse sollempnes ad populum*), a formulation that might indicate either Low or High Mass: ACF, Dipl. 392 (18 November 1231), in Giovanni Lami, *Sanctae Ecclesiae Florentinae Monumenta*, 4 vols. (Florence: Angelo Salutatae, 1758), vol. 3, 1653.

[3] The term *missa conventualis* appears in the Aretine constitutions, in Ubaldo Pasqui, *Documenti per la storia della città di Arezzo nel medio evo,* 4 vols. (Florence: G.P. Vieusseux, 1899, 1904, 1916, 1937), vol. 2, no. 623, con. 3, 365 (21 October 1263).

[4] Mores, fol. 1v, in Toker, *On Holy Ground,* 268; Marica S. Tacconi, *Cathedral and Civic Ritual in Late Medieval and Renaissance Florence: The Service-Books of Santa Maria del Fiore* (Cambridge: Cambridge University Press, 2005), 98–99.

High Mass rarely encountered their bishop, for whom the archpriest or another canon substituted as celebrant on all but the most important occasions.[5] The service was truly "conventual" in that it belonged to the canons.

On the most solemn feasts of the year, High Mass was nonetheless a public spectacle involving the bishop, clergy, and laity in a ritual of association designed to encourage and represent unity. Few occasions outshone the feasts of saints buried in the cathedral since the early Middle Ages. Canons mandated the participation of clerics from all churches of the city and suburbs, underscoring the submission of daughter institutions to the *ecclesia matrix* and adding welcome voices to their choir. In a reversal of usual practice, they encouraged congregants at Low Mass to return for High Mass.[6] In Lucca, this too became an obligation. As early as the eighth century, miracles that unfolded at the crypt of St. Regulus reportedly prompted a decree that all Lucchese were to worship at the cathedral on his day.[7] Canons carefully prepared their churches for the influx of lay people. On the *dies natalis* of St. Zenobius (25 May), newly cleaned lamps illuminated the Florentine cathedral. Garlands of laurel and myrtle hung from the saint's altar and the wall dividing the nave and crypt, which had been enlarged to resemble that of San Miniato by 1230 (fig. 5.3). The bishop, chapter, and visiting clergy sang Mass in this monumental space, but it nonetheless failed to accommodate all the clerics, for whom extra seats were placed in the east end of the nave and in unusual proximity to the congregation.[8]

For clergy and laity alike, High Mass presented a drama of which the protagonist was understood to be the bishop. The earliest and most influential proponent of this reading was the Carolingian liturgist Amalarius of Metz, who focused his attention on the second half of the service, the Liturgy of the Eucharist (table 6.1). Just as the bread and wine were similar to Christ's body, so the celebrant resembled Christ, and the sacrifice before

---

[5] The Aretine constitutions, in Pasqui, *Documenti*, vol. 2, no. 623, con. 4, 365–366 (21 October 1263), stipulated that the bishop might celebrate High Mass at the cathedral whenever he wished. They nonetheless imply that his presence was rare, for they deputize the primicer (i.e., cantor) to oversee the service on feasts of the Sanctorale and Sundays during Advent and Lent and his fellow canons to do so on other Sundays. Infrequent references to the bishop in the Tuscan ordinals reinforce the impression that the bishop celebrated High Mass on only the most solemn of feasts. So too does the instruction in Mores, fol. 9, in Toker, *On Holy Ground*, 277, that a sermon be delivered to the populace on the feast of Sts. Phillip and James (1 May) by the prelate, "if he is in the city, and if not, let it be done by any of the canons" (*pulsentur omnia signa ad predicationem episcopi, si est in civitate, vel si non est, fiat per aliquem canonicorum*). That a bishop might be away on this particular feast, which had acquired great importance since the Florentines' acquisition of St. Phillip's arm in 1205, hints at the regularity of his absence on less solemn occasions.

[6] On the feasts of the Nativity and Epiphany, the Sienese admonished those who attended Low Mass to return "as is the usual custom" (*ut more solito*) for High Mass on such important feasts: OOES, pt. 1, ch. 46, 42, and ch. 71, 65.

[7] See chapter 2, this volume.

[8] Ritus, fol. 83, in Toker, *On Holy Ground*, 236; and Mores, fols. 9v–10, in Toker, *On Holy Ground*, 278, of which both directed that the cathedral canons follow the same order of services on the anniversary of St. Zenobius's translation to Santa Reparata (26 January) (fols. 73 and 8, respectively, in Toker, *On Holy Ground*, 227 and 276).

TABLE 6.1
THE STRUCTURE OF HIGH MASS (ITALICS DENOTE INVARIABLE TEXTS)

	Sung Texts	Recited/Spoken Texts	Selected Ritual Actions
Liturgy of the Word	Introit		Censing of the altar (celebrant)
	Kyrie		
	Gloria		
		Collect (celebrant)	
		Epistle (subdeacon)	
	Gradual		
	Alleluia		Procession to the pulpit (ministers)
	Sequence		
		Gospel (deacon)	
		Sermon (celebrant)	
	Credo		
Liturgy of the Eucharist	Offertory	Secret (celebrant)	Acceptance of oblations / Preparation of bread and wine (celebrant and ministers)
		Preface (celebrant)	
	Sanctus		
		Canon (celebrant)	Elevation of the Host (celebrant)
	Agnus Dei		Communion (celebrant and ministers)
	Communion		
		Postcommunion (celebrant)	
		Ite missa est (deacon)	

the altar recalled his sacrifice on the cross.⁹ In the twelfth century, Honorius amplified this interpretation by likening the Mass to classical drama. In a passage entitled *De tragoediis* and later paraphrased by Sicardo of Cremona, he cast the celebrant as a tragedian who "represents Christ's battle to the Christian people with his gestures in the theater of the church and impresses upon them the victory of His redemption."¹⁰ The dramatic role offered the bishop an opportunity to occupy center stage at his cathedral but not as a lord and builder. Instead, he was an *alter Christus* whose authority was sacramental. Indeed, some prelates acquired an aura of sanctity via their particularly affecting performances: Anselmo II of Lucca, that uncompromising reformer whose canons drove him into exile, purportedly moved congregants closer to God by finishing his celebration of Mass in tears.¹¹ That a bishop communicated the significance of his performance through ritual action and heightened emotion ensured the intelligibility of the drama even among the unlettered.

The bishop's prescribed role at High Mass complemented that of the canons as overseers of the liturgy and projected an image of collegiality that belied their often adversarial relationship in central medieval Tuscany. Rubrics in the Florentine and Sienese ordinals facilitate a reconstruction of the textual, musical, and ritual details of the service while extensive quotations from Sicardo of Cremona's *Mitralis* in the latter *ordo* illuminate the clergy's allegorical interpretation of it.¹² If the bishop, as related below, was the protagonist of the Liturgy of the Eucharist, members of the chapter dominated the Liturgy of the Word, a division of labor explicitly acknowledged neither by medieval liturgists nor, thus far, by modern commentators but one nonetheless crucial to the

---

⁹ Amalarius of Metz, "Liber Officialis," in *Amalarii Episcopi Opera Liturgica Omnia*, ed. Ioanne Michaele Hanssens (Vatican City: Biblioteca Apostolica Vaticana, 1948), prooemium, ch. 8, 14, on which see Donnalee Dox, "Roman Theatre and Roman Rite: Twelfth-Century Transformations in Allegory, Ritual, and the Idea of Theatre," in *The Appearances of Medieval Rituals: The Play of Construction and Modification*, ed. Nils Holger Peterson et al. (Turnhout: Brepols, 2004), 37.

¹⁰ Honorius, *Gemma Animae*, bk. 1, ch. 83, in PL, vol. 172, col. 570: "Sic tragicus noster pugnam Christi populo Christiano in theatro ecclesiae gestibus suis repraesentat, eique victoriam redemptionis suae inculcat." Cf. Sicardo of Cremona, *Mitralis de Officii*, ed. Gábor Sarbak and Lorenz Weinrich (Turnhout: Brepols, 2008), bk. 3, ch. 9, 218. The classic treatment of *De tragoediis* is O. B. Hardison, *Christian Rite and Christian Drama in the Middle Ages: Essays in the Origin and Early History of Modern Drama* (Baltimore: Johns Hopkins University Press, 1965), 39–41, although see also Dox, "Roman Theatre," 35–36, 42–48. While acknowledging theatrical elements in the Mass, Karl Young, *The Drama of the Medieval Church*, 2 vols. (Oxford: Oxford University Press, 1933), vol. 1, 79–111, takes a critical view of Amalarius's and Honorius's interpretations of that service due, in large part, to his comparatively narrow definition of drama.

¹¹ Reports of Bishop Anselmo II's affective celebration of Mass appear not in the *Vita metrica Sancti Anselmi* of Bishop Rangerio of Lucca, discussed in chapter 4 this volume, but rather in the *Vita Anselmi episcopi Lucensis* (BHL 536), in MGH, SS, vol. 12, nos. 29 and 31, 21 and 22, on which see Louis Hamilton, *A Sacred City: Consecrating Churches and Reforming Society in Eleventh-Century Italy* (Manchester: Manchester University Press, 2010), 72–74.

¹² Ritus, fols. 102v–107, in Toker, *On Holy Ground*, 254–257; *OOES*, pt. 2, chs. 1–86, 402–487; cf. Sicardo, *Mitralis*, bk. 3, 126–221.

meaning of the High Mass. During its first half, two canons served as the prelate's faithful ministers, the deacon and subdeacon, and recited the great scriptural readings of the Mass while their colleagues sang its most ornate plainsong, often with polyphonic elaboration. Such musical performances cast the canons as the inheritors of the musical expertise attributed to cantors in the early Middle Ages and, more broadly, underscored their role as guardians of the mother church. The target audience was (yet again) the congregation, which, like the bishop and canons, had its prescribed part as active participants in the drama.

If the aforementioned roles fell to the bishop and canons as they celebrated High Mass on any solemn feast, the chants and readings proper (or specific) to a day further inflected the meaning of that service by engaging with the significance of a particular occasion. In three instances, as we shall see, such liturgical items rendered High Mass a particularly pointed exaltation of the bishop as divinely inspired celebrant and the canons as his faithful ministers, due to the self-referentiality of their texts. First, the Dedication of the Church memorialized the consecration of the Tuscan cathedrals, tacitly evoking the traditional role of the bishop as lord and builder while overtly exalting the varieties of song—celestial, clerical, congregational—that resounded through the edifices. Second, the *dies natalis* of St. Martin presented its universally venerated saint as a local Tuscan protector and foundational model of episcopal sanctity. Third, in an inversion of St. Martin's feast, the *dies natalis* of St. Donatus of Arezzo depicted its local bishop as an object of universal veneration. Like St. Martin, moreover, St. Donatus illustrated the ability of any bishop to reveal the power of the Christian faith through the liturgy. As related in their respective hagiography, St. Martin and St. Donatus had performed their greatest miracles as celebrants at Mass, miracles that in turn found prominent expression in the plainsong and iconography of the Tuscan cathedrals. On all three aforementioned feasts, the presiding bishop thus emerged as the protagonist of a drama that glorified his ecclesiastical office and sacramental authority. He was nonetheless surrounded by an indispensible supporting cast of canons who chanted the plainsong and orchestrated the ritual that gave High Mass its meaning.

THE CLERGY AND POPULACE CONVENE

On a feast of a saint buried in the cathedral, High Mass often began with a procession around the cloister or from a nearby church that signaled to the clergy and laity alike the significance of the relics of which the presence had provoked the celebration of this solemn liturgy. On the *dies natalis* of St. Zenobius, for example, the bells called all Florentines to Santa Reparata, where the bishop delivered a sermon.[13] Next, the assembly proceeded to the baptistery, where the clergy sang the brief hour of terce while the bishop

---

[13] Ritus, fol. 83, and Mores, fol. 10, in Toker, *On Holy Ground*, 236–237 and 278, respectively.

and his ministers—the deacon, subdeacon, and two acolytes—donned their vestments. The latter properly attired, clergy and populace processed back to the cathedral, the cross and candle bearers in front and the senior canons and bishop at the end. On other feasts and in other Tuscan cities, clerics bore relics of the saint whose feast they commemorated and sang a long, melismatic chant known as a responsory proper to the night office of matins.[14] The Florentines diverged from such conventions by leaving St. Zenobius's body in the crypt of Santa Reparata and singing a responsory specific to Pentecost, a variable feast that fell shortly before or after the *dies natalis* of their patron. *Iam non dicam* quotes Christ's decision, related in John 15:15, to call his disciples "friends and not servants," an apposite sentiment given that Zenobius, as noted by both Florentine ordinals, "was our apostle."[15] The procession ended as the clergy took its position either in the choir or (as in Florence) around an altar related to the saint in question.

The High Mass that followed constituted a drama of which the audience was the laity, which nonetheless played a more active role than the term "audience" might otherwise imply. Both the clergy and the laity had their parts to play. The cathedral canons sang the plainsong belonging to the Mass Proper and the Mass Ordinary. The chants of the former were specific to the feast, those of the latter set invariable texts (table 6.1). Congregants were to be neither passive listeners to such music nor unresponsive observers to the ritual unfolding behind the choir screen. They probably understood many of the sung and (especially) recited texts: the distinction between liturgical Latin and the vernacular was not so great in Italy during the central Middle Ages.[16] At prescribed moments they knelt, crossed themselves, recited the *Pater noster* and the *Ave Maria*, and responded *Deo gratias* to prompts from the bishop or deacon.[17] Few if any would have known the texts (much less the melodies) of the Proper, but many doubtless sang or spoke the chants of the Ordinary, particularly the simple litanies, the *Kyrie eleison* and *Agnus Dei*.[18] A Lucchese servant girl named Zita (†1278), renowned for her piety,

---

[14] On the feast of Sts. Phillip and James (1 May), for instance, the cathedral chapter of Florence carried the arm of St. Phillip on their procession to High Mass: Mores, fol. 9v, in Toker, *On Holy Ground*, 277. Similarly, on the feast of St. Regulus (1 September), the Lucchese bore their martyr's body in a reliquary as they processed around the cathedral cloister: *OOL*, fol. 61.

[15] Ritus, fol. 83; Mores, fol. 10.

[16] Christopher Page, *The Christian West and its Singers: The First Thousand Years* (New Haven: Yale University Press, 2010), 401–402.

[17] Augustine Thompson, *Cities of God: The Religion of the Italian Communes, 1125-1325* (University Park: Pennsylvania State University Press, 2005), 255–258. For similar practices in late medieval England, see Eamon Duffy, *The Stripping of the Altars: Traditional Religion in England 1400-1580* (New Haven: Yale University Press, 1992), 117–121.

[18] The Sienese *ordo* directed that laymen and women chant the *Kyrie eleison* at the morning hour of lauds during the Paschal Triduum: *OOES*, pt. 1, ch. 140, 123. Honorius, *Gemma Animae*, bk. 1, ch. 19, in PL, vol. 172, col. 550, likewise ordered the populace to sing the *Kyrie* while the clergy chanted the longer and more complicated *Credo* at Mass. Sicardo reported that in certain dioceses the laity did so as clerics sang the *Gloria* and *Sanctus*: *Mitralis*, bk. 3, ch. 4, 165. Cf. Thompson, *Cities of God*, 257–258, on the singing of the Mass Ordinary by the laity.

reportedly played her part with particular diligence, reciting prayers with great concentration and avoiding eye contact, much less words, with fellow worshipers. She even chose a position among the men in the right side of the nave in order to avoid the chatter and gossip of the women in the left.[19] The laity thus formed a large and (more or less) engaged audience for the drama to unfold.

THE LITURGY OF THE WORD

The first half of Mass, the Liturgy of the Word, culminated in a series of biblical readings and ornate plainsong that began with the Epistle and ended with the Gospel. As related below, this progression was the theological and musical fulcrum of High Mass, its scripture and plainsong laden with symbolism. It bestowed upon individual canons the roles of lamenting penitents, Christ, and, most prominently, angelic singers. Moreover, the scripture and chant underscored the canons' oversight of the liturgy: the recitation, singing, and ritual fell to members of their community while the bishop remained a largely passive observer. When the deacon, subdeacon, acolytes, cantor (or his substitute), and handpicked soloists played their roles with the requisite solemnity and skill, they undoubtedly impressed their bishop and lay audience with their expertise in singing and liturgical custom.

The Epistle and Gospel not only framed the progression of readings and plainsong but also established the trajectory of this movement from lesser to greater through their diverse literary character and performance. While the Epistle usually derived from the Apostles' letters, it was nonetheless associated with the Old Testament readings of the early Christian Mass and thus anticipated the Gospel from the New Testament.[20] Additional factors signaled to the congregation the hierarchy between the two readings. The subdeacon recited the epistle to a simple tone, while the deacon, the Gospel to a more ornate one. At the cathedrals of Florence and Siena, the former stood on a low wooden pulpit in the presbytery, facing east and away from the populace; the latter ascended the loftier marble pulpit affixed to the choir screen, facing northwest toward the nave, as seen in San Miniato in Florence (fig. 5.3).[21] Elsewhere, double-lectern pulpits

---

[19] *Vita Sancti Zitae* (*BHL* 9019), in *AS*, April, vol. 3, no. 18, 503. Women were thought to be particularly prone to frivolities at Mass. See, for instance, the canon issued by Pope Eugene II at his aforementioned council of Rome in 826 and preserved in the codex of San Martino of Lucca, BCL, 124, fol. 193, in Mansi, *Sacrorum Conciliorum*, vol. 14, 1008, con. 35. There the pontiff instructed priests to urge their flock to worship at church only for the sake of prayer rather than for "dancing, singing filthy words, and dancing in the manner of pagans" (*balando, verba turpia decantando, coros tenendo ac ducendo, similitudinem paganorum peragendo*) as women were wont to do on the *dies natales* of saints and other high feasts.

[20] *OOES*, pt. 2, ch. 49, 450–451; Sicardo, *Mitralis*, bk. 3, ch. 3, 146–147.

[21] While Ritus, fol. 103v, in Toker, *On Holy Ground*, 255, notes only that the subdeacon recited the Epistle "from above" (*desuper*) the high altar, *OOES*, pt. 2, ch. 49, 450, identifies the location as a smaller pulpit next to the altar. On the variability of the positions for the delivery of the two readings, see Joseph

provided a single site for both readings but preserved the hierarchy through their iconography. One survives *in situ* in the pieve of San Cristoforo of Barga, which preserves the arrangement of a low choral enclosure and no crypt once found in the cathedrals of Lucca and Pisa (fig. 5.4). On its pulpit, an Old Testament prophet supports the smaller lectern for the Epistle, a tetramorph the larger one for the Gospel (fig. 6.1).[22] Finally, the preeminence of the Gospel was reflected in the ritual that preceded its recitation but not that of the Epistle. Having received the bishop's blessing, the deacon processed from the presbytery through the choir and to the ambo while accompanied by the acolytes and subdeacon, who bore candles and censer, respectively. He positioned himself within the pulpit with cerifers to his left and right and the censer behind him.[23] The deacon greeted the faithful with the words of Christ's seventy-two disciples, "peace be to this house" (Luke 10:5), thus making, noted Sicardo, the "listeners attentive to hearing the Lord's word, for which reason he faces them. With their hearts turned toward the Lord and their faces toward the deacon, the people respond 'Et cum spiritu tuo.'"[24] All were to stand with great reverence even as they had been allowed to sit for the Epistle.[25]

Both the general importance and the hierarchical relationship of the twin readings found musical expression in two intervenient chants likewise laden with symbolism. The Gradual and Alleluia featured the most ornate melodies of the Mass Proper. Both comprised melismatic verses sung by small ensembles of able singers drawn from the choir. The latter included a distinctive melisma, or "jubilus," on the final syllable of its invariable first word ("Alleluia") (e.g., ex. 6.3). The Sienese *ordo* provided detailed prescriptions and glosses that reveal how the performance of these chants underscored their symbolic resonance in Siena and throughout Tuscany. According to the ordinal, two clerics chanted the Gradual loudly and slowly (*gradatim*) from the stairs (*gradibus*)

---

[21] A. Jungmann, *The Mass of the Roman Rite: Its Origins and Development*, trans. Francis A. Brunner, 2 vols. (New York: Benziger, 1951–1955), vol. 1, 411–419.

[22] Gigetta Dalli Regoli, "Coerenza, ordine e misura di una maestranza: Il pulpito di Barga e i Guidi," *Arte medievale* series II, 6 (1992): 91–111; Antonio Milone and Guido Tigler, "Catalogo dei pulpiti romanici Toscani," in *Pulpiti medievali toscani. Storia e restauri di micro-architetture. Atti della Giornata di studio, Accademia delle Arti del Disegno, Firenze, 21 giugno 1996*, ed. Daniela Lamberini (Florence: Leo S. Olschki, 1999), 159. Dalli Regoli suggests that the figure supporting the smaller lectern is perhaps Moses or Aaron (p. 102) while Milone and Tigler identify him as St. Christopher. The latter likewise provide overviews and bibliographies on the Romanesque marble pulpits that once stood in the cathedrals of Pisa (p. 164) and Pistoia (pp. 180–181). The first was moved to the cathedral of Cagliari in 1311 or 1312; fragments of the second now appear in the crypt of its home church.

[23] Ritus, fols. 103v–104, in Toker, *On Holy Ground*, 255; *OOES*, pt. 2, chs. 51–52, 453–454.

[24] *OOES*, pt. 2, ch. 52, 454: "in quo auditores reddit attentos ad audiendum verbum Domini, unde stat versus ad eos, cui populus conversis cordibus ad Dominum, et vultibus ad diaconum dicit: Et cum spiritu tuo, quasi orans, ut fit Dominus cum spiritu ejus." Cf. Sicardo, *Mitralis*, bk. 3, ch. 4, 156–157.

[25] Ritus, fol. 104v, in Toker, *On Holy Ground*, 255; and *OOES*, pt. 2, ch. 49, 451, and ch. 53, 455; cf. Sicardo, *Mitralis*, bk. 3, ch. 3 and ch. 4, 147 and 161. The *Vita Anselmi episcopi Lucensis*, in MGH, SS, vol. 12, no. 79, 34, likewise underscores the importance of standing during the recitation of the Gospel. It tells how Countess Matilda of Tuscany died of fever while struggling to remain on her feet during this portion of the Mass.

FIGURE 6.1. Pulpit, San Cristoforo of Barga (saec. XII$^{3/4}$; attr. Guido Bigarelli da Como) (Alinari / Art Resource, NY).

that divided the choir from the presbytery, the deliberate tempo underscoring their labors "in laments of penitence" and struggles to "climb (*gradi*) from one virtue up to the next." Afterward, the cantor joined his subordinates and all three ascended to the pulpit to sing the Alleluia with organum, thus amplifying its joyous (rather than penitential) character.[26] The custom of reserving polyphony for the Alleluia and of singing the chant from the pulpit were distinctively Italian, but they nonetheless resonated with the traditional association of the chant with angelic choirs. Quoting Sicardo, the Sienese *ordo* cast the cantor and his deputies as "perfect and contemplative [ones] who sing the Alleluia harmoniously in the pulpits and whose place is in heaven. They are not men but angels."[27] The handpicked soloists

---

[26] *OOES*, pt. 2, ch. 50, 452; cf. Sicardo, *Mitralis*, bk. 3, ch. 3, 148–152.
[27] *OOES*, pt. 2, ch. 50, 452: "Alii sunt perfecti et contemplativi, qui Alleluia in pulpitis concinunt, quorum conversatio est in celis. Non est hominum sed angelorum." Cf. Sicardo, *Mitralis*, bk. 3, ch. 3, 152. That few if any transalpine liturgists allude to the practice of singing the Alleluia in the pulpit suggests that Sicardo was describing an indigenous Italian practice, one that was in turn prescribed elsewhere in the Tuscan ordinals.

hence underscored the transition from the Epistle to the Gospel by assuming the role first of humble penitents and second of angelic choristers. The conclusion of the Gospel in turn marked the end of the canons' virtuosic performance, which so dominated High Mass that less scrupulous lay people felt at liberty to depart directly thereafter.[28]

THE LITURGY OF THE EUCHARIST

Having recited the Gospel, the deacon ceded the stage to the bishop, who ascended the pulpit, delivered his sermon, and intoned the statement of faith, the Credo. The Liturgy of the Eucharist then officially began as the clergy sang the Offertory and the prelate and his ministers prepared the bread and wine at the altar, concluding with the prayer, "Receive, Lord Holy Father, this oblation" (*Suscipe Domine Sancte Pater hanc oblationem*). It now fell to the laity to make its offerings: in Siena, the bishop received the donations while standing at the right side of the altar, but elsewhere he entered the nave to do so.[29] This moment constituted the most direct encounter between the bishop and his flock, and underscored the status of the cathedral as a holy storehouse. Because the bishop had recently descended from the pulpit, Sicardo compared the oblations to the Israelites' offerings for the Tabernacle following Moses's descent from Mount Sinai (Exod. 35:20–39).[30]

The Sienese sang the Alleluia from the pulpit on principal feasts of the Temporale (Nativity, Epiphany, Easter, Ascension, and Pentecost) (*OOES*, pt. 1, ch. 437, 392) while the Pistoiese evidently reserved the practice for the Nativity (OOPist2, fol. 9v). The Florentines sang all three intervenient chants—the Gradual, Alleluia, and Sequence—from the pulpit on the principal temporal and Marian feasts, All Saints, the Dedication of the Church, and the feasts "of our patrons" such as St. Zenobius (Ritus, fol. 98v). By contrast, at Notre Dame of Paris, soloists sang both the Gradual and Alleluia *cum organo* on solemn feasts but from the center of the choir rather than the pulpit: Craig Wright, *Music and Ceremony at Notre Dame of Paris, 500-1550* (Cambridge: Cambridge University Press, 1989), 341. On the broader association of the Alleluia with angelic choirs in the Middle Ages, see Margot Fassler, *Gothic Song: Victorine Sequences and Augustinian Reform in Twelfth-Century Paris* (Cambridge: Cambridge University Press, 1993), 31.

[28] Sicardo of Cremona noted the "perverse custom of the laity to withdraw after the singing of the Gospel" as one reason why some bishops perhaps delivered their sermon before rather than after that reading. Sicardo, *Mitralis*, bk. 3, ch. 4, 163: "Alicubi etiam ante evangelium predicate, forte ex prava consuetudine laicorum cantato evangelio recedentium." Congregants' departure after the scriptural readings was hardly a new phenomenon, in opposition to which Caesarius of Arles (469/470–542) dedicated an entire sermon: Germain Morin, ed. *Sancti Caesarii Arelatensis Sermones*, 2 vols. (Turnhout: Brepols, 1953), vol. 1, no. 73, 306–309, cited in Joseph Dyer, "*Psalmi ante sacrificum* and the Origin of the Introit," *Plainsong and Medieval Music* 20 (2011): 97.

[29] Thompson, *Cities of God*, 251. Cf. *OOES*, pt. 2, ch. 57, 459; and Ritus, fol. 104v, in Toker, *On Holy Ground*, 255, of which the latter prescribes only that "the priest, if he shall be called, goes with the subdeacon or another as is necessary in order to receive the oblation of the people" (*tunc sacerdos, si vocabitur, vadit cum subdiacono vel alio ad hoc necessario recipere oblationem populi*).

[30] Sicardo, *Mitralis*, bk. 3, ch. 5, 168; cf. *OOES*, pt. 2, ch. 57, 460.

The acceptance of oblations in turn preceded the core of the Liturgy of the Eucharist, one that equaled if not surpassed in its theatricality the Liturgy of the Word. Standing before the high altar, the bishop recited the Preface, a brief prayer involving a call and response with the populace. He proceeded on to the Eucharistic Prayer, or Canon, which he recited in a hushed voice. Paraphrasing Honorius, Sicardo noted that it marked a crucial moment in the dramatic representation of Christ, as the latter was a lamb led to his sacrifice in silence.[31] Only toward the end of the lengthy prayer did the bishop barely raise his voice to signal its ending to the deacon. By the thirteenth century, the moment of transubstantiation marked by Christ's words earlier in the Canon—"for this is my Body" (*hoc est enim Corpus meum*) and "for this is the chalice of my Blood" (*hic est enim calix Sanguinis mei*)—came to overshadow the conclusion of the prayer. During the course of the Duecento, Italians adopted the transalpine custom of marking the pivotal moment with the Elevation of the Host.[32] Because general communion occurred as rarely as once a year, the Elevation offered lay men and women more frequent access to the Eucharist through a kind of "sacramental viewing."[33] In Lucca, the altar was to be fully illuminated and the Host and chalice to be censed continually so that the populace might perceive the miraculous transformation.[34] With the Elevation of the Host, the bishop amplified his role as the mediator by which the central mystery of the Mass unfolded.

If the cathedral chapter and bishop thus emerged as the respective protagonists of the Liturgy of the Word and of the Eucharist, proper readings and plainsong tailored the meaning of their performances to a particular feast. These survive in six service books compiled for Tuscan cathedrals (table 6.2).[35] The graduals preserve the canonical chants

---

[31] Sicardo, *Mitralis*, bk. 3, ch. 9, 218; cf. Honorius, *Gemma Animae*, bk. 1, ch. 83, in PL, vol. 172, col. 570.

[32] Thompson, *Cities of God*, 252–253; Miri Rubin, *Corpus Christi: The Eucharist in Late Medieval Culture* (Cambridge: Cambridge University Press, 1991), 49–63.

[33] Rubin, *Corpus Christi*, 63–65; cf. Duffy, *The Stripping of the Altars*, 95–102; and Jungmann, *The Mass*, vol. 2, 361–365. OOES, pt. 1, ch. 46, 42, ch. 197, 177, ch. 247, 234, prescribed general communion on Nativity, Easter, and Pentecost, respectively (on which see Thompson, *Cities of God*, 270). Its compiler, Oderigo, further noted that in some other dioceses the populace took communion on Maundy Thursday (OOES, pt. 1, ch. 149, 130). Indeed, this was the custom in Florence: Ritus prescribed general communion on Nativity (fol. 10), Maundy Thursday (fol. 36v), and Easter (fol. 46). The remaining Tuscan ordinals do so only on Easter: OOP, fol. 29v and OOPist2, fol. 28v. In what was perhaps a local custom, the Lucchese segregated the congregation such that women took communion in the cathedral and men in the cloister: OOL, fol. 32v.

[34] MDL, vol. 7, 55 (12 March 1253).

[35] James Vincent Maiello, "On the Manufacture and Dating of the Pistoia Choirbooks," *Plainsong and Medieval Music* 19 (2010): 21–33, dates the Pistoiese graduals, ACPist, C119 and C120 to between 1108 and 1127. Edward B. Garrison, *Studies in the History of Mediaeval Italian Painting*, 4 vols. (Florence: L'Imprenta, 1953–1962), vol. 3, 237–240, dates the Lucchese gradual, AVPist, R69, to the first quarter of the twelfth century on the basis of its illuminations and identified its provenance as Lucchese due to the appearance of a proper mass in honor the titular of its cathedral, St. Martin of Tours (on which more will be said below). More recently, Giacomo Baroffio, "Frammenti di richerche II (Un importante graduale troparlo lucchese: Pistoia, Archivio Vescovile, R 69)," *Philomusica On-Line* 5 (2006) has dated the manuscript to the first half of the twelfth century on the basis of its musical and literary script. He likewise confirms Garrison's identification

TABLE 6.2
SERVICE BOOKS FOR THE MASS

Manuscript	Type	Date	Provenance
ACPist, C119	Gradual	1108–1127	San Zeno of Pistoia
ACPist, C120	Gradual	1108–1127	San Zeno of Pistoia
AVPist, R69	Gradual	saec. XII$^{1/4}$	San Martino of Lucca
BCT, 52.11	Missal	saec. XIII	Diocese of Arezzo
ACPist, C121/Seville, Zayas Private Collection, 2, fols. 8-8v	Troper	1108–1127	San Zeno of Pistoia
BGV, L.3.39	Troper	ca. 1120	Cathedral of Volterra

(or formularies) of the Mass Proper, of which the five genres (Introit, Gradual, Alleluia, Offertory, and Communion) had been codified by the eighth century. The missal in turn supplements the chants with proper readings and prayers. Finally, the tropers contain tropes (i.e., introductions and/or interpolations to the aforementioned canonical chants) and sequences (i.e., a distinct genre of chant), which represent a subsequent layer to the Mass Proper developed in the centuries after 800. Collectively, these service books permit detailed reconstructions of High Mass on three feasts—the Dedication of the Church and the *dies natales* of St. Martin and St. Donatus—on which the proper chants, readings, and prayers underscored the musical and dramatic riches of the service at which they were sung. The invariable ritual actions of the Mass were surely significant to the entire congregation; however, these proper Latin texts, whether spoke or sung, inflected the meaning of this solemn liturgy in ways likely intelligible only to a smaller, more learned community—namely the bishop, cathedral chapter, visiting clergy, and the most of educated of lay people.

---

of its provenance by noting that its series of twenty-three post-Pentecostal Alleluias does not conform to the those in the aforementioned Pistoiese graduals. That the series in AVPist, R69 accords precisely with that preserved in the gradual compiled for San Martino of Lucca shortly after 1394, ODL, 10, fols. 7v–115v, on which see Benjamin Brand, *Liturgical Ceremony at the Cathedral of Lucca, 1275-1500*, Ph.D. diss., Yale University, 2006, 152–160, confirms the Lucchese provenance of the manuscript and disproves the alternate hypothesis of a Pistoiese origin set forth in Silvia Rondini, "Il graduale III.R.69 dell'Archivio Vescovile di Pistoia," *Bullettino Storico Pistoiese* 59 (2007): 53–56. Finally, on the provenance and dating of the Aretine missal, BCT, 52.11, see *Le graduel romain: Édition Critique* (Solesmes: Abbaye Saint-Pierre de Solesmes, 1957), vol. 2, 142. The majority of the Pistoiese troper survives as ACPist, C121, but two of its original fascicles are preserved in the private library of Rodrigo de Zayas in Seville: Lance Brunner, "Two Missing Fascicles of Pistoia C. 121 Recovered," in *Cantus Planus: Papers Read at the Fourth Meeting, Pécs, Hungary, 3–8 September 1990* (Budapest: Hungarian Academy of Sciences Institute for Musicology, 1990). On the dating and provenance of BCV, L.3.39, see Federica Checcacci, "I tropi d'introito in un codice volterrano del'XI-XII secolo (Volterra, Bibl. Guarnacci, L.3.39)," *Rivista internazionale di musica sacra* 20 (1999): 79–80.

THE DEDICATION OF THE CHURCH

Among the feasts of the liturgical year, few pertained more directly to local ecclesiastical history than the Dedication of the Church. As the anniversary of the consecration of the cathedral, it differed from most sanctoral feasts in commemorating a ritual act, a consecration, rather than a saint's martyrdom or translation.[36] As documented in sermons recited by the cathedral chapter at the night office of matins, the original consecrations featured such diverse protagonists as popes (in Lucca), the cathedral canons, and civic consuls (in Pisa).[37] Although conditions surrounding these original events, as related below, shaped the details of ritual practice of the Dedication Mass, the proper chants and readings made no overt references to these historical figures (table 6.3). Instead, they sounded more universal themes that amplified the association of the Liturgy of the Word with the cathedral canons and the Liturgy of the Eucharist with the bishop. The first part of the Mass focused on the varieties of music, celestial and earthly, that resounded through the church, underscoring the canons' role as guardians of the musical expertise long identified with the cantor. The second invoked biblical precedents for episcopal builders, recalling the early medieval figure of the *dominus et constructor*. Although the chants and readings eschewed the particulars of local history, they thus evoked, however indirectly, the traditional roles of Tuscan bishops and cathedral chapters.

The laity flocked to the *ecclesia matrix* for High Mass on the Dedication of the Church, attracted not only by copious indulgences but also by the outdoor processions by which the bishop, chapter, and diocesan clergy signaled the beginning of the service to their fellow citizens.[38] This rite often laid the proverbial foundation for the subsequent solemnities. The Florentines and Lucchese proceeded to and from their baptistery and around their cloister, respectively, singing plainchant that anticipated two biblical episodes featured at Mass: Solomon's blessing of the Temple and the hospitality offered to Christ by the tax collector, Zaccheus (table 6.3). In Pisa, more unusually, the route and accoutrements of the *processio missae* acquired historical overtones, recalling the

---

[36] The Florentines commemorated not one but two consecrations: on 6 November, they memorialized Bishop Andrea's dedication of the High Altar of the cathedral to St. Reparata in the late ninth century (Ritus, fol. 96, in Toker, *On Holy Ground*, 249; cf. chapter 2, this volume) and on 4 November, its rededication by Bishop Giovanni da Velletri following the reconstruction of the east end of the church around 1230 (Mores, fol. 12, in Toker, *On Holy Ground*, 280; cf. chapter 5, this volume).

[37] The canons typically derived the first six (of nine) lessons at matins from a local sermon and the subsequent three from a homily on the Gospel reading from Mass, Luke 19:1–10 (on which more will be said below). See *OOL*, fol. 63; *OOP*, fol. 51v; *OOES*, pt. 1, ch. 427, 385; and Ritus, fol. 96v, in Toker, *On Holy Ground*, 249. On the surviving examples of such sermons from Lucca and Pisa, see chapter 4, this volume.

[38] Such indulgences were usually established at the consecration of the cathedral, e.g., in Lucca (Pietro Guidi, "Per la storia della cattedrale e del Volto Santo," *Bollettino storico lucchese* 4 [1932]: 183); and in Pisa (Giuseppe Scalia, "La consacrazione della cattedrale pisana," *Bollettino storico pisana* 61 [1992]: 13). In Siena, the canons ordered local rectors to remind their flock of the spiritual benefits of attending Mass: *OOES*, pt. 1, ch. 428, 385.

TABLE 6.3
MASS FOR THE DEDICATION OF THE CHURCH

	Chant	Textual Source	Theme(s)	Diocese	Sources for variable items
Processio	R. *Benedic, Domine*	2 Chron. 6	Solomon's blessing of the Temple	Florence	*Ritus*, fol. 97
Misse	A. *Zachaee, festinans*	Luke 19:5–6	Zaccheus's hospitality to Christ	Lucca	*OOL*, fol. 63
Liturgy of the Word	Tr. *Organicis Christo*		Organum sung on the Dedication of the Church	Florence	*Ritus*, fol. 97; BGV, L.3,39, fol. 41v
	Tr. *Invisiblis Deus*		Lofty position of the Lord's house; biblical lords and builders; congregational singing on the feast of the Dedication of the Church	Pistoia	ACPist, 121, fols. 77–77v
	In. *Terribilis est locus iste*	Gen. 28:17	Jacob's ladder	All	
	Gr. *Locus iste*	Gen. 28:17	God enthroned in heaven; angelic choirs	All	
		4 Ezra 8:21-24			
	Ep. *Vidi sanctam civitatem*	Rev. 21:1–5	God enthroned in the New Jerusalem	All	
	Al. *Fundata est*	Isa. 2:2	Lofty position of the Lord's house	Lucca	*OOL*, fol. 63;
				Siena	*OOES*, pt. 1, ch. 428, 385
	Al. *Hec est domus Domini*		Sound foundations of the Lord's house	Arezzo	BCT, 52-11, fols. 268v–269

(Continued)

	Chant	Textual Source	Theme(s)	Diocese	Sources for variable items
	Al. *Sancti tui Domine*		The Lord's saints praise Him	Siena	*OOES*, pt. 1, ch. 428, 385
	Se. *Ad templi huius*		Lofty position of the Lord's house; angelic choirs; congregational singing on the feast of the Dedication of the Church	Pistoia Florence	ACPist, C121, fols. 77v–78v; BGV, L.3.39, fols. 41v–42v; Ritus, fol. 97; *OOVE*, fols. 91v–92
	Go. *Ingressus Iesus*	Luke 19:1–10	Zaccheus's hospitality to Christ	All	
Liturgy	Of. *Domine Deus*	1 Chron. 29:16–18	Israelites' offerings for the Temple	All	
of the Eucharist	Co. *Domus mea*	Matt. 21:13	Cleansing of the Temple	All	

unusually prominent role of the city's consuls in the consecration of the cathedral.[39] The procession began at San Sisto in the Piazza of the Seven Streets, the seat of the communal government. It proceeded according to the concession that Pope Gelasius II had made at his consecration of the cathedral in 1118. Clerics progressed on horseback rather than on foot, their steeds on loan from the commune. At the head of the procession rode six clergymen disposed two-by-two, clothed in white copes and carrying standards; at its conclusion rode the archbishop, whose horse was clad in a radiant white cloth.[40] The significance of the plainsong chanted in procession in Florence and Lucca was undoubtedly lost on many of the lay onlookers, but the civic religion so prominent in the course and trappings of the Pisan procession was unmistakable to all.

The selection of readings and formularies for the Dedication of the Church varied little from one diocese to another with the exception of the Alleluia; however, the precise location of the service within the church was more flexible and shaped congregants' perception of High Mass owing to the particular symbolic and historical associations of that space.[41] Originally composed for the consecration of Santa Maria ad Martyres in Rome around 609, the canonical chants drew their texts from the Bible, as was customary, but followed, more unusually, the order of books in the Old and New Testaments.[42] Mass typically occurred at the main altar unless there was a historical reason to do otherwise. In Florence, the bishop, chapter, and diocesan clergy worshiped in the baptistery in recollection of the original dedication of the cathedral complex to John the Baptist. This arrangement sacrificed the public character of the Mass for its symbolism because the smaller space restricted the number of lay men and women who could attend.[43] In Lucca, by contrast, many congregants in the nave enjoyed an unfettered view of the Mass, which unfolded at the side altar of St. Lucine, where Bishop Anselmo I had consecrated the church in 1070 (fig. 4.2).[44] As in the Pisan procession, the historical resonances of

---

[39] See chapter 4, this volume.

[40] *OOP*, fol. 51v. Gelasius's institution of the procession appears in the Pisan sermon: Scalia, "La consacrazione," 13.

[41] The variability in liturgical assignment of the Alleluia was typical of that liturgical genre in general: David Hiley, *Western Plainchant: A Handbook* (Oxford: Oxford University Press, 1993), 131.

[42] Susan Rankin, "*Terribilis est locus iste*: The Pantheon in 609," in *Rhetoric Beyond Words*, ed. Mary Carruthers (Cambridge: Cambridge University Press, 2010), 287–291. James W. McKinnon, *The Advent Project: The Later Seventh-Century Creation of the Roman Mass Proper* (Berkeley: University of California Press, 2000), 187–190, by contrast, argues that the mass formularies were originally composed later in the seventh century for the Dedication of the Church rather than the consecration of Santa Maria ad Martyres. Their texts appear in four of the six earliest surviving graduals from the ninth and early tenth centuries: René Jean Hesbert, *Antiphonale Missarum Sextuplex* (Rome: Herder, 1967), no. 100, 118–119. On the scriptural sequence formed by formularies, see Rankin, "*Terribilis*," 292–293.

[43] *Ritus*, fol. 96v. On the original dedication of the entire cathedral complex to John the Baptist, see chapter 2, this volume.

[44] *OOL*, fol. 63. On the consecration of San Martino of Lucca by Anselmo I, see chapter 4, this volume.

the Dedication echoed most conspicuously in the ritual rather than in the textual or musical dimension of its liturgy.

The readings and formularies of High Mass nonetheless alluded to their ritual context as the Introit, Epistle, and Gradual anticipated the Alleluia by painstakingly establishing the image of the angelic choirs traditionally associated with that song of joy. *Terribilis est locus iste* introduces the celestial scene by setting Jacob's exclamation after he had awoken from his dream of a ladder to heaven. Next, the Epistle develops it with a vision of the New Jerusalem in which God sits on his throne. Finally, *Locus iste*, typically sung by soloists from the choir, echoes the Introit with its incipit but it immediately redefines the referent of "this place" as the New Jerusalem: the remainder of its text derives from yet another vision of God enthroned and surrounded by angels, whose presence in the literary image anticipates the actual performance of the Alleluia by soloists with organum and often from the pulpit. The Gradual intensifies the association between celestial and earthly singers by describing the angels as a "choir" rather than a "host" (*exercitus*), as per the scriptural source. Nevertheless, the cathedral chapter and diocesan clergy might have been forgiven for comparing their entire clerical assembly, rather than the handpicked soloists, to the *chorus angelorum*.

The selection of Alleluia, the only variable formulary of the Dedication Mass, often reinforced the theme of angelic song but sometimes introduced a new one capable, in one instance, of underscoring the status of the cathedral as a treasury of relics. The Lucchese and Sienese adopted Alleluia *Fundata est,* which celebrates the lofty position of God's house above mountain peaks and thus recalls the depiction of the church as the New Jerusalem.[45] The Aretines favored Alleluia *Hec est domus Domini*, which stressed the stable foundations rather than the altitude of the cathedral.[46] The most distinctive choice belonged to the Sienese, who prescribed as an alternative to *Fundata est* the Alleluia *Sancti tui Domine*. Usually assigned to the *dies natales* of Roman martyrs, its celebration of unnamed saints offers no overt reference to the Dedication of the Church. The chant nonetheless alludes to the relics of saints buried in the cathedral upon its original consecration, none more so than St. Crescentius, the Roman martyr brought to Santa Maria Assunta in the eighth century.[47] It evoked the image of the cathedral as a holy treasury so prominent in the original rite of consecration but otherwise absent from the Dedication Mass.

---

[45] Karlheinz Schlager, *Alleluia-Melodien*, 2 vols. (Kassel: Bärenreiter, 1968 and 1987), vol. 1, 189–190. While *OOL*, fol. 63, prescribes Alleluia *Fundata est, OOES*, pt. 1, ch. 428, 385, allowed the option of either Alleluia *Fundata est* or Alleluia *Sancti tui Domine*.

[46] Schlager, *Alleluia-Melodien*, vol. 1, 200–201.

[47] The Pistoiese gradual, ACP, C120, is typical in assigning this Alleluia to the feasts of the following Roman martyrs: Sts. Fabian and Sebastian (fol. 97v), Sts. Tiburtius and Valerian (fol. 107), Sts. Alexander and his Companions (fol. 110), and Sts. Gordianus and Epimachus (fol. 110v). The singing of Alleluia *Sancti tui Domine* also resonated with the sermon delivered at Low Mass on the Dedication of the Church in Siena, one in which the celebrant reminded the populace of the relics preserved in the cathedral upon its consecration: *OOES*, pt. 1, ch. 428, 385. On the translation of St. Crescentius from Rome to Siena, see chapter 2, this volume.

With the conclusion of the Alleluia, the literary themes of the readings and formularies pivoted from celestial song to ones more resonant with the bishop, thus anticipating the transition from the Liturgy of the Word to that of the Eucharist. The Gospel recounts Zaccheus's hospitality to Christ, an episode understood to symbolize the purification of the church but that also illustrated the importance of charity. According to Luke 19:8, the wealthy tax collector immediately donated half of his possessions to the poor, an apt model for the congregation as it prepared to make its oblations to its mother church. The musical accompaniment to preparation of the altar and the alms-giving, the Offertory, identifies a more relevant precedent for charitable giving, setting David's description of the Israelites' offerings for the construction of the Temple.[48] The Communion also focuses on the Temple while privileging its religious function over its material needs by reference to Christ's expulsion of the money changers, as recounted in Matthew 21:13. The prominence of single authoritative figures such as David and Christ, rather than angelic choirs in the Gospel and the final two formularies of High Mass, resonates with the reenactment of the bishop of the Savior's crucifixion during the Liturgy of the Eucharist.

The readings and formularies for High Mass on the Dedication of the Church thus depicted Tuscan cathedrals as two holy sites, thereby amplifying the dual associations of any High Mass with the canons and the bishop. Collectively, the Introit, Epistle, Gradual, and Alleluia likened it to the New Jerusalem and, by extension, its chapter and visiting clergy to the choir of angels that stood before God's throne. Together, the Gospel, Offertory, and Communion evoked the Temple of the earthly Jerusalem and underscored the temporal and spiritual foundations of the church. As related below, the clergy elaborated these themes by singing tropes and sequences, additions to the Mass Proper that often served as glosses to the canonical chants and varied considerably from one region to another.[49] Of the three accretions documented in Tuscany, one was locally composed while the other two came from Aquitaine and Benevento. These musical imports reflect the broader blend of transalpine and southern Italian repertoires of tropes and sequence in Tuscany, an expression of the artistic, cultural, and economic exchanges facilitated by the pilgrimage routes running north and south through the region.[50] All three chants feature distinctive musical and literary styles that reflect their

---

[48] *Domine Deus* originally featured two verses that recounted Solomon's consecration of the Temple (1 Chron.: 1–3 and 8–12): Rankin, "*Terribilis*," 299. By the twelfth and thirteenth centuries, however, such verses had passed out of use in Tuscany and beyond, a process of abbreviation that characterized the broader repertory of medieval Offertories: Hiley, *Western Plainchant*, 121.

[49] Alejandro Planchart, "On the Nature of Transmission and Change in Trope Repertories," *Journal of the American Musicological Society* 41 (1988): 215–249, especially 219–220, explores the regional character of trope repertoires while Lori A. Kruckenberg, *The Sequence from 1050-1150: Study of a Genre in Change*, Ph.D. diss., University of Iowa, 1997, 86–139, stresses the division of the earliest sequences into East and West Frankish traditions.

[50] For overviews of the tropes and sequences preserved in Tuscan manuscripts and prescribed in Tuscan ordinals, see Massimiliano Locanto, "La tradizione dei tropi liturgici a Pistoia nel XII secolo. Uno sguardo

diverse provenances and elaborated aforementioned themes sounded in readings and formularies of the Dedication Mass.

Imported from southern Italy, the Introit trope *Organicis Christo* projects a vivid soundscape, celebrating the art of improvised polyphony emblematic of the musical expertise of Tuscan cathedral chapters (ex. 6.1).[51] It comprises an introduction and three subsequent interpolations to the canonical Introit, *Terribilis est locus iste*. In typical Beneventan style, these are in hexameter verse and can be read independently from the base chant: only indirectly do they amplify Jacob's sense of awe ("How terrible is this place!") by recounting the organum resounding throughout the courts of a "thundering" God.[52] The musical vocabulary—"organal voices," "polyphonic songs," and "vocal polyphony"—was not uncommon to Introit tropes and, in this literary context, describes celestial rather than earthly music. Like the image of the angels' choir cited in the Gradual, these words nonetheless anticipate the singing of the Alleluia with organum from the pulpit later in the Mass and, by extension, exalts the trained soloists among the cathedral canons responsible for this virtuosic art.

Although the Introit trope *Invisibilis Deus* was likely composed in Pistoia, it resembles its northern counterparts in adopting the function of a commentary on its canonical chant and, more broadly, on the entire service of High Mass to follow (ex. 6.2).[53] The lengthy introduction of *Invisibilis Deus* foreshadows the principal themes of High Mass in the manner of a gloss rather than introducing new ones, as does *Organicis Christo*. The introduction first anticipates the heavenly visions in the Introit, Epistle, and Gradual listed in table 6.3 by situating God's dwelling place "in the extreme height of the pole." It next anticipates the undercurrents of episcopal authority in the Liturgy of the Eucharist by naming three authoritative builders—Moses, Solomon, and Peter—of whom the second built the Temple of Jerusalem cited in the Offertory and Communion. The remainder of

---

d'insieme sul manoscritto Pistoia, Archivio capitolare, C. 121," *Musica e storia* 14 (2006): 402–421; Giulio Cattin, "Novità dalla cattedrale di Firenze: Polifonia, tropi, e sequenze nella seconda metà del XII scolo," *Musica e storia* 6 (1998): 7–29; Checcacci, "I tropi d'introito," 81–102; and Brunner, "Two Missing Fascicles," 8–9. James Borders, "The Northern and Central Italian Trope Repertory and Its Transmission," in *Atti del XIV Congresso della Società Internazionale di Musicologia*, ed. Angelo Pompilio (Turin: EDT 1990), 543–553, illustrates the "international" character of the repertory of tropes in Italian sources in general.

[51] BGV, L.3.39, fol. 41v, presents *Organicis Christo* in unheightened notation that does not indicate precise pitches. Hence ex. 6.1 draws on the version of the trope preserved in the two oldest extant sources from Benevento, of which both date from before 1050 and are transcribed in Alejandro Planchart, ed. *Beneventanum Troporum Corpus. Tropes of the Proper of the Mass from Southern Italy, A.D. 1000-1250* (Madison, WI: A-R Editions 1989), vol. 2, no. 75, 205–211. My translation of the text of *Organicis Christo* is likewise based on Planchart's (vol. 1, pp. 71–72).

[52] Alejandro Planchart, "About Tropes," *Schweizer Jahrbuch für Musikwissenschaft* 2 (1982): 131, notes the tendency of Beneventan tropes to present such "continuous discourse" rather than integrating the text of their base chants.

[53] On the provenance of *Invisibilis Deus*, see Locanto, "La tradizione," 457. Ex. 6.2 is based on the version of the trope preserved in ACPist, 121, fols. 77-77v.

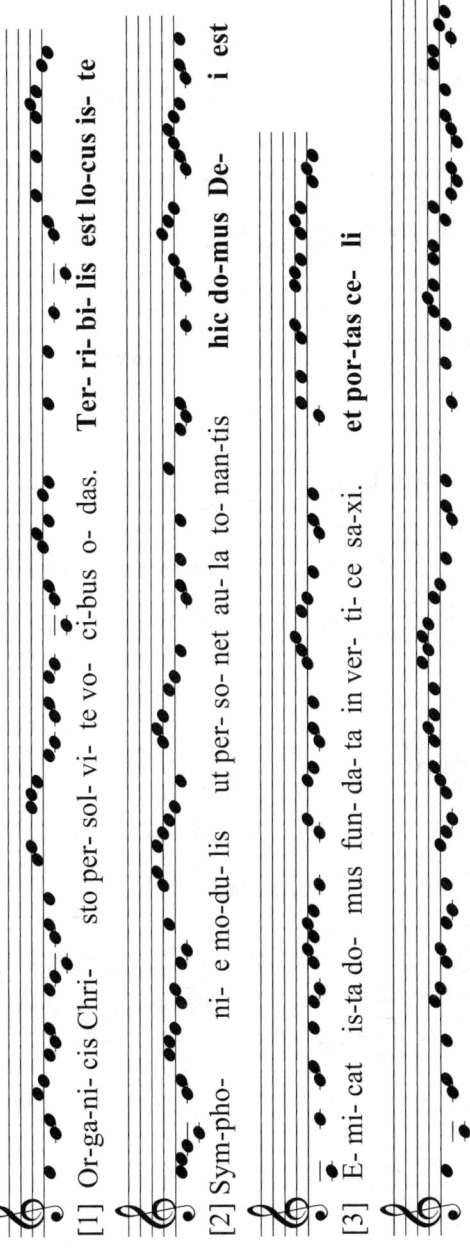

EXAMPLE 6.1. *Organicis Christo*. Trope of *Terribilis est locus iste* (Introit for the Dedication of the Church).

EXAMPLE 6.2. *Invisibilis Deus*. Trope of *Terribilis est locus iste* (Introit for the Dedication of the Church).

Invisibilis Deus glosses the Introit by integrating the text of that canonical chant into its discourse: the trope recasts Jacob's exclamation as praises rendered unto God with "one voice" rather than the "polyphonic songs" of *Organicis Christo*. In so doing, it strikes an inclusive tone that resonated with the status of High Mass on such solemn feasts as rituals of association. Even as it comments on its base chant, *Invisibilis Deus* thus evokes music that belongs to neither the angels nor the soloists of the cathedral chapter but instead to a generic "you" or "we" suggestive of the entire Christian community, clergy and lay.

The music of the Pistoiese trope underscores its literary function by amplifying rather than merely matching the melodic style of the original Introit. While *Organicis Christo* adopts the neumatic declamation of *Terribilis est locus iste*, *Invisibilis Deus* employs frequent melismas and scalar (or stepwise) motion (e.g., **supra**). The former repeatedly echoes the melodic incipit of the canonical chant: a descent from d to A and immediate ascent to d (**Christo, vocibus, Symphonie**, and **In que domo**) (ex. 6.1). This descending leap reinforces the plagal (i.e., lower) range of the Introit by emphasizing the fourth below the final (d). The latter, by contrast, shares little motivic material with the canonical chant and its rare melodic echoes of *Terribilis est locus iste* are relegated to the interpolations (ex. 6.2).[54] Far from confirming the plagal orientation of the Introit, *Invisibilis Deus* emphasizes the fifth above the final, of which the latter is transposed to a. Both textually and musically, the Pistoiese but not the Beneventan trope most closely resembles a gloss, expanding and amplifying the literary and melodic features of its base chant.

The third and final addition to the Mass formularies, the Aquitanian sequence, *Ad templi huius*, exemplifies the conventions of its genre and underscores the theme of celestial song embodied in the angelic choir.[55] It comprises prose couplets and features syllabic declamation, thus accommodating far more text than the Mass formularies. *Ad templi huius* begins with an exhortation that the congregation render joyous praise on this feast but proceeds to focus on loftier matters. One couplet recalls the Alleluia *Fundata est* by situating the church "atop the summits of mountains" while others allude to the Epistle, Revelation 21:1–5, by naming the edifice a New Jerusalem and "homeland of Angels."[56] Subsequent references to "unceasing voices" and "holy songs" that resound on high recall the angels' choir.[57] The prominence of the celestial imagery in *Ad templi huius* accords

---

[54] For instance, "**In** quo omnis" foreshadows "**hic domus** Dei" with an ascent from g to d'.

[55] *Ad templi huius* had been in wide circulation in Italy since the early eleventh century as indicated by its manuscript sources: Lance Brunner, "Catalogo delle sequence in manoscritti di orgine italiana anteriori al 1200," *Rivista Italiana di Musicologia* 20 (1985): 208–209. It is edited in James Borders and Lance Brunner, eds., *Early Medieval Chants from Nonantola*, 4 vols. (Madison, WI: A-R Editions, 1996-1999), vol. 4, 69–71; and *AH*, vol. 7, no. 223, 243–244. On the style and structure of such early sequences, see Richard L. Crocker, *The Early Medieval Sequence* (Berkeley: University of California Press, 1977), 370–391.

[56] BGV, L.3.39, fols. 41v–42: "Fundata enim est domus ista supra cacumina montium. | Et exaltata est supra omnes colles structura deifica.... Haec est illa caelestis aula angelorum patria."

[57] BGV, L.3.39, fols. 42–42v: "Sunt maiestates chori virtutes atque prestant gloriari oportet agmina sancta. | Indefessas voce laude persultant agmina.... Denique omnis eum mortalis laudet homo in excelsis decantans carmina sancta."

with the history of its genre. Sung directly after the Alleluia, its sequences were believed to have originated in the ninth century via the addition of new text to its melismatic jubilus, and indeed they often served as commentaries on that angelic song.[58] *Ad templi huius* was thus the ideal vehicle to reinforce the theme of the *chorus angelorum* already prominent in the Dedication Mass.

At High Mass on the Dedication of the Church, the historical associations of the day ceded to more general themes of music making and pious giving that heightened the associations of the Liturgy of the Word with the canons and the Liturgy of the Eucharist with the bishop. The first theme in turn encompassed angelic song, earthly polyphony, and jubilation of a unified clergy and laity. If such rhetoric would have been lost on the many congregants unable to glean the significance of the recited and sung Latin proper to the day, it nonetheless evoked two practical concerns of the cathedral canons. The angels' chorus offered a model, however stylized, for their chapter, which was expected to maintain a level of musical and liturgical expertise befitting their church. The joyous, singing congregation evoked the energized lay assemblies that, one hoped, would flock to the *ecclesia matrix* on any solemn feast. The idealized images of heavenly and mundane song were hardly isolated from the history of the Tuscan cathedrals.

Nevertheless, the readings and formularies of High Mass on the Dedication of the Church were less concerned with the bishop than those of other sanctoral feasts. On two such occasions, by contrast, these liturgical items explicitly thematized the bishop's prominence in the Liturgy of the Eucharist. The most distinctive to Tuscany was the *dies natalis* of St. Donatus of Arezzo, the only Tuscan saint honored with mass propers before the late thirteenth century. Sung throughout the region, these chants deemphasized St. Donatus's relationship with his city and amplified his similarities with an object of universal veneration, St. Martin of Tours. The saints' hagiography, plainsong, sculpture, and manuscript illumination amplify the image of episcopal virtue already prominent in the Mass by casting these two holy men not as lords and builders but instead as model prelates through whom God had revealed the mysteries of the Eucharist. A nuanced evaluation of the Mass Proper for St. Donatus thus depends on an equally close reading of the celebration of Martinmas in Tuscany.

ST. MARTIN

Although St. Martin's *dies natalis* (11 November) numbered among the important sanctoral feasts in every Tuscan diocese, it acquired particular significance in those of Lucca

---

[58] Thus Sicardo of Cremona observed that "the sequence is so called because it follows the neuma [i.e., melisma] of the jubilus" (*sequentia vero dicitur, quia neumam iubili sequitur*): Sicardo, *Mitralis*, bk. 3, ch. 3, 149; cf. *OOES*, pt. 2, ch. 52, 452. On the function of early sequences as commentaries on the Alleluia, see Fassler, *Gothic Song*, 38–47.

and Pistoia, where he had been patron of the cathedral in the early Middle Ages. While this dignity had passed to St. Zeno in the latter city, the bishop of Tours remained the titular of a side altar in its mother church.[59] The cathedral canons of Lucca and Pistoia, as related below, both commemorated St. Martin as a model of episcopal sanctity, but in strikingly different ways. The Lucchese fashioned complementary visual and musical programs with sculpture located in the portico of their church and mass formularies imported from southern Italy. The Pistoiese, by contrast, sang a single Frankish sequence that focused on the saint's status as an object of universal veneration and as a local patron. The former approach underscored St. Martin's Eucharistic miracle as a crucial sign of his holiness, a focus that undoubtedly reshaped the perception of the local bishop at High Mass. In presiding over the body and blood of Christ, the Tuscan prelate recalled not only the crucified Savior but also the divinely inspired bishop of Tours.

Since the early Middle Ages, St. Martin had numbered among the most influential exemplars of episcopal virtue. Clerics in Tuscany and beyond knew of him through the Life and *Letter to Bassula* written by his disciple, Sulpicius Severus, who had promoted his mentor as a universal and distinctly new model of sanctity.[60] Sulpicius's Martin was an ascetic whose holiness was revealed through neither magnificent building projects nor a heroic martyrdom but, instead, by his integrity and miracles in life.[61] As bishop, he continued to dress as a modest hermit and founded a second monastery where he might escape the hustle and bustle of the cathedral.[62] St. Martin became a model for such prelates as St. Fridian, who had likewise died a peaceful death and to whom the Lucchese ascribed the dedication of their cathedral to the former saint.[63] A revised Life of St. Fridian of the

---

[59] Natale Rauty, *Il culto dei santi a Pistoia nel medioevo* (Florence: SISMEL - Edizioni del Galluzzo, 2000), 233–237 (on St. Martin) and 331–334 (on St. Zeno). The Florentines claimed that St. Martin's relics lay in the altar of Thomas Becket in Santa Reparata (Tacconi, *Cathedral*, 118) but did not celebrate his feast with greater solemnity than befitted any other any other day of its rank (Ritus, fol. 97v, in Toker, *On Holy Ground*, 250).

[60] For instance, the passionary of San Martino of Lucca, BCL, P† (saec. XII$^{2/4}$) preserves the *Vita Sancti Martini* (*BHL* 5610) and *Epistola ad Bassulam* (*BHL* 5613) (fols. 178v–182v), as well as selections from Gregory of Tours's account of St. Martin's postmortem miracles and translation to the basilica of Saint-Martin of Tours in the fifth century (*BHL* 5619–5622) (fols. 182v–184): Baudouin de Gaiffier, "Catalogue des passionaires de la Bibliothèque Capitulaire de Lucques," in *Recherches d'hagiographie latine* (Brussels: société des Bollandistes, 1971), 123, nos. 110 and 111, respectively. The second volume of the passionary of San Zeno of Pistoia, BCR, 719, preserves an even larger collection of hagiographic material concerning St. Martin. In addition to the aforementioned writings of Gregory of Tours (fols. 195v–196v) and Sulpicius's *Vita* (fols. 177v–182v), it contains all three of the latter's letters (*BHL* 5611–5613) (fols. 182v–184v) and his three dialogues (*BHL* 5614–5616) (fols. 184v–195v): Albert Poncelet, *Catalogus codicum hagiographicorum latinorum bibliothecarum Romanarum praeter quam Vaticanae* (Brussels: n.p., 1909), 243.

[61] Allan Scott McKinley, "The First Two Centuries of Saint Martin of Tours," *Early Medieval Europe* 14 (2006): 175–182; Clare Stancliffe, *St. Martin and His Hagiographer: History and Miracle in Sulpicius Severus* (Oxford: Oxford University Press, 1983), 149–159.

[62] *Vita Sancti Martini*, ch. 10, trans. Sulpicius Severus, "Writings," in *The Fathers of the Church. Volume 7*, trans. Bernard M. Peebles (New York: Fathers of the Church, 1949), 116–117.

[63] The ascription of the building of San Martino to St. Fridian appears in the *Translatio Sancti Reguli I*, quoted in chapter 2 this volume, n. 42.

eleventh century recast its subject as a hermit whose upright mores moved the Lucchese to elect him their bishop.⁶⁴ Inspiration for this revision to the saint's dossier surely came from such Tuscan eremites as Romualdo, who had established his famous hermitage at Camaldoli in 1012. Writing at the turn of the twelfth century, however, Bishop Rangerio of Lucca identified the titular of his cathedral as the salient precedent: "As was Martin, so was Fridian—both of their poverty was complete."⁶⁵ This object of universal veneration was seen to have inspired the Lives of local saints even as he elicited devotion in his own right.

The distinctive character of St. Martin's holiness as witnessed in his thaumaturgy and poverty was the central theme in the mass formularies sung on saint's feast in Lucca. Preserved in the twelfth-century gradual of San Martino, these chants had originated in southern Italy and evidently did not circulate in other Tuscan dioceses.⁶⁶ Their texts derive from the *Epistola ad Bassulam*, which focuses on St. Martin's final days and thus reflects Sulpicius's search for a model of virtuous death less violent than the example provided by early Christian martyrs.⁶⁷ Hence the Introit quotes St. Martin's announcement to his followers of his imminent passing while the Gradual sets their lamentations in response to this tragic news.⁶⁸ The Alleluia recounts his constant prayer while on his deathbed, the Offertory his willingness either to live or to die according to the wishes of God. Of the five canonical chants of the Mass Proper, only the Communion departs from Sulpicius's letter, presenting a plea to St. Martin for intercession.

Just as the mass formularies drew their text from a venerable literary source, so the Alleluia and Offertory derived their melodies from older models. The latter chant is an adaptation of the Offertory *Dextera Domini*, often assigned to third Sunday after the Epiphany.⁶⁹

---

⁶⁴ See the *Vita Sancti Fridiani III*, ch. 1, in Gabriele Zaccagnini, *Vita Sancti Fridiani: Contributi di storia e di agiograpfia lucchese medievale* (Lucca: Fazzi, 1989), 155, which Zaccagnini dates to the eleventh century (p. 63).

⁶⁵ *Vita Metrica Sancti Anselmi*, in MGH SS, vol. 30, 1248, vv. 4380–4381: "Qualis Martinus, qualis fuit et Phrigianus, | Quorum paupertas nullius indiguit." On Romualdo and his hermitage at Camaldoli, see chapter 3, this volume.

⁶⁶ AVPist, R69, fols. 175v–176. Cf. Alejandro Planchart, "The Geography of Martinmass," in *Western Plainchant in the First Millennium: Studies in the Medieval Liturgy and its Music*, ed. Sean Gallagher et al. (2003), 145, on the provenance of the mass formularies and pp. 147–150 for a transcription of them from Benevento, Archivio Capitolare, 40, fols. 135v–138v. Planchart was evidently unaware of the Lucchese source for the chants, for it does not appear in his list of the few northern Italian manuscripts in pp. 140–141.

⁶⁷ In this respect, the mass formularies resemble the antiphons and responsories sung at the office hours on the *dies natalis* of St. Martin. Indeed, the Introit shares its text with the responsory *Beatus Martinus obitum* (*CAO* 6217), the Gradual with the responsory *Dixerunt discipuli* (*CAO* 6463), the Alleluia with the responsory *Oculis ac manibus* (*CAO* 7310) and antiphon of the same incipit (*CAO* 4111), and the Offertory with the antiphon *O virum ineffabilem* (*CAO* 4094). On the focus of St. Martin's office on the saint's death and its broader historical significance, see Ruth Steiner, "Matins Responsories and Cycles of Illustrations of Saints' Lives," in *Diakonia: Studies in Honor of Robert T. Meyer*, ed. T. Halton and J. Williman (Washington DC: Catholic University of America Press, 1986), 326–328.

⁶⁸ AVPist, R69, fol. 175v. Cf. Sulpicius Severus, *Epistola ad Bassulam*, in PL, vol. 20, cols. 181–182.

⁶⁹ Martha Van Zandt Fickett, *Chants for the Feast of St. Martin of Tours*, Ph.D. diss., Catholic University of America, 1983, 52.

EXAMPLE 6.3. Alleluia *Oculis ac manibus* (Alleluia for the *dies natalis* of St. Martin).

The former is similarly related to the Alleluia for High Mass on the feast of the Nativity, *Dies sanctificatus*, one of the oldest Roman Alleluias and a model for many chants of that genre (ex. 6.3).[70] As illustrated in the Martinian reworking *Oculis ac manibus*, the melody is largely confined to the relatively narrow ambitus between C and a; the emphasis on f and frequent oscillation between d and f establish the plagal rather than authentic mode. Typical of the genre is the large-scale and only slightly varied repetition of musical material (denoted by brackets) in the portion invariably sung by soloists, the verse.[71] In both iterations of the phrase, a melisma falls on a stressed syllable of text (***manibus***) and (***oratione***) and in the second it provides a felicitous and (perhaps intentional) aural counterpart to St. Martin's assiduous prayer.

If the Mass Propers sung at San Martino focused almost exclusively on the saint's death, the sculptural *vita* that adorned that church provided a complementary image of him that likewise emphasized his distinctive sanctity. Executed between 1233 and

---

[70] Ex. 6.3 is based on AVPist, R69, fols. 175v-176. It does not include *Alleluia Dies sanctificatus* because the relationship of that older chant to *Alleluia Oculis ac manibus* is not essential to the present argument. See Schlager, *Alleluia-Melodien*, vol. 1, 120–122, for an edition of *Alleluia Dies sanctifiactus*.

[71] Hiley, *Western Plainchant*, 132–136.

FIGURE 6.2. St. Martin and the Pauper (saec. XII$^{1/2}$) (Scala / Art Resource, NY). The original sculpture (pictured here) is currently affixed to the retrofaçade of San Martino. A later copy now stands in its original position on the façade of that church (see Fig. 5.2).

1250, and perhaps by Lombard master Guido Bigarelli, it comprises a statue placed above the central arch of the façade as well as four panels in mezzo-relievo that flank the central door in the portico (figs. 6.2, 6.3, and 6.4).[72] This program is the earliest surviving pictorial Life of St. Martin in Italy, and there existed few if any visual precedents for the panels. The selection of the scenes and their iconographic details surely fell to the canons rather than to Guido, of whom the former retained control over the Opera di Santa Croce until 1276 and would have drawn on the available literary sources such as Sulpicius's *vita*.[73] With one prominent exception, on which more will be said below, the episodes derive from writings of Sulpicius preserved in the canons' passionary, and they depict St. Martin as a generous Christian, fervent monk, miraculous healer, and, most important, liturgical celebrant. Yet far from neutrally representing the scenes as related

---

[72] On the attribution and dating of the sculptural program of San Martino, see chapter 5, this volume.

[73] On the relationship between the canons of San Martino and Opera di Santa Croce, see chapter 5, this volume.

Public Drama in the Mass   171

FIGURE 6.3. Life of St. Martin (ca. 1233–1250). Portico of San Martino, Lucca (north panel) (Scala / Art Resource, NY).

FIGURE 6.4. Life of St. Martin (ca. 1233–1250). Portico of San Martino, Lucca (south panel) (Scala / Art Resource, NY).

by Sulpicius, the sculpture reshapes them in ways that exalt the local bishop and the canons, and thus betray the influence of those latter clerics.

The sculptural Life begins with a demonstration of its protagonist's virtue with St. Martin and the Pauper (fig. 6.2). Still a young soldier in the Roman army, the protagonist encounters a poor man before the gates of Amiens. St. Martin cuts his cloak into two halves, of which one he offers to the pauper to ward off the winter cold.[74] Unlike the scenes depicted in the portico, the gesture of charity had been a frequent object of visual depiction since the tenth century, presumably because it was a pivotal moment in St. Martin's spiritual development.[75] In a dream later that night, he discovered that the pauper was in fact Christ and he resolved to convert to Christianity. The Lucchese further underscored the importance of charity as one of St. Martin's virtues by means of their civic ritual. On the saint's *dies natalis*, their commune paid a tailor to clothe the statue, but only after a horseman had borne the garments through the city streets for all to behold.[76] By the fifteenth century, red and white became their standard colors, and the clothes were donated to an actual pauper at the conclusion of the festivities.[77]

The continuation of the Life in the portico begins and ends with scenes that depict St. Martin as a thaumaturge and together underscore his transformation from a monk to a bishop (figs. 6.3 and 6.4). All four panels feature clearly visible inscriptions (translated below in parentheses) that facilitate their identification by literate viewers. The first panel depicts St. Martin's resuscitation of a catechumen at the monastery that he founded near Poitiers, before his episcopal election ("Martin makes the dead monk live").[78] According to Sulpicius, this miracle marked a turning point in the development of his cult: "already held to be a saint, he was now regarded as powerful in wonders and truly apostolic."[79] The final panel shows St. Martin's exorcism of a young slave, which illustrates his evangelical fervor as well as his thaumaturgic power: the saint drives a demon from the possessed, whose owner, a Roman proconsul, pledges to convert to Christianity ("Blessed Martin, you save him tormented by the demon").[80] The two panels' identical *mise-en-scène* draws attention to smaller differences that underline St. Martin's rise through the ecclesiastical ranks. In both panels, he stands at center left, attended by two companions and facing the young object of God's mercy. In the second, however, his companions

---

[74] *Vita Sancti Martini*, ch. 3, in Severus, "Writings," 106–108.

[75] The oldest surviving depictions of St. Martin and the Pauper are perhaps those that appear in earliest extant sources for the Sacramentary of Fulda (ca. 975–990), Göttingen, Universitätsbibliothek, theol. 231, fol. 113, and Udine, Biblioteca Capitolare, 1 (olim 76, V), fol. 70: Eric Palazzo, *Les sacramentaires de Fulda: Etude sur l'iconographie et la liturgie à l'époque ottonienne* (Münster: Aschendorff, 1994), 93–95.

[76] ASL, Statuti del Comune di Lucca, 5, p. 136 (30 November 1342).

[77] ASL, Statuti del Comune di Lucca, 10, fol. 144v (18 October 1446).

[78] "Martinus monachum defunctum vivere fecit." Cf. *Vita Sancti Martini*, ch. 7, in Severus, "Writings," 112–114.

[79] *Vita Sancti Martini*, ch. 7, in Severus, "Writings," 114.

[80] "Demone vexatum salvas Martine beate." Cf. *Vita Sancti Martini*, ch. 17, in Severus, "Writings," 125–126.

are canons rather than monks, St. Martin wears episcopal regalia instead of a monastic habit, and he carries a bishop's crosier rather than a book. When juxtaposed, the dual images thus exalt the episcopal office by implying that St. Martin forsook his monastic vocation in favor of that greater honor. This contradicted Sulpicius, who, as noted previously, claimed that his subject preferred the dress and habits of a hermit even after having become a bishop.[81]

The second panel likewise celebrates episcopal authority as it depicts St. Martin's consecration as bishop. While its inscription sustains the impression that he forsook his monastic calling ("You, Martin, have been called from a monk to bishop"), its orderly and symmetrical scene of six clerics effaces the rowdy yet perceptive citizens whom Sulpicius placed at the Mass of Consecration.[82] The lay people had elected St. Martin over the vocal opposition of visiting bishops, who derided the candidate's shabby appearance. Since the ninth century, episcopal elections had become the purview of emperors and later of cathedral canons. Accordingly, pictorial hagiography usually treated a bishop's consecration rather than his election.[83] As told by Sulpicius, however, God signaled his approval of the popular vote. A large, boisterous congregation at Mass blocked the cleric assigned to read the Epistle from reaching the presbytery. A layman thus grabbed the psalter and recited the verse to which he randomly opened, one that implicitly condemned one of St. Martin's bitterest critics among the bishops. The Lucchese panel, by contrast, follows iconographic convention by presenting a scene of clerical harmony free of popular tumult and (one presumes) the saint's detractors.[84]

The third panel echoes St. Martin and the Pauper in its celebration of its protagonist's care for the poor while introducing his priestly duty as liturgical celebrant. Among the episodes included in the sculptural *vita* of St. Martin, only this one depended on a literary source other than Sulpicius's Life. It depicts an episode first recounted in that author's second Dialogue. One day the bishop of Tours wore a rough tunic too small to cover his arms, one that his miserly archdeacon had purchased for him after St. Martin had given his regular tunic to a pauper. God recognized the bishop's charity by making a ball of fire appear above his head while he celebrated Mass ("Fire appears above the head of Martin as he offers up the holy sacrifices").[85] The miracle had captured the imagination of Gregory of Tours,

---

[81] *Vita Sancti Martini*, ch. 10, in Severus, "Writings," 116–117.

[82] "De monacho presul es tu Martine vocatus." Cf. *Vita Sancti Martini*, ch. 9, in Severus, "Writings," 115–116, from which the remainder of the paragraph draws.

[83] Cynthia Hahn, *Portrayed on the Heart: Narrative Effect in Pictorial Lives of the Saints from the Tenth to the Thirteenth Century* (Berkeley: University of California Press, 2001), 135–136; and Barbara Fay Abou-El-Haj, *The Medieval Cult of Saints: Formations and Transformations* (Cambridge: Cambridge University Press, 1994), 38–39. On canonical elections of local bishops in Tuscany, see chapter 5, this volume.

[84] A similar scene of ecclesiastical unity appears, for instance, in the Consecration of St. Martin that belongs to the pictorial Life executed in stained glass at the cathedral of Chartres in the early thirteenth century and reproduced in Colette Manhès, *Les vitraux narratifs de la cathédrale de Chartres: Étude iconographique* (Paris: Léopard d'or, 1993), fig. 20.

[85] "Ignis adest capiti Martino sacra litanti." Cf. *Dialogus II*, chs. 1–2 (*BHL* 5615), in Severus, "Writings," 201–203.

who included it in a pictorial Life commissioned for his renovated cathedral in the late sixth century and supplemented with inscriptions by Venantius Fortunatus.[86] In the Middle Ages, it nonetheless found more enthusiasts among liturgists than artists and their patrons, owing to the prominence of the liturgy as its background. Johannes Beleth included a summary and analysis of the miracle, arguing that, *pace* Sulpicius, St. Martin's equality with the Apostles was revealed by the fiery globe rather than the saint's aforementioned raising of the catechumen. His discussion in turn provided the basis for that of Sicardo of Cremona.[87]

Correlations between Beleth's text and the Lucchese panel suggest that the former, and not Sulpicius's Dialogue, was the literary source for the latter.[88] The saint's pose agrees with the twelfth-century liturgist, who noted that the globe of fire appeared not as St. Martin blessed the altar, as per Sulpicius, but rather as he raised his arms and recited the Preface to the Canon (table 6.3).[89] Before the widespread adoption of the Elevation of the Host, this gesture marked the culmination of a bishop's performance at Mass. According to Honorius Augustodunensis, just as his outstretched arms recalled Christ crucified, so the spoken Preface to be followed by the silent Canon evoked His cries from the cross.[90] In the portico, St. Martin faces west and thus toward the populace, a departure from liturgical and iconographic convention that places the viewers in the position of the Touraine congregants who beheld the

---

[86] MGH, AA, vol. 1, pt. 1, bk. 10, no. 6, 237–238, on which see Michael Roberts, *The Humblest Sparrow: The Poetry of Venantius Fortunatus* (Ann Arbor: University of Michigan Press, 2009), 193–195; and Brian Brennan, "Text and Image: 'Reading' the Walls of the Sixth-Century Cathedral of Tours," *Journal of Medieval Latin* 6 (1996): 77–81. Brennan (p. 78) argues that the painting ornamented the apse of the cathedral. With his inscription, Venantius conflated the Eucharistic miracle portrayed in the portico of San Martino with another one recounted by Sulpicius, according to whom a man perceived St. Martin's hand to be covered in jewels during the bishop's celebration of Mass: *Dialogus III*, ch. 10, in Severus, "Writings," 238.

[87] Johannes Beleth, *Summa de ecclesiasticis officiis*, ch. 163, ed. Heribert Douteil (Turnhout: Brepols, 1976), 320–321; Sicardo, *Mitralis*, bk. 9, ch. 52, 676–677. Cf. Jacobus de Voragine, *The Golden Legend*, trans. Granger Ryan and Helmut Ripperger (New York: Arno, 1969), 670, which likewise cites Beleth's account of St. Martin's Eucharistic miracle.

[88] The cathedral canons perhaps knew Beleth's *Summa* directly, for their ordinal integrated extensive quotations from that text. Alternatively, they could have drawn on Sicardo's revision of Beleth's discussion of the Eucharistic miracle from the copy of the former's *Mitralis* in their possession by 1239 (see chapter 5, this volume).

[89] St. Martin likewise adopts the posture of an orant in the depiction of his Eucharistic miracle in a sacramentary from the abbey of Weingarten in Swabia, New York, Morgan Library, M.711, fol. 124v (saec. XII$^{4/4}$–XIII$^{1/2}$), reproduced in Hanns Swarzenski, *The Berthold Missal, the Pierpont Morgan Library Ms 710 and the Scriptorium of Weingarten Abbey* (New York: Pierpont Morgan Library, 1943), fig. 122. By contrast, he leans toward the altar with his clasped hands on its cloth in the pictorial Life executed in stained glass at the cathedral of Bourges ca. 1210–1215, reproduced in Louis Grodecki, *Les vitraux du Centre et des Pays de la Loire*, ed. Louis Grodecki, Françoise Perrot, and Jean Tarlon (Paris: Editions du Centre national de la recherche scientifique, 1981), no. 7.

[90] Honorius, *Gemma Animae*, bk. 1, ch. 83, in PL, vol. 172, col. 570; cf. Sicardo, *Mitralis*, bk. 3, ch. 9, 218. Subsequent Italian pictorial Lives of St. Martin, by contrast, situate the miracle at the moment of his Elevation of the Host, thus reflecting the universal adoption of the practice. The most prominent example is found in the fresco cycle executed by Simone Martini ca. 1312–1319 in the Chapel of St. Martin in the lower church of San Francesco of Assisi, reproduced in Andrew Martindale, *Simone Martini: Complete Edition* (New York: New York University Press, 1988), no. 4, 174–181.

fire above his head.⁹¹ As a result, all Lucchese might contemplate the miracle despite the fact that Sulpicius had written that only a select few—a virgin, a priest, and three monks—had discerned the globe. This contradiction suggests, once again, that the liturgical commentary of Johannes Beleth was the primary literary source for the sculptural Life of St. Martin.

Nevertheless, the Lucchese panel went beyond Beleth's account of the miracle in its casting of the cathedral canons as supporting actors in the drama of the Mass. Disposed (yet again) with perfect symmetry, each figure is identifiable by carefully wrought liturgical vestments. St. Martin himself wears a narrow, Y-shaped band, or pallium, around his neck, an attribute typically reserved for the pope but often bestowed upon bishops in Italian iconography of the period.⁹² To his right stand the deacon and subdeacon: the former wears a dalmatic with its distinctive, wide sleeves, the latter a tunic with its narrow ones. They carry (one presumes) an evangeliary and epistolary containing their readings. To St. Martin's left stands the archpriest and acolyte, of whom the first wears a cope (or pluvial) fastened with a clasp, the prescribed vestment when he assisted the bishop at High Mass.⁹³ The archpriest is old and bearded, befitting his authority as the second-ranking member of the chapter after the archdeacon. He aids his bishop at this crucial moment: with his right hand he secures the page of the missal on which he indicates the Preface proper to the day. The ministers' presence beside St. Martin found precedent in neither the literary sources nor earlier images; however, it was the sort of scene familiar to anyone who had attended a High Mass and it conveyed a sense of collegiality between bishop and canons, as did that solemn rite.

The Eucharistic miracle emerges as the most significant scene in a sculptural Life that reshaped Sulpicius's narrative and thus privileges the episcopate and cathedral chapter. The relevance of the episode to the local ecclesiastical politics was clearest on the *dies natalis* of

---

⁹¹ More typical is the depiction of the Eucharistic Miracle at the cathedral of Bourges (cited above, n. 89), where the scene is viewed from the south as St. Martin faces east and with his back toward a solitary minister and five laymen who stand behind a choir screen. The altar frontal executed in the second half of the thirteenth century and now preserved the Museo de Arte de Cataluña in Barcelona: Jaon Sureda, *La pintura románica en Cataluña* (Madrid: Alianza, 1981), no. 87, 341–342, similarly shows St. Martin from the south as he faces east and is attended by two ministers. In the absence of a survey of medieval representations of the Mass, an examination of publically available images in the Romanesque style from the Index of Christian Art suggests that the posture of the celebrant *versus populum* seen in the portico of San Martino was indeed rare. That this continued to be the case from the fourteenth through the sixteenth centuries is suggested by the images examined in James McKinnon, "Representations of the Mass in Medieval and Renaissance Art," *Journal of the American Musicological Society* 31 (1978): 21–52.

⁹² Charles Buchanan, *A Late Eleventh-Century Illustrated Hagiographic Lectionary from Lucca (Biblioteca Capitolare, Passionario C): Expression of Ecclesiastical Reform*, Ph.D. diss., University of California, Santa Barbara, 1997, 138–139.

⁹³ *OOES*, pt. 2, ch. 9, 410. By the twelfth century, the cope had likewise become associated with the cantor, who nonetheless discharged his duties from the choir rather than the assisting the bishop at the altar as prescribed in *OOES*, pt. 2, ch. 17, 418. Hence the bearded cleric in the mezzo-relievo in the portico of San Martino is surely the archpriest rather than the cantor.

its protagonist.[94] In Lucca, the bishop's prescribed role began on the previous evening at vespers, when, in an exceptional move, he substituted for the cantor by donning the chief singer's white cope and intoning the introductory versicle as well as subsequent readings and chants of the office. On the following morning, the bishop's part aligned with the sculptural relief when he celebrated High Mass. The formularies, as noted above, complemented the visual program by focusing exclusively on St. Martin's virtuous death. As the bishop raised his arms and recited the Preface, he represented not only Christ on the Cross but also St. Martin's reenactment of the crucified savior. The Lucchese prelate and ministers perhaps faced west toward the populace to complete the concordance between image and liturgical action. At San Martino, the cathedral canons aligned music, text, ritual, and sculpture to construct a distinct portrait of episcopal sanctity, one that involved their own number as supporting actors and privileged, *inter alia*, the bishop's sacramental authority over his role as *dominus et constructor*.

If the Lucchese clergy employed diverse media to convey their message, the Pistoiese used a single chant, a sequence, to commemorate St. Martin's life and death. The latter adopted a set of mass formularies sung throughout central and northern Italy on the feasts of various bishop saints.[95] These chants emphasized the dignity of the episcopal office and the fidelity of its incumbent to God, of which the latter reinforced the Epistle of the day, a paean to the steadfast priest who upholds holy law.[96] The Pistoiese also chanted an Introit trope from Aquitaine, though this too derived from the commons. Like another Introit trope, *Invisibilis Deus* (see ex. 6.2), it frames the text of the canonical chant as the musical praises rendered unto St. Martin by the congregation.[97] The exploration of St. Martin's life and death thus fell to *Sacerdotem Christi Martinum* (ex. 6.4), a tenth-century East Frankish sequence in wide circulation in Italy and beyond.[98] Like the sculptural Life at San Martino,

---

[94] The following account of the feast of St. Martin draws on the prescriptions for his *dies natalis* in *OOL*, fol. 64, which remains incomplete due to the mutilation of the manuscript and thus concludes with the end of lauds.

[95] The two Pistoiese graduals prescribe the following chants: *Statuit ei* (Introit), *Inveni David* (Gradual), Alleluia *Beatus vir sanctus, Veritas mea* (Offertory), and *Fidelis servus* (Communion): ACPist, C119, fols. 135v–136, and ACPist, C120, fols. 109v–110. Only the Alleluia was in fact proper to the feast of St. Martin. It acknowledges his home city of Tours and affirms his place in heaven. Cf. Planchart, "The Geography," 40–41, on the diffusion of these formularies throughout central and northern Italy.

[96] Both the Epistle and Gospel for Martinmas appear in the Aretine missal, BCT, 52.11, 52.11, fols. 352v–353. The Epistle presents a pastiche from Eccles. 44:16 to 45:20, while the Gospel, Luke 12:35–40, sets Christ's admonishment that all watch and prepare for his coming. The missal preserves the same formularies as do the Pistoiese graduals with one exception, preserving the Communion *Beatus servus* rather than *Fidelis servus*.

[97] *Inclitus hic rutilo* appears in one of two fascicles that once belonged to the Pistoiese troper, ACPist, C121: Seville, Zayas Private Collection, 2, fols. 8–8v; cf. Brunner, "Two Missing Fascicles," 12. ACPist, C121, fol. 77, identifies the trope by its text incipit and assigns it to the common of confessor bishops. Alejandro Planchart, *The Repertory of Tropes at Winchester*, 2 vols. (Princeton, NJ: Princeton University Press, 1976), vol. 2, no. 167, 171, lists seven French sources from the late tenth, eleventh, and twelfth centuries, of which all assign the trope the feast of St. Martial of Limoges.

[98] Brunner, "Catalogo," 259. *AH*, vol. 53, no. 181, 294–297, provides an edition of the text of *Sacerdotem Christi Martinum* and a list of its manuscript sources throughout Europe. Cf. Borders and Brunner, *Early Medieval*

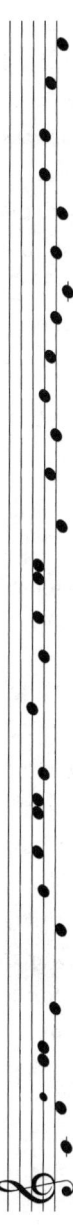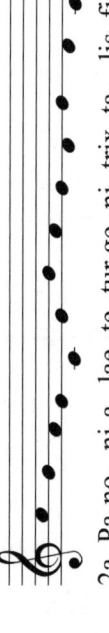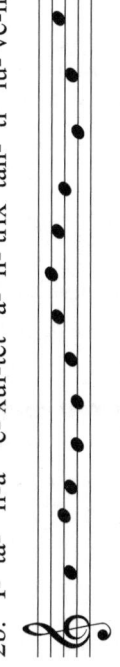

EXAMPLE 6.4. *Sacerdotem Christi Martinum* (Sequence for the *dies natalis* of St. Martin) (first three of nine verses)

the chant recounts the miracles through which St. Martin's holiness was revealed; however, it concomitantly thematizes both the local and universal characters of his cult, an appropriate topic for a work with broad appeal and one composed far from the saint's burial site.

Sacerdotem Christi Martinum conforms to the literary and musical conventions evident in the sequence for the Dedication of the Church, *Ad templi huius*, discussed in the previous section. Its melody sets in an almost entirely syllabic fashion nine unrhyming and irregular couplets. The introductory element setting the first three words ("Martin, Christ's priest") is fairly typical of the genre but acquires particular significance by emphasizing St. Martin's priestly office. The remainder of the first couplet attributes musical praises of St. Martin to the universal church, and the last makes a plea for his intercession on the part of an unnamed congregation. The second and third couplets elaborate on the geographical breadth of his cult by explaining its appeal in various regions. Verses 2a and 2b are the shortest in the entire sequence and note that Panonia (in present-day Hungary) was the place of St. Martin's birth, Italy that of his youth as a Roman soldier. Verses 3a and 3b are much longer and argue for the universality of the saint's cult: all Christians, we learn, might enjoy his patronage despite the claims of the French on his episcopate and of Tours on his relics. The contrasting melodies of the second and third couplets are not atypical of sequences in general, but further a broader literary aim in this instance by throwing this message into high relief. Both couplets begin on the reciting tone (a) and conclude with a similar approach to the final (d). Yet the second is confined to the fifth between those two pitches; the third, by contrast, rises to the octave above the final, introducing a higher tessitura between a and d' similarly emphasized in subsequent verses (not transcribed). As they sang through this triumphant ascent to d' not once but twice with the performance of verses 3a and 3b, such Italian clerics as the cathedral canons of Pistoia made their own claim to the cult of St. Martin.

The remainder of *Sacerdotem Christi Martinum* explores the distinctive nature of its subject's holiness by emphasizing his virtuous conduct and miracles as originally recounted by Sulpicius Severus. Like the sculptural Life at San Martino, it begins with St. Martin's signature act of charity before the gates of Amiens (verse 4b) and proceeds to his healing of the sick, exorcism, and raising of the dead (verses 6a and 6b). In the place of St. Martin's consecration, the sequence lauds another act of episcopal authority, his destruction of pagan shrines (verse 7a), which provides a dramatic foil for the bishop's celebration of the Catholic liturgy as illustrated in the Eucharistic miracle (verse 7b).[99] Finally, it celebrates St. Martin's virtuous death by citing his pious prayer in the days

---

Chants, vol. 4, 365–367, for an edition of the music and text as it appears in the late eleventh-century troper from Nonantola, BCR, 1741, fols. 121–122v. Ex. 6.4 is based on Seville, Zayas Private Collection, 2, fols. 9v-11.

[99] *Sacerdotem Christi Martinum* evidently draws on the inscription of Venantius Fortunatus, for it cites the light that encircled his bare arms rather than the ball of fire as per Sulpicius Severus's account (see above, n. 86).

before his passing (verses 8a and 8b). The chant borrows the phrase "with eyes and hands raised to heaven" (*oculis ac manibus in celum*) from Sulpicius's *Letter to Bassula*, one also employed in the Alleluia sung at San Martino (see ex. 6.3).

In Pistoia and Lucca, then, High Mass on the *dies natalis* of St. Martin acquired particular importance owing to the dedication of their cathedrals to that holy bishop. In both cities, as throughout western Christendom, St. Martin was a model of episcopal sanctity distinct from that offered by early Christian martyrs, as well as famous bishop builders such as his contemporary, St. Ambrose. The Pistoiese and Lucchese nonetheless followed different approaches in commemorating the bishop of Tours: the former imported a northern sequence that emphasized St. Martin's dual role as local patron and object of universal veneration; the latter chanted southern Mass formularies that complemented the exceptional sculptural Life at their church. In Lucca, moreover, the most poignant of the miracles ascribed to St. Martin was the ball of fire that appeared above his head. God's recognition of his charity not only rendered him an "equal of the Apostles" but also added Martinian overtones to the Christological ones associated with the local bishop's performance at High Mass.

The cult of St. Martin was a model for those of local bishop saints in and beyond Tuscany. The Lucchese, as noted above, amplified the similarities between St. Fridian and St. Martin in a revised Life of the former. The Florentines surely thought of the Touraine bishop as they processed to their cathedral on the *dies natalis* of their episcopal father and "apostle," Zenobius.[100] Upon entering Santa Reparata, they sang the same Introit, Gradual, Offertory, and Communion as did the Pistoiese on St. Martin's feast, similarly modifying the first chant with tropes.[101] Nevertheless, affinities with the bishop of Tours were most evident in St. Donatus of Arezzo, whose local relic cult was the only one to spread throughout and beyond the region, and who was thus a quasi-universal figure analogous to St. Martin. He was likewise exceptional in Tuscany for eliciting proper mass formularies, products of local Aretine initiative of which the texts nonetheless cast St. Donatus as an object of broad veneration. Moreover, the plainsong focused on a Eucharistic miracle redolent of St. Martin's own, yet one that underscored with even greater clarity the role of the episcopal celebrant at High Mass as vessel for divine power and the status of the cathedral canons as his faithful ministers.

ST. DONATUS

Alone among the saints buried in medieval Tuscany, St. Donatus became an object of universal veneration throughout the region. With little exaggeration did the cathedral canons of Florence rank his *dies natalis* (7 August) among the "principal feasts that are celebrated by

---

[100] See above, n. 15.
[101] Ritus, fol. 83, in Toker, *On Holy Ground*, 236.

the entire Christian populace with great devotion."[102] The spread of St. Donatus's cult had begun by the late sixth century, as illustrated in his inclusion in three sources that identified the saint as an Aretine bishop but not a martyr: the earliest comprehensive martyrology, the *Martyrologium Hieronymianum*, the collection of prayers (or sacramentary) ascribed to Pope Gelasius I (492–496), and the *Dialogues* of Gregory the Great.[103] By the early eighth century, there circulated a Passion identifying St. Donatus as a pious Roman youth who had fled the persecutions of Julian the Apostate (†363) and found refuge in Arezzo, where he was elected bishop and martyred at approximately thirty years of age.[104] The *passio* in turn shaped the accounts of St. Donatus in the influential martyrologies of Bede (ca. 731) and Ado of Vienne (†875), by whose lifetime Arezzo had become a waystation for emperors and kings who wished to venerate its martyr's relics.[105] His unique prominence among Tuscan saints throughout and beyond the region found expression in ancient and wealthy suburban basilicas dedicated to him in Lucca and Siena, as well as in the altar that purportedly contained his relics in the cathedral of Pistoia.[106] No less than Peter Damian acknowledged St. Donatus's importance in a sermon delivered at San Donato on its titular's feast. The eleventh-century ecclesiastical reformer concluded by proclaiming that "the omnipotent God desired to illuminate the entire Tuscan community" through the Aretine martyr.[107]

---

[102] Ritus, fol. 98v, in Toker, *On Holy Ground*, 251: "Precipua feasta dicuntur que a toto christiano populo magna devotione celebrantur."

[103] *Martyrologium Hieronymianum*, in *AS*, November, vol. 2, pt. 1, 102; H. A. Wilson, ed. *The Gelasian Sacramentary* (Oxford: Oxford University Press, 1894), 189; and Pope Gregory I, *Dialogues*, ed. Adalbert de Vogüé, trans. Paul Antin, 3 vols. (Paris: Éditions du Cerf, 1978, 1979, and 1980), vol. 2, bk. 1, no. 7, 68–69. Pierluigi Licciardello, *Agiografia aretina altomedievale: Testi agiografici e contesti socio-culturali ad Arezzo tra VI e IX secolo* (Florence: SISMEL - Edizioni del Galluzzo, 2005), 229–243, surveys the early history of St. Donatus's cult.

[104] *Passio Sancti Donati I*, in Corrado Lazzeri, *La donazione del tribuno romano Zenobio al vescovo d'Arezzo San Donato (sec. IV)* (Arezzo: Reale Accademia Petrarca, 1938), 117–121, on which see chapter 2, this volume. According to this narrative, St. Donatus was the same age or perhaps slightly younger than Julian (b. 331/332) and was martyred in 362.

[105] The martyrologies appear in PL, vol. 94, cols. 1000–1001, and vol. 123, cols. 320–321, respectively. See chapter 3 this volume, on the imperial and royal custom of venerating St. Donatus.

[106] On the development of San Donato of Lucca, first documented in 760 and located due west of the city before its destruction in the first decade of the sixteenth century, see Domenico Corsi, "La Canonica di S. Donato di Lucca e le constitutzioni dei Canonici del 26 maggio 1322," in *Scritti in onore di Mons. Giuseppe Turrini* (Verona: Accademia di Agricoltura Scienze e Lettere di Verona, 1973), 167–216. San Donato of Siena numbered among the six ancient "cardinal churches" located in the Sienese suburbs and enclosed within the new ring of city walls constructed in the twelfth century: Michele Pellegrini, *Chiesa e città: Uomini, comunità e istituzioni nella società senese del XII e XIII secolo* (Rome: Herder, 2004), 347–348. On the altar of St. Donatus in San Zeno of Pistoia, see OOPist2, fol. 63r: "in festo beati Donati, de cuius reliquiis sunt in altari beati Proculi."

[107] Peter Damian, *Sermones*, ed. Giovanni Lucchesi (Turnhout: Brepols, 1983), sermon 38, no. 11, 239: "per quos, tamquam geminos superni luminis oculos, omnipotens Deus totius Tusciae corpus voluit illustrare." The present sermon was one of four that Peter Damian delivered in honor of local Aretine martyrs, of whom the others were Sts. Laurentinus, Pergentinus, Flora, and Lucilla. Together, these sermons underscore the author's fervent devotion to the holy treasure of Arezzo: Giovanni Lucchesi, "Il sermonario di S. Pier Damiani," *Studi Gregoriani* 10 (1975): 65.

The broad appeal of St. Donatus's cult is likewise evident in the diffusion of his mass formularies, products of local Aretine initiative nonetheless intended for wider adoption. They belong to the program of reform and rebuilding promoted by Bishops Elemperto and Alberto between 986 and 1023, one that included the reinstitution of the Rule of Aachen among the canons, the rebuilding of the cathedral and canonry, and the laying of the foundations of the new martyrium of San Donato at Pionta. As depicted in a revised Passion attributable to one of the reformed canons, St. Donatus now resembled the current Aretine prelates as builder and imperial client.[108] This second *passio* was the textual source for the Mass Proper, which in turn derived its melodies from older formularies sung on other feasts.[109] First recorded in a cathedral sacramentary compiled between 1015 and 1025, the plainsong (like the *passio*) was undoubtedly the canons' work and predated the episcopate of Bishop Teodaldo (1023–1036) and the arrival of his client, the celebrated choirmaster, Guido of Arezzo.[110] That the chants make no reference to the building project ascribed to St. Donatus in the revised Passion suggests (once again) that Tuscan canons had little interest in celebrating in song their episcopal father as a *dominus et constructor*. Yet it also accords with their evident desire for a broader audience for the plainsong, which makes no mention of Arezzo and portrays St. Donatus as patron of an unidentified congregation. Indeed, by the twelfth century and probably much earlier, the formularies were sung in dioceses throughout the region and beyond.[111]

---

[108] See chapter 3, this volume.

[109] Mario Sironi, "La Messa di San Donato," in *Codex Angelicus 123. Studi sul graduale-tropario bolognese del secolo XI e sui manoscritti collegati*, ed. Maria Teresa Rosa-Barezzani and Giampaolo Ropa (Cremona: Una cosa rara, 1996), 319–322, identifies the melodic sources for the mass formularies while Brian Møller Jensen, "'Magni presulis celebrans Doanti diem sollemnem': Bishop Donatus of Arezzo in Roma, Bibl. Angelica 123," *Rivista internazionale di musica sacra* 22 (2000): 125–133, explores their liturgical and interpretative significance. Sironi, "La Messa" (pp. 326–333) provides a transcription of the Mass of St. Donatus based on its earliest manuscript sources; Eun Ju Kim, "La messa di San Donato nella tradizione aretina," *Rivista internazionale di musica sacra* 21 (2000): 143–147, offers one based on an Aretine choirbook, ACA, Duomo H, fols. 63–65v (ca. 1300).

[110] The Aretine sacramentary, BAV, Vat. Lat. 4772, fols. 112v–113, identifies the incipits of the canonical chants of the Mass Proper. For the dating of the sacramentary, see Licciardello, *Agiografia aretina*, 424–425. Giovanni Alpigiano, "Alcune precisazioni sulla Messa di San Donato," *Rivista internazionale di musica sacra* 25 (2004): 124–126; and Licciardello, *Agiografia aretina*, 323–325, correct the *terminus ante quem* of 980 proposed for the Mass Proper by Sironi, "La Messa," 322–323. That the formularies were not the work of Guido finds further support in the derivation of their melodies from older models and consequent failure to conform to the rules of musical composition outlined in chs. 11, 13, and 15 of his *Micrologus*, Joseph Smits van Waesberghe, ed., *Guidonis Aretini Micrologus* (n.p.: American Institute of Musicology, 1955), 139–146, 150–157, and 162–177.

[111] The earliest surviving source for the complete chants is the Bolognese gradual, Rome, Biblioteca Angelica, 123, fols. 129–129v (1029–1039), in *PM*, vol. 18. The Tuscan sources for the Mass Proper are ACPist, C119, fols. 123v–124, and C 120, fols. 99v–100; AVPist, R69, fol. 155–156; and BCT, 52.11, fols. 325–326v. Sironi, "La Messa," 311, provides a more comprehensive list of manuscript source for the mass formularies but does not include the Lucchese gradual, AVPist, R69. The ordinals of Pistoia and Siena also illustrate the dissemination of the formularies throughout Tuscany by identifying the Introit by its incipit: OOPist2, fol. 63, and

Through their text and music, the Aretine formularies elaborated contrasting readings at High Mass, celebrating St. Donatus's dual status as martyr and bishop. The Epistle, Wisdom 3:1–9, evokes the passing of martyrs from this world and their glorious rewards in the next.[112] The Gospel, Luke 12:35–40, was assigned to feasts of such bishops as St. Martin and sets Christ's words to his followers to prepare for his second coming.[113] As on the Dedication of the Church, the Gradual and Alleluia sustain the theme of the Epistle. The melody of the former derives from the Gradual, *Gloriosus Deus*, sung on the feast days of Roman martyrs, thus underscoring the Aretine bishop's Roman lineage and his heroic sacrifice. The Alleluia celebrates the martyrdom of the saint and his companion by proclaiming, "Today blessed Donatus and Hylarian migrate to the Lord."[114] The word *today* conflates the time of the execution with that of the chanting of the Alleluia, a convention characteristic of nonbiblical liturgical texts and dubbed the *hinc et nunc* ("here and now").[115]

The second, even more prominent theme of the mass formularies was the dignity of St. Donatus's episcopal office to which the Gospel alluded, one that undoubtedly redounded on the image of the bishop as the virtuous celebrant at High Mass. It in turn underscored the affinities between this Aretine saint and St. Martin, as did the widespread diffusion of their cults. According to both versions of his Passion, St. Donatus, like St. Martin, was a committed ascetic and evangelizing bishop who performed miraculous acts of healing upon his flock; however, it was his signature miracle, which unfolded at his first episcopal Mass, that most distinctly recalled the Touraine bishop. According to St. Donatus's first Passion, this service attracted not only Christians but also pagans.[116] Unlike the Eucharistic miracle of St. Martin, one of the bishop's ministers played a supporting role: when the deacon, Antimus, offered Christ's blood to the faithful, the pagans surged forward and knocked from his hand the chalice, which shattered as it hit the pavement. St. Donatus comforted a distressed Antimus, a compassionate gesture between a bishop and minister that surely appealed to cathedral canons eager to cast their relationship with their prelate as collegial. St. Donatus instructed Antimus to collect the fragments, before which the bishop knelt and implored the Lord to repair

---

OOES, pt. 1, ch. 379, 344. Among the Tuscan cathedral canons, only the Florentines expressly proscribed the singing of such proper chants: Ritus, fol. 89v, in Toker, *On Holy Ground*, 242.

[112] BCT, 52.11, fols. 325–325v; cf. Ritus, fol. 66v, in Toker, *On Holy Ground*, 221, which identifies Ws. 3:1–9 as the first of six possible selections for the Epistle on the feasts of multiple martyrs. Another selection prescribed in the Florentine ordinal was Heb. 11:33–39, which the Sienese in turn recited on the feast of St. Donatus: *OOES*, pt. 1, ch. 379, 344.

[113] BCT, 52.11, fol. 326; cf. n. 96 above for the Gospel on the feast of St. Martin, as well as Ritus, fol. 66, which identifies Luke 12:35–40 as the third of five possible selections for the Gospel of the feast of a bishop. The Sienese, by contrast, recited Luke 10:16 ff.: *OOES*, pt. 1, ch. 379, 344.

[114] BCT, 52.11, fol. 326: "Alleluia. Beatus Donatus et Hylarianus hodie migrarunt ad Dominum."

[115] Kruckenberg, "The Sequence," p. 267, n. 42.

[116] *Passio Sancti Donati I*, in Lazzeri, *La donazione*, 128.

the vessel so that all in attendance might know God's dominion over heaven and earth. After St. Donatus had returned to his feet and presented the chalice made whole to the deacon, the faithful rejoiced and seventy-nine of the pagans converted to Christianity. If the Eucharistic miracle of St. Martin had illustrated God's approval of an act of charity, this one thus revealed the power of the Christian faith as worked through a new bishop. Already by the seventh century, it was the definitive sign of St. Donatus's sanctity, long before the twelfth-century liturgist Johannes Beleth had deemed the globe of fire to have rendered St. Martin the equal of the Apostles.[117]

With the revised *Passio Sancti Donati*, the cathedral canons of Arezzo provided a longer account of the miracle of the chalice, of which the immediate resonance they amplified by updating its details to conform to contemporary liturgical practice. The Passion underscored the dramatic character of the liturgical service by explaining that the pagans rushed toward Antimus out of curiosity for the spectacle of the holy sacrifice. It likewise provided greater detail concerning the liturgy: Antimus lay the fragments of the chalice not, as per the original Passion, on an unnamed vestment belonging to St. Donatus, but instead on the bishop's amice, or neck cloth.[118] Finally, the second *Passio* reflected a heightened concern for pastoral care by transforming the entire episode into an opportunity for lay instruction.[119] St. Donatus's words of comfort to his deacon became an exhortation to the congregation: "Brother Antimus and dearest children, grieve not, but instead take strength in the Lord, knowing that the judgment of the Governor permits not a plotter of the human sort to do such a thing without cause: for that steward, who uses evil for good, can change your sadness into joy."[120] St. Donatus completed his lesson by lifting up the miraculously repaired chalice in order to show the assembly of Christians and pagans the efficacy of faith. The ritual actions of the late Antique bishop resonated with those of his medieval counterparts: his gesture

---

[117] In his brief description of the Aretine saint, Gregory the Great cited neither St. Donatus's miracles of healing nor his heroic martyrdom, but instead described him as he "who restored a broken chalice" (Gregory I, *Dialogues*, vol. 2, bk. 1, no. 7, 68–69). Peter Damian likewise devoted a far greater portion of his aforementioned sermon on Donatus's feast to the saint's repair of the chalice than to his other miracles: Damian, *Sermones*, sermon 38, nos. 5–6, 235–236.

[118] Celebrants had worn the amice at Mass since the eighth century as first documented in Ordo Romanus I (saec. VII^{ex}-VIII^{in}), in Michel Andrieu, *Les Ordines Romani du Haut Moyen Age*, 5 vols. (Louvain: Spicilegium Sacrum Lovaniense, 1931–1961), vol. 2, 78. See Cyril E. Pocknee, *Liturgical Vesture: Its Origins and Development* (London: Mowbray, 1960), 18.

[119] Note, however, that pastoral care was not among the primary concerns of eleventh-century reformers: Colin Morris, *The Papal Monarchy: The Western Church from 1050 to 1250* (Oxford: Oxford University Press, 1989), 100.

[120] *Passio Sancti Donati II*, in Giovanni Alpigiano and Pierluigi Licciardello, *Officium Sancti Donati I: L'ufficio liturgico di san Donato di Arezzo nei manoscritti toscani medievali* (Florence: Edizioni del Galluzzo, 2008), ch. 11, nos. 7–8, 371: "Anthime frater et dilectissimi filii, tristari nolite, sed confortamini in Domino, scientes non sine causa tale aliquid insidiator humani generis permissus est facere Gubernatoris iudicio. Ipse enim dispensator, qui malo bene utitur, potest tristitiam vestram mutare in gaudium."

anticipated the Elevation of the Host by which Tuscan bishops similarly demonstrated the power of Christian belief.

Just as the Eucharistic miracle acquired heightened resonance in the revised Passion, so it became a dominant theme of the mass formularies sung on the feast of St. Donatus. The Introit and Gradual integrate St. Donatus's prayer to God into their pleas for intercession. Hence that bishop's words now belong to the congregation gathered in celebration on his feast: in emulation of St. Donatus, the faithful address God as "the omnipotent one who elevates the broken and repairs the shattered."[121] Moreover, the longest of the formularies, the Offertory, *Confractum vitreum*, cites the repaired vessel as the first of three miracles performed by St. Donatus after his episcopal election (ex. 6.5). The second and third miracles named in the Offertory were new to the revised Passion and depict St. Donatus as defender of his city: the heroic bishop slays a menacing dragon and purifies the well polluted by it. Nevertheless, the conspicuous absence of any reference to Arezzo in the chant undercuts the potential for civic overtones that often accompanied the image of the *defensor civitatis*. *Confractum vitreum* instead concludes on a note of universal celebration by lauding the martyrdom of the bishop and his companion, Hylarian.[122] With their proper liturgy for High Mass on the feast of St. Donatus, the Aretines thus sacrificed an opportunity to articulate their exclusive claims to their saint's cult in order to emphasize his appeal to all Christians.

The derivation of the melody of *Confractum vitreum* from *Stetit angelus*, an Offertory sung on the feast of another dragon slayer, St. Michael (29 September), constitutes the richest example of musical borrowing among the mass formularies. The latter chant was an unusually florid model that provided a fitting musical vehicle for the celebration of St. Donatus's death.[123] The melismatic declamation and wide ambitus of *Stetit angelus* (and thus of *Confractum vitreum*) rival those of the preceding Gradual and Alleluia. Particularly

---

[121] BCT, 52.11, fol. 325: "*Domine* Hiesu Christe, *qui confracta erigis* omnipotens, gregem tuum protege in die hac beatorum Donati et Hylariani piissimis precibus quorum festa colimus. V. *Da letitiam plebi tue congregate in nomine sancto tuo* Domine." Italics denote the text drawn from the *Passio Sancti Donati II*, ed. Alpigiano and Licciardello, *Officium Sancti Donati*, ch. 11, no. 12, 372. Cf. Jensen, "'Magni presulis,'" 125–126. The quotation in the Gradual, by contrast, is more fleeting but nonetheless distinctive: "Sancte pater Donate, cunctas [sic] coram te consistimus, ora pro omni qui convenit populo. V. *Aufer* plebi *tristitia[m]* impetrans populo veniam tuis sanctis precibus" (BCT, 52.11, fol. 325v).

[122] The Aretine sacramentary, BAV, Vat. Lat. 4772, fol. 113, includes four alternative post-communion prayers not included in the missal, BCT, 52.11, fol. 326v. Two echo the Introit, Gradual, and Offertory by citing St. Donatus's Eucharistic miracle: "God, you who deigned to restore the fragments of the cup in the hands of your martyr and bishop, blessed Donatus" (*Deus, qui in beati Donati martyris tui atque pontificis manibus poculi fraugmenta restaurare dignatus es*).

[123] Ex. 6.5 is based on ACPist C119, fol. 124 (for *Confractum vitreum*) and fols. 134-134v (for *Stetit angelus*). *Stetit Angelus* itself derived its melody from the older Offertory, *Viri Galilaei* (for the Ascension), which was in turn the model for a third Offertory, *Iustorum animae* (from the common of martyrs): Ruth Steiner, "Some Questions about the Gregorian Offertories and their Verses," *Journal of the American Musicological Society* 19 (1966): 173–174. Sironi, "La Messa," 321, identifies *Iustorum animae* as the source for *Confractum*

EXAMPLE 6.5. Comparison of *Confractum vitreum* and *Stetit angelus* (Offertories for the *dies natalis* of St. Donatus of Arezzo and the feast of St. Michael).

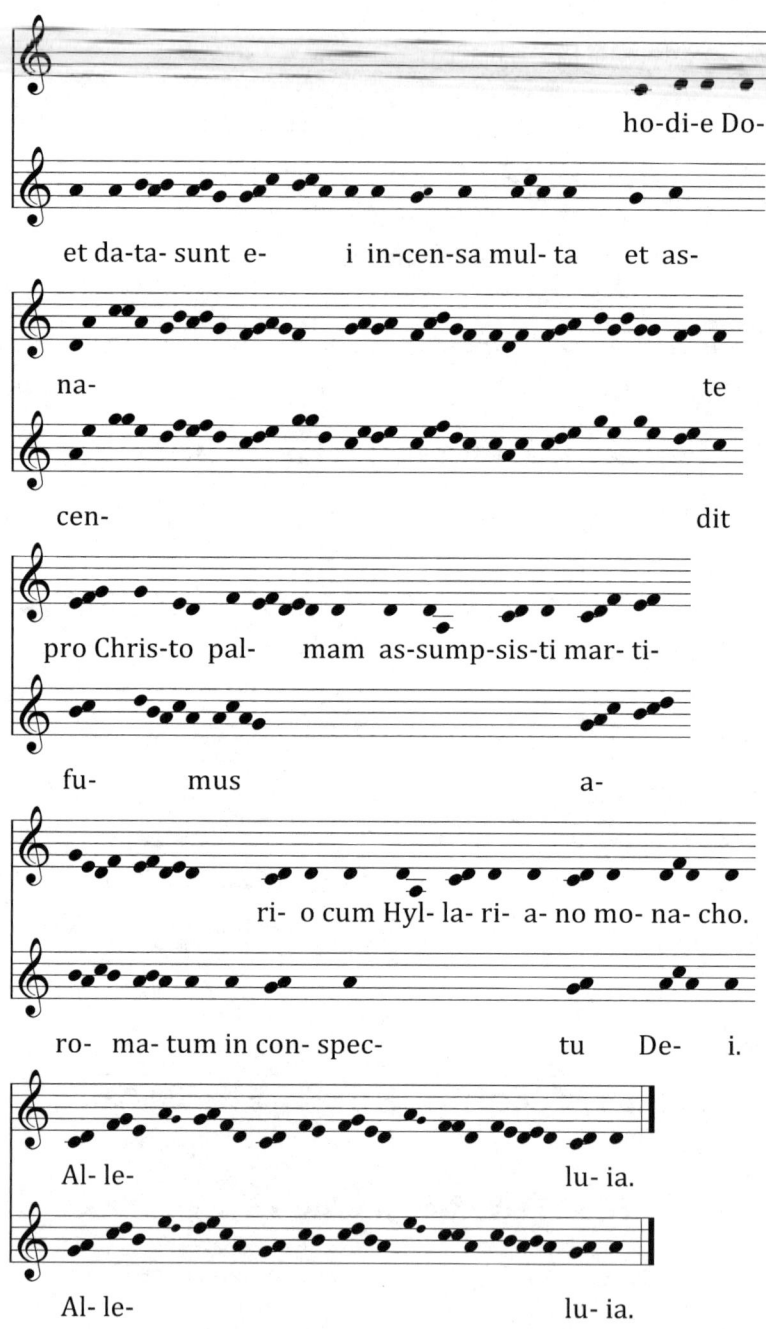

EXAMPLE 6.5. (*Continued*)

striking in this respect is the melodic gesture that precedes the longest melisma of the chants: the traversal of an entire octave with only two intervening pitches on **et ascendit** (*Stetit angelus*) and on **hodie Dona***te* (*Confractum vitreum*).[124] Although idiomatic to Offertories based on d, this gesture amplifies the meaning of text in both chants, albeit in different ways. In *Stetit angelus*, the dramatic ascent sets the word *ascendit* in a straightforward case of musical pictorialism; however, in *Confractum vitreum*, it punctuates the transition from a discussion of the saint's miracles to that of his martyrdom. The brief recitation on the final (d), though not in and of itself unusual, allows the subsequent melisma to fall on the stressed syllable (*Dona***te**). Moreover, this simple melodic gesture emphasizes via its repeated pitches the word *hodie*, and hence the *hinc et nunc* that conflates the days of execution and of celebration. By setting the saint's name, the melisma becomes a musical emblem for that Aretine bishop and a celebration of his victory even in death.

If the melody of *Stetit angelus* underscored St. Donatus's martyrdom, its text resonated with his Eucharistic miracle. The Offertory for St. Michael draws its text from Apocalypse 8:3–4, which describes the appearance of an angel before an altar with censer in hand after the opening of the seventh seal.[125] The well-known collection of biblical commentary, the *Glossa ordinaria*, offered two interpretations of this passage: either the angel signifies Christ, or he represents the celebrant and the altar Christ.[126] That the verses from Apocalypse 8 and their gloss were indeed relevant to the Eucharistic miracle of St. Donatus finds confirmation in the details of musical borrowing in *Confractum vitreum*. The first and second phrases derive from *Stetit angelus* and set words that allude to the liturgical ceremony evoked by the text of the older chant. The third phrase, which begins with *signaculo*, in turn narrates the defeat of the dragon and is newly composed. In this

---

vitreum; and Alpigiano, "Alcune precisazioni," 123, argues that the composer of the Aretine offertory drew not on a single chant but the entire melodic family formed by *Viri Galilaei, Iustorum animae*, and *Stetit Angelus*. Two pieces of evidence nonetheless confirm that *Confractum vitreum* was based on *Stetit angelus* alone. First, *Iustorum animae* evidently did not belong to the liturgies of the Tuscan dioceses, as it does not appear in the graduals or missal of the region (see table 6.2) and is not prescribed in the Tuscan ordinals. Second, *Viri Galilaei* and *Iustorum animae* employ a shorter version of their final phrase than do *Stetit angelus* and *Confractum vitreum*, which suggests only the third chant (and not the first two) could have been the model for the fourth (ex. 6.5).

[124] Steiner, "Some Questions," 174.

[125] "*Stetit angelus* iuxta aram templi *habens turibulum aureum* in manu sua *et data sunt* ei *incensa multa et ascendit fumus* aromatum in conspectu *Dei*. Alleluia." The divergences between *Stetit angelus* and the Vulgate indicate that the former likely drew its text from one of the earlier Latin translations of the New Testament (i.e., the *Vetus latina*): Rebecca Maloy, *Inside the Offertory: Aspects of Chronology and Transmission* (Oxford: Oxford University Press, 2010), 82–84.

[126] The *Glossa ordinaria* includes an interlinear gloss that interprets the angel as Christ and a marginal one that explains, "the angel stood before the altar, prepared to sacrifice in the manner of a priest. Or Christ, who offers himself, [is] the altar, on which the church offers praises to God" (*Stetit angelus ante altare paratus immolare, ad similitudinem sacerdotis, vel Christus [est] altare qui se obtulit, et super quem ecclesia offerto Deo preces*). See Karlfried Froehlich, Margaret T. Gibson, and Adolph Rusch, eds., *Biblia Latina cum glossa ordinaria: Facsimile Reprint of the Editio Princeps Adolph Rusch of Strassburg 1480/81*, 4 vols. (Turnhout: Brepols, 1992), vol. 4, 559.

instance, the insertion of new music underscores the absence of textual resonances between the two Offertories.[127] By so juxtaposing the Passion of St. Donatus with the book of the Apocalypse, *Confractum vitreum* thus casts the celebrant as an angelic, Christ-like figure, whether he be St. Donatus celebrating his first episcopal Mass or a Tuscan bishop commemorating the Aretine saint's feast.

Through musical and literary intertextuality, *Confractum vitreum* became the linchpin of mass formularies by celebrating St. Donatus as heroic martyr and an authoritative bishop through whose celebration of the liturgy God's power was revealed. The latter role obtained visual expression, moreover, in the Lucchese gradual of the early twelfth century (fig. 6.5). The inhabited initial ornamenting the Introit for St. Donatus follows his revised Passion by presenting him as one who died an old man. The bearded saint wears an alb and chasuble and holds a book, the customary trappings of bishops depicted in illuminated manuscripts from medieval Lucca. This portrayal stands in stark contrast, however, with that of the passionary of San Martino datable to the same period. Although the manuscript transmits the revised Passion, it accords with the first one by depicting the protagonist as a young man guided by his companion, Hylarian (fig. 6.6).[128] Neither image makes explicit reference to the reparation of the chalice, but the first one underscores the bishop's role as mediator between God and his flock in a manner similar to the Eucharistic miracle: he makes the sign of blessing in emulation of God's right hand, which blesses him from above.[129] The differences between the depictions of St. Donatus in turn parallel the liturgical function of the text and music that they accompany: the first illumination ornaments plainsong sung at High Mass, the second a Passion recited at the night office. In the spoken and sung liturgy, as well as manuscript illumination, this late Antique bishop is a divinely empowered celebrant and thus a model for contemporary bishops in Lucca and throughout Tuscany.

That iconography, hagiography, and plainsong in commemoration of this Aretine saint spread to such other Tuscan centers as Lucca reflected the universality of such ideals as sacramental authority and heroic martyrdom exemplified in St. Donatus. Like St. Martin, he offered medieval prelates throughout and beyond the region a model of comportment while his relationship with Antimus illustrated the impression of collegiality between bishops and canons that the latter strove to convey at Mass in general. The wide circulation of the formularies, moreover, surely depended on their avoidance of local

---

[127] Jensen, "'Magni presulis,'" 132, parses the text of *Confractum vitreum* such that "ad crucis signaculum" [sic] belongs to the preceding phrase. Nevertheless, the strong cadence at the end of the second phrase (*calicem*) suggests that the composer understood these words to describe Donatus's defeat of the dragon. Neither of the saint's Passions mentions the sign of cross in relation to either miracle.

[128] The depiction of Donatus as either a young man (as per his first Passion) or an old one (as per the second) remained common throughout the twelfth century: Licciardello, *Agiografia aretina*, 243–245.

[129] Buchanan, *A Late Eleventh-Century*, 129–130 and 139, on the motifs of the right hand of God and of the book, respectively, in Lucchese manuscript illumination.

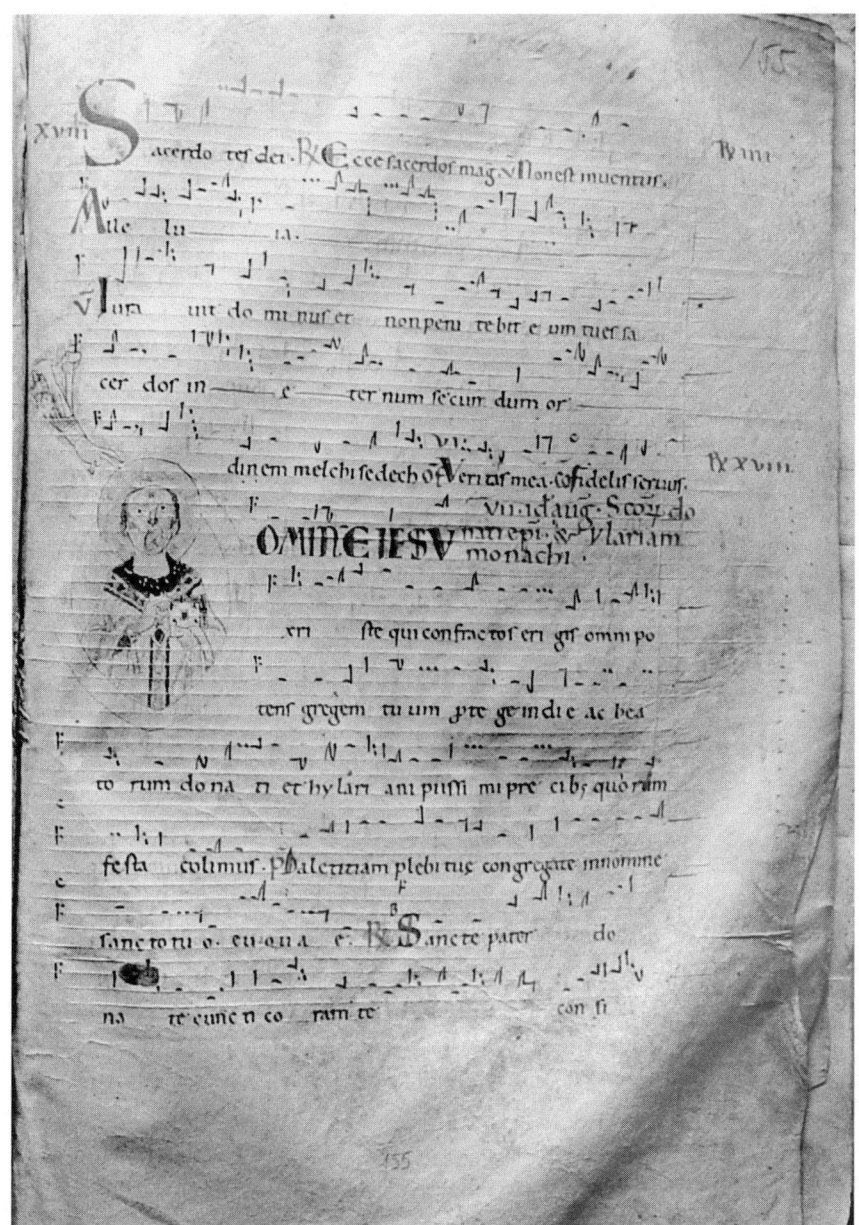

FIGURE 6.5. St. Donatus, AVPist, R69, fol. 155 (saec. XII[1/4]) (photo by author).

themes, a hypothesis that finds support in the fate of a sequence, *Laudes Deo digna*. Although it survives as an *unicum* in a Bolognese gradual of 1029–1039, the chant is clearly Aretine.[130] Much like the sequence for St. Martin, *Sacerdotem Christi*, it recounts

---

[130] Rome, Biblioteca Angelica, 123, fols. 143–144, of which an edition of the text appears in Jensen, "'Magni presulis,'" 137–138.

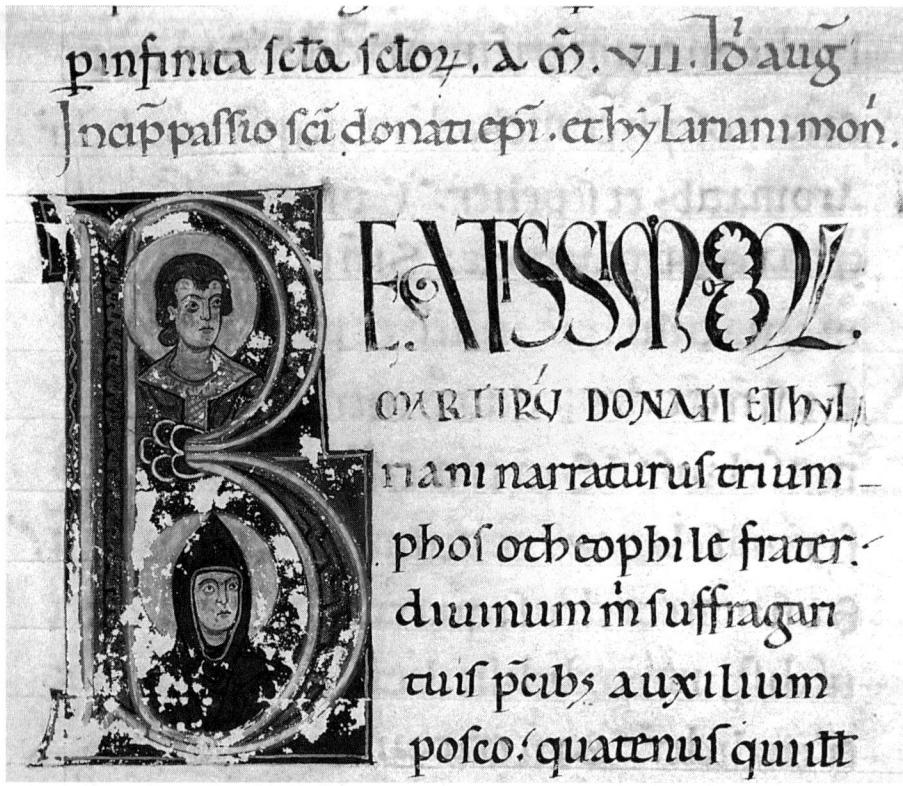

FIGURE 6.6. St. Donatus (above) and St. Hylarian (below), BCL, P†, fol. 41v (saec. XII[2/4]).

a selection of St. Donatus's virtues and miracles, of which the reparation of the chalice merits the greatest attention. In contrast with the mass formularies, however, *Laudes Deo digna* emphasizes the local character of the miracle: "the Aretine fatherland rejoices, having been illuminated by his intercession," owing to the reparation of the chalice.[131] Such expressions of local pride rendered *Sacerdotem Christi* less relevant in other dioceses and explains its conspicuous absence from other Tuscan liturgies. By contrast, the mass formularies presented a model of episcopal sanctity that served the interests of both bishops and cathedral canons throughout the region.

* * * * *

In central medieval Tuscany, High Mass was a public drama in which the bishop and cathedral canons performed distinct roles before congregants who flocked to their mother church. The former recalled Christ's crucifixion, as well as the Eucharistic miracles of St. Martin and St. Donatus on the feasts of those two holy bishops; the latter embodied the angelic choirs associated with the Alleluia. In so doing, bishops and

---

[131] Rome, Biblioteca Angelica, 123, fol. 243v: "Gaudet Aretina patria | eius optentu lustrata, | Quia calix fructus ruerat, | quem levita sacer obtulerat."

canons projected an image of collegiality that obscured the often adversarial relationship between them. In marked contrast, as related in Chapter 7, the liturgy of the Divine Office was not a ritual of association intended to bring clergy and laity together but instead was more private and local in character. In Florence, Arezzo, and Lucca, the cathedral chapters and their rivals composed plainsong for office hours in honor of the preeminent saints buried in their churches. Unlike the standardized mass formularies, as well as the imported tropes and sequences, such chant rarely circulated outside its home diocese. It also engaged in greater detail the peculiarities of the heroic lives and deaths of its respective saints in the manner of a narrative rather than a drama. This plainsong, sung by the clergy for the greater glory of its saints and for its own edification, constitutes the most enduring musical monument to the relic cults of medieval Tuscany.

7

Sacred Narrative in the Divine Office

TO EVEN THE most educated and pious of lay people of medieval Tuscany, the Divine Office was a far more abstruse liturgy than the Mass and better left to the clergy. Even Ranierius of Pisa, a merchant's son literate in Latin and skilled in song, followed only with difficulty its complex series of readings, psalmody, and plainsong. He spent day and night in prayer at the church of the Holy Sepulcher during a pilgrimage to Jerusalem, leaving only when the Armenian monks recited their office because he did not understand their language. At long last, "God opened his ears so that he might hear, and he understood their office better than he had ever comprehended that of the Latins."[1] For especially devout members of the lower classes, by contrast, the Divine Office was less a ritual to be understood and more a backdrop to mystical reveries. Zita, the Lucchese servant girl discussed in Chapter 6, typically rose in the middle of the night and visited the nearby church of San Frediano. As its Augustinian canons celebrated the long and complicated hour of matins, she stood alone in the nave and "poured forth her tears, filled the place with groans, beat her breast with her hand or a stone, and at sundry times conferred with God all the secrets of her inmost thought."[2] Ranierius's and Zita's regular attendance at the night office underscored their sanctity precisely because it was so exceptional, as the majority of their lay brethren did well to attend Mass.[3]

---

[1] *Vita Sancti Ranierii* (BHL 7084), in Réginald Grégoire, *San Ranieri di Pisa (1117-1160) in un ritratto agiografico inedito del secolo XIII* (Pisa: Pacini, 1990), no. 30, pp. 127–128, ll. 650–659: "Cumque diu hoc fecisset, Deus audiendi ei aurem aperuit, apertiusque eorum intellexit officium quam nunquam fecerat Latinorum."

[2] *Vita Sancte Zite* (BHL 9019), in *AS*, April, vol. 3, no. 17, 503: "spargebat lacrymas, locum replebat gemitibus, tundebat manu vel lapide pectora, et cogitationis occultæ secreta cuncta cum Deo multifarie conferebat."

[3] Augustine Thompson, *Cities of God: The Religion of the Italian Communes, 1125-1325* (University Park: Pennsylvania State University Press, 2005), 243–244, identifies Ranierius as one of a number of lay

If the reigning metaphor for the Mass was drama, that for the Divine Office was work. The Rule of St. Benedict coined the phrase, *opus Dei*, and made clear that the "work of God" was the primary responsibility of a monk.[4] Yet the significance of the term was hardly figurative: comprising a daily round of eight services (or hours), the Divine Office was a grueling exercise in communal prayer. Brothers were to encourage each other's faithful execution of it while remaining mindful that God was always watching and judging them. Not without reason did Benedict quote Psalm 2:11, "Serve ye the Lord with fear."[5] The Rule of Aachen likewise underscored the exertion necessitated by the *opus Dei*, warning that canons who tirelessly spent their days dealing with worldly matters rarely had the stamina for the praying and singing of the Divine Office.[6] At Mass, the metaphor of drama implicitly acknowledged the bishop as the central protagonist, the chapter as the supporting cast, and the congregation as the audience. At the Office, by contrast, that of work encouraged a role neither for the local prelate, who joined the canons in celebrating the Divine Office only rarely, nor for such extraordinarily pious lay men and women as Ranierius and Zita who managed to attend.[7] The *opus Dei* belonged to the corporate religious community, namely the cathedral chapter.

As celebrated throughout medieval Tuscany, the Divine Office situated the major liturgical obligations in the hours around dawn and dusk, leaving the daytime relatively free for the fulfillment of pastoral duties or the celebration of Mass or votive services. On solemn feasts, it began on the previous evening with first vespers, continued in the early morning with the night office (or matins) and the morning office (or lauds), proceeded through the little hours of prime (6:00 AM), terce (9:00 AM), sext (12:00 PM), and none (3:00 PM), and concluded with another round of evening offices, second vespers,

---

saints whose Lives cite their attendance at matins as a sign of their heightened piety. Sicardo of Cremona in turn underscored the unusualness of such lay men and women when he observed that the clergy did not bother to name the source of the lessons at matins because the laity was not normally present. By contrast, the deacon and subdeacon so identified the Gospel and Epistle, respectively, at Mass for the benefit of the congregation: *OOES*, pt. 2, ch. 32, 433; cf. Sicardo of Cremona, *Mitralis de Officii*, ed. Gábor Sarbak and Lorenz Weinrich (Turnhout: Brepols, 2008), bk. 4, ch. 4, 249. Cf. late medieval England, where clerical authorities expected the laity to attend matins, as well as Mass and evensong (i.e., vespers) on more than fifty annual feasts: Eamon Duffy, *The Stripping of the Altars: Traditional Religion in England 1400-1580* (New Haven: Yale University Press, 1992), 156.

[4] Timothy Fry, *RB 1980: The Rule of St. Benedict* (Collegeville, MN: Liturgical Press, 1981), ch. 43, 242.

[5] Fry, *RB*, ch. 19, 216. Cf. ch. 22, p. 218, on the encouragement with which monks were to rouse themselves in preparation for matins.

[6] MGH C, vol. 2, pt. 1, no. 131, 408.

[7] The bishop presided over the hours whenever he wished, but the rarity with which the Tuscan ordinals cite his presence at the Office suggests that he participated in it even more infrequently than in Mass. In his place served the archpriest, provost, or another canon designated the weekly-duty priest (*canonicus hebdomadarius*), a practice codified in the Aretine capitular constitutions: Ubaldo Pasqui, *Documenti per la storia della città di Arezzo nel medio evo*, 4 vols. (Florence: G. P. Vieusseux, 1899, 1904, 1916, 1937), vol. 2, no. 623, 365–366, con. 4 (21 October 1268).

and compline. The distributions of currency prescribed in the capitular constitutions of Arezzo and Lucca quantified the importance of the hours relative to each other and to High Mass. Absence from the combined night and morning office elicited the largest penalty, followed by Mass and vespers, and finally the little hours and compline.[8]

Matins and lauds merited the greatest remuneration by virtue of their combined complexity and length. Like every hour of the Divine Office, the former began when the senior resident canon recited two short versicles with their responses. Thereupon followed a hymn, the call to prayer known as the invitatory (Psalm 94, *Venite exultemus*), and finally the core of the night office, the nocturn. It began with three psalms framed by their respective antiphons, relatively brief chants that usually featured syllabic or neumatic declamation. The second consisted of three pairs of lessons and responsories, of which the latter were longer, melismatic chants comprising two parts, respond and verse. Monastic institutions followed a more demanding cursus by which a nocturn comprised four responsories and lessons. The night office consisted of only one nocturn on normal weekdays (i.e., ferial days) and feasts of lesser rank, but three nocturns on Sundays and solemn (i.e., high) feasts.[9] That festal matins lasted approximately two hours illuminates an aforementioned episode from the tenth-century Passion of St. Alexander of Fiesole. Having chanted the night office with their bishop, Romano, before the martyr's tomb, the majority of clerics returned home to sleep, exhausted from their exertions.[10] By the central Middle Ages, however, the conclusion of matins offered no such respite for the clergy, who proceeded directly on to lauds at sunrise. This morning office comprised a hymn, five psalms but six antiphons, of which the last framed the Song of Zechariah, the Benedictus (Luke 1:66–79), the first of three "Gospel" antiphons sung at the Divine Office.

Matins and lauds presented a rich opportunity for spiritual contemplation without the potentially disruptive presence of the laity, albeit one that necessitated a veritably heroic effort. On temporal (i.e., Christological) feasts, responsory texts might comment

---

[8] Aretine canons forfeited five *denarii* for their absence from matins, three for Mass or vespers, and one each for the five remaining hours of the day: Pasqui, *Documenti*, vol. 2, no. 623, 365, con. 3 (21 October 1268). Their Lucchese counterparts adopted a similar scheme, forfeiting four *denarii* for matins, two for Mass, and two for vespers: ACL, LL 40, fol. 31v, con. 5 (1 April 1281). That they made no mention of the little hours or compline suggest that these services were the purview of smaller, more informal groups of clerics, as was likely the case at the cathedral of Verona: James Borders, *The Cathedral of Verona as a Musical Center in the Middle Ages*, Ph. D. diss., University of Chicago, 1983, 330 and 334. Finally, the constitutions issued by Bishop Ardingo of Florence, or the *Leges ardinghi*, prescribed the canons' celebration of every hour of the Divine Office but similarly threatened financial penalties for their absence only from matins, Mass, and vespers: ACF, Dipl. 392 (18 November 1231), in Giovanni Lami, *Sanctae Ecclesiae Florentinae Monumenta*, 4 vols. (Florence: Angelo Salutatae, 1758), vol. 3, 1653.

[9] On the structure of matins, see David Hiley, *Western Plainchant: A Handbook* (Oxford: Oxford University Press, 1993), 25–27; and Andrew Hughes, *Medieval Manuscripts for the Mass and Office: A Guide to their Organization and Terminology* (Toronto: University of Toronto Press, 1982), 53–66.

[10] See chapter 2, this volume.

on the biblical and patristic works recited as lessons like a gloss or exegesis.[11] On sanctoral (i.e., saints') feasts, as related below, the responsories more likely formed narratives that paralleled and distilled the hagiographic texts recited as lessons. In both cases, music underscored the divergent functions of the two genres: lessons were set to simple reciting tones and responsories to ornate melodies akin to the Gradual and Alleluia of the Mass.[12] Yet clerics' appreciation of such theological and literary subtleties obviously depended on their attendance at the night office, which was not a foregone conclusion. In Lucca, the cathedral canons required their servants to set their clock such that matins would end precisely at sunrise. Servants were to rouse the chapter by ringing the bells not once but three times, with an interval between each peal that allowed its members to proceed to the choir with dignity. The young acolytes evidently had the most difficulty in rising at the requisite hour: one was to wake the others by shouting and, if necessary, by shaking them.[13] It is little wonder that Sicardo of Cremona compared the participants to soldiers called to battle by the sound of trumpets.[14]

The dominant hour of the remainder of the Divine Office was vespers, which resembled lauds in its liturgical structure but Mass in its social character. The little hours of prime, terce, sext, and none each comprised only a hymn, a paired antiphon and psalm, chapter, versicle, and prayer. Compline was nearly as brief as these four hours with four psalms framed by a single antiphon and a second, Gospel antiphon paired with the Song of Simeon, the Nunc dimittis (Luke 2:29–32). Vespers, by contrast, was more substantial,

---

[11] The night office was thus an example of what Susan Boynton characterized as "performative exegesis" in her "Performative Exegesis in the Fleury *Interfectio puerorum*," *Viator* 29 (1998): 44. While first employing the term to describe liturgical drama, Boynton subsequently explored its relevance to matins in her *Shaping a Monastic Identity: Liturgy and History at the Imperial Abbey of Farfa, 1000-1125* (Ithaca, NY: Cornell University Press, 2006), 64–80. On the exegetical character of the medieval liturgy in general, see Robert Lagueux, *Glossing Christmas: Liturgy, Music, Exegesis, and Drama in High Medieval Laon*, Ph.D. diss., Yale University, 2005, 199–207; and William T. Flynn, *Medieval Music as Medieval Exegesis* (Lanham, MD: Scarecrow, 1999).

[12] On solemn occasions, the Tuscan cathedral chapters often sang the third, sixth, and/or ninth responsory with organum, thus amplifying their musical difference from the lessons while concomitantly underscoring the formal division of the nocturns. See, for instance, the instances of polyphonic improvisation prescribed in the Lucchese and Sienese ordinals and inventoried in Agostino Ziino, "Polifonia nella cattedrale di Lucca durante il XIII secolo," *Acta musicologica* 47 (1975): 20–21; and Gemma Gonzato, "Alcune considerazioni sull' 'Ordo Officiorum Ecclesiae Senensis,'" in *Le Friuli, 22-24 agusto 1980*, ed. C. Corsi and P. Petrobelli (Rome: Torre d'Orfeo, 1989), 282–289.

[13] ACL, LL 40, fol. 39v, con. 5 (14 March 1284) (on the setting of the clock and ringing of the bells) and ACL, LL 43, fol. 192, con. 7 (25 June 1294) (on the acolytes' rising for matins).

[14] Sicardo, *Mitralis*, bk. 4, ch. 1, 224. Cf. *OOES*, pt. 2, ch. 2, 404, which employs the common metaphor, used throughout the Middle Ages, of church bells as battle trumpets. Cf. John H. Arnold and Caroline Goodson, "Resounding Community: The History and Meaning of Medieval Church Bells," *Viator* 43 (2012): 118–121. So demanding were the night and morning offices that each canon, chaplain, and acolyte might absent himself once every week without penalty: ACL, LL 40, fol. 32v, con. 21 (1 April 1281). The choirboys enjoyed an even greater reprieve, presumably on account of their youth, for they attended the night office only on the most solemn occasions: ACL LL 40, fol. 40, con. 10 (14 March 1284).

featuring a hymn, five antiphons and psalms, and a Gospel antiphon paired with the Song of Mary, the Magnificat (Luke 1:46–55). Conveniently positioned at the end of the workday, it drew a substantial lay audience not unlike High Mass on solemn feasts.[15] Indeed, on such occasions, the canons strengthened the affinities of vespers with that morning service in ways that rendered this evening office a more extravagant performance. Their soloists sang longer or more elaborate chants such as responsories, Alleluias, and sequences, of which the second and third derived from the Liturgy of the Word. They often performed these melodies with polyphonic elaboration and sometimes from the pulpit, as was likewise the case at Mass.[16]

On the feasts of most saints, Tuscan canons sang from the *commune sanctorum*, corpora of antiphons and responsories appropriate to any holy man or woman of a given profile (e.g., a martyr, bishop, or virgin). Nevertheless, for the *dies natales* of the most venerated saints buried in their churches, these clerics composed a cycle of such plainsong proper to the day and known as an "Office."[17] As illustrated in this book's appendices, a sanctoral Office included antiphons, responsories, and (occasionally) hymns sung at the three principal hours of the day. It typically began at first vespers on the previous evening: the five antiphons belonged to the day before the feast, the hymn and Magnificat antiphon to the feast itself. It continued with the antiphons and responsories for matins and lauds, and concluded with the Magnificat antiphon for second vespers. In the absence of proper antiphons for vespers, the clergy employed those of lauds, exploiting the parallel structure of the two hours. The Tuscan ordinals identify particular Offices by the incipits of key chants; however, the full texts and melodies of the plainsong survive in three other medieval service

---

[15] Frequent references to the populace at vespers in the Tuscan ordinals confirm its public character. Cf. the foundation of Pope Leo IV (847–855) that vespers would be celebrated "publically" at San Paolo fuori le mura in Rome by the resident clergy and papal schola on the feast of its titular saint: Louis Duchesne and Cyrille Vogel, eds., *Le Liber pontificalis*, 2nd. ed., 3 vols. (Paris: E. de Boccard, 1955), vol. 2, ch. 105, no. 12, 108.

[16] The Lucchese, for instance, substituted an Alleluia and sequence for the hymn on twelve temporal and ten sanctoral feasts as prescribed in *OOL*: Martino Giusti, "L'*Ordo Officiorum* della Cattedrale di Lucca," in *Miscellanea Giovanni Mercati* (Vatican City: Biblioteca Apostolica Vaticana, 1946), 538, n. 75. The Pisans regularly substituted a sequence for the hymn on at least nine occasions: *OOP*, fol. 8v (Nativity), fol. 9 (St. Stephen and St. John the Evangelist), fol. 10v (Octave of Nativity), fol. 11v (Epiphany), fol. 30 (Easter), fol. 33v (Ascension), fol. 34v (Pentecost), fol. 46v (St. John the Baptist) of which the third, fifth, and sixth prescriptions mention the use of the organ as accompaniment. The Pistoiese regularly inserted a sequence after the chapter and sang it polyphonically from their pulpit on the five highest feasts of the Temporale: OOPist2, fol. 10 (Nativity), fol. 13v (Epiphany), fol. 36v (Ascension), fol. 29 (Easter), and fol. 39 (Pentecost). Finally, the Sienese ordinal (following Sicardo of Cremona) noted that while some religious communities sang single responsories at each of the clerical hours of the day save lauds, the Sienese did so only at vespers on solemn occasions and with polyphonic embellishment: *OOES*, pt. 2, ch. 81, 483; Sicardo, *Mitralis*, bk. 4, ch. 8, 278. Cf. *OOES*, pt. 1, ch. 438, 393, for the feasts on which this occurred.

[17] Henceforth, "Divine Office" will denote the entire cycle of daily hours for which the clergy was responsible, "night," "morning," or "evening office" the individual hours of matins, lauds, and vespers, respectively. "Office" or "*Officium*" will indicate the cycle of proper antiphons and responsories composed for a given feast, e.g., the Office of St. Minias or the *Officium Sancti Miniatis*.

books. Two twelfth-century antiphoners preserve the antiphons and responsories. One was compiled for the monastery of Santa Maria di Pontetetto near Lucca and the other for the cathedral of Florence.[18] An eleventh-century breviary likely of Aretine origin but later used at the cathedral of Lucca supplements these chants with lessons, thus facilitating an analysis of both plainsong and readings.[19]

Chapter 7 presents a detailed analysis of the five extant Offices composed for saints buried in the cathedrals or suburban martyria of the region. Without exception, these Offices honored bishops and martyrs of late Antiquity and the early Middle Ages—Sts. Minias and Zenobius (in Florence), St. Donatus (in Arezzo), and Sts. Fridian and Regulus (in Lucca)—whose cults had once been championed by episcopal lords and builders. And although they remain anonymous, they were undoubtedly the work of the canons (or monks) resident at their saint's shrines.[20] With the mass formularies for St. Donatus examined in chapter 6, these Offices comprise the lions' share of indigenous sacred music to survive from medieval Tuscany and thus testify to the particular power of early medieval relic cults to inspire the composition of plainsong. They in turn offer an implicit rebuke to newer objects of popular devotion that came to prominence in the twelfth century—St. Ansanus (in Siena), the Volto Santo (in Lucca), and St. James (in Pistoia)—and for whom their respective cathedral chapters either adopted widely circulating Offices or drew from the *commune sanctorum* rather than fashioning truly local liturgies.

The following analysis illustrates how historical developments of the tenth and eleventh centuries outlined in part I prompted the creation and shaped diverse features of

---

[18] BCL, 603 (saec. XII$^{1/4}$) and AAF, n.s. (saec. XII^{med}), on the dating and provenance of which see Edward B. Garrison, *Studies in the History of Mediaeval Italian Painting*, 4 vols. (Florence: L'Imprenta, 1953–1962), vol. 2, 223–224; and Marica S. Tacconi, *Cathedral and Civic Ritual in Late Medieval and Renaissance Florence: The Service-Books of Santa Maria del Fiore* (Cambridge: Cambridge University Press, 2005), 80–83, respectively. Keith Glaeske, Charles Downey, and Lila Collamore, eds., *The Twelfth-Century Antiphoner of Firenze, Curia Arcivescovile: A CANTUS Index* (Washington, DC: Benjamin T. Rome School of Music, Catholic University of America Press, 1994) inventories the contents of AAF, n.s., while Giovanni Alpigiano, "L'antifonario fiorentino e la sua epoca," *Rivista internazionale di musica sacra* 23 (2002): 171–186, explores the historical context of its compilation. On 22 February 2007, AAF, n.s. was reported stolen from the archiepiscopal archives of Florence. It was recovered only days later, albeit without fols. 180–184, in which the *Officium Sancti Miniatis* is preserved. My analysis of this Office thus depends on my examination of a black-and-white microfilm of the antiphoner produced before its theft.

[19] BCL, 605 (saec. XI). While a twelfth-century *ex libris* indicates that the breviary belonged to the cathedral of Lucca (fol. 1), the predominance of Aretine saints (i.e., Donatus, Hylarian, Flora, and Lucilla) and the absence of Lucchese saints (i.e., Fridian and Regulus) from the Sanctorale points to an Aretine origin for the manuscript. See Giovanni Alpigiano and Pierluigi Licciardello, *Officium Sancti Donati I: L'ufficio liturgico di san Donato di Arezzo nei manoscritti toscani medievali* (Florence: Edizioni del Galluzzo, 2008), 26, for a discussion of the manuscript and relevant bibliography.

[20] The Tuscan Offices thus differed from their transalpine counterparts, which were often ascribed to particular individuals who wished to be remembered as authors and composers by their religious community: Christopher Page, *The Christian West and its Singers: The First Thousand Years* (New Haven: Yale University Press, 2010), 407.

the Tuscan Offices. As argued below, their composition typically occurred at discrete historical moments rather than over broader periods of time.[21] It usually accompanied the revision of the saint's Passion or Life and, like the rewriting of such hagiography, coincided with one or more of the following events: the translation of relics, the rebuilding of a church, and the reform of resident clergy.[22] Moreover, Offices often complemented (and in some cases shaped) the architecture or ornamentation of the basilicas in which they were sung, thus revealing the coordination of aural and visual media similar to that uncovered in chapter 6. Finally, rivalries between urban cathedrals and suburban martyria contributed to the creation of new Offices illustrated by the earliest of their number, the *Officium Sancti Miniatis*, probably fashioned around 900 in connection with its saint's translation from San Miniato to Santa Reparata of Florence. The remaining Tuscan Offices likely date from the eleventh century and similarly reflect their precise geographical origins while nonetheless evoking the priorities of ecclesiastical reform and an emerging civic consciousness characteristic of that period. Once again, Tuscan liturgies were a prism that refracted the ideals and realities of ecclesiastical politics in the Middle Ages.[23]

If the Offices reflect the particularities of their respective geneses, they likewise demonstrate how composers selected and manipulated their texts in accordance with the diverse social characters of the Divine Office to a degree acknowledged neither by medieval liturgists nor by modern scholars. Antiphons and hymns for the public hour of vespers evoke the attendant populace in the manner of mass formularies, setting pleas for intercession or calls to prayer that often praise their holy protagonists. Such "panegyric" plainsong often lauds miracles by which saints acted as protectors of the entire city, or *defensores civitatis*, casting them as civic patrons in the mold of more popular objects of veneration to emerge in the late eleventh and twelfth centuries.[24] In 1094, the count of Caiazzo (near Capua) commissioned the Benedictine monks of Montecassino

---

[21] My reconstruction of the genesis of proper Offices thus differs from that of Roman Hankeln, "'Properization' and Formal Changes in High Medieval Saint's Offices: The Offices for Saints Henry and Kunigunde of Bamberg," *Plainsong and Medieval Music* 10 (2001): 20, who envisions a process by which "new chants were *gradually* added as, for example, when a complete block of responsories or antiphons was inserted as a group, until finally all the requirements of the liturgy came to be supplied by an especially composed repertory" (italics added). With the exception of the *Officium Sancti Miniatis*, of which the composition unfolded in not one but two phases, there is no evidence that the Tuscan Offices were composed in such piecemeal fashion.

[22] The concurrence between the revision of hagiography and the composition of Offices was typical of northern Europe, as well as Tuscany: Page, *The Christian West*, 412.

[23] On the political dimensions of medieval plainsong in general and sanctoral Offices in particular, see Roman Hankeln, "A Blasphemous Paradox? Approaches to Socio-Political Aspects of Medieval Western Plainchant," in *Political Plainchant?: Music, Text, and Historical Context of Medieval Saints' Offices*, ed. Roman Hankeln (Ottawa: Institute of Mediaeval Music, 2009), 1–5.

[24] I respectfully borrow the terms "panegyric" and "historical" to describe medieval Offices from Christina E. A. Marshall, *Late Medieval Liturgical Offices in Acrostic Form: A Catalogue and Study*, Ph.D. diss., University of Toronto, 2006, 15.

to write a Life and compose "some chants and melodies of sweet praises" for a newly discovered saint, "in order that all faithful, who convene to celebrate his feast, might pray more festively in his honor on that day."[25] This desire to incite public veneration with proper plainsong undoubtedly lay behind the vespers chant of the Tuscan Offices. Some (though not all) lay men and women would have certainly grasped the generally direct and inclusive rhetoric of its texts, which evoked the voice of the entire Christian community, clerical and lay, thus casting vespers as a ritual of association not unlike the Mass.

The antiphons and responsories for the private hours of matins and lauds, by contrast, sounded a more intimate tone by retelling the dramatic lives and deaths of their protagonists and thus earning the widely used epithet "history" (*historia*). Such narrative or "historical" chant typically quoted the appropriate *vita* or *passio*, parsing such hagiographic texts in ways that reflected the particular interests of the religious foundation responsible for its composition. For instance, in a possible sign of the periodic tensions between bishops, on the one hand, and cathedral chapters or monasteries, on the other, the Offices make no reference to the building projects ascribed to late antique or early medieval bishops in the related Lives and Passions. While the *Officium Sancti Donati* went furthest in telling a coherent story of its saint, every night and morning office featured narrative elements largely free of the inclusive, panegyric rhetoric typical of vespers. Here, the implied community was not the entire congregation but, rather, the canons or monks whose arduous celebration of the matins and lauds signaled their commitment to the *opus Dei*. By singing and (one hoped) contemplating the virtues, miracles, and exploits of their holy patron, they engaged in a process of spiritual edification not unlike that prompted by the reading of hagiography.

If the Tuscan Offices were thus deeply embedded in the ecclesiastical politics and literary culture of their particular churches and cities, they nonetheless illustrate a broader engagement with transalpine models of plainsong. The first layer of the *Officium Sancti Miniatis*, as we shall see, presents a faithful adaption of the venerable conventions of "Gregorian" chant, a fusion of Frankish and Roman plainsong ascribed to Gregory the Great and imposed throughout the Carolingian Empire in the late eighth and ninth centuries.[26] In the early tenth century, there emerged a new generation of Frankish Offices of which the influence in Italy has gone almost entirely unnoticed. If the Aretine and (even more) the Lucchese Offices betrayed the influence of these northern works, their Florentine counterparts evince an equally "post-Gregorian" style more indebted to

---

[25] Giovanni Orlandi, "Vita Sancti Mennatis: Opera inedita di Leone Marsicano," *Rendiconti: Classe di lettere e scienze morali e storiche* 97 (1963): 580, quoted in Page, *The Christian West*, 436: "Ut autem fideles quique populi, ad eius convenientes colemnia, haberent unde se eadem die in eius laudibus festivius exercerent, non illa tantum que luculentissimo tanti presulis [i.e., Gregory the Great] stilo digesta fuerant, congestis undecumque sententiis compententibus ampliari et spatiari poposcerat, sed et cantus insuper aliquot et laudum suavium melodias rogaverat valde devotus inde componi."

[26] Page, *The Christian West*, chs. 14, 15, and 16, presents a recent, wide-ranging, and particularly imaginative discussion of the origins and dissemination of Gregorian chant, on which the bibliography is otherwise vast.

the teachings of Guido of Arezzo and less to transalpine precedent. The Tuscan offices thus reveal not only an evolving adaption of northern models in the form of Gregorian and post-Gregorian plainsong but also the rise of indigenous musical techniques amid the liturgies inspired by local relics.

ST. MINIAS

The literary foundation of the first Tuscan Office was the Passion of St. Minias, a text in circulation by the late ninth century and one grounded in the conventions of the most venerable hagiography of Latin Christendom. It resembled the ancient *Gesta martyrum* of Rome in its exclusive focus on the trial and execution of it subject.[27] According to the narrative, St. Minias fell victim to the persecutions of Emperor Decius (249–251), whose soldiers capture the young Christian in the woods outside of Florence during their sovereign's residence in that city. Their young captive steadfastly refuses to sacrifice to the pagan gods and valiantly undergoes various tortures. The Passion narrates the trial with the concision typical of the *gesta* but appears increasingly circular as one episode begins to resemble another. For instance, not once but twice does Decius command, "let there be brought a wild beast more horrible than any other, so that it might devour him."[28] His minions procure first a leopard and second a lion, of which St. Minias dispatches the former with a prayer to God and the latter with the sign of Christ. Such miraculous acts of survival predictably infuriate the emperor and lead to St. Minias's execution and burial atop the Monte Fiorentino, located south of the Arno and the future site of his shrine, San Miniato al Monte.

The *Officium Sancti Miniatis* comprises two chronological layers, of which the first has nine antiphons and responsories for matins and five antiphons for lauds (appendix I). Without exception, these chants draw their texts from the related Passion, albeit in ways that amplify rather than clarify its circularity. Those of the first nocturn of matins establish the expectation of a linear narrative, relating Decius's persecution of Christians in Rome, arrival in Florence, and first encounter with St. Minias. Yet the coherence dissolves as the subsequent antiphons and responsories relate vignettes from the trial with overlap, repetition, and lack of sequence. Table 7.1 illustrates such recurrence, as well

---

[27] Among earliest and most prominent *gesta* were those dedicated to the second-century martyrs Polycarp, Ptolemaeus, and Lucius, and Justin, in *The Acts of the Christian Martyrs*, trans. Herbert Musurillo (Oxford: Oxford University Press, 1972), 5–21, 38–41, and 42–61, respectively. While Hippolyte Delehaye, *The Legends of the Saints: An Introduction to Hagiography*, trans. V. M. Crawford (Notre Dame, IN: University of Notre Dame Press, 1961) remains the classic study of the *gesta*, see also Timothy D. Barnes, "Pre-Decian Acta Martyrum," *Journal of Theological Studies* 19 (1968): 509–531; and Gary A. Bisbee, *Pre-Decian Acts of Martyrs and Commentarii*, ed. Margaret R. Miles and Bernadette J. Brooten (Philadelphia: Fortress 1988).

[28] *Passio Sancti Miniatis I*, BLF, Edili 139, fol. 202v, *AS*, October, vol. 11, col. 429: "Adducatur fera crudelis et pessima, ut eum devoret." Compare this account of St. Minias's felling of the leopard with that of the lion quoted in table 7.1.

TABLE 7.1
TEXTUAL BORROWING FROM THE *PASSIO SANCTI MINIATIS I* INTO THE *OFFICIUM SANCTI MINIATIS* (ITALICS DENOTE TEXT COMMON TO THE PASSION AND THE OFFICE)

Officium Sancti Miniatis	Passio Sancti Miniatis I	Officium Sancti Miniatis
M-R5		M-R7
Beatus Christi miles Minias liberatus exiit ab igne. Videns autem Decius quod fuerat *factum* iussit presentari *feram orribilem* ad *devorandum illum.*	Beatus miles Christi Minias liberatus exiit ab igne. Videns autem Decius imperator quod factum est, dixit: Adducatur fera omnium ferarum orribilis et devoret illum, et superabimus eum.	*Cum vidisset beatus Minias* bestiam, *signo crucis contra eam facto, in ictu oculi* coram eo *extincta est.*
M-V5		
Statimque preparatus est leo cordium, quem *cum vidisset beatus Minias signo crucis contra eam facto in ictu oculi ipsa fera extincta est.*	Statimque preparatus est leo cordius. Et cum vidisset eum beatus Minias, signo crucis contra eum factum, in ictu oculi ipsa fera extincta est.	
M-R5		M-R7
Blessed knight of Christ, Minias, exited, liberated from the fire. Seeing what had happened, Decius ordered that a horrible *wild beast* be presented to devour him.	The blessed knight of Christ, Minias, exited, liberated from the fire. Seeing what had happened, emperor Decius said, "let there be brought a wild beast [more] horrible than any other and he will devour him and we shall defeat him."	*When blessed Minias saw* the beast, with *the sign of the cross* having been *made,* it *was killed in the blink of an eye* before him.
M-V5		
And immediately a "leo cordium" *was prepared*, [and] *when blessed Minias saw it,* with *the sign of the cross* having been *made against it, that beast was killed in the blink of an eye.*	And immediately a "leo cordius" was prepared. And when blessed Minias saw it, he made the sign of the cross against it and that beast was killed in the blink of an eye.	

as the process by which the composer compressed key passages from the Passion into libretti suitable for singing.²⁹ Introducing St. Minias's defeat of the lion, *Beatus Christi miles* (M-R5) condenses some unnecessary verbiage, including the noun *emperor* and the direct speech attributed to Decius. Both *Statimque preparatus* (M-V5) and *Cum vidisset* (M-R7), by contrast, quote the subsequent passage with little modification, replicating in the series of matins responsories the verbal repetition so prominent in the Passion.

Statimque preparatus also reveals a marked lack of literary discernment on the part of the composer of Layer 1. Its text preserves the nonsensical phrase, "lion of hearts" (*leo cordium*), found in the Florentine recension of the *passio*, one that was likely the result of a twofold error that occurred at some earlier date in the copying of the Passion. First, one scribe mistook the second wild beast to threaten Minias as the leopard that appears earlier in the narrative; second, another scribe miscopied "leopardus" as "leo cordius."³⁰ Drogone, the first abbot of the Benedictine monastery at San Miniato al Monte, was more alert to this and other textual infelicities than the composer of *Statimque preparatus*. In his revised *Passio Sancti Miniatis* (ca. 1018), he criticized the original Passion for its rough literary style and wondered why the older one "calls the lion a 'leo cordium.'"³¹

A far more conspicuous peculiarity of Layer 1 suggests that its composer was a canon of Santa Reparata. None of the antiphons and responsories mention the saint's execution and subsequent burial atop the Monte Fiorentino, as related in his original Passion. In so doing, the chants not only ignore the seminal moment in the life of any martyr—namely his or her heroic death in the name of Christ—but also minimize the significance of St. Minias's original shrine on the mount. Only the clerics of Santa Reparata would have had a motive to do so. In 898, as related in chapter 2, their church had acquired relics of that saint from San Miniato al Monte, transforming itself into the center of his cult until the foundation of the hilltop shrine as a Benedictine monastery in 1018. That the first layer of the Office of St. Minias originated at the canonry of Santa Reparata rather than the monastery likewise accords with two of its defining characteristics. The Office follows a secular rather than monastic cursus—that is, nine rather than twelve responsories—and draws its texts from the first Passion rather than the revision later penned by Abbot Drogone. With its failure to narrate the life of St. Minias to its inevitable

---

²⁹ I borrow the term "libretto" to describe such modification of biblical or hagiographic texts from James W. McKinnon, *The Advent Project: The Later Seventh-Century Creation of the Roman Mass Proper* (Berkeley: University of California Press, 2000), e.g., 104. The text of the *Passio Sancti Miniatis I* presented in table 7.1 derives from the cathedral passionary of Florence, BLF, Edili 139, 202v, which features textual variants that accord more closely with the antiphon and responsory texts than does the version in *AS*, October, vol. 11, col. 429.

³⁰ The misreading was an old one, for "leo cordius" appears not only in the cathedral passionary of Florence, BLF, Edili 139, 202v (quoted in table 7.1) but also the ninth-century passionary, Rome, Biblioteca Nazionale, Farfa 29, fol. 151.

³¹ *Passio Sancti Miniatis II*, BLF, Mugell., 13, fol. 234v: "Bestiam nimie iubet adduci crudelitatis quam is cuius scripta pedetemptim sequor leo cordium vocat."

conclusion, namely his execution and burial, the oldest plainchant in his honor thus reveals itself to be the work of cathedral canons intent on reinforcing their claims to his relics at the expense of his original shrine.

The history of the cathedral and its chapter in turn elucidates the chronology of Layer 1 of the Office. The late ninth century offers a plausible historical moment in which the *Officium Sancti Miniatis* might have emerged. It witnessed the promotion of Santa Reparata by the energetic bishop, Andrea, via the building of an annular confessional and the acquisition of the relics of St. Zenobius.[32] The late tenth century and early eleventh centuries are far less plausible moments for the composition of the Office. The former saw the decline and near disbanding of the chapter, the latter its renewal but promotion of St. Zenobius rather than St. Minias as its patron.[33] Hence the first layer of the *Officium Sancti Miniatis* surely belongs to that earlier period of activity and perhaps dates from as early as 898.

The relative antiquity of the first layer of the Office and the conservatism of its literary source in turn mirrors its musical organization and style, which is grounded in venerable conventions of the Gregorian (or classical) plainsong imposed throughout the Carolingian Empire. Gregorian antiphons heavily favor three of the eight possible modes (1, 7, and 8), a restricted distribution to which those of the *Officium Sancti Miniatis* conform. Its responsories are similarly traditional, adding only Mode 4 to their mix.[34] Equally suggestive of Gregorian principles is the melodic construction of the individual chants of the Office. Its antiphons belong to "tune families," which are groups of antiphons that are in the same mode and share a basic melodic plan that nonetheless varies from one member to another. Its responsories, by contrast, employ smaller (but equally traditional) formulae that are used in many other responsories of the same mode and achieve greater fixity.[35] Hence neither genre presents adaptations of single preexisting chants in the manner of the mass formularies studied in chapter 6. Instead, they draw on a stock of melodic material common to many classical melodies in a given mode.[36]

---

[32] See chapter 2, this volume.

[33] See chapters 3 and 4, this volume.

[34] On the modal distribution of Gregorian antiphons and responsories, see Willi Apel, *Gregorian Chant* (Bloomington: Indiana University Press, 1958), 138.

[35] On the melodic construction of Gregorian antiphons and responsories, see most recently László Dobszay and Janka Szendrei, eds., *Antiphonen*, 3 vols. (Kassel: Bärenreiter, 1999), vol. 1, 22–25; Jean-François Goudesenne, *Les Offices historiques ou historiae composés pour les fêtes des saints dans la province ecclésiastique de Reims (775-1030)* (Turnhout: Brepols, 2002), 153–210; and Kate Helsen, "The Use of Melodic Formulas in Responsories: Constancy and Variability in the Manuscript Tradition," *Plainsong and Medieval Music* 18 (2009): 61–75.

[36] Other composers of medieval Offices indeed adapted discrete, preexisting melodies to new texts in a procedure known as contrafacture. Nine responsories for St. Olav of Norway (saec. XII$^{2/2}$), for instance, were based on those for St. Augustine (saec. XII$^{1/2}$): Roman Hankeln,"St. Olav's Augustine-Responsories: Con trafactum Technique and Political Message," in *Political Plainchant?: Music, Text, and Historical Context*

The forging of the antiphons from Gregorian tune families involved the manipulation of melodic gestures and cadences to underscore both the syntax and the semantics of their texts, a subtle process of adaptation that reinforced the perceived antiquity of these chants. The most prominent family among the antiphons of Layer 1 features a melodic incipit that immediately signals Mode 1 with a leap from final to reciting tone framed by lower and upper neighbors (c, d, a, b) (ex. 7.1).[37] *Tunc iratus* (M-A9) adheres to the usual phrase structure exemplified in *Tecum principium* but includes an uncommonly neumatic ascent to the reciting tone (***militem***) that distinguishes the verb from the direct object and accentuates the figure of St. Minias as "Christ's knight." *Tunc imperator* (L-A3) typifies the same tune class, a fact that reinforces its textual affinities with *Tunc iratus*. Both chants begin with the emphatic "tunc," feature Decius as their subject, and recount his "order" (*iussit*) that St. Minias be tortured. *Tunc imperator* nonetheless begins with a low introductory phrase that further dramatizes the telltale ascent to b' (***fornace***).[38] Thereafter, it adheres more closely than does *Tunc iratus* to the phrase structure seen in *Tecum principium*. Yet again, cadences underscore the particular syntax of the text: the third phrase concludes with a subtonal cadence rather than one approached from above as is typical (***proicit***), thus dividing one sentence of the text from the other. Hence the melodies of *Tunc iratus* and *Tunc imperator* and, by extension, all of the antiphons of Layer 1, serve as effective vehicles for their local Florentine texts even as they maintain an eminently Gregorian sound.

The responsories of Layer 1 of the *Officium Sancti Miniatis* are likewise models of Gregorian propriety. In keeping with the conventions of their genre, they were longer as well as more melismatic and formulaic than the antiphons. *Ministri presidis* (M-R2) and *Beatus Christi* (M-R5), for instance, belong to the largest class of classical responds in Mode 8 (ex. 7.2).[39] They have precisely the same sequence of six fixed phrases, which are occasionally extended to accommodate longer texts via recitation on such structural

---

of Medieval Saints' Offices, ed. Roman Hankeln (Ottawa: Institute of Mediaeval Music, 2009), 171–199; and Roman Hankeln, "Texting Techniques in St. Olav's Augustine-Responsories," in *Studies in Medieval Chant and Liturgy in Honour of David Hiley*, ed. Terence Bailey and László Dobszay (Ottawa: Institute of Mediaeval Music, 2007), 275–293. A more proximate example, geographically if not chronologically, is the Florentine Office of St. Zenobius (ca. 1513), of which approximately one-third of the melodies derive from chants sung on seven related feasts: Tacconi, *Cathedral*, 231–241.

[37] The transcription of *Tecum principium* in ex. 7.1 is based on AAF, n.s., fol. 24. *Beatus Xistus* (M-A2), *Nulla maleficia* (M-A7), *Tunc iratus* (M-A9), and *Tunc imperator* (L-A3) belong to the tune family inventoried in Walter Howard Frere, *Antiphonale Sarisburiense: A Reproduction in Facsimile of a Manuscript of the Thirteenth Century* (London: London: Plainsong and Medieval Music Society, 1901), vol. 1, 66–67 (Ib); and Dobszay and Szendrei, *Antiphonen*, vol. 1, nos. 1168–1266, 82–135 (C).

[38] *Tunc imperator* belongs to the tune sub-family inventoried in Dobszay and Szendrei, *Antiphonen*, vol. 1, nos. 1258–1266, 129–135 (C6).

[39] On the tune class exemplified by *Ministri presidis* (M-R2) and *Beatus Christi* (M-R5), see Frere, *Antiphonale Sarisburiense*, vol. 1, 52–55 (VIIa); Kate Helsen, *The Great Responsories of the Divine Office: Aspects of Structure and Transmission*, Ph.D. diss., University of Regensburg, 2008, 247–252.

EXAMPLE 7.1 *Tecum principium* (Nativity, V2-A1), *Tunc iratus* (*Officium Sancti Miniatis*, M-A9) and *Tunc imperator* (*Officium Sancti Miniatis*, L-A3).

EXAMPLE 7.2. Comparison of *Beatus Christi miles* (*Officium Sancti Miniatis*, M-R5) and *Ministri presidis* (*Officium Sancti Miniatis*, M-R2).

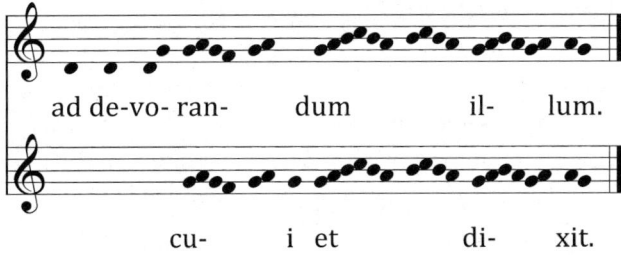

EXAMPLE 7.2. *(Continued)*

pitches as the final (g), the second above (a), or the reciting tone (c'). The phrases in turn form three pairs, or periods, typical of classical responds. The medial cadences of the first and third period are invariably off the final (*miles* and *orribilem*; *eum* and *tribunalibus*), but the concluding cadence of the second might provide a measure of tonal stability by falling on the final (*igne* but not *Cesari*).⁴⁰ Even more formulaic than the responds were the paired verses (not transcribed here), which adhere to one of eight recitation tones assigned to each mode.

The *Officium Sancti Miniatis* thus originated via not one but two processes of adaptation that reinforced its perceived antiquity. The texts of its first layer derived from yet amplified the cyclical character of a Passion that was itself modeled upon the esteemed *Gesta martyum* of Rome; the melodies were scrupulous adaptations of the tune families and fixed formulae of the venerable corpus of Gregorian plainsong. If indeed the first layer of the Office of St. Minias dates from as early as 898, moreover, it constitutes not only one of the oldest examples of Italian plainsong composed outside of Rome but also a precocious witness to the fluency of the Florentine clergy in the Gregorian chant disseminated by the Carolingians a century earlier.⁴¹ Yet whatever its precise dating, the *Officium Sancti Miniatis* constituted via its text and music a clear evocation of Rome. In this respect, it mirrored the relic translations and annular confessionals that had

---

⁴⁰ Helsen, "The Use," 62.
⁴¹ An analogous case is the Venetian Office of St. Mark, which David Hiley, "The Offices Sung in San Marco, Venice. Stylistic Layers in Plainchant for Local Saints," in *Sine musica nulla disciplina... Studi in Onore di Giulio Cattin*, ed. Franco Bernabei and Antonio Lovato (Padua: Il poligrafo, 2006), 131–136, dates to the tenth century on the basis of its thoroughly Gregorian style. In their fidelity to Gregorian models, these Italian Offices mirrored the "Carolingian basilical Offices" composed north of the Alps from approximately 750 to 840 and so named in Goudesenne, *Les Offices*, 213–222; cf. Jean-François Goudesenne, "A Typology of Historiae in West Francia (8-10 c.)," *Plainsong and Medieval Music* 13 (2004): 22–23. Indeed, these early Frankish Offices proved influential in northern Italy and were perhaps so in Tuscany: Jean-François Goudesenne, "*Historiae* from *Alta Italia* and their Frankish Models: A Progressive 'Romanisation' by the Carolingian Franks (750–950)," in *Political Plainchant?: Music, Text, and Historical Context of Medieval Saints' Offices*, ed. Roman Hankeln (Ottawa: Institute of Mediaeval Music, 2009), 19–20.

characterized the development of relic cults throughout early medieval Tuscany and were likewise inspired by the Eternal City.

Nevertheless, the development of St. Minias's cult did not end with his translation to the cathedral and nor did the evolution of this Office.[42] Although Otto II purportedly acquired the saint's relics and transferred them to Metz in 970, Bishop Ildebrando of Florence claimed to have rediscovered them along with those of other martyrs atop the Monte Fiorentino nearly fifty years later. Likely inspired by the royal abbey dedicated to St. Denis, he sought to transform the shrine into a pilgrimage site by adding an outer crypt to the dilapidated church, a structure evocative of the one built at Saint-Denis by its celebrated abbot, Hilduin (†840). He also established a Benedictine monastery with the support of his aristocratic patron, Emperor Henry II. The foundation provided the impetus for three related developments: the immediate elaboration of its titular's dossier via the revised Passion of St. Minias by its first abbot, Drogone; the enlargement (perhaps not long after) of the *Officium Sancti Miniatis*; and the rebuilding of the entire church from the late eleventh century.

The revised Passion provided the literary justification for Ildebrando's project by bolstering the claims of San Miniato to possess St. Minias's relics and rendering the saint more appealing to ecclesiastical reformers of the eleventh century. Drogone preserved the sequence of events related in the original *passio* with one major exception designed to discount reports of previous translations of St. Minias from the saint's original home. St. Minias, he claimed, was executed not atop the Monte Fiorentino but, rather, at a site north of the Arno, whence the decapitated martyr bore his own head to the mount in the manner of the most famous cephalophore, St. Denis: "With the miraculous, admirable indication, [St. Minias] declared that he wished to await the Day of Judgment in that place."[43] If the postmortem journey virtually precluded his purported translations either to Santa Reparata or to Metz, more subtle innovations evoked the very hermits and monks who vociferously criticized Ildebrando for corruption and incontinence. Drogone depicted St. Minias not as a blank slate, as had the first Passion, but as an evangelizer and ascetic who gathered together followers to fast and pray atop the Monte Fiorentino. The author also embellished the tortures inflicted upon St. Minias and emphasized the protagonist's manly (*viriliter*) triumph over them, employing a gendered vocabulary common to reformist hagiography of the eleventh century.

The promotion of St. Minias extended from the revised Passion to new plainsong with which the monks of San Miniato amplified the original Office likely composed around 900. The Florentine antiphoner presents eight chants—five vespers antiphons, two Gospel antiphons, and a responsory—distinct from the remainder of the Office

---

[42] The present paragraph summarizes the discussion of Ildebrando's foundation at San Miniato in chapter 3, this volume.

[43] *Passio Sancti Miniatis II*, BLF, Mugell., 13, fol. 136: "Ibique se ultimum examinis diem prestolari velle mirandis evidentissimisque indiciis declaravit."

in their literary character and musical style (appendix I). Their attribution to the Benedictine monks hinges on the textual sources for the respond. *Pretiosus Christi* draws its first phrase from a responsory from a ninth-century Office of St. Denis, confirming the importance of the transalpine martyr as a model for St. Minias. Its subsequent one derives from the revised Passion in the form of St. Minias's final prayer before his execution.[44] Its verse in turn features new text in the form of the Lord's reply but recalls Drogone's gendered vocabulary by praising the saint's "virile combat."[45] In accordance with the monastic cursus of their night office, the monks likely composed two more responsories. Following the narrative trajectory established by *Pretiosus Christi* (M-R10) and likewise mirrored in the Office of St. Denis, these would have related St. Minias's execution and selection of his gravesite via his postmortem perambulation. But because the antiphoner was copied for the cathedral rather than San Miniato, its scribe declined to include these chants because the depiction of the saint as a cephalophore supported the monks' claims to his relics.

If the new responsory introduced a biographical episode noticeably lacking in the original Office, the antiphons sounded a panegyric tone in accordance with their performance at the public hour of vespers. While the Gospel antiphons set a call to prayer by an unidentified community that "cultivates the protection of the most blessed martyr, Minias," those for vespers channel the voice of the monks.[46] *Martyrialis honor* (V2-A2) pleads for St. Minias to intercede on behalf of "we the monks" while *Tripudio cuncti* (V2-A4) urges "all brothers" to celebrate his feast with a "magnificent dance."[47] *Lucida pre reliquis* (V2-A5) addresses the saint as "nurturing father" (*pater alme*), an epithet that was often used to describe bishops and abbots but not martyrs, and was most appropriately expressed by the monks.[48] The chant also sets a rare instance of poetry, an elegiac couplet that conveyed a distinct impression of erudition.[49] Finally, the remaining

---

[44] See chapter 3, this volume.

[45] M-R10: "Pretiosus Christi martyr *Minias* in agone novissimo *dicens gratias tibi ago spes certantum quod me vincere fecisti tiranum. Iube precor modo in pace recipi spiritum meum.*" M-V10: "Vox de caelo facta est veni dilecte meus Minias accipe coronam quam viriliter certando acquisisti ad quam ipse laetus respondit."

[46] V-Am: "Beatissimi Miniatis martirris patrocinia colimus, fidei amore complectimur, multiplici veneramur affectu, cuius fides claruit in passione, et virtus fulget in gloria alleluia." L-Ab: "Almum hunc diem caelebremus colentes festa seculi laudando Miniatem martrrem Christo canamus gloriam."

[47] V2-A2: "Martyrialis honor Minias monachos tege pro nos." V2-A4: "Tripudio cuncti gaudeamus magnifico fratres in hac celebri Miniatis festivitate qui meruit eternam patriam feliciter adipisci."

[48] While the appellation, *pater alme*, appears in neither Passion of St. Minias, it serves as the incipt of the matins hymn for the episcopal father of Florence, St. Zenobius (appendix II). Nevertheless, its most prominent appearance in the liturgy is as the incipit of a responsory from a German office for St. Benedict, *Alme pater qui praescius*, inventoried in "Cantus: A Database for Latin Ecclesiastical Chant," http://publish.uwo.ca/~cantus/.

[49] V2-A5 "Lucida pre reliquis fueras, pater alme, lucerna; | est quoque fama tui [sic] lucida pre reliquis." I thank Leofranc Holford-Strevens for calling my attention to its poetic form. Around 1100, Bishop Rangerio of Lucca made similar use of elegiac couplets in his rhymed Life of St. Anselmo II, on which see chapter 4, this volume. For an analogous case from north of the Alps, see two of the verse epistles by Magister Leonin of

antiphons shift attention to the laity who undoubtedly flocked to San Miniato on the feast of its titular. *Adesto tibi* (V2-A1) asks St. Minias to intercede for "his subjects, the Florentines," and *Uterque sexus* (V2-A3) calls on "men and women of every age" to honor his passing.[50] Such rhetoric was surely understood by many of the attendant faithful and reflected the monks' desire to promote their patron saint beyond the walls of their monastery by casting him as protector of all Florentines.

The new chants of the *Officium Sancti Miniatis* became a vehicle not only for the aspirations of the monks of San Miniato but also for a post-Gregorian musical style. *Pretiosus Christi* (M-R10) eschews the periodic phrase structure and fixed formulae typical of classical responsories in favor of the principle of internal development (ex. 7.3). The second and third phrases are elaborations of the first: each begins by circling around the final (g) before ascending to the reciting tone (c'). The new responsory likewise eschews the modal clarity provided by Gregorian formulae and blends the authentic (high-range) and plagal (low-range) modes based on g in a procedure known as commixture. Its initial descent to d and emphasis on c firmly establish the plagal Mode 8; however, its elevated tessitura and recitation on d' in the fourth and fifth phrases imply the authentic Mode 7. Eschewing the simple recitation tones typical of classical responsories with an original melody, the verse confirms the authentic rather than the plagal mode with its high tessitura and prominent leaps of a fifth from g to d' (***vox*** and ***accipe***). All these features distinguished *Pretiosus Christi* from not only Gregorian plainsong but also the relatively traditional melodies of one of its textual sources, the ninth-century Office of St. Denis.[51] If the monks of San Miniato had access to a notated version of this transalpine liturgy, they nonetheless chose not to emulate its musical style.

The new antiphons of the *Officium Sancti Miniatis* likewise evince an equally distinctive post-Gregorian style, one cultivated by the canons of Santa Reparata and the monks of San Miniato. The chants exceed the modal distribution of classical plainsong by favoring Modes 4 and 6, and avoid the old tune classes to which the antiphons of the first layer so faithfully adhere. Their cadences are unusually restricted and in some chants fall exclusively on the final, a distinctly non-Gregorian procedure promoted in the 1020s by Guido of Arezzo for the sake of modal clarity.[52] Also distinctive is their narrow ambitus, relatively florid declamation, and repetition of entire phrases within individual melodies, of which the third approach likewise garnered Guido's approval.[53] *Martyrialis*

Paris: Bruce Holsinger and David Townsend, "The Ovidian Verse Epistles of Magister Leoninus," *Journal of Medieval Latin* 8 (2000): 389–423.

[50] V2-A2: "Adesto tibi subiectis Minias almifice Florentinis opem ferens caelestem assidue." V2-A4: "Uterque sexus et aetas omnis laudem concrepent Miniatis qui caelorum regna scandit hodie."

[51] For an edition of the Office of St. Denis, see Jean-François Goudesenne, ed., *L'office romano-franc des Saints Martyrs Denis, Rustique, et Eleuthère* (Ottowa: The Institute of Medieval Music, 2002).

[52] Joseph Smits van Waesberghe, ed. *Guidonis Aretini Micrologus* (n.p.: American Institute of Musicology, 1955), ch. 11, 140.

[53] Smits van Waesberghe, *Guidonis Aretini Micrologus*, ch. 15, 167–168.

EXAMPLE 7.3. *Pretiosus Christi* (*Officium Sancti Miniatis*, M-R10) and *Vox de caelo* (*Officium Sancti Miniatis*, M-V10).

honor (V-A3) illustrates all but this last trait and evinces striking similarities to its counterpart in the *Officium Sancti Zenobii* (ex. 7.4).[54] They occupy an identical position in their respective offices, feature a similar melodic profile, and present the same series of

---

[54] *Beatissimi Miniatis* (V-Am) presents something of an exception among the antiphons of Layer 2 of the *Officium Sancti Miniatis*. It is in Mode 1 and constitutes an extremely free elaboration of the Gregorian tune

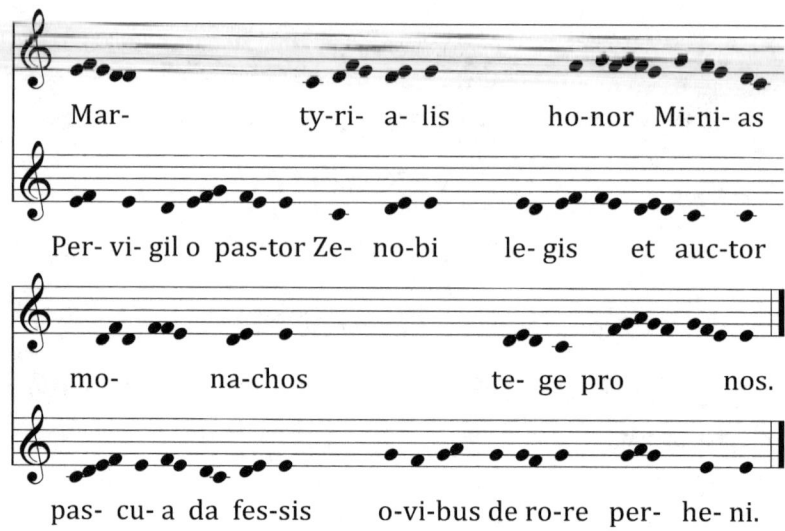

EXAMPLE 7.4. *Martyrialis honor* (*Officium Sancti Miniatis*, V-A3) and *Pervigil o pastor* (*Officium Sancti Zenobii*, V-A3).

four cadences. The first and third are subtonal on the final (e) and the second is open on c. The two antiphons exemplify the musical similarities between the two Florentine offices that, as illustrated below, suggest the emergence of a style characteristic of their city, one particularly indebted to Guido of Arezzo and not to the most prominent ultramontane models of post-Gregorian chant.

When did the monks of San Miniato compose the new plainsong in honor of their titular saint? While its dependence on the revised Passion provides an approximate *terminus post quem* of 1018, its preservation in the Florentine antiphoner indicates a rough *terminus ante quem* of 1150. Its marked similarities with the *Officium Sancti Zenobii* nonetheless suggest a narrower window of time. The two Florentine offices, as argued below, likely date from the same period, the third and fourth decades of the eleventh century. Extending this hypothesis, the creation of the new antiphons and responsories for St. Minias perhaps followed hard on the footsteps of the revised *Passio Sancti Miniatis* (one might further speculate) under the supervision of Abbot Drogone. This scenario accords with the frequent and well-documented concurrence of such literary and liturgical projects north of the Alps.[55] It also suggests that the expanded Office of St. Minias not only anticipated but also shaped the reconstruction and decoration of San Miniato, a project that communicated the same themes—the saint's bodily presence

---

family exemplified by *Tunc imperator* (L-A3) (see ex. 7.1). Nevertheless, its use of internal repetition as well as its devotional text place the antiphon squarely with Layer 2.

[55] Page, *The Christian West*, 412.

atop the Monte Fiorentino and his status the preeminent patron of Florence—sounded in the new plainsong.

As the monks continued to promote their saint with the rebuilding of their church, they emphasized not only his bodily presence but also his role as civic patron of Florence at the expense of such rivals as John the Baptist. The construction of the edifice unfolded in two building campaigns, one in the final third of the eleventh century and another in the second quarter of the twelfth. The first incorporated the outer crypt built by Ildebrando, transforming it into a monumental hall that intimated the presence of St. Minias's relics as had the now lost responsories that presumably narrated the saint's postmortem selection of his gravesite (fig. 5.3).[56] The second campaign yielded the marble façade, which features a polychrome, geometrical design similar to that of the baptistery of San Giovanni completed earlier in the twelfth century. The correspondence denoted competition rather than emulation: in the mosaic of the early thirteenth century, the Virgin and St. Minias flank Christ enthroned, the martyr occupying a position of honor normally reserved for St. John (fig. 7.1). The martyr emerges as the preeminent intercessor for the Florentines, whose city he faces below, in a visual analogue to the vespers antiphons that likewise cast him as a civic patron. Correspondences between image and music continue inside the basilica, where the apse mosaic completed in 1297 repeats this substitution of St. Minias for St. John while reinforcing the message of the crypt and of the aforementioned responsories. The depiction of Christ the Judge recalls St. Minias's intention, as related by Drogone, to remain atop the Monte Fiorentino until the Day of Judgment (fig. 7.2).

If the façade and apse mosaics thus drew on the revised Passion and echoed the second layer of the Office, they also elaborated St. Minias's dossier in such a way as to distinguish its subject from St. John and St. Zenobius. Both mosaics portray St. Minias as a young blond, clothed in a blue tunic and a red or gold mantle, and presenting a crown to Christ. The titulus in the apse (*Sanctus Miniatus Rex Erminie*) confirms that the portrayal reflected the belief that St. Minias was not the local hermit described by Drogone but, rather, an Armenian king who fell victim to the Decian persecutions while traveling through Tuscany.[57] The embellishment of the saint's background endowed him with

---

[56] On the significance of such monumental hall crypts, see chapter 5, this volume. The remainder of the paragraph summarizes Scott B. Montgomery, "*Quia venerabile corpus redicti martyris ibi repositum*: Image and Relic in the Decorative program of San Miniato al Monte, Florence," in *Images, Relics, and Devltional Practices in Medieval and Renaissance Italy*, ed. Sally J. Cornelison and Scott B. Montgomery (Tempe: Arizona Center for Medieval and Renaissance Studies, 2005), 12–13 and 16–17, concerning the visual program of San Miniato.

[57] While the purportedly royal lineage of St. Minias was thus undoubtedly propagated by the monks of San Miniato, it nonetheless found its earliest expression in the illuminated passionary from San Martino of Lucca, BCL, P†, fol. 158v (saec. XII$^{2/4}$). Like other early martyrs pictured in Lucchese manuscripts, St. Minias is brown haired, bearded, and clothed in a green tunic and red mantle. Suggestive of his aristocratic lineage, however, is the golden broach, bejeweled cuff, and lilies, all imperial attributes usually reserved for

FIGURE 7.1. Façade Mosaic, San Miniato al Monte, Florence (saec XII[in]) (Album/Art Resource, NY).

a lineage more noble than that of a local Florentine aristocrat such as St. Zenobius.[58] It concomitantly amplified the longstanding imperial associations of St. Minias's shrine in contradistinction with St. John, whose cult was squarely identified with the Florentine commune in the twelfth and thirteenth centuries.[59]

---

aristocrats or soldiers. Moreover, St. Minias holds what appears to be a crown. On the iconographic conventions concerning early martyrs and the characteristic attributes of the empire, see Charles Buchanan, *A Late Eleventh-Century Illustrated Lectionary from Lucca*, Ph.D. diss., University of California, Santa Barbara, 1997, 127–132 and 305, respectively.

[58] While the *Vita Sancti Zenobii I*, in *AS*, May, vol. 6, ch. 3, no. 2, col. 58, noted that its subject was "of noble origin" (*carnis origine nobilis*), a late twelfth-century revision, *Vita Sancti Zenobii II*, BLF, Pluteo 27.1, fol. 140, in Giovanni Lami, *Charitonis et Hippophili hodeoporicon*, 4 vols. (Florence: Viviani, 1741–1754), 549, described him as "born of a noble Florentine family" (*ut erat ex nobili Florentinorum progenie natus*).

[59] See introduction to part II. The notion that St. Minias was a king perhaps stemmed from his own description of himself as a "soldier and servant of Christ" (*Dixi iam tibi quia ego sum Minias, miles et servus Christi*),

FIGURE 7.2. Apse Mosaic, San Miniato al Monte, Florence (1297) (Nicolo Orsi Battaglini/Art Resource, NY).

The efforts of the monks of San Miniato to promote Florence's first martyr as its preeminent protector naturally found little support among the cathedral canons. The latter maintained their claims to possess St. Minias's relics into the eleventh century, when they evidently abandoned his cult in favor of that of St. Zenobius (on which more below).[60] Neither ordinal of Santa Reparata signaled the presence of St. Minias's relics in his church. Moreover, the Ritus classified his *dies natalis* only among the second-ranking, or "principal" (*precipua*) feasts, rather than the "highest" (*summa*) ones,

---

as told in the *Passio Sancti Miniatis I*, BLF, Edili 139, fol. 202v, in *AS*, October, vol. 11, col. 429. The phrase may mean that the protagonist was a member of the Roman army. Alternatively, it might simply illustrate the common metaphor for a Christian, the *miles Christi*. Finally, Robert Davidsohn, *Storia di Firenze*, trans. Giovanni Battista Klein, 7 vols. (Florence: Sansoni, 1956–1965), vol. 1, 59, n. 1, argues instead that the transformation of St. Minias into an Armenian king resulted from the conflation of the Latin "Erminia," its derivative proper name, "Herminias," and the abbreviated form "Minias." Such an argument based on etymology does not preclude the political one offered here.

[60] That the cathedral canons continued to believe they possessed St. Minias's relics finds confirmation in the now-lost "Rituale antico" of the eleventh century, which names them among the inventory of holy treasure preserved in Santa Reparata: ASF, Carte Strozziane, II, 56, fol. 22v.

such as the Dedication of the Church or the feast of such "patrons" as St. Zenobius.[61] On St. Minias's *dies natalis*, the canons chanted the expanded Office issued by their rivals (with the exception of the now-lost responsories) but recited the original Passion, rejecting Drogone's narrative and thus the literary vehicle for the promotion of San Miniato as the uncontested site of St. Minias's relics.[62] Finally, they made a more public gesture of disapproval by declining to worship at the suburban basilica on its titular's feast, an honor accorded to seven local churches over the course of the liturgical year.[63] Instead, the canons remained at Santa Reparata, chanting first and second vespers as well as Mass in the crypt, surely in recollection of the relics of St. Minias once believed to have been interred there.[64]

In its literary and musical character, then, the *Officium Sancti Miniatis* reflects the evolution of its saint's cult over two centuries. Its first layer resulted from his translation to the cathedral around 900, its second from the foundation of the monastery of San Miniato in 1018. The former amplified the circularity of a Passion itself based on the ancient *Gesta martyrum* and adopted the venerable conventions of Gregorian plainsong. The latter drew text from the *passio* by Drogone, as well as the Office of St. Denis. It reflected the monks' desire to promote St. Minias as a civic patron and forged a new style of plainsong independent of the strictures of classical conventions. Despite the musical and artistic glories of San Miniato, however, its titular never became a preeminent Florentine patron, an honor that fell to John the Baptist and secondarily to St. Zenobius.

---

[61] Ritus, fols. 98v–99, in Franklin Toker, *On Holy Ground: Liturgy, Architecture, and Urbanism in the Cathedral and Streets of Medieval Florence* (Turnhout: Brepols, 2009), 251.

[62] Both the cathedral passionary, BLF, Edili 139, fols. 202–203v (saec. XII$^{2/4}$), and lectionary, BLF, Edili 147, fols. 251–254 (1447–1453), preserve the *Passio Sancti Miniatis I*. On the dating and provenance of these manuscripts, see Rossana E. Guglielmetti, *I testi agiografici latini nei codici della Biblioteca Medicea Laurenziana* (Florence: SISMEL - Edizioni del Galluzzo, 2007), 94–95 and 146, respectively; as well as Knut Berg, *Studies in Tuscan Twelfth-Century Illumination* (Oslo: Universitetsforlaget, 1968), no. 69, 268 (for the first manuscript only). By contrast, the cathedral canons of Pisa, Pistoia, and Siena evidently adopted the *Passio Sancti Miniatis II*, for their ordinals prescribe proper lessons but chants from the Common of Multiple Martyrs in accordance with Drogone's novel assertion that St. Minias was martyred with his followers rather than alone: OOP, fol. 52; OOPist1, fol. 63; and Giovanni Crisostomo Trombelli, ed., *Ordo Officiorum Ecclesiae Senensis ab Oderico eiusdem Ecclesiae canonicus anno MCCXIII compositus* (Bologna: Longhi, 1766), pt. 1, ch. 416, 375.

[63] Ritus, fol. 95, in Toker, *On Holy Ground*, 248. By contrast, the cathedral chapter chanted Mass at the following Florentine churches on the feasts of their titulars: Sant'Andrea (Ritus, fol. 68v and Mores, fols. 5v–6, in Toker, *On Holy Ground*, 223 and 273); Santa Lucia di Massa Pagani (Mores, fol. 6, in Toker, *On Holy Ground*, 273), Santo Stefano (Ritus, fol. 11v and Mores, fol. 7, in Toker, *On Holy Ground*, 170 and 274); San Pancrazio (Ritus, fol. 82v and Mores, fol. 9v, in Toker, *On Holy Ground*, 236 and 278); San Pietro Maggiore (Ritus, fol. 86v and Mores, fol. 10v, in Toker, *On Holy Ground*, 239 and 278); Sant'Apollinare (Ritus, fol. 88v and Mores, fol. 10v, in Toker, *On Holy Ground*, 241 and 279); Santa Felicita (Ritus, fol. 88v and Mores, fol. 10v, in Toker, *On Holy Ground*, 242 and 279).

[64] Mores, fol. 11v, in Toker, *On Holy Ground*, 280. Tacconi, *Cathedral*, 125, by contrast, calls attention to the parallel locations of the altars of St. Minias and St. Zenobius in San Miniato and Santa Reparata, respectively, and speculates that the cathedral canon's practice of worshiping in their own crypt "may have been a symbolic action intended to parallel the adoration of [St. Minias] in the crypt of San Miniato."

Suggestive of St. Minias's diminished stature in the late Middle Ages were the liturgical reforms undertaken by the cathedral chapter in 1301, as a result of which its canons substituted his proper Office with chants from the *commune sanctorum*.[65] By the late Middle Ages, their efforts had long since shifted to their own spiritual father, St. Zenobius.

ST. ZENOBIUS

In its structure, literary themes, and musical style, the *Officium Sancti Zenobii* mirrored the second layer of its counterpart for St. Minias. Sung on the holy bishop's *dies natalis* (25 May) and the anniversary of his translation (26 January), it included six antiphons and a responsory for first vespers, of which the former were sung again at lauds and second vespers and the latter at matins (appendix II). Like the additions to the *Officium Sancti Miniatis*, as related below, the plainsong suited the public character of the evening office by promoting its protagonist as a civic patron, albeit by evoking a solitary supplicant rather than the collective citizenry. Exceptional among the Tuscan Offices, by contrast, were the three proper hymns for St. Zenobius sung at the principal hours of the day. They acquired the narrative role typically played by the antiphons and responsories of matins and lauds, underscoring St. Zenobius's power as a miraculous healer in life and in death. Following the likely completion of the Office in the 1030s, the canons of Santa Reparata embellished this portrayal by revising his Life and commissioning an altarpiece that provided visual expression to the musical and literary narratives. In so doing, they recast St. Zenobius as an acquirer of relics while underscoring their own importance in local religious life by giving newfound prominence to his clerical ministers.

The inclusion of the *Officium Sancti Zenobii* in the Florentine antiphoner establishes a *terminus ante quem* for its composition of ca. 1150; however, the ultimate origins of the Office lie in the revival of St. Zenobius's cult more than a century earlier.[66] In the 1030s, the cathedral canons had obtained financial independence from their bishop, taken an unusually active role in the reconstruction of Santa Reparata, and undoubtedly

---

[65] The liturgical reforms were part of the synodal legislation issued by Bishop Antonio degli Orsini of Florence (1309–1321) in Richard C. Trexler, *Synodal Law in Florence and Fiesole, 1306-1518* (Vatican City: Biblioteca Apostolica Vaticana, 1971), 266, on which see Tacconi, *Cathedral*, 69–71. The monks of San Miniato presumably continued to sing the *Officium Sancti Miniatis*, perhaps even after the cessation of their community to the abbey of Monte Oliveto Maggiore in 1373. The enduring appeal of the Office is confirmed by its appearance in a later addition to a breviary of the Florentine Badia, Oxford, Bodleian, Canonici liturg. 392, fols. 333–333v, 339–339v, and 341–341 (saec XV^med) and an antiphoner of the parish church of San Miniato tra le torre, Oxford, Bodleian, Canonici liturg. 379, fols. 11v–16v (1452). The Office also appears in the breviary, BLF, Conv. soppr. 457, fols. 455v–458 (saec. XV) compiled for a Benedictine monastery in Florence. That it contains sumptuous illuminations for the feasts of St. Benedict and St. Francis but no illumination for St. Minias suggests that its provenance was not San Miniato al Monte.

[66] The remainder of the paragraph summarizes the discussion of St. Zenobius's cult presented in chapter 4, this volume.

encouraged their guest, Lorenzo of Amalfi, in writing the first Life of its most prominent saint, St. Zenobius. While the author cast the protagonist as a beneficent healer of his flock, he also underscored the holiness of the rebuilt cathedral. Echoing the account of the purported rediscovery of St. Minias's relics in the foundation charter of San Miniato (1018), he declared the body of St. Zenobius "that most precious gem" and a gift to the Florentine populace from God, as he related its own transfer to the cathedral during which the saint's bier touched a tree that immediately bloomed. Lorenzo concluded with two miracles of exorcism and curing worked by the deceased bishop upon supplicants before his altar.

The *Officium Sancti Zenobii* combined the voices of such petitioners with similar expressions of civic pride of which the intensity was unique among the Tuscan Offices. The focus was on first vespers, which the cathedral canons celebrated in the crypt of Santa Reparata, requiring the clergy of the city to join them and decorating the church with garlands of laurel and myrtle as they would do for High Mass.[67] This exercise in public veneration demanded a full complement of proper chants rather than a single Magnificat antiphon typically reserved for first vespers. *O gemma fulgens presulum* (V-R) and *Hac subiens regnum* (V-Am) set pleas for intercession for the saint's Florentine subjects, the former, as noted in chapter 4, in concert with the image of St. Zenobius as a precious gem taken from the *Vita Sancti Zenobii*. *Gaudet membellis* (V-A5) proclaims that the entire city rejoices in their possession of his relics. *O pater et pastor* (V-A2) and *Votivo presul peteris* (V-A4), by contrast, adopt a more personal tone with their interjectory, "I pray" (*queso*). They thus identify their speaker as a single supplicant not unlike those whose petitions before St. Zenobius's altar were recorded by Lorenzo. Indeed, the latter antiphon illustrates the devotional habits that the canons aimed to inculcate among the attendant populace: "Bishop, you who are besought with a votive drachma, beg, I pray, that Jesus Christ be kind to us."[68] Throughout the evening office, St. Zenobius thus emerged as the good "father" and "pastor" to his "flock" in an exceptional use of civic rhetoric that far surpassed even that of the Office of St. Minias.

The public festivities on the eve of St. Zenobius's feast did not end with the conclusion of first vespers but continued on to a service known as a vigil, which presented readings and plainchant from matins at an hour and in an abbreviated format more convenient for the laity.[69] Unlike vespers, the vigil combined chants proper to the saint's *dies natalis* with ones drawn from other feasts in order to underscore St. Zenobius's broader significance for his city. A single antiphon, *Zenobi mundo* (V-A1), framed five psalms and gave voice to the collective petition that he "not spurn the vows of your Florentines."[70] Three

---

[67] Mores, fols. 9v–10, in Toker, *On Holy Ground*, 278. On the celebration of High Mass on the *dies natalis* of St. Zenobius, see chapter 6, this volume.

[68] V-A4: "Votivo presul peteris qui dragmate Ihesu[m] pro nobis Christum queso deposce benignum." I thank Leofranc Holford-Strevens for his assistance in translating this text.

[69] On the vigils, which were celebrated throughout Tuscany on the feasts of important saints, see Benjamin Brand, "The Vigils of Medieval Tuscany," *Plainsong and Medieval Music* 17 (2008): 23–54.

[70] V-A1: "Zenobi mundo fulgens prelucide cuncto Florentinorum ne spernas vota tuorum."

lessons drawn from the Life authored by Lorenzo of Amalfi framed two responsories. The first, *Beatus vir*, derived from the common of saints' feasts during Eastertide, while the second, *Iam non dicam*, was borrowed from the office of Pentecost. It cast the disciples as Christ's "friends and not servants" and thus reflected St. Zenobius's status as a local Florentine apostle.[71]

If the second layer of the *Officium Sancti Miniatis* and the *Officium Sancti Zenobii* both cast their saints as civic patrons, their antiphons and responsories evinced equally important musical similarities that perhaps reflect the geographic proximity of the two communities responsible for their creation. Both Offices employed a post-Gregorian style redolent of the teachings of Guido of Arezzo. As illustrated by the comparison between *Martyrialis honor* and *Pervigil o pastor*, the antiphons for St. Zenobius resemble the newer ones for St. Minias in their florid declamation, restricted number of cadential pitches, and preference for Modes 4 and 6 (ex. 7.4). The responsories for the two saints, *O gemma fulgens presulum* and *Pretiosus Christi*, likewise share key formal and stylistic features but also diverge in ways that suggest the preferences of their diverse composers (see ex. 7.3 and 4.1, respectively). Both eschew the periodic phrase structure and fixed formulae typical of Gregorian responsories. Both restrict their principal cadences to the final and feature verses set to distinct melodies rather than simple tones. *O gemma fulgens presulum* differs from *Pretiosus Christi*, however, in setting a pair of rhyming couplets in accentual verse characteristic of late medieval offices. It also employs unusually florid declamation, which serves to underscore the prayer (***ora***) requested of St. Zenobius. The melismas often feature melodic cells repeated (***Florentie*** and ***ora***) or transposed and slightly varied (***presulum***), highly structured roulades entirely atypical of classical responsories. If *Pretiosus Christi* had exceeded Gregorian norms through its modal instability, *O gemma fulgens presulum* did so via its ornate melodic surface.

Indeed, the musical resemblances between the second layer of the *Officium Sancti Miniatis* and the entirety of the *Officium Sancti Zenobii* suggest a process of imitation if not outright appropriation between the cathedral chapter and monastery of San Miniato. Given that approximate dating of their hagiography—the revised Passion of St. Minias was written around 1018, the Life of St. Zenobius around 1039—one might well suppose that the martyr's Office likewise predated the bishop's. The resonances of the Florentine chant with Guido's prescriptions nonetheless point to a more intriguing possibility. The choirmaster's patron, Bishop Teodaldo of Arezzo (1023–1036), was an ally of the cathedral canons, of whom one remembered him as a "glorious and most reverent bishop of good memory," for having consecrated the altar of John the Evangelist in the south apsidiole their church (fig. 4.1).[72] The canons perhaps learned of Guido's teachings

---

[71] The Florentine clergy likewise chanted *Iam non dicam* in procession to High Mass on St. Zenobius's feast (see chapter 5, this volume).

[72] See chapter 4, this volume.

through their connection with Teodaldo and applied them (albeit selectively) to the Office of St. Zenobius sometime in the 1030s. According to this hypothesis, the monks of San Miniato in turn borrowed the distinctive musical style forged by their adversaries at the cathedral in expanding the Office of their own titular saint.

Whatever the relationship between the two Florentine Offices, the canons of Santa Reparata distinguished theirs by including hymns, which served the narrative function played by the antiphons and responsories in the other Tuscan Office by tracing the protagonist's career and postmortem miracles in condensations of his Life. All three feature strophes comprising pairs of rhyming couplets of the sort encountered in *O gemma fulgens presulum* (V-R). And in accordance with the conventions of their genre, each was sung in largely syllabic fashion to simple melodies.[73] Much like the sequence at Mass, moreover, each hymn begins by extolling the musical praises rendered unto its saint before proceeding to a narrative section.[74] In *Almi patris Zenobii* (M-H), the singers identify themselves as "comrades" (*socii*), surely an allusion to the clergy given its performance at the private hour of the matins. *Psallat chorus fidelium* (L-H) evokes a generic "choir of the faithful," while *Letetur urbs Florentia* (V-H) signals the public character of vespers with its evocation of the entire city. The disparate incipits underscore the different topics and functions of the three hymns. The first two briskly recount St. Zenobius's life and translation without civic rhetoric; the third focuses on a single miracle at his altar before concluding with a plea that the saint secure the place for all Florentines among the "citizens of heaven."

Almi patris Zenobii (M-H) and *Psallat chorus fidelium* (L-H) are largely neutral summaries of Lorenzo of Amalfi's *Vita Sancti Zenobii*. The first begins with the subject's noble lineage, classical education, and precocious reputation for virtue. It continues with his election as bishop and his vision of St. Ambrose in the old cathedral of San Lorenzo, which the Milanese prelate had consecrated.[75] Much like the Life, the matins hymn devotes greatest attention to two miracles performed by St. Zenobius before his death, namely the raising of two boys from the dead. With *Psallat chorus fidelium*, the narrative omits the saint's death and proceeds directly to his translation from San Lorenzo to Santa Reparata. The hymn tells of the miraculously flowering tree and St. Zenobius's

---

[73] The cathedral hymnal, BLF, Edili 131, fols. 180v–182, provides a melody for *Letetur urbs Florentia* (V-Am) but not for the remaining hymns of St. Zenobius's Office. The original, neumatic notation pertaining to the first line of its poetry has been replaced by a new musical incipit notated in square notation, but the subsequent three lines retain their original musical notation. The remaining hymns for St. Zenobius were undoubtedly sung to another melody preserved in the hymnal, perhaps that associated with *Letetur urbs Florentia*.

[74] On the literary conventions of the sequence, see the discussions of *Sacerdotem Christi Martinum* for St. Martin and *Laudes Deo digna* for St. Donatus in chapter 6, this volume.

[75] Cf. *Vita Sancti Zenobii I*, ch. 1, in *AS,* May, vol. 6, col. 59. St. Zenobius's vision of St. Ambrose in prayer is first reported in Paulinus's *Vita Sancti Ambrosii* (*BHL* 377), in PL, vol. 14, col. 44.

unwillingness to enter his new home before the foundation of a cathedral chapter. If the first of these two miracles had provoked a celebration of Florentine glory in the Life, the hymn more soberly interprets it as a sign of the additional miracles that St. Zenobius would perform in the future cathedral.

Letetur urbs Florentia (V-H) distinguishes itself from the preceding hymns with its civic rhetoric and its focus on a single miracle, the exorcism of a boy before the altar of St. Zenobius. While it is the only chant of the *Officium Sancti Zenobii* to draw words or phrases from the Life, it nonetheless expunges a key detail.[76] According to Lorenzo of Amalfi but not the hymn, the boy's mother relied on the aid of the cathedral canons, who led her son to the altar only with great difficulty owing to the aversion of the demon inside him. In accordance with the public character of vespers, the omission shifts attention to the laity as the woman and her son become the focus of the miracle. It likewise anticipates the personal prayers of the second and fourth vespers antiphons, of which the first is particularly redolent of a mother's concern: "O father and shepherd, look after your flocks, that is your own children, I pray, with the expansive protection of heaven."[77] Such plainsong depicts an intensely personal and charged relationship between a single Florentine supplicant and her patron saint, albeit one sung by a grand assembly of clergy before an unusually large lay audience.

Constructed upon the literary foundation of the *vita* by Lorenzo of Amalfi and the musical one of the post-Gregorian style of plainsong distinctive of Florence, the *Officium Sancti Zenobii* signals the aspirations of the cathedral canons to attract supplicants to the tomb of their holy bishop and to render him the preeminent protector of their city. Following its likely completion in the 1030s, the clerics turned to literary and visual media to further this agenda. Later in the twelfth century, there was written a second Life of St. Zenobius that reflected the canons' interests. It transformed its protagonist into an acquirer of relics, promoted Santa Reparata as the religious center of Florence, and amplified the profile of his clerical ministers.[78] The revised *vita* neither enjoyed the wide circulation of the original nor replaced that text as matins lessons on the feast of its

---

[76] L-H: "*Quidam puer italicus* | tanto *perustus febribus* | ut nocte quarter decies | ei potus vix sufficeret." Italics denote the text drawn from the *Vita Sancti Zenobii I*, ch. 3, in *AS*, May, vol. 6, col. 61.

[77] V-A2: "O pater et pastor gregibus natisque peramplo presidio propriis prospice queso poli." I thank Leofranc Holford-Strevens for his assistance in translating this text.

[78] *Vita Sancti Zenobii II*, in Lami, *Charitonis et Hippophili hodeoporicon*, 548–566, of which the introduction spuriously ascribes the text to St. Ambrose's successor to the bishopric of Milan, Simplicianus (397–400). On the dating of the revised Life, see Maureen C. Miller, "The Saint Zenobius Dossal by the Master of the Bigallo and the Cathedral Chapter of Florence," *Haskins Society Journal* 19 (2007): 72–76, which convincingly refutes its dating to the ninth century by Anna Benvenuti, "Stratigrafie della memoria: Scritture agiographiche e mutamenti architettonici nella vicenda del 'Complesso cattedrale' fiorentino," in *Il bel San Giovanni e Santa Maria del Fiore: Il centro religioso di Firenze dal tardo antico al Rinascimento*, ed. Domenico Cardini (Florence: Le lettere, 1996), 99–102. Miller's argument rests in part on the critique of the revised Life by Lami, *Charitonis et Hippophili hodeoporicon*, 521–547, as well as that author's aforementioned edition of the text.

protagonist; however, it shaped the narrative program of an altarpiece executed for St. Zenobius's altar around 1230.[79]

The new *Vita Sancti Zenobii* enshrined the status of Santa Reparata as the mother church, suggesting, however anachronistically, that it had played this role during its protagonist's lifetime at the turn of the fifth century and partly due to his efforts. It thrice referred to the future cathedral as the *ecclesia maior* and noted that the church was dedicated to the Holy Savior in likely emulation of the original titular of the Lateran in Rome.[80] While Lorenzo had mentioned the urban basilica only in connection with St. Zenobius's translation and postmortem miracles, the second Life cast it as a setting for one of the saint's exorcisms.[81] It likewise told how St. Zenobius obtained for San Salvatore the bodies of two unidentified martyrs from the pope in Rome, a dubious claim as the earliest known translation of relics from the Eternal City to Tuscany date from the eighth century.[82] The purported transfer of holy treasure from Rome nonetheless resonated with contemporary politics as Florence formed an alliance with the papacy with its entrance into the newly formed Tuscan League in 1197.[83]

The revised Life of St. Zenobius similarly underscored the relationship of Florence with Milan while amplifying its subject's credentials as a translator of relics. According to Paulinus's *Vita Sancti Ambrosii* (422), Ambrose had founded Florence's first cathedral, San Lorenzo, in which he had interred the bodies of two Bolognese martyrs, Vitalis and Agricola.[84] In order to ensure the subsequent preeminence of Santa Reparata vis-à-vis San

---

[79] The single surviving manuscript source for the *Vita Sancti Zenobii II* to predate 1300 is a passionary compiled for St. Zenobius's first burial site, the suburban basilica of San Lorenzo, BLF, Pluteo 27.1, fols. 141–143 (saec. XII[med]): Miller, "The Saint Zenobius Dossal," 75–76; Guglielmetti, *I testi agiografici*, 663–668; and Berg, *Studies*, no. 35, 244. A marginal note to the prescription for the *translatio* of St. Zenobius in Ritus confirms that the cathedral canons continued to recite the Lorenzo's *vita*: "Pro legenda eius require in passionali in legenda predicti sancti Zenobii ab eo loco ubi dicit *Vellem preterea* etc" (fol. 73). The incipit, "Vellem preterea" marks the end of the account of St. Zenobius's life and thus the transition to that of his death and translation in the *Vita Sancti Zenobii I*, ch. 2, in *AS*, May, vol. 6, col. 61.

[80] Benvenuti, "Stratigrafie," 98–99. That Santa Reparata had been dedicated to the Holy Savior was an article of faith among the cathedral canons during this period. Mores, fol. 12, ordered that the bells peal three times on the feast of the Holy Savior, "because it was once the head of this church" (*pro sancto Salvatore, vicibus iiijor campanas, quia olim fuit caput istius ecclesie*). Ritus, fols. 97–97v, prescribes the integration of the office of the Holy Cross with that of the martyr, St. Theodore, on that same feast, likely a result of the belief, first documented in the fifteenth century, that a bishop named Teodoro had consecrated the church of the Holy Savior in 321: Tacconi, *Cathedral*, 90–92.

[81] *Vita Sancti Zenobii II*, BLF, Pluteo 27.1, fol. 140, in Lami, *Charitonis et Hippophili hodeoporicon*, 560.

[82] *Vita Sancti Zenobii II*, BLF, Pluteo 27.1, fol. 139v, in Lami, *Charitonis et Hippophili hodeoporicon*, 557–558. The earliest documented precedents for the translation of Roman relics to Tuscany was the translation of St. Crescentius by Bishop Ansifredo of Siena in the 750s (see chapter 2, this volume).

[83] Davidsohn, *Storia*, vol. 1, 912–919.

[84] *Vita Sancti Ambrosii*, ed. PL, vol. 14, no. 29, col. 39. A notice in the aforementioned passionary of San Lorenzo, BLF, Pluteo 27.1, fol. 129v, transcribed in Guglielmetti, *I testi agiografici*, 667; Lami, *Charitonis et Hippophili hodeoporicon*, 575–576, similarly tells how St. Ambrose deposited the relics of Sts. Vitalis and Agricola, as well as those of St. Mark the Pope, in that extramural basilica.

Lorenzo, the cathedral canons claimed, by the eleventh century, to possess some of the very relics that had cemented the Milanese bishop's reputation as a builder. These belonged to four martyrs—Nazarius, Celsus, Gervasius, and Protasius—whom Ambrose had translated to two newly built basilicas outside the walls of Milan.[85] It nonetheless fell to the revised *Vita Sancti Zenobii* to explain how portions of their holy bodies had arrived in Florence. According to the narrative, St. Zenobius was traveling through the mountains not far from his city in order to consecrate a church. While en route, he encountered legates bearing the gifts of the aforementioned relics from Ambrose. Seeing that one of them had died, St. Zenobius held and kissed the martyr's casket before returning the deceased legate to life.[86] With a single episode, the revised Life thus underscored the alliance between Florence and Milan, buttressed the status of Santa Reparata as *ecclesia matrix*, and celebrated St. Zenobius as an authoritative bishop who, like Ambrose, consecrated churches and translated relics for the benefit of his flock.

Although the revised Life of St. Zenobius thus cast its protagonist in the guise of a traditional lord and builder, it concomitantly underscored the emergence of an independent cathedral chapter in the central Middle Ages.[87] Like many *vitae* of holy bishops written in the eleventh century, the first Life had depicted St. Zenobius as a solitary figure unaided by subordinates. The second one, by contrast, featured two new characters, the archdeacon St. Eugenius and the subdeacon, St. Crescentius, whose relics had resided in Santa Reparata since the eleventh century.[88] The ministers assisted St. Zenobius in matters of ecclesiastical administration and in his performance of at least one miracle, the sort of collegial interaction that (ideally) occurred between bishops and cathedral canons. With the archdeacon and subdeacon, moreover, the revised Life yet again underscored the rise of the future cathedral as the mother church. Upon their deaths, St. Zenobius interred them in Santa Reparata even as he expressed his own desire to be buried, in traditional fashion, in his then-current seat of San Lorenzo.[89]

---

[85] Ambrose documented his translation of Sts. Nazarius and Celsus to the Basilica of the Apostles in 386 in a letter to his sister, in PL, vol. 16, no. 22, cols. 1019–1026. In his *Vita Sancti Ambrosii*, Paulinus writes of this event in his as well as of Ambrose's translation of Sts. Gervasius and Protasius to Sant'Ambrogio (olim Basilica Ambrosiana): in PL, vol. 14, nos. 32–33, cols. 38–39, and no. 14, cols. 31–32, respectively. In their now-lost *Rituale antico* of the eleventh century, the cathedral canons named all four saints, one after another, in the list of relics preserved in Santa Reparata: ASF, Carte Strozziane, II, 56, fol. 23. Marginal notes to Ritus, fols. 84v and 88v similarly indicate the presence of such treasure.

[86] *Vita Sancti Zenobii II*, BLF, Pluteo 27.1, fol. 141, in Lami, *Charitonis et Hippophili hodeoporicon*, 565.

[87] The following three sentences draw on Miller, "The Saint Zenobius Dossal," 78–80.

[88] Indeed, St. Eugenius is the subject of a new Life appended to the revised *Vita Sancti Zenobius: Vita Sancti Eugenii* (BHL 2682), BLF, Pluteo 27.1, fols. 141–143v, in Lami, *Charitonis et Hippophili hodeoporicon*, 566–575. The now-lost *Rituale antico* named Sts. Eugenius and Crescentius among the list of relics preserved in Santa Reparata and identifies them as St. Zenobius's ministers: ASF, Carte Strozziane, II, 56, fol. 22v.

[89] *Vita Sancti Zenobii II*, BLF, Pluteo 27.1, fol. 143, in Lami, *Charitonis et Hippophili hodeoporicon*, 573.

FIGURE 7.3. Altarpiece of St. Zenobius (ca. 1230; attr. Master of the Bigallo). Museo dell'Opera del Duomo, Florence (Scala/Art Resource, NY).

The canons' promotion of St. Eugenius and St. Crescentius continued with the altarpiece of St. Zenobius likely commissioned upon the enlargement of his crypt by 1230 (fig. 7.3).[90] In the center of the panel, the archdeacon and deacon flank their bishop to the left and right. In the four corners, they appear behind him in each of the narrative scenes, the former clothed in a blue cope (or pluvial), the latter in a gold-colored alb. Each scene illustrates a miracle related in the proper hymns sung before the altarpiece on the *dies natalis* and *translatio* of its saint. In the upper and lower left, St. Zenobius returns to life a boy who had been entrusted to him by his mother.[91] In the upper right, he similarly raises a deceased boy discovered by a band of Florentine citizens at the city gate, while below he exorcises a young boy.[92] The hymns perhaps inspired the selection of scenes and undoubtedly contributed, with the altarpiece, to the broader depiction of St. Zenobius as a healing thaumaturge. By casting St. Eugenius and St. Crescentius as

---

[90] Miklòs Boskovits, *The Origins of Florentine Painting, 1100-1270*, trans. Robert Wolf (Florence: Giunti, 1993), 90. Cf. pp. 292–303 for a physical description of the altarpiece and relevant bibliography.

[91] Cf. M-H: "After he opens the locks of death, he resuscitates the boy and delivers him to the mother from whom he had taken [the boy] in hand" (*Mortis claustra post reserat | nam puerem resuscitat | Quem matri tradit unici [sic] | a qua sumperat mutuo*).

[92] Cf. M-H: "Not long after the carriage, he returns another [boy] to the citizens in the middle of the northern entrance to the city." (*Non multo post curriculo | alium donat civibus | in porte urbis medio | que respicit settentrio*). Miller, "The Saint Zenobius Dossal," 76–77, convincingly argues against the contention of Boskovits, *Origins of Florentine Painting*, 292, that the third scene depicts the resurrection of the Milanese legate as told in the *Vita Sancti Zenobii II*, BLF, Pluteo 27.1, fol. 141, in Lami, *Charitonis et Hippophili hodeoporicon*, 565. She cites in support of her identification the diminutive proportions of the prone figure and the absence of the relics sent to Florence by St. Ambrose. Note that the fourth and final scene of the altarpiece follows the revised Life rather than the original one and *Letetur urbs Florentia* (V-H). While the first describes the miracle as occurring before St. Zenobius's death, the second and third place it at his altar in Santa Reparata: *Vita Sancti Zenobii II*, BLF, Pluteo 27.1, fols. 139v–140, in Lami, *Charitonis et Hippophili hodeoporicon*, 559–560.

consistent witnesses to their bishop's miracles, moreover, the altarpiece exceeded even the revised *vita* in portraying the Florentine prelate not as a solitary hero but one assisted by his faithful ministers. In this respect, it resembles the contemporaneous Life of St. Martin in the portico of San Martino of Lucca, which similarly insists on the presence of its subject's ministers at his Eucharistic miracle (fig. 6.4).

The altarpiece marked the latest chapter in remarkably successful efforts to promote St. Zenobius as an alternative to St. Minias as a civic patron of Florence. Having begun in the 1030s with the reconstruction of the cathedral and the writing of the *Vita Sancti Zenobii*, it continued with the composition of St. Zenobius's Office, the revision of his Life, and the rebuilding of his crypt. As an episcopal father, shepherd, healer, and exorcist whose cult was based in the burgeoning city-center, St. Zenobius was naturally a more persuasive candidate than St. Minias as Florentine protector. Although he never displaced John the Baptist as the preeminent object of local civic pride, his cult flourished into the Renaissance. Far from abandoning his Office as they did that of St. Minias, the cathedral canons fashioned an entirely new one in the fourteenth century.[93] Yet despite the rivalry between San Miniato and Santa Reparata, the liturgies for their respective titulars evinced marked similarities—namely the civic overtones and distinctive style of post-Gregorian chant, one evocative of the teachings of Guido of Arezzo. In both respects, the Florentine Offices proved unique in Tuscany: their Aretine and Lucchese counterparts proved more historical than panegyric in their literary character and more indebted to northern models of new plainsong.

ST. DONATUS

The *Officium Sancti Donati* belongs to the ambitious program of renewal pursued by three Aretine bishops from 987 to 1036. Elemperto rebuilt the extramural cathedral and its canonry and reformed its chapter; Alberto and Teodaldo oversaw the construction of the basilica of San Donato, which expressed the fidelity of their bishopric to the empire through its centralized plan.[94] Their rebuilding of their cathedral complex found a literary expression in St. Donatus's Passion and an aural one in the mass formularies composed for the saint's *dies natalis* by 1025. The Office surely originated from this same phase of creative activity: like the canonical chants of the Mass Proper, it drew its

---

[93] This late medieval Office of St. Zenobius appears in the fourteenth-century breviary from the cathedral of Florence, BLF, Edili 117, fols. 283v–286v, and is inventoried in Tacconi, *Cathedral*, 223–226. On the broader development of the saint's cult after 1300, see Blake Wilson, "Music, Art, and Devotion: The Cult of St. Zenobius at the Florentine Cathedral during the Early Renaissance," in *Il "Cantate Domino." Musica nei secoli per il duomo di Firenze. Atti del Convegno Internazionale di Studi (Firenze, 23-25 maggio 1997)* ed. Piero Gargiulo, Gabriele Giacomelli, and Carolyn Gianturco (Florence: Edifir, 2001), 17–36.

[94] See chapter 3, this volume.

texts from the revised *passio* and circulated throughout Tuscany.⁹⁵ Yet while the former self-referentially focused on St. Donatus's signature miracle, his repair of the chalice at Mass, and were adaptations of venerable models of Gregorian plainsong, the latter retold the entire story of his career with a coherence exceptional among the Tuscan Offices and made measured use of a new melodic style.

Inspiration for the narrative turn and post-Gregorian style of the *Officium Sancti Donati* came from a new generation of Frankish Offices to emerge in the tenth century.⁹⁶ The cathedral canons of Florence were enthusiastic adopters (if not emulators) of such ultramontane liturgies: their antiphoner includes five of them, of which all are connected with universal cults.⁹⁷ The oldest were probably the Offices for the *inventio* of St. Stephen by Stephen of Liège (†920) and for St. Peter by Hucbald of Saint-Amand (†930); however, equally if not more popular in Tuscany was the Office of St. Nicholas composed around 960 by Reginold, a future bishop of Eichstätt.⁹⁸ Among the innovative features of such Offices was their arrangement of antiphons and responsories according to an ascending modal order analogous to the narrative sequence typically formed by

---

⁹⁵ Alpigiano and Licciardello, *Officium Sancti Donati*, 11. On the mass formularies for St. Donatus, see chapter 6, this volume. The dioceses of Lucca, Pistoia, and Siena adopted the Office of St. Donatus: *OOL*, fol. 58v, OOPist1, fol. 58; and *OOES*, pt. 1, ch. 379, 344. More enigmatic is the case of Florence: while Ritus, fol. 89v, in Toker, *On Holy Ground*, 242, indicates that the cathedral canons sang from the Common of One Martyr on St. Donatus's *dies natalis*, the saint's Office appears in their antiphoner, AAF, n.s., fols. 153v–155v.

⁹⁶ Page, *The Christian West*, 383–441; Goudesenne, *Les Offices*, 223–249; Goudesenne, "A Typology," 24–25; David Hiley, "Style and Structure in Early Offices of the Sanctorale," in *Western Plainchant in the First Millennium: Studies in the Medieval Liturgy and its Music*, ed. Sean Gallagher et al. (Burlington: Ashgate, 2003), 157–179; Richard L. Crocker, "Matins Antiphons at St. Denis," *Journal of the American Musicological Society* 39 (1986): 441–490; and Ritva Jonson [Jacobsson], *Historia: Études sur la genèse des offices versifiés* (Stockholm: Stockholm: Almqvist & Wiksel, 1968).

⁹⁷ AAF, n.s., fols. 25–28v (St. Stephen), 28v–31v (John the Evangelist), 143–145 (St. Peter), 156–159 (*inventio* of St. Stephen), 200v–206v (St. Nicholas), of which all appears among the "progressive" Offices inventoried in Hiley, "Style and Structure," 167–169. Likewise "modern" was the Office of St. Vincent, which was added to the original corpus of the Florentine antiphoner sometime in the early thirteenth century (fols. 266–267v and 227v).

⁹⁸ Of the six "progressive" Offices in the Florentine antiphoner, for instance, the Sienese adopted only those for St. Stephen, St. John, St. Nicholas, and St. Peter as prescribed in their ordinal: *OOES*, pt. 1, ch. 50, 47–48, ch. 53, 50, ch. 302, 277, and ch. 362, 332. The Lucchese, by contrast, adopted the Offices of St. Stephen, St. John, St. Nicholas, all of which appear in the monastic antiphoner from their diocese, BCL, 603, fols. 24v–27, 27–30v, and 37v–40. Transcriptions of Hucbald's Office of St. Peter appear in Yves Chartier, "L'oeuvre musicale d'Hucbald de Saint-Amand: Les Compositions et le traité de musique," in *Cahiers d'études médiévales* (Saint-Laurent, Québec: Bellarmin, 1995), 291–299; and Rembert Weakland, "The Compositions of Hucbald," *Études grégoriennes* 3 (1959): 161–162, of which the latter (pp. 158–159) discusses its circulation in northern Italy in the eleventh century. Antoine Auda, *L'école musicale liégeoise au Xe siècle: Étienne de Liège* (Brussels: Lamertin, 1923), 58–66, provides an edition (music and text) of Stephen's Office for the *inventio* of Stephen. Charles W. Jones, *The Saint Nicholas Liturgy and its Literary Relationships (Ninth to Twelfth Centuries)* (Berkeley: University of California Press, 1963), 14–41, provides one (text only) of the Office of St. Nicholas and, in pp. 69–37, ascribes it to Reginald.

the plainsong and lessons.[99] Also novel were the expansive melodies that, in the case of the antiphons, conformed to new tune classes distinct from those of their Gregorian predecessors. These were the elements adopted, to varying degrees, by the composer of Aretine and Lucchese Offices.

That the *Officium Sancti Donati* features the strict narrative sequence (but not the modal ordering) typical of the northern Offices mirrored the breadth and variety of its literary source (appendix III).[100] The Passion begins with its protagonist's childhood in Rome, where he studied with St. Pigmenius together with Julian the Apostate. It proceeds to detail St. Donatus's early adulthood: having fled his former schoolmate's persecution of Christians, the hero settles in Arezzo, where he becomes a hermit under the guidance of the monk, Hylarian, and distinguishes himself as a healer, exorcist, and evangelizer. His reputation for holiness paves the way for his election as bishop, in which capacity St. Donatus forges an alliance with the Christian emperor, Theodosius, and defends Arezzo from the dangers of a dragon and a poisoned well.[101] He likewise makes provisions for his burial in a small oratory atop the hill at Pionta. Finally, the Passion concludes with the trial and execution of Sts. Donatus and Hylarian by an imperial prefect eager to ingratiate himself to the invading king of the Goths, Radagasius (†406). It thus casts its protagonist as an evangelizer, thaumaturge, ascetic, *defensor civitatis*, and defender of Christianity.

The *Officium Sancti Donati* transformed this wide-ranging story into a multi-layered narrative. As related in chapter 3, the Magnificat antiphons for first and second vespers related the protagonist's defeat of a dragon and purification of a well, which established his credentials as a *defensor civitatis* and thus accorded with the public character of the evening office.[102] The core elements of the narrative, however, remained the matins

---

[99] Indeed, Stephen of Liège drew attention to the relationship between modal order and narrative sequence in the lessons (albeit not in the plainsong) in his dedicatory preface to his Office of St. Lambert: "thereafter, new responsories and antiphons are added according to the genuine reason of the art of music, in which series of tones [i.e., the modes] responds to the order of the lessons" (*Exinde musicae artis ratione authentica subnectuntur cum antiphonis responsoria nova, in quibus ordini lectionum series respondet tonorum*) (PL, vol. 132, col. 645). On modal ordering in medieval Offices, see Jean-François Goudesenne, "Nouvelles perspectives sur le rôle des abbayes de Saint-Amand, de Saint-Thierry de Reims et de l'oeuvre d'Hucbald dans l'ordonnancement régulier des modes dans la composition musicale (850–900)," *Études grégoriennes* 30 (2002): 127–152; Andrew Hughes, "Modal Order and Disorder in the Rhymed Office," *Musica Disciplina* 37 (1983): 29–51; and Michel Huglo, *Les tonaires. Inventaire, analyse, comparaison* (Paris: Heugel, 1971), 127–152.

[100] In its lack of modal ordering, the *Officium Sancti Donati* resembles the sanctoral Offices composed in northern Italy from the ninth to the twelfth century: Goudesenne, "*Historiae*," 17.

[101] That the *Passio Sancti Donati II* so portrayed its protagonist as both an imperial ally and defender of his city resulted from the conflation of St. Donatus of Arezzo with the homonymous fourth-century bishop of Evorea (in western Greece): Pierluigi Licciardello, *Agiografia aretina altomedievale: Testi agiografici e contesti socio-culturali ad Arezzo tra VI e IX secolo* (Florence: SISMEL - Edizioni del Galluzzo, 2005), 309–316.

[102] Note that six of the ten Tuscan sources for the *Officium Sancti Donati* included the antiphon *Confractum namque vas*, which they variously assigned to the liturgical function of V-Am, L-Ab, and V2-Am: Alpigiano

lessons and responsories, of which the inclusion in the Aretine breviary facilitates a textual analysis not possible for the remaining Tuscan Offices.[103] The codex denotes the exact division of St. Donatus's Passion into lessons (as antiphoners do not) and shows how they were paired with responsories. Nearly every responsory not only quotes extensively from its lesson but also distills its essential elements, a procedure that yields a narrative sequence within the series of chants (appendix III). For instance, *Dum Iulianus* (M-R2) and *Secutus dicente* (M-V2) focus exclusively on St. Donatus's own flight from Rome, eschewing the narrative excursus concerning Hylarian's travels in *Nam Gazeos fugiens* (M-Lx2). The creation of such plainchant thus involved a process of editing by which the author identified the most salient elements of the saint's biography.

Nevertheless, a sensitivity to the private character of matins distorted the story formed by the responsories in one telling instance. *Eodem vero tempore* (M-Lx6) narrates two miracles—the slaying of the dragon and purification of the well—that cast St. Donatus as a defender of Arezzo. Such accomplishments, as we have seen, were deemed more appropriate for public hour of vespers, due (one presumes) to their civic resonance. *Cum augustus* (M-R6) thus ignores the dragon in favor of St. Donatus's raising of Eufrosina, a miracle related in the fourth rather than the sixth lesson.[104] This disjunction between *Eodem vero tempore* and *Cum augustus* not only breaks the relationship of distillation that normally characterizes responsory/lesson pairs but also disrupts the narrative sequence of the responsories. *Cum beatus Donatus* (M-R5) relates the miracle of the chalice, an episode that occurred after the raising of Eufrosina in the original Passion. Hence considerations of social context evidently trumped those of narrative coherence.

The story formed by the matins and lauds antiphons in turn reinforces and complements that of the responsories. Both *Stans beatus Donatus* (M-A6) and *Eufrosina adiuro te* (M-V6), for example, set St. Donatus's command that the dead Eufrosina reveal where she had hidden misbegotten funds. And the entire series of both antiphons and the responsories culminate with chants that cite the "angelic" or "heavenly" choirs that "exalt" the ascent of Sts. Donatus and Hylarian to heaven. By contrast, *Antime frater* (M-A9) supplements the account of the miracle of the chalice in the previous nocturn by setting the protagonist's gentle remonstration to his deacon, Antimus, who had dropped that vessel at Mass. Other antiphons allude to less miraculous elements of St. Donatus's

---

and Licciardello, *Officium Sancti Donati*, 66. This chant departed from *Ignis ardore* and *Sancti Donati sputum* in that its text related the miracle of the chalice, on which see chapter 6, this volume.

[103] On the dating and provenance of BCL, 605, see above, n. 19.

[104] While all seven eleventh- and twelfth-century sources for the *Officium Sancti Donati* preserved the sequence of responsories shown in appendix III, one manuscript of the thirteenth century, the antiphoner of the cathedral, ACA, Duomo A, fols. 84v–85v (saec. XIII[ex]), reverses the order of *Cum augustus receptus* and *Cum beatus Donatus*, thus modifying the series of responsories to preserve the narrative sequence: Alpigiano and Licciardello, *Officium Sancti Donati*, 100. Given the late date and exceptional reading of the Aretine source, it seems plausible that its reading is not authentic to the original office.

biography that nonetheless underscore his piety and commitment to ecclesiastical hierarchy. *Hylarianus monachus* (M-A4) narrates his zealous asceticism while *Sathirus episcopus* (M-A7) and *Iulius urbis Rome* (M-A8) trace his ascent through the ecclesiastical ranks from deacon to priest and finally to bishop. With the antiphons, responsories, and lessons, the combined night and morning offices thus presented three parallel narratives that variously synthesized, duplicated, and complemented each other.

If the *Officium Sancti Donati* resembled the new Frankish Offices of the tenth century in its coherent narrative structure, it made more sparing yet strategic use of their novel melodic style. Unlike its Florentine counterparts, it shows no trace of Guido of Arezzo's influence—hardly surprising given that his arrival at Pionta in the mid-1020s likely postdated its composition. Of the antiphons of matins and lauds, only one departed from Gregorian models. Perhaps not coincidentally, *Antime frater* (M-A9) is the only antiphon to allude to St. Donatus's Eucharistic miracle, which emblematized a bishop's sacramental authority and obtained great prominence in the mass formularies sung on the saint's feast (ex. 7.5). With its initial ascent from the final, g, to the reciting tone, d', *Antime frater* adheres to conventions of the traditional tune family exemplified by *Illuminata Siranna* (M-A5).[105] Rather than proceeding to a recitation first on d' and then on c', however, it then divides what would normally be a third phrase into two with a subtonal cadence on d' (*carissime*). With its subsequent ascent to and emphasis on the octave above the final (g'), it renders that pitch a true melodic goal and outlines the upper tetrachord (a collection of four notes) of the modal octave (d' to g'). This gesture expands the ambitus of the chant to a ninth and underscores the St. Donatus's admonition that Antimus not give himself up to grief. It was atypical of old Gregorian tune families but characteristic of the newly expansive melodic style of much Frankish plainsong. Inspiration for the *Antime frater* perhaps came from transalpine Offices such as the *Officium Sancti Nicolai*, of which the matins antiphon, *Pontifices almi*, similarly exploits the entire modal octave with its third phrase, "Nicolaum tunc presulum."[106]

Among the responsories of the *Officium Sancti Donati*, a single chant showcased the distinction between old and new melodic styles. Most of the responds employ the fixed formulae typical of Gregorian responsories and all their verses are set to the traditional tones.[107] Yet two responds are modeled upon a single chant rather than constructed from a

---

[105] See Frere, *Antiphonale Sarisburiense*, vol. 1, 72 (VIIb); and Dobszay and Szendrei, *Antiphonen*, vol. 3, nos. 7001–7017, 851–857 (A5), on the tune family to which *Illuminata Siranna* (M-A5) belongs; and Dobszay and Szendrei, *Antiphonen*, vol. 3, nos. 7171–7202, 934–951 (C1), on that to which *Antime frater* (M-A9) adheres. Cf. Alpigiano and Licciardello, *Officium Sancti Donati*, 181, which associates *Antime frater* with one particular member of the latter family, namely *Videntes stellam*.

[106] The transcription of the third phrase of *Pontifices almi* in ex. 7.5 derives from BCL, 603, fo. 138v. Other northern offices present more florid examples of such antiphons in Mode 7, including *Cornelius centurio* (*Officium Sancti Petri*, M-A7) and *In jejuniis et orationibus* (*Officium Inventionis Sancti Stephan*, M-A7).

[107] Four responds employ Gregorian formulae in exemplary fashion: *Puer Donatus* (M-R1) belongs to the class "Ia," *Dum Iulianus* (M-R2) to the class "VIIIa," *Cum beatus Donatus* (M-R7) and *Data est lex* (M-R8) to the class "IIa" inventoried in Frere, *Antiphonale Sarisburiense*, vol. 1, 17–18, 52–55, and 5–7, respectively.

EXAMPLE 7.5. *Illuminata Siranna* (*Officium Sancti Donati*, M-A5), *Antime frater et levita* (*Officium Sancti Donati*, M-A9), and the third phrase of *Pontifices almi* (*Officium Sancti Nicolai*, M-A7).

repertoire of conventional phrases (ex. 7.6). *Cum beatus Donatus* (M-R5) follows virtually note-for-note the Gregorian respond for the first Sunday of Advent, *Montes Israel*; *Hodie cum exultatione* (M-R9) is a looser adaptation that omits the fourth phrase of this same

---

Meanwhile, *Siranna utroque* (M-R3) and *Asterius Apruniani* (M-R4) are looser adaptations of classes "IIIb" and IIIa" inventoried in Frere, *Antiphonale Sarisburiense*, vol. 1, 30–31. Finally, *Cum augustus* (M-R6) does not fall into any of the tune classes inventoried by Frere.

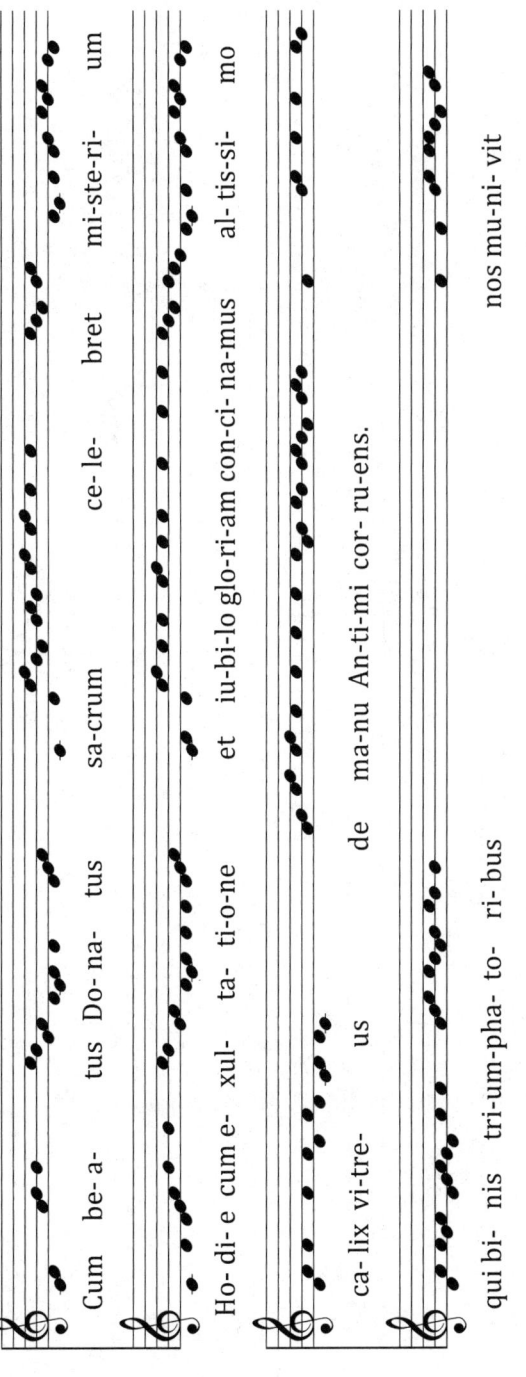

EXAMPLE 7.6. Comparison between *Cum beatus Donatus* (*Officium Sancti Donati*, M-R5) and *Hodie cum exultatione* (*Officium Sancti Donati*, M-R9).

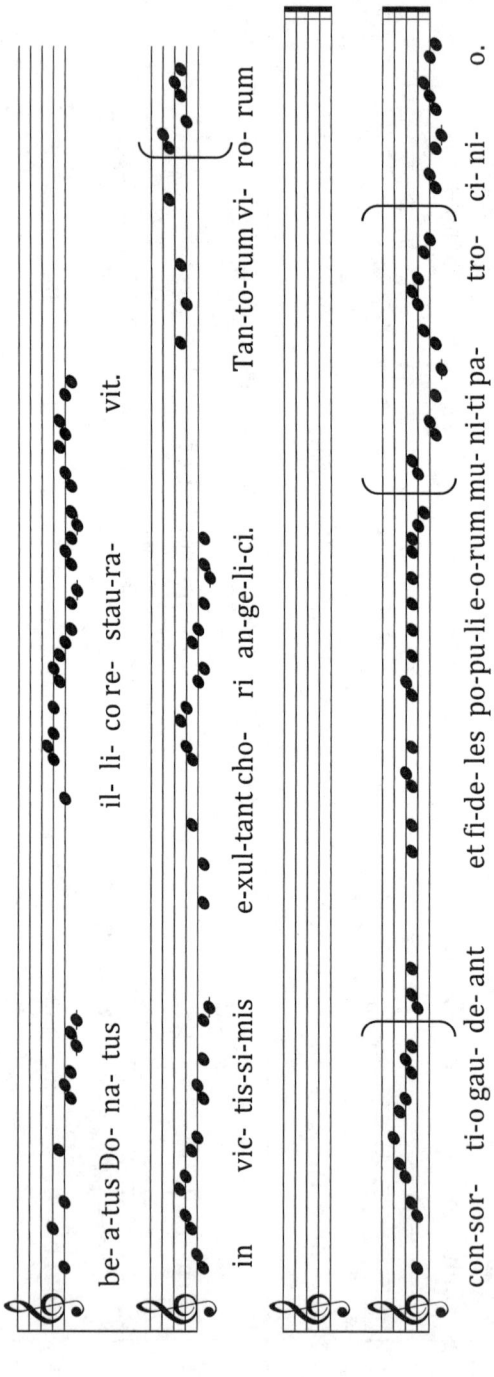

EXAMPLE 7.6 (*Continued*)

model and adds two more.[108] The resulting coda renders *Hodie cum exultatione* the longest of the nine responsories, befitting its position at the conclusion of matins and its status as the only chant of the night office to set an invitation to song. Moreover, the coda introduces a post-Gregorian melodic style distinct from the previous material. Its ascents to the octave above the final (*virorum* and *consortio*) exceed the narrow ambitus of *Montes Israel* and thus of *Cum beatus Donatus*, tracing the upper tetrachord of the modal octave in manner similar to *Antime frater* (M-A9). The accompanying emphasis on the fifth between g and d′ via a leap (*virorum*) and scalar motion (*consortio*) is foreign to the entire corpus of Gregorian responsories in Mode 1.[109] Finally, the last phrase exemplifies the principal of internal development atypical of classical responsories as it elaborates and transposes the penultimate one. Like *Antime frater, Hodie cum exultatione* thus illustrates the targeted use of newer, Frankish styles in what otherwise sounds like a traditional Gregorian Office.

Just as the first layer of the *Officium Sancti Miniatis* marked the emulation of Gregorian plainsong around 900, so the *Officium Sancti Donati* witnesses the reception of post-Gregorian models from north of the Alps roughly one century later. Its antiphons and responsories form parallel narratives in accordance with the breadth and variety of their literary foundation, the revised Passion of St. Donatus, and in imitation of the French and German Offices of the tenth century. Their occasionally expansive melodies likewise reveal a musical engagement with transalpine developments befitting a saint whose shrine attracted the veneration of Carolingian and Ottonian emperors and whose bishops were loyal and unabashed clients of such sovereigns. The influence of ultramontane models proved even more pronounced in the Offices composed for St. Fridian and St. Regulus in Lucca later in the eleventh century.

STS. FRIDIAN AND REGULUS

The Lucchese Offices illustrate even more clearly than their Florentine counterparts the often tense relationships between suburban martyria and urban cathedrals, for literary differences between the two liturgies reflect the divergences in the development of their saints' cults. The *Officium Sancti Fridiani*, as related below, was the work of a new community of Augustinian canons at San Frediano and is largely panegyric, exalting

---

[108] *Montes Israel* appears in the Florentine Antiphoner, AAF, n.s., fol. 2. It belongs to a small collection of responsories modeled on the responsory *In medio ecclesie* for St. John the Evangelist and inventoried as class "Ig" in Frere, *Antiphonale Sarisburiense*, vol. 1, 22. The particular melodic correspondences between *Cum beatus Donatus* (M-R5) and *Hodie cum exultatione* (M-R9) and *Montes Israel* confirm that the first two are indeed modeled directly upon the third one.

[109] Few Gregorian formulae outline the fifth from g to d′ and those that do employ stepwise motion rather than a leap of a fifth in the manner of *Hodie cum exultatione* as illustrated in the appendix, "Transcription of Mode 8 Standard Elements," to Helsen, "The Great Responsories" as well as in Frere, *Antiphonale Sarisburiense*, vol. 1, 52–28.

its subject as defender of the city that he had once guided as its bishop. The *Officium Sancti Reguli,* by contrast, was issued by the reformed urban canons of San Martino; its chants are strictly historical as befits a martyr whose relationship with Lucca began long after his death with his translation to San Martino in 780. Preserved in the Lucchese antiphoner of the first quarter of the twelfth century, these two Offices adopted similar musical approaches, thus mirroring the affinities between their Florentine counterparts. Both Lucchese Offices include antiphons but not responsories, employ music as a pointed rhetorical device, and adopt the melodic style of Frankish Offices. In this last respect, they befitted a city prominently positioned on the main pilgrimage from northern Europe to Rome, the Via Francigena.

The *Officium Sancti Fridiani* emerged from the resurgence of its saint's cult promoted by the Augustinian canons resident at San Frediano since the 1040s and who garnered a grant of papal immunity from Alexander II (i.e., Bishop Anselmo I) in 1068.[110] The church had previously been administered by a rector appointed by the local bishop, whose control of the basilica found expression in the second Life of St. Fridian.[111] If that *vita* had celebrated Bishop Giovanni I for having interred its protagonist in a newly built confessional, a third, expanded Life issued in the eleventh century reflected the interests and ideals of the Augustinians.[112] The revised narrative curtailed Giovanni's role by ascribing the discovery of St. Fridian's relics to a local laywoman.[113] Furthermore, it promoted San Frediano as a holy site independent of the bishopric by recounting miracles that the saint had performed from his confessional upon pilgrims traveling on the Via Francigena.[114] Finally, like the revised Passion of St. Minias of Florence, the *vita* appealed to the sensibilities of the eleventh century by recasting its protagonist as a hermit. In an emphatic endorsement of poverty, it tells how St. Fridian heeded Christ's pronouncement, "every one of you that doth not renounce all that he possesseth, cannot be my disciple" (Luke 14:33). The saint abandoned his hermitage to become bishop of Lucca only at the insistence of the local clergy and populace and with great reluctance.[115]

This elaboration of St. Fridian's background provides the key connection between the revised Life and the Office (appendix IV). *Dum in suis temporibus* (M-A1) refers to the saint's hermitage as a "retreat" (*latebra*) in which he prayed to the Lord. *Sprevisti pauperem* (M-A5), moreover, seemingly alludes to the saint's departure from his native

---

[110] PL, vol. 146, no. 62, cols. 1346–1347 (13 October 1068), on which see Enrico Coturri, "La canonica di S. Frediano di Lucca dalla Prima Istituzione (metà del sec. xi) alla unione alla congregazione riformata di Fregionaia (1517)," *Actum Luce* 3 (1974): 58.

[111] On the early history of San Frediano and the *Vita Sancti Fridiani II* (*BHL* 3175), see chapter 2, this volume.

[112] *Vita Sancti Fridiani III* (*BHL* 3175b), in Gabriele Zaccagnini, *Vita Sancti Fridiani: Contributi di storia e di agiografia lucchese medievale* (Lucca: Fazzi, 1989), 151–198, who dates the revised Life to eleventh century (p. 63).

[113] *Vita Sancti Fridiani III*, ch. 9, in Zaccagnini, *Vita*, 185–186.

[114] *Vita Sancti Fridiani III*, chs. 11–16, in Zaccagnini, *Vita*, 189–198, on which see Zaccagnini, *Vita*, 75–79.

[115] *Vita Sancti Fridiani III*, ch. 1, in Zaccagnini, *Vita*, 155.

Ireland and his self-imposed poverty: "you, Fridian, a pauper, spurned your countrymen and followed Christ."[116] The text derives from the fourth verse of a sequence, *Dilecte Deo*, composed in honor of the titular saint of the Frankish monastery of St. Gall by the prominent author and composer, Notker Balbulus (†912).[117] The quotation hints at ultramontane contacts cultivated by the Lucchese and facilitated by the Via Francigena. Those familiar with the northern sequence surely discerned similarities between St. Fridian and St. Gallus other than their eremeticism. Subsequent stanzas of *Dilecte Deo* relate its subject's foundation of Notker's monastery and thus recall St. Fridian's own foundation of San Frediano. Such intertextual subtleties aside, the most obvious points of reference for *Dum in suis temporibus* and *Sprevisti pauperem* were contemporary ideals of reformed monasticism that shaped the revised Life of St. Fridian.

The dominant image of the protagonist of the *Officium Sancti Fridiani* is nonetheless that of the *defensor civitatis*. Seven antiphons present pleas for intercession, though without reference to St. Fridian's part as "father" or "shepherd," or the civic rhetoric so prominent in the *Officium Sancti Zenobii*. Four more depart from such panegyric by citing St. Fridian's signature miracle that had won him an approving reference in the *Dialogues* of Gregory the Great.[118] According to his first and third Lives, the Lucchese had long sought to divert the Serchio River to the north of their city because it regularly overflowed its banks and destroyed their crops. Faith accomplished what engineering could not when St. Fridian traced a new course with a hoe and commanded the Serchio to follow his lead.[119] *Sancte Frigiane* (V-Am) provided the most prominent citation of the miracle in the sung liturgy due to its length and position at the beginning of the Office. Disposed into five irregular rhyming lines, its text suggests an unusual penchant for rhymed prose, which is atypical of Gregorian plainsong and appears in one other antiphon for St. Fridian but in none of the other Tuscan Offices. Moreover, it is the only chant of the *Officium Sancti Fridiani* to quote the account of the deviation of the Serchio in the saint's *vita*, which it combines with a plea for intercession.[120] Hence *Sancte*

---

[116] M-A5: "Sprevisti pauperem pauper Dominum sequens et patriantibus Frigiane."

[117] Editions of *Dilecte Deo* appears in AH, vol. 53, no. 149, 246–249 (text only), and Richard L. Crocker, *The Early Medieval Sequence* (Berkeley: University of California Press, 1977), 264–265 (music and text). The sequence circulated in northern Italy by at least the eleventh century, as illustrated by its three Italian sources: Lance Brunner, "Catalogo delle sequence in manoscritti di orgine italiana anteriori al 1200," *Rivista Italiana di Musicologia* 20 (1985): 225.

[118] V-Am, M-A8, M-A9, and L-A3 of the *Officium Sancti Fridiani* refer to the miracle in question. Cf. the account in Gregory I, *Dialogues*, ed. Adalbert de Vogüe, trans. Paul Antin, 3 vols. (Paris: Editions du Cerf, 1978, 1979, 1980), vol. 1, bk. 9, nos. 1–3, 286–289.

[119] *Vita Sancti Fridiani I and III*, ch. 5, in Zaccagnini, *Vita*, 175–179, provide roughly the same account of the deviation of the Serchio, the *Vita Sancti Fridiani II*, ch. 5, in Zaccagnini, *Vita*, 174–178, a much abbreviated one.

[120] V-Am: "*Sancte Frigiane* confessor Christi | *magnam* gratiam meruisti | fluminis impetum removisti | et *a periculo populum liberasti* | intercede pro nobis ad Dominum cui fidem plenam [h]abuisti." Italics denote the text drawn from the *Vita Sancti Fridiani I and III*, ch. 5, in Zaccagnini, *Vita*, 179. The other antiphon from the *Officium Sancti Fridiani* to employ rhymed prose is M-A8: "Vexillum leva ferebat | Christi signum faciebat | dextera imperabat | fluvio sanctus ut sequeretur latex cor astro dederat signum."

Frigiane provided a distinctive vehicle for the portrayal of its saint as defender of his city, one that characterized the entire office.

While the Office of St. Fridian integrates panegyric and historical elements in its portrayal of its subject as defender of his (unnamed) city, that of St. Regulus presents exclusively narrative ones based on (but rarely quoted from) a seventh-century Passion.[121] Given the relatively antiquity of the *passio*, its relationship with the *Officium Sancti Reguli* does not illuminate the dating or authorship of the Office. Nevertheless, the latter was surely composed by a cathedral canon and perhaps in the first decade of the twelfth century, when Bishop Rangerio translated the relics of St. Regulus to their current location in the east end of San Martino and (one suspects) revised the saint's Translation.[122] According to this hypothesis, the *Officium Sancti Reguli* would have marked the contribution of the cathedral chapter to a larger project: the revival of the cult of St. Regulus through literary, musical, and architectural means.

The Passion had promoted its subject as a model of three holy types: defender of Catholic doctrine, virtuous hermit, and heroic martyr.[123] It begins with St. Regulus's time as archbishop of Africa, when he struggles to stem the Arian heresy that had flourished since the Vandal conquest in the fifth century. This challenge surely left no time for the building projects and thaumaturgy usually ascribed to holy bishops. Tacitly acknowledging the appeal of Arianism in early Lombard Italy, the Passion adopts an unusually didactic tone, its lengthy passages excoriating the Arians' anti-Trinitarian beliefs.[124] The narrative pace quickens as St. Regulus and his companions escape the threats of their opponents, enduring a stormy voyage across the Mediterranean to Tuscany, where the protagonist becomes a hermit. News of his (unspecified) miracles attract the attention of the king of the Goths, Totila, whose soldiers demand that St. Regulus appear before their lord. Upon his refusal, they summarily behead him, after which the martyr picks up his own head and walks to his preferred burial site north east of Populonia (fig. 1.1).

The *Officium Sancti Reguli* tells the story of its subject's life and death no less than three times and without a single reference to Lucca, a profusion of narrative cycles that perhaps explains why the cathedral canons recited lessons from the Common of One Martyr rather than the *passio* (appendix V).[125] The first narrative sequence unfolds via the matins antiphons, of which the first four trace the subject's biography to his eremeticism

---

[121] Only two antiphons of the *Officium Sancti Reguli* quote from the Passion, *Iste pater Africe* (M-A1) and *Tyrannus ira plenus* (M-A9).

[122] See chapter 4, this volume.

[123] The remainder of the paragraph summarizes the *Passio Sancti Reguli*, chs. 1–9, in Manlio Simonetti, "Note sulla tradizione agiografica di S. Regolo di Populonia," in *Atti del convegno "Il Paleocristiano della Tuscia," Viterbo, Palazzo dei Papi, 16-19 giugno 1979* (Viterbo: Consorzio per la gestione delle bibliotheche comunale degli ardenti e provinciale "Anselmo Anselmi," 1981), 119–125.

[124] Simonetti, "Note sulla tradizione," 116.

[125] *OOL*, fol. 60v.

and the last concludes with his execution. The composer initially underscored this trajectory by situating the first three antiphons in ascending modal sequence, an ultramontane technique that he thereafter abandoned. The fifth through eighth antiphons further confuse the story by returning to St. Regulus's defense of Catholicism and his eremitic life. *Maris undas mitigans* (M-A6), moreover, amplifies the saint's credentials as a thaumaturge by casting him as an exorcist, which finds no support from the Passion. Less confused is the second narrative of the Office, one formed by the antiphons sung at lauds and again at vespers. Most unusual, however, is the third story, one told in the three Gospel antiphons, which present none of the usual pleas for intercession or calls to prayer. *Laudanda est Trinitas* (V-Am) adopts the didacticism of the *passio*, exalting the Trinity and its defenders without mention of the protagonist. *Beatus Regulus* (L-Ab) recounts his heartfelt refusal to appear before Totila, *Hodie sacer sumus* (V2-Am) his execution and the events to unfold thereafter. Hence the story of St. Regulus's life and death becomes a structural device, marking the conclusion of the principal hours of the Divine Office.

Although many of the lay people who attended second vespers on the feast of St. Regulus probably followed the narrative of its antiphons with great difficulty, they found a visual aid in the thirteenth-century mezzo-relievo in the portico of San Martino (fig. 7.4; cf. fig. 5.2).[126] Situated just to the south of the pictorial Life of St. Martin and above the door that leads directly to St. Regulus's altar, it displayed to both lettered and unlettered the most dramatic moments of his Passion. The lintel depicts the confrontation of St. Regulus and his companions with a band of Arians. The former carry books and are dressed in clerical garb; the latter bear arms and are clothed in classical tunics. The striking imagery overshadows the parchment rolls summarizing their opposing theologies: "I, Regulus, assert that the Father, Son and the Holy Ghost have always been lord," and "we Arians say that the son of God relinquished his divine origin."[127] The tympanum shows St. Regulus kneeling before his executioner, clothed in episcopal regalia notwithstanding his eremeticism. The detail underscores the subject's archiepiscopal office and betrays the influence of the cathedral canons, who likewise exalted the episcopate in ways clear to the lettered and unlettered in the nearby pictorial Life of St. Martin (figs. 6.3 and 6.4).[128]

If the Lucchese Offices offer different literary approaches, they share key musical strategies suggesting that they were composed in the same period—from the mid-eleventh to the early twelfth century—and that one provided inspiration for the other in the manner of their Florentine counterparts. Both the *Officium Sancti Fridiani* and the

---

[126] On the execution of the mezzo-relievo, see chapter 5, this volume.

[127] "Ego Regulus assero semper fuisse dominum patrem et filium et spiritum sanctum." "Nos ariani dicimus filium dei initium in divinitate abuisse."

[128] See chapter 6, this volume.

FIGURE 7.4. Life of St. Regulus (ca. 1233-1250). Portico of San Martino, Lucca (photo by author).

Officium Sancti Reguli employ melodic gestures that underscore the rhetoric of the text in particularly prominent ways. For example, the two Offices make frequent use of a Gregorian tune class in Mode 1 that begins with a descent to the subtonic and a modest ascent to the third or fourth above the final.[129] In four of six instances in the Lucchese Offices, the melodic incipit underscores a textual one, either "Bishop Fridian" or "Blessed Regulus," encountered in none of their remaining antiphons (ex. 7.7). Because the six antiphons belonged to two different feasts and were not sung consecutively, one after another, only those responsible for their performance (i.e., the canons of San Martino and San Frediano) and the more discerning listeners in attendance would have been likely to notice the similar beginnings of these chants. In this understated melodic gesture, these individuals would have heard an aural equivalent of these common appellations—Bishop Fridian, Blessed Regulus—in a manner encountered in no other Tuscan Office.[130]

---

[129] Dobszay and Szendrei, *Antiphonen*, vol. 1, nos. 1267–1379, 135–194 (D); and Frere, *Antiphonale Sarisburiense*, vol. 1, 67–68 (1f), of which examples include M-A4, M-A7, L-A1, and L-A3 from the *Officium Sancti Fridiani*, L-A1 and L-Ab from the *Officium Sancti Reguli*, and M-A4, L-A2, and V2-Am from the *Officium Sancti Donati*.

[130] The only point of comparison among the Tuscan Offices is the use of the same tune class (though not the same melodic incipit) to underscore the similar textual incipits of *Tunc iratus* (M-A9) and *Tunc imperator* (L-A3) in the *Officium Sancti Miniatis* (ex. 7.1).

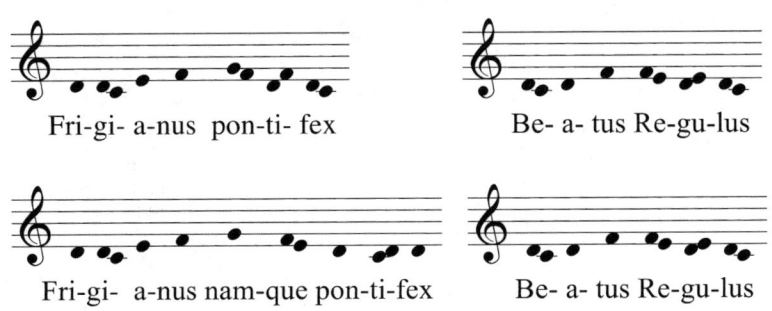

EXAMPLE 7.7. Incipits of Four Antiphons: *Frigianus pontifex* (*Officium Sancti Fridiani*, M-A7), *Frigianus namque pontifex* (*Officium Sancti Fridiani*, L-A1), *Beatus Regulus* (*Officium Sancti Reguli*, L-A1), and *Beatus Regulus* (*Officium Sancti Reguli*, L-Ab).

Musical rhetoric found a far more accessible vehicle in the final antiphon of the *Officium Sancti Reguli* (ex. 7.8). By far the longest chant of the two Lucchese Offices, *Hodie sacer sumus* was sung at the public hour of vespers and was modeled upon the "Hodie" antiphons that adorned the Magnificat on ancient temporal, Marian feasts, and sanctoral feasts. These models usually comprise two, three, or (in one instance) four sentences that summarize the significance of the feast. Each begins with the word *today*, which invokes the *hinc et nunc* (here and now) by conflating the historical events with the moment of celebration.[131] *Hodie sacer sumus* presents four sentences that narrate St. Regulus's martyrdom, his postmortem perambulation, the angel's appearance to his disciples and the pleading of his tormented executioners, and finally his ascent to heaven. Its melody recalls one particular "Hodie" antiphon, *Hodie Simon Petrus*, in adhering to the largest Gregorian tune family in Mode 1, thereby befitting a saint once buried in an annular confessional modeled on that of St. Peter's.[132] Yet *Hodie sacer sumus* exceeds that venerable Petrine chant in its length and use of escalating rhetoric to underscore the repetition of *today*. The first *hodie* elicits but a modest rise to the final (d), an initial gesture found in other "Hodie" antiphons and one that may have ultimately derived from Byzantine hymns (*stichēra*).[133] The second *hodie* provokes a stepwise one to the reciting

---

[131] Anne Walters Robertson, "From Office to Mass: The Antiphons of Vespers and Lauds and the Antiphons before the Gospel in Northern France," in *The Divine Office in the Latin Middle Ages: Methodology and Source Studies, Regional Developments, Hagiography, Written in Honor of Professor Ruth Steiner*, ed. Margot Fassler and Rebecca A. Baltzer (Oxford: Oxford University Press, 2000), 312–313; and Egon Wellesz, *Eastern Elements in Western Chant: Studies in the Early History of Ecclesiastical Music* (Boston: Byzantine Institute, 1947), 141–149. The texts of the 'Hodie' antiphons appear in *CAO* 3088-3124. On the *hinc et nunc*, see chapter 5, this volume.

[132] Dobszay and Szendrei, *Antiphonen*, vol. 1, no. 1165, 79–80 (B5). Three examples of this tune family appear in ex. 7.1. On the annular confessional built for St. Regulus by Bishop Giovanni I of Lucca in 780, see chapter 2, this volume.

[133] Michel Huglo and Joan Halmo, "Antiphon," *Grove Music Online*, ed. L. Macy (accessed 16 August 2007), http://www.grovemusic.com.

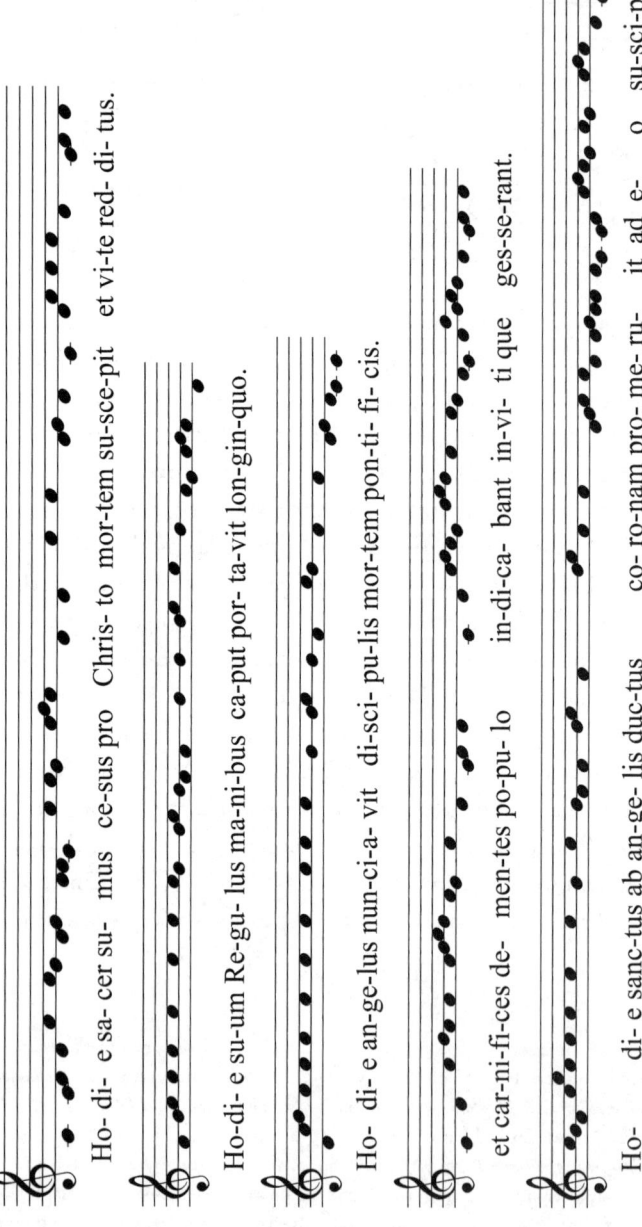

EXAMPLE 7.8. *Hodie sacer sumus* (*Officium Sancti Reguli*, V2-Am).

tone (a), and the third a leap from the final to reciting tone and upper neighbor, precisely the gesture characteristic of its prominent tune class. The fourth iteration disposes of the final altogether and begins with a melismatic flourish on a. Modeled upon some of the most prestigious chants of the old Gregorian repertoire, *Hodie sacer sumus* nonetheless presents a relatively unusual case of escalating musical rhetoric accessible to all in attendance.

The Lucchese Offices also signal their mutual affinities via their equally distinctive and strategic use of the new, post-Gregorian style characteristic of Frankish chant. If the *Officium Sancti Donati* employed this style in a single antiphon, *Antime frater* (see ex. 7.5), the *Officii Sancti Reguli* and *Sancti Fridiani* adopted it in antiphons of a single mode, namely Mode 2. The second mode had obtained little favor among Gregorian antiphons but greater prominence among newer ones owing to the technique of modal ordering, which dictated that the second matins antiphon be in Mode 2. *Laudanda est trinitas* (*Officium Sancti Reguli*, V-Am) illustrates the key features of the small corpus of Gregorian antiphons in the second mode: a narrow range and emphasis on the subtonic (c), final (d), and reciting tone (f) through recitation and cadences (ex. 7.9).[134] *Ejectus a*

EXAMPLE 7.9. *Laudanda est Trinitas* (*Officium Sancti Reguli*, V-Am) and *Ejectus a propriis* (*Officium Sancti Reguli*, M-A2).

---

[134] Dobszay and Szendrei, *Antiphonen*, vol. 2, nos. 2001–2118, 331–390 (A); and Frere, *Antiphonale Sarisburiense*, vol. 1, 69 (IId). Other instances of this Gregorian tune family include *Ignis ardore* (*Officium Sancti Donati*, V-Am).

propriis (*Officium Sancti Reguli*, M-A2) is one of five remaining Lucchese antiphons in Mode 2 that exemplify a single Frankish tune family.[135] Its cadential scheme is less varied than *Laudanda est trinitas* and, in the absence of the traditional emphasis on the reciting tone, it employs descending leaps to A and ascent to the final d (*a propriis* and *transfretavit maria*) to signal its plagal orientation. The emphasis on the lower tetrachord results in a newly expansive melody and recalls the establishment of the upper one in another Tuscan antiphon in the Frankish style, *Antime frater* (ex. 7.5).

Probably composed in the eleventh or early twelfth century, the Offices of St. Fridian and St. Regulus witness the adoption of Frankish musical conventions but nonetheless evince literary differences with each other that underscore the positions of their respective saints in Lucca. St. Fridian was a *defensor civitatis* long buried at his suburban martyrium; St. Regulus was a relatively new arrival to the city, one interred in its religious heart, the cathedral, but whose heroic deeds had all unfolded beyond its walls. In the twelfth century, these saints in turn became proxies for the hostilities that broke out between their respective churches. The Augustinians garnered a reputation for clerical discipline and forged an alliance with the papacy, accruing great wealth, extensive network of dependent churches, and an unusual degree of autonomy from the local bishopric.[136] By so challenging the preeminence of San Martino as the mother church, they likewise garnered the resentment of the cathedral chapter. Relations reached a nadir in 1171, when Pope Alexander III (1159–1181) rebuked the canons of San Martino for proclaiming that St. Fridian lay in their church rather than in his extramural martyrium, and for threatening to excommunicate those who worshiped at San Frediano on the saint's feast.[137] Under papal pressure, they relinquished such dubious claims but did not cease to promote St. Regulus as an object of civic veneration at the expense of St. Fridian.

A primary vehicle for the advancement of the African archbishop and martyr were the vigils sung at San Martino on the eve of his *dies natalis*, which resembled, in their social character and political function, the one chanted for St. Zenobius at Santa Reparata of Florence.[138] The cathedral canons underscored the solemnity of their vigil, chanting a service of three nocturns rather than the usual one and enlisting the rare participation of the bishop. He presided over the service while the canons sang the nine matins

---

[135] Dobszay and Szendrei, *Antiphonen*, vol. 2, nos. 2119–2152, 391–405 (E), of which the Lucchese examples are *Obtine nobis* (*Officium Sancti Fridiani*, M-A3), *Lucane nampe crassante* (*Officium Sancti Fridiani*, L-A2), *Clementissime Christi* (*Officium Sancti Fridiani*, V2-Am), *Ejectus a propriis* (*Officium Sancti Reguli*, M-A2), and *Telluris Italice* (*Officium Sancti Reguli*, M-A4). Frankish Offices often feature this tune class in their second matins antiphon, e.g., *Dum adhuc paene vigilaret vir* (*Officium Inventionis Sancti Stephani*, M-A2), *Postquam domi puerilem* (St. Nicholas, M-A2), and *Ait Petrus principibus* (*Officium Sancti Petri*, M-A2).

[136] Diana Webb, *Patrons and Defenders: The Saints in the Italian City-States* (London: Tauris Academic Studies, 1996), 72; and Coturri, "La canonica," 59–68.

[137] PL, vol. 200, no. 781, 716–717 (8 January 1171).

[138] The following two paragraphs summarize *OOL*, fol. 61, of which Brand, "The Vigils of Medieval Tuscany," 41–44, provides a more detailed examination.

antiphons of the *Officium Sancti Reguli* and responsories from the *commune sanctorum*. If such plainsong did not construe St. Regulus as a common object of worship as did the proper chants for St. Zenobius, ecclesiastical ceremony did precisely that. For the cathedral canons required the entire city clergy to gather at San Martino to celebrate a second vigil directly after theirs. At this service, representatives from the major Lucchese basilicas recited individual lessons with the conspicuous exception of the canons of San Frediano, who either did not wish or were not allowed to take such a prominent role in honoring the patron saint of their rivals. The twin vigils of nine lessons each were exceptional in Tuscany; they not only responded to the crowds of lay men and women who flocked to the cathedral on the eve of St. Regulus's feasts but also signaled the subjugation of the entire Lucchese clergy to its mother church. Congregants perceived the scene of shared worship with unusual clarity, for custom demanded that fifty candles burnt atop the low choral enclosure in which the visiting clerics worshiped.[139]

Despite the wealth and fame of San Frediano in the twelfth century, the cathedral canons were ultimately successful in marginalizing the cult of its titular. Much like the *Officium Sancti Miniatis*, the Office of St. Fridian passed out of use by the late thirteenth century.[140] Meanwhile, the cathedral canons continued to chant the *Officium Sancti Reguli* and organize their vigils in St. Regulus's honor even as the commune organized horse races and other public celebrations on his feast.[141] An African martyr who had never visited Lucca in life had surpassed in the local pantheon of saints a bishop once celebrated for his many building projects and defense of the city. As in Florence so in Lucca, urban basilicas proved more propitious sites than suburban ones for the promotion of relic cults.

*****

---

[139] See the agreement between the cathedral chapter and the Opera del Duomo in 1274, of which the latter was responsible for the maintenance of the cathedral edifice and the provision of candles: ASL, Opera di Santa Croce, 3, fol. 17, in Graziano Concioni, "San Martino di Lucca: La cattedrale medioevale," *Rivista di archeologia, storia, costume* 22 (1994), 43.

[140] Two Lucchese antiphoners, BCL, 602, fols. 205–205v (saec. XII$^{3/4}$), and BCL, 599, fols. 339–339v (saec. XIII), preserve the Magnificat antiphons for first and second vespers but none of the remaining antiphons inventoried in appendix IV. Moreover, neither the late-thirteenth-century antiphoner of San Frediano, Lucca, San Frediano, Guardaroba, D, nor the antiphoner of San Martino, ODL, 4 (saec XV^{ex}) preserve the *Officium Sancti Fridiani*.

[141] ODL, 4, fols. 94v–115 (saec XV^{ex}), preserves the Office of St. Regulus (fols. 94v–115), which had come to include proper responsories for matins, in Benjamin Brand, ed., *Historia Sancti Reguli* (Ottawa: Institute for Medieval Music, 2009) and analyzed in Benjamin Brand, "John Hothby and the Cult of St. Regulus at Lucca," *Early Music History* 27 (2008): 32–38. As codified in the first communal statues, issued in 1308, civic officials were to sponsor two horse races on the martyr's feast in the fields directly to the west of Lucca. Indeed, the *dies natalis* of St. Regulus was one of three feasts on which the commune appointed its twelve best heralds to guard the cathedral against the excesses of revelers. See ASL, Statuti del Comune di Lucca, 1, 47 and 13 (1308), respectively.

If the Offices of medieval Tuscany lie at the heart of the musical history of the region as they constitute the majority of its locally composed music, these liturgies also illuminate in graphic detail the religious and political forces that shaped them. Their creation was intimately tied to the key events in the development of their respective relic cults, whether it be the translation of St. Minias to Santa Reparata in the late ninth century, the building of San Donato in the 1020s, or the formation of the Augustinian canonry at San Frediano in the eleventh century. They also reflected the enduring rivalries between urban cathedrals and suburban martyria, a product of the sacred topography forged in the early Middle Ages by episcopal lords and builders who translated some but not all relics *intra muros*. By setting historical and panegyric texts as appropriate to the public or private character of a service, their composers cast their saints not only as exemplars of holy virtue but also as civic patrons as the expense of those of their competitors. Yet the Tuscan Offices were not simply products of local conditions; instead, they reflected the ongoing adoption of transalpine literary and musical conventions, initially in the form of Gregorian plainsong and subsequently via a new generation of Frankish Offices. They are not simply musical artifacts but also historical ones that illustrate various ways in which relic cults fostered the intersection of local devotion and politics with transregional liturgical cultures.

With its two-part organization, this book has aimed to reveal the broader historical significance of all the liturgies studied therein, including the consecration of the Tuscan cathedrals and the mass and office rites sung within the walls of these great churches. All three liturgies were the ultimate result of historical developments behind which stood the figure of the *dominus et constructor*. As demonstrated in part I, ambitious prelates such as Giovanni I and Anselmo I (in Lucca), Andrea and Ildebrando (in Florence), and Elemperto, Alberto, and Teodaldo (in Arezzo) amplified their own authority via campaigns to promote local relic cults. Through a wide variety of means that necessitate a holistic, interdisciplinary approach from the modern scholar—the writing of hagiography, the foundation and reform of cathedral chapters, the construction and consecration of tombs and churches, and the singing of plainchant—bishops cast themselves as magnanimous patrons of ecclesiastical building, steadfast protectors of relics, and virtuous upholders of clerical discipline. In so doing, most bishops sanctified the urban core of their cities, transforming intramural cathedrals into treasuries of holy relics intended to attract the veneration and thus the oblations of the faithful from near and far. Others favored the old extramural shrines, thus encouraging rivalries between urban cathedrals and suburban basilicas. In the eleventh century, the rise of monastic reformers, an invigorated papacy, and autonomous cathedral chapters all contributed to curtailing the influence of the bishops. Yet Tuscan relic cults and, by extension their liturgies, had already acquired their essential geography and much of their individual character, owing to the efforts of episcopal lord and builders.

As the focus shifted from the historical context to the musico-liturgical texts in part II, the bishops ceded center stage to the cathedral canons. From the late eleventh century, as we learned, these clerics wielded unprecedented influence over their church, styling themselves as the protectors of its liturgy, its relic cults, and, by extension, its prerogatives as the *ecclesia matrix*. Through often acrimonious negotiations, they divided the income of the mother church with their bishop and its *opera*, of which the later evolved into an instrument for lay influence at the cathedral. The canons concomitantly embraced the emergence of popular objects of veneration such as the Holy Face (*Volto Santo*) and St. James. They nonetheless signaled their preference for older, episcopal cults via the performance of proper liturgies that belonged to the campaigns of relic promotion. The plainsong and ritual of the Mass reflected the widely perceived theatricality of that public service, underscoring the bishops' pastoral and sacramental authority as well as their ostensibly collegial relationship with the canons. The proper Offices, by contrast, were more varied in their tone, signaling public veneration (at vespers) or private, clerical edification (at matins and lauds). Celebrated for centuries after their composition, these mass and office liturgies reinforced and arguably inspired literary and visual programs devoted to their saints. Meanwhile, they remained tributes, however indirect, to the bishops who had laid the foundations of the cults to which their music and ritual belonged.

Finally, Tuscan relic cults reveal the manifold ways in which local, regional, and supra-regional forces combined to influence their hagiographic, artistic, architectural, and liturgical dimensions. Although these cults were local phenomena that reflected the particularities of their respective cities and dioceses, they were nonetheless shaped by external influences from within and beyond the region. Bishops and cathedral chapters attended the consecrations of their neighbors' cathedrals, commemorated the feasts of their neighbors' saints, and occasionally sang their neighbors' plainsong. Such interactions inevitably fueled competition as ecclesiastical and civic officials adopted the strategies of their Tuscan counterparts in promoting local saints via hagiography, architecture, and liturgy. Meanwhile, the Carolingian (and later Holy Roman) Empire and Rome offered compelling models, musical and otherwise, that were initially mutually reinforcing but later conflicting. In the eighth and ninth centuries, the building of an annular confessional and the copying of the *Liber Pontificalis* signaled the ecclesiastical preeminence of the pope and the political dominion of his Carolingian allies. The subsequent antagonism between the empire and the papacy rendered untenable such dual symbolism. Hence emerged the cults of St. Donatus and St. Minias, who became philo-imperial objects of veneration via the details of their rewritten Passions, the plans and decoration of their rebuilt churches, and textual as well as musical features of their plainsong. Tuscan relic cults and their liturgies thus belong not only to the local bishops and canons whose stories this book tells but also to larger religious and political histories that inspired and shaped the creative endeavors of such men on behalf of their local saints.

Appendix I

OFFICIUM SANCTI MINIATIS (NORMAL TYPE DENOTES LAYER 1; BOLD TYPE DENOTES LAYER 2).[*]

Genre	Mode	Incipit	Summary of Text
V-Am	**1**	***Beatissimi Miniatis***	**Call to celebration on Minias' feast.**
M-A1	8	*Imperante Decio*	Decius persecutes Christians.
M-A2	1	*Beatus Xistus*	Pope Sixtus II and his deacon, Lawrence, are martyred.
M-A3	8	*Dumque Decius*	Decius arrives in Florence and his men discover Minias.
M-R1	1	*Cum venisset Decius*	Decius arrives in Florence and his men discover Minias.
M-V1	1	*Percontatusque*	Minias identifies himself as a Christian.
M-R2	8	*Ministri presidis*	Decius's men present Minias to Decius.

(*Continued*)

---

[*] Appendix I presents the *Officium Sancti Miniatis* as it appears in AAF, n.s., fols. 180v–184, from which all quotations and transcriptions of the Office derive. The scribe identified *Almum hunc diem* as the Benedictus antiphon for lauds with the rubric "in evangelio" (fol. 183v). That he marked the subsequent antiphon, *Adesto tibi*, with a large initial suggests that this and the remaining four antiphons belong to vespers.

Appendix I

Genre	Mode	Incipit	Summary of Text
M-V2	8	Tu es Minias	Decius accuses Minias of preaching Christianity.
M-R3	4	Preses dixit	Decius orders Minias to sacrifice to Roman gods.
M-V3	4	Bonisque omnibus	Decius promises that Minias will prosper thereafter.
M-A4	1	Dum agnovisset	Decius's men present Minias to Decius.
M-A5	8	Quo vocaris nomine	Decius asks Minias his name.
M-A6	8	Interrogabat Decius	Decius accuses Minias of being Christian.
M-R4	7	Sanctus Minias	Minias proclaims not to fear Decius' tortures.
M-V4	7	Quoniam tormenta	Minias likens Decius's tortures to ocean waves.
M-R5	8	Beatus Christi	An angel protects Minias in the oven.
M-V5	8	Statimque preparatus	Minias defeats a lion with the sign of Christ.
M-R6	7	Beatus Minias	Minias is not swayed by Decius's treasure.
M-V6	7	Quoniam dii tui	Minias ridicules the Roman gods as stupid and mute.
M-A7	1	Nulla maleficia	Minias proclaims that he follows only God.
M-A8	7	Thesaurus	Minias is not swayed by Decius's treasure.
M-A9	1	Tunc iratus Decius	Decius orders that Minias face the lion.
M-R7	4	Cum vidisset	Minias defeats a lion with the sign of Christ.
M-V7	4	Beatus Minias	Minias claims victory over the lion.
M-R8	4	Ministri presidis	Decius's ministers plead that Minias sacrifice to their gods.
M-V8	4	Et extendens	Minias prays to God for support.
M-R9	1	Gratias ago tibi	Minias thanks God for sending the angel to him in the oven.
M-V9	1	Ananias Azarias	Minias thanks God for sending the angel to him in the oven.
M-R10	**7/8**	***Pretiosus Christi***	**Minias prays to God before his execution.**
M-V10	**7**	***Vox de caelo***	**God answer's Minias's prayer.**
L-A1	8	Decius dixit	Decius orders Minias to sacrifice to Roman gods.

Genre	Mode	Incipit	Summary of Text
L-A2	7	*Minias dixit*	Minias proclaims not to fear Decius's tortures.
L-A3	1	*Tunc imperator*	Decius orders that Minias be placed in the oven.
L-A4	4	*Sanctus Minias*	Minias prays to God for support.
L-A5	7	*Minias dixit*	Minias ridicules the Roman gods.
L-Ab	**6**	***Almum hunc diem***	**Call to celebration on Minias's feast.**
[V2-A1]	6	*Adesto tibi*	Plea to Minias for intercession for the Florentines.
[V2-A2]	4	*Martyrialis honor*	Plea to Minias for the monks' protection.
[V2-A3]	4	*Uterque sexus*	Call to prayer for laymen and women of all ages.
[V2-A4]	6	*Tripudio cuncti*	Call to celebration for all "brothers" (i.e., monks).
[V2-A5]	6	*Lucida pre reliquis*	Minias's renown outshines that of others.

Appendix II

OFFICIUM SANCTI ZENOBII.*

Genre	Mode	Incipit	Summary of Text
V-A1	1	*Zenobi mundo*	Plea for intercession on behalf of the Florentines.
V-A2	7	*O pater et pastor*	Plea for protection.
V-A3	4	*Pervigil, o pastor*	Plea for consolation.
V-A4	6	*Votivo presul*	Plea for intercession.
V-A5	8	*Gaudet membellis*	Florence rejoices in the relics of Zenobius and Reparata.
V-R	8	*O gemma fulgens presulum*	Plea for intercession on behalf of the Florentines.
V-V	8	*Ne tibi subiectis*	Plea for protection from plague.
V-H	8	*Letetur urbs*	A boy is exorcised before Zenobius's altar.
V-Am	2	*Hac subiens renum*	Plea for consolation.
M-H	—	*Almi patris*	Summary of Zenobius's life.
L-H	—	*Psallat chorus*	Zenobius is translated to Santa Reparata.

* Appendix II presents the *Officium Sancti Zenobii* as it appears in AAF, n.s., fols. 128–128v (for the antiphons and responsory) and the hymnal of the cathedral, BLF, Edili 131, fols. 180v–182 (saec. XIV) (for the hymns). All quotations and transcriptions of the Office derive from these two manuscripts. Ritus, fols. 82v–83 and fol. 73 prescribes the Office by the incipits of its chants for St. Zenobius's *dies natalis* and his *translatio* respectively.

Appendix III

OFFICIUM SANCTI DONATI.*

Genre	Mode	Incipit	Summary of Text
V-Am	2	*Ignis ardore*	Donatus purifies the well.
M-A1	8	*Puer Donatus*	Donatus is expelled from home for having become a Christian.
M-A2	8	*Pigmenius presbyter*	Pigmenius teaches Donatus theology.
M-A3	7	*Crassante Iuliani*	Donatus's parents die in the persecution of Julian the Apostate.
M-Lxi	--	*Beatissimorum martyrum*	Donatus is educated in Rome. Julian becomes emperor and begins his persecutions. Hylarian flees his native Gaza to escape them.
M-R1	1	*Puer Donatus*	Pigmenius teaches Donatus theology.
M-V1	1	*Hic ne infructuosus*	Donatus converts his parents to Christianity.

(*Continued*)

---

* Appendix III presents the antiphons and responsories of the *Officium Sancti Donati* as they appear in the antiphoner, AAF, n.s., fols. 153v–156, and the lessons as preserved in the breviary, BCL, 605, 215v–224v. While the assignment of regular antiphons for matins and lauds is largely stable across the ten surviving manuscript sources of Tuscan provenance, that of the Gospel antiphons is more variable: Alpigiano and Licciardello, *Officium Sancti Donati*, 66–67.

Genre	Mode	Incipit	Summary of Text
M-Lx2	--	Nam Gazeos fugiens	Hylarian travels from Gaza to Sicily, Cyrpus, and finally to Arezzo. Meanwhile, Donatus's parents die in Julian's persecutions and Donatus flees to Arezzo, where he becomes a hermit under the tutelage of Hylarian. The blind Siranna seeks to be cured by Hylarian.
M-R2	8	Dum Iulianus	Donatus flees Rome and arrives in Arezzo.
M-V2	8	Secutus dicente	Donatus heeds Christ's dictum to flee persecution.
M-Lx3		Quo audito, Hylarianus	Donatus cures Siranna of blindness, she converts to Christianity and donates property to charity, after which bishop Satyrus baptizes her.
M-R3	3	Siranna utroque orbata	Donatus cures the blind Siranna.
M-V3	3	Idola sua tradidit	Siranna forsakes her idols and donates her property to the poor.
M-A4	1	Hylarianus monachus	Donatus becomes an ascetic under Hylarian's guidance.
M-A5	7	Illuminata Siranna	Donatus cures the blind Siranna and converts her to Christianity.
M-A6	1	Stans beatus Donatus	Donatus raises Eufrosina from the dead.
M-Lx4	--	Eodem quoque tempore	Donatus exorcises Apronianus's son, Asterius, is consecrated first a deacon then priest by Bishop Satyrus, and raises Eustasius's wife, Eufrosina from the dead.
M-R4	3	Asterius Apruniani	Apronianus pleads with Donatus to exorcise his son, Asterius.
M-V4	3	Miserere mei	Apronianus pleads with Donatus to exorcise his son, Asterius (cont.)
M-Lx5	--	Post multum vero temporibus	Donatus is elected bishop upon Satyrus's death, and is consecrated by Pope Julius in Rome. He miraculously repairs the shattered chalice at his first episcopal mass.
M-R5	1	Cum beatus Donatus	Donatus repairs the broken chalice at Mass.
M-V5	1	Colligens itaque	Hylarian collects the fragments of the chalice.

Officium Donati

Genre	Mode	Incipit	Summary of Text
M-Lx6	--	Eodem vero tempore	Donatus defeats a dragon threatening Arezzo, purifies one well and discovers another, and appears before Emperor Theodosius.
M-R6	1	Cum augustus	Eustasius seeks Donatus's aid in raising his wife, Eufrosina, from the dead.
M-V6	1	Eufrosina adiuro te	Donatus raises the dead Eufrosina.
M-A7	8	Sathirus episcopus	Bishop Satyrus ordains Donatus as priest.
M-A8	1	Iulius urbis Rome	Pope Julius consecrates Donatus as bishop.
M-A9	7	Antime frater	Donatus repairs the broken chalice at Mass.
M-Lx7		Tunc regina precedens	Donatus exorcises Theodosius's daughter, in return for which they donate land on which he might build his burial church for the salvation of their souls.
M-R7	2	Cum beatus Donatus	Donatus tells Theodosius that it is not him but God who will save his daughter.
M-V7	2	Theodosius augustus	Theodosius pleas for Donatus to exorcise his daughter.
M-Lx8		Puella vero non recedebat	Donatus instructs Theodosius's daughter in theology, returns to Arezzo, and raises from the dead a man wrongfully accused of being a debtor. In order to demonstrate God's power to local aristocrats, who petition Theodosius, Donatus makes it rain. The latter takes possession of his burial site.
M-R8	2	Data est lex inpiorum	Quadratianus tries Donatus and Hylarian for magic.
M-V8	2	Data est lex	Quadratianus tries Donatus and Hylarian for magic (cont.).
M-Lx9		His itaque gestis	Radagasius, king of the Goths, invades Italy and persecutes Christians. Quadratianus tries Donatus and Hylarian for magic.
M-R9	1	Hodie cum exultatione	Call to celebrate the heroic martyrdom of Donatus and Hylarian.
M-V9	1	Hylarianus monachus	Quadratianus executes Donatus and Hylarian.
L-A1	6	Sancti Donati imperator	Theodosius pleads that Donatus exorcise his daughter.

(Continued)

Genre	Mode	Incipit	Summary of Text
L-A2	1	*Sancto Donato intrante*	Donatus exorcises Emperor Theodosius's daughter.
L-A3	7	*Oravit Donatus*	Donatus walks through the miraculously created rain without becoming wet.
L-A4	1	*Sacrificent daemonibus*	Donatus refuses to sacrifice before false gods.
L-A5	8	*Ora sanctorum*	Quadratianus executes Donatus and Hylarian.
L-Ab	4	*Caelorum chorus*	Donatus and Hylarian take their place in heaven while celestial choirs rejoice.
V2-Am	1	*Sancti Donati*	Donatus defeats the dragon.

Appendix IV

OFFICIUM SANCTI FRIDIANI.*

Genre	Mode	Incipit	Summary of Text
V-Am	7	*Sancte Fridiane*	Fridian deviates the Serchio river; plea for intercession.
M-A1	8	*Dum in suis*	Fridian seeks a retreat for his spiritual meditations.
M-A2	7	*Sancte Frigiane*	Plea for intersession.
M-A3	2	*Obtine nobis*	Plea for intercession.
M-A4	1	*Qui multis*	Plea for intercession.
M-A5	8	*Sprevisti pauperem*	Fridian leaves his homeland and embraces poverty.
M-A6	1	*Meruisti coronam*	Plea for intercession.
M-A7	1	*Frigianus pontifex*	Plea for intercession on the part of the populace.
M-A8	8	*Vexillum leva*	Fridian deviates the Serchio river.
M-A9	4	*Qui maris*	Fridian deviates the Serchio river.
L-A1	1	*Frigianus namque*	Fridian's virtue is a model for his followers.
L-A2	2	*Lucane nampe*	[Text obscured in manuscript.]

(Continued)

---

* Appendix IV presents the *Officium Sancti Fridiani* as it appears in BCL, 603, fols. 219–220, from which all quotations and transcriptions of the Office derive. Damage to fol. 219v has rendered some of the text and music of the lauds antiphons unintelligible, as is indicated in brackets.

Genre	Mode	Incipit	Summary of Text
L-A3	1	*Qui missus Domini*	Fridian deviates the Serchio river.
L-A4	1	*Beatus Frigianus*	[Text obscured in manuscript.]
L-A5	8	*Factus patre*	[Text obscured in manuscript.]
L-Ab	2	*O signe Frigiane*	[Text obscured in manuscript.]
V2-Am	2	*Clementissime Christi*	Plea for intercession (first-person plural).

Appendix V

OFFICIUM SANCTI REGULI.[*]

Genre	Mode	Incipit	Summary of Text
V-Am	2	*Laudanda est Trinitas*	Celebration of the Holy Trinity.
M-A1	1	*Iste pater Africe*	Regulus struggles against Arian heresy.
M-A2	2	*Ejectus a propriis*	Regulus is forced into exile.
M-A3	3	*Liquid rura Aeolis*	Regulus and his companions weather the stormy journey to Italy.
M-A4	2	*Telluris Italice*	Regulus becomes a hermit and performs miracles.
M-A5	3	*Presul coarguit*	Regulus struggles against Arian heresy.
M-A6	6	*Maris undas mitigans*	Regulus calms unsettled waters, tames wild animals, and expels demons.
M-A7	8	*Regulus repulit*	Regulus struggles against Arian heresy.
M-A8	5	*Hic speculator*	Regulus becomes a hermit.
M-A9	7	*Tyrannus ira plenus*	Regulus is martyred.

(*Continued*)

---

[*] Appendix V presents the *Officium Sancti Reguli* as it appears in BCL, 603, fols. 200–200v, from which all quotations and transcriptions of the Office derive. See also the critical edition, Brand, *Historia Sancti Reguli*.

Genre	Mode	Incipit	Summary of Text
L-A1	1	*Beatus Regulus*	Regulus struggles against Arian heresy.
L-A2	8	*Coniunctis sibi*	Regulus is forced into exile with two bishops and three priests.
L-A3	1	*Dum transfretarent*	Regulus and his companions weather the stormy journey to Italy.
L-A4	8	*Prostratus in oratione*	Regulus prays for safe passage to Italy.
L-A5	8	*Antistes sanctus*	Regulus arrives in Tuscany and becomes a hermit.
L-Ab	1	*Beatus Regulus*	Regulus refuses to appear before Totila.
V2-Am	1	*Hodie sacer sumus*	Regulus is martyred, proceeds to his chosen burial site, and ascends into heaven.

REFERENCES

MANUSCRIPTS AND ARCHIVAL DOCUMENTS

AAF, n.s.
ACA, Dipl. 694
ACA, Duomo A
ACA, Duomo H
ACF, Dipl. 310/16
ACF, Dipl. 328/C16
ACF, Dipl. 392
ACF, Dipl. 406/C17
ACF, Dipl. 434
ACF, Dipl. 447/C22
ACF, Dipl. 533 (21 July 1280)
ACF, Dipl. 534/C29
ACF, P238
ACFie, II.B.1
ACFie, XXII, 1
ACL, Dipl. +8
ACL, Dipl. BB 44
ACL, Dipl. S 160
ACL, LL 32
ACL, LL 38
ACL, LL 40
ACL, LL 43
ACL, LL 45
ACL, LL 46

ACP, C150
ACP, Dipl. 728
ACP, Dipl. 800
ACP, Dipl. 842
ACPist, C102 (= OOPist2)
ACPist, C114 (=OOPist1)
ACPist, C117
ACPist, C119
ACPist, C120
ACPist, C121
ASF, Diplomatico, Capitolo della cattedrale di Pistoia (2 August 1227)
ASF, Diplomatico, Capitolo della cattedrale di Pistoia (8 July 1290).
ASF, Carte Strozziane II
ASL, Opera di Santa Croce, 3
ASL, Statuti del Comune di Lucca, 1
ASS, Diplomatico, Archivio dell'Opera Metropolitana (4 March 1284)
ASS, Diplomatico, Archivio dell'Opera Metropolitana (27 April 1288)
AVPist, R69
BAV, Vat. Lat. 4772
BAV, Vat. Lat. 6453
BCIS, G.V.8 (= OOES)
BCL, B
BCL, C
BCL, D
BCL, G
BCL, P†
BCL, 47
BCL, 124
BCL, 490
BCL, 599
BCL, 602
BCL, 603
BCL, 605
BCL, 607
BCL, 608 (=OOL)
BCL, 626
BCR, 719
BCT, 52.11
Benevento, Archivio Capitolare, 40
BGV, L.3.39
BLF, Conv. soppr. 457
BLF, Edili 131
BLF, Edili 139
BLF, Edili 147

BLF, Mugell. 13
BLF, Pluteo 20.30
BLF, Pluteo 27.1
Bologna, Biblioteca Universitaria, 1758 (= OOP)
Florence, Archivio dell'Opera di Santa Maria del Fiore, I.3.8 (= Mores)
Florence, Biblioteca Riccardiana, 3005 (= Ritus)
ODL, 4
ODL, 10
Oxford, Bodleian, Canonici liturg. 379,
Oxford, Bodleian, Canonici liturg. 392
Rome, Biblioteca Angelica, 123
Rome, Biblioteca Nazionale, Farfa 29
Seville, Zayas Private Collection, 2

PRINTED BOOKS

Abou-El-Haj, Barbara Fay. "Audiences for the Medieval Cult of Saints." *Gesta* 30 (1991): 3–15.
Abou-El-Haj, Barbara Fay. *The Medieval Cult of Saints: Formations and Transformations.* Cambridge: Cambridge University Press 1994.
The Acts of the Christian Martyrs. Translated by Herbert Musurillo. Oxford: Oxford University Press, 1972.
Alpigiano, Giovanni. "Alcune precisazioni sulla Messa di San Donato." *Rivista internazionale di musica sacra* 25 (2004): 121–131.
Alpigiano, Giovanni. "L'antifonario fiorentino e la sua epoca." *Rivista internazionale di musica sacra* 23 (2002): 171–186.
Alpigiano, Giovanni, and Pierluigi Licciardello. *Officium Sancti Donati I: L'ufficio liturgico di san Donato di Arezzo nei manoscritti toscani medievali.* Florence: Edizioni del Galluzzo, 2008.
Ambrosini, Riccardo. "Le iscrizioni del Duomo e della Curia." *Rivista di archeologia, storia, costume* 26 (1998): 7–24.
Andrieu, Michel. *Les Ordines Romani du Haut Moyen Age.* 5 vols. Louvain: Spicilegium Sacrum Lovaniense, 1931–1961.
Angelini, M., M. V. De Bellis, Elisabetta De Minicis, P. Robino, N. Scarpignato, and M. R. Valazzi. "L'uso e la diffusione delle cripte nell'Europa carolingia." In *Roma e l'età carolingia. Atti delle giornate di studio, 3- maggio 1976*, 319–323. Rome: Multigrafica, 1976.
Apel, Willi. *Gregorian Chant.* Bloomington: Indiana University Press, 1958.
Argenziano, Raffaele. *Agli inizi dell'iconografia sacra a Siena: Culti, riti e iconografia a Siena nel XII secolo.* Florence: Edizioni del Galluzzo, 2000.
Argenziano, Raffaele. "Corpi sancti e immagini nella Siena medievale: I santi patroni." *Bullettino senese di storia patria* 60 (2004): 214–239.
Arnold, John H., and Caroline Goodson. "Resounding Community: The History and Meaning of Medieval Church Bells." *Viator* 43 (2012): 99–130.
Ashley, Kathleen M., and Pamela Sheingorn. *Writing Faith: Text, Sign and History in the Miracles of Sainte Foy.* Chicago: University of Chicago Press, 1999.
Auda, Antoine. *L'école musicale liégoise au Xe siècle: Étienne de Liège.* Brussels: Lamertin, 1923.

Baracchini, Clara, and Antonino Caleca. "Il duomo di S. Martino in Lucca: Urbanistica, architettura, arredo fisso." In *Il duomo di Lucca*, edited by Clara Baracchini and Antonino Caleca, 9–61. Lucca: Baroni, 1973.

Barcellona Scorza, Francesco. "Un martire locale: Ansano." In *I santi patroni senesi*, edited by Franca Lea Consolino, 10–33. Siena: Accademia Senese degli Intronati, 1991.

Barnes, Timothy D. "Pre-Decian *Acta Martyrum*." *Journal of Theological Studies* 19 (1968): 509–531.

Baroffio, Giacomo. "Frammenti di richerche II (Un importante graduale troparico lucchese: Pistoia, Archivio Vescovile, R 69)." *Philomusica On-Line* 5 (2006).

Baroffio, Giacomo. "Sanctorum Officia. Ufficiature liturgiche del Santorale tramandate in fonti italiane." *Rivista internazionale di musica sacra* 21 (2000): 263–295.

Barrow, Julia. "Chrodegang, his Rule and its Successors." *Early Medieval Europe* 26 (2006): 201–212.

Barrow, Julia. "William of Malmesbury's Use of Charters." In *Narrative and History in the Early Medieval West*, edited by Elizabeth M. Tyler and Ross Balzaretti, 67–89. Turnhout: Brepols, 2006.

Barsotti, Riccardo, ed. *Gli antichi inventari della cattedrale di Pisa*. Pisa: Istituto di storia dell'arte, Universita di Pisa, 1959.

Bauer, Franz Alto. "La frammentazione liturgica nella chiesa romana del primo medioevo." *Rivista di Archeologia Cristiana* 75 (1999): 385–446.

Beleth, Johannes. *Summa de Ecclesiasticis Officiis*, edited by Heribert Douteil. Turnhout: Brepols, 1976.

Beiche, Michael. "Discantus/Diskant." In *Handwörterbuch der musikalischen Terminologie*, edited by Hans Heinrich Eggebrecht. Stuttgart: Franz Steiner, 1997.

Benvenuti, Anna. "Il *Bellum Fesulanum* e il mito delle origini fiorentine." In *Un archivio, una diocesi: Fiesole nel medioevo e nell'età moderna*, edited by Maura Borgioli, 23–39. Florence: L.S. Olschki, 1996.

Benvenuti, Anna. "Giovanni Gualberto e Firenze." In *I Vallombrosani nella società italiana dei secoli XI e XII: Primo colloquio vallombrosano, Vallombrosa 3-4 settembre 1993*, edited by Giordano Monzio Compagnoni, 83–112. Florence: Edizioni Vallombrosa, 1995.

Benvenuti, Anna. "Stratigrafie della memoria: Scritture agiografiche e mutamenti architettonici nella vicenda del 'Complesso cattedrale' fiorentino." In *Il bel San Giovanni e Santa Maria del Fiore: Il centro religioso di Firenze dal tardo antico al Rinascimento*, edited by Domenico Cardini, 95–127. Florence: Le lettere, 1996.

Benvoglienti, Bartolomeo. *Trattato de l'origine et accrescimento de la citta di Siena. Composto da M. Bartolomeo Benvoglienti proposto di Siena, e professor di filosofia & teologia. A l'Illustriss. et reverendiss. Cardinale Sforza Legato di Bologna e Romagna*. Translated by Fabio Benvoglienti. Rome: Giuseppe degli Angeli, 1571.

Berg, Knut. *Studies in Tuscan Twelfth-Century Illumination*. Oslo: Universitetsforlaget, 1968.

Berti, Giovanni Felice. *Cenni storico-artistici per servire di guida ed illustrazione alla insigne Basilica di S. Miniato al Monte e di alcuni dintorni presso Firenze*. Florence: Baracchi, 1850.

Bertini, Luca. *Peredeo vescovo di Lucca*. Pisa: Pacini, 1973.

Betti, P. Umberto. "Il maestro Ardengo, vescovo di Firenze." *Divinitas* 9 (1965): 161–170.

Bini, Telesforo. "Di chi promovesse la reidificazione della Cattedrale di Lucca dal 1060 al 1070." *Atti della Reale Accademia Lucchese di Scienze, Lettere e Arti* 7 (1860): 179–197.

Birch, Debra J. *Pilgrimage to Rome in the Middle Ages: Continuity and Change*. Woodbridge, Suffolk, and Rochester, NY: Boydell Press, 1998.

Bisbee, Gary A. *Pre-Decian Acts of Martyrs and Commentarii*. Edited by Margaret R. Miles and Bernadette J. Brooten. Philadelphia: Fortress, 1988.

Blomquist, Thomas W., and Maureen F. Mazzaoui, eds. *The "Other Tuscany": Essays in the History of Lucca, Pisa, and Siena during the Thirteenth, Fourteenth, and Fifteenth Centuries*. Kalamazoo: Medieval Institute Publications, Western Michigan University, 1994.

Boesch, Sofia. "Giovanni Gualberto e la vita comune del clero nelle biografie di Andrea da Strumi e di Atto da Vallombrosa." In *La vita comune del clero nei secoli XI e XII. Atti della settimana di studio, Mendola, settembre 1959*, 228–235. Milan: Vita e pensiero, 1962.

Borders, James. *The Cathedral of Verona as a Musical Center in the Middle Ages*. Ph. D. diss., University of Chicago, 1983.

Borders, James. "The Northern and Central Italian Trope Repertory and Its Transmission." In *Atti del XIV Congresso della Società Internazionale di Musicologia*, edited by Angelo Pompilio, 543–553. Turin: EDT, 1990.

Borders, James, and Lance Brunner, eds. *Early Medieval Chants from Nonantola*. 4 vols. Madison, WI: A-R Editions, 1996–1999.

Boskovits, Miklòs. *The Origins of Florentine Painting, 1100-1270*. Translated by Robert Wolf. Florence: Giunti, 1993.

Bowen, Lee. "The Tropology of Mediaeval Dedication Rites." *Speculum* 16 (1941): 469–479.

Boynton, Susan. "Performative Exegesis in the Fleury *Interfectio puerorum*." *Viator* 29 (1998): 39–64.

Boynton, Susan. *Shaping a Monastic Identity: Liturgy and History at the Imperial Abbey of Farfa, 1000-1125*. Ithaca, NY: Cornell University Press, 2006.

Brand, Benjamin, ed. *Historia Sancti Reguli*. Ottawa: Institute of Mediaeval Music, Canada: Institute for Medieaval Music, 2009.

Brand, Benjamin. "John Hothby and the Cult of St Regulus at Lucca." *Early Music History* 27 (2008): 1–45.

Brand, Benjamin. *Liturgical Ceremony at the Cathedral of Lucca, 1275-1500*. Ph.D. diss., Yale University, 2006.

Brand, Benjamin. "The Vigils of Medieval Tuscany." *Plainsong and Medieval Music* 17 (2008): 23–54.

Brennan, Brian. "Text and Image: 'Reading' the Walls of the Sixth-Century Cathedral of Tours." *Journal of Medieval Latin* 6 (1996): 65–83.

Brocchieri, Ercole. "Sicardo di Cremona e la sua opera letteraria." *Annali della Biblioteca Governativa e Libreria Civica di Cremona* 11 (1958): 1–115.

Brown, Peter. *Power and Persuasion in Late Antiquity: Towards a Christian Empire*. Madison: University of Wisconson Press, 1992.

Brunner, Lance. "Catalogo delle sequence in manoscritti di orgine italiana anteriori al 1200." *Rivista Italiana di Musicologia* 20 (1985): 191–276.

Brunner, Lance. "Two Missing Fascicles of Pistoia C. 121 Recovered." In *Cantus planus: Papers Read at the Fourth Meeting, Pécs, Hungary, 3-8 September 1990*, 1–19. Budapest: Hungarian Academy of Sciences Institute for Musicology, 1990.

Buchanan, Charles. "Evidence of a Scriptorium at the Reformed Canonry of S. Frediano in Lucca." *Scriptorium* 57 (2003): 3–26.

Buchanan, Charles. *A Late Eleventh-Century Illustrated Hagiographic Lectionary from Lucca (Biblioteca Capitolare, Passionario C): Expression of Ecclesiastical Reform*. Ph.D. diss., University of California, Santa Barbara, 1997.

Buchanan, Charles. "Spiritual and Spatial Authority in Medieval Lucca: Illuminated Manuscripts, Stational Liturgy and the Gregorian Reform." *Art History* 27 (2004): 723–744.

Buchanan, Charles S. "An Illustrated Romanesque Hagiographic Lectionary (Lucca: Biblioteca Capitolare, Passionario C): Inspiration, Formulation, and Reception." *Studies in Iconography* 28 (2007): 111–69.

Calderoni Masetti, Anna Rosa. "Anselmo da Baggio e la cattedrale di Lucca." *Annali della Scuola Normale Superiore di Pisa, Serie III* 1 (1977): 91–116.

Calderoni Masetti, Anna Rosa. "L'abside maggiore del duomo, dalle origini al Quattrocento." In *La tribuna del Duomo di Pisa, capolavori di due secoli*, edited by Roberto Paolo Ciardi, 13–28. Milan: Electa, 1995.

Camici, Cecilia, and Debora Giorgi, eds. *La Cattedrale di San Romolo a Fiesole e lo scavo archeologico della cripta*. Florence: A. Pontecorboli, 1995.

"Cantus: A Database for Latin Ecclesiastical Chant." http://publish.uwo.ca/~cantus/.

Cardini, Domenico. "Ipotesi sulle fasi trasformative del Centro religioso dalla formazione della cinta difensiva carolingia alla sua sostituzione." In *Il bel San Giovanni e Santa Maria del Fiore: Il centro religioso di Firenze dal tardo antico al Rinascimento*, edited by Domenico Cardini, 129–157. Florence: Le lettere, 1996.

Cattaneo, Enrico. "Il battistero in Italia dopo il Mille." In *Miscellanea Gilles Gerard Meersseman*, 171–196. Padua: Antenore, 1970.

Cattin, Giulio. "Novità dalla cattedrale di Firenze: Polifonia, tropi, e sequenze nella seconda metà del XII secolo." *Musica e storia* 6 (1998): 7–36.

Cattin, Giulio. "'Secundare' e 'Succinere.' Polifonia a Padova e Pistoia nel duecento." *Musica e storia* 3 (1995): 41–121.

Caturegli, Natale, ed. *Le carte arcivescovili pisane del secolo 13*. 4 vols. Rome: Istituto storico italiano per il Medio Evo, 1974-1993.

Caturegli, Natale. *Regestum pisanum*. Rome: Istituto storico italiano per il Medio Evo, 1938.

Cavazzini, Laura. "La decorazione della facciata di San Martino a Lucca e l'attività di Guido Bigarelli." In *Medioevo: Le officine. Atti del Convego internazionale di* Studi, Parma, *22-27 settembre 2009*, 481–493. Milan: Electa, 2010.

Ceccarelli Lemut, Maria Luisi. "Santi nei Mediterraneo dalla Sardegna a Pisa." *Bolletino Storico Pisano* 74 (2005): 201–208.

Cecchelli, Margherita. "La cripta semianulare vaticana e le sue derivazioni romane." In *L'Orbis Christianus Antiquus di Gregorio Magno*, edited by Letizia Ermini Pani, 105–120. Rome: Società alla Biblioteca vallicelliana, 2007.

Cervelli, Iacopo Lazzareschi. "L'arredo scultoreo." *Rivista di archeologia, storia, costume* 26, no. 2-4 (1998): 25–86.

Chartier, Yves. "L'oeuvre musicale d'Hucbald de Saint-Amand: Les Compositions et le traité de musique." In *Cahiers d'études médiévales*. Saint-Laurent, Québec: Bellarmin, 1995.

Checcacci, Federica. "I tropi d'introito in un codice volterrano del'XI-XII secolo (Volterra, Bibl. Guarnacci, L.3.39)." *Rivista internazionale di musica sacra* 20 (1999): 76–116.

Chinball, Marjorie. "Charter and Chronicle: The Use of Archive Sources by Norman Historians." In *Church and Government in the Middle Ages: Essays Presented to C. R. Cheney on his 70th*

Birthday, edited by Christopher Nugent Lawrence Brooke, 1–17. Cambridge: Cambridge University Press, 1976.

Cignoni, Francesco. "L'officiatura di San Donato vescovo di Fiesole (†876). Edizione e studio." *Rivista internazionale di musica sacra* 24 (2003): 46–131.

Cignoni, Francesco. "Le officiature dei santi Alessandro e Romulo, vescovi di Fiesole. Edizioni e studio." *Rivista internazionale di musica sacra* 22, no. 2–290 (2001).

Claussen, M. A. *The Reform of the Frankish Church: Chrodegang of Metz and the Regula Canonicorum in the Eighth Century*. Cambridge: Cambridge University Press, 2004.

Cohn, Samuel K. *The Cult of Remembrance and the Black Death: Six Renaissance Cities in Central Italy*. Baltimore: Johns Hopkins University Press, 1992.

Collavini, Simone. "Da società rurale periferica a parte dello spazio politico lucchese: S. Regolo in Gualdo tra VIII e IX secolo." In *"Un filo rosso." Studi antichi e nuove richerche sulle orme di Gabriella Rossetti in occasione dei suo settanta anni*, edited by Gabriella Garzella and Enrica Salvatori, 231–247. Pisa: ETS, 2007.

Colledge, Edmund, and J. C. Marler. "*Céphalologie*: A Recurring Theme in Classical and Medieval Lore." *Traditio* 37 (1981): 411–426.

Concioni, Graziano. *Contributi alla storia del Volto Santo*. Pisa: ETS 2005.

Concioni, Graziano. "San Martino di Lucca: La cattedrale medioevale." *Rivista di archeologia, storia, costume* 22 (1994): 1–453.

Concioni, Graziano. *Vescovi e canonici a Lucca tra Longobardi e Franchi*, Saggi e Richerche. Pisa: ETS 2007.

Constitutiones Sacri Capituli Metropolitanae Senensis Ecclesiae. Siena: Luca Bonetto, 1579.

Cooper, Kate. "The Martyr, The Matrona and the Bishop: The Matron Lucina and the Politics of Martyr Cult in Fifth- and Sixth-Century Rome." *Early Medieval Europe* 8, (1999): 297–319.

Corbin, Solange. *Die Neumen*. Cologne: Arno Volk, 1977.

Corsi, Domenico. "La Canonica di S. Donato di Lucca e le constitutzioni dei Canonici del 26 maggio 1322." In *Scritti in onore di Mons. Giuseppe Turrini, 167–216*. Verona: Accademia di Agricoltura Scienze e Lettere di Verona, 1973.

Coturri, Enrico. "La canonica di S. Frediano di Lucca dalla Prima Istituzione (metà del sec. xi) alla unione alla congregazione riformata di Fregionaia (1517)." *Actum Luce* 3 (1974): 47–80.

Cowdrey, H. E. J. "The Gregorian Papacy and Eremetical Monasticism." In *San Bruno e la Certosa di Calabria. Atti del convegno internazionale di studi per il IX centenario della Certosa di Serra S. Bruno. Squillace, Serra S. Bruno, 15-18 settembre 1991*, edited by Pietro De Leo, 33–54. Catanzaro: Soveria Mannelli, 1995.

Cowdrey, H. E. J. "Pope Gregory VII and the Bishoprics of Central Italy." *Studi Medievali* 34 (1993): 51–64.

Cowdrey, H. E. J. "The Structure of the Church, 1024-1073." In *The New Cambridge Medieval History. Vol. 4: c. 1024-c. 1198*, edited by David Luscombe and Jonathan Riley-Smith, 229–267. Cambridge: Cambridge University Press, 2004.

Crocker, Richard L. *The Early Medieval Sequence*. Berkeley: University of California Press, 1977.

Crocker, Richard L. "Matins Antiphons at St. Denis." *Journal of the American Musicological Society* 39 (1986): 441–490.

Crook, John. *The Architectural Setting of the Cult of Saints in the Early Christian West, c.300-1200*. Oxford: Oxford University Press, 2000.

Crosby, Sumner McKnight. *The Royal Abbey of Saint-Denis from its Beginnings to the Death of Suger, 475-1151*. Edited by Pamela Z. Blum. New Haven: Yale University Press, 1987.

Cushing, Kathleen G. *Papacy and Law in the Gregorian Revolution: The Canonistic Work of Anselmo of Lucca*. Oxford: Oxford University Press, 1998.

D'Accone, Frank. *The Civic Muse: Music and Musicians in Siena During the Middle Ages and the Renaissance*. Chicago: University of Chicago Press, 1997.

D'Accone, Frank. *A Documentary History of Music at the Florentine Cathedral and Baptistery During the Fifteenth Century*. Ph.D. diss., Harvard University, 1960.

D'Accone, Frank. "The Sienese Rhymed Office for the Feast of Sant'Ansano." In *L'ars nova italiana del Trecento: Atti del congresso internazionale "L'Europa e la musica del Trecento", Certaldo, Palazzo Pretorio, 19-20-21 luglio 1984*, edited by Giulio Cattin and Patrizia Dalla Vecchia, 21–40. Certaldo: Edizioni Polis, 1992.

Dale, Thomas E. A. *Relics, Prayer, and Politics in Medieval Venetia: Romanesque Painting in the Crypt of Aquileia Cathedral*. Princeton, NJ: Princeton University Press, 1997.

Dalli Regoli, Gigetta. "Coerenza, ordine e misura di una maestranza: Il pulpito di Barga e i Guidi." *Arte medievale* series II, 6 (1992): 91–111.

Dameron, George W. "The Cult of St. Minias and the Struggle for Power in the Diocese of Florence, 1011-1018." *Journal of Medieval History* 13 (1987): 125–141.

Dameron, George W.. *Episcopal Power and Florentine Society, 1000-1320*. Cambridge, MA: Harvard University Press, 1991.

Davidsohn, Robert. *Storia di Firenze*. Translated by Giovanni Battista Klein. 7 vols. Florence: Sansoni, 1956–1965.

Davis, Raymond. *The Book of Pontiffs (Liber Pontificalis): The Ancient Biographies of the First Ninety Roman Bishops at AD 715*. 3rd ed. Liverpool: Liverpool University Press, 2010.

De Angelis D'Ossat, Guglielmo. "Il 'Duomo Vecchio' di Arezzo." *Palladio* 27 (1978): 4–46.

De Blaauw, Sible. *Cultus et Decor: Liturgia e architettura nella Roma tardoantica e medievale*. Translated by Maria Beatrice Annis. 2 ed. 2 vols. Vatican City: Biblioteca Apostolica Vaticana, 1994.

De Minicis, Elisabetta, and Alessandra Molinari. "I nuovi scavi sulla collina del Pionta ad Arezzo: Una cittadella vescovile tra alto e bassomedioevo. Notizie preliminari." *Archeologia Medievale* 30 (2003): 299–332.

"Decretum Gratiani." In *Corpus iuris canonici*, edited by Emil Albert Friedberg. Leipzig: Bernhardus Tauchnitz, 1879.

Delehaye, Hippolyte. *The Legends of the Saints: An Introduction to Hagiography*. Translated by V. M. Crawford. Notre Dame, IN: University of Notre Dame Press, 1961.

Delumeau, Jean. *Arezzo: Espace et sociétés, 715-1230*. Rome: École française de Rome, 1996.

Dobszay, László, and Janka Szendrei, eds. *Antiphonen*. 3 vols. Kassel: Bärenreiter, 1999.

Doig, Allan. *Liturgy and Architecture from Early Church to the Middle Ages*. Burlington: Ashgate, 2008.

Dox, Donnalee. "Roman Theatre and Roman Rite: Twelfth-Century Transformations in Allegory, Ritual, and the Idea of Theatre." In *The Appearances of Medieval Rituals: The Play of Construction and Modification*, edited by Nils Holger Peterson, Mette Birkedal Bruun, Jeremy Llewellyn, and Eyolf Østrem, 33–48. Turnhout: Brepols, 2004.

Duchesne, Louis, and Cyrille Vogel, eds. *Le Liber pontificalis*. 2nd ed., 3 vols. Paris: E. de Boccard, 1955.

Duffy, Eamon. *The Stripping of the Altars: Traditional Religion in England 1400-1580*. New Haven: Yale University Press, 1992.

Dyer, Joseph. "*Psalmi ante sacrificum* and the Origin of the Introit." *Plainsong and Medieval Music* 20 (2011): 91–121.

Ela Consolino, Franca. "Un martire 'Romano': Crescenzio." *Bullettino senese di storia patria* 97 (1990): 34–48.

Ermini Pani, Letizia. "La fasi altomedievali." In *La chiesa dei Santi Giovanni e Reparata in Lucca: Dagli scavi archeologici al restauro*, edited by Giovanna Piancastelli Politi Nencini, 49–77. Lucca: Fazzi, 1993.

Fabbri, Lorenzo, and Marica Tacconi, eds. *I libri del duomo di Firenze codici liturgici e biblioteca di Santa Maria del Fiore (secoli XI-XVI)*. Florence: Centro Di: 1997.

Falaschi, Emma. *Carte dell'Archivio Capitolare di Pisa 1 (930-1050)*. Rome: Edizioni di storia e letteratura, 1971.

Fassler, Margot. *Gothic Song: Victorine Sequences and Augustinian Reform in Twelfth-Century Paris*. Cambridge: Cambridge University Press, 1993.

Fassler, Margot. "The Office of the Cantor in Early Western Monastic Rules and Custom Rites: A Preliminary Investigation." *Early Music History* 5 (1985): 29–51.

Fassler, Margot. *The Virgin of Chartres: Making History Through Liturgy and the Arts*. New Haven: Yale University Press: 2010.

Fassler, Margot, and Rebecca A. Baltzer, eds. *The Divine Office in the Latin Middle Ages: Methodology and Source Studies, Regional Developments, Hagiography, Written in Honor of Professor Ruth Steiner*. Oxford: Oxford University Press, 2000.

Ferrali, Sabatino. *L'Apostolo S. Jacopo il maggiore e il suo culto a Pistoia*. Pistoia: Opera dei Santi Giovanni e Zeno, 1979.

Ferrali, Sabatino. *Fasti e nefasti di un monumento: Appunti di storia della cattedrale di Pistoia*. Pistoia: Tip. Pistoiese, 1956.

Fickett, Martha Van Zandt. *Chants for the Feast of St. Martin of Tours*. Ph.D. diss., Catholic University of America, 1983.

Flint, Valerie I. J. "The Career of Honorius Augustodunensis. Some Fresh Evidence." *Revue Bénédictine* 82 (1972): 63–86.

Flint, Valerie I. J. "Place and Purpose in the Works of Honorius." *Revue Bénédictine* 87 (1977): 97–127.

Flynn, William T. *Medieval Music as Medieval Exegesis*. Lanham, MD: Scarecrow, 1999.

Foley, Edward. "The 'Libri Ordinarii'." *Ephemerides liturgicae* 102 (1988): 129–137.

Fonesca, Cosimo Damiano. "Canoniche regolari, capitoli cattedrali, e 'cura animarum'." In *Pievi e parrocchie in Italia nel basso medioevo (sec. XIII-XV). Atti del VI convegno di storia della chiesa in Italia (Firenze, 21-25 Settembre 1981)*, 257–278. Rome: Herder, 1984.

Fonesca, Cosimo Damiano. "Il capitolo di San Martino e la riforma canonicale nella seconda metà del sec. XI." In *Sant'Anselmo vescovo di Lucca (1073-1086). Nel quadro delle trasformazioni sociali e della riforma ecclesiastica*, edited by Cinzio Violante, 51–64. Rome: Istituto Palazzo Borromini, 1992.

Fonesca, Cosimo Damiano. "'Ecclesia matrix' e 'Conventus civium': L'ideologia della Cattedrale nell'età comunale." In *La Pace di Costanza, 1183. Un difficile equilibrio di poteri fra società italiana ed impero. Milano-Piazenza, 27-30 aprile 1983*, 135–149. Bologna: Cappelli, 1984.

Foot, Sarah. "Reading Anglo-Saxon Charters: Memory, Record, or Story?" In *Narrative and History in the Early Medieval West*, edited by Elizabeth M. Tyler and Ross Balzaretti, 39–65. Turnhout: Brepols, 2006.

Fortunio, Agostino. *Historiarum Camaldulensium, libri tres*. 3 vols. Florence: Bibliotaeca Sermartelliana, 1575.

Francesconi, Sara. "Storia della miniatura a Pistoia dall XII al metà del XIII secolo." Tesi di laurea, University of Pisa, 2008.

Franciotti, Cesare. *Historia delle miracolose imagini e delle vite dei santi, i corpi dei quali sono nella città di Lucca*. Lucca: Ottavio Guidoboni, 1613.

Frere, Walter Howard. *Antiphonale Sarisburiense: A Reproduction in Facsimile of a Manuscript of the Thirteenth Century*. London: Plainsong and Medieval Music Society, 1901.

Froehlich, Karlfried, Margaret T. Gibson, and Adolph Rusch, eds. *Biblia Latina cum glossa ordinaria: Facsimile Reprint of the Editio Princeps Adolph Rusch of Strassburg 1480/81*. 4 vols. Turnhout: Brepols, 1992.

Fry, Timothy. *RB 1980: The Rule of St. Benedict*. Collegeville, MN: Liturgical Press, 1981.

Fuller, Sarah. "Early Polyphony." In *The New Oxford History of Music. The Early Middle Ages to 1300*, rev. ed., edited by Richard Crocker and David Hiley, 485–556. Oxford: Oxford University Press, 1990.

Gaiffier, Baudouin de. "Catalogue des passionaires de la Bibliothèque Capitulaire de Lucques." In *Recherches d'hagiographie latine*, 77–124. Brussels: Société des Bollandistes, 1971.

Ganz, David. "The Ideology of Sharing: Apostolic Community and Ecclesiastical Property in the Early Middle Ages." In *Property and Power in the Early Middle Ages*, edited by Wendy Davies and Paul Fouracre, 17–30. Cambridge: Cambridge University Press, 1995.

Garrison, Edward B. *Studies in the History of Mediaeval Italian Painting*. 4 vols. Florence: L'Imprenta, 1953–1962.

Geary, Patrick J. *Furta Sacra: Thefts of Relics in the Central Middle Ages*. 2nd ed. Princeton, NJ: Princeton University Press, 1990.

Geary, Patrick J. *Living with the Dead in the Middle Ages*. Ithaca, NY: Cornell University Press, 1994.

Ghignoli, Antonella, ed. *Carte dell'Archivio di Stato di Siena: Opera Metropolitana (1000-1200)*. Siena: Accademia senese degli intronati, 1994.

Giannarelli, Elena. "Savino, Bartolomeo e l'alternanza dei patroni." *Bullettino senese di storia patria* 97 (1990): 64–83.

Giorgi, Andrea, and Stefano Moscadelli. *Costruire una catatedrale: L'Opera di Santa Maria di Siena tra XII e XIV secolo*. Munich: Deutscher Kunstverlag, 2005.

Giusti, Martino. "Le elezioni del vescovo di Lucca specialmente nel secolo XIII." *Rivista di storia della chiesa in Italia* 6 (1952): 205–230.

Giusti, Martino. "L'*Ordo Officiorum* della Cattedrale di Lucca." In *Miscellanea Giovanni Mercati*, 523–566. Vatican City: Biblioteca Apostolica Vaticana, 1946.

Glaber, Rodulfus. *The Five Books of the Histories*. Translated by John France. Oxford: Oxford University Press, 1989.

Glaeske, Keith, Charles Downey, and Lila Collamore, eds. *The Twelfth-Century Antiphoner of Firenze, Curia Arcivescovile: A CANTUS Index*. Washington, DC: Benjamin T. Rome School of Music, Catholic University of America Press, 1994.

Gonzato, Gemma. "Alcune considerazioni sull' 'Ordo Officiorum Ecclesiae Senensis'." In *Le polifonie primitive in Friuli e in Europa. Atti del congresso internazionale (Cividale del Friuli, 22-24 augusto 1980)*, edited by C. Corsi and P. Petrobelli, 247–293. Rome: Torre d'Orfeo, 1989.

Goodson, Caroline J. *The Rome of Pope Paschal I (817-824): Papal Power, Urban Renovation, Church Rebuilding and Relic Translation*. Cambridge: Cambridge University Press, 2010.

Goudesenne, Jean-François. "*Historiae* from *Alta Italia* and their Frankish Models: A Progressive 'Romanisation' by the Carolingian Franks (750–950)." In *Political Plainchant?: Music, Text, and Historical Context of Medieval Saints' Offices*, edited by Roman Hankeln, 13–29. Ottawa: Institute of Mediaeval Music, 2009.

Goudesenne, Jean-François. "Nouvelles perspectives sur le rôle des abbayes de Saint-Amand, de Saint-Thierry de Reims et de l'oeuvre d'Hucbald dans l'ordonnancement régulier des modes dans la composition musicale (850-900)." *Études grégoriennes* 30 (2002): 127–152.

Goudesenne, Jean-François, ed. *L'office romano-franc des saints Martyrs Denis, Rustique, et Eleuthère*. Ottawa: The Institute of Medieval Music, 2002.

Goudesenne, Jean-François. *Les Offices historiques ou historiae composés pour les fêtes des saints dans la province ecclésiastique de Reims (775-1030)*. Turnhout: Brepols, 2002.

Goudesenne, Jean-François. "A Typology of Historiae in West Francia (8-10 c.)." *Plainsong and Medieval Music* 13 (2004): 1–31.

Le graduel romain: Édition Critique. Solesmes: Abbaye Saint-Pierre de Solesmes, 1957.

Grégoire, Réginald. *San Ranieri di Pisa (1117-1160) in un ritratto agiografico inedito del secolo XIII*. Pisa: Pacini, 1990.

Gregory I, Pope. *Dialogues*. Edited by Adalbert de Vogüé. Translated by Paul Antin. 3 vols. Paris: Éditions du Cerf, 1978, 1979, and 1980.

Grier, James. "Adémar de Chabannes, Carolingian Musical Practices, and 'Nota Romana.'" *Journal of the Americal Musicological Society* 56 (2003): 43–98.

Grodecki, Louis. *Les vitraux du Centre et des Pays de la Loire*. Edited by Louis Grodecki, Françoise Perrot, and Jean Tarlon. Paris: Editions du Centre national de la recherche scientifique, 1981.

Guerra, Almerico, and Pietro Guidi. *Compendio di storia ecclesiastica lucchese dalle origini a tutto il secolo XII*. Lucca: Cooperativa Artigiana Editrice, 1924.

Guerrini, Roberto, ed. *Sotto il duomo di Siena: Scoperte archeologiche, architettoniche e figurative*. Siena: Silvana, 2003.

Guglielmetti, Rossana E. *I testi agiografici latini nei codici della Biblioteca Medicea Laurenziana*. Florence: SISMEL - Edizioni del Galluzzo, 2007.

Guidi, Pietro. "Per la storia della cattedrale e del Volto Santo." *Bollettino storico lucchese* 4 (1932): 169–186.

Guidi, Pietro. *Tuscia*. 2 vols. Vatican City: Biblioteca Apostolica Vaticana, 1932.

Guidi, Pietro, and O. Parenti, eds. *Regesto del capitolo di Lucca*. 3 vols. Rome: Ermanno Loescher, 1910–1933.

Guidi, Pietro, and Ermenegildo Pellegrinetti. *Inventari del vescovato, della cattedrale e di altre chiese di Lucca*. Rome: Poliglotta vaticana, 1921.

Gurrieri, Francesco, Luciano Berti, and Claudio Leonardi. *La Basilica di San Miniato al Monte a Firenze*. Florence: Giunti Barbèra, 1988.

Haggh, Barbara. "Foundations or Institutions? On Bringing the Middle Ages into the History of Medieval Music." *Acta Musicologica* 68 (1996): 87–128.
Hahn, Cynthia. *Portrayed on the Heart: Narrative Effect in Pictorial Lives of the Saints from the Tenth to the Thirteenth Century*. Berkeley: University of California Press, 2001.
Hamilton, Louis. *A Sacred City: Consecrating Churches and Reforming Society in Eleventh-Century Italy*. Manchester: Manchester University Press, 2010.
Hamilton, Sarah. "The Early Pontificals: The Anglo-Saxon Evidence Reconsidered from a Continental Perspective." In *England and the Continent in the Tenth Century. Studies in Honour of Wilhelm Levison (1876-1947)*, edited by David Rollason, Conrad Leyser, and Hannah Williams, 411–428. Turnhout: Brepols, 2010.
Hankeln, Roman. "A Blasphemous Paradox? Approaches to Socio-Political Aspects of Medieval Western Plainchant." In *Political Plainchant?: Music, Text, and Historical Context of Medieval Saints' Offices*, edited by Roman Hankeln, 1–11. Ottawa: Institute of Mediaeval Music, 2009.
Hankeln, Roman, ed. *Political Plainchant?: Music, Text, and Historical Context of Medieval Saints' Offices*. Ottawa: Institute of Mediaeval Music, 2009.
Hankeln, Roman. "'Properization' and Formal Changes in High Medieval Saint's Offices: The Offices for Saints Henry and Kunigunde of Bamberg." *Plainsong and Medieval Music* 10 (2001): 3–22.
Hankeln, Roman. "St. Olav's Augustine-Responsories: Contrafactum Technique and Political Message." In *Political Plainchant?: Music, Text, and Historical Context of Medieval Saints' Offices*, edited by Roman Hankeln, 171–199. Ottawa: Institute of Mediaeval Music, 2009.
Hankeln, Roman. "Texting Techniques in St Olav's Augustine-Responsories." In *Studies in Medieval Chant and Liturgy in Honour of David Hiley*, edited by Terence Bailey and László Dobszay, 275–293. Ottawa: Institute of Mediaeval Music, 2007.
Hardison, O. B. *Christian Rite and Christian Drama in the Middle Ages: Essays in the Origin and Early History of Modern Drama*. Baltimore: Johns Hopkins University Press, 1965.
Harper, John. *The Forms and Orders of Western Liturgy from the Tenth to the Eighteenth Century*. Oxford: Oxford University Press, 1991.
Heene, Katrein. "Audire, legere, vulgo: An Attempt to Define Public Use and Comprehensibility of Carolingian Hagiography." In *Latin and the Romance Languages in the Early Middle Ages*, edited by Roger Wright, 146–163. University Park, PA: Pennsylvania State University Press, 1996.
Heinzelmann, Martin. *Translationsberichte und andere Quellen des Reliquienkultes*. Turnhout: Brepols, 1979.
Helsen, Kate. *The Great Responsories of the Divine Office: Aspects of Structure and Transmission*. Ph.D. diss., University of Regensburg, 2008.
Helsen, Kate. "The Use of Melodic Formulas in Responsories: Constancy and Variability in the Manuscript Tradition." *Plainsong and Medieval Music* 18 (2009): 61–75.
Herrick, Samantha Kahn. "Studying Apostolic Hagiography: The Case of Fronto of Périgeux, Disciple of Christ." *Speculum* 85 (2010): 235–270.
Hesbert, René. *Antiphonale Missarum Sextuplex*. Rome: Herder, 1967.
Hesbert, René. *Corpus Antiphonalium Officii*. 6 vols. Rome: Herder, 1975.
Hiley, David. "The Offices Sung in San Marco, Venice. Stylistic Layers in Plainchant for Local Saints." In *Sine musica nulla disciplina... Studi in Onore di Giulio Cattin*, edited by Franco Bernabei and Antonio Lovato, 123–136. Padua: Il poligrafo, 2006.

Hiley, David. "Style and Structure in Early Offices of the Sanctorale." In *Western Plainchant in the First Millennium: Studies in the Medieval Liturgy and its Music*, edited by Sean Gallagher, James Haar, John Nádas, and Timothy Striplin, 157–179. Burlington: Ashgate, 2003.

Hiley, David. *Western Plainchant: A Handbook*. Oxford: Oxford University Press, 1993.

Hiscock, Nigel. "The Ottonian Revival: Church Expansion and Monastic Reform." In *The White Mantle of Churches: Architecture, Liturgy, and Art Around the Millennium*, edited by Nigel Hiscock, 1–28. Turnhout: Brepols, 2003.

Holsinger, Bruce, and David Townsend. "The Ovidian Verse Epistles of Magister Leoninus." *Journal of Medieval Latin* 8 (2000): 389–423.

Horn, Walter. "Romanesque Churches in Florence. A Study in their Chronology and Stylistic Development." *Art Bulletin* 25 (1943): 112–131.

Hughes, Andrew. *Medieval Manuscripts for the Mass and Office: A Guide to their Organization and Terminology*. Toronto: University of Toronto Press, 1982.

Hughes, Andrew. "Modal Order and Disorder in the Rhymed Office." *Musica Disciplina* 37 (1983): 29–51.

Huglo, Michel. *Les tonaires. Inventaire, analyse, comparaison*. Paris: Heugel, 1971.

M. Huglo and Joan Halmo. "Antiphon," *Grove Music Online*, ed. L. Macy. Accessed 16 August 2007. http://www.grovemusic.com.

Iogna-Prat, Dominique. *Agni immaculati: Recherches sure les sources hagiographieques relatives à Saint Maieul de Luny (954-994)*. Paris: Cerf, 1988.

Jacobson, Werner. "Saints' Tombs in Frankish Church Architecture." *Speculum* 72 (1997): 1107–1143.

Jaeger, C. Stephen. "The Courtier Bishop in the *Vitae* from the Tenth to the Twelfth Century." *Speculum* 58 (1983): 219–325.

Jansen, Katherine L., Joanna Drell, and Frances Andrews, eds. *Medieval Italy: Texts in Translation*. Philadelphia: University of Pennysylvania Press, 2009.

Jensen, Brian Møller. "'Magni presulis celebrans Doanti diem sollemnem': Bishop Donatus of Arezzo in Roma, Bibl. Angelica 123." *Rivista internazionale di musica sacra* 22 (2000): 119–139.

Jones, Charles W. *The Saint Nicholas Liturgy and its Literary Relationships (Ninth to Twelfth Centuries)*. Berkeley: University of California Press, 1963.

Jonson [Jacobsson], Ritva. *Historia: Études sur la genése des offices versifiés*, Studia Latina Stockholmiensia 15. Stockholm: Almqvist & Wiksel, 1968.

Jung, Jacqueline Elaine. "Beyond the Barrier: The Unifying Role of the Choir Screen in Gothic Churches." *Art Bulletin* 82 (2000): 622–657.

Jungmann, Joseph A. *The Mass of the Roman Rite: Its Origins and Development*. Translated by Francis A. Brunner. 2 vols. New York: Benziger, 1951–1955.

Kehr, Paul Fridolin. *Regesta Pontificum Romanorum. Italia Pontificia*. 10 vols. Berlin: Weidmann, 1908.

Keller, Hagen. "Origine sociale e formazione del clero cattedrale dei secoli XI e XII nella Germania e nell'Italia settentrionale." In *Le istituzioni ecclesiastiche della 'societas christiana' dei secoli XI-XII. Diocesi, pievi, parrocchie. Atti della VI settimana internazionale di studi (Milano, 1-7 settembre 1974)*, 137–159. Milan: Vita e pensiero, 1977.

Kemp, Eric Waldram. *Canonization and Authority in the Western Church*. Oxford: Oxford University Press, 1948.

Kim, Eun Ju. "La messa di San Donato nella tradizione aretina." *Rivista internazionale di musica sacra* 21 (2000): 143–147.

Klapisch-Zuber, Christiane. "San Romolo: Un vescovo, un lupo, un nome alle origini dello stato moderno." *Archivio Storico Italiano* 155 (1997): 3–48.

Kruckenberg, Lori A. *The Sequence from 1050-1150: Study of a Genre in Change*. Ph.D. diss., University of Iowa, 1997.

Kurze, Wilhelm. "Nobiltà toscana e nobiltà aretina " In *I ceti dirigenti in Toscana nell'età precommunale. Atti del I Convegno, Firenze, 2 dicembre 1978*, 257–265. Pisa: Pacini, 1981.

Lagueux, Robert. *Glossing Christmas: Liturgy, Music, Exegesis, and Drama in High Medieval Laon*. Ph.D. diss., Yale University, 2005.

Lami, Giovanni. *Sanctae Ecclesiae Florentinae Monumenta*. 4 vols. Florence: Angelo Salutatae 1758.

Lami, Giovanni. *Charitonis et Hippophili hodeoporicon*. 4 vols. Florence: Viviani, 1741–1754.

Landes, Richard Allen. *Relics, Apocalypse, and the Deceits of History: Ademar of Chabannes, 989-1034*. Cambridge, MA: Harvard University Press, 1995.

Lazzeri, Corrado. *Guglielmino Ubertini, vescovo di Arezzo (1248-1289) e i suoi tempi*. Florence: Libreria editrice fiorentina, 1920.

Lazzeri, Corrado. *La donazione del tribuno romano Zenobio al vescovo d'Arezzo San Donato (sec. IV)*. Arezzo: Reale Accademia Petrarca, 1938.

Leigh Choate, Tova Ann. *The Liturgical Faces of Saint Denis: Music, Power, and Identity in Medieval France*. Ph.D. diss., Yale University, 2009.

Leyser, Henrietta. *Hermits and the New Monasticism: A Study of Religious Communities in Western Europe, 1000-1150*. New York: St. Martin's, 1984.

Licciardello, Pierluigi. *Agiografia aretina altomedievale: Testi agiografici e contesti socio-culturali ad Arezzo tra VI e IX secolo*. Florence: SISMEL - Edizioni del Galluzzo, 2005.

Locanto, Massimiliano. "La tradizione dei tropi liturgici a Pistoia nel XII secolo. Uno sguardo d'insieme sul manoscritto Pistoia, Archivio capitolare, C. 121." *Musica e storia* 14 (2006): 381–477.

Lohse, Tillman. "Stand und Perspektiven der *Liber ordinarius*-Forschung." In *Liturgie in mittelalterlichen Frauenstiften*, edited by Klaus Gereon Beuckers, 215-255. Essen: Klartext Medienwerkstatt, 2012.

Lorenzo of Amalfi. *Opera*. Edited by Francis Newton, MGH Q 7. Weimar: H. Böhlaus Nachf, 1973.

Lucchesi, Giovanni. "Il sermonario di S. Pier Damiani." *Studi Gregoriani* 10 (1975): 9-67.

Lucchesini, Cesare. *Della storia letteraria del ducato lucchese*. 2 vols. Lucca: Francesco Bertini, 1825–1831.

Magini, Maria Clotilde. "Cryptes du haut Moyen age en Italie: Problèms de typologie du IX jusqú au début du XI siècle." *Cahiers Archeologiques* 28 (1979): 41–85.

Maiello, James Vincent. "On the Manufacture and Dating of the Pistoia Choirbooks," *Plainsong and Medieval Music* 19 (2010): 21–33.

Maloy, Rebecca. *Inside the Offertory: Aspects of Chronology and Transmission*. Oxford: Oxford University Press, 2010.

Manhès, Colette. *Les vitraux narratifs de la cathédrale de Chartres: Étude iconographique*. Paris: Léopard d'or, 1993.

Mansi, Giovanni Domenico. *Sacrorum Conciliorum Nova et Amplissima Collectio*. 31 vols. Venice: Antonio Zatta, 1759–1798.

Mansi, Giovanni Domenico, ed. *Stephani Baluzii Tutelensis Miscellanea*. 4 vols. Lucca: Vincentius Junctinius, 1761.

Marchetti, Mino. *Liturgia e storia della chiesa di Siena nel XII secolo: I calendari medioevali della chiesa senese*. Siena: Istituto storico diocesano di Siena, 1991.

Maroni, Alfredo. *Prime comunità cristiane e strade romane nei territori di Arezzo—Siena—Chiusi (dalle origine al secolo VIII)*. 3rd ed. Siena: Cantagalli, 2001.

Marshall, Christina E. A. *Late Medieval Liturgical Offices in Acrostic Form: A Catalogue and Study*. Ph.D. diss., University of Toronto, 2006.

Martimort, Aimé-Georges. *Les "Ordines," les Ordinaires et les Cérémoniaux*. Turnhout: Brepols, 1991.

Martindale, Andrew. *Simone Martini: Complete Edition*. New York: New York University Press, 1988.

Masini, Paolo. "Magister Johannes Beleth: Ipotesi di una Traccia Biografica." *Ephemerides Liturgicae* 107 (1993): 248–259.

Mattei, Antonio Felice. *Ecclesiae Pisanae Historia*. 2 vols. Lucca: Leonardo Venturini, 1768–1772.

Maxwell, Robert A., ed. *Representing History, 900-1300: Art, Music, History*. University Park: Pennsylvania State University, 2010.

McClendon, Charles B. "Church Building in Northern Italy around the Year 1000: A Reappraisal." In *The White Mantle of Churches: Architecture, Liturgy, and Art Around the Millennium*, edited by Nigel Hiscock, 221–232. Turnhout: Brepols, 2003.

McKinley, Allan Scott. "The First Two Centuries of Saint Martin of Tours." *Early Medieval Europe* 14 (2006): 173–200.

McKinnon, James. *The Advent Project: The Later Seventh-Century Creation of the Roman Mass Proper*. Berkeley: University of California Press, 2000.

McKinnon, James. "Representations of the Mass in Medieval and Renaissance Art." *Journal of the American Musicological Society* 31 (1978): 21–52.

McKitterick, Rosamond. *The Frankish Church and the Carolingian Reforms, 789-895*. London: Royal Historical Society, 1977.

McLynn, Neil B. *Ambrose of Milan: Church and Court in a Christian Capital*. Berkeley: University of California Press, 1994.

Méhu, Didier. "*Historiae* et *Imagines* de la consécration de l'église au moyen âge." In *Mises en scène et mémoires de la consécration de l'église dans l'occident médiéval*, edited by Didier Méhu, 15–48. Turnhout: Brepols, 2008.

Melucco Vaccaro, Alessandra, ed. *Arezzo. Il colle del Pionta. Il contributo archeologico alla storia del primitivo gruppo cattedrale*. Arezzo: Provincia di Arezzo, Progetto archeologia, 1991.

Metz, Amalarius of. "Liber Officialis." In *Amalarii Episcopi Opera Liturgica Omnia*, edited by Ioanne Michaele Hanssens, 9–109. Vatican City: Biblioteca Apostolica Vaticana, 1948.

Miccoli, Giovanni. "Ecclesiae primitivae forma." *Studi medievali* (1959): 470–498.

Miller, Maureen C. *The Bishop's Palace: Architecture and Authority in Medieval Italy*. Ithaca, NY: Cornell Unversity Press, 2000.

Miller, Maureen C. "The Saint Zenobius Dossal by the Master of the Bigallo and the Cathedral Chapter of Florence." *Haskins Society Journal* 19 (2007): 65–81.

Milo, Yoram. *Tuscany and the Dynamics of Church Reform in the Eleventh Century*. Ph.D. diss., Stanford University, 1979.

Milone, Antonio. "Il Duomo e la sua facciata." In *Il Duomo di Pisa*, edited by Adriano Peroni, 191–206. Modena: F.C. Panini, 1995.

Milone, Antonio, and Guido Tigler. "Catalogo dei pulpiti romanici Toscani." In *Pulpiti medievali toscani. Storia e restauri di micro-architetture. Atti della Giornata di studio, Accademia delle Arti del Disegno, Firenze, 21 giugno 1996*, edited by Daniela Lamberini, 157–191. Florence: Leo S. Olschki, 1999.

Monaco, Giorgio, Lucia Bertolini Campetti, and Silvia Meloni Trkulja. *Museo Nazionale di Villa Guinigi, Lucca: La villa e le collezioni*. Lucca: Ente provinciale per il turismo, 1968.

Montgomery, Scott B. "*Mittite capud meum. . . ad matrem meam ut osculetur eum*: The Form and Meaning of the Reliquary Bust of Saint Just." *Gesta* 36 (1997): 48–64.

Montgomery, Scottt B. "*Quia venerabile corpus redicti martyris ibi repositum*: Image and Relic in the Decorative Program of San Miniato al Monte, Florence." In *Images, Relics, and Devotional Practices in Medieval and Renaissance Italy*, edited by Sally J. Cornelison and Scott B. Montgomery, 7–25. Tempe, AA: Arizona Center for Medieval and Renaissance Studies, 2005.

Morin, Germain, ed. *Sancti Caesarii Arelatensis Sermones*. 2 vols, Corpus Christianorum Series Latina. Turnhout: Brepols, 1953.

Morris, Colin. *The Papal Monarchy: The Western Church from 1050 to 1250*. Oxford: Oxford University Press, 1989.

Moscadelli, Stefano, ed. *L'Archivio dell'Opera della Matropolitana di Siena*. Munich: Bruckmann, 1995.

Mosiici, Luciana, ed. *Le carte del monastero di S. Miniato al Monte (secoli IX-XII)*. Florence: Leo S. Olschki, 1990.

Muratori, Ludovico Antonio. *Rerum italicarum scriptores*. 25 vols. Milan: Typ. Societatis Palatinae, 1723–1751.

Nanni, Luigi. "La canonica della cattedrale senese nei secoli XI-XII." In *La vita comune del clero nei secoli XI e XII. Atti della settimana di studio, Mendola, settembre 1959*, 255–259. Milan: Vita e pensiero, 1962.

Nardi, Carlo. "La fortuna di Ambrogio nelle memorie medioevali di Zanobi, vescovo di Firenze." In *Le radici cristiane di Firenze*, edited by Anna Benvenuti, Franco Cardini, and Elena Giannarelli, 77–116. Florence: Aliena 1994.

Nelson, Janet L. "Charles the Bald and the Church in Town and Countryside." In *The Church in Town and Countryside: Papers Read at the Seventeenth Summer Meeting and the Eighteenth Winter Meeting of the Ecclesiastical History Society*, edited by Derek Baker, 103–118. Oxford: Oxford University Press, 1979.

Noble, Thomas F. X. "A New Look at the *Liber Pontificalis*." *Archivium Historiae Pontificiae* 23 (1985): 347–358.

North, William. "The Fragmentation and Redemption of a Medieval Cathedral: Property, Conflict, and Public Piety in Eleventh-Century Arezzo." In *Conflict in Medieval Europe: Changing Perspectives on Society and Culture*, 109–130. Aldershot: Ashgate, 2003.

Orlandi, Giovanni. "Vita Sancti Mennatis: Opera inedita di Leone Marsicano." *Rendiconti: Classe di lettere e scienze morali e storiche* 97 (1963): 467–490.

Osheim, Duane J. *An Italian Lordship: The Bishopric of Lucca in the Late Middle Ages*. Berkeley: University of California Press, 1977.

Paatz, Walter, and Elisabeth Valentiner Paatz. *Die Kirchen von Florenz, ein kunstgeschichtliches Handbuch*. 6 vols. Frankfurt: V. Klostermann, 1952–1955.

Page, Christopher. *The Christian West and its Singers: The First Thousand Years*. New Haven: Yale University Press, 2010.

Palazzo, Eric. "The Image of the Bishop in the Middle Ages." In *The Bishop Reformed: Studies of Episcopal Power and Culture in the Central Middle Ages*, edited by John S. Ott and Anna Trumbore Jones, 86–91. Aldershot: Ashgate, 2007.

Palazzo, Eric. *Les sacramentaires de Fulda: Etude sur l'iconographie et la liturgie à l'époque ottonienne*. Münster: Aschendorff, 1994.

Palisca, Claude V., ed., and Warren Babb, trans. *Hucbald, Guido, and John on Music*. New Haven: Yale University Press: 1978.

Parker, Elizabeth C. "Architecture as Liturgical Setting." In *The Liturgy of the Medieval Church*, edited by Thomas J. Heffernan and E. Ann Matter, 273–326. Kalamazoo: Medieval Institute Publications, Western Michigan University, 2001.

Parkes, Henry. "Questioning the Authority of Vogel and Elze's *Pontifical Romano-Germanique*." In *Understanding Medieval Liturgy: Essays in Interpretation*, edited by Sarah Hamilton and Helen Gittos. Aldershot: Ashgate, forthcoming.

Parsons, Anscar. *Canonical Elections*. Washington, DC: Catholic University of America, 1939.

Pasqui, Ubaldo. *Documenti per la storia della città di Arezzo nel medio evo*. 4 vols. Florence: G.P. Vieusseux, 1899, 1904, 1916, and 1937.

Patitucci Uggeri, Stella. "La via Francigena in Toscana." In *La via Francigena e altre strade della Toscana medievale*, edited by Stella Patitucci Uggeri, 9–134. Florence: All'Insegna del Giglio, 2004.

Pecchiai, Pio. *L'opera della Primaziale pisana. Notizie storiche e documenti. Elenco degli Operai. Regesto di diplomi a tutto il XIV secolo*. Pisa: F. Mariotti, 1905.

Pejrani Baricco, Luisella. "I risultati dell'indagine archeologica sulla chiesa abbaziale di Fruttuaria: Prime considerazioni." In *Dal Piemonte all'Europa: Esperienze monastiche nella società medievale*, edited by Renato Bordone, 587–606. Turin: Deputazione subalpine di storia patria - regione Piemonte, 1988.

Pellegrini, Michele. *Chiesa e città: Uomini, comunità e istituzioni nella società senese del XII e XIII secolo*. Rome: Herder, 2004.

Pelt, Jean Baptiste. *Etudes sur la cathédrale de Metz: Textes extraits principalement des registres capitulaires (1210-1790)*. Metz: Imprimerie du Journal de Lorrain, 1930).

Peroni, Adriano. "Architettura e decorazione." In *Il Duomo di Pisa*, edited by Adriano Peroni, 13–147. Modena: F.C. Panini, 1995.

Peroni, Adriano, ed. *Il Duomo di Pisa*. 3 vols. Modena: F.C. Panini, 1995.

Peroni, Adriano. "Funzionalità architettonica, configurazione e arredo dell'area liturgica: Il caso del duomo di Pisa." In *Medioevo: La chiesa e il palazzo*, edited by Arturo Carlo Quintavalle, 369–383. Milan: Electa, 2007.

Peter Damian. *Letters, 91-120*. Translated by Owen J. Blum. Washington, DC: Catholic University of America Press, 1998.

Peter Damian. *Sermones*, edited by Giovanni Lucchesi. Turnhout: Brepols, 1983.

Petrucci, Amadeo. "Il codice n. 490 della Biblioteca Capitolare di Lucca: Un problema di storia della cultura medievale ancora da risolvere." *Actum Luce* 2 (1973): 159–175.

Piattoli, Renato. *Le carte della canonica della cattedrale di Firenze (723-1149)*. Rome: Istituto storico italiano per il Medio Evo, 1938.

Picard, Jean-Charles. *Le Souvenir des évêques: Sépultures, listes épiscopales et culte des évêques en Italie du Nord des origines au Xe siècle*. Rome: École Française de Rome, 1988.

Planchart, Alejandro. "About Tropes." *Schweizer Jahrbuch für Musikwissenschaft* 2 (1982): 125–135.

Planchart, Alejandro, ed. *Beneventanum Troporum Corpus. Tropes of the Proper of the Mass from Southern Italy, A.D. 1000-1250*. Madison, Wis.: A-R Editions, 1989.

Planchart, Alejandro. "The Geography of Martinmass." In *Western Plainchant in the First Millennium: Studies in the Medieval Liturgy and its Music*, edited by Sean Gallagher, James Haar, John Nádas, and Timothy Striplin, 119–156. Burlington: Ashgate, 2003.

Planchart, Alejandro. "On the Nature of Transmission and Change in Trope Repertories." *Journal of the American Musicological Society* 41 (1988): 215–249.

Planchart, Alejandro. *The Repertory of Tropes at Winchester*. 2 vols. Princeton, NJ: Princeton University Press, 1976.

Plumpe, Joseph C. "Ecclesia Mater." *Transactions and Proceedings of the American Philological Association* 50 (1939): 535–555.

Pocknee, Cyril E. *Liturgical Vesture: Its Origins and Development*. London: Mowbray, 1960.

Poggiaspalla, Fermino. *La vita comune del clero*. Rome: Storia e Letteratura, 1968.

Polanichka, Dana M. "Transforming Space, (Per)forming Community: Church Consecration in Carolingian Europe." *Viator* 43 (2012): 79–98.

Politi Nencini, Giovanna Piancastelli. "Le ultime fasi costruttive del Battistero." In *La chiesa dei Santi Giovanni e Reparata in Lucca: Dagli scavi archeologici al restauro*, edited by Giovanna Piancastelli Politi Nencini, 133–149. Lucca: M. P. Fazzi, 1993.

Poncelet, Albert. *Catalogus codicum hagiographicorum latinorum bibliothecarum Romanarum praeter quam Vaticanae*. Brussels: n.p., 1909.

Quilici, Brunetto. *La chiesa di Firenze nei primi decenni del secolo XIII*. Florence: Salesiana, 1965.

Rankin, Susan. "Between Oral and Written: Thirteenth-Century Italian Sources of Polyphony." In *Un millennio di polifonia liturgica tra oralità e scrittura*, edited by Giulio Cattin and F. Alberto Gallo, 75–95. Bologna: Il mulino, 2002.

Rankin, Susan. "*Terribilis est locus iste:* The Pantheon in 609." In *Rhetoric Beyond Words*, edited by Mary Carruthers, 281–310. Cambridge: Cambridge University Press, 2010.

Rapp, Claudia. *Holy Bishops in Late Antiquity: The Nature of Christian Leadership in an Age of Transition*. Berkeley: University of California Press, 2005.

Rasmussen, Niels Krogh. *Les pontificaux du haut moyen âge: Genèse du livre de l'évêque*. Edited by Harcel Maverlas. Leuven: Spicilegium Sacrum Lovaniense, 1998.

Raspini, Giuseppe. *San Romolo vescovo di Fiesole*. Florence: Giampiero Pagnini, 1997.

Rauty, Natale. *L'antico palazzo dei vescovi a Pistoia: Storia e restauro*. 2 vols. Florence: Leo S. Olschki, 1981.

Rauty, Natale. *Il culto dei santi a Pistoia nel medioevo*. Florence: SISMEL - Edizioni del Galluzzo, 2000.

Rauty, Natale, ed. *Regesta Chartarum Pistoriensium: Canonica di S. Zenone Secolo XII*. Pistoia: Società Pistoiese di Storia Patria, 1995.

Rauty, Natale. "Società, istituzioni, politica nel primo secolo dell'autonomia comunale." In *Storia di Pistoia. L'età del libero comune. Dall'inizio del XII alla metà del XIV secolo*, edited by Giovanni Cherubini, 1–40. Florence: Felice Le Monnier, 1998.

Repsher, Brian V. *The Rite of Church Dedication in the Early Medieval Era*. Lewiston, NY: Edwin Mellen, 1998.

Reynolds, Roger E. "The Ritual of Clerical Ordination of the Sacramentarium Gelasium Saec. VIII: Early Evidence from Southern Italy." In *Rituels mélanges offerts à Pierre-Marie Gy, o.p.*, edited by Paul De Clerck and Eric Palazzo, 437–445. Paris: Editions du Cerf, 1990.

Riché, Pierre. *Education and Culture in the Barbarian West: From the Sixth through the Eighth Century*. Translated by John Contreni, J. Columbia: University of South Carolina Press, 1976.

Ridolfi, Enrico. *L'arte in Lucca studiata nella sua cattedrale*. Lucca: Canoventti, 1882.

Roberts, Michael. *The Humblest Sparrow: The Poetry of Venantius Fortunatus*. Ann Arbor: University of Michigan Press, 2009.

Robertson, Anne Walters. "From Office to Mass: The Antiphons of Vespers and Lauds and the Antiphons before the Gospel in Northern France." In *The Divine Office in the Latin Middle Ages: Methodology and Source Studies, Regional Developments, Hagiography, Written in Honor of Professor Ruth Steiner*, edited by Margot E. Fassler and Rebecca A. Baltzer, 300–323. Oxford: Oxford University Press, 2000.

Rondini, Silvia. "Il graduale III.R.69 dell'Archivio Vescovile di Pistoia." *Bullettino Storico Pistoiese* 59 (2007): 37–58.

Ronzani, Mauro. *Chiesa e civitas di Pisa nella seconda metà del secolo 11: Dall'avvento del vescovo Guido all'elevazione di Daiberto a metropoita di Corisca, 1060-1092*. Pisa: GISEM-ETS, 1997.

Ronzani, Mauro. "Da aula cultuale del vescovo a 'Ecclesia Major' della città: Note sulla fisonomia istituzionale e la rilevanza pubblica del Duomo di Pisa." In *La cattedrale e la città nel medioevo: Atti della giornata di studio Pisa, giugno 1991*, 79–83. Pisa: Pacini, 1993.

Ronzani, Mauro. "Dall'*edificatio ecclesiae* all' 'Opera di S. Maria': Nascita e primi sviluppi di un'istituzione nella Pisa dei secoli XI e XII." In *Delle fabbriche cittadine fino all'inizio dell'età moderna. Atti della tavola rotonda, Villa I Tatti, Firenze, 3 aprile 1991*, edited by Margaret Haines and Lucio Riccetti, 1–70. Florence: Leo S. Olschki, 1996.

Ronzani, Mauro. "La 'plebs' in città. La problematica della pieve urbana in Italia centro-settentrionale fra IX e il XIV secolo." In *Chiesa e città: Contributi della Commissione italiana di storia ecclesiastica comparata aderente alla Commission international d'histoire écclesiastique comparée al XVII Congresso internazionale di scienze storiche (Madrid, 26 agosto-2 settembre 1990)*, edited by Cosimo Damiano Fonseca and Cinzio Violante, 23–43. Galatina: Congedo, 1990.

Ronzani, Mauro. "Vescovi, canoniche e cattedrali nella 'Tuscia' dei secoli X e XI: Qualche considerazione a partire dall'esempio di Fiesole." In *Un archivio, una diocesi: Fiesole nel medioevo e nell'età moderna*, edited by Maura Borgioli, 3–21. Florence: Leo S. Olschki, 1996.

Ronzani, Mauro. "Vescovi, capitoli e strategie famigliari nell'Italia comunale." In *Storia d'Italia. Annali 9. La Chiesa e il potere politico dal medioevo all'età contemporanea*, edited by Giorgio Chittolini and Giovanni Miccoli, 103–148. Turin: Einaudi, 1986.

Rossetti, Gabriella. "Origine sociale e formazione dei vescovi del 'Regnum Italiae' nei secoli XI e XII." In *Le istituzioni ecclesiastiche della "Sociatas Christiana" dei secoli XI e XII: Diocesi, pievi e parrochie. Atti della VI settimana di studio, Milano 1-7 settembre 1974*, 57–88. Milan: Vita e pensiero, 1977.

Rotelli, Elena. *Il capitolo della cattedrale di Firenze dalle origini al XV secolo*. Florence: Firenze University Press, 2005.

Rubin, Miri. *Corpus Christi: The Eucharist in Late Medieval Culture*. Cambridge: Cambridge University Press, 1991.

Savigni, Raffaele. *Episcopato e società cittadina a Lucca: Da Anselmo II (†1086) a Roberto (†1225)*. Lucca: S. Marco 1996.

Scalia, Giuseppe. "Ancora intorno all'epigrafe sulla fondazione del duomo pisano." *Studi Medievali* 10 (1970): 483–519.

Scalia, Giuseppe. "La consacrazione della cattedrale pisana." *Bollettino storico pisana* 61 (1992): 1–31.

Scaravelli, Irene. "Giovanni da Besate." In *Dizionario Biografico degli Italiani*, 716–718. Rome: Istituto della Enciclopedia italiana, 2000.

Schiaparelli, Luigi. *Codice diplomatico Longobardo*. 2 vols, Fonti per la storia d'Italia 62–63. Rome: Istituto Storico Italiano, 1929–1933.

Schiaparelli, Luigi. *Il codice 490 della Biblioteca Capitolare di Lucca e la scuola scrittoria lucchese (sec. VIII-IX)*. Vatican City: Biblioteca Apostolica Vaticana, 1924.

Schlager, Karlheinz. *Alleluia-Melodien*. 2 vols. Kassel: Bärenreiter, 1968 and 1987.

Schmidt, Tilmann. *Alexander II (1061-1073) und die römische Reformgruppe seiner Zeit*. Stuttgart: Hiersemann, 1977.

Schneider, Fedor, ed. *Regestum Senese*, Regesta Chartarum Italiae 8. Rome: Ermanno Loescher, 1911.

Schwarzmaier, Hansmartin. *Lucca und das Reich bis zum Ende des 11. Jahrhunderts: Studien zur Struktur einer Herzogstadt in der Toskana*. Tübingen: M. Niemeyer, 1972.

Seidel, Max. "Tradizione e innovazione. Note sulle scoperte architettoniche nel duomo di Siena." In *Sotto il duomo di Siena: Scoperte archeologiche, architettoniche e figurative*, edited by Roberto Guerrini, 35–83. Siena: Silvana, 2003.

Severino, Gabriella. "La 'Vita metrica' di Anselmo da Lucca scritta da Rangerio: Ideologia e genere letterario." In *Sant'Anselmo vescovo di Lucca (1073-1086). Nell quadro delle trasformazioni sociali e della riforma ecclesiastica*, edited by Cinzio Violante, 223–271. Rome: Istituto Palazzo Borromini 1992.

Severus, Sulpicius. "Writings." In *The Fathers of the Church. Volume 7*, 101–254. Translated by Bernard M. Peebles. New York: Fathers of the Church, 1949.

Sicardo of Cremona. *Mitralis de Officii*, edited by Gábor Sarbak, and Lorenz Weinrich. Turnhout: Brepols, 2008.

Silva, Romano. *La basilica di San Frediano a Lucca: Immagine simbolica di Roma Cristiana*. Lucca: Maria Pacini Fazzi, 2010.

Silva, Romano. "Chiese e cappelle palatine in Toscana: Origine e tradizione." *Prospettiva* 24 (1981): 31–37.

Silva, Romano. "La datazione del Volto Santo di Lucca." In *La santa croce di Lucca: Il Volto Santo: Storia, tradizione, immagini: Atti del Convegno, Villa Bottini, 1-3 Marzo 2001*, 76–81. Lucca: Editori dell'Acero, 2003

Silva, Romano. "*Dilexi decorem domus tuae*: Il ruolo dell'episcopato nello sviluppo dell'architettura in Toscana dall'XI secolo alla prima metà del XII." *Arte medievale* 10 (1996): 23–38.

Silva, Romano. "La ricostruzione della cattedrale di Lucca (1060-1070): Un esempio precoce di architettura della riforma gregoriana." In *Sant'Anselmo vescovo di Lucca (1073-1086). Nel quadro delle trasformazioni sociali e della riforma ecclesiastica*, edited by Cinzio Violante, 297–309. Rome: Istituto Palazzo Borromini, 1992.

Simonetti, Adele. "Santi cefalofori altomedievali." *Studi medievali* 28 (1987): 67–121.

Simonetti, Adolfo. "Alberto I Marchese di Toscano e il saccheggio di Narni nell'878." *Bollettino della Deputazione di Storia Patria per l'Umbria* 7 (1901): 1–17.

Simonetti, Manlio. "Note sulla tradizione agiografica di S. Regolo di Populonia." In *Atti del convegno "Il Paleocristiano nella Tuscia," Viterbo, Palazzo dei Papi, 16-19 giugno 1979*, 107–130. Viterbo: Consorzio per la gestione delle bibliotheche comunale degli ardenti e provinciale "Anselmo Anselmi," 1981.

Sironi, Mario. "La Messa di San Donato." In *Codex Angelicus 123. Studi sul graduale-tropario bolognese del secolo XI e sui manoscritti collegati*, edited by Maria Teresa Rosa-Barezzani and Giampaolo Ropa, 311–333. Cremona: Una cosa rara, 1996.

Smith, Christine. "East or West in 11th-Century Pisan Culture: The Dome of the Cathedral and its Western Counterparts." *Journal of the Society of Architectural Historians* 43 (1984): 195–208.

Smith, Julia. *"Aedificatio Sancti Loci*: The Making of a Ninth-Century Holy Place." In *Topographies of Power in the Early Middle Ages*, edited by Mayke De Jong, Frans Theuws, and Carine Van Rhijn, 361–396. Leiden: Brill, 2001.

Smith Julia. "Old Saints, New Cults: Roman Relics in Carolingian Francia." In *Early Medieval Rome and the Christian West: Essays in Honour of Donald A. Bullough*, edited by Julia M. H. Smith, 317–339. Leiden: Brill, 2000.

Smits van Waesberghe, Joseph, ed. *Guidonis Aretini Micrologus*. N.p.: American Institute of Musicology, 1955.

Stancliffe, Clare. *St. Martin and His Hagiographer: History and Miracle in Sulpicius Severus*. Oxford: Oxford University Press, 1983.

Steiner, Ruth. "Matins Responsories and Cycles of Illustrations of Saints' Lives." In *Diakonia: Studies in Honor of Robert T. Meyer*, edited by T. Halton and J. Williman, 317–332. Washington DC: Catholic University of America Press, 1986.

Steiner, Ruth. "Some Questions about the Gregorian Offertories and their Verses." *Journal of the American Musicological Society* 19 (1966): 162–181.

Strunk, W. Oliver, and Leo Treitler, eds. *Strunk's Source Readings in Music History (Revised Edition)*. New York: W. W. Norton, 1998.

Sureda, Jaon. *La pintura románica en Cataluña*. Madrid: Alianza, 1981.

Susi, Eugenio. "Strategie agiografiche altomedievali in un leggendario di Farfa." *Christianesimo nella Storia* 18 (1997): 277–302.

Swarzenski, Hans. *The Berthold Missal, the Pierpont Morgan Library Ms 710 and the Scriptorium of Weingarten Abbey*. New York: Pierpont Morgan Library, 1943.

Tabacco, Giovanni. "Canoniche Aretine." In *La vita comune del clero nei secoli XI e XII. Atti della settimana di studio, Mendola, settembre 1959*, 245–254. Milan: Vita e pensiero, 1962.

Tacconi, Marica S. *Cathedral and Civic Ritual in Late Medieval and Renaissance Florence: The Service-Books of Santa Maria del Fiore*. Cambridge: Cambridge University Press, 2005.

Tangari, Nicola, ed. *Musica e liturgia a Monatecassino nel medioevo. Atti del Simposio internazionale di studi (Cassino, 9-10 dicembre 2010)*. Rome: Viella, 2012.

Testini, P., G. Cantino Wataghin, and L. Pani Ermini. "La cattedrale in Italia." In *Actes du XI Congrès international d'archéologie chrétienne*, 5-229. Rome: École française de Rome, 1989.

Thacker, Alan. "*Loca Sanctorum*: The Significance of Place in the Study of Saints." In *Local Saints and Local Churches in the Early Medieval West*, edited by Alan Thacker and Richard Sharpe, 1–43. Oxford: Oxford University Press, 2002.

Thompson, Augustine. *Cities of God: The Religion of the Italian Communes, 1125-1325*. University Park: Pennsylvania State University Press, 2005.

Tigler, Guido. "Maestri lombardi del Duecento a Lucca: Le sculture della facciata del duomo." In *I magistri commacini: Mito e realtá del medioevo lombardo. Atti del XIX Congresso internazionale di studio sull'alto medioevo, Varase-Como, 23-25 ottobre 2008*, 827–935. Spoleto: Fondazione Centro italiano di studi sull'alto medioevo, 2009.

Tigler, Guido. *Toscana romanica*. Milan: Jaca Book, 2006.

Tirelli Carli, Matilde. *Carte dell'Archivio Capitolare di Pisa 3 (1076-1100)*. Rome: Edizioni di storia e letteratura, 1977.

Toker, Franklin. "A Baptistery Below the Baptistery of Florence." *Art Bulletin* 58 (1976): 157–168.

Toker, Franklin. *Archeological Campaigns Below the Florence Duomo and Baptistery, 1895-1980*. Turnhout: Brepols, 2013.

Toker, Franklin. "Excavations Below the Cathedral of Florence." *Gesta* 14 (1975): 17–36.

Toker, Franklin. "A Gap in the Liturgical History of Florence Cathedral, and a Byzantine Casket Rich Enough to Fill It." In *Arte d'Occidente: Studi in onore di Angiola Maria Romanini*, edited by Antonio Cadei, Marina Righetti Tosti-Croce, Anna Segagni Malacart, and Alessandro Tomei, 767–779. Rome: Edizioni Sintesi Informazione, 1999.

Toker, Franklin. *On Holy Ground: Liturgy, Architecture, and Urbanism in the Cathedral and the Streets of Medieval Florence*. Turnhout: Brepols, 2009.

Töpfer, Bernhard. "The Cult of Relics and Pilgrimage in Burgundy and Aquitaine at the time of the Monastic Reform." Translated by János Bak. In *The Peace of God, Social Violence and Religious Response in France around the Year 1000*, edited by Thomas Head and Richard Landes, 41–57. Ithaca, NY: Cornell Unversity Press, 1992.

Töpfer, Bernhard. "Reliquienkult und Pilgerbewegung zur Zeit der Klosterreform im burgundische-aquitanischen Gebiet." In *Vom Mittelalter zur Neuzeit: Zum 65. Geburtstag von Heinrich Sprömberg*, edited by Hellmut Kretzschmar, 420–439. Berlin: Rütten & Loening, 1956.

Trexler, Richard C. *Synodal Law in Florence and Fiesole, 1306-1518*. Vatican City: Biblioteca Apostolica Vaticana, 1971.

Tristano, Caterina, and Alessandra Molinari, eds., *Arezzo: Il Pionta. Fonti e materiali dall'età classica all'età moderna*. Arezzo: Rotary Club, 2005.

Trombelli, Giovanni Crisostomo, ed. *Ordo Officiorum Ecclesiae Senensis ab Oderico eiusdem Ecclesiae canonicus anno MCCXIII compositus*. Bologna: Longhi, 1766.

Ughelli, Ferdinando. *Italia Sacra*. 8 vols. Rome: Bernardino Tano, 1644–1662.

Van Dam, Raymond. *Saints and Their Miracles in Late Antique Gaul*. Princeton, NJ: Princeton University Press, 1993.

Van Der Ploeg, Kees. *Art, Architecture, and Liturgy: Siena Cathedral in the Middle Ages*. Groningen: Egbert Forsten, 1993.

Van Engen, John. "The 'Crisis of Cenobitism' Reconsidered: Benedictine Monasticism in the Years 1050-1150." *Speculum* 61 (1986): 269–304.

Vecchi, Giuseppe. "L'insegnamento e la pratica musicale nella comunità dei canonici (sec. XI - XII)." In *La vita comune del clero nei secoli XI e XII. Atti della settimana di studio, Mendola, settembre 1959*, 26–39. Milan: Vita e pensiero, 1962.

Verrando, Giovanni Nino. "I due leggendari di Fiesole." *Aevum* 74 (2000): 443–491.

Villani, Giovanni. *Nuova Cronica*. 3 vols. Parma: Fondazione Pietro Bembo, 1990.

Violante, Cinzio. "Appunti per lo studio delle canoniche regolari a Pisa al tempo della riforma gregoriana." In *Studi in onore di Mons. C. Castiglioni*, 253–264. Milan: Dott. A Giuffrè, 1957.

Violante, Cinzio, and Cosimo Damiano Fonesca. "Ubicazione e dedicazione delle cattedrali dalle origini al periodo romanico nelle città dell'Italia centro-settentrionale." In *Il romanico pistoiese nei suoi rapporti con l'arte romanica dell'Occidente. Atti del primo convegno internazionale di studi medioevali di storia e d'arte, Pistoia, Montecatini Terme, 27 settembre-3 ottobre 1964*, 303–346. Pistoia: Ente provinciale per il turismo, 1966.

Vogel, Cyrille, and Reinhard Elze. *Le Pontifical romano-germanique du dixième siècle*. 3 vols. Vatican City: Biblioteca Apostolica Vaticana, 1963–1972.

Von Fischer, Kurt. "Das Kantorenamt am Dome von Siena zu Beginn des 13. Jahrhunderts." In *Festschrift Karl Gustav Fellerer zum sechzigsten Geburtstag am 7. Juli 1962*, 155–160. Regensburg: Bosse, 1962.

Von Fischer, Kurt. "Die Rolle der Mehrstimmigkeit am Dome von Siena zu Beginn des 13 Jahrhunderts." *Archiv für Musikwissenschaft* 18 (1961): 167–182.

Voragine, Jacobus de. *The Golden Legend*. Translated by Granger Ryan and Helmut Ripperger. New York: Arno, 1969.

Vroom, Wim. *Financing Cathedral Building in the Middle Ages: The Generosity of the Faithful*. Translated by Elizabeth Manton. Amsterdam: Amsterdam University Press, 2010.

Ward-Perkins, Bryan. *From Classical Antiquity to the Middle Ages: Urban Public Building in Northern and Central Italy, AD 300-850*. Oxford: Oxford University Press, 1984.

Weakland, Rembert. "The Compositions of Hucbald." *Études grégoriennes* 3 (1959): 155–162.

Webb, Diana. "The Holy Face of Lucca." *Anglo-Norman Studies* 9 (1986): 228–237.

Webb, Diana. *Patrons and Defenders: The Saints in the Italian City-States*. London: Tauris Academic Studies, 1996.

Webb, Diana. "St. James in Tuscany: The Opera di San Jacopo of Pistoia and Pilgrimage to Compostela." *Journal of Ecclesiastical History* 50 (1998): 207–234.

Weinrich, Lorenz. "Der *Ordo officiorum Senensis ecclesie* des Oderigo und Sicards *Mitralis de officiis*." *Sacris Erudiri* 42 (2002): 375–389.

Wellesz, Egon. *Eastern Elements in Western Chant: Studies in the Early History of Ecclesiastical Music*. Boston: Byzantine Institute, 1947.

Whitehead, Christina. "Columnae... sunt episcopi. Pavimentum... est vulgus: The Symbolic Translation of Ecclesiastical Architecture in Latin Liturgical Handbooks." *The Medieval Translator / Traduire au Moyen Age* 8 (2003): 29–37.

Wickham, Chris. *Courts and Conflict in Twelfth-Century Tuscany*. Oxford: Oxford University Press, 2003.

Wickham, Chris. *Early Medieval Italy: Central Power and Local Society 400-1000*. Totowa, NJ: Barnes & Noble, 1981.

Wickham, Chris. "Economic and Social Institutions in Northern Tuscany in the 8th Century." In *Istituzioni ecclesiastiche della Toscana medieovale*, 7–34. Galatina: Congedo, 1980.

Wickham, Chris. *Framing the Early Middle Ages: Europe and the Mediterranean, 400-800.* Oxford: Oxford University Press, 2005.

Wickham, Chris. *The Inheritance of Rome: A History of Europe from 400 to 1000.* London: Penguin, 2009.

Wickham, Chris. "Topographies of Power: Introduction." In *Topographies of Power in the Early Middle Ages,* edited by Mayke De Jong, Frans Theuws, and Carine Van Rhijn, 1–8. Leiden: Brill, 2001.

Willis, G. G. *Further Essays in Early Roman Liturgy.* London: Society for Promoting Christian Knowledge, 1968.

Wilson, Blake. "Music, Art, and Devotion: The Cult of St. Zenobius at the Florentine Cathedral during the Early Renaissance." In *Il "Cantate Domino." Musica nei secoli per il duomo di Firenze. Atti del Convegno Internazionale di Studi (Firenze, 23-25 maggio 1997)* edited by Piero Gargiulo, Gabriele Giacomelli, and Carolyn Gianturco, 17–36. Florence: Edifir, 2001.

Wilson, H. A., ed. *The Gelasian Sacramentary.* Oxford: Oxford University Press, 1894.

Wood, Susan. *The Proprietary Church in the Medieval West.* Oxford: Oxford University Press, 2006.

Wright, Craig. *Music and Ceremony at Notre Dame of Paris, 500-1550.* Cambridge: Cambridge University Press, 1989.

Yawn, Lila. "The Italian Giant Bible, Lay Patronage and Professional Workmanship (11th-12th Centuries)." In *Les usages sociaux de la Bible, XIe-XVe siècles,* 162–255. Paris: Laboratoire de Médiévistique Occidentale de Paris, 2011.

Young, Karl. *The Drama of the Medieval Church.* 2 vols. Oxford: Oxford University Press, 1933.

Zaccagnini, Gabriele, ed. *Vita Sancti Fridiani: Contributi di storia e di agiografia lucchese medievale.* Lucca: Fazzi, 1989.

Ziino, Agostino. "Polifonia nella cattedrale di Lucca durante il XIII secolo." *Acta musicologica* 47 (1975): 16–30.

INDEX

Aaron, 151n22
acolytes, 33, 144, 149–151, 175, 195
Adalbert I, Margrave, 43
Adalbert II, Margrave, 49, 50n22
Ademar of Chabannes, 53n32
Ado, of Vienne, 35n64, 85n41, 180
Agatha, Saint, 88, 132
Agnes, Saint, 88, 132
Agnus Dei, 146, 149
Agricola, Saint, 222
Alberto, Bishop of Arezzo, 54–58, 61, 90n53, 181, 225, 244
Aldobrandini, Roberto, 141n109
All Saints, Feast of, 126n47, 153n27
Alexander I, Pope, 87, 160n47
Alexander II, Pope. *See* Anselmo I, Bishop of Lucca
Alexander III, Pope, 242
Alexander of Fiesole, Saint, 14–15, 36–39, 51–52, 70, 194
Alleluia (plainsong), 146, 151–152, 155, 159–162, 166, 190, 195–196 (*see also individual chants*)
Amalarius of Metz, 123, 145–147
Ambrose, Saint
   as builder, 11, 30, 32, 179, 223
   and St. Zenobius, 76, 220, 222–223, 224n92

Andrea, Bishop of Florence, 39–41, 49, 78, 131, 156n36, 203
angels
   choirs of, 150, 152–153, 156–158, 160–162, 165–166, 228
   in hagiography, 26, 29, 32, 64, 65n77, 239
Angilram, Bishop of Metz, 140n103
Ansanus, Saint, 18–19, 20n11, 25, 42, 71, 127–131, 135–136, 197
Anselmo I, Bishop of Lucca, 84–102, 112, 131–132, 140, 159, 234
Anselmo II, Saint, 84, 97–98, 99n92, 147
Ansifredo, Bishop of Siena, 17–19, 25, 27, 35, 131
Antimus, Deacon, 182–183, 228–229
antiphoners, 110, 197, 228
antiphons (*see also individual chants*)
   in the Divine Office, 194–196, 198–199
   Gospel, 194–196, 208–209, 237
   Hodie, 239–240
   modal distribution, 203, 241
   modal order, 226–227, 237, 241
   in the rite of consecration, 10, 33, 94–96
   tune families, 203–204, 229, 238–242
Antonio delgi Orsini, Bishop, 217n65
Apollinaris, Saint, 88, 132n71

285

apostles, 132–133, 150, 174, 179
  ideal of, 48, 51, 73, 75, 77, 86, 97
Aquitaine, 53n32, 127n52, 161, 165, 176
archdeacon, 142, 175, 193n7 (*see also individual archdeacons*)
archpriest, 130, 141–142, 145, 175, 193n7, 193n7 (*see also individual archpriests*)
Ardingo, Bishop of Florence, 120, 138–139, 194n8
Arezzo, 1–2, 17–19, 47–49, 54–61, 179–190, 225–233 (*see also individual bishops, churches, and saints*)
Arian heresy, 26n32, 36n66, 236–237
Arno River, 5, 38–39, 41, 62, 64, 200, 208
Arrigo, chaplain, 137n89
Ascension, Feast of the, 122n32, 153n27, 184n123, 196n16
Attone, Bishop of Florence, 72, 74–77, 81n29, 83–84
Attone, Bishop of Pistoia, 111n5
Augustine, Saint, 116n14, 142, 203n36
Ave Maria, 149
Azzo, hermit, 68

Babbino, Abbot of San Frediano, 28n39
baptism, 95, 108–109
Badia, Florence, 217n65
baptismal parishes. *See* pievi
baptisteries, 109 (*see also individual churches*)
Bede, Saint, 26n31, 47, 180
Beleth, Johannes, 108, 123, 174–175, 183
Benedict IX, Pope, 75–76, 86
Benedict, Saint, 209n48, 217n65
  Rule of, 66, 72, 82, 193
Benedictus (Song of Zechariah), 194
Benevento, 161–162, 165
Bertha, Margravine, 49
Bigarelli, Guido, 90n54, 133, 152, 170, 225
bishops (*see also individual bishops*)
  as builders, 10–11, 22, 29–35, 54–61, 63, 65–66, 68–70, 87–101
  as celebrants at Mass, 147–150, 153–154, 173–176, 182–190
  as defenders of the church, 2, 10–11, 36–43, 50–52
  as ecclesiastical reformers, 54–55, 67–69, 74–76, 91–92, 97–98, 138–139
  as founders of cathedral chapters, 47–48, 50–51

  as imperial clients, 10, 36–41, 47–57, 62–67, 74–76, 85–86
  participation in the Divine Office, 37, 193–194, 242–243
  as translators of relics, 18, 25–28, 32, 37, 40–41, 58–61, 63, 85–86
Blaise, Saint, 88, 132n71
Blancardo, Archdeacon, 91–92, 131
Bonfilio, Bishop of Siena, 137n89
Bono, Bishop of Pisa, 137n89
Bono, Bishop of Siena, 130n64, 135
breviaries, 110, 197, 228
Burchard of Worms, 107n1, 122–123
Buschetto, architect, 102–103, 112

Caesarius of Arles, 153n27
Cagliari, 103, 151n22
Caiazzo, 198
Camaldoli, hermitage of, 1, 66, 68, 72, 83, 168
candles, offerings of, 108–109, 131, 135
Canon (prayer), 146, 154, 174
canons (*see also individual churches*)
  absenteeism, 139
  chapters, 44–54, 136–143
  and civic relic cults, 129–130, 132–134
  conflict with their bishop, 97–98, 135–137
  and the Divine Office, 193, 245
  as guardians of liturgical tradition, 112–123
  prebends, 137, 139–140
  role at Mass, 147–153, 162, 166, 175–176, 190–191
  social origins, 45, 112–113, 136
cantor, 116–120, 122, 148, 150, 152, 156, 175n93, 176 (*see also individual cantors*)
Carolingians. *See individual kings and emperors*
Cassius, Saint, 43
catacombs, 19, 27, 31
cathedrals. *See individual churches*
Cavalcante, priest, 141n105
Celsus, Saint, 223
cephalophores. *See* saints
chaplains, 137, 140–142, 144, 195n14
Charlemagne, 31, 36, 44, 56
  conquest of Italy, 5, 24, 35
  donation to San Miniato al Monte, 41, 62–63
Charles the Bald, Emperor, 39–40, 49, 51, 57n47
charters, 13, 36, 38, 46–48, 51–53, 62–63, 67–69, 71, 74–75

Index

choirboys, 2, 116, 142, 144, 195n14
choirs (architectural), 124, 126, 149–152 (see also individual churches)
Christopher, Saint, 151n22
Città di Castello, 17
Cluny, Monastery of, 72, 81–84
Clusina, 17
Collect (prayer), 146
communes, 74, 97, 99, 104–105, 109, 111, 142, 159, 172, 214, 243
commune sanctorum, 176, 184n123, 196–197, 216n62, 217, 219, 226n95, 236, 243
communion, 146, 154
Communion (plainsong), 146, 155, 161, 168, 179 (*see also individual chants*)
compline, 194–195
confessionals. See crypts, annular
commixture, 210
Conrad II, Emperor, 53n29, 60n54, 76n13, 85
consecration of a bishop, 173, 178
consecration of a church, 9–11, 58–61, 92–97, 103–104, 156
constitutions. See canons
Cornelius, Saint, 85n41
Corsica, 104
Credo, 146, 149n14
Crescentius, Saint, 19, 25, 27, 131, 160
Crescentius of Florence, Saint, 223–224
crypts, 112, 127, 131 (*see also individual churches*)
    annular, 31–32, 37, 55, 101, 124, 203, 207, 239
    hall, 41n82, 55–56, 65–66, 70, 124, 208
    monumental, 124–126

Damian, Peter, 66, 140, 180, 183n117
David, King, 161
Davino, chaplain, 142
deacons, 148–151, 153–154, 175, 193n3 (*see also individual deacons*)
Decius, emperor, 41, 200–202, 204
Dedication of the Church, Feast of, 95n71, 135n80, 153n27, 155–166, 216
Deodericus, Bishop, 62n63
Denis, Saint, 61, 64–66, 208, 210
diplomas. See charters
discant. See organum
Divine Office, 192–245
    narrative in, 199–202, 209, 220, 226–229, 236–237
    structure of, 193–196

Dofana. See Sant'Ansano, Dofana
Dominus et constructor (*see* bishops)
Donatus of Arezzo, Saint, 13, 18, 47–48, 54–60, 70–71, 81, 84n36
    Mass, 166, 179–190, 197, 225
    Office, 56–59, 199, 225–233, 241
Donatus (of Evorea), Saint, 227n101
Donatus (of Fiesole), Saint, 38–39, 52
Drogone, Abbot, 63–65, 76, 202, 208–209, 212–213

Easter, Feast of, 104n111, 140n103, 153n27, 154n33, 196n16, 219
ecclesia matrix, ideal of, 34–35, 107–109, 111, 121–123, 129, 138–139, 145
Edmund, Saint, 88, 132n71
elevation of the Host, 146, 154, 184
Elemperto, Bishop of Arezzo, 54–59, 61, 66, 90n53, 181, 225, 244
Enrico, cantor, 117
Ephysius, Saint, 103
Epimachus, Saint, 160n47
Epiphany, Feast of, 145n6, 153n27, 168, 196n16
Epistle (reading), 146, 150–151, 153, 160–162, 165, 173, 176, 182
Eufrosina, 228
Eugene II, Pope, 126n51, 150n19
Eugenius, Saint, 223–224
Eusebius, Saint, 35n64
Exaltation of the Cross, Feast of, 131, 135, 135n80

Fabian, Saint, 160n47
Farfa, Abbey of, 6n
Fausta, Saint, 43
Felice, Bishop of Lucca, 28n39, 43n90
Fiesole, 19–20, 36–39, 50–52, 67–71 (*see also individual churches, bishops, and saints*)
Flora, Saint, 180n107, 197n19
Florence, 39–42, 61–67, 72, 74–84, 200–225 (*see also individual churches, bishops, and saints*)
Francis, Saint, 217n65
Fridian, Saint, 18, 22–23, 28–30, 32–33, 70, 77n19, 81, 103, 108, 167–168, 179
    Office of, 233–243

Gallus, Saint, 235
Gelasius I, Pope, 45n8, 180
Gelasius II, Pope, 104–105, 159

Gerardo, primicer, 58
Gerardo, Bishop of Florence, 81n29, 83n34, 84n37, 86
Gervasius, Saint, 223
Gesta martyrum, 200, 216
Giovanni I, Bishop of Lucca, 21–37, 40, 42, 77, 85–86, 90n53, 98–100, 108, 128, 234
Giovanni II, Bishop of Lucca, 84–86, 89–90, 95
Giovanni da Velletri, Bishop of Florence, 125, 156n36
Glaber, Rodulfus, 12, 53, 59
Gloria, 146, 149n14
Glossa ordinaria, 187
Gordianus, Saint, 160n47
Gospel (reading), 146, 150–151, 153, 161, 182
Gradual (plainsong), 146, 151–152, 155, 195 (*see also individual chants*)
graduals, 110, 154–155, 188–189
Gratian, canonist, 121
Great Persecution, 18
Gregory I, Pope, 31–32, 47, 180, 183n117, 199, 235
Gregory II, Pope, 24n24
Gregory VII, Pope, 73, 76, 86, 97
Gregory, Bishop of Tours, 32–33, 167n60, 173–174
Grimaldo, Bishop of Pisa, 50n19
Gualberto, Giovanni, 72–75, 83, 86n44
Gualfredo, Bishop of Siena, 128–129
Gualfredo, Count, 60n54
Guasperto, Gastald of Siena, 17–18, 42, 128
Guasperto, Rector of San Frediano, 28n39
Guidetto da Como, 112
Guido, Archbishop of Pisa, 102
Guido of Arezzo, 1–2, 181, 200, 210–212, 219, 229

Hadrian I, Pope, 24n23
hagiographic lectionaries. *See* passionaries
hagiography (*see also individual saints*)
    civic rhetoric in, 26, 79, 99–100, 105
    genres of, 13–14
    literary conventions of, 14, 19–20, 26–29, 32
    as a literary source for plainsong, 57–58, 79–80, 168, 178, 184, 198–202, 208, 212, 220, 227–228, 234–237
Henry II, Emperor, 52–53, 62–64, 66–67, 69, 208
Henry III, Emperor, 61
Henry IV, Emperor, 61, 97, 99n88, 102
Hilaria, Saint, 87–89, 98, 126, 132–133

Hildebrand, Archdeacon. *See* Gregory VII, Pope
Hilduin, Abbot of Saint Denis, 64–66
hinc et nunc, 182, 187, 195, 239
History of the Custodians of Arezzo, 47, 54–56, 60, 90n53, 134
Holy Saturday, Feast of, 120n24, 124n45, 135n80
Holy Savior, Florence. *See* San Lorenzo, Florence
Holy Sepulcher, Jerusalem, 192
Honorius II, anti-pope, 93
Honorius II, Pope, 128
Honorius III, Pope, 137
Honorius Augustodunensis, 123, 147, 154, 174
hospitals, 73, 83–84, 90, 142
Hucbald of Saint-Amand, 226
Hugh, King, 48–50, 53
Hylarian, Saint, 182, 184, 188, 197n19, 227–228
hymns (*see also individual chants*)
    Byzantine (*stichēra*), 239
    in the Divine Office, 194–196, 198
    in procession, 27, 43, 59, 129

Ildebrando, Bishop of Florence, 61–68, 72, 76, 78–79, 124, 208, 213
Immone, Bishop of Arezzo, 58n50
Introit, 146, 155, 168, 176, 179 (*see also individual chants*)
invitatory, 194
Ite missa est, 146

Jacob, patriarch, 157, 160, 162, 165
Jacopo, Bishop of Fiesole, 61, 67–71, 74–76, 88n49
Jacopo, Bishop of Lucca, 28, 33–36, 108
James, Saint, 127, 133–134, 197
James (the Just), Saint, 145n5, 149n14
Jason, Saint, 87–89, 98, 126, 132–133
Jerusalem, literary image of, 10, 96, 157, 160–161, 165
John VII, Pope, 43
John XII, Pope, 50
John XVIII, Pope, 84n37
John XIX, Pope, 1
John, Saint (the Baptist), 23, 39n76, 40–41, 132, 159, 196n16
    as civic patron, 109, 131, 213, 216, 225
John, Saint (the Evangelist), 83, 132, 196n16, 219, 226n97, 233n108

jubilus, 151, 166
Julian the Apostate, Emperor, 18, 57, 180, 227
Justin, Saint, 200n27
Juvenal, Saint, 43

Kyrie, 10, 146, 149n18

laity
  depredation of ecclesiastical property, 12, 38, 46, 50, 52
  ecclesiastical foundations, 115, 141–142
  Latin, knowledge, 149, 166, 192
  participation in the liturgy, 9–10, 57–61, 134, 148–150
  promotion of relic cults, 127–135
Lambert, Saint, 227n99
Lamberto, Archpriest, 91–92, 131
Lamberto di Specioso, 103n104
Lateran, Rome, 222
lauds, 193–196, 199
Laurentius, Saint, 180n107
Lawrence, Saint, 29
Leo IV, Pope, 126n51, 128, 196n15
Leo IX, Pope, 84
Leonin of Paris, 209n49
lessons, matins, 15, 17, 156n37, 194–195, 221
Liber pontificalis, 11, 24–25, 27, 31–33, 85n41
Lorenzo of Amalfi, 76–79, 81–82, 218–221
liturgical commentaries, 122–123 (*see also* individual authors)
Liturgy of the Eucharist. *See* Mass
Liturgy of the Word. *See* Mass
Liutprand, King, 17–18, 22–24
Lives (*vitae*). *See* hagiography
Lothair I, Emperor, 36, 44, 47–48
Louis the Pious, Emperor, 44, 47, 128
Lucca, 22–35, 84–101, 103–104, 131–133, 167–176, 233–243 (*see also* individual bishops, churches, and saints)
Lucilla, Saint, 180n107, 197n19
Lucine, Saint, 85–86, 88–90, 94–98, 159
Lucius, Saint, 200n27

Maginardo, architect, 56
Magnificat (Song of Mary), 196, 218, 239
Mainz, 9n1, 42
Malavolti, Rinaldo, 141n109, 142n114
Mantua, 93
Mark, Saint, 207n41

Mark, Pope, 222n84
Martin, Saint, 32–34, 88, 107–108, 132–133, 135n80, 154n35, 182–183, 189, 225, 237
  Mass of, 166–179
  as model of episcopal sanctity, 167–168, 176, 179
  sculptural Life, 15, 169–175
martyria, extramural, 19–23, 35–40, 49, 61–71, 233
Mary, Virgin, 33, 88, 104, 108, 121, 130, 132–133, 213
Mass
  dramatic character, 145–149, 154–155, 175, 183, 193, 245
  Liturgy of the Eucharist, 153–156, 158, 161–162, 166
  Liturgy of the Word, 146–147, 150–154, 156–157, 161, 166, 196
  Low, 134, 144–145
  public character, 134, 145–156, 173–174
  remuneration for, 140, 194
  Requiem, 142
Matilda of Tuscany, Countess, 97, 102n99, 151n25
matins (night office), 68, 134, 192–196
  private character, 37, 79, 192–195, 199
  remuneration for, 140, 194
Maundy Thursday, Feast of, 154n33
Maurus, Saint, 87–89, 98, 126, 132–133
Metz, 62, 64, 208
Michael, Saint, 88, 132, 184–187
Minias, Saint, 18, 41–42, 49, 61–67, 76, 78, 124, 225
  Office, 65–66, 197–220, 243
Minor Litanies, 122n32, 135n80
miracles, 29, 58
  cephalophores. *See* saints
  exorcism, 172, 178, 218, 221–222, 227
  Eucharistic, 167, 173–175, 178–179, 182–184, 187–188, 190, 225–226, 228–229
  healing, 21, 77, 182, 218, 227
  protection of a city, 57–58, 184, 187, 188n127, 227–228, 235–236
  raising of the dead, 172, 178, 220, 224
  and relic translations, 27–28, 32–33, 77–78, 128–129, 220–221
  at a saint's tomb, 20–21, 28, 35, 37, 60, 77, 129, 218, 220–221, 234
missals, 110, 155, 176n95
monastery, proprietary, 66–67
Monte Oliveto Maggiore, Abbey of, 217n65
Montecassino, Abbey of, 6n, 76, 198
Moses, 89, 151n22, 153, 162

Narni, 43
Nativity, Feast of the, 145n6, 153n27, 154n33, 169, 196n16, 205
Nazarius, Saint, 223
neumes, unheighted, 94
Nicholas, Saint, 131n65, 226
Nicholas I, Pope, 35n64
Nicholas II, Pope. *See* Gerardo, Bishop of Florence
night office. *See* matins
none, 193, 195
nocturn, 194
Normans, 38–39, 52
Notker Balbulus, 235
Notre Dame, Paris, 153n27

oblations, 10–11, 20–21, 45, 60, 109, 123, 129–130, 134–136, 158, 161
    at Mass, 146, 153–154
Oderigo, Canon, 118, 121–122
Odilo, Abbot of Cluny, 76, 82
offerings. *See* oblations
Offertory (plainsong), 146, 153, 155, 168, 179 (*see also individual chants*)
Olav, Saint, 203n36
opere, 103, 105, 109, 111–112, 115, 133–136, 143 (*see also individual churches*)
opus Dei, 193, 199
ordinals, 4, 109–110, 115–123, 147
Ordo ad benedicandam ecclesiam, 9–11, 92, 94–96
organum, 119–120, 140n103, 152, 157, 162, 195n12, 196
Otto I, Emperor, 50, 52n29
Otto II, Emperor, 51, 52n29, 53, 62, 75n10, 208
Otto III, Emperor, 53n29, 55
Ottonians. *See individual emperors*

Paganello, Bishop of Lucca, 138, 139n99
Palmerio, chaplain, 141n105
Panonia, 178
Pantaleon, Saint, 25, 27–28, 31
Pascentius, archdeacon, 30n46
passionaries, 14–15, 33, 188, 190
Passions (*passiones*). *See* hagiography
Pater noster, 149
Paul I, Pope, 27, 32
Paulinus of Milan, 11, 76, 222, 223n85
Pavia, 36, 39, 102, 138

Pentecost, Feast of, 149, 153n27, 154n33, 196n16, 219
Peppin, King, 31
Peredeo, Bishop of Lucca, 23–25, 29
Peregrinus, 35n64
Pergentinus, Saint, 180n107
Perpetuus, Bishop of Tours, 32–33
Peter, Saint, 18–19, 31, 33, 35n64, 52, 69–71, 101, 162, 226, 239
Phillip, Saint, 145n5, 149n14
plainsong (*see also individual chants and genres*)
    Gregorian style, 199–200, 203–207, 219, 229, 235, 238–241, 244
    historical/narrative, 198–199, 225–229, 234, 236
    panegyric, 198–199, 209, 233, 235–236
    post-Gregorian style, 199–200, 210–212, 219–220, 226–227, 299–233, 241
Pietro, Archbishop of Pisa, 104
Pietro, Bishop of Arezzo, 48, 51
pievi, 23, 29, 137
Pigmenius, Saint, 227
pilgrims and pilgrimage, 12, 18, 20–21, 26, 30–31, 38, 60, 65, 70, 73, 134, 192
    to Rome, 6, 38, 161, 234
Pisa, 102–105, 156, 159 (*see also individual bishops, churches, and saints*)
Pistoia, 133–134, 176–179 (*see also individual bishops, churches, and saints*)
Polycarp, Saint, 200n27
polyphony. *See* organum
Pontianus, Saint, 35
popes and the papacy (*see also individual popes*)
    alliance with the Carolingians, 6–7, 24
    as builders, 11, 25, 31–32
    and ecclesiastical reform, 73, 75–76, 84, 86, 92, 97–98
Populonia, 5, 21, 25, 43, 236
Postcommunion (prayer), 146
Potitus, Saint, 103
prebends. *See* canons
Preface (prayer), 146, 154, 174–176
prime, 144, 193, 195
primicer. *See* cantor
provost. *See* archdeacon
Protasius, Saint, 223
pulpits, 150–153, 162, 196. *See also individual churches*

processions, 68, 92, 111n104, 122n32, 129, 132–133
    before Mass, 148–149, 156–159
psalms, singing of
    in procession, 27, 43, 129
    in the Divine Office, 37, 194–196
Ptolemaeus, Saint, 200n27

Quid significent, 92–93, 95–97

Radagasius, King, 227
Raimbaldo, Bishop of Fiesole, 67–68
Rainaldo, *operaio*, 112
Rangerio, Bishop of Lucca, 105, 126, 131–132
    Sermo in dedicatione ecclesie Sancti Martini,
        88–89, 91–93, 96, 98, 101
    Translatio Sancti Reguli II, 99–101, 236
    *Translatio Sanctorum Reguli, Iasonis, Mauri,
        et Hilarie*, 98, 101
    Vita Metrica Sancti Anselmi, 5–6, 22–23,
        84–85, 87–92, 97–101, 168, 209n49
Ranieri, Count of Tuscany, 59
Ranierius, Saint, 117n19, 192–193
Regulus, Saint, 18, 25–32, 43, 85–86, 88, 98–101,
    103–104, 126, 132–133, 145
    as a cephalophore, 20–21, 26, 64
    Office, 197, 233–234, 236–243
    sculptural life, 15, 237
reform movements
    monastic, 66–69, 72–73, 81–84, 92, 102, 208,
        234–235, 244
    papal, 86, 92, 97, 102
Reginold, Bishop of Eichstätt, 226
relics. *See* bishops, miracles, *and individual
    saints*
Reparata, Saint, 23, 40, 109, 118n19
responsories, 149, 194–197, 199, 228 (*see also
    individual chants*)
    formulaic construction, 203, 210, 219,
        229–230
    modal distribution, 203
    modal ordering, 226–227
Rogation Days. *See* Minor Litanies
Rolando of Florence, Canon, 83
Rolando of Pisa, Deacon, 117n19, 118, 120–121
Romano-German Pontifical (PRG), 9–12, 58,
    92, 94
Romano, Bishop of Fiesole, 14, 36–37, 43, 77, 194
Rome. *See* popes and papacy *and individual
    churches*

Romualdo, Saint, 66, 68–73, 83, 168
Romulus, Saint, 18, 67, 69–70
Rule of Aachen, 44–48, 51–52, 54, 69, 73, 75,
    86, 102, 137, 181, 193
    and the office of cantor, 116, 120, 122
Rule of St. Benedict. *See* Benedict, Saint

saints (*see also individual saints*)
    ascetics and hermits, 66, 72, 167–168, 173,
        182, 208, 227, 229, 234–237
    cephalophores, 20, 26, 64, 208–209, 236
    civic patrons, 109, 198, 213, 216–221, 225
    defenders of Catholic doctrine, 19,
        236–238
    defensores civitatis, 58, 184, 198, 227–228,
        235–236, 242
    evangelizers, 18, 19, 58, 64, 70–71, 128, 182,
        208, 227
    healers, 19, 26, 170–172, 217–218, 220,
        223–225, 227
    thaumaturges (*see* miracles)
Saint-Denis, Paris, 64–66, 208
Saint-Martial, Limoges, 53n32, 60n56
Saint-Martin, Tours, 167n60
Salvo, chaplain, 117n19
San Alessandro, Fiesole, 20, 37–38, 42, 51
San Alessandro Maggiore, Lucca, 87
San Bartolomeo, Fiesole (old cathedral), 19–20,
    37–39, 51, 68–69, 71, 75n12
San Concordio, Lucca, 137n89
San Cristoforo, Barga, 5, 126–127, 151–152
San Donato, Arezzo, 1–2, 56–61, 63, 81, 83,
    90n53, 93, 134–135, 180–181, 225
San Donato, Lucca, 180
San Donato, Siena, 180
San Francesco, Assisi, 174n90
San Frediano, Lucca, 6, 22–23, 26, 28–35, 43,
    77n19, 110
    Augustinian canons, 6, 192, 233–234, 238,
        242–243
San Giorgio, Sorbano del Giudice, 121
San Giovanni, Florence (baptistery), 39–40,
    81n29, 109, 144, 148–149, 156, 159, 213
San Giovanni, Lucca (baptistery), 23, 40, 109n9,
    156
San Giovanni, Pisa (baptistery), 109
San Giovanni, Pistoia (baptistery), 109n9
San Lorenzo, Florence (old cathedral), 11, 39,
    40, 49, 77, 220, 223

San Martino, Lucca (cathedral), 23–35, 85–98, 102–104, 130, 197
  altar of Sts. Jason, Maurus, and Hilaria, 88–89, 98, 126, 132–133
  altar of St. Lucine, 88–89, 95–98, 159
  altar of St. Regulus, 88, 98, 101, 132–133, 236
  canons, 49, 88, 91–92, 94–98, 104, 107, 111, 123, 132–140, 147, 170, 175–176, 195, 234, 236–238, 242–243
  chapel of the Holy Cross, 88, 131–133
  crypt, 30–31, 88, 98, 101, 104, 126, 239, 145
  façade, 112, 114, 169–170
  opera, 111, 133, 135, 170
  portico, 90, 98, 102, 112, 114, 133, 167, 169–176, 225, 237–238
San Miniato al Monte, Florence, 41, 61–68, 72, 74–75, 110, 200, 202, 216–220, 225
  apse mosaic, 213–215
  crypt, 65–66, 124–125, 145, 213
  façade, 213–214
  monks, 62, 65–66, 208–217, 220
  pulpit, 150
San Miniato tra le torre, Florence, 217n65
San Pancrazio, Florence, 216n63
San Pietro, Fiesole. *See* San Bartolomeo, Fiesole (old cathedral)
San Pietro in Gerusalemme, Fiesole. *See* San Alessandro, Fiesole
San Pietro in Vincoli, Rome, 34
San Pietro Maggiore, Florence, 216n63
San Pietro Maggiore, Lucca, 87
San Regolo, Gualdo, 5, 25–26, 29
San Romolo, Fiesole (cathedral), 20, 68, 75n12, 93, 109n9, 110
San Sisto, Pisa, 159
San Vitale, Ravenna, 56
San Zeno, Pistoia (cathedral), 110, 155, 167, 180
  canons, 133–134, 136, 142, 178
  chapel of St. James, 133–134
  pulpit, 151n22
Sanctus, 146, 149n14
Sant'Apollinare, Florence, 216n63
Sant'Andrea, Florence, 216n63
Sant'Andrea in Percussina, 118n19
Sant'Ansano, Dofana, 5, 17–18, 128, 131
Santa Felicta, Florence, 216n63
Santa Lucia di Massa Pagani, 216n63
Santa Maria, Fiesole, 20, 68
  canons, 50–52, 68–69

Santa Maria ad Martyres, Rome, 159
Santa Maria Assunta, Pisa (cathedral), 102–105, 108, 110, 121, 126, 141–142, 151, 159–160
  canons, 49, 53, 102–105, 113n9, 136–137
  façade, 112–113
  opera, 111, 135
  pulpit, 151n22
Santa Maria Assunta, Siena (cathedral), 108, 110, 121, 128–131, 141n109
  altar of St. Ansanus, 127n51, 130, 135
  altar of St. Savinus, 130, 135
  atrium, 112n6, 125n46
  canons, 128–130, 135
  crypt, 124–125, 131
  opera, 111, 135
Santa Maria del Fiore, Florence, 81, 102
Santa Maria, Pontetetto, 197
Santa Maria in Via, Lucca, 141n107
Santa Maria Maggiore, Rome, 34
Santa Prassede, Rome, 89n52
Santa Reparata, Florence (cathedral), 39–40, 49, 81–82, 109–110, 144–145, 148–149, 179, 208
  altar of St. John the Evangelist, 82–84
  altar of St. Thomas Becket, 82, 167n59
  canons, 53, 64, 74–84, 136, 138–139, 144–145, 159, 179, 202–203, 210, 215–226
  crypt, 125, 131, 136, 145, 149, 203, 216, 218
  hospital, 83–84
  pulpit, 150
Santa Reparata, Lucca (old cathedral), 23, 25–26, 31, 40
Santo Stefano, Florence, 216n63
Ss. Jacopo e Filippo, Lucca, 35
Ss. Maria e Stefano, Arezzo (cathedral), 60, 66, 70, 90n53, 110, 225
  canons, 47–50, 54–55, 57–60, 134–136, 138, 181–183
  crypt, 55–56
Ss. Vincenzo e Anastasio, Lucca, 117
Sardinia, 103–104
Savinus, Saint, 130, 135
Sebastian, Saint, 160n47
Secret (prayer), 146
Senesius, Saint, 87
Sequence (plainsong), 146, 155, 161, 165–166, 196 (*see also individual chants*)
sequentiaries, 110
Serchio River, 5, 235

sermon, at Mass, 146, 153
Severus, Sulpicius
    Dialogi, 173–175, 178n89
    Epistola ad Bassulam, 167–168, 179
    Vita Sancti Martini, 167, 169–170, 172–173
sext, 193, 195
Sicardo, of Cremona, 97, 118n19, 123, 147, 151–154, 174, 195, 196n16
Sigezone, cantor, 116n15
Siena, 17–20, 128–131. *See also individual churches and saints*
Silvestro, chaplain, 141n106-107
Simone Martini, 174n90
Simplicanus, Bishop of Milan, 221n78
Solomon, King, 69, 87–90, 156–157, 161n48, 162
Song of Mary. *See* Magnificat
Song of Simeon. *See* Nunc dimittis
Song of Zechariah. *See* Benedictus
Speyer, 102
St. Gall, Monastery of, 235
St. Peter's, Rome, 19, 31, 38, 50, 87, 93, 101–102
Stabile, Bishop of Arezzo, 17–18, 42
Stephen, Bishop of Liège, 226, 227n99
Stephen, Saint, 29, 55, 196n16, 22
Stephen II, Pope, 17–18, 24n24, 131
Suaverico, Primicer, 116n15
subdeacon, 148–151, 153n27, 175, 193n3
suffrage, 132–134

Teodaldo, Bishop of Arezzo, 1–3, 54–61, 66, 77, 90n53, 181, 225
    and Santa Reparata, Florence, 83–84, 219–220
Teodoro, Bishop of Florence, 222n80
terce, 144, 193, 195
Theodore, Saint, 222n80
Theodosius I, Emperor, 57–58, 227
Thomas Becket, Saint, 167n59
Tiburtius, Saint, 160n47
Tolomeo of Lucca, 92–93
Totila, King, 236
Tours, 21, 35, 167n95, 178
Translations (*translationes*). *See* hagiography
tropes (plainsong), 155, 161–162, 179 (*see also individual chants*)
tropers, 110, 155, 178n89
Tuscany
    Lombard Duchy, 5, 22
    dioceses, 4–6

Ubaldo, Archbishop of Pisa, 136–137, 141n105
Ubertini, Guglielmino, Bishop of Arezzo, 138, 141n105
Ugolino, cantor, 116n15
Urban II, Pope, 104n112

Valerian, Saint, 160n47
Vallombrosa, Monastery of, 72, 83
Vatican. *See* St. Peter's, Rome
Venantius Fortunatus, 174, 178n89
versicles, 132, 176, 194–195
vespers, 195–196
    participation of the bishop, 176
    public character, 58, 79–80, 198–199, 209–210, 217–218, 220–221, 239–241
    remuneration for, 140, 194
vestments, 2, 33, 149, 159, 175–176, 183, 188, 224, 237
Via Cassia, 6, 47
Via Francigena, 6, 234–235
Victor II, Pope, 84n37, 86
vigil, 130, 134, 218–219, 242–243
Vikings, 36, 42, 49
Villani, Giovanni, 69
Vincent, Saint, 29, 226n97
Vincentius, Saint, 35n64
Vinizzone, Bishop of Fiesole, 50–51
Visconti, Frederico, Archbishop of Pisa, 121n30
Vitalis, Saint, 222
Volterra, 17, 155
Volto Santo, 127, 131–133, 135, 197
votive services, 142, 193

Walprando, Bishop of Lucca, 23–24, 28n39, 29
Wandelbert of Prüm, 26n31
Wilielmo, Bishop of Arezzo, 54n33

Zachary, Pope, 17–18
Zaccheus, 156–158, 161
Zeno, Saint, 134n77, 167
Zenobio, Bishop of Fiesole, 50–52, 61, 68–69, 71, 73
Zenobio, Bishop of Pisa, 50n19
Zenobius, Saint, 18, 39–42, 45, 49, 76–82, 131, 136, 145, 148–149, 179, 203, 213–217, 242
    altarpiece, 15, 222, 224
    office, 79–80, 197, 211–212, 217–221, 224–225, 242–243
Zita of Lucca, 149–150, 192–193

INDEX OF MANUSCRIPTS

Arezzo, Archivio Capitolare (ACA)
    Duomo A: 228n104
    Duomo H: 181n109

Bologna, Biblioteca Universitaria. 1758 (OOP): 117n19, 118, 121n17

Fiesole, Archivio Capitolare (ACFie)
    II.B.I: 52n27
    XXII, I: 52n27
Florence, Archivio Arcivescovile (AAF), n.s.: 79n28, 197, 204n37, 208–209, 212, 217, 226, 226n95, 226n97, 233n108
Florence, Archivio dell'Opera di Santa Maria del Fiore, I.3.8 (Mores): 117n19, 118, 139n96
Florence, Biblioteca Laurenziana (BLF)
    Conv. soppr. 457: 217n65
    Edili 117: 225n93
    Edili 131: 220n73
    Edili 139: 63n68, 64n70, 202n29-30, 216n62
    Edili 147: 216n62
    Mugell. 13: 63n67
    Pluteo 20.30: 87n45
    Pluteo 27.1: 39n77, 222n79
Florence, Biblioteca Riccardiana, 3005 (Ritus): 118, 119n21, 157–158, 215

Lucca, Biblioteca Capitolare (BCL)
    B: 86n42
    C: 33n61, 33–34
    D: 33n61
    G: 86n42
    P†: 89n50, 99n88, 167n59, 170, 188, 190, 213n57
    124: 107-108, 126n51, 150n19
    490: 24, 27n34, 85n41
    599: 243n140
    602: 243n140
    603: 197, 226n98, 234
    605: 94n70, 197, 228
    607: 92, 94
    608 (OOL): 118, 119n21, 156
Lucca, Opera del Duomo (ODL)
    4: 243n140
    10: 155n35
Lucca, San Frediano, Guardaroba, D: 243n140
Oxford, Bodleian Library
    Canonici liturg. 379: 217n65
    Canonici liturg. 392: 217n65

Pisa, Archivio Capitolare (ACP), C150: 104n109
Pistoia, Archivio Capitolare (ACPist)
    C102 (OOPist2): 118
    C114 (OOPist1): 118
    C119: 154n35, 155, 176n95, 181n111, 184n123
    C120: 154n35, 155, 160n47, 176n95
    C121: 155, 158, 176n97
Pistoia, Archivio Vescovile (AVPist), R69: 154n35, 155, 168–169, 188–189

Rome, Biblioteca Angelica, 123: 181n111
Rome, Biblioteca Casanatense (BCR)
    719: 99n88, 167n60
    1741: 178n98
Rome, Biblioteca Nazionale, Farfa 29: 63n68, 202n30

Seville, Zayas Private Collection, 2: 155, 176n97
Siena, Biblioteca Comunale degli Intronati (BCIS), G.V.8 (OOES): 118, 130n61

Toledo, Biblioteca Capitolare (BCT), 52.11: 155

Vatican City, Biblioteca Apostolica Vaticana (BAV)
    Vat. Lat. 4772: 181n110, 184n122
    Vat. Lat. 6453: 26n31
Volterra, Biblioteca Guarnacci (BGV), L.3.39: 155, 157–158, 162n51

INDEX OF PLAINSONG

Boldface type indicates musical examples.

Ad templi huius (sequence), 158, 165–166, 178
Adesto tibi (antiphon), 210, 249
Ait Petrus principibus (antiphon), 242n135
Alleluia. Beatus vir sanctus, 176n95
Alleluia. Dies sanctificatus, 169
Alleluia. Fundata est, 157, 160, 165
Alleluia. Hec est domus Domini, 157, 160
Alleluia. Oculis ac manibus, 168n67, **169**, 179
Alleluia. Sancti tui Domine, 158, 160
Alme pater qui praescius (antiphon), 209n48
Almi patris (hymn), 209n48, 220, 224n91–92 251
Almum hunc diem (antiphon), 209n46, 249
Antime frater (antiphon), **228-230**, 233, 241–242, 255
Asterius Apruniani (responsory), 230n107, 254

Beatissimi Miniatis (antiphon), 209n46, 211n54, 247
Beatus Martinus obitum (responsory), 168n67
Benedic, Domine (responsory), 157
Beatus Christi miles (responsory), 201–202, **206-207**, 248
Beatus Regulus (antiphon), 237, **239**, 260
Beatus vir (responsory), 219

Clementissime Christi (antiphon), 242n135, 258
Confractum namque vas (antiphon), 227n102
Confractum vitreum (offertory), **184-188**
Cornelius centurio (antiphon), 220n106
Cum augustus (responsory), 228, 230n107, 255
Cum beatus Donatus (responsory), 229n107, 255
Cum beatus Donatus sacrum (responsory), 228, **230-233**, 254
Cum vidisset (responsory), 201–202, 248

Data est lex (responsory), 229n107, 255
Dextera Domini (offertory), 168
Dilecte Deo (sequence), 235
Dixerunt discipuli (responsory), 168n67
Domus mea (communion), 158
Domine Deus (offertory), 158, 161–162
Domine Hiesu Christe (introit), 184
Dum adhuc paene vigilaret vir (antiphon), 242n135

Dum in suis temporibus (antiphon), 234–235, 257
Dum Iulianus (responsory), 228, 229n107, 254

Ejectus a propriis (antiphon), **241-242**, 259
Eufrosina adiuro te (responsory verse), 228, 255

Fidelis servus (Communion), 176n95
Frigianus namque pontifex (antiphon), **239**, 257
Frigianus pontifex (antiphon), **239**, 257

Gaudet membellis (antiphon), 218, 251

Hac subiens regnum (antiphon), 218, 251
Hodie cum exultatione (responsory), **230-233**, 255
Hodie sacer sumus (antiphon), 237, **239-241**, 260
Hodie Simon Petrus (antiphon), 239
Hylarianus monachus (antiphon), 229, 254

Iam non dicam (responsory), 149, 219
Ignis ardore fatigatus (antiphon), 57n48, **58–59**, 60, 228n102, 241n134, 253
Illuminata Siranna (antiphon), **229-230**, 254
In jejuniis et orationibus (antiphon), 229n106
In medio ecclesie (responsory), 233n108
Inclitus hic rutilo (trope), 176
Inveni David (gradual), 176n95
Invisibilis Deus (trope), 157, 162, **164-165**, 167, 176
Iste pater Africe (antiphon), 236n121, 259
Iulius urbis Rome (antiphon), 229, 255
Iustorum animae (offertory), 184n123

Laudanda est Trinitas (antiphon), 237, **241-242**, 259
Laudes Deo digna (sequence), 189–190, 220n74
Letetur urbs Florentia (hymn), 220–221, 251
Locus iste (gradual), 157, 160, 160–162
Lucane nampe crassante (antiphon), 242n135, 257
Lucida pre reliquis (antiphon), 209, 249

Maris undas mitigans (antiphon), 237, 259
Martinus Abrahae sinu laetus (responsory), 79n28
Martyrialis honor (antiphon), 209, **211-212**, 249
Ministri presidis (responsory), 204, **206-207**, 242
Montes Israel (responsory), 230, 233

O virum ineffabiliem (antiphon), 168n67
Obtine nobis (antiphon), 242n135, 257

Oculis ac manibus (antiphon), 168n67
Oculis ac manibus (responsory), 168n67
O gemma clara martyrum (antiphon), 79n28
O gemma fulgens presulum (responsory), **79–80**, 218–220, 251
O pater et pastor (antiphon), 218, 221, 251
Organicis Christo (trope), 157, **162–163**, 165

Pervigil o pastor (antiphon), **211–212**, 219, 251
Pontifices almi (antiphon), **229–230**
Postquam domi puerilem (antiphon), 242n135
Pretiosus Christi (responsory), 65–66, **209–211**, 219, 248
Preciosus Domini (responsory), 65
Psallat chorus fidelium (hymn), 220, 251
Puer Donatus (responsory), 229n107, 253

Qui maris (antiphon), 235n118, 257
Qui missus Domini, 235n118, 25

Sacerdotem Christi Martinum (sequence), **176–179**, 189–190, 220n74
Sancte Frigiane (antiphon), 235–236, 257
Sancte pater Donate (Gradual), 184
Sathirus episcopus (antiphon), 229, 255
Secutus dicente (responsory verse), 228, 254
Siranna utroque (responsory), 230n107, 254
Sprevisti pauperem (antiphon), 234–235, 257
Stans beatus Donatus (antiphon), 228, 254

Statimque preparatus (responsory verse), 201–202, 248
Statuit ei (introit), 176n95
Stetit angelus, **184–187**
Sub altare Domini (antiphon), 96
Surgite sancti (antiphon), 94–95

Tecum principium (antiphon), **204–206**
Telluris Italice (antiphon), 242n135, 259
Terribilis est locus iste (introit), 157, 160, **162–165**
Tripudio cuncti (antiphon), 209, 249
Tunc imperator (antiphon), **204–206**, 212n54, 238n130, 249
Tunc iratus (antiphon), **204–206**, 238n130, 248
Tyrannus ira plenus (antiphon), 236n121, 259

Uterque sexus (antiphon), 210, 249

Veritas mea (offertory), 176n95
Vexillum leva (antiphon), 235n118, 235n120, 257
Videntes stellam (antiphon), 229n105
Viri Galilaei (offertory), 184n123
Votivo presul peteris (antiphon), 218, 251
Vox de caelo (responsory verse), 209, **210–211**, 248

Zachaee, festinans (antiphon), 157
Zenobi mundo (antiphon), 218, 251